CW01617602

FACTFILE
Dictionary

FACTFILE Dictionary

John Grisewood

WHSMITH
EXCLUSIVE
· BOOKS ·

Editor Rachel Pilcher
Designer Ross George
Illustrator Ron Hayward Art Group
Picture Research Elaine Willis

Published in 1990 by
Grisewood & Dempsey Ltd
Elsley House
24–30 Great Titchfield Street
London W1P 7AD

The text in this edition
is revised from the
Pocket Dictionary, first
published in 1984 by
Kingfisher Books

Text © Grisewood & Dempsey 1984, 1990
Illustrations © Grisewood & Dempsey 1990

All rights reserved. No part of this
publication may be reproduced, stored in
a retrieval system, or transmitted, in
any form or by any means, electronic,
mechanical, photocopying, recording or
otherwise, without the prior
permission of the publishers.

Printed in Yugoslavia

ISBN 0-906279-81-X

The publishers would like to thank Jill Thomas for her
assistance in the production of this book.

Photographic Acknowledgements

The publishers wish to thank the following for supplying photographs for this book:

Page 29 Camera Press; 33 ZEFA; 45 Barnabys Picture Library; 51 Camera Press; 55 Ministry of Defence; 60 Barnabys Picture Library; 67 Courtesy, Ferranti; 91 The Mansell Collection; 108 Hulton-Deutsch Collection; 114 The Mansell Collection; 116 Courtesy, Salt Lake Bureau; 233 Shell Photo Library; 249 ZEFA; 260 Courtesy, Man Roland; 262 The Mansell Collection; 268 Courtesy, Minnesota Arrowhead; 271 Camera Press; 278 Courtesy, Italian Tourist Board; 291 Courtesy, Zimbabwe Tourist Office; 304 Allsport; 308 ZEFA; 311 Ann Ronan Picture Library; 317 Peter Clayton; 362 ZEFA; 365 Camera Press; 369 Camera Press; 389 Courtesy, Tektronix.

Contents

ABBREVIATIONS

These are the abbreviations used in this dictionary.

abbrev.	abbreviation
adj.	adjective
adv.	adverb
Austral.	Australian
conj.	conjunction
e.g.	for example
etc.	etcetera (Latin for 'and so on')
i.e.	id est (Latin for 'that is')
interj.	interjection
n.	noun
pl.	plural
pl.n.	plural noun
past part.	past participle
pron.	pronoun
Sc.	Scottish
USA	United States of America
vb.	verb

A

a, an the indefinite article, used before a noun. *A person. An apple.*
aardvark *n.* an African mammal that resembles an anteater.
aardwolf *n.* a burrowing animal from Africa that looks like a small hyena.
ab- abs- *prefix* meaning away from, without, e.g. **abnormal** different from what is normal.
abacus *n.* a frame with sliding beads, used for counting.
abandon *vb.* 1. stop doing something. *They had to abandon the game.* 2. leave and not return. *They had to abandon the ship.*
abbey *n.* church and other buildings where monks or nuns live; a great church.
abbot *n.* the man in charge of the monks in an abbey.
abbreviation *n.* a short way of writing either a word or a group of words. *Tom is an abbreviation of Thomas.*
abdicate *vb.* give up a position of power, usually that of king or queen. **abdication** *n.*
abdomen *n.* 1. the stomach (in people). 2. the rear part of the body (in insects).
abduct *vb.* kidnap, carry off. **abduction** *n.* **abductor** *n.* a person who abducts.
abhor *vb.* detest, feel hatred for. **abhorrence** *n.*
abject *adj.* miserable, degraded.
able *adj.* having the power or strength to do something. *Are you able to help me?* **ability** *n.*
aboard *adv.* on a ship, aircraft or train. *They went aboard the ship.*
abolish *vb.* stop or put an end to something, e.g. slavery.
abolitionists *n.* the name given to people in the 17th and 18th centuries who worked for the abolition of slavery.
abominable *adj.* disgusting, unpleasant.
aborigines (*abo*-**rij**-*in-ees*) *n. pl.* the first people who lived in a country, especially the first Australians.

Aborigine shield and boomerang.

abort *vb.* cause to miscarry; put an end to, e.g. spacecraft mission.
abortion *n.* operation to remove foetus from womb.
about 1. *adv.* more or less; roughly. *About an hour ago.* 2. *prep.* around; nearby. *There's a lot of hay fever about.*

above *prep*. overhead, higher than something.
abrasive 1. *adj*. having the property of grinding or smoothing down. 2. *adj*. (of a person) rude; upsetting people. 3. *n*. a substance that grinds or smooths.
abreast *adv*. side by side. *Keep abreast of me*.
abridge *vb*. shorten, condense.
abroad *adv*. in another country.
abrupt *adj*. sudden; hasty.
abscess *n*. a boil; a collection of pus.
absent *adj*. not there.
absolute *adj*. complete.
absolve *vb*. free someone from blame.
absorb *vb*. take in water or some other liquid. *A sponge absorbs water*. **absorbent** *adj*. & *n*.
abstain *vb*. hold back or restrain oneself from doing something, e.g. eating. **abstinence** *n*.
absurd *adj*. something that is ridiculous or comical.
abundance *n*. a plentiful quantity of something. **abundant** *adj*.
abuse *vb*. 1. use something wrongly. 2. be rude to someone. **abusive** *adj*.
abyss (*a*-**biss**) *n*. deep pit or gorge. **abysmal** *adj*. bottomless; (*casual*) very bad.
academy *n*. a higher or specialized school; society for art, science etc. **academic** *adj*. scholarly; theoretical.
accelerate (*ack*-**sel**-*erate*) *vb*. go faster. **acceleration** *n*. **accelerator** *n*. device (e.g. car pedal) for increasing speed.
accent (*ack-sent*) 1. *n*. local way of pronouncing a language. 2. *vb*. emphasize; stress.
accept (*ack*-**sept**) *vb*. receive or take something which is offered to you; agree to; believe.
access *n*. entrance, approach. **accessible** *adj*. that can be easily approached or reached.
accident (**ack**-*sident*) *n*. something that happens and is not expected, usually something bad; a mishap.
acclaim *vb*. praise; welcome.
accommodate *vb*. provide someone with a place in which to live. **accommodation** *n*. lodging.
accompany *vb*. 1. go along with someone or something, perhaps on a journey. 2. play a musical instrument alongside another instrument or voice. **accompaniment** *n*.

How a dropped ball accelerates. In the first second it travels 4.9m, in the next second 14.6m.

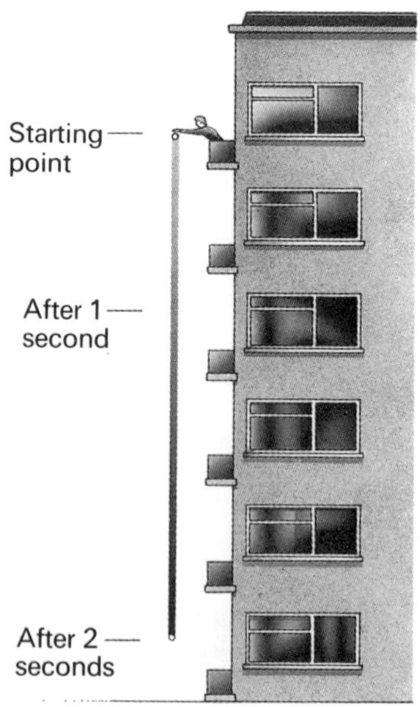

A modern accordion. The keyboard plays the tune and the buttons play chords.

accomplice *n.* helper, partner (particularly in crime).
accomplish *vb.* achieve, carry out. **accomplished** *adj.* skilled, talented. *She is an accomplished violinist.*
accord *vb.* agree; be consistent with.
according *adv.* (with, to) asserted by. *According to him the report is true.*
accordion *n.* musical instrument carried by means of a strap over the shoulder, played by pumping air from bellows, and fitted with keys like a piano.
account 1. *n.* a record of money owed, received, or paid. 2. *n.* a description or report of an event. 3. *vb.* explain, give reasons for.
accumulate *vb.* collect; pile up; continue gradually to increase. **accumulation** *n.*
accurate *adj.* correct and exact. **accuracy** *n.*
accuse *vb.* charge someone with wrongdoing.
accustom *vb.* make used to, familiar with.
ace *n.* 1. the name for 'one' in cards. *The ace of spades.* 2. Someone of great skill, such as an aircraft fighter pilot. 3. a successful unreturned service in tennis.
ache (rhymes with *cake*) *n.* a pain that goes on for a long time, like a toothache.
achieve *vb.* succeed; reach a goal or target. **achievement** *n.*
acid (*asid*) *n.* a substance which tastes sour, like vinegar. *Strong acids can burn you.* **acidic** *adj.*
acknowledge *vb.* admit to; recognize; accept something as one's own. **acknowledgement** *n.*
acme *n.* highest point or stage.
acne *n.* red spots on the skin, common among young people.
acorn *n.* the fruit or nut of an oak tree.

Acorn and oak leaf.

acoustics *n.* 1. the science of sound. 2. the effect of a building on sounds, particularly music, produced inside it. *The acoustics were so bad that I could not hear the orchestra properly.*
acquaintance (*ack*-**wain**-*tance*) *n.* person who is known, but who is not a close friend. **acquaint** *vb.* make aware or familiar. *Let me acquaint you with the facts.*

acquit *vb.* (in law) declare not guilty; set free.
acre (*aker*) *n.* a measure of land (4047 sq m or 4840 sq yds). *A football pitch has an area of about one and a half acres.*
acrobat *n.* a person who does balancing tricks, often in a circus. **acrobatics** *n. pl.*
acronym *n.* a word formed from the initial letters of other words, e.g. NATO, which stands for North Atlantic Treaty Organization.
across *prep.* from one side to the other. *Kate walked across the road.*
acrostic *n.* a set of words, often in the form of a poem, where the first letters of each line spell a word.
act 1. *n.* a thing done. *There are some acts you do every day.* 2. *vb.* behave; play a part or pretend. *He acts the part of a pirate in our play.* **acting** *n.* art of performing. 3. *n.* part of a stage play.
action *n.* 1. a deed. 2. a gesture. 3. a law suit.
active *adj.* busy, full of energy. **activity** *n.*

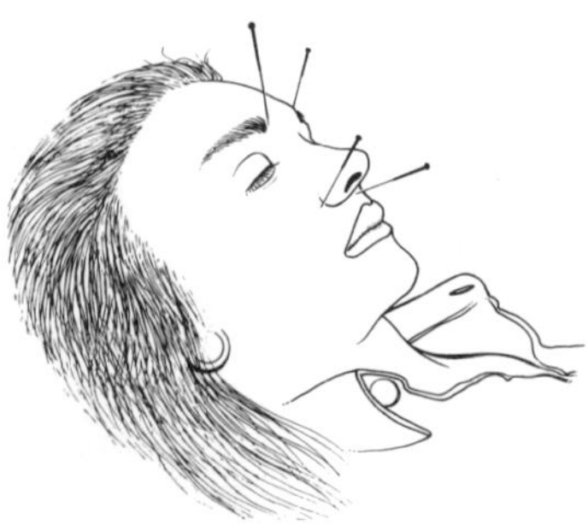

Acupuncture is an ancient Chinese medical treatment.

The adder is a poisonous snake.

actor *n.* person who acts in plays, in films or on TV.
actress *n.* woman who acts in a play or film or on TV.
actual *adj.* existing in fact; real.
acupuncture *n.* a medical treatment in which thin needles are used to puncture various parts of the body. Developed by the Chinese about 5000 years ago, it is still in use today.
acute *adj.* 1. sharp, penetrating. *He had an acute pain in his shoulder.* 2. coming to a crisis. *The situation is acute.*
AD *abbrev.* short for *Anno Domini* (Latin for 'in the year of Our Lord') used with dates after the birth of Christ.
ad- *prefix* (also **ac**- before c, **aff**-, **all**-etc.) meaning to, towards.
adapt *vb.* change something to make it more suitable for the purpose. **adaptation** *n.*
add *vb.* put things together to make more. *Colin added all the numbers together to find the total.* **addition** *n.*
adder *n.* a small poisonous snake found in northern countries; a viper.
addict *n.* a person who is obsessed with a habit –

especially drugs – almost beyond cure.

address *n.* 1. the place where a person lives and to which letters are sent. 2. a speech.

adenoids *pl. n.* small lumps at the back of the nose that help to prevent infection. When enlarged, they can make breathing through the nose difficult.

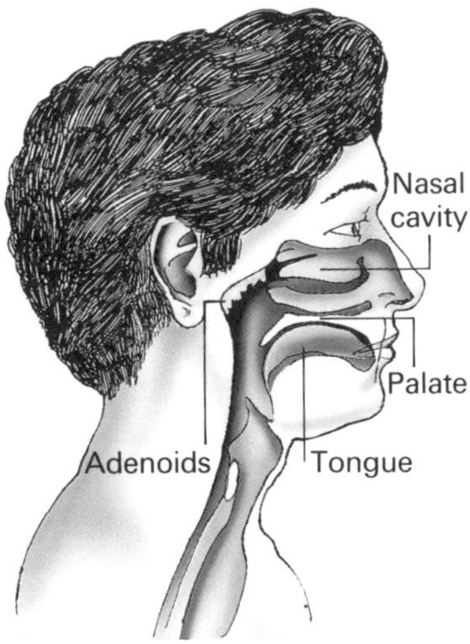

adequate *adj.* enough; sufficient.

adhere *vb.* stick to something. **adherence** *n.*

adhesive *adj.* sticky; able to stick to things. *Adhesive tape. n.* a substance that sticks things together; glue.

adjective *n.* a word that describes what something or somebody is like. (*The black cat.* 'Black' is an adjective. *The water is cold.* 'Cold' is an adjective). Most adjectives can be 'compared' (cold, colder, coldest).

adjourn (*ad*-**jern**) *vb.* postpone (a meeting), suspend, move elsewhere. **adjournment** *n.*

adjust *vb.* arrange; put in order. **adjustment** *n.*

administer *vb.* govern; run something. **administration** *n.*

admiral *n.* very senior officer in the navy.

admire *vb.* think well of something or somebody. **admiration** *n.* **admirable** *adj.* worthy of admiration; excellent.

admit *vb.* 1. allow to enter. 2. confess; own up as true. *He admits his mistake.* **admission** *n.* being allowed into somewhere; the money you pay to go in. **admissible** *adj.* what may be admitted or allowed.

admonish *vb.* warn, usually mildly.

ado (*a*-**do**) *n.* unnecessary fuss.

adobe (*ad*-**doh**-*be*) *n.* sun-dried brick; also building made of adobe.

adolescence *n.* the period of life when a person moves from childhood to adulthood.

adopt *vb.* 1. accept somebody else's child as a child of your own family. *The couple decided to adopt the boy.* 2. take up, accept (an idea etc.).

adore *vb.* worship; think highly of someone or something; love.

adorn *vb.* cover with ornaments. **adornment** *n.*

adult 1. *adj.* grown-up. *An adult person.* 2. *n.* a grown-up.

advance *vb.* move forward, proceed. *n.* a movement forward; a loan of money.

advantage *n.* gain; a better condition or circumstance.

advent *n.* the coming or arrival. *Ice cream sales increased with the advent of warmer weather.*
adventure *n.* exciting happening or experience.
adverb *n.* a word that tells us how, when or where something happens. Most adverbs have the ending *-ly*. (*They walked home slowly*. 'Slowly' is an adverb.)
adversary *n.* opponent.
adverse *adj.* hostile; unfavourable.
advertise *vb.* tell people about something you want to sell. *People advertise in newspapers, on television, or by sticking up posters.*
advertisement *n.* a printed notice in a newspaper or a message about goods or services on radio or TV.
advice *n.* something said to you to help you decide what to do. *We took our teacher's advice and borrowed the book from the library.*
advise *vb.* tell someone what you think they should do. *What do you advise me to do?*
aerial *n.* something through which radio and television signals are sent out or received.
aero- *prefix* meaning of air, aircraft, e.g. **aerobatics** stunts in aircraft.
aeronautics *pl. n.* the science of flight.
aeroplane (or **airplane**) *n.* a flying machine driven by an engine or engines.
aerosol *n.* a substance which can be sprayed under pressure from a container.
affair *n.* business; that which has to be done; love affair. (*pl.*) business in general. *The affairs of state.*

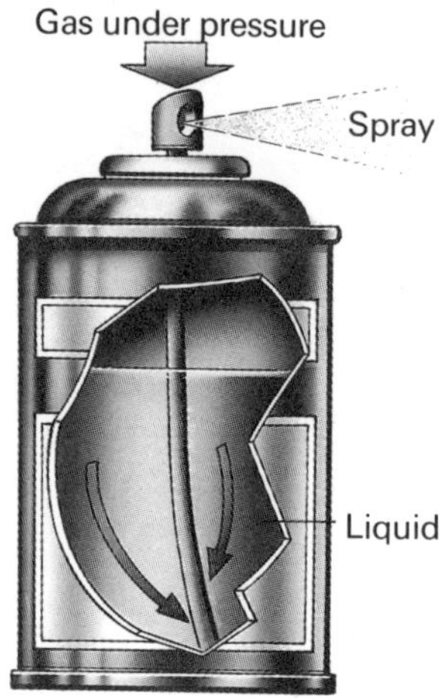

An aerosol can contains liquid and gas. A fine spray is released when the button is pressed.

affect *vb.* make someone or something different in some way. *The hot weather affects her health.* **affectation** *n.* insincere, pretentious manner.
affection *n.* a great liking.
affinity *n.* an attraction.
affirm *vb.* state positively, formally or confidently.
affix *vb.* attach; fasten to.
afflict *vb.* cause pain of body or mind. **affliction** *n.*
affluence *n.* wealth.
afford *vb.* have enough money to buy something. *He can't afford that car.*
afraid *adj.* 1. frightened. 2. sorry. *I am afraid this shop is closed.*
Afrikaans *n.* dialect of Dutch

spoken in South Africa.
aft *adj*. towards the stern of a ship or back of an aircraft.
after 1. *adv*. behind. *They followed after*. 2. *conj*. later in time. *After they left*. 3. used with other verbs: *Look after my bags* (take care of them); *He takes after his father* (he is like his father).
aftermath *n*. period following a disastrous event; the outcome.
afternoon *n*. the part of the day between morning and evening.
afterwards *adv*. later. *We watched TV and afterwards went out to a play*.
again *adv*. once more; another time.
against *prep*. 1. next to; resting on. *Put it up against the wall*. 2. in opposition to; versus. *Which team are we playing against?*
agate *n*. a semi-precious stone marked by bands of colour.
age 1. *n*. length of time a person has lived. 2. *n*. a length of time in history, such as the Stone Age and Bronze Age. 3. *vb*. to become older. *He has aged a lot since I last saw him*.
aged *adj*. (*aj-id*) very old.
agenda *pl. n*. list of things to be done at a meeting etc.
agent *n*. 1. someone working on behalf of someone else. 2. a spy. (A double agent is a spy who tries to serve both sides.) 3. the representative of a musician, artist, actor etc. *His agent has found him a wonderful part in a new play*.
aggravate *vb*. make worse; annoy. **aggravation** *n*. annoyance.
aggression *n*. an attack without cause or provocation. **aggressive** *adj*. eager to attack. **aggressor** *n*.
aghast *adj*. shocked, amazed.
agile *adj*. nimble, quick. **agility** *n*.
agitate *vb*. disturb, shake up; make nervous, stir up unrest. **agitation** *n*. **agitator** *n*.
agnostic *n*. a person who believes that nothing can be known about the existence of God.
ago *adj*. & *adv*. in the past; previously. *Ten years ago*.
agony *n*. great pain or suffering. **agonizing** *adj*.
agrarian *adj*. relating to farming and land management.
agree *vb*. say 'yes' to; consent. *If you agree, I will come too*.

The tractor is a vital piece of machinery in agriculture.

agriculture *n*. farming.
aground *adv*. (of ships) stranded on the bottom of shallow water. *The ship ran aground*.
ahead *adv*. in front. *Dad went ahead to get seats for us*.
aid *vb*. help. *n*. the help that is given.

Aids *n.* a disease which destroys the body's natural defences against infection. It stands for Acquired Immune Deficiency Syndrome.

aim 1. *vb.* point a weapon at something. 2. n. something you try to do. *Jane's aim was to learn French.*

air *n.* the mixture of gases we breathe. *vb.* expose to the air (to dry); make known. *They aired their views.*

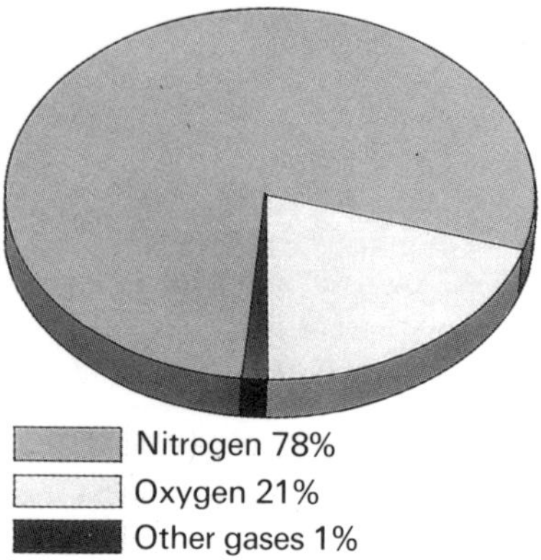

air conditioning *n.* system for cooling and cleaning the air in a building.

aircraft *n.* flying machine such as an aeroplane, an airship, a helicopter etc.

airline *n.* organization that owns and flies aircraft.

airport *n.* place where aircraft land and take off.

airscrew *n.* propeller of an aircraft.

airship *n.* a lighter-than-air craft that is powered and can be steered by its pilot. Airships are sometimes called 'dirigibles' from a French word meaning to 'steer'.

airtight *adj.* so tightly shut that air cannot get in or out.

aisle *n.* passage between rows of seats in a church, cinema, aeroplane etc.

ajar *adv.* partly open. *The door was ajar.*

akin *adj.* related, similar to.

alabaster *n.* a stone similar to marble.

alarm 1. *n.* a warning sound or signal. 2. *vb.* frighten; arouse to sense of danger.

albatross *n.* a large seabird that spends most of its time in the air over the oceans.

albino *n.* & *adj.* a person or animal without natural colouring matter (pigmentation) in skin, hair and eyes.

album *n.* 1. a blank book for keeping photographs, stamps etc. 2. a collection of songs (on a long-playing record).

alchemy *n.* medieval form of chemistry. **alchemist** *n.*

alcohol *n.* 1. the name of a group of chemical substances, mostly liquids. 2. strong drinks, such as beer, wine and spirits.

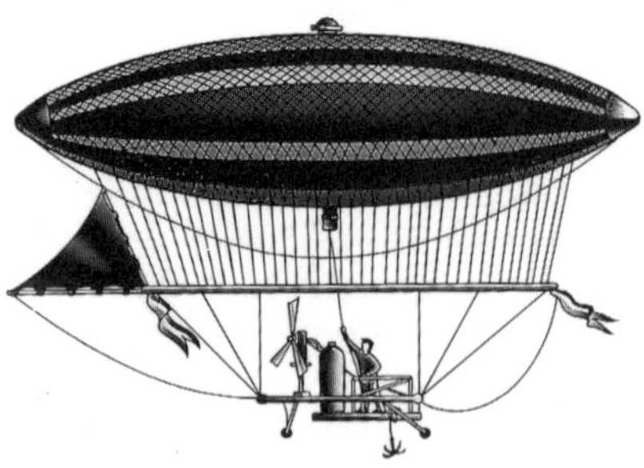

An early design for an airship. Airships flew before aeroplanes, but the gas-filled balloons often caught fire.

alcoholic *n*. person addicted to drinking alcohol.
alcove *n*. a recess in a wall.
alder *n*. a tree belonging to the birch family.
ale *n*. a kind of beer.
alert 1. *adj*. paying attention. 2. *vb*. attract someone's attention. 3. *n*. watchfulness. *Be on the alert*.
algae *pl*. *n*. a group of plants that includes seaweeds and other water plants.

Seaweeds like these are types of algae.

algebra *n*. a branch of mathematics in which letters are used to represent quantities.
alias *n*. an assumed name.
alibi *n*. a term used in law when a person or persons accused of a crime say that they were somewhere else at the time it was committed.
alien 1. *adj*. strange; foreign. 2. *n*. a stranger; a foreigner. **alienate** *vb*. turn away; make a stranger of.
align (al-ine) *vb*. bring into line. **alignment** *n*.
alike 1. *adj*. looking or acting the same. *People say my sister and I are very much alike*. 2. *adv*. in the same way. *We were always treated alike*.
alive *adj*. living; not dead.
alkali *n*. the name of a number of chemical substances, such as ammonia, which have the property of dissolving other substances, but which are distinct from acids.
all *adj*. each, every; the whole of something.
Allah *n*. the name of God among Muslims.
allegory *n*. story with a deeper meaning than the literal one.
allergy *n*. a bodily reaction to some normally harmless substance. *She has an allergy to eggs*. **allergic** *adj*.
alleviate *vb*. make easier, relieve. *The pill alleviated the pain*.
alley *n*. a short narrow passage between buildings.
alliance *n*. a union, especially of states, political parties etc.
alligator *n*. a reptile like a crocodile that lives in parts of the Americas and in China.
alliteration *n*. the same sound frequently repeated in a poem or sentence. *Peter Piper picked a peck of pickled peppers*.
allot *vb*. share out. **allotment** *n*. a share; a small plot of land for cultivation.
allow *vb*. let someone do something, permit. *He allows us to play in his garden*. **allowance** *n*. fixed sum (of money) allowed.
alloy *n*. a mixture of metals. *vb*. mix metals together.

allude *vb*. refer to briefly or indirectly. **allusion** *n*.
allure *n*. & *vb*. charm, have the power to attract.
alluvium *n*. sand, soil, gravel etc. washed down by a river.
ally (**al**-*eye*) *n*. a friend or a country that helps another.
almond *n*. a tree cultivated in warm climates for its edible nuts (almonds).
almost *adj*. very nearly; not quite.
alone *adj*. by yourself; with no one else.
along *prep*. the length of something; from end to end. *Jill walked along the path.*
aloud *adv*. in a voice that can be heard.
alpha (**al**-*fa*) *n*. the first letter of the Greek alphabet.
alphabet *n*. all the letters of a language arranged in order. **alphabetical** *adj*.
already *adv*. by this time; previously. *Have you finished your work already?*
also *adv*. as well as; in addition to something.
although *conj*. even if. *Although he was ill, he went to work.*
altar *n*. the table in a church with a cross on it; communion table.
alter *vb*. change something. *You should alter the dress to make it fit.*
alternate *vb*. happen by turn, one after the other.
alternative *adj*. & *n*. a choice between two things.
altitude *n*. height above the sea level. *The aircraft flew at a very high altitude.*
alto *n*. male singing voice of the highest pitch (above tenor).
altogether *adv*. completely, utterly.
aluminium *n*. a silvery metal which weighs less than most other metals. *Aluminium is used to make cooking pots and aircraft.*
always *adv*. at all times; all the time.
a.m. *abbrev*. the hours between midnight and noon from the Latin *ante meridiem* meaning 'before noon'. *Nine a.m. is 9 o'clock in the morning.*
amalgamate *vb*. combine, mix. **amalgamation** *n*.
amass *vb*. gather together; accumulate.
amateur *n*. a person who is keenly interested in sport, music or some other activity for pleasure, not for payment; unprofessional. **amateurish** *adj*. inexpert.

An ornate church altar.

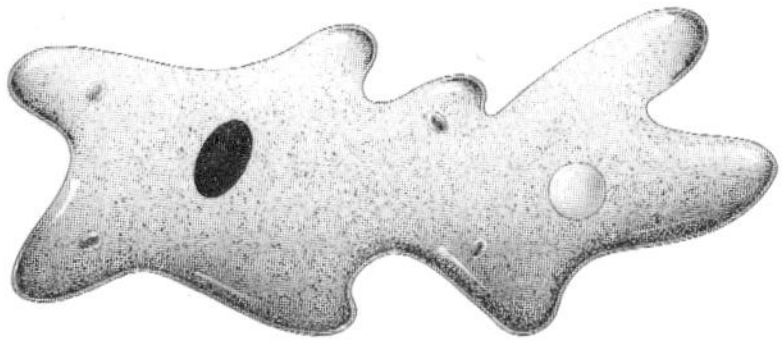

Amoeba, a simple, one-celled animal.

amaze *vb.* astonish, astound. **amazement** *n.*
ambassador *n.* a person who represents one country in another country.
amber *n.* a golden-yellow fossil resin from trees in prehistoric times; the colour of amber, used for the lights between green and red in traffic signals.
ambi- *prefix* meaning both, e.g. **ambidextrous** able to use both hands equally well.
ambition *n.* strong desire to succeed; the object of such desire. *Her ambition was to be a vet.* **ambitious** *adj.*
amble *vb.* walk at an easy pace.
ambulance *n.* a vehicle for carrying people who are ill or injured.
ambush *vb.* hide and wait for someone so that you can take them by surprise. *n.* hiding place for a surprise attack.
amen *n.* an expression used to show agreement, especially at the end of a prayer.
amend *vb.* correct, make improvements.
amethyst *n.* a semi-precious stone; a purple variety of quartz.
amicable *adj.* kindly, friendly.
ammonia *n.* a strong chemical, often used for cleaning purposes.
ammunition (*am-mu-***ni***-shun*) *n.* bullets and other things that are fired from guns.
amnesia *n.* loss of memory.
amnesty *n.* general pardon, especially of prisoners.
amoeba *n.* a one-celled animal that moves about by changing its body shape.
among *prep.* in the middle of; together with a group. Also **amongst**.
amorphous (*am-***or***-fuss*) *adj.* shapeless.
amoral *adj.* neither moral nor immoral; without a sense of morality.
amount *n.* total sum, quantity.
ampere *n.* a unit for measuring the strength of an electrical current.
ampersand *n.* the sign '&' which means *and.*
amphibian *n.* a member of a class of animals in between fish and reptiles that lives both in water and on land. *A frog is an amphibian.*

The frog (above) *and the newt* (below) *are both amphibians. They are at home both in water and on land, but must return to the water to breed.*

amphitheatre *n*. in Roman times an arena surrounded by tiers of seats, used for sporting events.

A Roman amphitheatre. Some, like the Colosseum in Rome, still stand today.

amphora *n*. (plural **amphorae** *pron. am-for-eye*) a Greek jar with two handles.

ample *adj*. enough, plenty.

amplifier *n*. electrical equipment used to make sounds louder. *vb*. **amplify**.

amputate *vb*. (surgical) cut off a limb. **amputation** *n*.

amuse *vb*. make someone smile or laugh. **amusement** *n*. **amusing** *adj*.

anachronism *n*. a person, event or thing that is historically/chronologically out of place. *Napoleon rode to Waterloo in a jeep*.

anaconda *n*. the longest and heaviest snake in the world. Some have reached 9 metres (30 ft) in length.

anaemia *n*. a lack of red blood cells. **anaemic** *adj*.

anaesthetic *n*. a drug used so that people do not feel pain during an operation.

anagram *n*. a word or phrase made up with the letters of another in a different order. *Alps is an anagram of slap*.

analyse *vb*. examine in detail, **analysis** (*pl*. **analyses**) *n*.

anarchy *n*. without government; disorder.

anatomy *n*. the science of the structure of the body, learned by dissection (cutting up) of dead bodies.

ancestor *n*. forefather, a person now dead from whom one is descended. *His ancestors lived in this house for hundreds of years*. **ancestral** *adj*. **ancestry** *n*.

anchor *n*. a heavy iron hook on a long chain. *An anchor is dropped into the water to stop a boat moving*. *vb*. secure a ship with an anchor.

anchovy *n*. small fish of the herring family and with a strong flavour.

ancient (**ayn**-shent) *adj*. very old or very long ago.

and *conj*. a link word expressing addition to what has gone before.

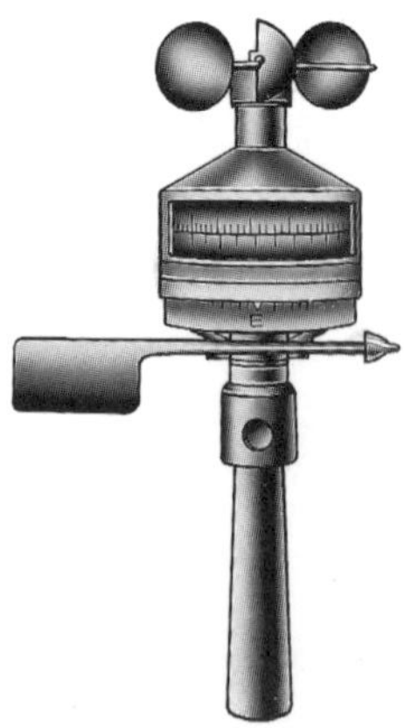

The anemometer, an instrument which measures wind speed.

anecdote *n.* a short story, account of an amazing or amusing nature.
anemometer *n.* instrument used to measure wind speed.
anemone (*an-em-on-ee*) *n.* cultivated or woodland flower of which there are many species.
angel *n.* a messenger from God. **angelic** *adj.*
anger *n.* bad temper, fury, rage. **angry** *adj.*
angle *n.* the space between two straight lines or surfaces that meet.
angler *n.* a person who fishes with hook and line as sport.
Anglican *n.* member of the Church of England or an episcopal church.
Anglo- *prefix* meaning English, e.g. **Anglo-French Treaty**.
anguish *n.* extreme distress.
animal *n.* any living thing that is not a plant.
animosity *n.* extreme dislike, hatred.
ankle *n.* the joint between the leg and the foot.
annex *vb.* seize, take possession of (territory). **annexe** *n.* additional building.
annihilate *vb.* destroy completely.
anniversary *n.* a day on which an event is remembered each year, like the anniversary of a wedding.
announce *vb.* tell; declare; make known; present (a person or event). *She announced that she was leaving at once.* **announcement** *n.* **announcer** *n.* (especially in radio) a person who reads the news.
annoy *vb.* make someone cross or angry, irritate.
annual 1. *adj.* happening every year. *Christmas is an annual event.* 2. *n.* a plant that lives for one year only.
annul *vb.* abolish, cancel.
anoint *vb.* smear with oil, especially in a religious ceremony.
anomaly *n.* exceptional or irregular condition.
anonymous *adj.* without (the author's) name. *This poem is anonymous.*
anorak *n.* a waterproof jacket, now usually made of plastic material, with a hood.
anorexia *n.* a chronic lack of appetite for food.
another *adj.* one more; a different one. *Have another glass of lemonade. That is quite another thing.*
answer 1. *n.* & *vb.* reply to a question. 2. *n.* the solution to a problem.
ant *n.* a small insect that lives with many other ants.

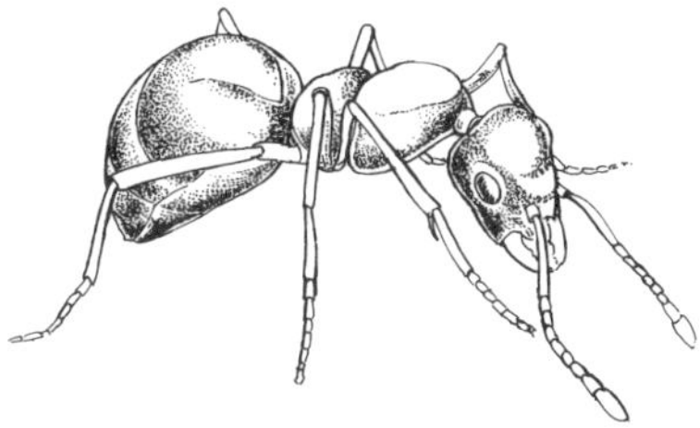

An ant. Because ants live in large colonies, they are called social insects.

antagonism *n.* hostility, dislike. **antagonist** *n.* opponent. **antagonize** *vb.* cause dislike, hostility.

The anteater lives in the tropical forests and swamps of South America.

Antarctic *adj.* & *n.* (of) the South Polar regions.

ante- *prefix* meaning before, e.g. **antenatal** before birth, **ante-room** a room leading into another room.

anteater *n.* a toothless mammal of South America. It has a tapering snout specially shaped for winkling out ants etc.

antelope *n.* an animal like a deer with long horns.

antenna (plural **antennae** pronounced *an*-**ten**-*ee*) *n.* 1. one of a pair of feelers on an insect's or a lobster's head. 2. an aerial.

anthropology *n.* the study of all aspects of people.

anti- *prefix* meaning against or opposed to, e.g. **anticlimax**, **anticlockwise**.

antibiotic *n.* a drug which helps destroy harmful bacteria. *Penicillin is an antibiotic.*

anticipate *vb.* 1. expect. *We did not anticipate that you would get here so quickly.* 2. do something first. *Do not anticipate the question before I have finished asking it.* **anticipation** *n.*

antifreeze *n.* a substance used to lower the freezing point of water in car engines.

antique (*ant*-**eek**) *adj.* very old. *n.* a very old object. *Antiques are often valuable.*

antiseptic *n.* & *adj.* a substance, such as chlorine, that kills certain kinds of germ. *The doctor cleaned the child's cut knee with an antiseptic.*

antithesis *n.* the opposite of something or contrast of ideas.

antler *n.* the branched horn of a deer.

antonym *n.* a word which has the opposite meaning to another. e.g. long, short.

anvil *n.* a block on which a blacksmith hammers metal into shape.

anxiety *n.* uneasy feeling of uncertainty. **anxious** *adj.*

any *adj.* some. *I haven't got any money.*

anybody *n.* (also **anyone**) any person; no matter who. *Can anybody tell me the time?*

Anzac *n.* & *adj.* Australian and New Zealand Army Corps in the 1914–18 War. **Anzac Day** 25 April.

apart *adv.* away from each other; distant. *Our houses are two kilometres apart.*

apartheid *n.* in South Africa the political system of total separation of Europeans from other races.

apartment *n.* a flat; a set of rooms in a building.

apathy *n.* lack of interest, indifference.

ape 1. *n.* a large monkey-like animal with no tail. 2. *vb.* imitate, mimic.

aperture *n.* opening or gap.

aphid *n.* tiny soft-bodied insect which does great harm to plants.

apologize *vb.* express regret for doing something wrong. **apology** *n.*

apostle *n.* any of the 12 chosen by Jesus Christ to preach the Gospel.

apostrophe (*a*-**pos**-*trofee*) *n.* a punctuation mark, like this ('). It is used when letters are left out (*don't* means *do not*) or when 's' is added to a word to show ownership. *That is John's bicycle.*

appal *vb.* horrify or shock greatly. *She was appalled by his rude behaviour.*

apparatus *n.* equipment for carrying out experiments.

apparent *adj.* obvious, clear.

apparition *n.* unusual or unexpected sight; a ghost.

appeal *vb.* 1. call for, make an earnest request. *The police appealed for witnesses to the crime.* 2. be attractive. *The idea appeals to me.*

appear *vb.* 1. come into sight. *A man appeared through the mist.* 2. seem to be. *A microscope makes things appear larger.* **appearance** *n.*

appease *vb.* calm, soothe.

appendicitis *n.* painful inflammation of the appendix.

appendix *n.* 1. part of the intestines. 2. addition to a book, at the end.

appetite *n.* the desire for food; hunger.

applaud *vb.* clap one's hands as a sign of enjoying something; praise. **applause** *n.*

apple *n.* the edible fruit of the apple tree.

appliance *n.* a piece of equipment for a special purpose. e.g. an attachment to a vacuum cleaner for cleaning difficult corners.

apply *vb.* 1. ask for something. *He applied for a job in the local factory.* 2. be relevant. *That rule does not apply in this case.*

appoint *vb.* choose someone to do a particular job.

appointment *n.* a time agreed for a meeting.

This aqueduct, the Pont du Gard in France, was built by the Romans.

appreciate *vb.* value highly, think much of; rise (in value). *Paintings appreciate rather than depreciate in value the longer you keep them.* **appreciative** *adj.* showing gratitude.

apprentice *n.* a person learning a craft or trade from an employer. **apprenticeship** *n.*

approach 1. *vb.* go near. *They approached the house.* 2. *n.* access; the means of getting to a place. *The approach to the house was through a wood.*

approve *vb.* express a good opinion of.

approximate *adj.* nearly correct. *I can give you the approximate cost.*

apricot *n.* an orange-yellow fruit with a big hard seed.

April *n.* the fourth month of the year.

apron *n.* a piece of cloth or plastic worn in front of and over clothes to keep them clean.

apse *n.* a semi-circular end to a church.

apt *adj.* suitable.

aptitude *n.* talent or ability.

aqualung *n.* breathing apparatus for swimming under water.

aquarium *n.* a place where fish and other water animals and plants are kept and studied. *aqua* is the Latin name for water.

aquatic *adj.* growing or living in water; taking place in or on water.

aqueduct *n.* a channel or pipe for carrying water, often a bridge, across a valley.

arc *n.* a curved line; part of a circle.

arcade *n.* row of arches supported by columns.

arch *n.* a curved structure of stones that can support a load, used to cover an opening such as a doorway, or the ceiling of a church.

arch- *prefix* meaning chief, principal, e.g. **archbishop, arch-villain**.

archaeology (**ark**-*i-ology*) *n.* the study of history through the things that people have made and built. **archaeologist** *n.*

archaeopteryx *n.* a prehistoric bird about the size of a crow, with teeth like a lizard.

archaic (*ar*-**kay**-*ik*) *adj.* ancient, no longer in use, antiquated.

archer *n.* a person who shoots with a bow and arrow.

archery *n.* the sport of shooting with a bow.

archipelago (*ark-i*-**pel**-*ago*) *n.* a group of islands; an area of sea containing many islands.

architecture *n.* style of buildings. **architectural** *adj.*

archives (**ark**-*ives*) *pl. n.* public records; place where the records are kept. **archivist** *n.* person who keeps the records.

Arctic *adj.* & *n.* (of) the North Polar regions.

ardour *n.* enthusiasm, warmth. **ardent** *adj.*

arduous *adj.* difficult to do.

area *n.* 1. the size of a surface. Areas are measured in units such as square metres, hectares, square yards and acres. *A football pitch is about 6000 square metres in area.* 2. part of a country or the world. *They come from the Detroit area.*

arena *n.* a sports stadium; originally the enclosed space in which the Ancient Roman games took place.

argue (*arg-yoo*) *vb.* dispute; give reasons why you support something. *They argue their case well.* **argument** *n.* reason put forward, **argumentative** *adj.* fond of arguing.

arid *adj.* dry; parched with heat.

arise *vb.* get up; come up for consideration.

aristocracy *n.* nobility.

arithmetic *n.* sums; the science of numbers.

ark *n.* 1. ship or large boat,

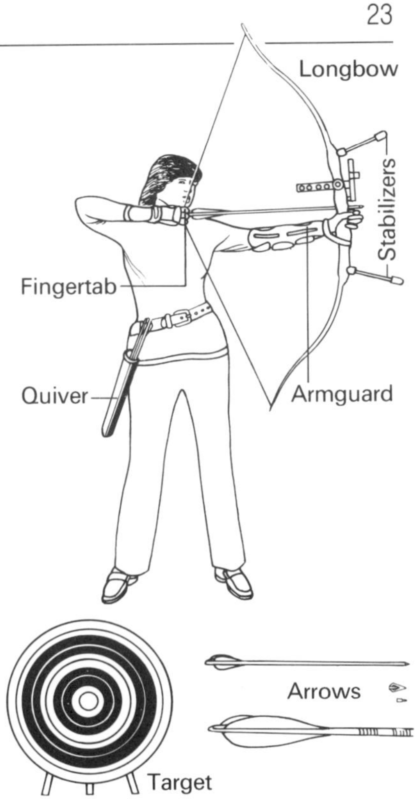

An archer uses a longbow to shoot arrows at a target.

particularly Noah's Ark. 2. the wooden chest in which the Jewish Tablets of the Law were kept (the Ark of the Covenant).

arm 1. *vb.* give weapons to. *They will arm the soldiers with the latest weapons.* 2. *n.* part of the body from the shoulder to the hand.

armada *n.* a Spanish word for a great fleet of armed ships.

armadillo *n.* a small South American mammal protected by a shell of bony scales.

armed forces *pl. n.* the army, navy and air force of a country.

armistice *n.* a truce, an agreement to stop fighting.

armour *n.* a covering, usually made of metal, that protects the body in battle.

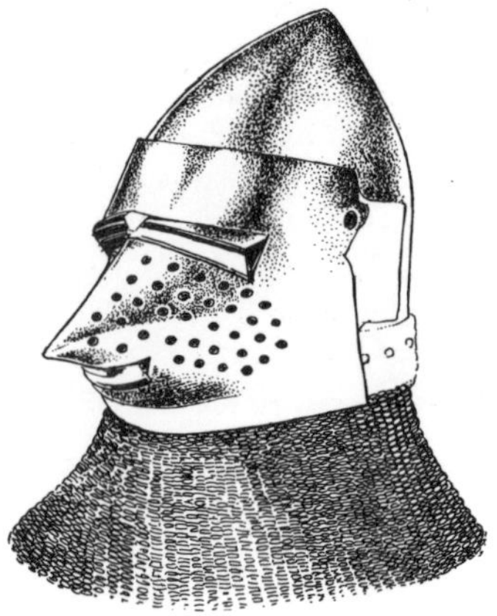

A helmet – part of a suit of armour.

army (plural **armies**) *n.* a large number of soldiers.

aroma *n.* a smell – usually pleasant or belonging to something in particular.

arose past of **arise**.

around 1. *adv.* on all sides. *She looked around but could see nobody.* 2. *prep.* in a circle; in all directions. *We walked around the old town.*

arouse *vb.* wake up, stir to action.

arrange *vb.* fix or organize something; put things in order. **arrangement** *n.*

array *n.* arrangement, display. *There was a lovely array of flowers on the table.*

arrest *vb.* take a suspected criminal into custody.

arrive *vb.* reach a place. *The train arrived at the station.* **arrival** *n.* reaching a place.

arrogant *adj.* exaggerating one's own importance; conceited; full of pride.

arrow *n.* a pointed stick that is shot from a bow.

arsenal *n.* a place where weapons and ammunition are stored or made.

arsenic *n.* a chemical element, a form of which (white arsenic) is extremely poisonous.

arson *n.* a name used in law for the crime of deliberately setting fire to property.

art *n.* drawing, painting and modelling, and the things that are made that way.

artery *n.* one of the tubes that carries blood from the heart to all parts of the body.

arthritis *n.* painful inflammation of a body joint causing severe stiffness.

arthropod *n.* group of animals which includes insects, spiders and crabs.

artichoke *n.* name applied to two different plants: (Jerusalem) plant with edible tuber; (globe) thistle-like plant, the flowerhead of which is eaten.

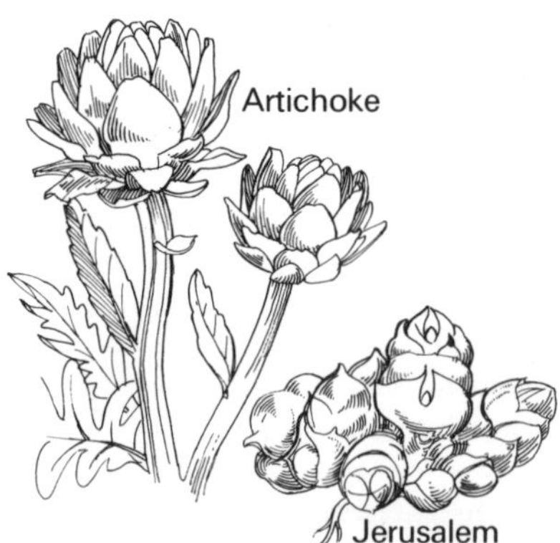

article *n*. 1. any object. 2. a passage in a newspaper, encyclopedia etc. 3. the words 'a, an' (indefinite article) and 'the' (definite article).
articulate *adj*. 1. clear and distinct of speech. *vb*. speak clearly. 2. having joints. *An articulated lorry*. *vb*. connect by joints.
artificial (*art-i-***fish***-el*) *adj*. not natural, made by people and machines; not grown. *Natural rubber comes from the juice of a tree, but artificial rubber is made from coal.*
artillery *n*. the big guns used by an army.
artist *n*. a person who draws, paints or carves. **artistic** *adj*.
as 1. *adv*. to the same extent. *Please do it as soon as possible.* (Also used in proverbial phrases. *The baby was as good as gold.*) 2. *conj*. because. *As she is sick, you will have to go.*
asbestos *n*. the name given to a group of minerals that occur naturally as fibres. Because asbestos does not burn, it is used for fireproof materials.
ascent *n*. the act of going up a slope or hill.
ascertain (*ass-sur-tane*) *vb*. find out, make sure.
ash *n*. 1. the powder that is left after something has been burned. 2. a tall tree with greyish bark and tough white wood.
ashamed *adj*. feeling guilty or disgraced.
ashet (*Sc.*) *n*. meat dish.
Ash Wednesday first day of Lent in the Christian Church.
aside *adv*. apart; on one side. *I shall put this book aside for you.*
ask *vb*. put a question, enquire; make a request. *She asked her boss for more pay.*
asleep *adj*. & *adv*. the state of sleeping; not awake. *They were all asleep in bed when the phone rang.*
asp *n*. a small poisonous snake.
aspect *n*. a view, a look; the direction in which a house faces.
asphalt *n*. a brown or black tarry substance, used for surfacing roads.
aspidistra *n*. indoor pot-plant with broad pointed leaves.

aspiration *n*. ambition. **aspire** *vb*. aim high.
aspirin *n*. a drug used to reduce pain.
ass *n*. a donkey, especially a wild one.
assassinate *vb*. murder a public figure. **assassin** *n*.
assault *vb*. attack someone. *n*. an attack.

assemble *vb*. collect together a number of people or things; put the parts of something together to make a whole. **assembly** *n*.
assent *vb*. agree. *n*. formal consent.
assert *vb*. declare, maintain.
assign *vb*. appoint; give someone their share. **assignment** *n*. a task.
assist *vb*. help someone. **assistance** *n*.
association *n*. a group of people or organizations that works together. **associate** *vb*. join, connect.
assorted *adj*. mixed, various.
assume *vb*. 1. take for granted as true. *We assume the facts are correct*. 2. take upon oneself. *She has assumed far too much responsibility*. **assumption** *n*.
assure *vb*. promise, make certain. *She assured me that she had posted the letter*.
asterisk *n*. a star-shaped mark (*), often used in books to refer to footnotes.
astern *adv*. at or behind the stern, or rear, of a boat.
asthma *n*. a medical condition which causes difficulty in breathing.
astonish *vb*. amaze; surprise.
astound *vb*. surprise, shock.
astray *adv*. in the wrong direction; lost. *My notes seem to have gone astray*.
astrology *n*. the study of the stars in order to predict the future.
astronaut *n*. a traveller in space.
astronautics *n*. the science of space travel.
astronomy *n*. the study of the Sun, planets, Moon and stars. **astronomer** *n*. a student or expert in astronomy.
astute *adj*. shrewd, crafty.
asylum *n*. refuge, shelter. Once a place for treating people with mental illness.
ate *vb*. past of **eat**.
atheist *n*. a person who does not believe that there is a God. **atheism** *n*. disbelief in God.
athlete *n*. someone who is good at sports or games that need strength or speed. **athletic** *adj*.
atlas *n*. a book of maps.
atmosphere *n*. the air around the earth.
atoll *n*. a coral island with a central lagoon, or lake.

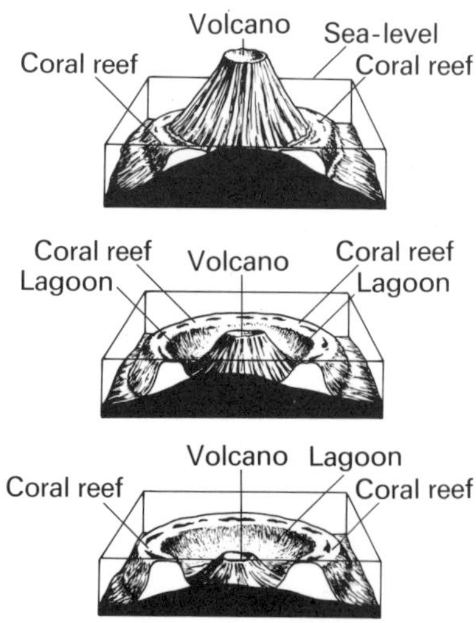

How coral reefs grow round a volcanic island to form an atoll.

atom *n*. the smallest particle of a chemical element.
atrocious *adj*. cruel, wicked; very bad. **atrocity** (*at*-**tross**-*ity*) *n*. wicked act; (*casual*) ugly object.

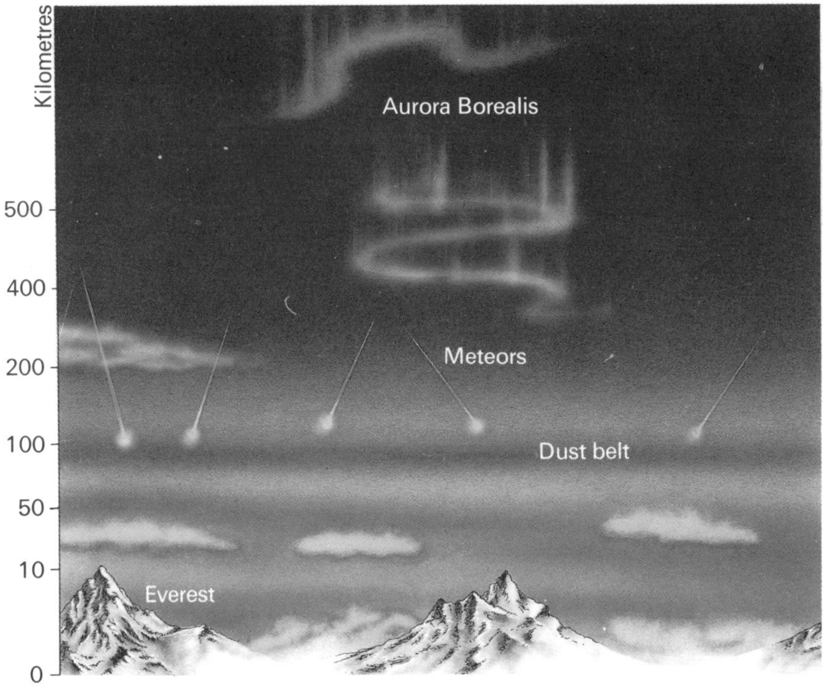

attach *vb.* fasten or join one thing to another.

attack *vb.* try to hurt a person or capture a place. *The soldiers planned to attack the castle.*

attain *vb.* reach, arrive at, accomplish. **attainment** *n.* accomplishment.

attempt *vb.* try to do something. *Jack will attempt the climb tomorrow.*

attend *vb.* 1. be present. **attendance** *n.* 2. give thought to. *Please attend to what I am saying.* **attention** *n.*

attic *n.* a room in the roof of a house.

attitude *n.* way of thinking, opinion.

attorney *n.* 1. (US) lawyer. 2. person authorized to act on behalf of someone else in legal matters etc.

The atmosphere gives us oxygen to breathe, it keeps the Earth's temperature at the right level and it shields us from most of the Sun's harmful rays. It also reflects most radio signals back to Earth.

attract *vb.* pull towards; have an appeal for. **attraction** *n.* **attractive** *adj.*

auction *n.* a public sale at which the asking price is raised until a buyer is found. *vb.* sell by auction. **auctioneer.** *n.*

audible *adj.* loud enough to be heard.

audience *n.* people who watch a play or listen to music together; a formal interview.

auditorium *n.* part of concert hall or theatre where audience sits.

August *n.* the eighth month of the year.

aunt *n.* the sister of your mother or father. Also your uncle's wife.
austere *adj.* stern; without luxury; severe. **austerity** *n.*
authentic *adj.* genuine, reliable.
author (**aw**-*ther*) *n.* a person who writes a book or a play.
authority *n.* 1. power over others. 2. an expert. *She was an authority on Shakespeare.*
auto- *prefix* meaning self, e.g. **automobile** (self moving).
autobiography *n.* the story of a person's life written by that person.
autograph *n.* someone's name written in their own handwriting. *Georgia collected the autographs of famous authors.*
automatic *adj.* working without being looked after, like an automatic washing machine.
automation *n.* the control by machine of the process of manufacturing goods.
automobile *n.* a motor car.
autopsy *n.* post-mortem, examination of a body after death.
autumn *n.* the season of the year between summer and winter. **autumnal** *adj.*
avail *vb.* help, benefit.
available *adj.* obtainable, ready to be used.
avalanche *n.* a great mass of snow and rocks sliding down a mountain.
avarice *n.* greed for wealth or gain.
avenge *vb.* take vengeance; get satisfaction for a wrong by punishing the wrongdoer.
avenue *n.* a road with trees on both sides; a broad street in a town.
average 1. *adj.* normal; usual. 2. *n.* a mathematical word. To find the average of 2, 4 and 6 you add them together and divide by 3. The answer is 4.
averse *adj.* opposed (*to*); unwilling.
aviary *n.* a place in which birds are kept, often a large cage or a building containing cages.
aviation *n.* (science) of flying in a powered plane.

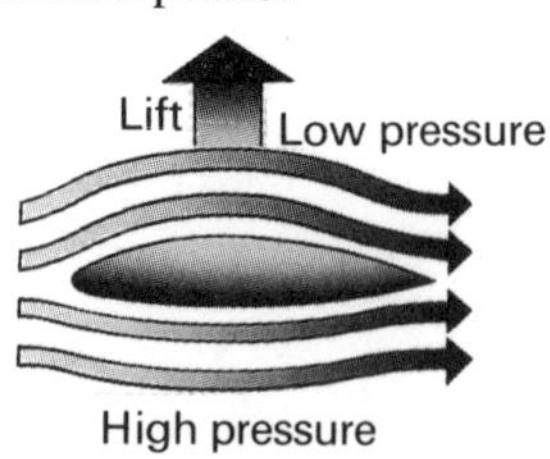

When the lift is greater than the weight of the aircraft it is lifted off the ground.

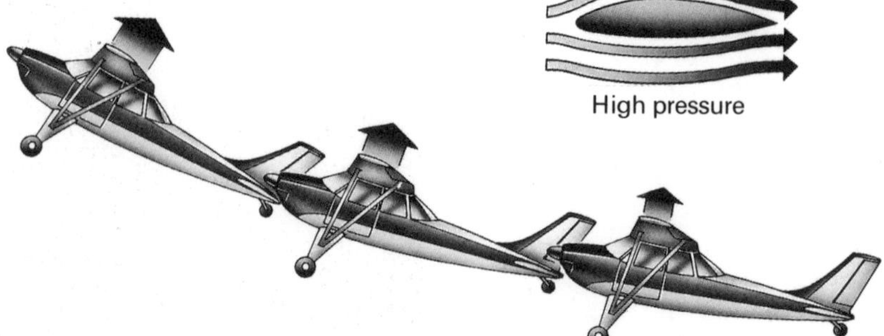

avid *adj*. eager, greedy.
avocado *n*. a pulpy green fruit with a large stone which grows on several kinds of tropical tree.

avoid *vb*. keep out of the way of someone or something; fail to do something. *She was deliberately avoiding him.*
await *vb*. wait for someone or something.
awake *adv*. not sleeping.
award *vb*. give someone a prize or distinction, *n*. a prize.
aware *adj*. conscious; knowing. *Aware of dangers.*
away *adv*. 1. at a distance; far off. *Do not throw it away.* 2. continuously. *Sing away.*
awe *n*. respect mixed with fear. *The soldier stood in awe of the general.*
awful *adj*. terrible; dreadful; nasty.
awkward *adj*. clumsy; uncomfortable; difficult.
awning *n*. covering, often of canvas, to protect against weather.
axe *n*. tool for chopping wood.
axle *n*. the rod on which a wheel turns.
ayatollah *n*. a Muslim religious leader.
azure *n*. & *adj*. the unclouded sky; sky-blue.

B

babble *n*. & *vb*. chatter, prattle.
baboon *n*. a large kind of monkey.
baby *n*. a very young child. also **babe**.
baby-sitter *n*. a person who is paid to look after a child or children while the parent(s) are out.
bachelor *n*. an unmarried man; someone who has taken a first university degree–*B.A.; B.Sc.* (Bachelor of Arts, Bachelor of Science etc).
back 1. *n*. the part of the body from the neck to the bottom. 2. *n*. the side opposite to the front. 3. *vb*. move backwards. *Ask her to back the car.* 4. *vb*. support. *I back your decision.* 5. *vb*. bet on *She backed a loser.*

The Ayatollah Khomeini.

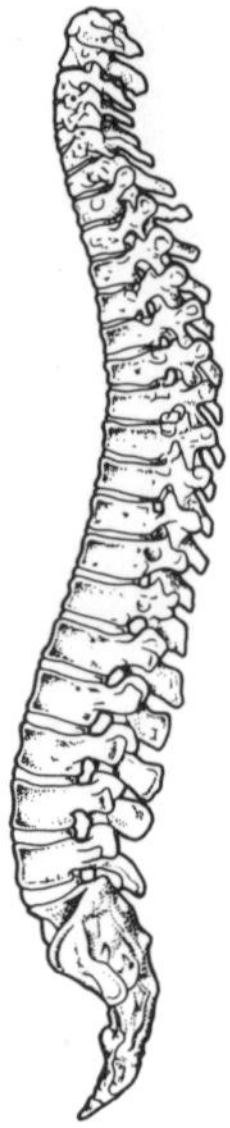

The backbone or spine is made up of 26 small bones called vertebrae. Down the centre runs the spinal cord.

backbone *n.* the bones that run down the back of a skeleton; the spine.
backcloth *n.* main part of stage scenery.
backer *n.* a supporter.
backgammon *n.* a game for two people played on a board with 15 light and 15 dark draughts which are moved according to the fall of dice.
background *n.* the part of a scene or picture that is behind all the rest or in the distance; a person's education etc.
backstage *adv.* behind the scenes at the theatre.
backward(s) *adv.* towards the back, opposite of forward(s). *adj.* directed backwards; slow in learning.
bacon *n.* smoked or salted meat from the back and side of a pig.
bacteria *pl. n.* tiny living things that can only be seen with a powerful microscope.
bad *adj.* not good, faulty, wicked.
badge *n.* something worn by a person, usually with a picture or message on it; an emblem. *Badges often show that a person belongs to a school or club.*
badger *n.* a dog-sized nocturnal mammal with white marks on its forehead and cheeks.
badly *adv.* incorrectly; to a serious extent. *The house badly needs repairing.*
badminton *n.* a game that is played with rackets, like tennis, but with a shuttlecock instead of a ball.
baffle *vb.* bewilder, mystify.
bag *n.* a sack or pouch; a handbag; the animals or birds a hunter has shot. *vb.* capture, seize.
baggy *adj.* hanging loosely.
bagpipes *n. pl.* a musical instrument with a windbag and pipes.
bail 1. *n.* money or other security given to free an accused person before their trial. *He was released on bail of £1000. vb.* (out) secure temporary release of; drop from aircraft by parachute (also spelled *bale*). 2. *n.* one of a pair of cross pieces on the top of the stumps in cricket. 3. *vb.* scoop water out of a boat.
bait *n.* food used to attract fish or animals so that they can be caught. *vb.* set a trap; tease.
baize *n.* woollen cloth, often green, used to cover a table.

bake *vb.* cook in the oven.
baker *n.* a person who makes cakes and bread and sells them. **bakery** *n.* a place where bread is baked and may be sold.
baking powder *n.* a white powder used in cooking to make cakes light and spongy.
balalaika *n.* Russian stringed instrument.

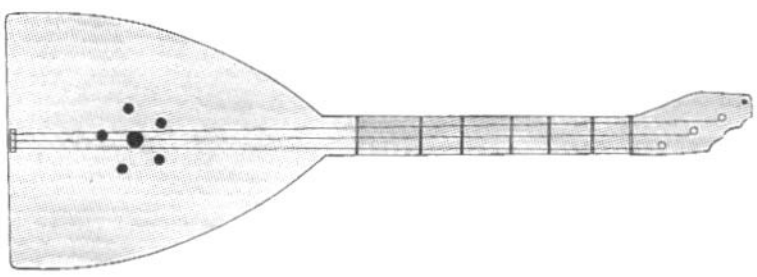

A balalaika has three strings.

balance 1. *vb.* keep steady. *Roger balanced the book on his head.* 2. *n.* an instrument for weighing.
balcony *n.* a platform or gallery attached to an outside wall.
bald (rhymes with *called*) *adj.* without hair. **baldness** *n.*
bale *n.* a large bundle. *vb.* pack into bundles.
ball *n.* 1. a round object, often used in games. 2. a dance.
ballad *n.* a simple poem or song that tells a story.
ballast *n.* a heavy material, such as sand or water, used to fill the storage areas of an empty cargo ship.
ballerina *n.* a female ballet dancer.
ballet (**bal**-*ay*) *n.* a stage show that usually tells a story with dance and music.
ballistics *pl. n.* the study of the movement of bullets, shells, and other projectiles.
balloon *n.* a bag of thin material filled with air or gas.
ballot *n.* a method of voting secretly.
ballpoint *adj.* & *n.* a kind of pen with a ball in place of a nib.
balm *n.* a healing ointment; a soothing influence. **balmy** *adj.* mild.
bamboo *n.* giant grass, growing in tropical lands.
ban 1. *n.* a prohibition; something that is forbidden. 2. *vb.* forbid; outlaw. *Cars are banned in the park.*
banal *adj.* commonplace, trite **banality** *n.*
banana *n.* a long, thin tropical fruit with a yellow skin when ripe.
band 1. *n.* a thin strip of material for fastening things together. 2. *n.* a group of people who do things together. 3. *vb.* a group of musicians.
bandage *n.* a strip of material for covering a wound. *vb.* tie up with a bandage.

Items made of bamboo.

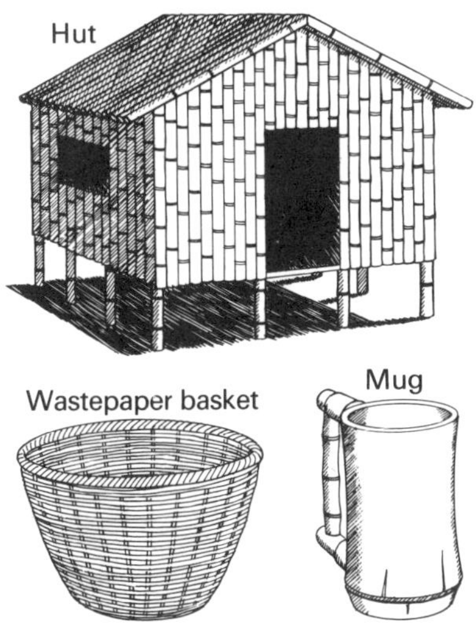

The bandicoot is a marsupial, a mammal which carries its young in a pouch.

bandicoot *n.* a rat-like marsupial of Australia and New Guinea.
bandit *n.* a robber, often working in a group or band.
bandy 1. *adj.* having curved legs. 2. *vb.* hurl from one person to another.
bang 1. *vb.* beat violently. 2. *n.* a sudden loud noise.
banish *vb.* send someone away from (a country); exile. **banishment** *n.*
banister(s) *n.* rail(s) up the sides of staircases.
banjo *n.* a stringed musical instrument that is similar to a guitar.
bank *n.* 1. sloping ground. 2. land along the side of a river. 3. a place where people keep money; a business that specializes in money. **banker** *n.* director of a bank.
bankrupt *n.* & *adj.* (someone) unable to pay debts. *vb.* make bankrupt.
banner *n.* a flag.
banns *pl. n.* official announcement of an intended forthcoming marriage and read out in church.
banquet (**bang**-*kwet*) *n.* a feast or official dinner with speeches.
bap (*Sc.*) *n.* a bread roll.
baptism *n.* the Christian ceremony of christening someone, usually a child, by pouring water on the forehead. **baptize** *vb.* give baptism.
bar 1. *n.* a long piece of hard material. 2. *n.* counter at which refreshments are served; a room with a bar serving drinks. 3. *vb.* to stop someone going through. *The man tried to bar our way into the park.*
barbarian *n.* a rough, uncivilized person. (In the Ancient World a barbarian meant someone who was neither Greek nor Roman.) **barbaric** *adj.* cruel. **barbarity** *n.* savage cruelty.
barbecue *n.* a frame for roasting meat etc; an outdoor party at which such food is cooked and served. *vb.* roast food on a barbecue.
barber *n.* a person who cuts men's hair.
bare 1. *adj.* naked; not covered. 2. *vb.* expose. *The dog bared its teeth.* 3. *adj.* empty. *The room looked bare without its furniture.* **barely** *adv.* only just, scarcely.
bargain 1. *n.* something bought cheap. 2. *vb.* haggle; argue over the price.
barge 1. *n.* a flat-bottomed boat used on canals and rivers. 2. *vb.* knock into.
baritone *n.* & *adj.* male singing voice between tenor and bass.
bark 1. *n.* & *vb.* the sharp noise made by a dog. 2. *n.* outer covering of a tree.
barley *n.* a cereal plant.

bar-mitzvah *n.* Jewish boy of 13; the religious ceremony for the boy.
barn *n.* a farm building for animals or for storing grain or hay.
barnacle *n.* a small sea creature with a soft body surrounded by hard, bony plates.
barometer *n.* an instrument for measuring air pressure.
baron *n.* a lord; a peer. (In Britain a baron is the lowest rank of the peerage.) **baroness** *n.* female peer in her own right or the wife of a baron.
baroque *n.* & *adj.* a heavily decorated European style of architecture, about 1600 to 1750.
barrack 1. *n.* a building where soldiers live. 2. *vb.* jeer.
barrage *n.* dam built across a river.
barrel *n.* 1. a container with curved sides. 2. the tube of a gun.

A batter prepares to bat in a game of baseball.

barren *adj.* bare, sterile; unable to bear offspring.
barricade *n.* a hastily built fortification across the road etc. *vb.* fortify in haste.
barrier *n.* a fence or rail; an obstacle.
barrister *n.* a lawyer who can plead in the higher courts.
barrow *n.* 1. a small cart, usually with one wheel, used in gardening. 2. a prehistoric burial mound.
barter *vb.* exchange goods for other goods without using money; swop.
base 1. *n.* the part of an object on which it stands. 2. *n.* a headquarters. 3. *vb.* establish, found.
baseball *n.* an American game played with a ball and bat by two teams of nine players each, who compete to score the greatest number of runs in nine innings.
basement *n.* a floor of a building below the ground.
bash *vb.* strike violently, smash.
bashful *adj.* shy.

basic *adj*. fundamental, forming the base.
basil *n*. an aromatic herb.
basilica *n*. a church in the form of a long oblong hall with apse at one end and two colonnades; a Roman Catholic church with special privileges.
basin *n*. 1. a container for holding water or other liquid; a bowl for washing one's hands. 2. (in geography) the land drained by a river.
basis *n*. (plural **bases**) foundation; principle.
basket *n*. a container, often made from cane. Some baskets are used for carrying shopping etc. Others are used for waste paper.
basketball *n*. a game in which two teams of five players each attempt to score points by throwing a ball through one of two metal rings placed above each end of a rectangular court.

Basketball players. The game is very popular in the USA.

bass *n*. 1. (rhymes with *case*) lowest male singing voice. 2. (rhymes with *mass*) a sea fish.
bassoon *n*. a large musical wind instrument that makes low notes.
bastard *n*. the child of unmarried parents (often used offensively).
baste *vb*. pour fat over roasting meat.
bat 1. *n*. a small mouse-like flying animal. 2. *n*. a piece of wood for hitting a ball. *vb*. hit a ball with a bat.
batch *n*. a number of cakes or loaves baked together; a group of things that come together. *We must answer this batch of letters*.
bath *n*. a large basin for washing the whole body; a swimming bath. *vb*. wash oneself in a bath.
bathe *vb*. swim or wash. **bather** *n*.
bathroom *n*. a room containing a bath, for washing.
bathyscaphe *n*. an underwater vessel for exploring the ocean depths.
batik *n*. an Eastern method of producing designs on cloth with the use of wax and dyes.
baton *n*. the stick a conductor uses to beat time for an orchestra.
batter 1. *vb*. hit very hard. 2. *n*. a mixture of flour, eggs and milk cooked to make pancakes etc.
battery (plural **batteries**) 1. *n*. a container for storing electricity. 2. *n*. two to six guns which work together.

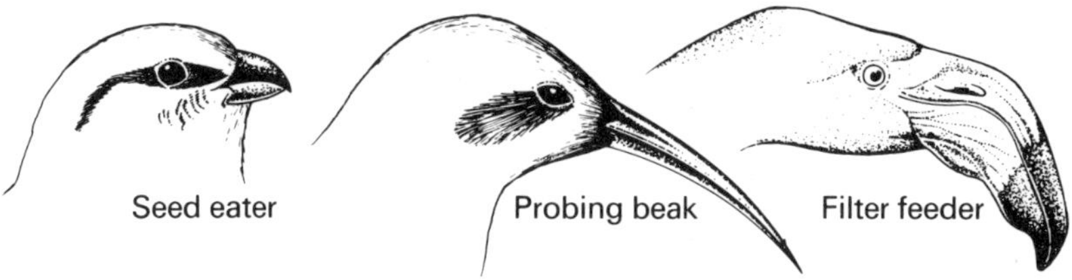

Birds' beaks are many different shapes and are suited to the type of food each bird eats.

battle *n.* a fight between two armies. *vb.* fight, struggle. *The wind was so strong, we had to battle against it.*
battleship *n.* a large, heavily armoured naval ship with batteries of guns.
bauxite *n.* a clay which is the chief source of the metal aluminium.
bay 1. *n.* part of the sea shore that makes a wide curve inward. 2. *n.* a kind of laurel. 3. *n.* a recess, e.g. a bay window. 4. *vb.* cry made by hounds. 5. *n.* & *adj.* reddish-brown horse.
bayonet *n.* a blade which can be attached to the end of a rifle.
bazaar (*be*-**zar**) *n.* 1. a market in Eastern countries. 2. a sale to raise money.
BC *abbrev.* time before Jesus Christ was born.
be *vb.* have some quality; exist. *When will you be free?*
beach *n.* the shore between the high and low tide marks; the edge of the sea or lake.
beacon *n.* a warning or signal light or fire.
bead *n.* a small piece of wood, glass or other material with a hole through it. *Beads are used to thread on string to make necklaces and other jewellery.*
beagle *n.* small hound used in hunting hares.
beak *n.* the hard outer part of a bird's mouth.
beaker *n.* a cup with no handle; a glass vessel used in chemistry.
beam 1. *n.* a big heavy bar used as a support in a building or in a ship. 2. *n.* a ray of light, like *the beam of a torch*. 3. *vb.* smile widely.
bean *n.* the fruit or seed of certain plants, eaten as food, and related to peas. *Broad beans; runner beans; French beans etc.*
bear 1. *n.* a large kind of furry mammal. 2. *vb.* tolerate, support or put up with something. *I can't bear the thought of it*. 3. *vb.* give birth to.
beard *n.* hair that grows on the lower part of a man's face.
bearing 1. *n.* way a person acts or moves. 2. *n. pl.* relative position. 3. *n.* part of a machine that supports moving parts and reduces friction.
beast *n.* an animal.
beat 1. *vb.* hit hard and often. *The cruel man beat the boy.* *n.* throb, pulse, rhythm. 2. *vb.* conquer or defeat. *John beat me at table tennis.*

beauty *n*. good looks, loveliness. *She was famous for her beauty*. **beautiful** *adj*. **beautify** *vb*.

beaver *n*. a furry, flat-tailed animal that lives on land and in the water.

became *vb*. past of **become**.

because *conj*. as a result of; for the reason that. *Do it because I say so*.

beckon *vb*. call by signs, make a silent signal.

become *vb*. grow to be. *He has become a strong athlete*.

bed *n*. 1. something to sleep on. 2. a place where flowers are planted. 3. bottom of the sea or river.

bedding *n*. sheets, blankets etc.; straw etc., for cattle to lie on.

bedeck *vb*. decorate, adorn.

bedouin *n*. a wandering desert tribe of Arabs.

bedroom *n*. a room with a bed or beds.

bee *n*. an insect that makes honey. People keep bees in a *beehive*.

beech *n*. a smooth, silvery-barked, glossy-leaved tree.

beef *n*. the meat of cattle. **beefy** *adj*. thick set, strong.

beehive *n*. a small box where bees are kept.

been *vb*. past participle of **be**.

beer *n*. a strong drink made from malted barley, flavoured with hops. *Ale and lager are both kinds of beer*.

beet *n*. a plant with an edible root, a variety of which is used to make sugar.

beetle *n*. an insect with hard wing covers.

before 1. *prep*. in front of. *Age before beauty*. 2. *conj*. at an earlier time; previous to. *They ran away before I could stop them*.

beg *vb*. ask someone for help, especially for money. **beggar** *n*. someone who begs.

began *vb*. past of **begin**.

begin *vb*. (**began** past; **begun** past part.) start doing something; commence. **beginning** *n*. **beginner** *n*.

behave *vb*. act in a particular way. *Sue behaved very badly at the party*. act well. *Try to behave*. **behaviour** *n*.

behead *vb*. cut someone's head off; execute someone in this way.

behind 1. *adv*. somewhere else; at the rear. *I left my book behind*. 2. *prep*. on the other side of something. *The burglar was hiding behind the curtain*.

beige *n*. & *adj*. a light brown colour.

being 1. *n*. a person. *A human being*. 2. *part*. in a certain state or situation. *Stop being so difficult*.

belch *vb*. let out wind from the stomach through the mouth; throw out smoke from a volcano.

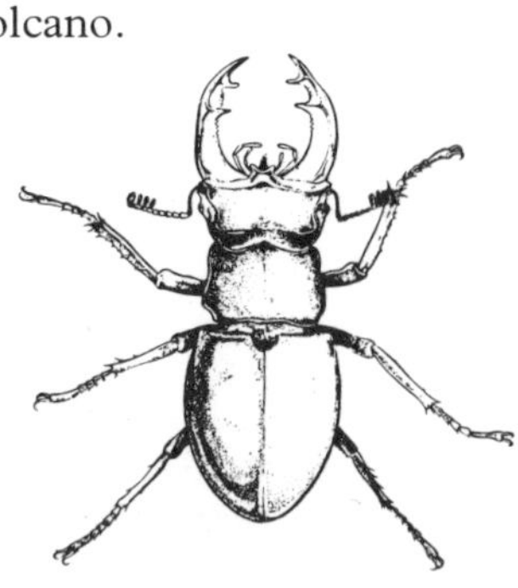

A stag beetle. There are more types of beetle than of any other insect.

A pair of bellows. These are used to pump air into a fire.

belfry *n*. bell tower.

believe *vb*. feel sure about the truth of something. **belief** *n*.

bell *n*. a hollow object which makes a musical sound when struck.

bellow *vb*. shout or roar; *n*. the noise made by a bull.

bellows *pl. n*. hand instrument for pumping air into a fire etc.

belly *n*. the stomach.

belong *vb*. be someone's property; be owned by someone. *Does this watch belong to you?*

belongings *pl. n*. possessions, one's property.

beloved 1. *n*. someone who is loved very much. 2. *adj*. much-loved.

below *prep*. & *adv*. underneath; lower than; beneath.

belt *n*. a strap of leather or other material worn around the waist; strap connecting wheels of machinery. *vb*. thrash, beat with a belt.

bemoan *v*. express sadness about something. *She bemoaned the loss of her purse.*

bench *n*. a long wooden seat, often without a back.

bend 1. *n*. a curve; not straight. 2. *vb*. curve over; lean over from upright.

bene- *prefix* meaning well.

benefactor *n*. someone who gives help.

benefit *n*. advantage. *She speaks perfect French because she has the benefit of living in France*; profit; pension, allowance. *vb*. do good to.

benign (*bi*-**nine**) *adj*. mild and gentle.

bent *vb*. past of **bend**.

bequeath *vb*. leave in a will. **bequest** *n*. what has been bequeathed.

beret (**ber**-*ray*) *n*. a round flat hat, common in France and Spain.

berry *n*. a small fruit with many seeds.

berserk *adj*. in a violent frenzy.

berth *n*. 1. a bunk or bed in a ship or train. 2. the place where a ship docks. *The ship was tied up at its berth.*

beside *prep*. at the side of, close to.

besides *adv*. as well; in addition.

besiege (*bi*-**seej**) *vb*. lay siege to a castle or fortress; to surround.

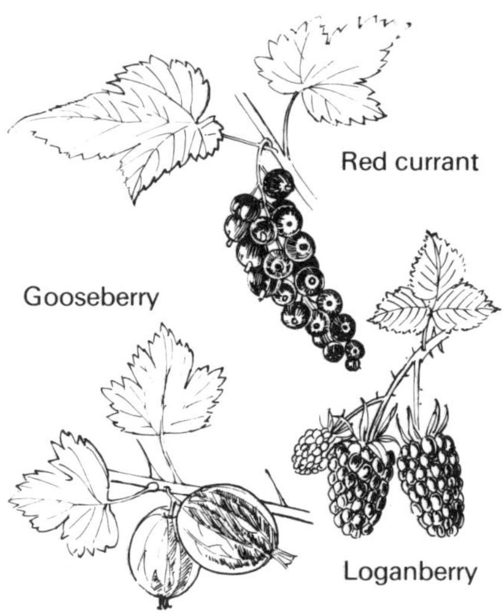

Types of berries.

best *adj*. of the finest quality; very good; excellent. *vb*. defeat, outwit.

bestial *adj*. like a beast; rude; cruel.

bet *vb*. & *n*. wager; put money on (a horse); assume something to be the case. *I bet you can't climb that wall.*

beta *n*. second letter of the Greek alphabet: ß.

betray *vb*. give someone up, or let them down; deceive. *The spy was betrayed to the enemy.* **betrayal** *n*.

better *adj*. improved; more suitable, recovering or having recovered health; *vb*. make better.

between *prep*. in the middle of. *The player kicked the ball straight between the goalposts.*

beverage *n*. any kind of drink. *Orangeade and beer are both beverages.*

beware *vb*. be warned. The sign said: *'Beware of the dog'*.

bewilder *vb*. confuse, puzzle, mystify. **bewildering** *adj*.

beyond *prep*. on the far side of. *Julia's house is beyond the church.*

bi- *prefix* meaning twice or double; appearing or occurring once in every two. e.g. **bilateral** with two sides, **bilingual** speaking two languages, **biped** two-footed animal etc.

bias *n*. a leaning towards, inclination; prejudice.

bib *n*. cloth or plastic shield placed under a child's chin to protect clothing.

Bible *n*. the sacred book of the Christian religion.

bicycle *n*. a two-wheeled vehicle powered by its rider.

bicker *vb*. quarrel in a pointless way.

bid 1. *vb*. offer to pay a price at an auction. 2. *n*. call (in card games). 3. *vb*. command.

bidet (*bee-day*) *n*. a low basin on which one sits to wash the lower part of the body. The word is French for 'pony'.

big *adj*. large; important.

bigot *n*. a person who obstinately sticks to a belief or opinion.

bikini *n*. a scanty two-piece bathing costume.

bill *n*. 1. a paper showing how much you owe for something you have bought. 2. a bird's beak.

billabong (*Austral.*) *n*. a stagnant pool or lake formed by an incomplete tributary of a river; an Aboriginal word meaning 'dead river'.

An Australian billabong.

A biplane is an aircraft with two sets of wings. Many of the earliest aircraft were biplanes, but these days there are only a few still flying.

billiards *n.* a game in which balls are struck by a cue into pockets at the edge of a flat table.

billion *n.* one thousand million (1,000,000,000). Sometimes used in Great Britain to mean one million million (1,000,000,000,000).

billycan (*Austral.*) *n.* a vessel of tin or enamel used as a kettle, or for cooking.

billygoat *n.* a male goat.

bin *n.* a container, such as a breadbin or dustbin.

binary *adj.* made up of two parts or units. In the binary arithmetic system only two numbers are used, 0 and 1.

bind *vb.* tie; make fast.

binding 1. *n.* book cover. 2. *adj.* obligatory.

bingo *n.* numbers game, also called housey-housey.

binoculars *n.* field glasses; an instrument to make things far away look closer. *You look through a pair of binoculars with both eyes.*

bio- *prefix* meaning life or of life.

biography *n.* the written story of a person's life.

biology *n.* the study of living things. **biologist** *n.*

biplane *n.* an aircraft with two sets of wings.

birch *n.* a tree with a slim trunk and branches, and a smooth bark.

bird *n.* the only feathered member of the animal kingdom, with front limbs adapted as wings.

birth *n.* coming into life; emergence of a child or animal from the body of its mother.

birth-control *n.* contraception, the prevention of pregnancy.

birthday *n.* the anniversary of a birth.

biscuit *n.* a small, flat, thin cake.

bisect *vb.* divide into two equal parts.

bishop *n.* 1. priest in charge of a diocese, or group of parishes. 2. a piece in chess.

bison *n.* a large, cow-like animal with a huge shaggy hump on its shoulders. In North America bison are often called buffalo.

bit *n.* 1. a small piece. 2. a metal bar that goes in a horse's mouth: part of the bridle. 3. single unit of information expressed in binary numbers, especially for computers.

bitch *n.* a female dog, fox or wolf.
bite *vb.* take a piece of something, usually food, with the teeth. *n.*
bitter *adj.* sharp, unpleasant taste; not sweet. **bitterness** *n.*
black 1. *n.* the darkest of all colours; the opposite of white. 2. *adj.* & *n.* belonging to the black-skinned groups of peoples.
blackball *vb.* vote against, exclude a candidate by putting a black ball in a ballot box.
blackberry *n.* the fruit of the bramble.
blackbird *n.* European songbird related to the thrush.
blackboard *n.* a board, usually painted black, which can be written on with chalk and is used for teaching.
black box *n.* electronic equipment on an aircraft which records details of the flight.
blackcurrant *n.* the small black fruit of a garden plant, much used to make drinks.
black hole *n.* the area in space where the pull of gravity is so strong that nothing can escape, not even light.
blackleg *n.* someone who continues to work when a strike is called.
black magic *n.* evil magic; witchcraft.
blackmail *n.* & *vb.* the crime of demanding money from someone in return for keeping something secret. *The man said that if I gave him £5 he would keep quiet about the window I broke. This was blackmail.* **blackmailer** *n.*
blackout *n.* temporary loss of consciousness.
black sheep *n.* scoundrel; member of a family who is a good for nothing.
blacksmith *n.* a person who works with iron and makes shoes for horses.
bladder *n.* the part of the body where liquid wastes gather before they are passed out.
blade *n.* the sharp cutting edge of knife, razor, sword etc.
blame *vb.* say that it was the fault of something or someone that something went wrong. *n.* responsibility for bad happening.
blanch *vb.* to make something white or pale in colour, or to become white.
blancmange (*blu*-**monj**) *n.* a kind of jelly or milk pudding.
bland *adj.* smooth; gentle, mild; dull.
blank *adj.* empty; with nothing written on it.
blanket *n.* a sheet of (usually thick) cloth used as a bed covering.
blare *vb.* make a loud noise; shout. *I can't hear you with that radio blaring.*
blaspheme *vb.* speak irreverently about God. **blasphemy** *n.*
blast *n.* a strong wind; the shock waves of an explosion.
blast furnace *n.* an enormous oven for producing iron from ore.
blast-off *n.* the moment when a rocket is launched into space.
blatant *adj.* noisy; obvious and obtrusive.
blaze 1. *n.* a white mark on the

face of an animal. 2. *vb.* to burn brightly.

blazer *n.* coloured jacket, often part of a school uniform.

blazon *n.* word used in heraldry for a coat of arms.

bleach 1. *vb.* to make white. 2. *n.* a chemical used to remove colour from things.

bleak *adj.* exposed, barren and often windswept.

bleat *vb.* & *n.* the cry of a sheep or goat.

bleed *vb.* lose blood.

bleep 1. *n.* a shrill noise at regular intervals. 2. *vb.* to make the sound of a bleep.

blemish *vb.* mark, spoil, *n.* stain; fault.

blend *vb.* mix two or more substances together; go well with something.

blenny *n.* a small fish with spiny fins.

bless *vb.* ask God to protect someone or something. **blessing** *n.*

blew *vb.* past of **blow**.

blight *n.* plant disease caused by fungus or insects.

blind 1. *adj.* not able to see. **blindness** *n.* 2. *n.* window cover. 3. *vb.* to make blind.

blindfold *adj.* & *adv.* having the eyes covered with a handkerchief etc. *vb.* cover eyes.

blink *vb.* shut and open eyes rapidly.

blinker *n.* leather flap on a bridle to prevent a horse seeing sideways.

bliss *n.* greatest happiness. **blissful** *adj.*

blister *n.* a swelling like a bubble on the skin, filled with a watery liquid.

blithe *adj.* happy or carefree. Usually used in poetry.

blitz *n.* & *vb.* attack from the air.

blizzard *n.* a snowstorm with very strong winds.

bloated *adj.* swollen, puffy.

A blast furnace is used to make iron. Iron ore is mixed with coke and limestone and then heated at a very high temperature.

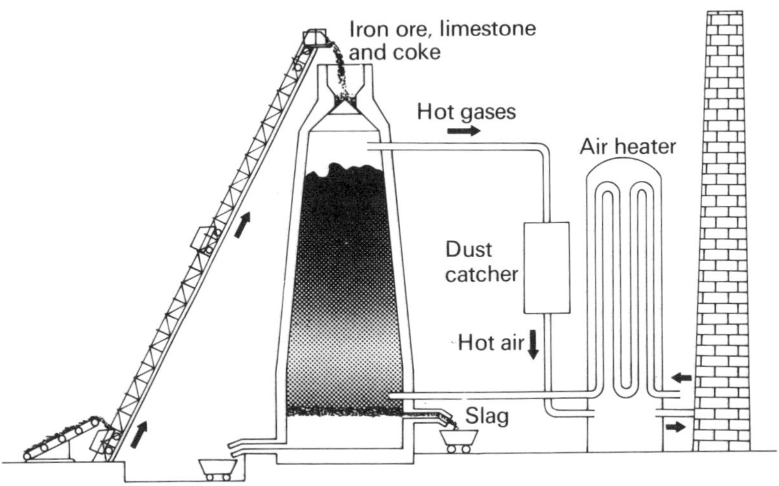

blob *n.* a drop; small round mass.

block 1. *n.* a large lump of something, e.g. wood or stone. 2. *n.* a large building of flats or offices. 3. *vb.* get in the way of. *A fallen tree can block a road.*

blockade *n.* cutting off of supplies to an enemy. *vb.*

blond *adj. n.* fair-haired or a fair-haired person. (When used of women: **blonde**.)

blood *n.* the red liquid that is pumped round our bodies by the heart.

bloodhound *n.* a large breed of dog, once used by the police for tracking criminals.

bloom *n.* flower; first freshness or beauty. *In the bloom of youth.* *vb.* bear blooms; flourish.

blossom *n.* flower or mass of flowers, especially on fruit trees.

blot *n.* an inky stain; a smudge or mark *vb.* make a blot on.

blouse *n.* a kind of loose shirt, usually worn by women.

blow 1. *n.* a hard knock. 2. *vb.* (past **blew**) make the air move. *The wind blows from the west.*

blubber 1. *n.* whale fat. 2. *vb.* weep. (shortened to **blub**).

blue *n.* & *adj.* the colour of a cloudless sky.

bluebell *n.* a name given to two different kinds of wild flower: the wild hyacinth and the harebell.

bluebottle *n.* a name given to several species of large fly, having a blue abdomen, and particularly attracted to rotting meat.

bluff 1. *vb.* deceive, make pretence. 2. *adj.* outspoken, blunt, frank and hearty.

blunder *n.* & *vb.* (make) a stupid mistake. *John made a blunder when he wrote 10 instead of 100.*

blunt *adj.* not sharp.

blur *n.* smudge; indistinct impression. *vb.* blot, obscure.

blurb *n.* publisher's description of a book, usually printed on the jacket.

blurt *vb.* speak out suddenly, in a rush.

blush *vb.* become red in the face because you are ashamed or shy.

boa 1. *n.* a family of large snakes, mainly from South America, which kill their prey by crushing it to death. 2. *n.* a long, tube-shaped scarf, made of fur or feathers, once worn by women.

boar (rhymes with *sore*) *n.* a male pig; wild pig.

board 1. *n.* a long flat piece of wood; a plank. 2. *n.* a flat piece of wood or card used for a special purpose. *A chess board is used for the game of chess.* 3. *n.* an authorized group of people, e.g. board of directors. 4. *vb.* get on to a ship, train or aircraft. *We must board the plane now.*

boast *vb.* talk about how good you think you are, brag.
boat *n.* a small or medium-sized vessel used for travelling on water. (The term 'ship' is used for larger vessels such as liners and warships.)
boater *n.* hard, flat straw hat.
boatswain (**bo**-*sun*) *n.* a senior member of a crew who controls the work of the rest of the crew.
bobble *n.* a small ball of material, often wool, used as a decoration.
bobby *n.* slang for a policeman.
body *n.* 1. the visible part of a person or animal. 2. a group of people. 3. the main part of something. 4. an astronomical object. *A star is sometimes called a heavenly body*. **bodily** *adj.* of the body.
bodyguard *n.* person employed to protect someone.
bog *n.* spongy ground, a marsh.
bog down *vb.* overwhelm with work.
bogus *adj.* false, sham.
boil 1. *vb.* heat a liquid until it bubbles and steams. 2. *n.* painful swelling on the body.
boisterous *adj.* noisy, lively.
bold *adj.* showing no fear.
Bolshevik *n.* a member of the Russian revolutionary party that seized power in 1917. **Bolshevism** *n.*
bolt 1. *n.* a metal fastening on a door or window. 2. *n.* a metal pin with a screw at one end that goes into a nut to fasten things. 3. *vb.* run away quickly.
bomb *n.* a container filled with explosive. *vb.* attack with bombs. **bomber** *n.* aircraft using bombs.
bombard *vb.* attack with gunfire; abuse.
bond *n.* 1. something that links or connects. *The close bond of friendship*. 2. a written promise to pay money or to carry out a contract.
bone *n.* the hard framework that supports the flesh and organs of all vertebrates (animals with backbones). *vb.* remove bones from. *She boned the fish.*
bonfire *n.* a big fire made in the open air.
bonnet *n.* 1. a woman's or baby's head-dress tied on by strings. 2. cover over engine of a car.

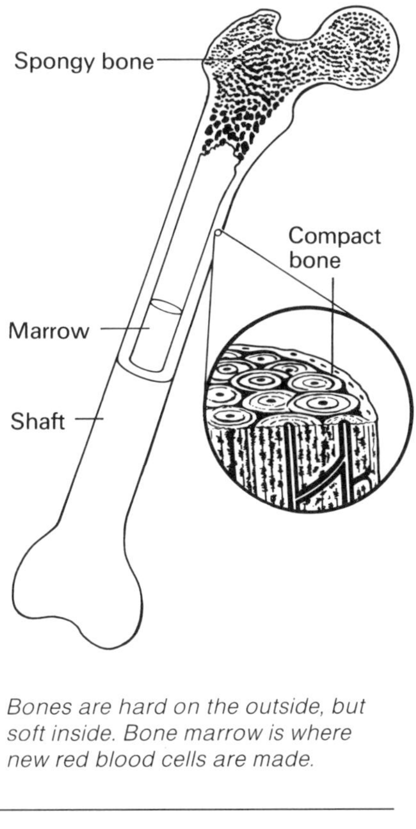

Bones are hard on the outside, but soft inside. Bone marrow is where new red blood cells are made.

bonny *adj*. pleasant, healthy-looking.

bonsai (*bon-sigh*) *n*. dwarf tree grown in a pot; an art which was developed in Japan.

bonus *n*. something extra; money paid in addition to wages or dividends.

book 1. *n*. pages of – usually – printed paper bound together in a cover. 2. *vb*. reserve a ticket or place.

bookkeeper *n*. a person who looks after business accounts and keeps them in order.

bookmaker *n*. someone who makes a living by taking bets on horse races etc.

bookworm *n*. 1. an avid reader. 2. a grub that eats holes in books.

boom *n*. 1. deep moaning sound *vb*. 2. period of great commercial activity. 3. a spar or pole attached at one end to a mast to stretch the foot of a sail.

boomerang *n*. a throwing stick used by Australian Aborigines for hunting. *vb*. recoil or come back like a boomerang.

boon *n*. benefit, blessing.

boost *vb*. help on (by shoving); raise voltage. **booster** *n*. auxiliary motor in a rocket.

boot 1. *n*. a sort of shoe that also covers the ankle and sometimes the leg. *vb*. kick. 2. *n*. where you put luggage in a car.

booty *n*. plunder, spoils.

border *n*. 1. the part near the edge of something. 2. the land near the line dividing two countries.

bore 1. *vb*. drill out; make a hole in. 2. *vb*. make someone weary with uninteresting conversation. *n*. a boring person; someone who does not know when they are not wanted. **boredom** *n*. 3. *n*. a hole inside a gun barrel.

borrow *vb*. get something from someone else which you use and then give back. The other person *lends* it to you.

bosom *n*. breast. **bosom friend** *n*. intimate friend.

boss *n*. 1. The chief person in an organization; the person you work for. 2. a stud or ornament in the centre of a shield.

botany *n*. the study of plants and the way they grow. **botanist** *n*.

botch *vb*. patch badly, make a bungle of something.

both *adj*. & *pron*. the two together. *She invited both of us to her party*.

bother *vb*. 1. worry, annoy. *n*. a nuisance. 2. take care. *Why should I bother to telephone?*

bottle *n*. a container, usually made of glass, in which liquid is kept. *vb*. put in bottles.

bottom *n*. 1. the lowest part of something. 2. a person's seat or backside. *adj*. lowest, last. *Bottom drawer*.

A cricket bowler in action.

bough *n*. the branch of a tree.
bought *vb*. past of **buy**.
boulder *n*. a large rock rounded by action of water etc.
bounce *vb*. spring up again like a ball that is dropped on the ground.
bound *vb*. past of **bind**.
boundary *n*. 1. the border or frontier of a country; a line separating one place from another. 2. the edge of a cricket field.
bounty *n*. gift, bonus.
bout (*bowt*) *n*. turn, attack, fit (of illness), round (in boxing match).
bovine *adj*. oxlike; stupid.
bow (rhymes with *low*) *n*. 1. a piece of wood curved by a tight string. *A bow is used for shooting arrows*. 2. a knot with loops. 3. a stick with long hairs attached to it, which is used for playing musical instruments like violins.
bow (rhymes with *cow*) 1. *n*. the front of a ship. 2. *vb*. & *n*. bend at the waist to greet an important person.
bowels *pl. n*. the part of the body where solid wastes gather; intestines.
bower bird *n*. a bird native to Australia and New Guinea.
bowl 1. *n*. a deep dish or basin. 2. *vb*. throw a cricket ball or roll a ball in the game of bowls. **bowler** *n*.
bowler *n*. 1. person bowling in cricket; player at bowls. 2. hard hat with round crown.
bowls *pl. n*. an outdoor ball game played on a smooth, flat lawn called a bowling green. Balls (bowls) of about 12.5 cm (5 in) in diameter are rolled as close as possible to a small white ball called the jack. **bowler** *n*.
box 1. *n*. a hollow, square container, often made of wood or cardboard. *vb*. put in a box. 2. *vb*. fight with the fists. 3. *n*. a small evergreen tree or shrub, having hard yellowish wood.
boxer *n*. 1. a person who fights with the fists; one who boxes; 2. a kind of dog related to the bulldog.

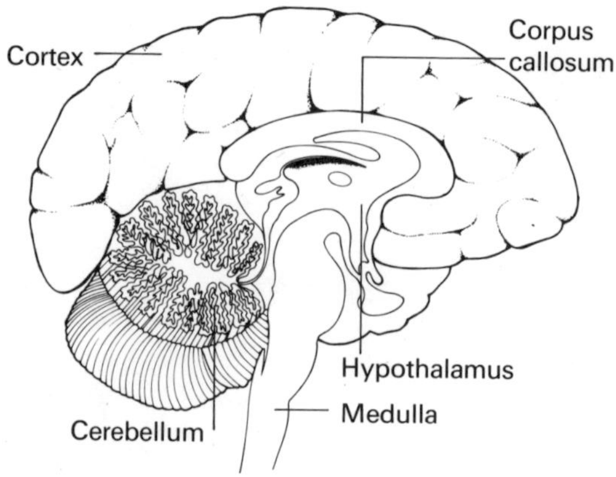

A human brain: the body's control centre.

boxing *n.* sport of fighting with fists.
Boxing Day *n.* the first weekday after Christmas Day, when boxes or presents are traditionally given.
boy *n.* a young male person.
boycott *vb.* refuse to speak to someone; have nothing to do with them; send to Coventry. *n.* the act of boycotting someone or something.
boyhood *n.* time of being a boy.
brace 1. *n.* a carpenter's tool. 2. *n.* a pair or couple especially of game. 3. *vb.* tighten, support, make firm.
bracelet *n.* a band worn round the arm or wrist.
bracing *adj.* invigorating.
bracken *n.* a kind of fern.
bracket *n.* 1. a support to hold a shelf. 2. one of a pair of marks ( ) used to enclose words or mathematical symbols. *vb.* enclose with brackets.
bradawl *n.* small tool used for boring.
brae (*Sc.*) *n.* a hill.
braid *vb.* plait, interlace.
braille (rhymes with *sail*) *n.* raised letters that a blind person can read by touching them.
brain *n.* the grey matter in the head which controls the work of the body, and with which you think; the intellect itself. **brainy** *adj.* clever.
brainwave *n.* clever idea.
braise *vb.* stew in a covered pan.
brake *n.* something that is pressed against a wheel to stop it turning. *vb.* apply the brake.
bramble *n.* a blackberry bush.
branch *n.* 1. one of the arm-like parts of a tree growing out of the trunk. 2. large stores and banks also have branches; separate buildings in different towns.
brand 1. *vb.* burn the owner's symbol on the hide of cattle with a hot iron. 2. *n.* a make of goods. 3. *n.* a poetic word for a sword.
brandish *vb.* wave about, especially a weapon.
brandy *n.* an alcoholic drink distilled from wine.
brass *n.* a bright, yellowish

The tuba is a brass instrument.

metal made by mixing copper and zinc.

brave 1. *adj*. fearless *vb*. meet boldly without fear. **bravery** *n*. 2. *n*. an American Indian warrior.

brawl *n*. a rowdy quarrel. *vb*. quarrel noisily.

brawn *n*. 1. muscular strength. 2. pickled chopped pork.

bread *n*. a food made from flour and baked in an oven.

breadth *n*. width, broadness, distance from side to side.

break 1. *vb*. smash. 2. *n*. a rest. *When she had finished her work, she had a break*. 3. *n*. in snooker or billiards, a series of scoring strokes.

break down *vb*. 1. (of a piece of machinery) to stop working. *n*. failure. 2. separate something into the parts it is made up of. *It's quite a big job, but if we break it down sensibly, we can do it*.

breaker *n*. heavy ocean wave which breaks on rocks or shore.

breakfast *n*. the first meal of the day, usually eaten in the early morning.

breakthrough *n*. major advance in science etc.

breakwater *n*. a structure built in the sea, usually near a harbour, to break the force of the waves.

bream *n*. a freshwater or sea fish.

breast (rhymes with *rest*) *n*. the milk-secreting organ in mammals; the chest of a person or an animal.

breathalyser *n*. device for measuring the amount of alcohol in the blood.

breathe (*breeth*) *vb*. take air into the lungs and let it out again. **breath** (*breth*) *n*. air drawn in and expelled by lungs.

breed 1. *n*. animals that produce others of exactly the same kind. *The Labrador is a breed of dog*. 2. *vb*. produce young ones.

breeze *n*. a gentle wind.

brevity *n*. briefness, shortness in speech or writing. *Brevity is the soul of wit*.

brewery *n*. a place where beer is brewed or made. **brew** *vb*. make beer.

bribe *n*. money or something offered to obtain some services – usually dishonest or illegal. *vb*. offer a bribe.

brick *n*. a block of hardened clay used in building.

bride *n*. a woman who is about to be married or who has just been married. **bridal** *adj*. of a bride or wedding.

bridegroom *n*. a man who is about to be married or who has just been married.

bridesmaid *n*. a girl who helps a bride at her wedding.

bridge *n.* 1. a structure that enables people or vehicles to cross a road, river or other obstacle. *vb.* span a space with a bridge. 2. platform on a ship for navigating etc. 3. the name of a card game for four players that is based on whist.

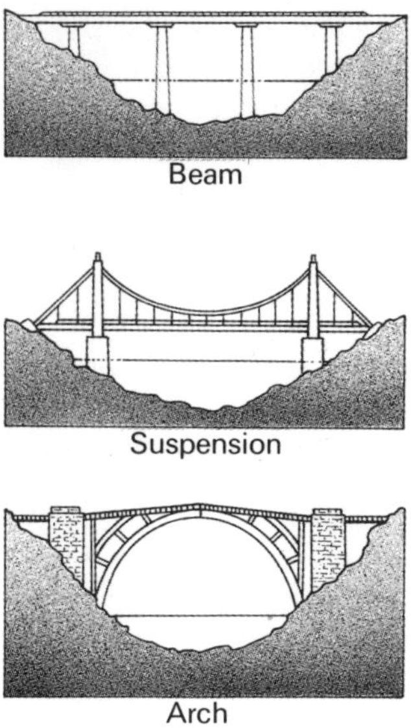

TYPES OF BRIDGE

bridle *n.* the harness that goes on a horse's head, including the reins.
brief 1. *adj.* lasting for a short time only. *The meeting was a brief one.* 2. *n.* an instruction, particularly to a lawyer.
brigand *n.* a robber.
bright (rhymes with *bite*) *adj.* 1. shiny, cheerful. 2. clever. **brightness** *n.*
brilliant 1. *adj.* very bright. *A brilliant star shone between the clouds.* 2. *adj.* very clever. **brilliance** *n.*
brim *n.* 1. the edge of a cup or container. *The bucket was full to the brim.* 2. the projecting edge of a hat.
bring *vb.* fetch or carry.
bring up *vb.* care for a child as it grows; to be sick.
brink *n.* the edge of something, such as a river or precipice.
brisk *adj.* lively, alert.
bristle 1. *n.* a short stiff hair. 2. *vb.* become angry.
brittle *adj.* easily snapped or broken.
broad *adj.* wide, a long way across.
broadcast 1. *vb.* & *n.* send out in all directions, particularly by radio or television. 2. *vb.* scatter seed.
broaden *vb.* make or become broader.
broccoli *n.* hardy variety of cauliflower.
brochure *n.* pamphlet or booklet.
brock *n.* a badger.
broke, broken *vb.* past and past part. of **break**.
bronchitis *n.* inflammation of the windpipe, resulting in coughing, wheezing and shortness of breath.

Broccoli is a vegetable with edible heads and stalks.

The mighty brontosaurus was up to 21m long and weighed as much as 30 tonnes, but it ate only plants.

brontosaurus *n.* a giant dinosaur which lived 150 million years ago.
bronze *n.* a reddish-brown metal made from mixing copper and tin.
Bronze Age the time between the Stone Age and the Iron Age when people made tools of bronze.
brooch (rhymes with *coach*) *n.* a piece of jewellery that is pinned on to clothing.
brood 1. *n.* birds produced at one hatch. *vb.* sit on eggs. 2. *vb.* meditate deeply; worry about.
brook *n.* a small stream.
broom *n.* 1. a brush with a long handle. 2. yellow flowered shrub.
broth *n.* a thin soup.
brother *n.* a son of the same parents as someone; member of a religious order, trade union etc.
brought *vb.* past of **bring**.
brow *n.* the forehead; top of a hill in a road. **browbeat** *vb.* bully.
brown *n.* & *adj.* the name of a dark colour between black and orange; the colour of earth.
brownie *n.* 1. a small friendly elf. 2. a junior Girl Guide.
bruise (*brooze*) *n.* a blue-black mark on the skin caused by a knock. *vb.* inflict bruises.
brunt *n.* the main force of an attack or shock.
brush *n.* 1. implement with bristles for sweeping, smoothing hair, cleaning teeth etc. *vb.* use a brush. 2. fox's tail.
brute *n.* an animal; unkind person. **brutal** *adj.* inhuman; unfeeling.
bubble *n.* a thin skin of liquid filled with gas.
buccaneer *n.* a pirate who plundered Spanish ships in America in the 17th and 18th centuries.
buck 1. *n.* a male deer or rabbit. 2. *vb.* (of a horse) kick up the heels.
bucket *n.* an open container with a handle, often used for carrying water.

The ladybird is a type of bug.

buckle *n.* & *vb.* a fastener, usually on a belt or strap; to fasten with a buckle.
bud *n.* a young flower or leaf before it opens. *vb.* sprout buds.
budge *vb.* move slightly; shift.
budgerigar *n.* a brightly coloured Australian bird, like a small parrot.
budget *n.* financial statement or forecast of revenue and expenditure. *vb.* (*for*) allow for in a budget.
buffalo *n.* in Asia, a kind of wild ox; in North America, a bison.
buffet (**buff**-*fay*) 1. *n.* refreshment bar; meal set out on a table from which people help themselves. 2. *vb.* (**buff**-*it*) strike, knock about *n.*
bug *n.* one of a group of insects with a mouth that can prick and suck.
bugle *n.* a musical instrument, usually made of brass or copper, similar to a trumpet but without the stops, and mainly used for military calls or signals.
build (rhymes with *milled*) *vb.* make something by putting different parts together. *This bird builds its nest from twigs and feathers.* **building** *n.* a structure with roof and walls.
building site *n.* the place where a building is being built.
built *vb.* past of **build**.
bulb *n.* 1. an electric lamp. 2. the roundish underground stem of some plants, like onions.
bulk *n.* a large quantity; large amount.
bulky *adj.* large and clumsy.
bull *n.* a male of the cattle family or a male elephant.
bulldog *n.* a powerful and courageous breed of dog (formerly used in the cruel sport of bull baiting).

bulldozer *n.* a heavy machine for clearing land.
bullet *n.* a piece of shaped metal made to be shot from a hand-gun.
bullion *n.* bars of gold or silver before being turned into coins etc.
bullock *n.* castrated bull.
bully *n.* a person who uses his or her strength to frighten other, weaker people. *vb.*
bulrush *n.* a tall plant that grows near water.
bumble *vb.* buzz or hum loudly.
bumble bee *n.* a large bee that hums noisily.

bump 1. *vb.* knock into something. *n.* a collision, a jolt. 2. *n.* a lump or swelling.
bumper 1. *adj.* large or abundant. *A bumper crop of wheat.* 2. *n.* the bars or fenders that protect the front and back of a motor car.
bun *n.* a kind of small round cake or bread roll.
bunch *n.* a number of things of the same kind together, like a *bunch of grapes. vb.* make into a bunch.
bundle *n.* a number of things wrapped up together. *vb.* tie into a bundle.
bung *n.* a stopper, often a cork, used to stop up a container.
bungalow *n.* a house with all its rooms on the ground floor.
bungle *vb.* blunder; do something awkwardly.
bunion *n.* lump or inflamed swelling on toe.
bunk *n.* a narrow bed fixed to the wall, often one above the other.
buoy (rhymes with *boy*) *n.* an anchored float marking a channel or a reef for ships. **buoyant** *adj.* apt to float; cheerful.
burble *vb.* murmur or speak in a rambling way.
burden *n.* & *vb.* a load; something difficult to bear.
bureau 1. *n.* a writing desk. 2. an office or department.
burglar *n.* a person who breaks into a house to steal. **burglary** *n.* **burgle** *vb.*
burial *n.* burying of a dead body; a funeral.
buried *vb.* past of **bury**.
burly *adj.* large and sturdy.
burn 1. *vb.* (past and past part. **burnt, burned**) destroy or damage something by fire. *n.* injury or mark caused by burning. 2. *n.* (*Sc.*) a brook; stream.
burrow *n.* a hole made in the ground by an animal as a home. *vb.* make or live in a burrow.
burst *vb.* break apart suddenly, or explode. *The balloon burst with a loud bang.*
burst in or **into** *vb.* rush in. *Jane burst into the room.*
bury *vb.* put something in the ground; hide away.
bus *n.* a motor vehicle for carrying large numbers of people (short for 'omnibus' – a Latin word meaning 'for all').
bush *n.* a shrub; a small thick tree.
bushman *n.* a native of the southern African deserts.

A smiling bushman of the Kalahari Desert.

business (**biz**-*ness*) 1. *n.* a shop or organization. 2. *n.* a person's work or occupation. *My father's business is running a bookshop.*
busker *n.* wandering musician or actor.
bust *n.* 1. a statue of a person's head and shoulders. 2. a woman's breast. 3. (*slang*) bankrupt; penniless. *They all lost their jobs when their company went bust.*
bustle *vb.* hurry (or make others hurry) about. *n.* excited activity.
busy (*bizzy*) *adj.* having a lot to do.
but *conj.* however; on the other hand.
butcher *n.* a person who kills or cuts up animals to sell their meat.
butler *n.* head manservant in a large house.
butt *vb.* to hit with the head.
butter *n.* a soft, yellow food made from fats contained in cream. *vb.* spread butter.
buttercup *n.* a small wild flower with yellow petals.
butterfly *n.* an insect with large colourful wings. Unlike the moth it flies during the daytime.

This beautiful swallowtail is one of the many different kinds of butterfly.

buttock *n.* one of the two fleshy parts of the bottom or backside.
button *n.* a small round object, made of plastic, leather, horn etc., and which is used for fastening clothes.
butty *n.* (N. Eng. dialect) a sandwich, snack.
buttress *n.* a prop, support built against a wall. *vb.* support, strengthen.

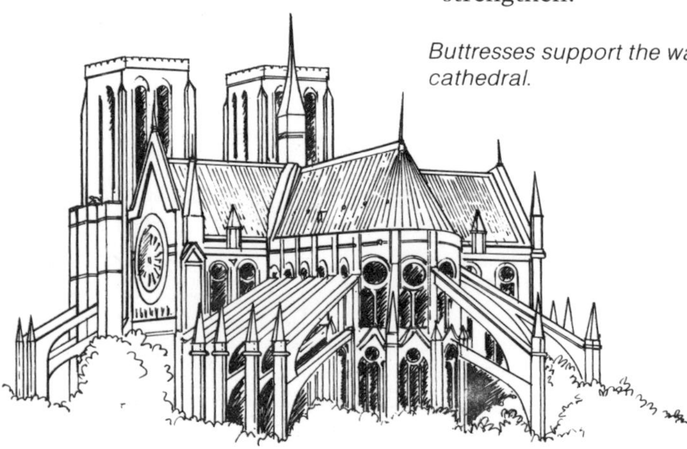

Buttresses support the walls of this cathedral.

buy *vb*. (past **bought**) purchase something; obtain goods in exchange for money.
buzz *vb*. make a noise like a bee.
buzzard *n*. the name of a family of birds of prey related to the falcon.
by *prep*. along; through; during; as a result of. *Little by little. By the way. By force.*
by-election *n*. an election held to fill a vacancy caused by death or resignation.
bystander *n*. a spectator.
byre *n*. cow shed.
byte *n*. a group of bits in a computer.

C

cab *n*. 1. a taxi. 2. the part of a lorry or locomotive in which the driver sits.
cabbage *n*. a vegetable with thick green leaves growing very close together.
cabin *n*. 1. a room in a ship or aircraft. 2. a hut; a simple house.
cabinet *n*. 1. a cupboard or similar piece of furniture. 2. the senior members of a government.
cable *n*. 1. a strong wire or rope; a bundle of telegraph wires. 2. an overseas telegram. *vb*. send a message by cable.
cackle *n*. noise made by a hen; silly talk; foolish laughter. *vb*.
cactus *n*. (plural **cacti**) a prickly desert plant with a thick green stem.

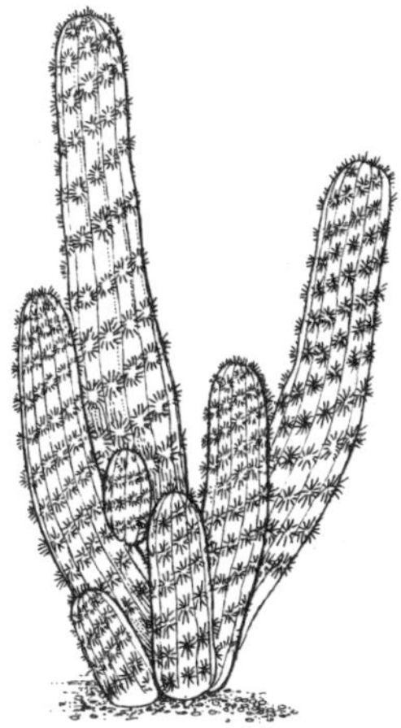

The cactus has a fleshy stem which saves water in the desert.

caddy *n*. 1. small box for holding tea. 2. (also caddie) person who carries clubs etc. for a golfer.
cadet *n*. a young person studying to become a member of the armed forces or the police.
cadge *vb*. beg; take advantage of someone's generosity.
café (**caf***fay*) *n*. a place where food and drink is sold; a small restaurant.
cage *n*. a box with bars in which birds or animals are kept. *vb*. keep in a cage.
cake *n*. a sweet kind of food made from flour, butter, eggs, sugar etc. and baked in an oven; a hard mass (of soap etc.).
calamity *n*. a disaster, terrible misfortune.

calcium *n.* a metallic chemical element (symbol *Ca*) present in many rocks and minerals such as limestone and gypsum. Calcium is also present in teeth and bones.

calculate *vb.* work out a sum, reckon. **calculation** *n.* **calculator** *n.* an electronic machine for doing sums.

calendar *n.* a list of the days, weeks and months of the year.

calf (rhymes with *half*) (plural **calves**) *n.* 1. a young cow, seal, elephant or whale. 2. the fleshy back part of the leg below the knee.

call *vb.* 1. shout, cry out; summon. *n.* 2. speak to on telephone. *n.* 3. name. 4. pay a short visit. *n.* **caller** *n.*

call box *n.* telephone kiosk.

call for *vb.* 1. demand. *The committee called for reforms.* 2. fetch. *I shall call for you on my way to the match.*

calligraphy (*kal*-**ig**-*raf-ee*) *n.* handwriting as an art.

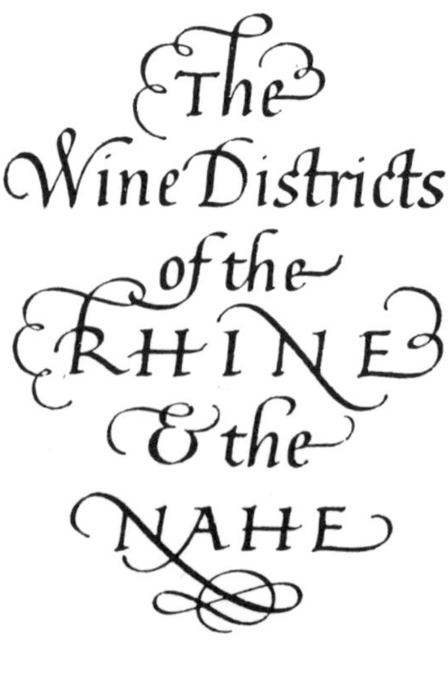

calling *n.* profession; occupation.

call off *vb.* decide not to do something that has been arranged. *The game was called off because the field was flooded.*

calm (rhymes with *arm*) *adj.* quiet, smooth. *vb.* soothe, make or become calm. *n.* stillness.

calorie *n.* a unit of heat. Calories are also used as a measure of the energy produced by food and drink. A person on a diet may need to count the calories in their food intake.

calve *vb.* give birth to a calf.

calypso *n.* West Indian song.

came *vb.* past of **come**.

camel *n.* an animal with a long neck and one hump or two on its back.

camellia *n.* evergreen shrub with beautiful rose-like flowers.

The camellia's beautiful flowers of pink, red or white, and glossy evergreen leaves make it a popular garden shrub. It blooms in early spring.

A camouflaged combat aircraft.

camera *n*. an instrument for taking photographs.
camouflage *vb*. & *n*. disguise of guns, ships, aircraft, and so on with paint, tree branches, or nets so that they cannot easily be seen.
camp 1. *n*. a place where people stay in tents or huts. 2. *vb*. live in a tent.
campaign *n*. a series of military or political operations, an organized programme. *vb*.
campus *n*. grounds of a college or university.
can 1. *vb*. be able to. *Can you run faster than me?* 2. *vb*. be allowed to. *You can come and go as you like*. 3. *n*. a metal container; a tin.
canal *n*. a man-made waterway for barges or for taking water to fields.
canary *n*. a small yellow, singing bird which is often kept in a cage as a pet. *adj*. colour of a canary.
canasta *n*. a card game of the rummy family.
cancel *vb*. cross out; bring to an end; call off. *The football match was cancelled*. **cancellation** *n*.
cancer *n*. a name give to a variety of serious diseases; a disease of the bodily cells; a growth or tumour.
candid *adj*. outspoken, sincere, frank. **candour** *n*.
candidate *n*. a person who seeks election or appointment; a person who sits any examination.
candle *n*. a stick of wax with a string or wick through the middle.
candlestick *n*. a holder for a candle.
candy *n*. crystallized sugar; (US) sweets.
cane *n*. the hollow, jointed stem of large reeds and grasses such as bamboo, used to make walking sticks and cane furniture. *vb*. beat with a cane.
canine *n*. of or belonging to a dog.
canister *n*. small box for holding tea etc.

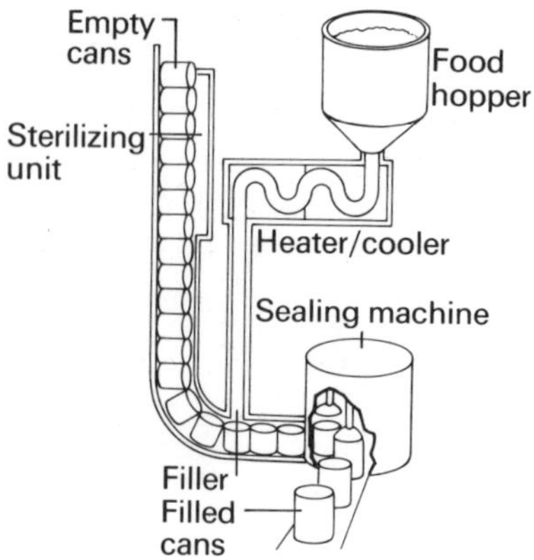

The canning process seals and sterilizes food.

cannibal *n.* human being who eats human flesh.
canning *n.* a way of preserving food by heating and sealing it in airtight containers. The heat kills any germs in the food. The airtight containers keep out bacteria that make it spoil.
cannon *n.* a big, heavy gun.
canny *adj.* shrewd.
canoe (*can*-**oo**) *n.* a light boat that is paddled through the water.
canon *n.* 1. a church dignitary. 2. a church decree, rule.
canopy *n.* a covering over a throne, bed etc.
canteen *n.* restaurant in a factory or office.
canter *n.* an easy gallop on horseback. *vb.*
canvas *n.* a coarse cloth used for tents and sails. Artists also paint on it.
canvass *vb.* go to people and ask them to vote for your political party etc. *We shall canvass for John Smith.*
canyon *n.* a deep gorge, usually cut through rock by a river (mainly US).
cap *n.* 1. a soft hat with a peak at the front. 2. a lid.
capable *adj.* able; competent.
capacity *n.* ability; the amount that can be held in something.
cape *n.* 1. a coat with no sleeves, worn over the shoulders. 2. a piece of land that juts out into the sea.
capital *n.* 1. the city where the government of a country works. 2. letters written like this: A, M, R, Z. 3. money with which business is started; accumulated wealth in stocks or shares etc.
capsize *vb.* overturn, especially in a boat.

A cannon is a large, long gun. Cannons were first used in battle in the Middle Ages. They fired big metal cannonballs.

capstan *n.* apparatus for winding in cables etc.
capsule *n.* 1. a small cylindrical case containing medicine. 2. part of a spacecraft.
captain *n.* 1. the officer in charge of a ship. 2. an army officer below a major and above a lieutenant.
caption *n.* the words near a picture which explain what it shows.
captivate *vb.* fascinate, charm.
captive *n.* a prisoner.

capture *vb.* take someone prisoner.
car *n.* a motor vehicle.
caramel *n.* burnt sugar used as a flavouring; a kind of toffee.
carat *n.* a measure of weight for precious stones; also used as a measure of the purity of gold.
caravan *n.* 1. a home on wheels, pulled by a car or horse. 2. a group of people travelling together across a desert.
carbon *n.* a non-metallic element that is found in all living things – both plant and animal. (Symbol – C.)
carbon dioxide *n.* a gas (CO_2) that occurs in small quantities in the atmosphere. People and animals breathe in oxygen and breathe out mainly carbon dioxide.
carbon monoxide *n.* a very poisonous gas (CO) with no smell, which is present in motor car exhaust fumes.
carburettor *n.* apparatus in motor engines for mixing air with petrol vapour for combustion.
carcass *n.* dead body of an animal.
cardboard *n.* extra thick card or paper.
cardiac *adj.* of the heart.
cardigan *n.* a knitted woollen jacket.
cardinal 1. *n.* a senior official in the Roman Catholic Church. 2. *adj.* & *n.* fundamental. The cardinal points of the compass are North, South, East and West.
care *n.* anxiety, concern, serious attention. *vb.* feel concern, anxiety for; feel affection for.
career 1. *vb.* go fast and perhaps dangerously. 2. *n.* the series of jobs or positions that people have during their working life. *He has spent his whole career as a teacher.*
care for *vb.* look after someone; love someone.
careless *adj.* not thinking about what one does.
caret *n.* mark (λ) showing where missing word should be placed in writing.
cargo *n.* (plural **cargoes**) goods carried by ship or aircraft.
caribou *n.* wild reindeer of North America.

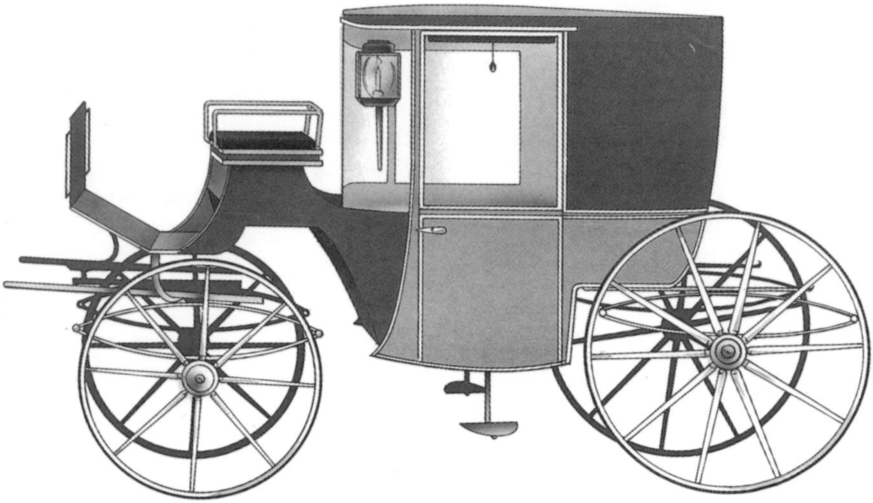

A closed horse-drawn carriage with windows to keep out the wind and rain. This model dates from the 1860s.

caricature *n.* an exaggerated or distorted drawing of someone which makes them appear ridiculous or absurd. Many political cartoons contain caricatures.

caries (rhymes with **bear**-*ease*) *n.* decay of tooth.

carnation *n.* a large, brightly coloured flower, related to the garden pink.

carnival *n.* a public occasion for making merry. *In New Orleans there is a famous carnival called Mardi Gras.*

carnivore *n.* an animal that eats meat.

carob *n.* an evergreen tree with sugary pods used as a substitute for chocolate.

carol *n.* a kind of song, usually religious, and sung at Christmas.

carp 1. *n.* large freshwater fish. 2. *vb.* find fault.

carpenter *n.* a person who makes things from wood.

carpet *n.* heavy floor covering of woven or knotted material.

carriage *n.* vehicle, usually with four wheels, pulled by horses; a coach for passengers on a train.

carrion *n.* the rotting body of an animal.

carrot *n.* a plant with an orange-red root which is used as a vegetable.

carry on *vb.* continue doing something.

cart *n.* a two-wheeled vehicle pulled by a horse, ox or other animal.

cartilage (**car**-*till-ij*) *n.* a material in the body similar to bone but lighter and more flexible. *You have pads of cartilage in your knee joints.*

cartography *n.* map drawing.

carton *n.* light box made of cardboard.
cartoon *n.* a funny drawing, often of people in politics. **cartoonist** *n.*
cartridge *n.* the case holding the explosive that fires a bullet.
carve *vb.* 1. shape a piece of wood or stone. 2. cut up meat to serve at a meal.
cascade *n.* waterfall. *vb.* fall like a cascade.
case *n.* 1. a box for carrying things or storing them. 2. an example; an instance. *There was a case of whooping cough in the class.* 3. a trial in a law court. *The man and woman in the case were found guilty.*
cash *n.* money in paper notes and coins. *vb.* exchange cheque etc. for money.
cashier *n.* the person who takes in and pays out money in a shop, hotel or other business.
cashmere *n.* wool from goats of Kashmir.
casino (*ka*-**seen**-*o*) *n.* public building for gambling.
cask *n.* a wooden barrel, often used for wines or spirits.
casket *n.* small case for jewels; (US) coffin.

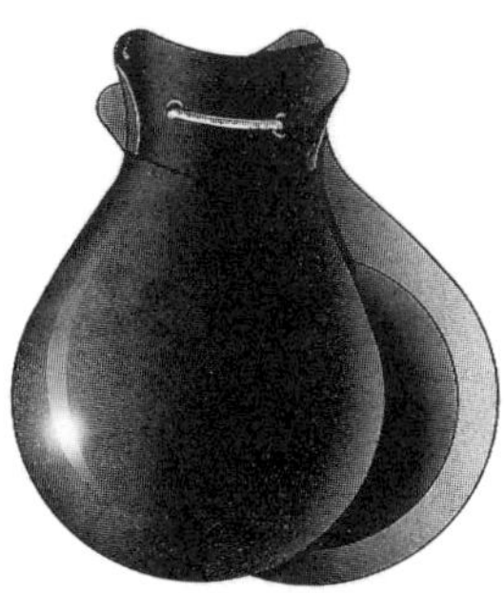

A pair of castanets.

The cassowary is a flightless bird.

casserole *n.* vessel in which food is both cooked and served.
cassette *n.* a container for holding magnetic tape used for recording.
cassock *n.* long robe, usually black, worn by clergymen.
cassowary *n.* a large flightless bird of New Guinea and Australia related to the ostrich and emu.
cast 1. *vb.* throw or fling. 2. *vb.* give parts in a play. 3. *n.* an impression or mould, generally done in plaster. *The police made a cast of the footprint.* **casting** *n.*
castanets *pl. n.* small wooden instruments held in the hand and clicked as an accompaniment to dance.
castaway *n.* a person left on a distant land, often after the ship has been wrecked.
castle *n.* a large building with thick walls, fortified against attack.
castrate *vb.* remove the testicles so that a male animal cannot mate and reproduce.

casual *adj.* accidental, by chance, *a casual meeting*; informal, *casual manners*.

casualty *n.* a person who is ill or injured. In warfare, casualties are soldiers who have been killed or wounded.

cat *n.* a small furry domestic animal with short ears and a long tail; any member of the cat family that includes lions, tigers and leopards.

catacombs *pl. n.* underground cemeteries containing passageways and crypts for burial of the dead.

catalogue (**cat**-*a-log*) *n.* a list of things, such as the pictures in an exhibition or the books in a library.

catalyst (**cat**-*a-list*) *n.* a substance that speeds up a chemical reaction but is left unchanged and so can be used several times for the process of catalysis.

catamaran *n.* a boat with two hulls joined together.

A catamaran.

catapult *n.* 1. a Y-shaped stick with a piece of elastic fixed to it. *A catapult is used for throwing small stones.* 2. an ancient weapon for throwing large stones. 3. a device for launching aircraft from an aircraft carrier.

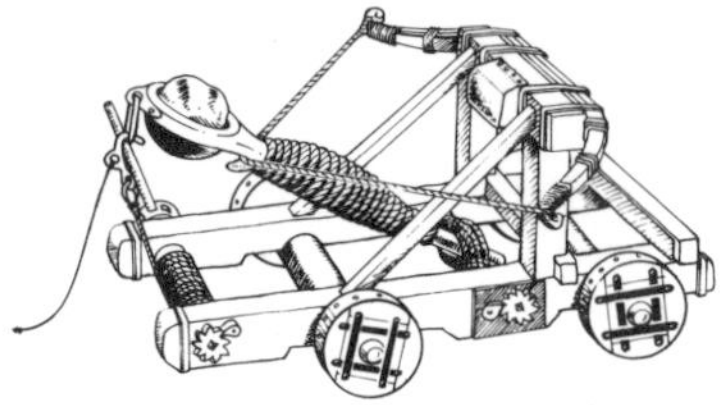

Catapults like this one were used in battle in the Middle Ages. They would attack the strong walls of cities and castles by throwing rocks at them to batter them down.

cataract *n.* 1. a waterfall. 2. a condition of the eye, affecting vision.

catarrh *n.* a runny nose; a cold in the head.

catastrophe *n.* a disaster.

catch 1. *n.* the lock or fastening

of a door. 2. *vb.* get hold of something or someone, perhaps after a chase. 3. *vb.* get a disease or illness. *I hope you don't catch my cold.*

category *n.* class or order of something.

caterpillar *n.* the larva stage in the growth of a butterfly or moth.

cathedral *n.* the main church of an area (diocese) in which a bishop or archbishop has his *cathedra* (Latin for 'chair').

catkin *n.* the hanging, fluffy flower of the hazel, and some other trees.

cattle *n.* heavily built grass-eating mammals which include all oxen and cows.

caught *vb.* past of **catch**.

cauliflower *n.* a kind of cabbage, the tightly-bunched flowers of which form whitish heads.

cause (rhymes with *saws*) 1. *vb.* make something happen. *My dog was the cause of the accident.* 2. *n.* a principle or ideal to which a person or group of persons is devoted. *Freedom is a noble cause.*

causeway *n.* a raised path through marshland or water.

caution 1. *n.* care; carefulness; *Proceed with caution.* 2. *vb.* warn (especially of the police).

cavalry *n.* soldiers who fight on horseback.

cave *n.* a hole in the side of a hill or under the ground.

caveman, cavewoman *n.* a person who lived in a cave, especially during the Stone Age.

caviar *n.* the eggs, or roe, of certain species of fish, especially the sturgeon, prized as a delicacy.

cavity *n.* hole, space within a solid body.

cease *vb.* stop.

cedar *n.* a large, spreading, evergreen coniferous tree.

cede (*seed*) *vb.* surrender, give up.

ceilidh (*kaylay*) *n.* (*Sc.*) an informal evening of song and story.

ceiling (*seeling*) *n.* the roof of a room.

celebrate *vb.* hold a party or other festivity in honour of an important event. **celebration** *n.*

celebrity *n.* famous, celebrated person.

celery *n.* a vegetable plant. It is the crisp stalks that are eaten.

cell *n.* 1. a small room in a monastery, convent or prison. 2. very small unit of living matter in animals and plants.

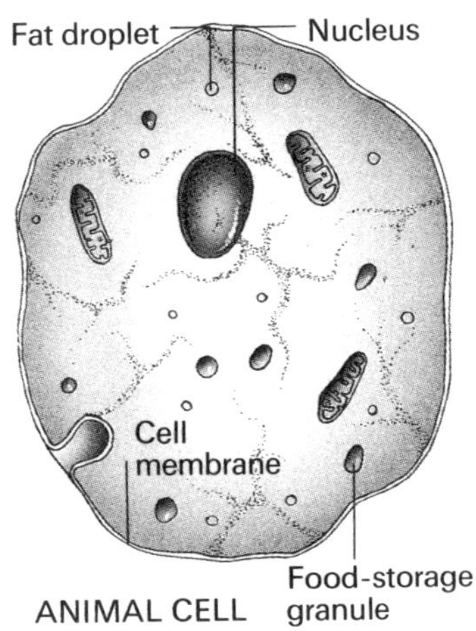

An animal cell. Every living thing is made up of tiny cells.

cellar *n.* an underground room for storing things.
cello (*chello*) *n.* a stringed instrument like a large violin. **cellist** *n.*
cellulose *n.* the substance that gives plants their rigidity or stiffness.
celsius *adj.* another name for centigrade scale on a thermometer, named after its inventor, Anders Celsius.
cement *n.* a grey powder that, when mixed with water, becomes hard.
cemetery *n.* a place (not a churchyard) where people are buried.
cenotaph *n.* monument to persons buried elsewhere.
census *n.* a counting of all the people in a country.
cent *n.* a coin used in many countries of the world. *There are 100 cents in a dollar.*
centaur *n.* an imaginary creature, half man and half horse.
centenary *n.* a hundredth anniversary. *It was the centenary of the writer's birth.*
centi – prefix meaning one hundred or one hundredth.
centigrade scale *n.* a temperature scale on which water freezes at 0°C and boils at 100°C.
centimetre *n.* a metric measure of length. *There are 100 centimetres in a metre.*
centipede *n.* a small creature with a long body and many legs.
central *adj.* at or near the centre. *Andy lives in central Birmingham.*
centre (rhymes with *enter*) *n.* the middle part or point of something.
centrifugal force *n.* an outward force produced by a body rotating in a circle.
centurion *n.* a Roman soldier in command of a *century* (100 men).

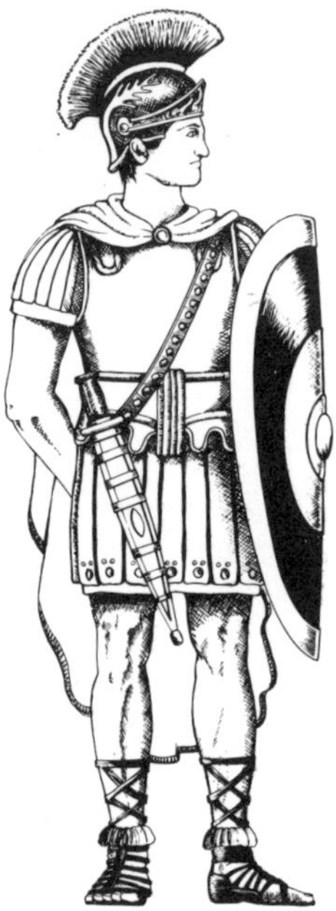

A Roman centurion in full armour. Centurions were the officers of the Roman army.

century *n.* 1. one hundred years. 2. company of soldiers in ancient Roman army. 3. a score of 100 runs at cricket.
ceramic *adj.* concerning pottery or **ceramics** *(pl.) n.*
cereal *n.* grain crops such as maize, rice or wheat used for food; breakfast food made from grain.

The chaffinch is a small song-bird, often seen in the garden. Like most finches, chaffinches are seed-eaters.

ceremony *n.* a dignified occasion; religious rite. *The wedding ceremony took place in an old church.* **ceremonial** *adj.* with ceremony, formal.

certain *adj.* 1. sure. *I am certain they will come soon.* 2. some. *Certain people are colour blind.* **certainty** *n.*

certificate *n.* a piece of paper that is proof of something. *Nicola was given a certificate to show she had swum five lengths of the pool.*

certify *vb.* declare officially.

chaff 1. *n.* husks of corn which need to be separated from the grain. 2. *vb.* make fun of someone (now slightly old-fashioned).

chaffinch *n.* small song-bird.

chain *n.* a line of rings joined together. The rings in a chain are called 'links'.

chair *n.* a piece of furniture for sitting on.

chairman *n.* a person who presides over a meeting. Also **chairwoman** and **chairperson**.

chalet (**shall**-*ay*) *n.* Swiss house of wood with overhanging roof.

chalk *n.* a kind of soft white rock; white material used for writing on a blackboard.

challenge *vb.* question, as a sentry; question truth of; invite to fight. *n.*

chameleon ('*ch*' spoken like *k*) *n.* type of tree lizard living mainly in Tropical Africa.

champagne (*sham*-**pain**) *n.* sparkling white wine.

champion *n.* the overall winner. *vb.* defend, uphold.

championship *n.* a competition to find the best person or team.

chance *n.* a possibility of something happening. *Leroy has a good chance of becoming champion, but Eric has no chance at all.*

chancel *n.* part of church near the altar used by choir and clergy.

chancy *adj.* risky.

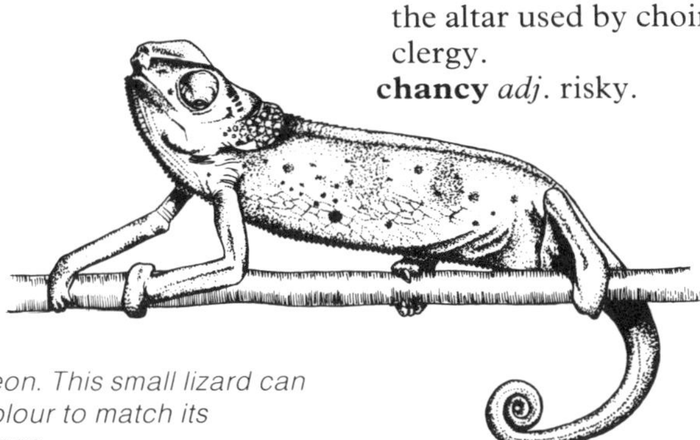

A chameleon. This small lizard can change colour to match its surroundings.

chandelier *n.* a holder for a number of lights which hangs from the ceiling.
change 1. *vb.* make something different. *The girls changed their clothes.* 2. *n.* the money given back when you give too much money for something you are buying. *I bought a loaf of bread and the assistant gave me change from my pound.*
channel *n.* 1. a narrow strip of water joining two seas. 2. a narrow passage for water to run through. *vb.*
chant *vb.* recite in a half-singing style; intone. *n.*
chaos (**kay**-*oss*) *n.* utter confusion. *adj.* chaotic.
chap *n.* man, boy, fellow.
chapel *n.* a small church, or part of a large church.
chaperon (**shap**-*er-on*) *n.* an older woman in charge of a girl at parties etc. *vb.*

A two-wheeled horse-drawn chariot.

chaplain *n.* clergyman attached to an institution or the armed forces.
chapter *n.* one section of a book.
char 1. *vb.* scorch. 2. *n.* a cleaning woman (short for charwoman). 3. *n.* a slang word for tea. 4. *n.* a fish in the trout family.
character *n.* 1. the things that make you the person you are. *Margaret's character was so pleasant that everyone liked her.* 2. one of the people in a book or play. *Little Red Riding Hood is a character in a story.*
charade (*sha*-**raad**) *n.* game in which syllables of a word are acted out separately, the whole word being guessed at by the audience.
charcoal *n.* a form of carbon made by heating wood with little air present.
charge 1. *vb.* rush forward and attack. 2. *vb.* ask a certain price for something. 3. **be in charge** *vb.* be responsible for. *Simon was left in charge of the department while the manager was out.*
charger *n.* a horse used by cavalry in war.
chariot *n.* a vehicle used for fighting and racing long ago. **charioteer** *n.* driver of a chariot.
charity *n.* help and kindness given to others.
charlatan *n.* a person who pretends to be something he or she is not. Often used of someone who pretends to have expert knowledge of a subject.
charm *n.* something that has magic power. *He carried a rabbit's foot charm.* **charming** *adj.* very attractive; delightful.
chart *n.* 1. a sea map for sailors, showing the sea depth, the position of buoys, rocks etc. 2. information shown by a diagram or graph.

chase *vb.* run after and try to catch.
chasm (*'ch'* spoken like *k*) *n.* wide hollow, gap.
chaste *adj.* pure.
chat *vb.* & *n.* talk in a friendly way. **chatty** *adj.*
château (**sha**-*tow*) *n.* the French word for castle.
chatter *vb.* 1. talk non-stop about unimportant things. 2. (of teeth) rattling together from fear or cold.
chauffeur (**show**-*fur*) *n.* someone paid to drive their employer's car.
chauvinism *n.* exaggerated and blind patriotism; passionate support for a cause.
cheap *adj.* not expensive; low in price (and therefore with a suggestion of poor quality). **cheapen** *vb.* make or become cheap.
cheat *vb.* act dishonestly in order to help oneself. *n.* one who cheats.
check *vb.* 1. make sure that something is right. *Did you check that all the windows were closed?* 2. stop or hold back for a short time. *He was checked in the goal area, but still managed to shoot.* 3. *n.* a pattern made up of squares, usually on material.

checkers *pl. n.* (US) the game of draughts.
cheek 1. *n.* the fat part of your face on either side of your mouth. 2. *n.* sauce, impudence. **cheeky.** *adj.*
cheer *vb.* 1. make happy; comfort. 2. shout joyfully.
cheerful *adj.* looking and feeling happy.
cheerless *adj.* dull and miserable.
cheese *n.* a food made from milk.

Stilton

Edam

cheetah *n.* a spotted feline animal found mostly in East Africa. It is the world's fastest mammal.
chef (*sheff*) *n.* a head cook who is in charge of a large kitchen.
chemical (**kem**-*ical*) *n.* a substance used in chemistry.
chemist (**kem**-*ist*) *n.* 1. a person who is trained in chemistry. 2. a person who makes and sells medicines.
chemistry *n.* a branch of science that is about what substances are made of and how they work together.

The cheetah looks like a big cat. It can run 110 km/h for short bursts when hunting its prey.

Chessspieces.

cheque (*check*) *n.* a piece of paper which, when filled in and signed, tells a bank to pay money to someone.
cherish *vb.* value highly, treat with affection.
cherry *n.* the small round fruit of the cherry tree.
chess *n.* a game for two people, each with 16 pieces (chessmen), played on a board of 64 black and white squares.
chest *n.* 1. a large strong box with a lid. 2. the upper part of the front of one's body.
chestnut *n.* a large tree with prickly fruits containing shiny, red-brown nuts (chestnuts).
chew *vb.* crush food in your mouth with your teeth.
chic (*sheek*) *adj.* elegant, very smart.
chick *n.* a baby bird.
chicken *n.* a young hen. *adj.* (*slang*) cowardly.
chicken-pox *n.* a disease that causes red itchy spots on the skin.
chief 1. *n.* a ruler or leader. 2. *adj.* most important; main. *Farming is the chief industry in many countries.*
chilblain *n.* a painful swelling that sometimes forms on people's hands and feet in cold weather.
child *n.* young person (plural **children**).
chill 1. *vb.* cool. 2. *n.* a cold or fever. **chilly**. *adj.*
chime *n.* set of tuned bells. *vb.*
chimney *n.* a structure in a building that allows the smoke from a fire to escape.
chimpanzee *n.* an African ape.

A chestnut tree with its prickly fruit. The red-brown nuts are sometimes called 'conkers'.

chin *n.* the lowest part of the face, below the mouth.
china *n.* fine clay baked and glazed, made into plates, cups and so on.
chink *n.* 1. narrow opening, gap. 2. sound of glasses or coins hitting together. *vb.*
chintz *n.* glazed cotton cloth printed with flower patterns.
chip *n.* 1. a small piece broken off something. 2. a tiny electronic device, usually made

A microchip small enough to fit through the eye of a needle.

of silicon, that holds a circuit with thousands of transistors.

chipmunk *n.* a small member of the squirrel family.

chips *pl. n.* slices of fried potato.

chiropodist (*ki*-**rop**-*o-dist*) *n.* person who treats feet (corns and toe-nails, for example).

chisel *n.* a sharp tool used for shaping wood, stone etc. *vb.* cut or shape with a chisel.

chivalry (**shiv**-*al-ree*) *n.* medieval system of knighthood; gallantry, courage etc.

chive *n.* herb related to the onion.

chlorine *n.* a yellow-green poisonous, choking gas used in the manufacture of bleach, hydrochloric acid; small quantities are used to kill germs in drinking water (symbol Cl).

chlorophyll ('*ch*' spoken as *k*) *n.* green colouring matter found in plants' cells.

chocolate *n.* food or drink made from the ground and roasted beans from the cacao tree.

choice *n.* the act of choosing.

choir (*kwire*) *n.* a group of people trained to sing together.

choke 1. *vb.* not able to breathe because of something in your throat or lungs. 2. *vb.* block something up. 3. *n.* a control on a motor car that helps it start when the engine is cold.

choose *vb.* make a choice between two or more possibilities; to come to a decision.

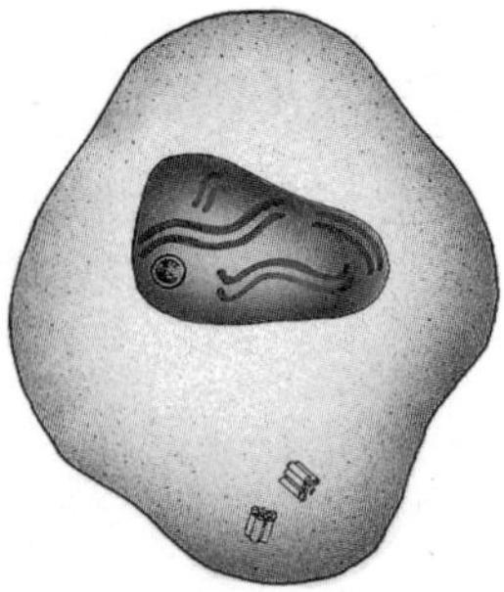

Chromosomes are found in all cells.

chop 1. *vb.* cut into pieces, often with an axe. 2. *n.* a thick slice of meat with a bit of bone in it.
chopsticks *pl. n.* a pair of sticks held in one hand and used by the Chinese for eating.
chord (*kord*) *n.* group of musical notes sounded together.
chore *n.* job about the house; dull, unenjoyable work.
choreography (*ko-ree-***og***-rafee*) *n.* the art of arranging the steps and movements of a ballet. **choreographer** *n.*
chorus (**kaw**-*rus*) *n.* choir, band of singers; part of a song that everyone sings after a solo part. **choral** *adj.* of, sung by, choir or chorus.
christen *vb.* give a name to and receive into the Christian Church; baptize. *Our baby was christened Angela by the priest.* **christening** *n.*
Christian *n.* a believer in and follower of the teachings of Jesus Christ.
Christianity *n.* the religion that was started by Jesus Christ.
Christmas *n.* the festival on 25 December celebrating the birth of Jesus.
chromium *n.* a hard white metal that does not rust (symbol Cr).
chromosome *n.* tiny thread-like structure, several of which occur in a cell nucleus and contain genes (hereditary instructions).
chronic *adj.* (of diseases) lasting, recurring; (*casual*) bad, boring.
chronicle (**kron**-*ic-al*) *n.* record of events in the order they happened. *vb.* write a chronicle.
chronometer *n.* a very accurate clock used as a navigational instrument to determine longitude at sea or in the air.
chrysalis *n.* a stage in the development of an insect between caterpillar and adult. *The caterpillar turned into a chrysalis, and then it became a butterfly.*
church *n.* a building used by Christians for worship (from a Greek word meaning 'belonging to the Lord').
churchyard *n.* the land surrounding a church, usually used as a burial ground.

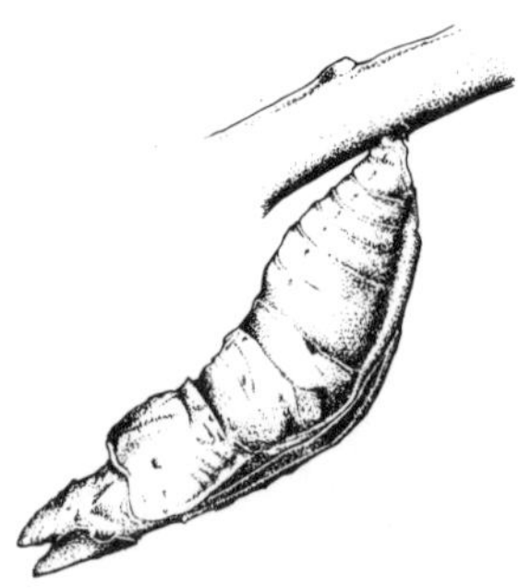

In time, a chrysalis like this will hatch into a butterfly.

churn *n.* vessel for making butter. *vb.* stir or agitate violently.

chutney *n.* flavouring for food, usually made from mangoes, chillies, and other ingredients.

cider *n.* an alcoholic drink made from apple juice.

cigar *n.* tobacco rolled in a tobacco leaf for smoking.

cigarette *n.* a small roll of tobacco in thin paper for smoking.

cinder *n.* piece of partly burned coal or wood.

cine-camera *n.* a camera for taking moving pictures.

cinema *n.* a theatre where moving pictures are shown.

cinnamon *n.* a spice from the bark of the Ceylon laurel tree; light yellow brown colour of cinnamon.

Cinnamon bark is used as a spice.

cipher see **code.**

circa *prep.* a Latin word meaning about and used mainly with dates. It is usually abbreviated to *c.* e.g. *c.* 1782.

circle *n.* a round flat shape, the line about this shape.

circuit *n.* 1. a circular journey. 2. a racetrack.

circular 1. *adj.* in the shape of a circle; round. 2. *n.* a letter or other document sent to a number of people.

circulate *vb.* move or send round. **circulation** *n.* 1. movement of blood round the body. 2. number of copies of a newspaper sold.

circum *prefix* (*sur-come*) round, about, e.g. **circumnavigate** sail around; **circumstances** everything surrounding an act, event etc.

circumcision *n.* the cutting away of the foreskin of the penis. This is practised by many religions, but is especially important to the Jews.

circumference *n.* the distance around the outside of a circle.

circus *n.* a travelling show with clowns, animals and acrobats, usually held in a tent.

citadel *n.* fortress protecting a city.

citizen *n.* 1. a person who lives in a town or city. 2. a person who has every right to live in a particular country. *She was an American citizen.*

city *n.* a large or important town.

civil engineering *n.* the branch of engineering that deals with man-made structures.

civilian *n.* a person who is not in one of the fighting services. *adj.*

civility *n.* politeness, kindness.

civilization *n.* a group of people in an advanced stage of development. **civilize** *vb.* make cultured, enlighten. **civilized** *adj.* living in a well-organized way.

claim *vb*. 1. say that something is yours. *You should claim your prize*. 2. say that something is a fact. *He claims that he can lift great weights*.
clammy *adj*. damp and sticky.
clamour *vb*. & *n*. (make) loud demand, noisy outcry.
clamp 1. *n*. a metal object for holding things in place. 2. *vb*. fasten with a clamp.
clan *n*. a group of families who claim to share the same ancestor.
clap *vb*. applaud by smacking one's hands together.
clapper *n*. tongue or striker of bell.

claret *n*. a red wine from Bordeaux in France. Also its colour.
clarify *vb*. make clear; explain.
clarinet *n*. a musical wind instrument with a single reed.
clarity *n*. clearness.
clash 1. *n*. a loud noise; the noise made by banging cymbals. 2. *vb*. (of colours) go badly together.
clasp 1. *n*. a fastening, such as a buckle or brooch. 2. *vb*. hold tightly. *They clasped hands*.
class *n*. a group of the same kind of people, like children who are taught together. *I go to the class at the ballet school*.

Clematis flowers.

classic *adj*. & *n*. 1. established quality of excellence, especially in art; 2. of ancient Greece and Rome and their culture.
classical *adj*. of ancient Greece or Rome.
clause (*klawz*) 1. *n*. part of a sentence. 2. *n*. section in a document.
claustrophobia (*klaws-tro-* **foab**-*ia*) *n*. fear of being in enclosed spaces.
claw *n*. a pointed nail on an animal's foot.
clay *n*. a soft kind of earth that goes hard when baked.
clean *adj*. not dirty; bright. *vb*. remove dirt from something.
clear *adj*. easy to see through. *The glass was clear;* easy to understand. *The meaning of the word was quite clear*; free from obstacles. *Before you cross, see that the road is clear*. *vb*. make or become clear.
clematis *n*. a climbing shrub.

clement *adj*. showing mercy; gentle, mild, soft. **clemency** *n*.

clerk (rhymes with *dark*) *n*. a person who works in an office writing things down.

clever *adj*. bright; intelligent.

cliché (**klee**-*shay*) *n*. commonplace, unoriginal expression or idea etc.

cliff *n*. a very steep high bank, especially by the sea.

climate *n*. the usual weather of a place over a long period of time.

climax *n*. the high point of a piece of music, drama; an expedition or holiday etc. *The climb to the top of the castle walls formed the climax of the school visit.*

climb *vb*. go up, sometimes using both hands and feet to hold on. *n*.

Sailing clippers carried goods across the seas during the 19th century. They were the fastest ships ever built until then.

cling *vb*. hang on to something.

clinic *n*. a doctor's surgery; a small hospital.

clip 1. *n*. a fastener or device for holding things together. *vb*. 2. *vb*. cut with scissors, cut short.

clipper *n*. a fast sailing ship of the mid-1800s.

cloak (rhymes with *poke*) *n*. a loose coat with no sleeves; a long cape.

cloakroom *n*. a place to leave your coat.

clock *n*. a machine for telling the time.

clockwise *adj*. going round in the same direction as the hands of a clock. **anti-clockwise** – going round in the opposite direction to the hands of a clock.

clockwork *n*. worked by a spring that is wound up.

clod *n*. 1. lump of earth. 2. lout, blockhead.

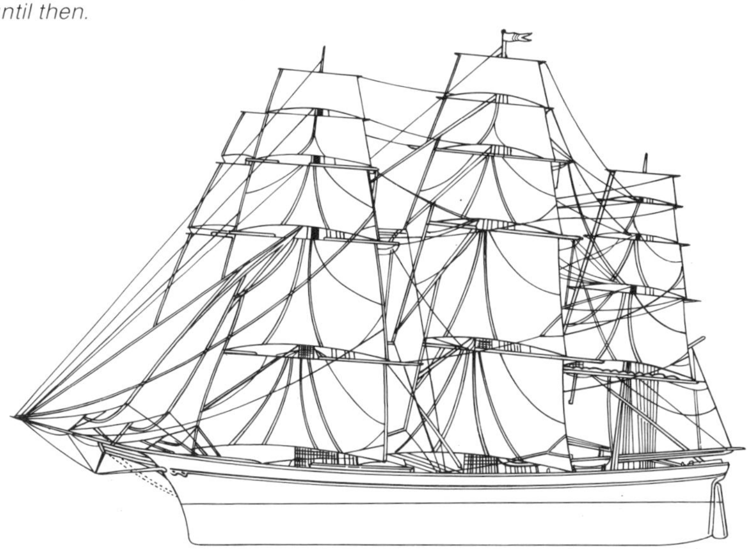

clog 1. *vb.* choke, fill up or obstruct. 2. *n.* a wooden shoe, especially in the Netherlands.
cloister *n.* covered way (arcade) open on one side and overlooking a quadrangle.
close 1. *adj.* (rhymes with *dose*) nearby; narrow. 2. *vb.* (rhymes with *nose*) shut; bring to an end.
cloth *n.* a material made by weaving fibres such as wool, linen or nylon.
clothes *pl. n.* things to wear. **clothes-horse** *n.* frame to dry clothes on.
cloud *n.* great clusters of tiny water droplets in the air.

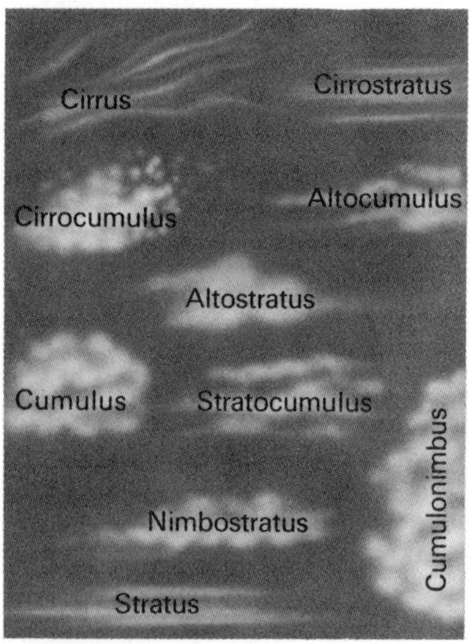

Cloud types can be recognized by their shapes.

cloudburst *n.* heavy rainstorm.
clout *n.* heavy swinging blow with the hand; to have power.
clove *n.* the dried bud of the clove tree, used as a spice.
cloven *adj.* divided, e.g. cloven hoof of ruminants.
clover *n.* a small green plant, usually with three leaves, which often grows in fields. The flowers are usually red or white. Widely cultivated as animal fodder.
clown *n.* a person who does funny things in a circus.
club *n.* 1. a heavy stick with which to hit things. 2. a group that people can join to do things together. *We have a chess club in our school.*
cluck *vb.* & *n.* sound made by a hen.
clue *n.* something that helps you to solve a puzzle.
clumsy *adj.* heavy and awkward.
clung *vb.* past of **cling**.
cluster *n.* number of things growing closely together; a group or bunch. *vb.*
clutch 1. *vb.* seize or grab eagerly. *n.* a firm hold. 2. *n.* device for engaging and disengaging gears etc. 3. *n.* set of eggs.
coach 1. *n.* a four-wheeled horse-drawn carriage; a single-decker bus. 2. *vb.* & *n.* teach someone, especially a sport. *n.* someone who helps others to prepare for examinations.
coal *n.* a black mineral that burns slowly and gives out heat.
coarse *adj.* rough; not fine.
coast *n.* land along the edge of the sea.
coat *n.* 1. an article of clothing with sleeves that covers the top half of the body; an overcoat. 2. a covering. *That door needs another coat of paint.*
coax *vb.* persuade gently.

cobbler *n.* a person who mends shoes.
cobra *n.* a poisonous snake that can expand its neck into a hood.
cobweb *n.* a fine web made by a spider.
cock *n.* a male bird, especially a farmyard fowl.
cockatoo *n.* a crested parrot.
cockerel *n.* a young cock bird.
cockle *n.* a kind of shellfish.
cockney *n.* a person from the East End of London.
cockpit *n.* the area where the pilot sits in an aircraft; the driver's seat in a racing car. (Originally an enclosed space for contests between fighting cocks.)
cocoa *n.* chocolate powder made from the seeds of the cacao tree.
coconut *n.* large oval, hard-shelled fruit of the coconut palm.
cocoon *n.* covering made by a caterpillar to protect itself during the chrysalis stage.
cod *n.* a large sea fish eaten as a food.
code *n.* 1. a secret system of writing; cipher. 2. a set of rules. *We should all learn the Highway Code*. 3. a signalling system.
co-education *n.* education of boys and girls together.
coffee *n.* a drink made from the roasted and ground beans of the coffee plant.

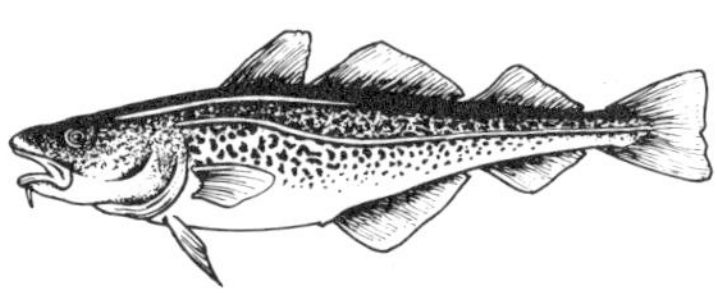

The cod is a large, edible fish.

Metal cogs fit together to drive a gear wheel round.

coffer *n.* box or chest for storing money etc.
coffin *n.* a box in which a dead person is buried or cremated.
cog *n.* one of the teeth around the rim of a gear wheel.
coil *vb.* & *n.* wind something in circles or spirals. *The old electric fire had two coils of wire that gave off heat*.
coin *n.* a piece of metal, usually of a uniform size and design, used as money.
coincide *vb.* happen at the same time; agree exactly. **coincidence** *n.* combination of events happening by chance.
coke *n.* what is left of coal after the gases have been removed by heating.
cold 1. *adj.* not hot. 2. *n.* a kind of illness which gives people a runny nose and causes sneezing and a sore throat.
collaborate *vb.* work together (with), co-operate. **collaboration** *n.*
collage (**koll**-*arj*) *n.* a picture made up of pieces of cloth, paper or other materials.
collapse *vb.* fall down; fall to pieces; *n.* breakdown. **collapsible** *adj.* folding.

collar *n.* part of a shirt or other clothing that goes around the neck; a leather band around an animal's neck.
colleague *n.* a fellow worker; fellow official.
collect *vb.* gather or bring together. *We collect coins*; gather from a number of people. *They went round the houses to collect money for charity*.
college *n.* a place where people go to study after secondary school; part of a university.
collide *vb.* bump into something by mistake. **collision** *n.*
collie *n.* a long-haired breed of sheepdog, originally from Scotland.
collier *n.* a coal miner; a ship that carries coal.
collision *n.* a striking together of moving bodies.
colloquial *adj.* everyday, familiar language.
colon *n.* 1. the large intestine. 2. punctuation mark (:).
colonel (**kern**-*el*) *n.* a senior rank in the army, below that of brigadier, but above lieutenant-colonel.
colony *n.* 1. a group of settlers in a new country who are still governed by their country of origin; the country where the settlers live. *Hong Kong is still a British colony*. 2. a group of people or animals that live together. *He came upon a large colony of bees*. **colonial** *adj.* **colonize** *vb.*
colossal *adj.* gigantic, huge.
colossus *n.* a statue much larger than life-size.
colour *n.* red, blue, green etc.

A collie is a type of sheepdog.

vb. apply paint, crayon etc.
colt *n.* a young male horse.
column *n.* a tall round pillar composed of a base, a shaft and a capital top. The capital is often decorated.

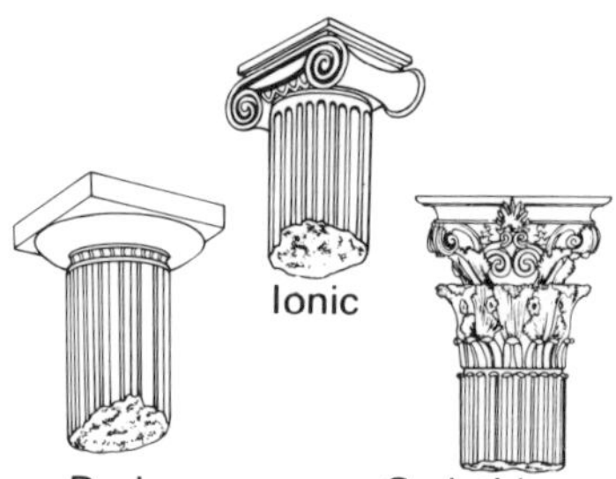

Columns were widely used in Greek and Roman architecture. There are three types of column: Doric, Corinthian and Ionic.

coma *n.* an unnatural, heavy and prolonged sleep.
comb *n.* & *vb.* a small object with 'teeth' used by people for making their hair tidy.
combat *n.* & *vb.* fight; battle.
combine *vb.* join together.
combine-harvester *n.* a large farm machine that cuts grain and threshes it.

combustion *n.* another word for burning, a chemical reaction that produces light and heat. **combustible** *adj.*

come *vb.* arrive; draw near. *'Come' is the opposite of 'go'.*

come about *vb.* happen. *It came about that we all met at the beach.*

come across *vb.* find something when you do not expect to. *I came across your letter when I was tidying my desk.*

comedy *n.* a funny play. **comedian** *n.* a stage or TV entertainer who tells jokes.

comet *n.* a body of (probably) ice and gas, which looks like a star but moves around our Sun.

come to *vb.* 1. total cost of several things. *When it is all added together it will come to £17.43.* 2. recover consciousness. *He has just come to after his operation.*

comfort *vb.* help someone who is unhappy. *Sandra comforted the little girl until her mother arrived.* **comfortable** *adj.*

comic 1. *adj.* funny. 2. *n.* a children's paper with strip pictures.

comma *n.* a punctuation mark like this, (,) that is used to show a pause in writing.

command 1. *vb.* order someone to do something. 2. *n.* be in charge of. *Napoleon took command of the whole army.*

commence *vb.* begin. **commencement** *n.*

comment *n.* & *vb.* a remark made about someone or something; an observation. **commentary** *n.* continuous comments on some happening, esp. when it is taking place, e.g. a football commentary.

commerce *n.* trade. *adj.* concerned with trade.

commercial *n.* broadcast advertisement.

commit *vb.* 1. do, carry out. 2. hand over, entrust.

committee *n.* a small group of people who are appointed by a larger group of people to run the larger group's affairs. *Our club's committee meets once a month.*

common *adj.* usual, normal; often seen. *A thrush is a very common bird.*

common sense *n.* good, ordinary, sensible thinking.

A comet looks like a star but moves in orbit around the Sun. The long tail is made up of gas and dust. The most famous comet is Halley's Comet.

communicate *vb.* pass on information or feelings to other people. **communication** *n.* the passing of information from one person to another.

communion *n.* 1. an act of sharing; fellowship. 2. Christian celebration of the Lord's supper.

communiqué (*kom*-**mune**-*ik-aye*) *n.* an official announcement.

Communism *n.* a political system which believes that all property should be held in common.

Karl Marx was the founder of Communism in the 19th century.

community *n.* all the people who live in a place.

commuter *n.* a person who travels some distance daily to and from work. **commute** *vb.*

compact (*kom*-**pact**) *adj.* & *vb.* packed closely together; easy to handle.

companion *n.* a friend; someone who goes with you.

company *n.* 1. an organization in business to make, buy or sell things. 2. visitors in your house.

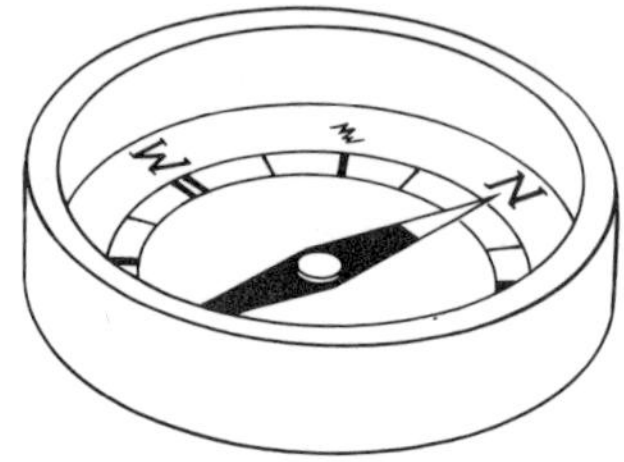

A compass has a needle that points to the North, so you can work out in which direction you are going.

compare *vb.* look at things to see how alike or unlike they are. *Roger compared the two chairs and decided to buy the larger one.* **comparison** *n.*

compartment *n.* marked off division of an enclosed space (box, railway carriage etc).

compass *n.* an instrument that shows direction and used for finding the way.

compasses *pl. n.* an instrument for drawing circles or for measuring.

compassion *n.* having pity or sorrow for the sufferings of another. **compassionate** *adj.*

compatible *adj.* able to get along together. *Bob and Sue are friends because they are compatible.*

compel *vb.* force, make or urge someone to do something.

compensate *vb.* make up for (the loss of etc.). **compensation** *n.* something given to make up for.

compère (com-*pair*) *n.* person who introduces entertainers in a variety show etc.

compete *vb.* take part in a contest. *All the girls will compete in the race.* **competition** *n.* a contest in

which a number of people take part to see who is the best.
competent *adj*. able, efficient, qualified. **competence** *n*.
complain *vb*. say that you are not pleased with something. **complaint** *n*. a grievance, protest; bodily illness.
complete 1. *adj*. whole; the full number. *When the party was complete it numbered 16 boys.* 2. *vb*. finish. *It will take three months to complete the new school.*
complex *adj*. complicated, difficult to understand. **complexity** *n*.
complexion *n*. colour and appearance of the skin, especially of the face.
complicated *adj*. made up of many different parts; difficult to understand. **complicate** *vb*. make complicated, entangle. **complication** *n*. complicated state; new illness developing in the course of another.
compliment *n*. & *vb*. praise, flattery, formal greeting.
comply *vb*. do as asked or commanded.
compose *vb*. write a story or make up a piece of music. **composer** *n*. a person who makes up music.
compound *n*. something made up of separate parts or elements. *vb*. mix or combine into a whole.
comprehend *vb*. understand; include. **comprehensible** *adj*. intelligible. **comprehensive** *adj*. all-inclusive.
comprise *vb*. include, consist of.
compromise *n*. a settlement of differences by meeting half way, each side giving up part of its claim. *vb*.
computer *n*. an electronic calculating machine that stores and processes information (data) and works with enormous speed.

A modern computer has several different components.

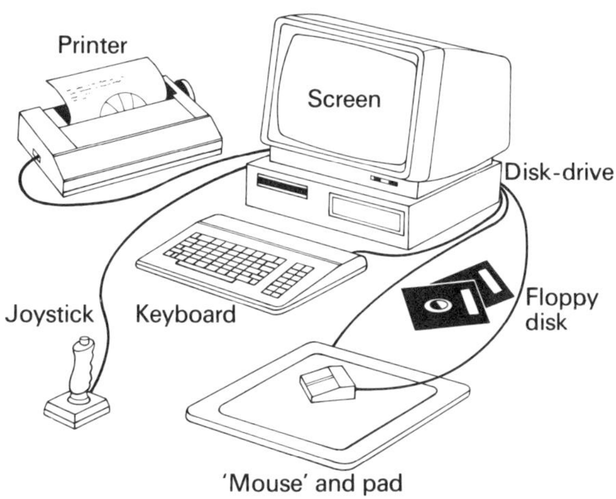

comrade *n.* a friend; a companion.
concave *adj.* a surface that curves inwards, like the inside of a saucer.
conceal *vb.* hide.
concede (*con*-**seed**) *vb.* give up; grant; allow.
conceive (*con*-**seeve**) *vb.* become pregnant.
concentrate *vb.* bring together; compress; focus attention on.
concentration *n.* the act of concentrating or giving one's attention to.
conception *n.* 1. becoming pregnant. 2. idea.
concern *vb.* have to do with; cause a feeling of responsibility. *I am concerned about your bad tooth. n.* what one is interested in; a business.
concerning *prep.* about, with regard to; regarding.
concert *n.* a musical entertainment.
concise *adj.* made shorter; abbreviated. *A concise encyclopedia.*
conclude *vb.* bring to an end; come to an opinion. *He concluded she was right.* **conclusion** *n.* ending; final opinion. **conclusive** *adj.*
concrete *n.* a hard building material made of cement, sand, gravel and water.
condemn *vb.* pronounce someone or something guilty or unfit for use. *The judge condemned the criminal to five years in prison.*
condense *vb.* 1. make something more solid; shorten. *She condensed the story by cutting out some unnecessary sentences.* 2. Change from a gas into a liquid. *The steam condensed into water.*

Concave and convex lenses.

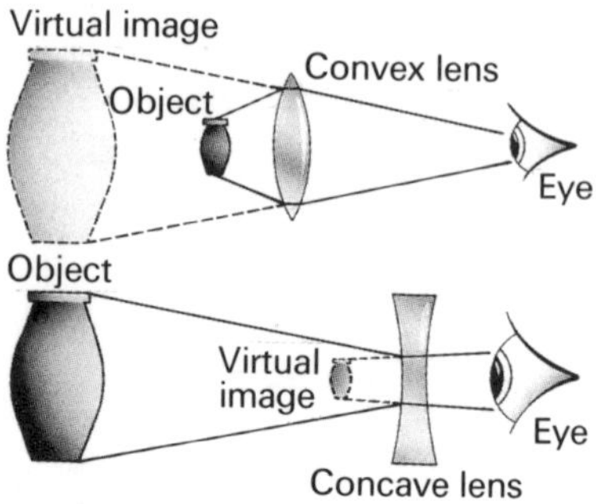

condition *n.* 1. state of being, health. *She is in no fit condition to go dancing.* 2. provision, specification. *You may go on condition you finish your homework first.*
conduct 1. *vb.* (*kon*-**duct**) lead, manage; direct a performance, orchestra etc. 2. *n.* (**kon**-*duct*) direction, behaviour. *His conduct was terrible.*
conductor *n.* 1. a person who leads a group of singers or musicians; a person who collects fares on a bus or train. 2. any material that allows electricity to pass through it is called a conductor. Metals are good conductors. Substances that do not conduct electricity are called insulators.
cone *n.* 1. solid body with a round bottom and a pointed top. 2. the fruit of a fir or pine tree.
confess *vb.* admit to doing wrong; own up. **confession** *n.*
confetti *n.* tiny pieces of coloured paper thrown over a couple at their wedding.

confidence *n.* 1. feeling of certainty; a trust in one's own abilities. 2. thing told as a secret. **confident** *adj.*
confidential *adj.* private, secret.
confine *vb.* shut up, imprison; keep within limits. **confinement** *n.*
confirm *vb.* 1. establish more firmly; ratify. 2. admit to full membership of the Christian Church. **confirmation** *n.*

An evergreen conifer. This type is called a spruce.

confiscate *vb.* to take something away as a punishment. *The teacher confiscated his sweets because he ate them in class.*
conflict 1. *n.* a war or fighting; an argument. 2. *vb.* differ; disagree.
conform *vb.* follow the accepted customs and rules, comply.
confront *vb.* face, oppose.
confuse *vb.* mix up, throw into disorder; mistake one thing for another. **confusion** *n.*
congeal *vb.* freeze; become solid after cooling down.
conger *n.* a type of large eel found in the sea.
congratulate *vb.* tell someone you are glad that they have done well.
congregate *vb.* gather together in a crowd, or **congregation** *n.*
Congress *n.* the parliament of the United States of America.
conifer *n.* an evergreen tree with cones for fruit.
conjuror *n.* a person who performs tricks that look like magic. **conjure** *vb.*

Fir cones like this are the fruits of the conifer.

conker *n.* the nut of the horse chestnut tree.
connect *vb.* join things together. *This road connects our town to the main highway.* **connection** (**connexion**) *n.*
connoisseur *n.* well-informed person in matters of taste etc.
conquer (**con**-*ker*) *vb.* defeat an enemy, overcome. **conquest** *n.*
conquistador *n.* Spanish soldier-explorer of the 1500s.

1. Pegasus
2. Pisces
3. Aries
4. Cygnus
5. Lyra
6. Cepheus
7. Perseus
8. Auriga
9. Taurus
10. Orion
11. Lynx
12. Polaris
13. Ursa Minor
14. Hercules
15. Corona Borealis
16. Ursa Major
17. Gemini
18. Cancer
19. Leo
20. Virgo

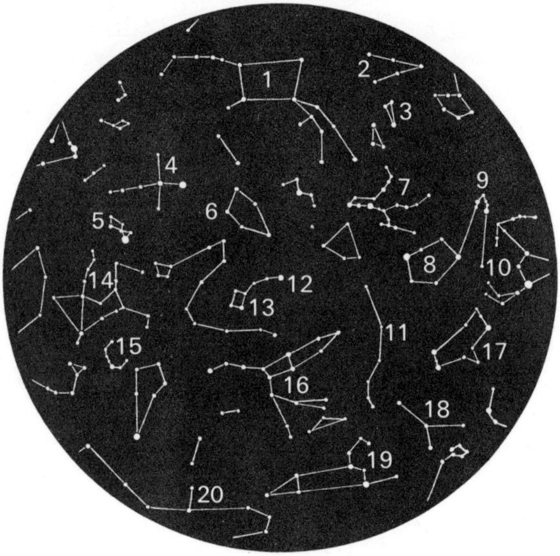

The constellations of the Northern Hemisphere.

conscience (**kon**-*shunz*) *n.* sense of right and wrong.

conscious (**kon**-*shuss*) *adj.* awake, alert, active.

consecrate *vb.* set apart; make holy; devote to. *He consecrated all his time to music.*

consent *vb.* agree to. *n.* permission. *You took the book without my consent.*

consequence *n.* outcome, result of something. *The consequence of his actions.*

conserve *vb.* keep something as it was without changing it. **conservation** *n.* looking after things so they are not spoiled or destroyed.

conservative *adj.* opposed to great change; cautious.

consider *vb.* think about. **consideration** *n.* quality of being thoughtful esp. of other people. **considerate** *adj.*

consist *vb.* be composed of.

consonant *n.* any letter of the alphabet except a, e, i, o, u, which are vowels.

conspire *vb.* plot secretly for an evil purpose.

constable *n.* a police officer.

constant *adj.* all the time.

constellation *n.* a group of stars which make a recognizable shape in the sky.

constitution *n.* 1. laws or rules by which a country, society etc. is governed. 2. a person's physical condition.

constrict *vb.* make narrow, compress. **constriction** *n.*

construct *vb.* build, fit together. **construction** *n.* **constructive** *adj.* creative, helpful.

consult *vb.* try to get advice or help from someone or from a book. **consultation** *n.*

consume *vb.* eat or drink; devour; destroy. *Fire consumed the building.*

contact *vb.* meet; join; get in touch with someone. *n.* a join; an electrical connection; a person whom you can get in touch with. *I have a good contact working in TV.*
contain *vb.* hold something. *This box contains all my belongings.* **container** *n.* a box, jar, pot or tin in which things are put.
contempt *n.* scorn, despising. *They have a contempt for authority.* **contemptible** *adj.*
contented *adj.* peaceful and satisfied.
contents 1. *n.* the things that are in something. *The contents of Rudolph's pockets were a penknife, a rubber band and two toffees.*
contest *n.* a competition; a fight.
continent *n.* one of the seven main land masses of the world: North America, South America, Asia, Africa, Europe, Australasia and Antarctica.
continue *vb.* go on being or doing. *We will continue collecting stamps.* **continual** *adj.* unceasing. **continuous** *adj.* uninterrupted, unbroken.
contour *n.* an outline; line on a map joining points of equal height.
contraception *n.* birth control, **contraceptive** *n.* device or drug which prevents conception.
contract (*kon*-**trakt**) 1. *vb.* grow smaller. *A heated metal bar contracts as it becomes colder.* **contraction** *n.* tightening of the muscles. 2. (**kon**-*trakt*) *n.* an agreement. *The butcher had a contract to deliver meat.*
contradict *vb.* go against person in what he or she says; deny, oppose. **contradiction** *n.* denial, inconsistency.
contrast *vb.* compare things and notice the differences. *n.* the difference shown by comparing different things.

The seven continents of the world.

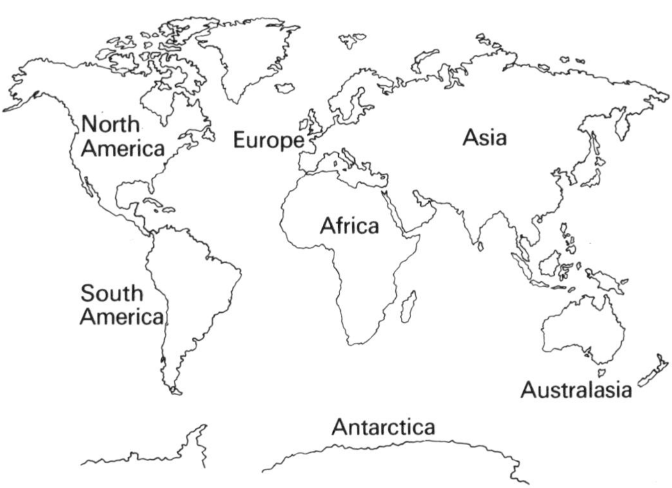

contribute *vb.* give (money etc.). *She contributed to a number of charities.* **contribution** *n.*

control *vb.* 1. be in charge of. 2. operate machinery. *n.* a lever, wheel or knob which is used to control machinery.

controversy *n.* dispute, argument.

convalescent *n.* & *adj.* regaining health after illness. **convalesce** *vb.*

convene *vb.* call a meeting, meet. **convention** *n.* formal assembly to discuss business etc.

convenient *adj.* suitable, handy. *Our new house is only two minutes from school. It is very convenient.*

convent *n.* a place where nuns live and work.

converge *vb.* come nearer together. *The two boats were converging rapidly and were in danger of colliding.*

conversation *n.* talk. **converse** *vb.*

convex *adj.* a surface that curves outwards, like an up-turned saucer.

convey *vb.* carry from one place to another; transmit sound etc.; lead.

convict 1. *n.* (**kon**-*vikt*) a criminal who has been sent to prison. 2. *vb.* (*kon*-**vict**) prove someone guilty of a crime.

convoy *n.* a group of merchant ships sailing together under naval escort.

cook *vb.* prepare food for table. *n.* a person who cooks.

cooking *n.* a way of making meals by heating food.

cool *adj.* rather cold; the opposite of warm.

co-operate *vb.* work with others to do something. *If we co-operate we will finish the job sooner.* **co-operation** *n.* **co-operative** *adj.* willing to help.

copper *n.* a reddish-brown metal. (symbol Cu).

copy *vb.* make something look exactly like something else. *n.* exact reproduction.

copyright *n.* the ownership of a piece of writing or other art form.

coral *n.* hard pink or white material made mainly in warm, shallow seas from the bodies of tiny animals.

cord *n.* a thin rope or stout length of string.

corduroy *n.* a cotton velvet fabric with ridges or 'wales' in the pile.

core *n.* the centre of, the middle part. *Our dog likes to eat the core of my apple.*

corgi *n.* a small Welsh breed of dog.

cork *n.* the light tough bark of the cork-oak tree; a bottle stopper made from cork.

corkscrew *n.* a tool for taking corks out of bottles.

The Welsh corgi is a dog with short legs and a long, pointed nose. Corgis were once used for herding cattle.

corm *n.* a bulb-like swelling on the stem of a plant underground. *A crocus grows from a corm.*
cormorant *n.* a sea bird.
corn *n.* grain. The seeds of wheat, oats, rye and barley; maize (corn-on-the-cob or Indian maize).
corner *n.* a point where two sides meet. *The front door is near the corner of the buiding.*
cornet *n.* a brass instrument similar to the trumpet.
cornflour *n.* finely ground maize, rice etc.
coronation *n.* the ceremony when a king or queen is crowned.
corpse *n.* dead human body.
correct *adj.* right; true; with no mistakes. *All my sums were correct today. vb.* put right any mistakes. *Our teacher corrects our exercise books every day.* **correction** *n.*
correspond *vb.* 1. be similar to. 2. exchange letters. **correspondence** *n.*

The cormorant is a fish-eating bird commonly found by the seashore.

corridor *n.* a long passage in a building.

Crocuses grow from corms.

corroboree (*ko*-**rob**-*o-ree*) *n.* a ceremonial dance of the Aborigines of Australia. Held at night by the light of bush fires.
corrode *vb.* wear away by the action of rust etc. **corrosion** *n.*
corrupt *vb.* spoil, influence badly. *adj.* evil, rotten. **corruption** *n.*
cosh *n.* truncheon or heavy stick used as a weapon. *vb.*
cosmetics *n.* beauty preparations for hair, skin etc. **cosmetic** *adj.*
cosmic rays *pl. n.* tiny particles that crash into the Earth's atmosphere from outer space.
cosmonaut *n.* (usually) a Russian astronaut.
cost 1. *n.* the amount one has to pay for something. 2. *vb.* cause the loss of. *His attempt to save the boy cost him his life.* **costly** *adj.* expensive.
costume *n.* clothes, especially the clothes worn by actors.
cot *n.* a small bed, usually with high sides, for a baby.

cottage *n.* a small house usually in the country.

cotton *n.* fibre from the seeds of the cotton plant.

couch *n.* a long, soft seat.

cougar *n.* another name for the puma, or mountain lion, a large member of the cat family native to the Americas.

cough (*koff*) *n.* & *vb.* a sudden and noisy rush of air from the lungs.

council *n.* a group of people who meet to take decisions.

counsel *n.* advice. *He gave Tom some wise counsel*; an adviser in Law. *vb.*

count 1. *vb.* add up. *Have you started to count the money yet?* 2. *n.* a European nobleman.

counter 1. *n.* a table or flat surface in a shop. 2. *n.* a small piece used in a board game. 3. *prefix* against, opposing, opposite, rival, e.g. **counteract** act in opposition to; **counter-balance** act against in equal strength. **counter-attraction** rival attraction.

countess *n.* wife of an earl or count.

country *n.* the whole land where people live. *France is the country of the French*; the land outside towns. *We like to walk in the country at weekends.*

county *n.* a part of the country with its own local government.

couple *n.* two; a pair. *vb.* join, link, connect together.

coupon *n.* detachable ticket which can be exchanged for something or used to apply for something.

courage *n.* bravery.

courier (**koo**-*ree-er*) *n.* messenger; person employed by a travel agency to conduct groups of travellers.

course *n.* 1. the direction in which something goes. *We followed the course of the river to its mouth.* 2. one of successive parts of a meal – *the sweet course*.

court *n.* 1. the place where trials are held. 2. the place where a king or queen lives, and the people who live there. 3. an area marked out for certain games, as a tennis court or squash court.

courteous (**kur**-*tee-us*) *adj.* polite, well mannered. **courtesy** *n.*

cousin *n.* the child of your aunt or uncle.

cover *vb.* put something over something else.

The cougar or mountain lion.

The coypu is a large rodent.

covering *n.* something that covers something. *Bark is the covering of a tree trunk.*
cow *n.* 1. a farm animal kept for its milk. 2. a female of the ox family or a female elephant, whale or seal.
coward *n.* a person who cannot hide fear and who lacks courage.
cowardice *n.* cowardly conduct. **cowardly** *adj.*
cowboy/cowgirl *n.* a person who looks after cattle on the American prairies.
cowslip *n.* plant of the primrose family.
coy *adj.* excessively shy.
coyote (*koy*-**oh**-*ti*) *n.* the wild dog of North America, resembling a small wolf.
coypu *n.* South American aquatic rodent whose fur is highly valued.
crab *n.* a marine animal with a hard shell and ten legs, two of which have large claws.
crack 1.*vb.* split; break. *Jack cracked a nut.* **cracked** *adj.* split, broken. 2. *n.* a sharp noise. 3. *n.* a split or small opening. *There is a crack in the cup.*
cracker *n.* 1. a small firework enclosed in a cylinder of coloured paper which snaps when the ends are pulled. 2. a crisp biscuit or wafer.
cradle *n.* a bed for a small baby, usually on rockers.
craft *n.* 1. skilled work with the hands. 2. a boat; an aircraft.
craftsman *n.* a skilled person who works at a craft.
cram *vb.* stuff into a small space.
cramp 1. *n.* sudden painful contraction of the muscles. 2. *n.* restrict; write too small.
crane (bird) *n.* a large water bird with long legs.
crane (machine) *n.* a machine that lifts and moves heavy things.
crash 1. *n.* & *vb.* a loud noise. 2. *n.* & *vb.* a collision. *Several cars were involved in the crash.*
crass *adj.* ignorant and stupid.
crate *n.* a large box made from thin pieces of wood.
crater *n.* 1. mouth of a volcano. 2. a hole in the ground made by the explosion of a bomb or shell.
crave *vb.* have a great desire for. **craving** *n.*

Cowslips flower in spring.

crawl 1. *vb*. move on all fours like a baby. 2. *n*. an overarm stroke in swimming.
crayon *n*. a kind of coloured pencil for drawing.
craze *n*. a general but passing fashion.
crazy *adj*. foolish, mad; eager for.
creak *n*. & *vb*. (make) harsh, squeaky sound.
cream *n*. the fatty part of milk. *n*. & *adj*. the colour of cream (yellowish white).
crease *n*. 1. a mark or line made in folding cloth, paper etc. 2. *n*. one of the white lines on a cricket pitch.

Ivy growing on the trunk of a tree. Ivy is a kind of creeper. It uses suckers to cling on to walls or fences or on to other plants.

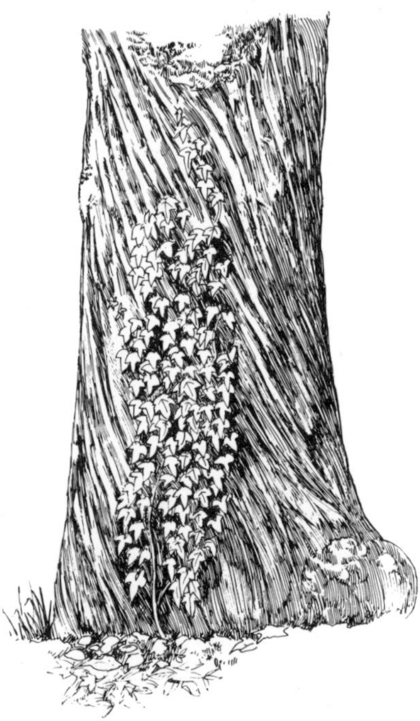

create *vb*. make something; bring something into existence. *Authors create characters for their stories*. **creation** *n*. the thing made or created.
creator *n*. 1. the person who creates. 2. the God who created the universe.
creature *n*. any living thing.
creed *n*. a statement or system of religious belief; general belief or opinion.
creek *n*. 1. a small inlet in the coastline. 2. a small river (Australia and USA). *up the creek* in trouble (slang).
creep *vb*. move along close to the ground; crawl; move stealthily.
creeper *n*. a plant that creeps along the ground or up the wall.
cremate *vb*. burn to ashes (especially dead bodies).
Creole *n*. & *adj*. person of European descent born in West Indies or Latin America; person of mixed Creole and Negro descent.
crêpe paper (crêpe rhymes with *grape*) *n*. a special sort of crinkly paper.
crept *vb*. past of **creep**.
crescent *n*. a curved shape like a new moon; a row of houses shaped like a crescent.
cress *n*. a family of plants, such as watercress, some of which are eaten in salads.
crest *n*. 1. tuft of hair or feathers on head of certain birds and animals. 2. device on a coat of arms. 3. highest point.
crew *n*. workers on a ship or aircraft.
crib *n*. 1. a baby's cot. 2. rack

for animal fodder. 3. translation of something in a foreign language. 4. *n.* a copy used for cheating in an examination.

cribbage *n.* a card game.

crick *n.* cramp or stiffness in the back of the neck.

cricket *n.* 1. a small insect like a grasshopper that leaps and makes a chirping noise. 2. an outdoor summer game played with bats and a ball by teams of eleven players.

express judgement on (work of art etc.); analyse; find fault with. **critic** *n.* person who criticizes, reviews a work of art etc. **critical** *adj.* fault-finding; concerning a crisis or risk. *a critical operation.*

croak *vb.* & *n.* (make) a harsh, hoarse sound of a frog, raven etc.

crochet (**kro**-*shay*) *n.* kind of knitting done with a hooked needle.

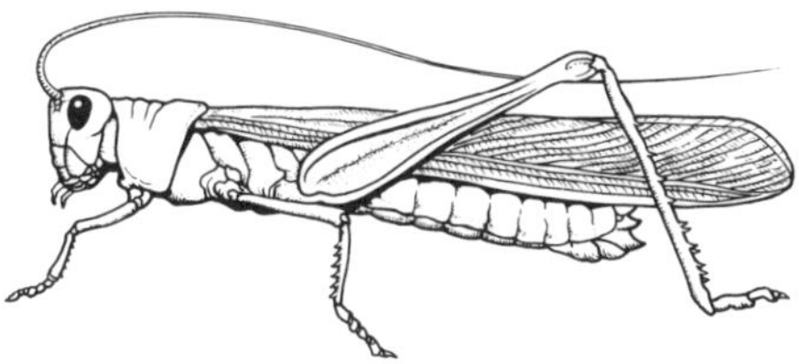

The cricket 'sings' by rubbing its wings together.

cried *vb.* past of **cry**.

crime *n.* something done that is against the law.

criminal *n.* someone who is guilty of a crime.

crimson *n.* & *adj.* a deep red colour.

cringe *vb.* shrink in fear.

crinkle *vb.* make something form wrinkles or folds.

crinoline *n.* a large stiff petticoat worn by 19th-century women.

cripple *n.* someone whose body is so badly hurt or deformed that they cannot do things easily. *vb.* disable, maim.

crisis *n.* a decisive point; a difficult time.

crisp 1. *adj.* dry and hard, but easy to break. 2. *n.* a potato flake.

criticize (**krit**-*is-ize*) *vb.*

crockery *n.* earthenware or china vessels–cups, plates etc.

crocodile *n.* a fierce, long reptile that lives in rivers.

crocus *n.* a small garden flower with yellow or purple petals.

croft *n.* a small house or farm, especially in the Highlands of Scotland.

crook *n.* 1. stick with a hooked top, used by shepherds. 2. cheat, swindler. *vb.* bend.

crooked *adj.* 1. not straight. 2. dishonest.

croon *vb.* sing or speak softly. **crooner** *n.*

crop 1. *n.* the plants that are gathered each year from a farm. 2. *vb.* cut short.

croquet (**krow**-*kay*) *n.* game played on a lawn in which balls are hit with a mallet through a series of hoops.

cross *n*. 1. the mark (X). 2. the wooden frame on which Jesus was crucified; the sign of the cross (†) as the symbol of the Christian faith.

crossbow *n*. spring-operated medieval weapon which fired an iron bolt.

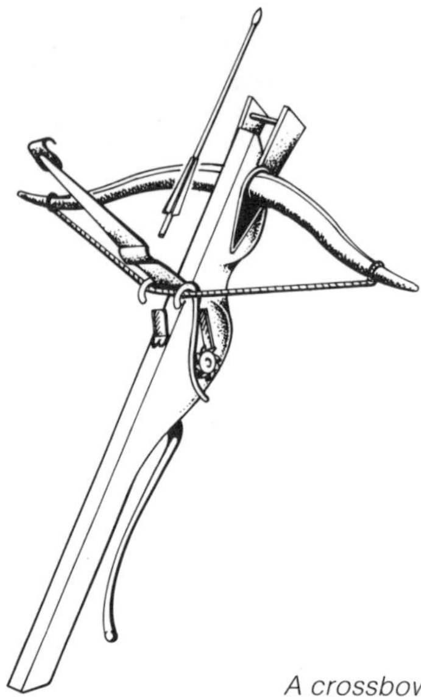

A crossbow.

crossing *n*. a place where people can go across the street. *It is safer to cross the road at the proper crossing.*

crossroads *n*. a place where two roads meet each other and cross.

crosswind *n*. blowing from the side.

crow 1. *n*. a large, black bird with a harsh cry. 2. *vb*. give a shrill cry like a cock. 3. *vb*. boast.

crowbar *n*. bar of iron used as a lever.

crowd *n*. a lot of people gathered together.

crown *n*. the headdress of a king or queen.

crucial *adj*. critical, decisive.

crucifix *n*. a figure or picture of Christ on the cross.

crude *adj*. rough, unfinished, raw, in natural state. **crudeness**, **crudity** *n*.

cruel *adj*. liking to give pain to others. **cruelty** *n*.

cruise *vb*. sail about for pleasure. **cruiser** *n*. warship designed for speed.

crumb *n*. a small scrap of bread or other food.

crumble *vb*. fall or break into small pieces.

crumpet *n*. soft round cake which is toasted and buttered.

crumple *vb*. crease carelessly; crush paper into a ball.

crunch *vb*. crush, grind noisily with the teeth; tread underfoot making noise of grinding gravel.

crusade *n*. & *vb*. a campaign or movement or undertaking to further a cause.

crush *vb*. 1. press on and break into pieces. *If you sit on the crackers you will crush them.* 2. defeat. *Napoleon went on to crush all his enemies.*

crust *n*. a hard, outer layer, like a crust of bread. **crusty** *adj*. having much crust; irritable.

crustacean *n*. one of a group of animals most of which have a hard shell and live in the sea.

crutch *n*. something that helps a lame person to walk.

cry *vb*. make a loud noise; weep or sob.

crypt *n*. the basement of a church; an underground place of worship.

cryptogram *n.* a message written in code.

crystal 1. *n.* a hard glass-like mineral. 2. *adj.* the shape which tiny pieces of many chemicals (such as salt) always take. 3. *n.* a kind of good quality, very clear glass.

A crystal.

cub *n.* 1. a young bear, lion, fox, tiger, or some other animal. 2. a junior Boy Scout.

cube *n.* a solid object with six equal sides. **cubic** *adj.* cube shaped.

cuckoo *n.* a family of birds that lay their eggs in the nests of other birds.

cucumber *n.* a long, narrow fruit, green outside, white inside.

cud *n.* food that cows and other ruminants bring back from their first stomach to chew again.

cuddle *vb.* hug. **cuddly** *adj.* pleasant to hug, like soft toys.

cue *n.* 1. a long rod for playing billiards, snooker etc. 2. signal for an actor to enter stage or start a speech.

cuff 1. *n.* the end of the sleeve. 2. *vb.* hit someone with the open hand. *n.*

culprit *n.* a guilty person.

cultivate *vb.* help plants to grow by preparing the soil well and looking after them.

culture *n.* type of civilization. **cultured** *adj.* well educated.

cunning *adj.* crafty; artful. *The fox is a cunning animal.*

cup *n.* an object used to contain drinks such as tea or coffee.

cupboard (*cub-erd*) *n.* a piece of furniture used for storing things.

curate *n.* assistant to a parish priest.

curb *n.* part of a bridle used to check or restrain a horse; a restraint. *vb.*

cure *vb.* 1. make well. 2. preserve some substances such as leather, tobacco and some meats by drying, smoking or salting them.

A cuckoo.

curious *adj*. 1. odd; strange. *Jane was wearing a very curious hat*. 2. wanting to find out about something. *I am very curious as to why she is wearing that hat*.

curlew *n*. wading bird with a long curved bill.

The curlew's long, curved bill helps it find food on the seashore.

curly *adj*. something that is twisted into shape like a spiral or coil, especially hair. **curl** *n*. & *vb*.

currant *n*. a small, seedless dried grape.

currency *n*. the money that is used in a country.

current *n*. air or water running in one direction.

current (electric) *n*. the movement or flow of electricity.

curriculum *n*. course of study.

curry *n*. a hot, spicy food, originally made in India and Pakistan.

curse *n*. asking that evil or punishment falls on a person. *vb*. swear.

curt *adj*. brief; short.

curtail *vb*. shorten, reduce.

curtain *n*. a piece of cloth used as a screen, particularly as a covering for windows.

curtsy *n*. old-fashioned gesture of respect made by women with bending of the knees. *vb*.

curve *n*. & *vb*. bend; a line that is not straight.

cushion *n*. an object like a small pillow, used for making a chair more comfortable. *vb*. protect (as if with cushions).

custard *n*. sauce made with milk and eggs or cornflour.

custody *n*. the state of being detained, often in gaol, while awaiting trial. **custodian** *n*. guardian, keeper.

custom *n*. the usual way of doing something. *It is the custom in some countries to kiss people on both cheeks when you meet them*. **customary** *adj*. usual.

customer *n*. a person who buys things from a shop or business, sometimes regularly.

cut *vb*. slice with a knife or other sharp objects. *Can I have a bandage? I've just cut my knee*.

cutlery *n*. knives, forks, spoons etc. used at table.

cyan *adj*. greenish blue colour.

cycle 1. *vb*. ride a bicycle. 2. *n*. a series of changes. *These pictures illustrate the life cycle of a frog*.

cyclone *n*. a violent storm with strong winds.

cygnet *n*. a young swan.

cylinder *n*. 1. a solid or hollow tube-shaped object. 2. the part of an engine in which the piston moves.

cymbals *n*. *pl*. a metal instrument consisting of two brass plates that are struck

A pair of cymbals. Cymbals are instruments used in the brass section of an orchestra.

against each other to make a clashing sound.

cynic (**sin**-*ik*) *n*. a person who sees no good in anything. **cynical** *adj*. sneering; disbelieving good in anything.

cypress (*sigh-press*) *n*. tall evergreen conifer with dark foliage.

czar (**tzar**) (*zar*) *n*. title of the former kings of Russia.

Nicholas II, the last Czar of Russia, ruled for 23 years. He was killed with his wife and children in 1918.

D

dab 1. *vb*. press repeatedly. *She dabbed at her eyes with a handkerchief to dry them.* 2. *n*. a kind of flatfish.

dabble *vb*. 1. splash about. 2. undertake in an amateurish way.

dachshund *n*. a small dog with a long body and short legs once used in Germany for hunting badgers.

daddy *n*. a word for 'father' used by children.

daffodil *n*. a tall yellow flower that grows in the spring.

daft *adj*. silly, foolish.

dagger *n*. a short, two-edged knife used as a weapon.

dahlia *n*. a brightly coloured family of garden flowers related to the daisy.

Dail (rhymes with *all*) the parliament of the Republic of Ireland.

daily 1. *adj*. something that happens every day. 2. *adv*. every day. 3. *n*. a daily newspaper. 4. *n*. a home help.

dainty *adj*. small, neat and elegant.

dairy *n*. a place where milk is kept and butter and cheese are made.

daisy *n*. a small wild flower with a yellow centre surrounded by white petals.

dale *n*. valley.

dam *n.* a thick wall of earth, rock or concrete for holding back water. *vb.* restrain with a dam.

damage *vb.* injure or do harm to something. *You will damage the gate if you swing on it. n.* harm, injury. *Little damage was done.*

damn *interjection* a curse; expression of anger *vb.* condemn.

damp *adj.* rather wet; soggy; not dry. *n.* moisture *vb.* moisten; smother.

damson *n.* a small, dark-red kind of plum.

dance *vb.* & *n.* move the feet and body in a rhythmical way, especially to music. **dancer** *n.* one who dances.

dandelion *n.* a wild flower with bright yellow petals.

dandruff *n.* scurf on skin of skull.

danger *n.* something that is likely to do harm to you. *The ice on the step is a danger to everyone.* **dangerous** *adj.*

dare *vb.* 1. be brave enough to do something, venture. *I wouldn't dare cross that road at night.* 2. ask someone to show how brave they are, defy. *I dare you to jump over the stream.* **daring** *adj.* & *n.*

dark 1. *n.* & *adj.* without light; night-time; gloomy. *I should go home before it gets dark.* 2. *adj.* not light in colour. 3. *adj.* having black or brown hair or skin. **darken** *vb.* make or become dark. **darkness** *n.* absence of light.

darling *n.* & *adj.* a dearly loved person; a pet.

darn *vb.* mend a hole in cloth by sewing threads across it. *n.*

dart 1. *vb.* move forward suddenly. 2. *n.* a small sharp-pointed arrow; a game in which darts are thrown.

dash 1. *vb.* rush; run quickly. 2. *n.* the punctuation mark (—). 3. *n.* a sprinkling. *A dash of sauce.*

dashing *adj.* showy.

data *pl. n.* (singular **datum**) facts or things known used as basis for calculating, reasoning etc. *There is little data to go on.*

date 1. *n.* the day, the month, the year, or all three together. *The date today is Friday, 13th July. vb.* mark with a date; become out of date, old-fashioned. **dateless** *adj.* timeless. 2. *n.* the sweet, sticky fruit that grows on a date palm, used in cake-making.

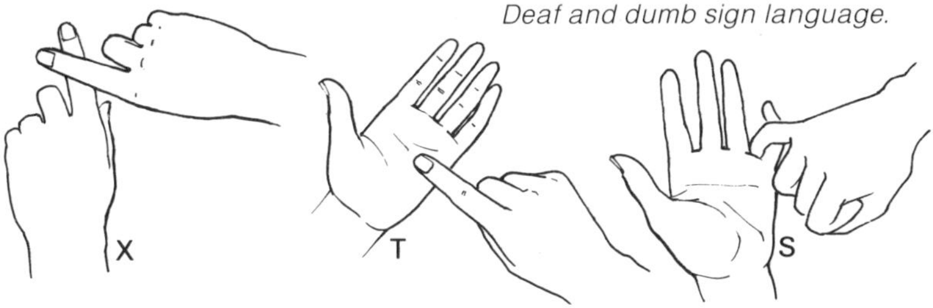

Deaf and dumb sign language.

daub *vb.* smear, paint badly.
daughter *n.* a person's female child. **daughter-in-law** *n.* wife of a person's son.
daunt *vb.* lessen the courage of, intimidate.
dawdle *vb.* move slowly, waste time.
dawn *n.* sunrise, daybreak. *vb.* begin to grow light.
day *n.* the time from midnight to the next midnight; also the part of the day from sunrise to sunset.
daytime *n.* the time when it is light; the opposite of night-time
daze *vb.* bewilder; confuse.
dazzle *vb.* shine very brightly; blind for a moment with a bright light. *It can be difficult to drive a car when the sun dazzles you.*
de- *prefix* meaning down, away, off, from, not, e.g. **decode**, **deduce**, **deform**, **degrade**.
deacon *n.* minor priest. **deaconess** (fem).
dead *adj.* no longer alive.
dead-heat *n.* a race in which two or more runners finish at exactly the same time.
deadlock *n.* inaction, the result of two sides being equally powerful.
deadly *adj.* causing death. *Deadly nightshade is a fatally poisonous plant.*
deaf *adj.* & *n.* not able to hear well or not at all. **deafen** *vb.*
deal *vb.* 1. tell about. *The book deals with butterflies and moths.* 2. give out. *It is your turn to deal the cards.*
deal in *vb.* buy and sell. *The butcher deals in meat.* **dealer** *n.* a person who buys and sells.
deal with *vb.* do whatever has to be done. *You tidy this room and I'll deal with the kitchen.*
dean *n.* head of a cathedral administration (chapter); head of a college or university. **deanery** *n.* dean's house; group of parishes under a dean.
dear *adj.* 1. greatly loved. 2. costing a lot of money; expensive.
dearth *n.* scarcity, lack of (especially of food).
death *n.* end of life; destruction. **deathly** *adj.* like death.
debase *vb.* lower the quality or value.
debate *vb.* discuss or argue in public. *n.* a formal discussion. **debatable** *adj.* something that can be disputed.
debris (**day**-*bree*) *n.* wreckage, broken pieces left after an accident.
debt (rhymes with *yet*) *n.* something that you owe someone.
decade *n.* a ten-year period.

decapitate *vb.* behead.
decathlon *n.* an Olympic sport, consisting of 10 track and field events.
decay *vb.* rot, go bad.
decease *vb.* die. **deceased** *n.* & *adj.* dead (person).
deceive (*de*-**seeve**) *vb.* make someone believe something that you know is not true; cheat. **deceit** *n.* trick. **deceitful** *adj.*
December *n.* the twelfth month of the year.
decent *adj.* modest; fairly good; kindly and tolerant.
decibel *n.* a unit of measurement of the intensity of sound.
decide *vb.* make up your mind about something.
deciduous *adj.* deciduous trees such as maples and poplars lose all their leaves in winter.

decimal *adj., n.* a way of writing fractions by using tens and tenths. Each place to the right of the decimal point stands for one tenth of the value of the place on its left; so 2.1 = 2 units + 1 tenth; 2.14 = 2 units + 1 tenth + 4 hundredths; 3.276 = 3 units + 2 tenths + 7 hundredths + 6 thousandths.
deck 1. *n.* the floor of a ship on which you walk. 2. *vb.* dress up; decorate.
declare *vb.* 1. make known publicly. *When we have all made an attempt, the teacher will declare the winner.* **declaration** *n.* a formal announcement. 2. (in cricket) to close innings before all team has batted.
decline *vb.* get smaller; go down (in quality). *Many theatres are suffering from declining audiences. n.*
decorate *vb.* 1. make more beautiful, clean and paint. 2. give someone a medal.
decoy (**dee**-*koy*) *n.* a model or other device to act as a trap for game birds etc. *vb.* (*di*-**koy**) entice, snare.
decrease *vb.* make something grow less.

decree *n.* an official order. *vb.* order.
deduce *vb.* arrive at a conclusion from the facts given.
deed *n.* something which is done, usually good or bad or brave.
deep *adj.* going a long way down. *The river is very deep near the bridge.* 2. wide. *The shelf was not deep enough.* 3.

Like cows, deer have hoofs and also chew the cud.

dark. *The dress was a deep red.*
deepen *vb.* make or to become deeper.
deer *n.* quick, graceful wild animals including moose, reindeer and red deer. The males have horns called antlers.
deface *vb.* spoil something by writing on it or in some other way, disfigure.
defeat *vb.* beat someone at a game or in battle. *n.* a lost battle or contest.
defect 1. *n.* (**dee**-*fekt*) fault, blemish. 2. *vb.* (*di*-**fect**) desert. **defector** *n.*
defend *vb.* guard or make safe.
defence *n.* resistance against attack; military fortifications, armaments; *A castle wall is a defence.* (in law) a defendant's case.
defer *vb.* 1. put off, postpone. 2. give in to another's opinion.
defiant *adj.* rebellious. **defy** *vb.* challenge. *I defy you to prove it.* **defiance** *n.* open rebellion.
deficient (*di*-**fish**-*ent*) *adj.* incomplete, insufficient.
define *vb.* explain the meaning of words; mark out limits. **definition** *n.*
definite *adj.* certain, without doubt.
definitive *adj.* decisive, final.
deform *vb.* spoil shape of.
defunct *adj.* dead, no longer existing.
defuse (**dee**-*fyuze*) *vb.* 1. remove the fuse from a bomb. 2. make something safe. 3. make a situation less dangerous, especially in politics.
degree *n.* 1. a unit of measurement for temperature or angles. It is often written like this: 10° means 10 degrees. 2. a title given by a university to someone who has passed an examination.
dehydrate (**dee**-*hi*-*drate*) *vb.* dry out the water from something. *Powdered milk is dehydrated.*
deity *n.* a god.
delay *vb.* make late or slow down; put off.
delegate *n.* a representative to a meeting etc. *vb.* send as a representative or assign responsibility to someone.
delete *vb.* cross out, erase.

deliberate *adj*. something that is done on purpose. *That was a deliberate foul.*
delicacy *n*. choice kind of food.
delicate *adj*. soft and not strong; dainty.
delicious *adj*. delightful to eat.
delightful *adj*. very pleasant.
deliver *vb*. 1. take things to a place where they are needed. *The boy delivers our newspapers every morning*. 2. give a speech. 3. help at the birth of a baby. *The doctor arrived in time to deliver the baby*. **delivery** *n*.
delta *n*. the triangle of land formed by rivers which have more than one mouth; fourth letter of Greek alphabet: Δ.
deluge *n*. a heavy rainstorm; a downpour. *vb*. flood.
demand *vb*. ask for something that you think is due to you. *I shall demand payment of the money now*. *n*. a request, urgent claim.
democracy *n*. a country in which the government is chosen by all the adult electors; this kind of government. *Denmark is a democracy*.
demolish *vb*. knock down. *They are demolishing the office block at the end of our street*. **demolition** *n*.
demon *n*. devil or evil spirit.
demonstrate *vb*. 1. show or explain something to others. 2. take part in a protest march or similar political activity.
den *n*. the hidden home of an animal.
denied *vb*. past of **deny**.
denim *n*. twilled cotton fabric.
denounce *vb*. speak critically or violently against.

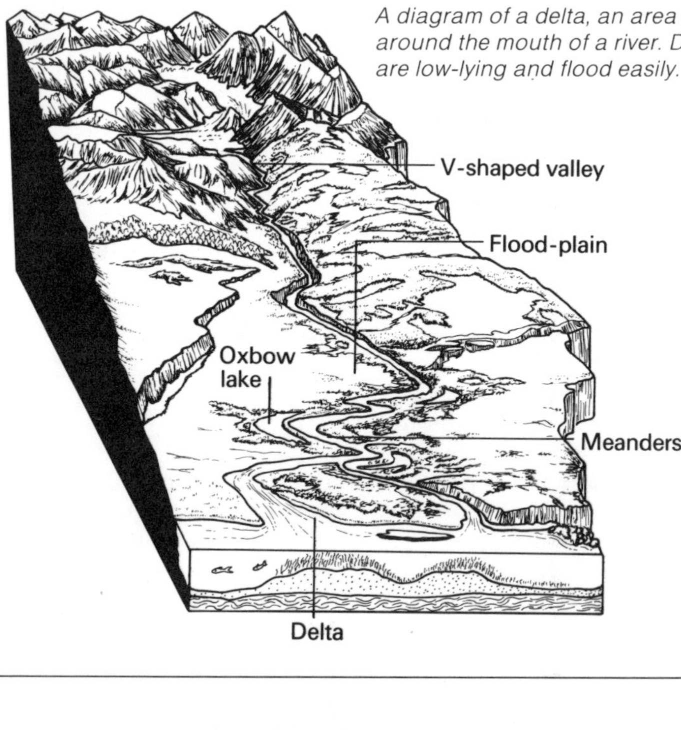

A diagram of a delta, an area of land around the mouth of a river. Deltas are low-lying and flood easily.

This derrick is a tall metal tower which houses oil-drilling equipment.

dense *adj*. thick. **density** *n*.
dent *n*. a mark or hole. *That car has a dent in its wing. vb. He dented the wing of his car.*
dental *adj*. of teeth or dentistry.
dentist *n*. a person who takes care of and treats teeth. **dentistry** *n*.
denture *n*. a set of false teeth.
deny (*den*-**eye**) *vb*. say that something is not true. **denial** *n*.
deodorant *n*. a substance which gets rid of smells.
depart *vb*. leave; go away. **departure** *n*.
department *n*. a separate part of a whole, e.g. a branch of government or business.
depend on *vb*. rely on someone for money or other things. *The child depends on us for all his needs.*
depict *vb*. describe, draw.
deplore *vb*. regret greatly, grieve. **deplorable** *adj*. regrettable, shocking.
deport *vb*. send out of the country; exile.
deposit *n*. a sum of money put down in advance of a larger payment. *They have put down a deposit on the holiday and will pay the rest before they go away. vb*. place; put a deposit down.
depot (**dep**-*owe*) *n*. a storehouse. (A railway station in the USA).
depreciate *vb*. fall in value. *The car depreciated by 20 per cent in three months.*
deprive *vb*. prevent from use or enjoyment; take away.
depth *n*. the distance from the top downward (how deep something is) or from the front to the back. *The depth of the shelf is just right.*
derrick *n*. 1. framework over a bore hole, e.g. an oil well. 2. a kind of crane, especially for unloading ships.
descend (*de*-**send**) *vb*. 1. go down. 2. come from, be derived from.
describe *vb*. say what something or somebody is like. *We can describe the man exactly.* **description** *n*. detailed account. **descriptive** *adj*.
desert (**dez**-*ert*) *n*. a large dry area of land where there is little water or rain.
desert (*dez*-**ert**) *vb*. abandon; leave behind. *Why did you desert us when we most needed you?*
deserve *vb*. be worthy of something. *You deserve the prize because of all your hard work.*

desiccate *vb*. dry up; preserve food by drying.
design (rhymes with *lime*) *vb*. make a plan or pattern for something. *n*. plan. **designer** *n*.
designate (**dez**-*ig-nate*) *vb*. appoint to job or post.
designedly *adv*. intentionally.
desire *vb*. want something very much. *n*. wish, longing. **desirable** *adj*. worth wanting; advisable.
desk *n*. a piece of furniture, like a table, for writing on.
despair *vb*. give up hope. *n*.
despise *vb*. look down on; think oneself superior. **despicable** *adj*. contemptible, unworthy.
dessert (*dez*-**ert**) *n*. the sweet course of a meal; a pudding.
destiny *n*. fate, pre-determined future.
destitute *adj*. & *n*. absolute poverty.
destroy *vb*. break up; make something useless. **destruction** *n*. **destructive** *adj*.
detach *vb*. remove something that was previously attached to something else.
detail *n*. a very small part of something.
detain *n*. hold someone up; make a person late.
detect *vb*. discover, find out. **detection** *n*.
detective *n*. a person who follows clues to find a criminal. *adj*. concerned with detection.
deter (*di*-**ter**) *vb*. discourage, hinder. **deterrent** *n*. something that deters as, for example, nuclear weapons.
detergent *n*. a substance which removes dirt; washing powder.
deteriorate *vb*. become worse in condition or quality. *Her health began to deteriorate after the accident*.
determined *adj*. with your mind firmly made up. *adj*. determination
detest *vb*. hate someone or something; loathe.
detonate *vb*. set off an explosion. **detonator** *n*. device for setting off an explosion.
detour *n*. roundabout way temporarily replacing a more direct route.
detract *vb*. (from) lessen the credit due to; belittle.
devastate *vb*. lay waste, destroy completely. **devastation** *n*.
develop *vb*. grow bigger and better. *A tadpole develops into a frog*. **development** *n*.
deviate *vb*. turn aside from main course.
device (*di*-**vise**) *n*. something made to do a particular thing.
devil *n*. an evil spirit; a demon. **devilish** *adj*. cruel; wicked.

A standard clock face. The dial is divided into 12 main sections for the hours and 60 small sections for the minutes.

devise (*di*-**vize**) *vb*. plan.
devote *vb*. set aside; give up. *Monks and nuns devote a large part of each day to prayer.* **devoted** *adj*. loyal, very affectionate. **devotion** *n*. great loyalty; love; (*pl*) prayers.
devour *vb*. eat something up whole. *The lions quickly devoured the antelope.*
devout *adj*. religious; pious; reverential.
dew *n*. the tiny drops of water that form on cool surfaces at night out of doors. **dewy** *adj*.
dexterity *n*. skill. **dextrous** *adj*.
diabetes *n*. a disorder in which too much sugar builds up in the blood.
diagnose *vb*. decide what illness someone is suffering from. *The doctor diagnosed measles.* **diagnosis** *n*.
diagonal *adj*. a straight line across a rectangular area from one corner to the opposite corner. *n*. an oblique line.
diagram *n*. a drawing that explains something. *The word 'diagonal' is explained here with a diagram.*
dial *n*. the face of a clock, watch or instrument; the numbered part of a telephone. *vb*. use the dial of a telephone.
dialect *n*. a form of a language which is slightly different from the usual one.
dialogue *n*. conversation in speech; the spoken part of a play; argument and exchange of views. *The dialogue between America and Russia continues.*
diameter *n*. a line right across a circle passing through the centre.
diamond *n*. 1. a very hard brilliant precious stone. 2. a four-sided figure with equal sides but no right angles.
diaper *n*. a baby's absorbent towel; a nappy (especially USA).
diary *n*. a book in which someone writes down what happens each day. **diarist** *n*. a person who keeps a diary, or notes down future engagements.
dice *pl. n*. (singular **die**) a small cube with one to six dots on its sides, used in games. *vb*. play with dice; cut into small cubes. *The cook diced the carrots.*
dictate *vb*. read aloud something to be written down. *She dictated letters to her secretary.*
dictator *n*. absolute ruler; a tyrant.
dictionary *n*. a book containing an alphabetical list of words with an explanation of their meaning or a translation of the words into another language.

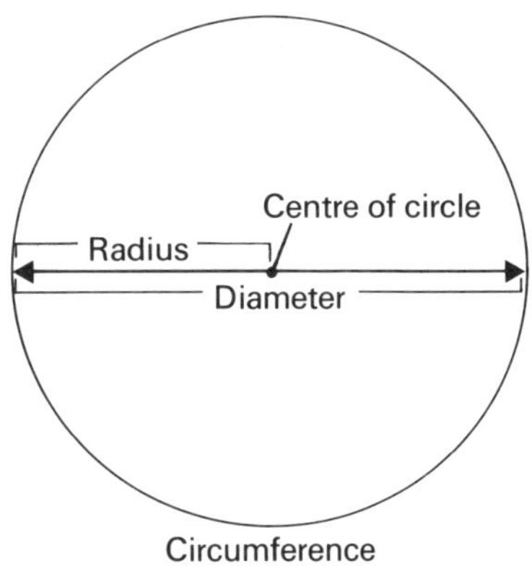

The diameter line runs across the centre of the circle, cutting it in half.

did *vb.* past of **do**.
didactic *adj.* means to instruct.
didgeridoo *n.* a musical wind instrument played by North Australian Aborigines.

die 1. *vb.* stop living; become dead. 2. *n.* the singular form of dice.
diesel engine *n.* an internal combustion engine that burns a certain kind of oil to supply power.

The diagram shows the four stages in the working of a diesel engine. Unlike a normal internal combustion engine, there is no spark. Instead ignition is caused by pressure on the air and oil mixture.

diet (**di**-*et*) *n.* the food you usually eat; special meals that some people have to make them healthy, and others have to help them lose weight. *vb.*
dif- *prefix* see **dis-.**
differ *vb.* be unlike; disagree. **difference** *n.* amount of unlikeness; a disagreement.
different *vb. adj.* separate; not the same, unlike.
difficult *adj.* hard; not easy. **difficulty** *n.* hard to overcome; an obstacle.
diffidence *n.* shyness; lack of self confidence.
diffuse (*di*-**fyuze**) *vb.* disperse; spread around.
dig *vb.* (past **dug**) make a hole in the ground; turn over the earth, usually with a spade.
digest *vb.* change the food you have eaten in such a way that your body can use it. **digestion** *n.* **digest** *n.* summary.
digit *n.* 1. a finger or toe. 2. a figure or number. *The number 100 contains three digits.*
digital *adj.* having figures or numbers. *A digital watch does not have hands, but shows the time in figures.*

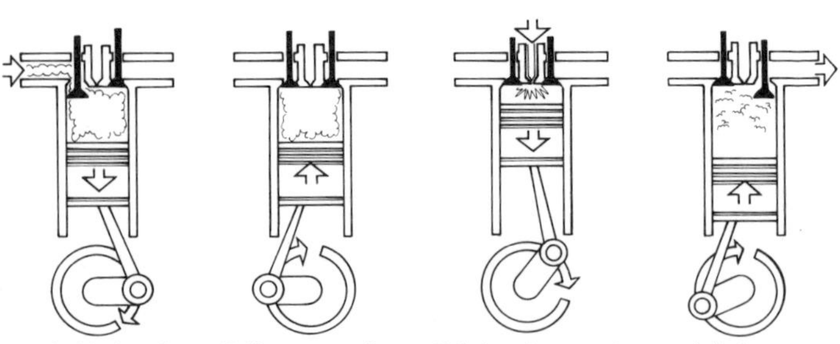

digitalis *n*. a drug made from leaves of foxgloves.
dignity *n*. a quality of worthy, estimable behaviour. **dignify** *vb*. do honour to.
dike (**dyke**) *n*. a ditch; a wall to keep the sea out of the surrounding land (especially in the Netherlands).
dilate (*dye*-**late**) *vb*. widen, expand, enlarge. *The pupils of the eyes dilate in the dark.*
dilemma *n*. a choice involving one of two unsatisfactory alternatives; having to choose the lesser of two evils.
dilute *vb*. water down, reduce strength of.
dim 1. *adj*. not bright. 2. *vb*. make or become darker.
dime *n*. US coin worth 10 cents.
dimension *n*. size, extent.
diminish *vb*. make or become less.
din *n*. a loud ugly noise.
dinghy *n*. a small, open boat.
dingo *n*. the wild dog of Australia.
dining-room *n*. the room in which meals are eaten.

The dingo is the Australian wild dog.

dinner *n*. the main meal of the day, usually eaten in the evening. **dine**. *vb*.
dinosaur *n*. one of a large group of prehistoric reptiles that became extinct millions of years ago.
diocese (**di**-*oss-ese*) *n*. district under control of a bishop.
dip *vb*. put something into a liquid and take it out again.
diphtheria *n*. dangerous infectious disease of the throat.
diplomacy *n*. the art of keeping good relations between countries; the use of charm or tact in relationships between people. **diplomat** *n*. official representative in diplomacy; skilled negotiator. **diplomatic** *adj*. tactful.
direct 1. *vb*. show or tell someone how to do something or go somewhere. 2. *adv*. the quickest way from one point to another. *This train goes direct to Montreal.*
direction *n*. the way from one place to another.
directly *adv*. very soon; in a direct way.
dirty *adj*. not clean; covered in **dirt** *n*.
dis- *prefix* that turns the main word into its opposite, usually negative, e.g. **disband**, **disbelieve**, **discolour**, **disconnect**, **discontinue**, **discourage**.
disable (*diss*-**ay**-*ball*) *vb*. make incapable through injury, cripple.
disagree *vb*. 1. quarrel, have different ideas about something. 2. have a bad effect. **disagreeable** *adj*. unpleasant.

Throwing the discus is one of the athletic events called field events. The discus is thrown with one hand.

disappear *vb.* vanish; be seen no more. **disappearance** *n.*
disappoint *vb.* make someone sad by not doing what they had hoped for; fail to fulfil expectations.
disarray *n.* confusion.
disaster *n.* a terrible accident. *Fifty people were killed in the disaster.* **disastrous** *adj.*
disc *n.* a flat circle, like a stereo record.
discern *vb.* see clearly with the mind. **discerning** *adj.*
disciple *n.* a follower. *Jesus left his disciples to carry on his work.*
discomfit *vb.* upset, defeat, throw into confusion.
discotheque (**disco**) *n.* a place where people dance to recorded music.
discover *vb.* find out something new.
discriminate *vb.* make or see differences between; make a distinction and single out, often for unfair treatment.
discus *n.* a heavy disc thrown in athletics competitions; the event in which it is thrown.
discuss *vb.* talk about something or someone with other people. **discussion** *n.*
disease *n.* illness.
disgrace *n.* shame; downfall. *vb.* bring shame upon.
disguise *n.* & *vb.* change what someone or something looks like. *His disguise was a mask and black cloak. He disguised himself.*
disgust *n.* strong loathing for.
dish *n.* a plate; a particular kind of food.
dishonest *adj.* lying or cheating; not honest.
disinfect *vb.* make something free from germs and disease. **disinfectant** *n.*
dislike *vb.* not like.
dismal *adj.* gloomy; feeble. *The players gave a dismal performance.*
dismay *vb.* & *n.* upset; fill with fear, despair.

dismiss *vb*. send away; order someone to leave their job. **dismissal** *n*.

disobedient *adj*. refusing to obey. *The girl did not do what her teacher told her. She was disobedient*. **disobedience** *n*. **disobey** *vb*.

display *vb*. show something off. *n*. an exhibition; show.

dispute (*dis*-**pyoot**) *vb*. quarrel, argue; call in question.

disregard *vb*. pay no attention to.

dissect *vb*. cut up a plant or dead animal in order to examine it scientifically.

dissident *n*. a person who disagrees with or opposes authority.

dissolve *vb*. mix something in a liquid so that it becomes part of the liquid. *Salt dissolves easily in water*.

distance *n*. the length between two points.

distant *adj*. far away.

distillation *n*. turn into steam or other vapour and then condense back into a liquid. *Brandy is made by the distillation of wine*.

distinct *adj*. clear; separate; different in kind.

distinguish *vb*. see differences between; make a distinction between; separate in classes. **distinguished** *adj*. famous, eminent.

distract *vb*. draw attention away; bewilder. **distraction** *n*. relaxation, amusement.

distress *vb*. cause unhappiness. *n*. great trouble, grief.

distribute *vb*. give each of a number of people a share of something. *Please distribute these books round the class*.

district *n*. part of a city or country.

disturb *vb*. interrupt or annoy someone; move something from its usual position. **disturbance** *n*.

ditch *n*. a narrow channel for water.

ditto *n*. (*abbrev*. **do**) the same; repeat statement etc.

dive *vb*. plunge into water head-first.

diver *n*. someone who dives; someone who goes deep into water for long periods by taking air with them or who has air pumped down from the surface.

divert *vb*. turn aside from; amuse.

divide *vb*. 1. separate, cut into parts; share. 2. find out how many times one number goes into another. *If you divide 8 by 2 the answer is 4*.

divine *adj*. of or like God or a god; sacred.

divorce *n*. & *vb*. the legal ending of a marriage.

do *vb*. (past **did**) carry out an action.

docile *adj*. easily led, teachable.

dock 1. *n*. a place in a habour where ships are loaded and unloaded. *vb*. bring ships into dock. 2. *n*. the place in a lawcourt where the prisoner stands.

doctor *n*. a person who treats sick people; also a graduate holding a degree. *vb*. treat medically; falsify.

doctrine *n*. religious or political beliefs or dogma.

document *n.* written information.
dodge *vb.* get quickly out of the way; duck. *The boy neatly dodged the snowball.*
dodgem *n.* a small car at a funfair, powered by electricity, whose driver bumps into other cars.
dodo *n.* a now extinct, giant flightless bird with stumpy legs.

doe *n.* a female deer or rabbit.
dog *n.* one of a family of mammals which includes wolves, jackals and foxes.
dogma *n.* a system of beliefs; authoritative doctrine. **dogmatic** *adj.* intolerant.
dole *n.* money paid to unemployed people.
doleful *adj.* sad and gloomy.
doll *n.* a small model of a person, usually for a child to play with.
dollar *n.* a banknote or coin used in many countries, including Australia, Canada, Hong Kong, the USA and New Zealand.
dolphin *n.* a small type of whale.
dolt *n.* a stupid, clumsy person.
dome *n.* a rounded roof like an upsidedown bowl.
domestic *adj.* to do with the home.
domesticated *adj.* word describing an animal that is used to living with people.
dominate *vb.* overshadow; exert control over.
domino *n.* (plural **dominoes**) one of 28 pieces marked with dots (or left blank) used in a game of dominoes.
don *n.* fellow or tutor in a college or university.
donate *vb.* make a **donation** (i.e. gift of money).
done *vb.* past part. of **do**.
donkey *n.* an ass; an animal of the horse family with long ears.
donor *n.* someone who gives something.
don't *vb.* contraction of **do not**.
doodle *vb.* draw in an absent-minded way. *n.* drawing done in this way.
doom *n.* destiny or fate. *vb.* condemn.
door *n.* a moveable panel (usually of wood or glass)

Many religious buildings such as mosques and churches have domed roofs.

which opens or closes the entrance to a room or building.
dormitory *n.* a bedroom for several people especially in a school or monastery.
dormouse *n.* a small gnawing rodent.
dorsal *adj.* on or of the back. *The shark has a dorsal fin.*
dose *n.* amount of medicine to be taken at regular times. *vb.* give medicine to.
dot *n.* small spot or point. *vb.* mark with a dot. *Dot the 'i's.*
double 1. *adj.* twice the amount. 2. *vb.* fold over into two layers. 3. *n.* a person exactly like someone else.
double-cross *vb.* betray.
doubt (rhymes with *out*) *vb.* feel unsure about something. *I doubt whether you are right. n.* feeling of uncertainty.
dough (rhymes with *go*) *n.* a mixture of flour and water for making bread or pastry.
doughnut *n.* a sweet doughy cake fried in fat. *Doughnuts are usually either round or shaped like a ring.*
dour (rhymes with *brewer*) *adj.* (Sc.) stubborn, grim, stern.
dove *n.* a bird related to the pigeon.
dovecote *n.* a house or loft for pigeons.
dowager *n.* widow of a titled person.
dowdy *adj.* drab, badly dressed.
down 1. *prep.* towards somewhere lower. *She went down the hill.* 2. *n.* very soft feathers.
downpour *n.* a heavy shower of rain.
downward(**s**) *adj.* towards a lower level.
doze *vb.* be half asleep.
dozen *n.* twelve.
drab *adj.* dull light brown; colourless.
drachma *n.* unit of Greek money.
drag *vb.* pull roughly along ground.
dragon *n.* a fierce legendary creature that breathed fire.
dragon-fly *n.* a brightly coloured insect with long wings that lives near water.

Dragonflies feed on insects.

drain *n.* a pipe that takes waste water away. *vb.* to take water away through pipes and ditches; empty. *When he gives a toast, they will all drain their glasses.*
drake *n.* a male duck.
drama *n.* an acted story; a play; the art of the theatre. **dramatic** *adj.* **dramatist** *n.* a person who writes plays.
drank *vb.* past of **drink**.
draper *n.* a person who deals in cloth.
drastic *adj.* severe.
draught (rhymes with *raft*) *n.* a flow of air, especially coming through a narrow gap in a door or window. **draughty** *adj.*

draughts (rhymes with *rafts*) *n.* a game played with pieces on a squared board.
draw *vb.* 1. make a picture or diagram with pen, pencil or crayon but not with paint. 2. the result of a game in which neither team nor player wins. 3. pull. *They draw water from the well.*
drawback *n.* a disadvantage.
drawbridge *n.* a bridge across a moat that could be pulled up when a castle was being attacked.
drawer *n.* a box-shaped part of a chest or cupboard that can be pulled open.
dread *vb.* fear terribly, especially before an event.
dreadful *adj.* terrible; unpleasant. (Originally 'inspiring dread'.) **dread** *n.* fear.
dreadlocks *pl. n.* long ringlets of hair worn notably by Rastafarians.

dream *n.* something that you think is happening during sleep. *vb.* experience a dream.
dreary *adj.* gloomy, tedious.
dredge *vb.* clear away sand and mud from under water.
dress 1. *n.* a single piece of clothing covering the body from the shoulders to the legs worn by women and girls. 2. *vb.* put on clothes. 3. *vb.* clean and trim wool, cloth, poultry etc.
dresser *n.* a piece of furniture like a cupboard with shelves above.
drew *vb.* past of **draw**.
drey *n.* a squirrel's nest.
dribble *vb.* 1. let saliva (spit) fall from corner of mouth. 2. in football, work ball forward with short taps and turns.
dried *vb.* past of **dry**.
drift *vb.* be carried slowly along by wind or water. *Without its engine, the ship will drift on to the rocks.*
drill *n.* 1. a pointed tool that is turned to bore holes. 2. exercises that are part of a soldier's training.
drink 1. *vb.* swallow water or other liquid. (past **drank**). 2. *n.* any liquid that is swallowed.
drip *vb.* fall in drops.
dripping *n.* fat melted from roasting meat.
drive 1. *vb.* steer a car or other vehicle. (past **drove**). 2. *vb.* strike a golf ball. 3. *n.* a road from the street to the front of a house.
drivel *n.* nonsensical talk. *vb.* talk foolishly.
driver *n.* the person who steers a car or other vehicle.
drizzle *n.* & *vb.* fine dense rain.
dromedary *n.* a fast camel with one hump.
drone *n.* a male bee or ant that does no work.
droop *vb.* hang down limply, wilt.

drop 1. *n.* a small amount of liquid, a raindrop. 2. *vb.* let something fall.

drop in *vb.* visit someone without telling them you are coming.

drought (rhymes with *out*) *n.* a long period of dry weather.

drove *vb.* past of **drive**.

drown *vb.* die by suffocation in water; drench.

drowsy *adj.* sleepy, not fully awake.

drug *n.* a medicine; a substance that takes away anxiety or pain. *vb.* make stupid with drugs; add drugs to food etc.

drum *n.* a round, hollow musical instrument with a skin stretched over a frame. *vb.* play a drum.

drunk 1. *adj.* having drunk too much alcohol. *People who drive when they are drunk are responsible for too many accidents.* 2. *n.* a person who habitually drinks too much. 3. *vb.* past part. of **drink**.

drupe *n.* fruit such as a plum with a stone contained in fleshy pulp.

dry *adj.* not wet; without water.

dual *adj.* making a pair, double (dual carriageway).

dubious (**dew**-*bius*) *adj.* doubtful, open to question.

duck 1. *n.* a web-footed water bird with a broad beak. 2. *vb.* bend down quickly to get out of the way of something. 3. *n.* a batsman's score of 0 at cricket.

duckling *n.* a young duck.

due *adj.* owing; merited; expected. *The plane is due at 10 o'clock.*

duet *n.* a piece of music for two performers.

dug *vb.* past of **dig**.

duke *n.* an important nobleman, next to a prince in rank. *A duke's wife is called a duchess.*

dull *adj.* not bright; not sharp; not interesting. *It is never dull when Mrs Perfect teaches our class.*

dumb *adj.* 1. not able to speak. 2. (*slang*) stupid.

dummy *n.* 1. model of a human figure. 2. teat for a baby to suck.

Drums vary in size, shape and sound.

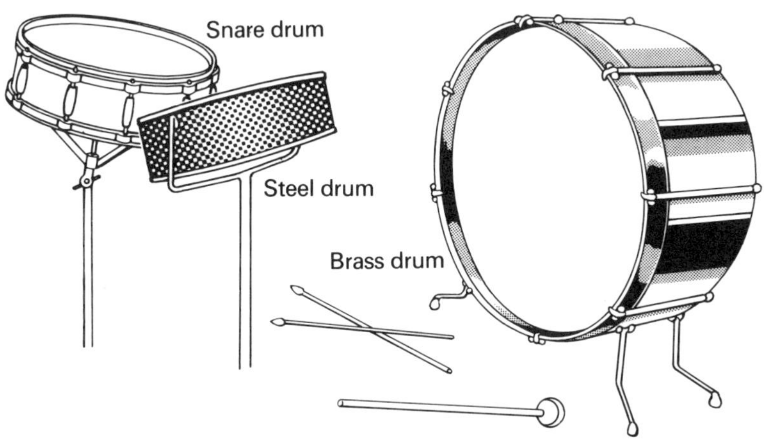

dump *vb.* put in a heap. *n.* rubbish tip; depot; (*casual*) a dull place.
dumpling *n.* small suet pudding.
dunce *n.* a person who is slow to learn.
dune *n.* a low hill of sand.
dung *n.* farmyard manure.
dungeon (**dun**-*jun*) *n.* an underground prison.
duplicate *vb.* make exact copy of.
durable *adj.* strong and long lasting.
during *prep.* 1. throughout. *The old man slept during the whole speech.* 2. some time in. *They arrived during the afternoon.*
dusk *n.* the time of evening when it is starting to get dark; twilight.
dust *n.* tiny grains of dirt.
dustbin *n.* a container for household rubbish.
dust-bowl *n.* a dry area (especially in the western Great Plains of the USA) which has many dust storms.
duty *n.* something that you must do. *The policeman's duty is to arrest the burglar.*
duvet (**doo**-*vay*) *n.* a bed covering, or quilt, filled with feathers or down.
dwarf *n.* a person, animal or plant that does not grow to full size.
dwell *vb.* 1. live somewhere. 2. write or speak at great length on.
dwindle *vb.* become smaller, grow less.
dye (rhymes with *lie*) *vb.* change colour of something by putting it in a special liquid called a **dye** (*n*).
dyke see **dike**.
dynamite *n.* a powerful explosive used for blasting.
dynamo *n.* a machine for making electricity. *The lamp on my bike is powered by a dynamo.*
dynasty *n.* a historical line of kings or queens.
dysentry (**dis**-*entry*) *n.* serious disease of the bowels.
dyslexia *n.* word blindness, inability to read easily.
dyspepsia *n.* indigestion, especially when chronic. **dyspeptic** *adj.*

A dust bowl in Texas.

E

each *adj*. every member of a group thought of separately. *He held a gun in each hand.*
eager *adj*. keen; enthusiastic. **eagerness** *n*.
eagle *n*. a large bird of prey.
ear *n*. 1. the organ, or part of the body with which we hear. 2. the grain on a stalk of corn.

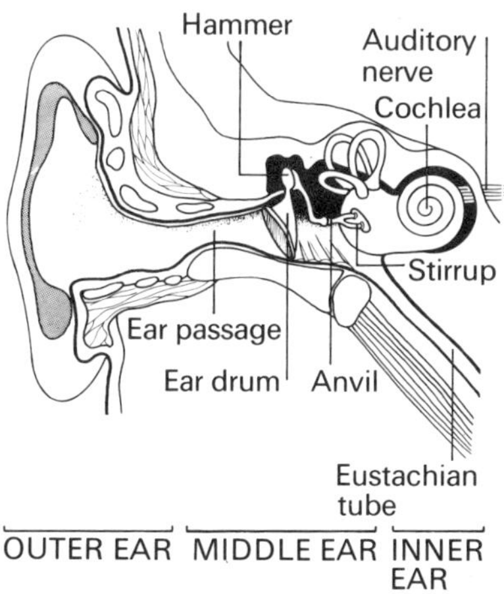

The main parts of the outer, middle and inner ear.

earache (**ear**-*ayk*) *n*. a pain in the ear.
earl *n*. the middle rank of the British peerage, between marquis and viscount. (The wife of an earl is called a countess.) **earldom** *n*.
early *adv*. & *adj*. soon; at the beginning (of the day). *She is an early riser.*
earn *vb*. 1. get something by working for it. 2. deserve. *She earns everyone's respect.*
earnest *adj*. serious; keen, but lacking in humour.
earnings *pl. n*. money earned.
ear-rings *pl. n*. ornaments worn in the ears.
earshot *n*. within hearing distance.
earth 1. *n*. the planet on which we live. 2. *n*. soil. **earthy** *adj*. of earth or soil; coarse. 3. *n*. hole of a fox. 4. *vb*. connect with earth.
earthquake *n*. a shaking movement of the surface of the Earth.
earthwork *n*. a mound of earth used as a fortification.
earwig *n*. insect with pincers at the end of its abdomen.
ease *n*. comfort; freedom from pain. *vb*. make easier; relieve from pain; relax.
easel *n*. a frame to hold up a picture or blackboard.
east *n*. & *adj*. the direction in which the Sun rises. *East winds blow from the east.* **eastward** *adv*. **eastern** *adj*.
Easter *n*. the day on which Christians remember the Resurrection of Jesus Christ.
easy *adj*. simple; not difficult.
easy-going *adj*. tolerant, not fussy.
eat *vb*. (past **ate**, past part. **eaten**) chew and swallow food.
eat away *vb*. destroy gradually.
ebb *n*. the tide flowing back from land to sea. *vb*.
ebony *n*. the name of various kinds of hard black wood. *adj*. the colour of ebony; black.

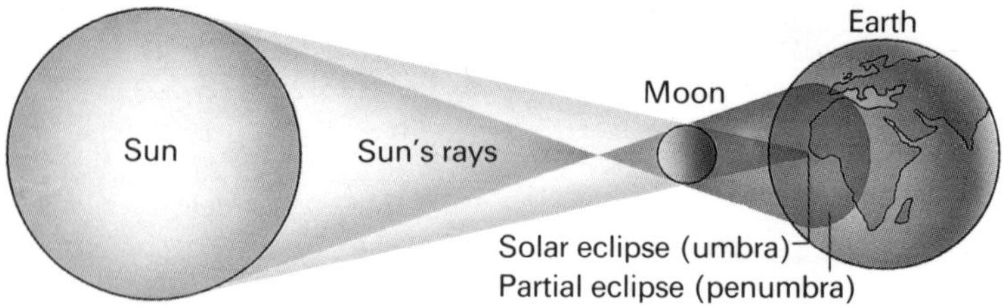

An eclipse of the Sun. This happens when the shadow of the Moon falls on the Earth. Total eclipses of the Sun are rare.

eccentric *adj*. odd, peculiar, *n*. a person with unusual habits or behaviour.

ecclesiastical *adj*. of or concerning the Church or clergy.

echo (*ecko*) *n*. & *vb*. a sound that is heard again when it bounces back or is reflected off something.

eclipse *n*. & *vb*. a time when the Sun's light is cut off because the Moon passes between the Earth and the Sun (an eclipse of the Sun); a time when the Moon's light is cut off because the Earth passes between the Sun and the Moon (an eclipse of the Moon).

ecology *n*. the study of the habits of living things, the places where they live and how they depend on each other. **ecological** *adj*. **ecologist** *n*.

economy *n*. 1. the management of a country's wealth. 2. a saving. *He is always trying to make false economies in our housekeeping*. **economical** *adj*. thrifty. **economize** *vb*. avoid expense.

eczema (**eks**-ma) *n*. a disease of the skin.

edge *n*. the part along the side or end of something. *The path ran round the edge of the field*.

edible *adj*. eatable.

edifice *n*. large building such as a church etc.

edify *vb*. teach and improve mentally.

edit *vb*. prepare a piece of writing for publication in a book, newspaper or magazine. **editor** *n*. a person who edits.

edition *n*. copies of a book or periodical printed at one time.

educate *vb*. teach or train. **education** *n*. **educational** *adj*.

Edwardian *adj*. belonging to the reign of Edward VII (1901–10).

eel *n*. a long slim fish with fins like narrow ribbons.

effect *n*. result or consequence of our action.

effeminate *adj*. womanish behaviour in a man.

efficient *adj*. capable, competent.

effigy *n*. image or likeness made in wood or stone.

effort *n*. hard work.

e.g. stands for two Latin words meaning 'for example'.

egg 1. *n*. one of the roundish objects that young birds, insects, fish and reptiles live inside before they are born; an important kind of food. 2. *vb.* **egg on** encourage.

egocentric *adj.* concerned with oneself; self-centred.

egotism *n.* selfishness.

eider *n.* a large sea duck, the soft down of which is used in eiderdowns (quilts or duvets).

eisteddfod (*I*-**stheth**-*vod*) *n.* (*Welsh*) a meeting of poets, musicians etc.

either *adj.* & *pron.* one or the other; one of two. *He will either come or he won't.*

eject *vb.* remove; send out, expel. **ejection** *n.* **ejector** *n.*

elaborate *adj.* done in great detail.

elastic *n.* & *adj.* a material that stretches out and then goes back to the same size. *A rubber band is elastic.*

elbow *n.* the joint between the upper and lower arm. *vb.* thrust, jostle.

elder 1. *adj.* older. *My elder brother was born before I was.* **elderly** *adj.* becoming old; past middle age. 2. *n.* an official of certain churches. 3. *n.* a tree with white flowers and black berries.

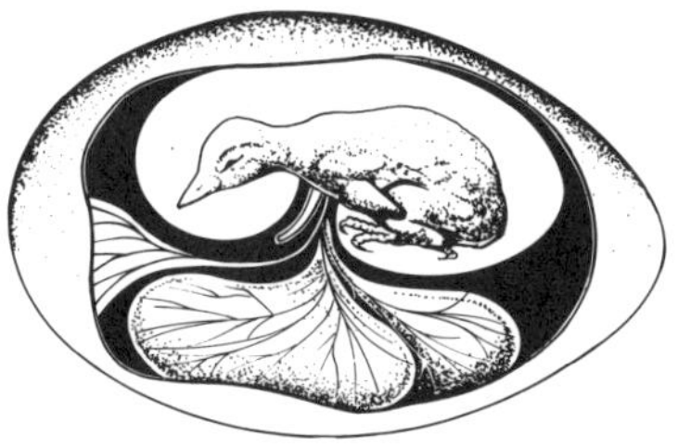

The shell of the egg protects the developing chick, while it feeds on the yolk. When it is ready, it will break the shell with its beak and hatch.

eldest *adj.* the first-born child in a family. *My eldest brother was born before my elder brother.*

election *n.* a time when people can choose by voting the men and women who will govern their town or country, society or club. **elect** *vb.* choose by voting. **elector** *n.* a person entitled to vote. **electorate** *n.* the mass or body of electors.

electric *adj.* worked by electricity.

electrician *n.* a person who works with electricity or electrical equipment.

electricity *n.* energy that is used to make heat and light and is used to drive some machines. Electricity moves along wires from generating stations to where it is needed. **electrify** *vb.* charge with electricity; change to working by electricity. *The railways will be electrified.*

electrocute *vb.* execute by using a powerful electric current.

electrode *n.* metal rod or plate through which electric current enters or leaves a battery etc.

electron *n.* small negatively charged subatomic particle.

electronics *n. pl.* the science that deals with things like television, radio and other pieces of apparatus that have devices such as transistors.

elegance *n.* refinement in taste; grace. **elegant** *adj.* tasteful.

elegy *n.* sad poem or song written usually for the dead.

element *n.* a substance that cannot be divided into simpler substances.

elementary *adj*. simple; introductory.

elephant *n*. the world's largest land mammal characterized by a long trunk and curved tusks made of ivory.

elevate *vb*. lift up, raise. **elevator** *n*. a lift (specially USA).

elf *n*. (plural *elves*) in story books, a small fairy.

élite (*ay*-**leet**) *n*. a select, privileged group; the best.

Elizabethan *adj*. belonging to the reign of Queen Elizabeth I.

elk *n*. the name for two large kinds of deer. The European elk is known as a moose in North America. The second kind is the American elk.

elm *n*. a broad-leaved tree, the leaves having zig-zag edges like the teeth of a saw.

elongate *vb*. stretch out, make longer.

The elm was once a very common tree, but many have been killed by Dutch elm disease in recent years.

elope *vb*. run away with a lover to get married without parental permission. *n*. **elopement**.

em- *prefix*. see **en-**.

emancipate *vb*. set free from control of another (social restraint, slavery etc.).

embankment *n*. the built-up bank of a river or lake; a bank so built to carry a road or a railway.

embargo *n*. a ban on trading for a time.

embark *vb*. get on board ship.

embarrass *vb*. make someone feel uncomfortable or ill at ease. **embarrassment** *n*.

embassy *n*. the building used by an ambassador and his staff.

embezzle *vb*. take property, money etc. that is not one's own but which has been put in one's charge.

emblem *n*. a badge, symbol.

embrace *vb*. take into the arms; accept; adopt (a cause).

embroidery *n*. decoration of cloth made by sewing a pattern of coloured stitches. **embroider** *vb*.

embryo (**em**-*bree-yo*) *n*. an animal in an early stage before it is born. **embryonic** *adj*.

emend *vb*. correct, remove errors. **emendation** *n*.

emerald *n*. a precious green stone.

emerge *vb*. come out; come to notice.

emergency *n*. a sudden happening that needs quick action.

emigrate *vb*. go away from your own country to live. **emigration** *n*.

eminent *adj*. distinguished;

The emu is the second largest bird.

standing above others because of some special quality.
emit *vb.* give out, send out.
emotion *n.* strong feeling (of love, hate etc.). **emotional** *adj.* agitated in feeling; easily moved by feelings.
emperor *n.* the male ruler of an empire. A female ruler is an **empress**.
emphasis (**em**-*fa-sis*) *n.* stress (e.g. on words) to show importance. **emphasize** *vb.* stress, underline; state strongly.
empire *n.* a group of countries under one ruler. *The Roman Empire spread all around the Mediterranean Sea.*
employ *vb.* 1. pay people to work. **employee** *n.* a person who works for wages. **employer** *n.* a person who employs others. **employment** *n.* 2. use. *I employ a fine pen to fill in the details.*
emporium *n.* a large shop (rather old-fashioned).
empty *adj.* having nothing inside; not full. *vb.* remove contents of. **emptiness** *n.*
emu *n.* a large Australian flightless bird.
en- prefix meaning to put into, on, effect, e.g. **enrage, enclose**. Before b, p and m, en becomes **em-**.
enable *vb.* make able.
enamel *n.* a very hard shiny paint; a hard, glass-like coating on metal saucepans, pottery or glass.
enchant *vb.* 1. put a magic spell on someone. 2. be very attractive to someone.
enclose *vb.* shut in on all sides. **enclosure** *n.* enclosed land.
encore (*on*-**kor**) *inter.* & *n.* shout of applause meaning *Again!* repetition of a song, etc.
encounter *vb.* meet someone. *n.* a casual meeting.
encourage *vb.* make someone feel able to do something; urge someone on. **encouragement** *n.*
encyclopedia *n.* a book or set of books that give you information about many subjects, and usually alphabetically arranged.
end *n.* the place where something stops; the edge or side of something. *vb.* to put a stop to. **endless** *adj.* without ending; incessant.

endeavour (*en*-**dev**-*er*) *vb*. try hard to do. *n*. an attempt.
endure *vb*. suffer, undergo (pain). **endurance** *n*. power to suffer, put up with.
enemy *n*. the people that one fights in time of war; someone you dislike.
energy *n*. the strength or power to do work; vigour; activity. **energetic** *adj*. *Machines have energy. The food we eat gives us energy.*
engage *vb*. 1. bind by promise. 2. hire. 3. (in) take part *in*. 4. begin fighting. 5. interlock. *He engaged the gear.*
engine *n*. a machine which changes energy into power or movement. *The train was pulled by its great engine.*
engineer *n*. 1. a person who plans and builds bridges, roads, machines and big buildings. 2. a person who looks after or works with engines.
engrave *vb*. cut a picture or writing into wood, steel or other hard substance. (An **engraving** (*n*) is a print made by this method.)
enigma *n*. a mystery, a riddle. **enigmatic** (-**al**) *adj*.
enjoy *vb*. get pleasure from. *I always enjoy going to the ballet.* **enjoyable** *adj*. **enjoyment** *n*.
enlarge *vb*. make or become bigger. **enlargement** *n*.
enlist *vb*. engage, take on (especially as a soldier).
enormous *adj*. very big.
enough *adj*. sufficient. *Have you had enough to eat?*
enquire see **inquire**
ensign *n*. a flag or badge.
ensue *vb*. happen afterwards.
ensure *vb*. make safe or certain. *Please ensure the door is locked.*
enter *vb*. go into place; record something (in a book); take part in a competition.
enterprise *n*. project or undertaking; an aptitude for taking on a project. *She showed great enterprise.*
entertain *vb*. 1. amuse people with a show. 2. have people as guests in your home. **entertainment** *n*. hospitality; performance (theatre etc.). **entertainer** *n*. professional singer, dancer etc.
enthusiasm *n*. great interest, zeal. **enthusiast** *n*. someone who is full of enthusiasm; a keen person.
entire *adj*. whole; complete.
entrance *n*. the place through which one enters or goes in.
entreat *vb*. beg, plead.
entry *n*. entrance; something

A 16th-century engraving by Stradnus, showing engravers at work inside a workshop.

entered in a book etc; a competitor in a race etc.
entwine *vb.* twist together.
envelop *vb.* cover completely.
envelope *n.* a paper covering for a letter; a wrapper.
environment *n.* surroundings; the place or kind of life surrounding an animal
envoy *n.* a diplomat lower in rank than an ambassador.
envy *n.* & *vb.* a feeling of wanting what someone else has; jealousy. **envious** *adj.* full of envy. **enviable** *adj.* exciting envy; desirable.
epic *n.* 1. a long poem that tells a story, such as Homer's *Odyssey*. 2. a historical film made at great expense with large numbers of actors.
epidemic *n.* a disease which a large number of people have at the same time.
epidermis *n.* the outer layer of skin.
epigram *n.* a short witty remark or poem.
epilepsy *n.* a nervous disease marked by repeated fits.
Epiphany (*i*-**pif**-*anee*) *n.* Christian feast (6 January) marking the visit of the Magi to Jesus.
episode *n.* one event in a series of events; one part of a film (etc.) serial. **episodic** *adj.*
epistle *n.* a letter (especially in the New Testament).
epoch *n.* an era, period marked by historic events.
equal *adj.* the same in size or number etc; a person of same rank. **equality** *n.* being equal. **equalize** *vb.* make even or equal.
equate *vb.* regard as equal.
equator *n.* an imaginary line around the middle of the Earth that is drawn on maps. **equatorial** *adj.* of, at or near the equator.
equestrian *adj.* to do with horse riding. *n.* a horse rider.
equine *n.* of or like a horse.
equinox *n.* the time of year in spring and autumn when the day and night are of equal length all over the world. The equinoxes happen about 21 March and 23 September.
equipment *n.* things needed to do something. **equip** *vb.* provide with things necessary (for fighting, playing games etc).
equitable *adj.* fair and just.
equivalent *adj.* the same or equal in force, value or meaning. *In 1988, £1.00 was the equivalent of about US $1.75.*
era *n.* period of time, particularly of history.
eradicate *vb.* uproot, destroy, wipe out, abolish.

The equator divides the world into the Northern and Southern Hemispheres.

Arches Park in Utah, North America, is a natural arch shaped by erosion.

erase *vb*. rub out, wipe off.
erect *vb*. raise up, build. *adj*. upright. **erection** *n*. building.
ermine *n*. the white winter fur of a species of weasel.
erosion *n*. the slow wearing away of the land by wind, water and other means. **erode** *vb*. gradually wear away.
erotic *adj*. arousing sexual desire, passion.
err *vb*. make a mistake; sin.
errand *n*. short journey to carry messages etc.
error *n*. mistake; something that is done wrongly.
erupt *vb*. burst out violently, shoot out lava etc.
eruption *n*. volcanic outbreak etc.
escalate *vb*. go up, increase by degrees.
escalator *n*. a moving staircase.
escape 1. *vb*. get away from or get free. *The lion escaped from its cage in the zoo*. 2. *n*. a leakage.
escapement *n*. part of the works of a watch or clock.
escort *vb*. accompany for protection.

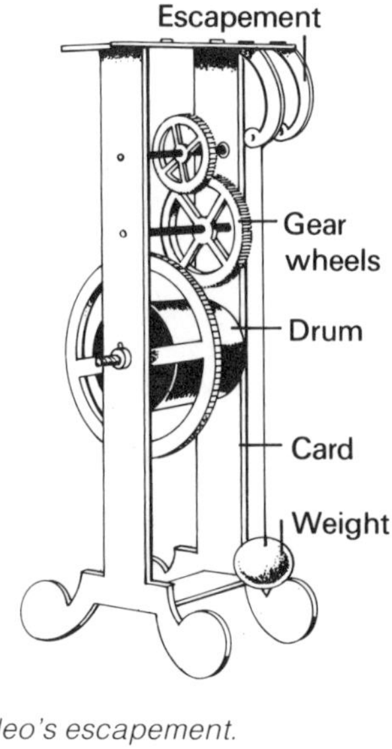

Galileo's escapement.

Eskimo *n.* (plural **Eskimos**) native people of the Arctic Circle.

especially *adj.* chiefly; more than normally. *I like raspberries, especially with cream.*

Esperanto *n.* an artificial language invented by the Russian L. L. Zamenhof in 1887.

espionage *n.* spying.

esquire (*es*-**kwire**) *n.* polite title added to a man's name when addressing a letter: *J. P. Jones Esq.*

essay *n.* a piece of writing. *You often have to write essays in exams.*

essence *n.* 1. the main quality of something. 2. a solution of a substance in oil, often used in cooking.

establish *vb.* settle or organize; set up. *The expedition established their base camp at the foot of the mountains.* **establishment** *n.*

estate *n.* an area of land that someone owns.

estimate *vb.* guess the size, weight or cost of something. *Can you estimate how tall that giraffe is?*

estuary *n.* the mouth of a large river.

etcetera *n.* (shortened as **etc.**) and so on; and other things. *Cats, cows, horses etc. are domestic animals.*

etch *vb.* draw on metal or glass by cutting lines with acid.

eternal *adj.* having no beginning or end; lasting forever. **eternity** *n.* infinite time; the after life.

ether (**ee**-*ther*) *n.* a liquid chemical, formerly used as an anaesthetic, the industrial uses of which include refrigeration.

ethnic *adj.* of race (people).

eucalyptus *n.* an Australian gum tree. Oil from the leaves is used as a medicine.

Eucharist (**yoo**-*kar-ist*) *n.* Christian service of Holy Communion.

eulogize *vb.* praise highly.

euphemism (**yoo**-*fem-izm*) *n.* the use of a mild or indirect word or expression in place of a harder, correct or true one. *He would not say 'dead' but always used the euphemism 'passed away'.*

evacuate *vb.* 1. empty. 2. withdraw from a dangerous place. **evacuee** *n.* a person who is removed.

evade *vb.* escape, get away; avoid something or someone on purpose. *She evaded the question.*

evangelist *n.* a writer of one of the Gospels (Matthew, Mark, Luke or John). **evangelism** *n.* the preaching of the gospel.

evaporate *vb.* turn from a liquid into a vapour or gas, usually because of heat. **evaporation** *n.*

even 1. *adv.* a word used to strengthen a statement. *He hasn't even read the book.* 2. *adj.* smooth; equal. 3. *adj.* divisible by 2. *Even numbers are the opposite of odd numbers.*

evening *n.* the time between afternoon and night.

event *n.* an important happening. **eventful** *adj.* full of incident.

eventually *adv.* in the end, at last.

ever *adv.* always; at all times. *They lived happily ever after.*

evergreen *n.* & *adj.* a tree that has green leaves all the year round.

every *adj.* each one, every individual member of a group thought of as making up the whole group.

everybody, everyone *pron.* each person; all the people.

everything *pron.* all things; each thing.

everywhere *adv.* in every place.

evict *vb.* turn out from, expel. **eviction** *n.*

evidence *n.* proof; particularly in a trial.

evil *n.* & *adj.* very bad, wicked.

evolution *n.* the process by which animals and plants develop and change over millions of years.

ewe (rhymes with *new*) *n.* a female sheep.

ex- *prefix* meaning out, from, beyond; formerly (ef- before f; e before many consonants).

exact *adj.* just right, perfectly correct.

exaggerate *vb.* make something sound bigger or smaller, or more or less important than it really is. **exaggeration** *n.*

exalt *vb.* praise. **exalted** *adj.* highly placed. *She has an exalted position in the government because she is minister of aviation.*

exam, examination *n.* 1. an important test to find out how much you know. 2. a close look at something.

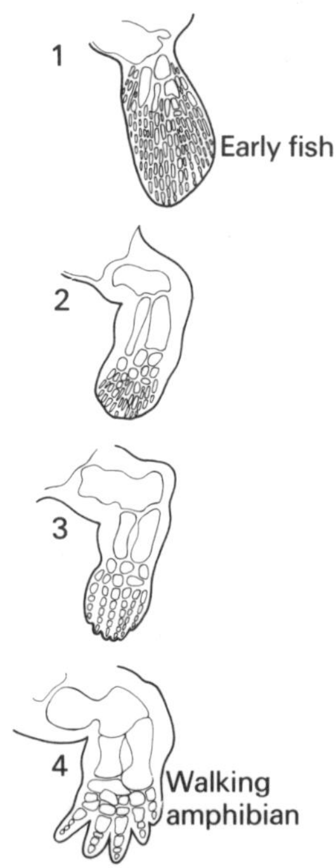

How the fin of an early fish might have developed into the leg of a primitive amphibian.

Marking out an archaeological site for excavation.

examine *vb.* look at something very carefully; inquire into; interrogate. **examiner** *n.*
example *n.* something which shows what something else is like or how it works. *This cake is a good example of my cooking.* a model; a warning to others.
exasperate *vb.* irritate, rouse to anger. **exasperation** *n.*
excavate *vb.* uncover by digging, unearth. *The archaeologist excavated several human bones.* **excavation** *n.*
exceed *vb.* go beyond. *It is dangerous to exceed the stated dose of this medicine.*
excellent *adj.* very good.
except *prep.* not included, omitting. *Everyone is here except John.*
exceptional *adj.* out of the ordinary, outstanding.
exchange *vb.* change one thing for another; swop.
excite *vb.* make someone look forward to something; thrill. **excitement** *n.*
exclude *vb.* shut out, keep out from. *He was excluded from the meeting.*
excursion *n.* short journey, pleasure trip.
excuse 1. *n.* an apology; a reason for not doing something, or for doing wrong. 2. *vb.* let someone off. *She was excused choir practice, as she has a cold.*
execute *vb.* put someone to death legally as a punishment.
exercise *n.* 1. work that helps to make the body strong and healthy. *vb.* 2. drill.
exert *vb.* bring into action; apply. **exertion** *n.* effort.
exhale *vb.* breathe out.
exhaust (*ex*-**awst**) 1. *vb.* use up completely; make very tired. 2. *n.* the part of an engine that lets out burned gases; the burned gases.
exhaustive *adj.* thorough, complete. *The police made exhaustive inquiries.*
exhibit *vb.* show something in public. *n.* the thing that is shown.
exhibition (*eks-i*-**bish**-*un*) *n.* a place or event where things are shown to the public, such as an art exhibition.
exile *n.* & *vb.* a person who has been forbidden by law to live in his or her own country. *He spent ten years in exile.*
exist *vb.* be or live. **existence** *n.*

exit *vb.* go out; leave. *n.* the place through which you go out; a direction in a play which tells an actor to leave the stage.
exodus *n.* the departure of a large group of people. (The Book of Exodus in the Bible deals with the departure of the Israelites from Egypt.)
exotic *adj.* brought in from abroad; unusual.
expand *vb.* get larger.
expanse *n.* a broad area. *An expanse of sky.*
expect *vb.* think that something will happen; look forward to. *I expect they will be here soon.*
expedition *n.* a group of people making a journey for a special reason, such as climbing a mountain.
expel *vb.* drive out, compel to leave.
expensive *adj.* costing a lot of money.
experience 1. *n.* something that happens to you, and from which you may learn. *Going to camp is a great experience.* 2. *vb.* feel; meet with. *They will experience great heat in the centre of Africa.* **experienced** *adj.*
experiment *n.* a test; a trial. *vb.* carry out a test.
expert *n.* someone who knows a lot about something.
expire *vb.* breathe out air; (breathe one's last breath) die.
expiry *n.* end, termination.
explain *vb.* show or make the meaning clear. **explanation** *n.* statement or fact that explains something, makes it clear. *So that is the explanation of the conjuring trick.*
explicit *adj.* stated or shown clearly.
explode *vb.* burst with a loud bang and, usually, great damage.
exploit 1. *n.* an adventure. 2. *vb.* develop or use profitably. *You must exploit your talent.*
explore *vb.* look carefully around a place where you have not been before; examine, discuss a possibility etc. **exploration** *n.*
explorer *n.* a person who travels to find out about places where people have not been before.

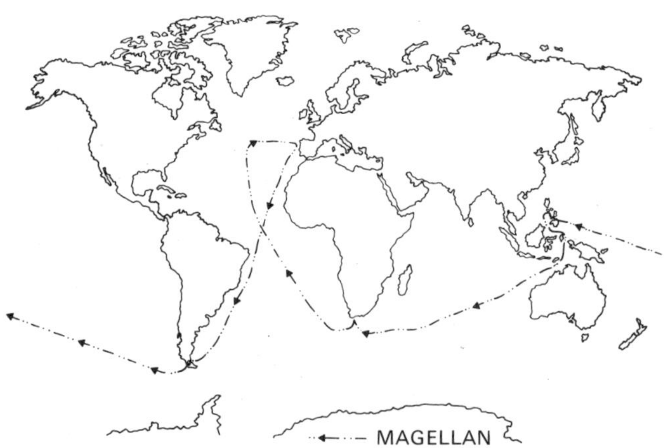

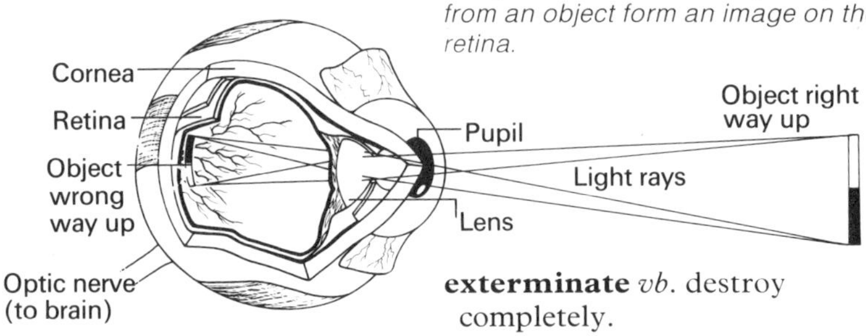

An eye in cross-section. Light rays from an object form an image on the retina.

explosion (*ex*-**plo**-*shun*) *n.* a loud noise when something explodes.
explosive *n.* anything such as dynamite used to make things explode or blow up.
exponent *n.* someone who explains or interprets.
export (*eks*-**port**) *vb.* sell goods to another country.
exports (*eks*-**ports**) *pl. n.* the goods that are exported.
expose *vb.* uncover; leave unprotected. *The troops were exposed to gunfire*; make public a villainy.
exposure *n.* the act of exposing, leaving unprotected; period of time light is allowed to fall on a sensitive emulsion in photography.
express 1. *vb.* explain something in words. *He has difficulty in expressing his meaning.* 2. *adj.* fast. *An express train.*
expression *n.* 1. a common form of words. 2. the look on a person's face.
extant *adj.* still living, existing.
extend *vb.* stretch out, lengthen; prolong.
exterior *n.* the outside (of a building).
exterminate *vb.* destroy completely.
external *adj.* outside.
extinct *adj.* a thing which was living is extinct when none of its kind is alive any more. *Dinosaurs have been extinct for millions of years.*
extinguish *vb.* put out, cause to stop. *The firemen extinguished the blaze.*
extra *adj.* more than usual. *You will need extra clothes because it's so cold.*
extraordinary *adj.* very unusual.
extravagance *n.* lavish wastefulness; wild.
extreme *adj.* very great or very far. **extremist** *n.* a person who holds strong uncompromising (political) views.
eye *n.* the organ, or part of the body, we use for seeing.
eyebrow *n.* the curve of hair above the eye.
eyelashes *pl. n.* the fringes of hair on the eyelids.
eyelid *n.* the flap of skin that covers the eye when it is closed.
eye-opener *n.* something which suddenly surprises you or makes you suddenly understand.
eyesight *n.* the ability to see.
eye-witness *n.* someone who sees an event happening.

F

fable *n.* a story that tries to teach us something. The characters are usually animals that talk.
fabric *n.* cloth.
fabulous *adj.* in a fable; marvellous, incredible.
façade (*fass-sard*) *n.* the front of a building; appearance given to other people.
face *n.* the front part of the head. *vb.* meet confidently and without fear.
facet *n.* one side of a cut gem.
facilitate *vb.* make easier; help.
facility *n.* ease; no difficulty in doing, learning etc.
facsimile (*fak*-**sim**-*ilee*) *n.* exact copy.
fact *n.* something that really happened, so people know that it is true. *It is a fact that William the Conqueror invaded England in 1066.*
factory *n.* a building where people and machines work together to make things.
factual *adj.* concerned with, containing fact.
fad *n.* a craze, passing enthusiasm.
fade *vb.* 1. lose colour. *Our curtains have faded in the sun.* 2. wither. *The flowers faded.* 3. disappear slowly. *Before long the ship faded from sight in the mist.*
Fahrenheit (**fa**-*ren-hite*) *n.* a thermometer scale in which the freezing point of water is 32° and the boiling point is 212°. It was invented by a German, Gabriel Daniel Fahrenheit (1686–1736).
fail *vb.* be unsuccessful.
failing *n.* weakness, defect, short-coming.
failure *n.* lack of success; omission: *failure in duty*.
faint 1. *adj.* weak; not clear. *We could hear a faint sound when we listened carefully.* 2. *vb.* become dizzy, with everything going black, so you may fall down; become unconscious.
fair 1. *adj.* acting in a just way, that is seen to be right. *Everyone should have a fair share of the cake.* 2. *adj.* light coloured. *Mary has fair hair and blue eyes.* 3. *adj.* (of weather) good. 4. *n.* a group of outdoor amusements, with sideshows and roundabouts.
fairly *adv.* moderately. *I know him fairly well.*
fairy *n.* an imaginary small creature with magic powers.
faith *n.* 1. a strong belief; trust. *I have complete faith in her.* 2. religion.
faithful *adj.* honest; trustworthy.
fake *n.* & *adj.* something that looks real but is not.
falcon *n.* a bird of prey related to the eagle.
fall *vb.* drop to the ground. *n.* 1. drop. 2. autumn (especially USA).
fall behind *vb.* fail to keep up with. *He has no money, so he will fall behind wih his rent.*

fall out 1. *vb.* quarrel. 2. *n.* radioactive dust settling after nuclear explosion.
fall through *vb.* fail to take place.
false *adj.* not true; not real.
falsetto *n.* & *adj.* male voice which is made artificially high.
falter *vb.* hesitate, stumble; lose courage.
fame *n.* being well-known or famous. *Her fame is world-wide.*
familiar *adj.* well-known.
family *n.* a group of people who are all related to each other.
famine *n.* a time when there is very little food in an area and people go hungry.
famous *adj.* well-known. *He is a famous musician.*
fan *n.* 1. a thing that moves the air and so makes you cooler. 2. a person who greatly admires someone famous; a supporter (short for *fanatic*).

The merlin is one of the smallest falcons. It flies fast on long, pointed wings.

fancy *vb.* imagine, picture to oneself; have a fancy for; take a liking to; be under a delusion. *He fancies he can fly.*
fanfare *n.* a flourish played on a trumpet, usually to introduce an important person.
fang *n.* a long, sharp tooth, especially the poison tooth of snakes such as vipers and cobras.

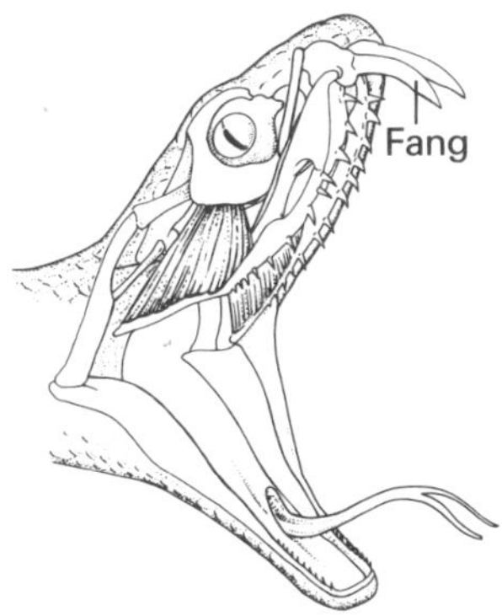

fantasy *n.* something, usually pleasant, that you imagine or dream about, but is not real.
far *adj.* a long way off.
farce *n.* an amusing kind of play, full of misunderstandings; an absurd situation.
fare *n.* 1. the price of travelling on a bus, train etc. 2. food and drink (now old-fashioned).
farewell *inter., n.* & *adj.* goodbye. *A farewell speech.*
farm *n.* land and buildings where crops are grown and animals reared. *vb.* use land to grow crops or rear animals.
farmer *n.*
farrago (*fa*-**rah**-*go*) *n.* a mixture.
farrier *n.* one who shoes horses, a blacksmith.

farrow *n.* litter of pigs. *vb.* give birth to pigs.
farther *adj.* (**further**) more distant.
farthest *adj.* (**furthest**) the most distant.
farthing *n.* former British coin worth a quarter of the former penny.
fascinate *vb.* attract, charm. **fascination** *n.*
Fascism *n.* a political belief and form of government in which a country has only one political party, and is ruled by a dictator.
fashion *n.* a way of dressing or doing things that most people like to copy at a certain time. *There was a fashion for huge sweaters last year.*
fast 1. *adj.* very quick. 2. *adv.* firmly fixed. *My boot was stuck fast in the mud.* 3. *vb.* eat no food for a time.
fasten *vb.* tie; fix firmly. **fastener** *n.* **fastening** *n.*
fat 1. *adj.* plump, fleshy and round. 2. *n.* the soft, oily part of the body of a person or an animal.
fatal *adj.* causing death or disaster. *A fatal accident.*
fate *n.* power which some believe determines events; destiny.
father *n.* a person's male parent.
fathom *n.* a nautical term used to measure the depth of water. A fathom equals 1.8 metres (6 ft). *vb.* sound depth of water; get to the bottom of (a problem etc.).
fatigue *n.* weariness; weakness in a metal. *vb.* tire.
fatty *adj.* containing fat.
fault (rhymes with *salt*) *n.* something that is not perfect; a mistake.
fauna (**fawn**-*a*) *n.* animal life of a district.
favour 1. *n.* an act of kindness or help. *Can you do me a favour by collecting my dress?* 2. *vb.* like one person or thing more than another.
favourite *adj.* & *n.* the best-liked person or thing.
fawn 1. *n.* a young deer. *adj.* fawn-coloured, yellowish brown. 2. *vb.* grovel, cringe (like a dog).
fear *vb.* feel frightened. *n.* the feeling of being frightened.
fearless *adj.* brave; without fear.
feast *n.* 1. a very grand meal. 2. a religious festival.
feat (*feet*) *n.* act or deed, especially showing strength or courage.
feather *n.* one of the many light coverings that grow on a bird's body.

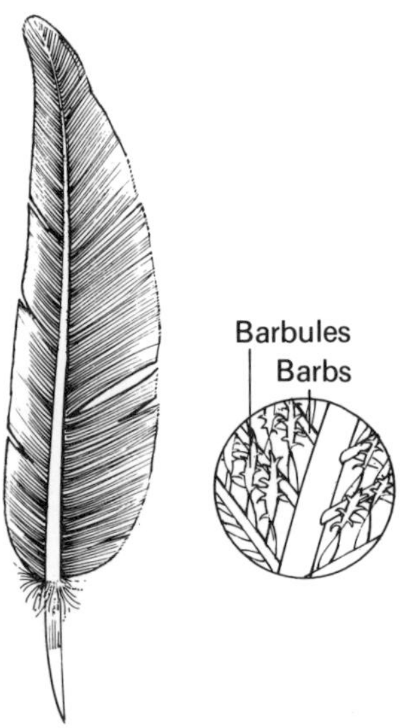

feature *n*. 1. one of the parts of the face. *Your nose is one of your features*. 2. an important part of something.

February *n*. The second month of the year.

fed *vb*. past tense and past part. of **feed**. *She was fed up with her job*. (*casual*) bored.

fee *n*. a payment made to someone for a professional service.

feeble *adj*. weak; indistinct.

feed *vb*. give food to a person or animal.

feel *vb*. be aware of something by touch; be conscious of; experience.

feeler *n*. the antenna of an insect, with which it touches or feels things.

feeling *n*. a sensation; an emotion; something that you know inside yourself, like knowing that you dislike someone. *A feeling of pain*.

feet *pl. n*. more than one foot.

feline *adj*. of cats or the cat family.

fell 1. *vb*. past of **fall**. *Jack fell down and broke his crown*. 2. *n*. a hill.

fellow *n*. a male person; a member of a learned society. *adj*. of the same class or kind. *A fellow countryman*.

felony *n*. serious crime such as murder.

felt 1. *vb*. past of **feel** 2. *n*. a kind of cloth made from bits of wool pressed together rather than woven.

female *n*. a woman; a girl; any animal that is not a male.

feminine *adj*. belonging to or characteristic of women.

feminist *n*. supporter of women's rights.

fen *n*. low-lying marshland or bog.

fence 1. *n*. a wooden or metal barrier. 2. *vb*. fight with special swords.

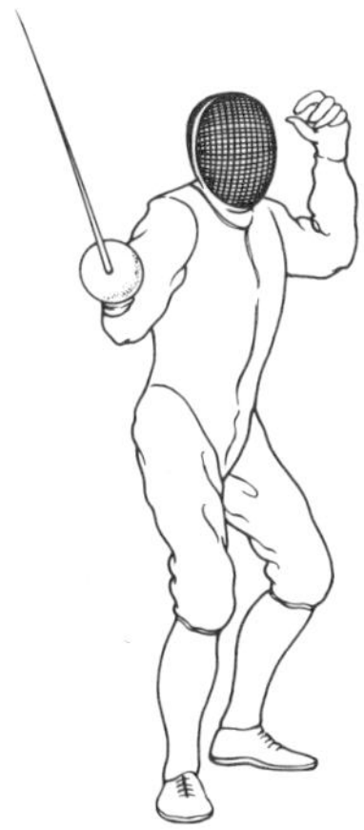

Fencers wear a mask and protective clothing when they fight.

fender *n*. protective frame round an open fireplace; fireguard. (*U.S*. car's bumper.)

fennec *n*. North African fox.

fennel *n*. a yellow-flowered herb.

ferment 1. *vb*. to go through a chemical change (fermentation) that results in the forming of bubbles of gas. 2. *n*. a state of agitation.

fern *n*. a plant with feathery leaves which does not produce flowers.

ferocious *adj*. fierce, cruel, savage.

ferret *n*. a small animal that can be trained to hunt rabbits and rats. *vb*. hunt with ferrets; rummage.

ferry *n.* a boat that carries people for short distances. *We crossed the river by the ferry.*

fertile *adj.* able to produce a lot of good crops. *The Nile valley is fertile.*

fertilize *vb.* 1. make fertile. 2. (of plants and animals) start to grow.

fervent *adj.* ardent, intense. **fervour** *n.* zeal.

fester *vb.* become sore and filled with pus.

festival *n.* a time for celebration– dancing, music and feasting.

fetch *vb.* collect something or bring it back.

fête (rhymes with *late*) *n.* a kind of open air party where there are games and things to buy. *A fête is usually organized to collect money for charity.*

fever *n.* an illness in which you have a high temperature. **feverish** *adj.*

few *adj.* not many, a small number. *He has few friends.*

fez *n.* brimless red felt hat worn by Muslims.

fiancé (*fi*-**on**-*say*) *n.* man to whom a woman is engaged to be married. (feminine: **fiancée**.)

fiasco (*fee*-**as**-*koh*) *n.* complete breakdown; mess.

fib *n.* small lie.

fibre (**fie**-*ber*) *n.* 1. a very fine thread. 2. material made from fibres.

fibula *n.* outer and smaller bone of the lower part of the leg.

fickle *adj.* changeable (especially in affections).

fiction *n.* a story that has been made up, that is not about real people or events.

fiddle 1. *n.* violin. *vb.* play a violin. 2. *n.* & *vb.* swindle.

fidget *vb.* move about restlessly.

field *n.* a piece of ground, often used for growing crops or keeping animals, and usually surrounded by a hedge or fence.

fierce *adj.* cruel and angry.

fiery *adj.* like fire, flaming; quick-tempered.

fiesta *n.* Spanish word for 'feast-day'. All Latin American countries hold fiestas, celebrating either religious or political events.

fig *n.* the soft, sweet fruit of a small-sized tree of the same name, which has large leaves.

fight *n.* a violent contest, either in battle or in some kinds of sport, e.g. boxing. *vb.* take part in a fight.

fighter *n.* aircraft designed for combat in the air.

fight shy of *vb.* avoid.

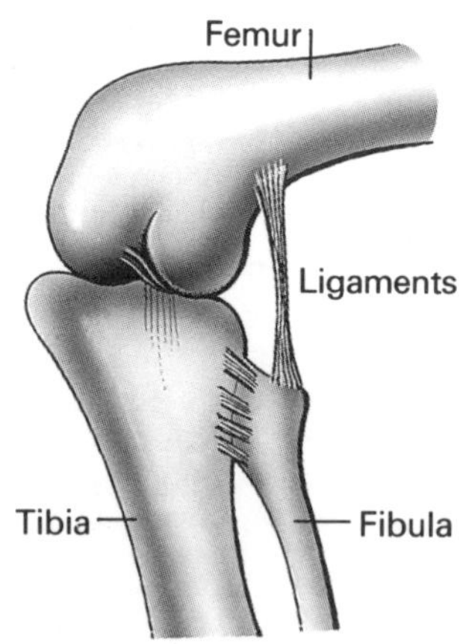

The fibula is the narrow bone on the right, below the knee joint.

figure *n.* 1. a sign for a number such as 5 or 9. 2. a diagram in a book. 3. the shape of the body. *The dancers have good figures.*

filament *n.* fine wire used in an electric light bulb.

file 1. *vb.* put in order in a box or holder (a file). 2. *n.* a metal tool with rough sides for smoothing surfaces.

fill *vb.* make something full. *Please, fill the kettle.* Occupy all the space.

filly *n.* a young female horse.

film *n.* 1. a thin covering. 2. a coated roll of plastic that can be placed in a camera and used to take photographs. 3. moving pictures that may be shown in a cinema. *vb.*

filter *vb.* strain a liquid through a fine mesh to remove impurities. *n.* a device for straining liquid.

filthy *adj.* very dirty.

fin *n.* part of a fish. *The fin helps the fish to swim and balance.*

final *adj.* the last.

finale (*fin*-**ah**-*lay*) *n.* final movement of symphony or other musical composition.

finally *adv.* at last.

finance *n.* the management of money matters. *vb.* provide money for. *He financed the play.*

finch *n.* a small bird belonging to a very large family of birds found almost everywhere except Australia.

find *vb.* discover or locate something.

find out *vb.* come to know something, discover. *Can you find out where he has gone?*

fine 1. *adj.* very thin or delicate. 2. *adj.* (of weather) good and clear. 3. *n.* money paid as a punishment.

finger *n.* one of the end parts, or digits, of the hand, including the thumb. *vb.* touch with the fingers.

fingerprint *n.* the mark left on something by the tip of your finger.

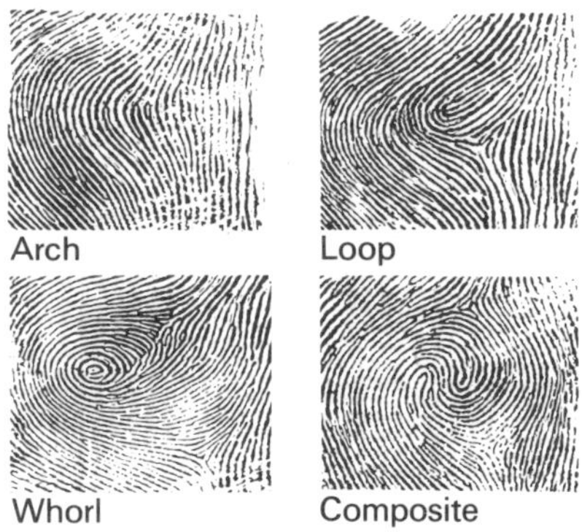

finish *vb.* & *n.* end something; complete a task.

fiord *n.* a long, narrow valley with steep sides along the coast, especially of Norway and Greenland.

fir *n.* an evergreen tree with needle-like leaves and fruit called cones.

fire 1. *n.* the bright light and heat that comes when something is burned. 2. *vb.* shoot a gun.

fire-engine *n.* a vehicle used by firefighters to put out fires by spraying water or foam on them.

fire-escape *n.* a way out of a burning building.

fire-fighter *n.* a person whose job it is to put out fires. *A fire-fighter goes to a fire in a fire-engine.*

fireplace *n.* the part of a room where a fire is or was made.
fire station *n.* a fire-fighter's head-quarters, where fire-engines are kept.
firewood *n.* small pieces of wood for use in a fire.
fireworks *n.* devices that burn with noise or pretty colours, like a rocket or a sparkler.
firm 1. *adj.* solid, hard, steady. 2. *n.* a business, company.
firmament *n.* the whole expanse of the sky with its stars and clouds.
first *adj.* & *adv.* number one in order; at the beginning.
first aid *n.* on-the-spot care of the victims of accidents or sudden illness.
fish 1. *n.* a cold-blooded vertebrate (backboned) animal that lives in water and breathes through gills. 2. *vb.* try to catch fish. **fishy** *adj.* of fish; smell of fish; suspicious.
fisherman *n.* person who catches fish.
fishmonger *n.* person who sells fish.
fission *n.* splitting or dividing into parts; the splitting of an atomic nucleus.
fist *n.* tightly closed hand.
fit 1. *adj.* in good health or physical condition. 2. *vb.* be suitable, the right size. *Are you sure that shoe fits you?* 3. *n.* a sudden, violent convulsion.
fix 1. *vb.* mend something. 2. *vb.* decide. *We will fix a date for the match.* 3. *n.* a difficult position. *We are in a fix.*
fixture *n.* 1. thing fixed in position (e.g. cupboard). 2. sporting event for which a date has been fixed.
flabbergast *vb.* astonish.
flabby *adj.* hanging loosely (especially of flesh); limp.
flaccid (**flass**-*sid*) *adj.* flabby, hanging loosely.
flag 1. *n.* a piece of coloured cloth with a pattern on it to show the country or organization to which it belongs. 2. *vb.* become tired. *In the last lap of the race she started to flag.*

The national flag of the United Kingdom is unofficially called the Union Jack.

flagon *n.* a large bottle (old-fashioned).
flagstone *n.* flat slab of stone for paving.
flair *n.* natural talent. *She has a flair for writing.*
flake *n.* a small, light piece of something, such as snow.
flamboyant *adj.* ornate, showy.
flame *n.* the burning gas from a fire.

flamingo *n.* a tropical bird, pink in colour, with long legs and neck.
flan *n.* an open tart.
flange *n.* projecting rim on wheel to keep it on a rail.
flank *n.* the side of certain things, especially animals. *vb.* stand at side of.
flannel *n.* soft woollen cloth.
flap 1. *n.* a piece of material that hangs down over an opening. 2. *vb.* make something move up and down. *The wind flapped the clothes on the line.*
flare *vb.* 1. blaze up (of fire). *n.* bright light. 2. spread outwards (e.g. a skirt).
flash *n.* a sudden burst of light. *vb.* reflect light.
flask *n.* a kind of bottle, particularly one for keeping liquids hot or cold.
flat 1. *adj.* level and smooth. 2. *n.* a separate home in a building, or block of flats.
flatter *vb.* please someone by praising them more than they deserve.
flatulence *n.* gas in the stomach or bowels.
flaunt *vb.* show off, make a great display of.
flautist *n.* flute-player.
flavour *n.* the taste and smell of food. *vb.* give flavour to; season.
flaw *n.* a defect or imperfection in something. *There is a flaw in your argument.*
flax *n.* a slender-stemmed plant with blue-flowers. The stems are used to make hemp. **flaxen** *adj.*
flea *n.* a small jumping insect that feeds on blood.

Flamingoes usually live together in large colonies on the edge of lakes and marshes. They eat tiny water creatures.

fleck *n.* speck of colour, light etc. *vb.* mark with flecks.
fledgeling *n.* a young bird that is just able to fly.
flee *vb.* run away from.
fleece *n.* a sheep's woolly covering.
fleet *n.* a number of ships under one leader.

The flax plant is used to make linen and linseed oil.

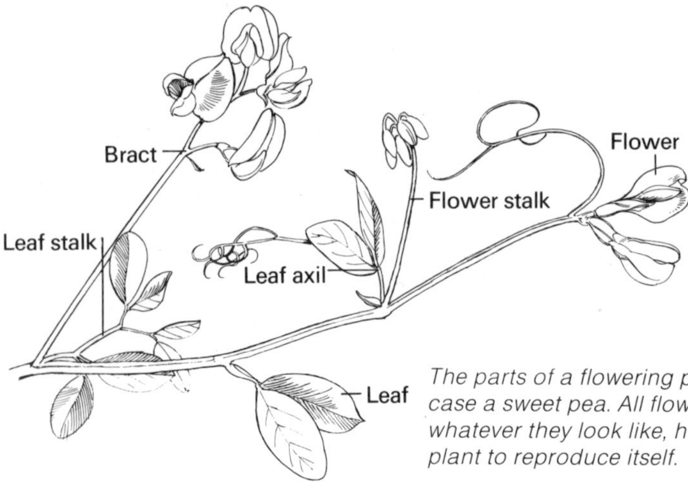

The parts of a flowering plant, in this case a sweet pea. All flowers, whatever they look like, help the plant to reproduce itself.

fleeting *adj*. passing by quickly. *A fleeting moment*.
flesh *n*. the soft part of the body covering the bones.
flew *vb*. past of **fly**.
flex *n*. electrical wire.
flexible *adj*. easily bent this way and that.
flicker *vb*. shine or burn, now bright, now faint.
flight (rhymes with *bite*) *n*. 1. the act of flying. 2. a journey in an aircraft. 3. running away from danger.
flimsy *adj*. light and frail.
fling *vb*. throw, hurl. *n*.
flint *n*. a glassy mineral that is a form of quartz.
flippant *adj*. to treat serious matters lightly.
flipper *n*. an arm-like part used by seals and other water animals to swim.
flirt (*flurt*) *vb*. play at courting a person.
float 1. *vb*. be held up in air or in water. 2. *n*. a piece of cork or wood on a fishing line or net.
flock *n*. a large group of animals, particularly sheep or birds.
flog *vb*. whip, thrash with a stick etc.
flood (*flud*) *n*. a lot of water that spreads over usually dry land. *vb*. cover with a flood.
floor *n*. 1. the part of the room on which one walks. 2. one level or storey of a building. *Nick lives on the second floor of the block of flats*.
flop 1. *vb*. throw oneself down clumsily and noisily. 2. *n*. utter failure. *The musical was a flop*.
flora *n*. plant life of a particular district.
florist *n*. a person or shop that sells flowers.
flounder 1. *n*. small flat fish. 2. *vb*. stumble, thrash about as if helpless in water; make a mess of things.
flour *n*. a powder made from grain and used in cooking.
flourish *vb*. prosper, thrive, be healthy. *The shop is flourishing*.
flow *vb*. move along as water does in a river. *n*. process of flowing.
flower *n*. the coloured part of a plant that produces seeds. *vb*.

flown *vb*. past part. of **fly.**
flu *abbr*. short for influenza.
flue *n*. smoke channel in a chimney.
fluff *n*. soft down, hair etc.
fluid *n*. any liquid or gas that can flow easily.
flung *vb*. past of **fling**.
flush *vb*. 1. blush. 2. clear out with sudden rush of water.
fluster *vb*. make confused or nervous; agitate.
flute *n*. a wind instrument with holes in the side. **flautist** *n*. flute-player.
flutter *vb*. flap wings quickly and nervously without flying.
fly 1. *vb*. move through the air; travel in an aircraft; depart suddenly. 2. *n*. one of a large group of winged insects.
fly-over *n*. a road bridge, usually on a motorway.
foal *n*. a young horse.
foam *n*. a white mass of small bubbles; froth.
focus *vb*. adjust the lens of a camera, telescope etc. in order to get a clear picture or view. *n*. distance from a lens at which the image is clear.
fodder *n*. food for cattle.
foe *n*. an enemy.
foetus (**feet**-*us*) *n*. the developing offspring (baby) in its mother's womb.
fog *n*. a thick mist that it is difficult to see through.
foil 1. *n*. metal plate rolled or beaten very thin. 2. *vb*. baffle, beat off attacks.
fold 1. *vb*. bend part of a thing back over itself. 2. *n*. part of material that is folded; a crease.
folder *n*. file, holder for papers.
foliage *n*. the leaves of plants.
folk (rhymes with *smoke*) *n*. people.
folklore *n*. popular beliefs, legends and customs.
follow *vb*. go after a person or thing; pursue. **follower** *n*.
folly *n*. foolishness, a stupid action.
fondle *vb*. caress, pet.
font *n*. a (usually stone) basin for holding water for baptism.
food *n*. what is eaten. **feed** *vb*.
foolish *adj*. without much sense; silly.
foot 1. *n*. the part of the leg on which we stand, below the ankle. 2. *n*. the bottom of something. *The foot of the page*. 3. *n*. a measurement of length (30.48 cm).
football *n*. a game played between two teams; the ball used to play football.

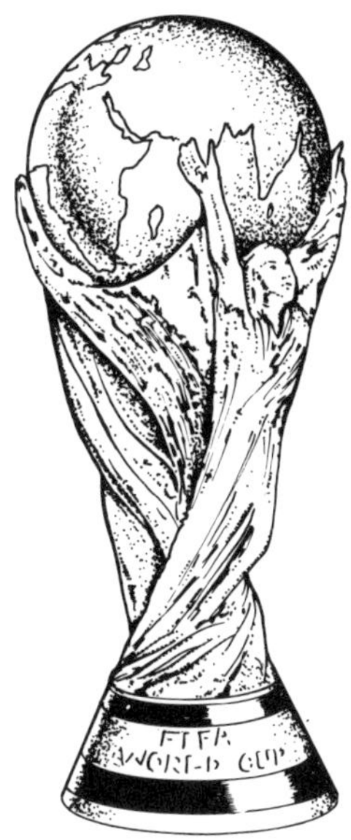

The World Cup is the world's most important football competition.

footlights *pl. n.* lights along the front of a theatre stage.
footnote *n.* note at the bottom of a printed page.
footprint *n.* the mark left by a foot in the ground.
footsteps *pl. n.* the sound of someone walking; footfalls. *I can hear footsteps on the stairs.*
for *prep.* 1. showing aim, direction. *Is this the coach for Hull?* 2. showing possession. *This letter is for you.* 3. showing preparation, purpose. *You must get ready for school.* 4. showing cause or reason. *He couldn't eat for laughing.*
forbid *vb.* (past **forbade**) prevent; prohibit. *I forbid you to tell lies.*
force 1. *vb.* make someone do something they do not want to. 2. *n.* power, strength. 3. *n.* a group of people who work together such as the police force.
ford *n.* a shallow place where a river can be crossed by walking across it.
fore- *prefix* meaning in front of, beforehand, near, e.g. **forecast**, **forehand**, **foreshadow**.
forecast *vb.* say what is likely to happen before it does. *n.* what is forecast. *The weather forecast is good.*
forehead *n.* the part of the face above the eyebrows.
foreign (**for**-*rin*) *adj.* from or of another country. **foreigner** *n.* a person from another country.
forest *n.* a large area of land covered thickly with trees.
forfeit (**for**-*fit*) *n.* & *adj.* & *vb.* thing lost through crime; penalty for crime or neglect.
forge *vb.* work metals by heating them, then hammering and rolling.
forgave *vb.* past of **forgive**.
forgery *n.* writing or a picture that is made to look as if someone else has done it; a false copy.
forget *vb.* (past **forgot**) fail to remember something.
forgive *vb.* (past **forgave**) stop being angry with someone for something they have done to you; pardon. **forgiveness** *n.*
fork *n.* a tool with two or more points for lifting food to the

Forts have been built since the Middle Ages and may be made of stone or wood as shown here.

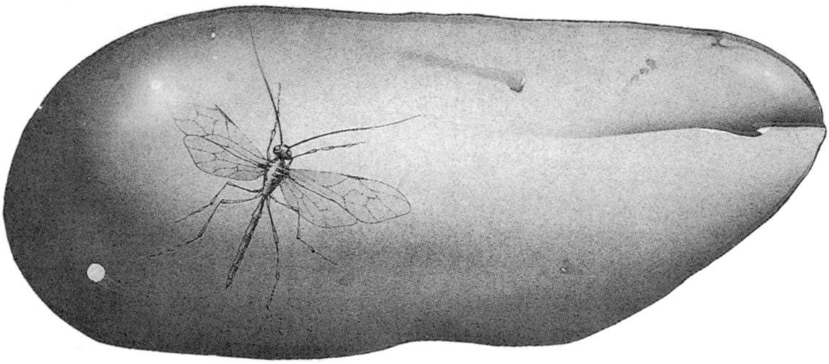

This fossil fly has been preserved in a piece of amber.

mouth; a large pronged tool for digging earth; a place where something divides. *Go on until you reach the fork in the road, and then keep to the left.*

form 1. *n.* the shape something has. 2. *n.* a printed paper with spaces where answers have to be filled in. 3. *n.* all the people in one year of a school. *I shall go into the second form next year.* 4. *vb.* make or turn into. *Water forms ice when it freezes.*

formal *adj.* following the rules, stiff, conventional.

format *n.* shape, size and style of a book etc.

formerly *adj.* in past times.

formidable *adj.* hard to cope with; to be dreaded.

formula *n.* 1. a rule or fact in sciences written in signs or numbers. *The chemical formula for water is H_2O.*
2. set of instructions for making up medicines etc.

forsake *vb.* (past **forsook**) desert, give up, abandon.

fort *n.* a strong building that can be defended.

forte (**for**-*tay* or *fawt*) *n.* a person's strong point. *Common sense is his forte.*

fortify *vb.* make a place strong so that it is difficult to attack.

fortnight *n.* a period of two weeks.

fortress *n.* a stronghold, fort.

fortunate *adj.* lucky, having or bringing good luck.

fortune *n.* 1. luck. 2. a lot of money. *James inherited a fortune from his Dad.*

forward 1. *adj.* in front of; at the front. 2. *n.* a position in football and other games.

fossil *n.* the remains of a prehistoric animal or plant that have turned to stone.

foster *vb.* bring up; encourage, promote.

foster-mother *n.* a woman who takes a child into her own home when the real parents cannot look after it. Also **foster-father, foster-parent**.

fought *vb.* past of **fight**.

foul *adj.* dirty, disgusting, bad. *He has a foul temper.*

found *vb.* 1. past of **find**. 2. establish, originate; **founder** *n.* person who starts a firm, institution etc.

foundations *pl. n.* the strong base of a building, usually below ground.

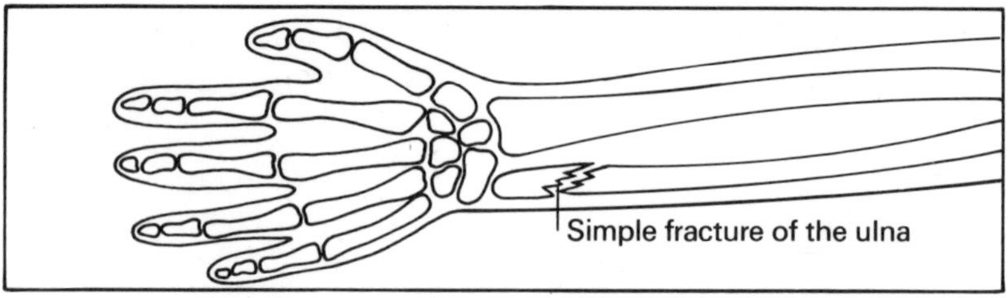

Any bone that is broken or cracked is said to be fractured. Old bones break more easily.

foundry *n.* a place where metals or glass are melted and moulded.
fountain *n.* an artificial structure with jets and basins of water; a spring of water.
foursome *n.* a group of four people.
fowl *n.* any bird, but particularly those kept for their eggs or meat.
fox *n.* a wild animal of the dog family with red-brown fur and a bushy tail. *vb.* deceive.
foxglove *n.* a tall plant with purple or white flowers; source of the drug digitalis.
foxy *adj.* crafty or cunning, like a fox.
foyer (**fwoi**-*ay*) *n.* entrance hall of an hotel, theatre etc. (U.S. lobby.)
fraction (frack-*shun*). *n.* a number that is less than a whole number. $\frac{1}{2}$ *(one half) and* $\frac{1}{4}$ *(one quarter) are fractions.* 2. a small part of something. *We only got a fraction of what we expected.*
fractious (*frack*-shus) *adj.* irritable and awkward.
fracture *vb.* & *n.* break; crack.
fragile *adj.* delicate; easily damaged.
fragment *n.* a small piece.
fragrant *adj.* sweet smelling.
frail *adj.* feeble; weak. **frailty** *n.*
frame *n.* 1. a number of pieces that fit together to give something its shape. *The frame of our tent is made up of two uprights with a pole going across between them.* 2. the border round the edge of a picture.
franc *n.* unit of currency in France, Belgium, Switzerland etc.
franchise *n.* right to vote, especially in parliamentary elections.
frank *adj.* open and honest.
frankfurter *n.* a type of sausage from Germany.
frankincense *n.* sweet-smelling resin burned as incense.
frantic *adj.* frenzied; excited with grief, pain, worry etc.
fraternal *adj.* brotherly.
fraud *n.* 1. a confidence trick or other crime that involves taking money by deceit. 2. a person who is not what he or she seems; a swindler.
fray *n.* a fight. *vb.* to wear out by rubbing, or to unravel at the edge (usually of fabric).
freak *n.* something odd or abnormal.
freckle *n.* a small brown mark on the skin.

free *adj*. 1. costing no money. 2. able to do what you want. *vb*. set at liberty, release.
freedom *n*. the state of being free, and able to do what you want.
freeze *vb*. turn from a liquid to a solid by lowering the liquid's temperature to below its freezing point. *As it freezes water turns into ice.*
freezer *n*. a box or cupboard kept very cold. *Food can be kept in a freezer for a long time.*
freight (rhymes with *late*) *n*. cargo, goods that are carried from one place to another.
freighter (rhymes with *later*) *n*. a ship or aircraft that carries freight.
frenzy *n*. violent rage, excitement.
frequency *n*. 1. repeated occurrence. 2. number of vibrations, waves, cycles per second.
frequent (free-*kwent*) *adj*. happening often. *vb*. (free-**kwent**) visit often.
fresco *n*. a painting made on freshly laid, still wet plaster. The greatest time of fresco painting was during the Renaissance in Italy.
fresh *adj*. new. *Start on a fresh page*. new and not preserved. *Fresh fruit and vegetables*.
fret 1. *n*. cut or sawn ornamental pattern in wood. 2. *n*. bar across fingerboard on a guitar etc. 3. *vb*. worry, grieve.
friction *n*. rubbing of two things together; the resistance something meets with when it rubs against something else.
Friday *n*. the name of the sixth day of the week, between Thursday and Saturday; named after Frigg, Norse goddess.
fridge *abbr*. short for refrigerator.
friend *n*. a person you know well and like. **friendship** *n*.
frieze *n*. ornamental band round top of wall.
frigate *n*. originally a sailing warship of the mid-18th century, today frigates are small escort destroyers in the Royal Navy. In the US Navy they are large guided-missile destroyers.
frighten *vb*. make afraid.
frill *n*. ornamental edging to dress; unnecessary extravagance.
fringe 1. *n*. ornamental border of loose threads. 2. *n*. hair brushed down on forehead and cut straight. 3. *adj*. not central, so less important.
fritter *vb*. waste time, money etc.
frivolous *adj*. silly, not serious. **frivolity** *n*.
frock *n*. a woman's or girl's dress (now rather old-fashioned).
frog *n*. a small, tail-less, web-footed amphibian.

Frogs feed on insects, grubs and slugs, which they catch with their long sticky tongues.

from *prep*. showing place or person from where something starts. *That letter is from my sister*.

front *n*. the part of something that faces forward.

frontier *n*. part of a country touching another country.

frost *n*. the powdery ice that covers everything when it is very cold.

froth *n*. foam; a collection of bubbles on the top of a liquid.

frown *vb*. & *n*. pull the eyebrows together when you are cross or thinking hard.

froze *vb*. past of **freeze**.

fruit (rhymes with *boot*) *n*. that part of a plant which has seeds in it and which is often eaten.

fry 1. *vb*. cook food in hot fat or oil. 2. *n*. *sing*. or *pl*. young fish.

fudge (*fuj*) *n*. a soft toffee.

fuel *n*. anything that is burned to make heat or to give energy, such as coal, oil, gas or wood.

There are more than 50,000 kinds of fungus, from tiny moulds to big toadstools. Some, like mushrooms, are good to eat; others are highly poisonous.

fulcrum *n*. the support on which a lever moves.

full *adj*. without space for more; the opposite of 'empty'.

fulmar *n*. a gull-like sea bird.

fumble *vb*. grope, use hands clumsily.

fumes *pl*. *n*. strong-smelling smoke.

fun *n*. amusement; a good time.

function (**funk**-*shun*) 1. *n*. the special work of a person or thing. *A hammer's function is to knock in nails*. 2. *vb*. do something. *This tool functions as a drill and as a screwdriver*.

fund *n*. a sum of money used for a charity or other purpose.

fundamental *adj*. basic, essential.

funeral *n*. the ceremony when someone who has died is buried.

fungus (plural **fungi**) *n*. a small plant with no leaves, flowers or green colouring (chlorophyll), such as a mushroom.

funk *n.* coward; state of fear. *vb.* try to get out of because of fear.
funnel *n.* a tube with a wide top and narrow bottom. *A funnel is used to pour liquid into a container with a narrow opening. vb.* use a funnel.
funny *adj.* 1. amusing; comical. *She read me a funny story.* 2. peculiar; odd. *He gave me a funny look.*
fur *n.* the soft, thick, hairy covering on some animals. **furry** *adj.*
furious *adj.* raging, very angry.
furnace *n.* a fire-place producing great heat.
furniture *n.* chairs, tables, beds, desks and other similar things. **furnish** *vb.*
furrow *n.* a straight, narrow cut made in the ground by a plough.
fury *n.* violent anger.

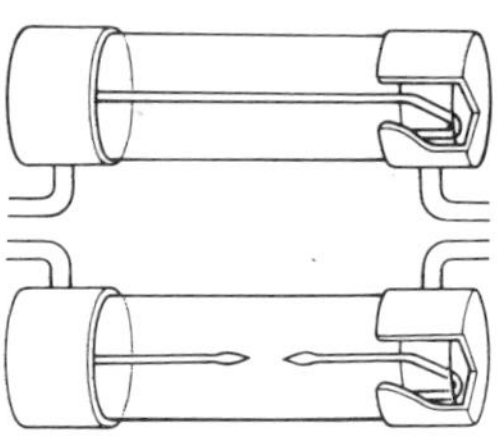

A cartridge fuse is fitted in ordinary household plugs. Too large a current melts the wire and breaks the circuit.

fuse 1. *n.* a safety device in an electric circuit. 2. *n.* a device that sets off explosions. 3. *vb.* join together by heat.
fuselage (**fyoo**-*se-larj*) *n.* the body of an aircraft.
fuss *n.* nervous excitement, bustle, bother. *vb.* worry, complain.
future *n.* the time yet to come.

G

gabardine *n.* a fine cloth used for dresses and raincoats.
gabble *vb.* talk too quickly, especially when reading aloud.
gable *n.* triangular part of outer house wall between the sloping sides of the roof.

gadget *n.* a small thing made to do a particular job.
Gaelic *n.* one of the ancient languages of the Celts. It reached Ireland from Europe, and spread to Scotland and the Isle of Man. In Eire it is an official language, but only five per cent of the people still use it. 'Clan' and 'loch' are Gaelic words.
gag 1. *n.* something tied round someone's mouth to stop them speaking. 2. *n.* a joke, funny story. *vb.* make gags. 3. *vb.* retch, choke.
gaga *adj.* senile.

gaggle *n.* a flock of geese.
gaiety *n.* cheerfulness, merrymaking.
gain (rhymes with *lane*) *vb.* win or reach. *Eric is sure to gain the prize.* *n.* addition, increase. *A gain in weight.*
gainsay *vb.* contradict, deny.
gala *n.* festivity.
galactic *adj.* of the galaxy.
galaxy *n.* a very large group of stars in outer space. *The Milky Way is a galaxy.*
gale *n.* a very strong wind.
gallant *adj.* brave, daring, courteous–especially of men to women.
galleon *n.* a large ancient Spanish sailing ship with a high stern.

A galleon usually had square sails on the foremast and main mast, and lateen sails on the mizzen mast.

gallery *n.* 1. a building where pictures or other works of art are shown. 2. the highest part of a theatre or church where people sit.
galley *n.* 1. an open sea-going vessel powered mainly by oars and used by Mediterranean nations from ancient times until the 1700s. 2. a ship's kitchen.
Gallic *adj.* relating to the Gauls; French.
gallon *n.* a liquid measure. *There are 8 pints in a gallon.*
gallop *n.* & *vb.* the fastest pace of a horse.
gallows *n.* wooden framework on which criminals used to be hanged.
galore *adv.* plenty. *At the party there was food and drink galore.*
galvanize *vb.* 1. to reduce the corrosion (rust) of iron and steel by coating it with a thin layer of zinc. 2. shock someone into doing something.
gambit *n.* opening move in a game of chess.
gamble *vb.* risk money in the hope of gaining more. **gambler** *n.* a person who gambles. **gambling** *n.*
gambol *vb.* frisk, jump about playfully. *The lambs gambolled in the field.*
game 1. *n.* a form of indoor or outdoor play, usually with rules. 2. *n.* wild animals that are hunted for food or for sport. 3. *adj.* ready; spirited.
gamma *n.* third letter of Greek alphabet: γ.
gamma rays *n. pl.* high frequency electromagnetic rays similar to, but more powerful than, X-rays. They can pass through iron 30 cm (1 ft) thick and are used in medicine against cancer.
gander *n.* a male goose.
gang *n.* a group of people working together.
gangster *n.* a member of a gang of criminals.
gangway *n.* 1. a moveable bridge between a ship and the

shore. 2. a passage between two rows of seats.

gannet *n.* large white sea-bird.

gaol (or **jail**) (rhymes with *male*) *n.* a prison where people who disobey the law are sent.*vb.* put in gaol.

gap *n.* 1. an opening; a space. 2. a space of time. *There was a long gap in the conversation.*

gape *vb.* stare, mouth open wide; be wide open.

garage *n.* a place where cars are kept or repaired. *vb.* put or keep in a garage.

garbage *n.* rubbish, waste, trash.

garden *n.* & *vb.* a piece of land for growing flowers, fruit or vegetables; to work in a garden. **gardener** *n.* a person who looks after a garden.

gargle *vb.* wash the throat by bubbling medicated liquid about in it. *n.* liquid used to gargle with.

gargoyle *n.* rainspout of a gutter often carved with grotesque figures.

garish *adj.* too bright or overcoloured.

garlic *n.* plant grown for its strong-tasting bulb, used as flavouring in cooking.

garment *n.* a piece of clothing.

garret *n.* room immediately below the roof of a house; an attic.

garrison *n.* body of troops stationed in a town or fortress. *vb.* occupy as a garrison.

garter *n.* 1. a band used to support a stocking. 2. the highest order of knighthood in the U.K. *Sir Winston Churchill was a Knight of the Garter.*

gas *n.* 1. any substance like air. *They filled balloons with helium gas because it is lighter than air.* 2. the gas used for heating. *We cook with gas in our house.*

gash *n.* a deep cut. *vb.*

gasoline see **petrol**.

gasp *vb.* struggle to breathe; breathe in short, sharp, quick breaths. *n.*

gastric *adj.* concerning the stomach.

gastronomy *n.* the art of good food and cooking.

gas turbine *n.* a efficient type of engine perfected in the 1930s and used largely in aircraft.

gate *n.* an outside door, often in a wall or fence.

gate-crash *vb.* attend a party etc. without having been invited. **gate-crasher** *n.*

gâteau (**gat**-*oh*) *n.* a rich cream cake.

gather *vb.* bring or come together, collect, pick. *Marian gathered a bunch of roses.*

Gargoyles are often in the form of monstrous human heads.

gaucho *n.* the South American cowboy of the pampas.
gauge (rhymes with *rage*) *n.* 1. an instrument for measuring. 2. the distance between a pair of railway lines; a standard measure. *vb.* measure exactly, estimate.
gaunt *adj.* lean, haggard.
gauze *n.* thin fabric of open texture.
gave *vb.* past of **give**.
gay *adj.* cheerful and full of fun. (*casual*) homosexual.
gaze *vb.* look at something for a long time. *n.* a fixed look.
gazelle *n.* slender sandy-coloured antelope found on dry grasslands in Africa and parts of Asia. Most species have a white streak on either side of the face, and the male gazelle has tall sweeping horns.
gazetteer *n.* geographical dictionary.
gear *n.* 1. a set of toothed wheels working together in a machine. 2. tackle; apparatus. 3. (*casual*) clothes.
geese *pl. n.* more than one goose.
geisha *n.* Japanese girl trained to entertain men.
gelatin (**jell**-*a-tin*) *n.* substance obtained from animal skins and bones. Gelatin is hard, transparent and tasteless, and consists mostly of protein; it forms a stiff jelly when dissolved in water. Gelatin is used in cooking and photography.
gelignite *n.* explosive used for blasting.
gem (*jem*) *n.* a jewel or precious stone.
gen (*casual*) *n.* information.
gene *n.* basic part of the heredity process.
genealogy *n.* a history of descent of persons and families from ancestors; pedigree.
general 1. *adj.* to do with most people or things. *There is a general feeling that dogs should be kept on leads in the street.* 2. *n.* a senior officer in the army.
generate *vb.* make, especially electricity.
generation *n.* all the people of about the same age. *I get on well with people of my mother's generation.*
generator *n.* a machine that produces electricity.
generous *adj.* ready to give freely and happily.
genesis *n.* origin, formation; the first book of the Old Testament.

genius (**jean**-*ius*) *n.* a particularly clever person.
gentile *n.* a person who is not a Jew.
gentle *adj.* quiet, mild or kind.
genuflect *vb.* bend the knee, specially in worship. **genuflexion** *n.*
genuine *adj.* real and true; authentic, not sham.
genus *n.* (plural **genera**) a biological grouping of plants or animals. In the Latin name of a species, the first word is the name of the genus. For example, the dingo of Australia is called *Canis dingo*. *Canis* is the name of the genus (the dog family). *Dingo* is the name of the species.
geo- *prefix* meaning earth, e.g. **geography**.
geography *n.* the study of the Earth and what happens to it.
geology *n.* the study of the Earth's history as shown in the rocks. **geological** *adj.* **geologist** *n.*
geometry *n.* the mathematical study of lines, surfaces, angles and solids. **geometric** *adj.*
Georgian *adj.* belonging to the reigns of King George I–VI.
geranium *n.* popular name for two groups of plants. One group, found wild in woodlands and also cultivated in gardens, has pink, purple or blue flowers. The other group, with scarlet, pink or white flowers, is often grown indoors or in greenhouses.
gerbil *n.* a small rodent (gnawing animal), also known as a desert rat, and popular as a pet.
geriatrics *n.* branch of medicine concerned with the health of the aged.
germ *n.* a microbe, especially one that makes people ill.
germinate *vb.* start to grow, especially of plants.
gesture *vb.* move the hand or head to show someone something. *She gestured towards the gate and everyone ran out. n.* an expressive movement.
get (past **got**, past part. **got**; past part. (USA) **gotten**). *vb.* 1. gain, become or achieve something. *What will you do if you get rich?* 2. go. *Get out of my sight.*
get away with *vb.* avoid the result of something you have done or not done. *I did my work badly, but I got away with it.*
get on *vb.* make progress.
get on with *vb.* have a friendly relationship with.
get one's own back *vb.* have one's revenge.

Geranium is the popular name for this widely grown pot plant. It is also called a pelargonium. Geraniums like this cannot survive the winter frosts outside.

When a geyser erupts, super-heated steam and water is pushed out of a crack in the ground in a powerful jet.

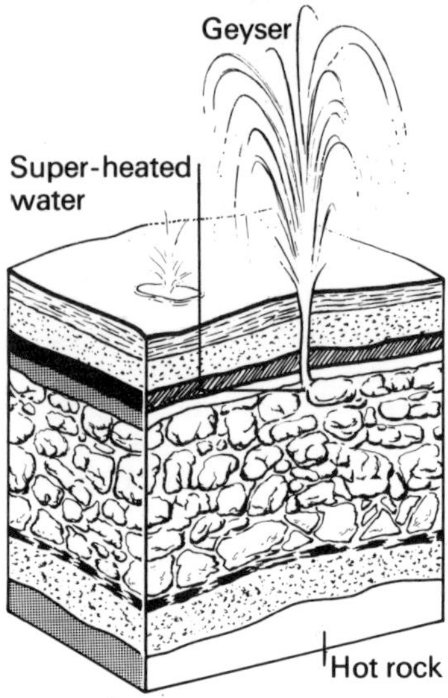

get over *vb.* recover. *Penny was getting over the loss of her cat.*
get rid of *vb.* throw away, shake off.
get through *vb.* pass an exam.
geyser *n.* a natural spring from which hot water and steam erupt, often at regular intervals; apparatus for heating water.
ghastly *adj.* horrible, terrifying.
gherkin *n.* a kind of small cucumber used for pickling.
ghetto *n.* quarter of a city where Jews were once forced to live; part of city–especially slums–lived in by a particular group of people.
ghost *n.* the spirit of a dead person that some people believe walks at night.
giant *n.* a huge animal or plant.
gibberish (g as in giant) *n.* confused or meaningless sounds or speech.
gibbon *n.* a long-armed tail-less ape.
giblets *pl. n.* liver, gizzard etc. of poultry removed before cooking.
giddy *adj.* dizzy; thoughtless.
gift *n.* a present, something that is given to someone. **gifted** *adj.* talented.
gig ('g' as in *give*) *n.* 1. light, two-wheel horse-drawn carriage. 2. public jazz, pop or rock performance.
gigantic (jye-**gan**-*tik*) *adj.* very large indeed.
giggle *vb.* laugh in a silly way. *n.*
gild *vb.* to cover with gold or gold colouring.
gill *n.* 1. ('g' as in *give*) a part on each side of a fish through which it breathes. 2. ('g' as in *giant*) a quarter of a pint.
gillie *n.* a person in Scottish Highlands who accompanies deerstalkers or people who go fishing.
gimlet *n.* a sharp pointed tool used to bore holes.
gimmick *n.* new and showy device. *Her kitchen was fitted with all the latest gimmicks*; some method of attracting attention especially for publicity purposes.
gin *n.* 1. snare, trap (for animals). 2. colourless alcoholic drink made from grain flavoured with juniper etc.
ginger 1. *adj.* & *n.* a reddish-brown colour. *He has ginger hair*. 2. *n.* the hot-tasting root of a plant, used as flavouring for ginger beer, gingerbread etc.

gingerly *adj.* delicately, timidly.
gingham ('g' as in *give*) *n.* cotton cloth with checked or striped pattern.
ginseng (g as in giant) *n.* a plant found in Asia. The root is used as a medicine.
gipsy see **gypsy**.
giraffe *n.* an African animal, with very long legs and neck.
girder *n.* beam, usually of steel.
girdle *n.* a belt or cord which goes round the waist. *vb.* to surround something with a girdle.
girl *n.* a female child; a young woman. **girlish** *adj.*
girth *n.* the leather or fabric band which holds a saddle on to a horse.
gist (*jist*) *n.* general meaning of a subject.
give *vb.* hand something over to someone else without payment.
give back *vb.* return something to someone.
give in *vb.* agree to something unwillingly. *Bill kept asking for another ice cream, and at last his father gave in.*
give out *vb.* announce, distribute. *Can you give out the programmes?*
give up *vb.* stop doing something. *My uncle will give up smoking on New Year's Day.*
gizzard *n.* bird's second stomach used for grinding food.
glacial *adj.* icy.
glacier *n.* body of ice that moves down valleys under the force of gravity. (Ice sheets are even larger bodies of ice.)
glad *adj.* pleased, happy.
glade *n.* an open space in a wood or forest.

Gladiators fought with a sword and shield or with a spear and net.

gladiator *n.* a man who fought, often to the death, for the entertainment of spectators in Ancient Rome.
glamour *n.* alluring charm often of false kind.
glance *vb.* look briefly at something. *He glanced at the newspaper and then put it aside.* *n.* a brief look.
gland *n.* an organ in the body which makes and secretes substances needed by the body.
glare 1. *vb.* look angrily at someone. 2. *n.* a strong continuous light.
glass *n.* 1. a hard, brittle material which can usually be seen through. 2. anything made of glass, such as a tumbler. 3. a mirror.
glasses *pl. n.* spectacles; lenses in frames to help you see better.
glaze 1. *n.* a mixture coated on pottery to give it a shiny surface. 2. *vb.* fit with glass or windows; coat pottery with glaze. **glazier** *n.* a person who glazes windows.
glean *vb.* gather corn left by harvesters; pick up facts here and there.

glide *vb.* move very smoothly.
glider *n.* an aircraft that flies without an engine.

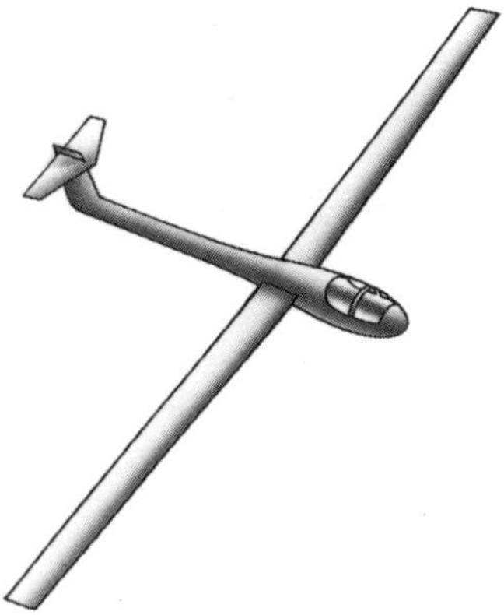

glimmer *n.* faint flickering light. *vb.*
glitter *vb.* shine brightly and reflect light. *The Christmas tree decorations glitter in the candlelight.*
global *adj.* world wide, general.
globe *n.* an object shaped like a ball, especially a map of the world shaped like this.
gloom *n.* dark, dismal; depression of the spirits. *The news filled him with gloom.* **gloomy** *adj.* dark, sullen.
glory *n.* splendour, fame; happiness of heaven. **glorious** *adj.* majestic; delightful.
gloss *n.* 1. smooth shiny coating. *gloss paint.* **glossy** *adj.* 2. a note or explanation in the margin of a book.
glossary *n.* a list, like a short dictionary, of special words used in a book.
glove *n.* a covering for the hand.
glow *vb.* shine with a bright, steady light.
glow-worm *n.* a beetle the wingless female of which emits a greenish light.
glucose *n.* a sweet substance made from grape sugar.
glue *n.* & *vb.* a sticky substance used for joining (gluing) things together.
glum *adj.* moody.
glut *n.* too great a supply.
glutton *n.* a very greedy person. **gluttony** *n.*
glycerine *n.* colourless, odourless, liquid alcohol, used in the making of perfume, cosmetics, explosives, antifreeze mixtures, and in medicine.
gnat (*nat*) *n.* a general name for any small, thin two-winged insect with long delicate legs, such as the mosquito.
gnaw (*naw*) *vb.* chew at. *Dogs love to gnaw bones.*
gnome (*nome*) *n.* a small goblin that lives under the ground.
gnu (*new* or *g-noo*) *n.* a large African oxlike antelope. Also known as wildebeest.
go (past **went**) *vb.* move from one place to another, travel, depart, turn, work, function etc.
goal (rhymes with *hole*) *n.* 1. the posts between which a ball must be sent in some games; points scored by doing this. 2. something you are trying to achieve or some place you are trying to reach.
goat *n.* an animal with horns, related to sheep.
gobble *vb.* 1. eat noisily and greedily. 2. make the noise of a turkey. *n.*
goblin *n.* a legendary ugly and usually evil spirit or fairy.

Gods and goddesses of ancient Egypt. Left to right: Ra, Isis, Anubis.

god *n.* a supreme being that is worshipped because people believe that it has control over their lives.
godchild (god-daughter, godson) *n.* one of whom one acts as sponsor at a Christian baptism, the sponsor being a **god parent** (**godmother** or **godfather**).
goddess *n.* a female god.
godly *adj.* pious.
go for *vb.* attack (usually animals).
goggles *pl. n.* large glasses that protect the eyes from water, wind or at work.
gold *n.* a precious, shiny yellow metal used for coinage, jewellery etc. (symbol Au).
golden *adj.* the colour of gold.
golden wedding *n.* 50th wedding anniversary.
goldfish *n.* an ornamental fish descended from a type of carp.
golf *n.* a game in which a small ball is driven by a club (stick) from hole to hole. **golfer** *n.*
gondola *n.* a narrow flat-bottomed boat, with curved prow and stern, used on the canals in Venice. **gondolier** *n.*
gone *vb.* past part. of **go**.
gong *n.* metal disc giving a ringing note when struck.
good (**better**, **best**) *adj.* 1. of high quality. *I'm reading a very good book.* 2. well behaved. *Be a good girl.*

An Egyptian gondola of 1375 BC.

goodbye *interj*. farewell; an expression of good wishes on parting.
Good Friday *n*. the Friday before Easter observed as the anniversary of the Crucifixion of Jesus.
goodness *n*. being good, virtue, excellence.
goods *pl. n*. 1. things that are bought and sold. 2. things that are carried on trains or trucks. *They took the goods off the truck and put them on the train.*
goose *n*. (plural **geese**) a large, web-footed water bird of the duck family.
gooseberry *n*. the edible fruit of the gooseberry bush.
gopher *n*. burrowing rodent (gnawing animal) of North America.
gore *vb*. pierce or wound with horns.
gorge 1. *n*. deep narrow valley. 2. *vb*. eat greedily.
gorgeous *adj*. magnificent, splendid; marvellous. *A gorgeous time.*
gorilla *n*. the largest of the apes.
gorse *n*. prickly yellow shrub.
gosling *n*. a young goose.
gospel *n*. one of the four books of the New Testament containing accounts of the life and teachings of Jesus.
gossip *vb*. chatter about other people and what they are doing. *n*. idle talk.
got *vb*. past and past part, of **get**.
go through *vb*. examine carefully.
gotten *vb*. (USA) past part. of **get**.
goulash *n*. highly seasoned Hungarian stew.
gourd *n*. large fleshy fruit of the cucumber family.

Decorative gourds.

govern *vb*. rule, control people or a country.
government *n*. the people who are chosen to rule or govern a country.
gown *n*. a woman's dress; a long flowing garment.
goy (plural **goyim**) Jewish name for gentile.
grab *vb*. seize quickly and roughly. *n*. an attempt to seize.
graceful *adj*. moving beautifully.
grade *vb*. arrange according to quality etc. *n*. rank, class, division.
gradient *n*. slope of a road, railway etc.
gradual *adj*. happening slowly. *The change was so gradual we hardly noticed it.*
graduate *vb*. take a degree at a university. *n*. holder of a degree.
graffiti *n*. (*graf*-**fee**-*tee*) words or drawings scribbled on a wall.
graft *vb*. cut part of one plant and join it to another so that it grows. *n*. (*surg*) transplant.

grain *n*. 1. the small, hard seeds of all plants like wheat, rice and maize. 2. the natural pattern in wood.

grammar *n*. the rules for using words and putting them together.

gramme (or **gram**) *n*. a small unit for measuring weight. *There are 1000 grammes in a kilogramme*.

granary *n*. a building where grain is stored.

grand *adj*. important, splendid.

grandchild (**grand-daughter**, **grandson**) *n*. the child of one's own child.

grandfather *n*. the father of a mother or father, also **grandad**, **grandpa**.

grandmother *n*. the mother of a mother or father, also **grandma**, **granny**.

grandstand *n*. rows of seats at a sports ground, usually covered.

granite *n*. a hard rock made largely of crystals of quartz and feldspar.

grant *vb*. allow, give. *He was granted a pension*. *n*. something granted, especially money.

grape *n*. a green or purple berry that grows in bunches on a vine.

Grasshoppers make a chirping noise by rubbing their legs against their wings. The long hind legs help them jump.

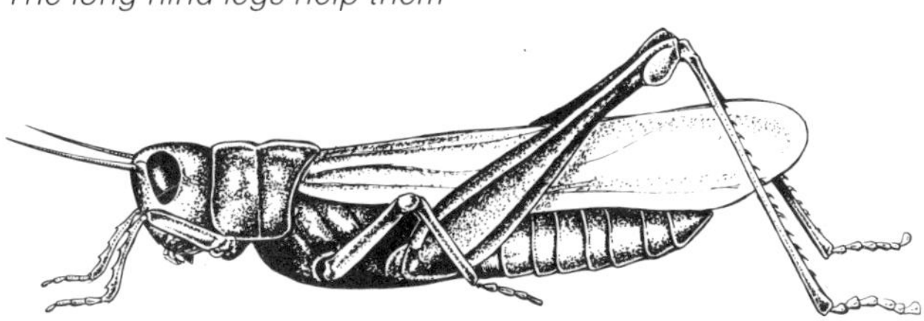

grapefruit *n*. a large yellow citrus fruit, often eaten for breakfast.

graph (rhymes with **laugh**) *n*. a diagram used to show how numbers and amounts compare.

grapple 1. *n*. a clutching instrument. 2. *vb*. seize, grip, fight.

grasp *vb*. hold tightly; understand. **grasping** *adj*. greedy.

grass *n*. a plant with thin green leaves grown on lawns and in fields.

grasshopper *n*. a small jumping insect which chirps.

grass-snake *n*. a common, harmless snake, also sometimes called the European water snake.

grate 1. *n*. iron frame in a fireplace. 2. *vb*. produce harsh noise by rubbing something on a rough surface.

grateful *adj*. feeling of thanks for something. *She was very grateful to the nurses who looked after her in hospital*.

grave 1. *n*. a hole in the ground in which a dead body is buried. 2. *adj*. serious, solemn.

gravel *n*. small stones used in the making of roads and paths.

graveyard *n.* a place where people are buried, near a church.
gravity *n.* 1. solemnity. 2. the force that pulls things together. *Gravity makes things fall.*
gravy *n.* hot sauce made with meat juices.
graze *vb.* 1. eat growing grass; (put out to) pasture. 2. scrape lightly. *n.*
grease *n.* any thick oily substance. *vb.* lubricate.
great *adj.* 1. large or heavy. *That's a great deal of money.* 2. important or famous. *He was a truly great man.*
Great Bear *n.* a constellation (*Ursa Major*) in the northern sky, made up of seven stars; 'the Plough'.

Ursa Major is the Latin name for the constellation called the Great Bear.

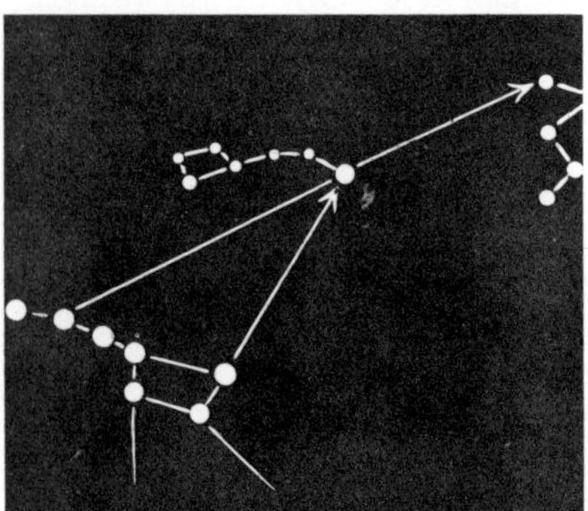

Great Dane *n.* large strong dog of German origin, despite its name. It is quiet and good-tempered but can be very fierce and so makes a good guard dog.
Grecian *adj.* Greek (*n.* and usual *adj.*).
greedy *adj.* selfishly fond of food, money or other things. **greed** *n.*
green 1. *n.* & *adj.* a colour like that of grass or leaves. 2. *n.* an open, grassy area.
greenbelt *n.* area of countryside around a town where building is restricted.
greengrocer *n.* a person who sells fruit and vegetables.
greenhouse *n.* a building with a glass roof and glass walls in which plants are grown.
greet *vb.* welcome. *She always greets me with a kiss.* **greeting** *n.*
grenade *n.* small explosive shell thrown by hand.
grew *vb.* past of **grow**.
grey *n.* & *adj.* colour midway between black and white.
greyhound *n.* fast-running dog with a slender body and long powerful legs. Greyhounds are used for hunting hares and for racing–in a greyhound race, the dogs chase a mechanical hare round an oval track.
grief (rhymes with *reef*). *n.* great sadness. **grieve** *vb.*
grim *adj.* severe, without joy.
grime *n.* dirt; squalor.
grin *n.* & *vb.* wide smile.
grind *vb.* 1. crush to a powder. *They grind wheat into flour at the mill.* 2. sharpen.
grip *vb.* & *n.* hold firmly.
grit *n.* 1. tiny pieces of stone or sand. 2. courage; staying power.
grizzly bear *n.* large bear from North America.
groan *vb.* make a deep sound of pain or sorrow. *n.* groaning sound.
grocer *n.* a person who sells

Grouse live in cold places, often on open moorland.

such foods as tea, sugar, cereals and jam.

groom 1. *vb.* & *n.* brush and clean a horse; a person who looks after a horse for someone else. 2. *n.* a bridegroom.

groove *n.* a long, narrow cut in a surface.

grope *vb.* feel one's way by touch, fumble.

gross 1. *adj.* large; fat; disgusting. 2. *adj.* (of prices, weights etc.) including all items. 3. *n.* twelve dozen (144).

grotesque *adj.* distorted style of decorative art using fantastic human and animal shapes.

grotto *n.* cave, often artificial.

ground 1. *n.* the surface of the Earth. 2. *n.* a sports field. 3. *vb.* past of **grind**.

group *n.* a number of people or things gathered together or belonging together. *vb.* form or fall into a group.

grouse 1. *n.* large game bird from the northern hemisphere which usually nests on the ground. There are about 30 species, mostly grey, brown or black in colour. 2. *vb.* grumble.

grow (past **grew,** past part. **grown**) *vb.* 1. become larger or taller. 2. live (of plants). 3. become. *They are growing old gracefully.*

growl *n.* & *vb.* a low, angry noise, as made by a dog.

grown up *n.* any person who is adult.

growth *n.* 1. the act of growing. 2. an abnormal tumour in the body.

grow up *vb.* stop being a child, attain maturity, become adult.

grub *n.* 1. the larva stage of an insect. 2. (*slang*) food. **grubby** *adj.* dirty.

grudge *vb.* envy, agree to do something unwillingly. *She grudged paying for it.*

grumble *vb.* complain in a cross way, protest. *n.* murmur, complaint.

grunt *vb.* & *n.* (make) a low noise like a pig.

guano *n.* rich manure made by the dung of sea-birds.

guarantee *n.* a promise to do something, especially to mend or replace something which goes wrong after it has been bought. *vb.* promise, answer for, secure. *This iron has a five-year guarantee.*

guard *vb.* protect someone or something. *The police will guard the exhibition of jewels. n.* a person who guards things.

guerrilla *n.* a fighter who does not belong to a country's organized army.

guess *vb.* decide without really knowing the facts. *He didn't know how to spell the word, so he made a guess. n.* opinion.
guest *n.* a person who is visiting another person's house or who stays in a hotel.
guide *vb.* show someone the way. *n.* a person who guides other people.
guided missile *n.* a rocket- or jet-propelled missile with an explosive warhead.
guilder *n.* the main unit of Dutch currency.
guillemot *n.* a sea bird.
guillotine *n.* an instrument for beheading people, named after a Dr Guillotin, first used in the French Revolution. *vb.* execute with guillotine.
guilty *adj.* having done something wrong. *The dog looked very guilty when we found the meat had gone.* **guilt** *n.*
guinea-pig *n.* small tail-less animal belonging to a family of South American rodents called cavies.
guitar *n.* a musical instrument with six strings which are plucked with the fingers. **guitarist** *n.* a guitar player.
gulf *n.* a large area of the sea almost surrounded by land.
gull *n.* a kind of large sea bird.
gullet *n.* food passage through the throat.
gulp *vb.* & *n.* swallow noisily and quickly.
gum *n.* 1. the pink flesh in which the teeth are set. 2. glue. 3. chewing gum.
gun *n.* a weapon that fires bullets or some other missile from a long tube open at one end; a firearm.
gunpowder *n.* an explosive made by mixing special amounts of charcoal, sulphur and saltpetre.
gunsmith *n.* maker of guns.
gurgle *vb.* & *n.* bubbling sound.
guru *n.* religious teacher, especially Sikh.
gush *vb.* flow out suddenly. *Water gushed through the door.*
gust *n.* suddent blast of wind.
gusto *n.* zest.
guts *pl. n.* 1. the intestines. 2. (*casual*) courage.
gutter *n.* a small channel for carrying off rainwater.
guttural *adj.* & *n.* sound formed in the throat; harsh, grating.
guy (rhymes with *lie*) *n.* 1. (*casual*) a man or boy. 2. a figure burned as Guy Fawkes on 5th November, Guy Fawkes Day. 3. a rope used to secure a tent.
guzzle *vb.* eat greedily.
gym or **gymnasium** *n.* a room for sports and training.
gymkhana *n.* a competition for horses and ponies and their riders.
gymnast *n.* a person who does exercises as a sport.
gymnastics *pl. n.* special exercises that help make the body fit.
gynaecology (guy-na-**kol**-*ojee*) *n.* branch of medicine treating diseases of women.
gypsy *n.* a member of a dark-haired group of wandering people.
gyroscope ('g' as in *giant*) *n.* a rapidly spinning wheel set in a frame which only touches another surface at one point.

H

habit *n.* 1. something that a person or animal does so often they do not think about it. 2. a monk's robe.

habitat *n.* the place where an animal or plant normally lives.

hacienda *n.* large estate or farm in Spanish South America.

hack 1. *vb.* chop roughly. 2. *vb.* cough harshly. 3. *n.* hired riding horse. 4. *n.* dull tedious work or person.

had *vb.* past of **have**.

haddock *n.* a sea fish, related to the cod, and important as food.

hag *n.* ugly old woman.

haggard *adj.* lean and with hollow eyes.

haggis *n.* a Scots dish made of minced meat and oatmeal, wrapped in the stomach of a sheep and boiled.

haggle *vb.* argue over the price of something.

ha-ha 1. *interj.* expressing laughter or sudden discovery. 2. *n.* boundary fence sunk in ditch.

haiku (*hy-koo*) *n.* three-line Japanese poem of 17 syllables.

hail 1. *n.* frozen rain. *vb.* fall as hail. 2. *vb.* greet someone by calling out to them.

hair *n.* a thread-like substance growing out of the skin of mammals.

hairdresser *n.* someone who cuts and looks after other people's hair.

hairy *adj.* covered in hair; similar to hair.

hake *n.* a sea fish, related to the cod, and eaten as food.

hale *adj.* healthy, energetic. *The swimmers look hale and hearty.*

half *n.* (plural **halves**) one of the two equal parts of something.

halibut *n.* a large flatfish of the North Atlantic and North Pacific.

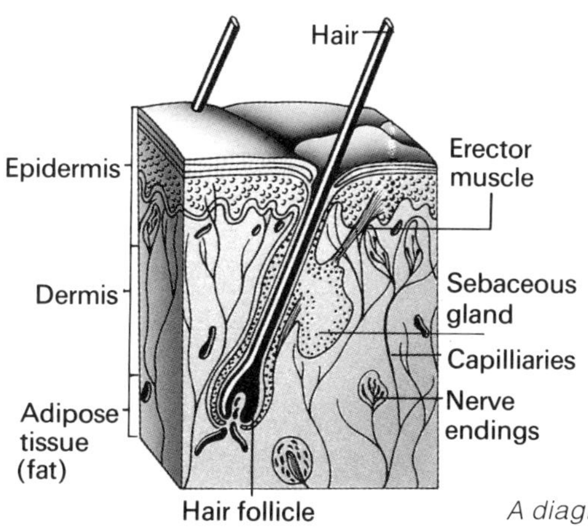

A diagram of a hair shaft.

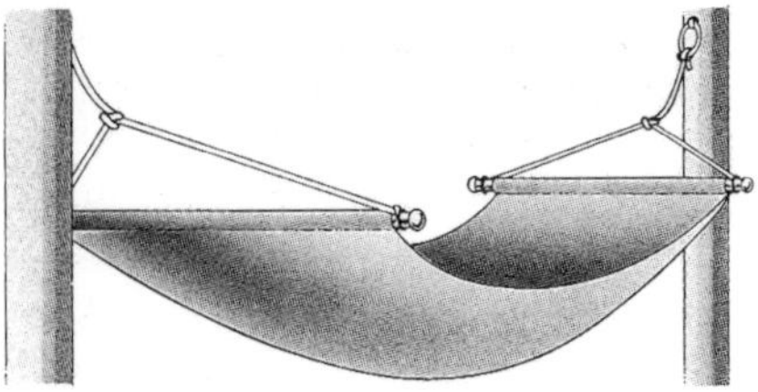

A hammock is a hanging bed slung between two fixed points.

halitosis *n.* foul-smelling breath.

hall *n.* 1. the entrance room of a house. 2. a large room for meetings, plays and other activities.

hallmark *n.* mark on gold or silver showing place of origin etc.

Halloween *n.* a festival held on 31 October, the day before All Saints' Day. (Halloween roughly means 'holy evening'.) People once believed that ghosts, demons and witches roamed about on Halloween night.

halo (**hay**-*low*) *n.* a circle of light around something.

halt *vb.* & *n.* stop.

halter *n.* rope with headstall for leading a horse.

halve *vb.* divide into two equal parts.

ham *n.* 1. salted or smoked meat from a pig's thigh. 2. (*slang*) inexpert but showy performer.

hamburger *n.* a round cake of chopped beef inside a bun, eaten hot.

hamlet *n.* small village, usually without a church.

hammer *n.* a tool for driving in nails or breaking things. *vb.* strike with a hammer.

hammock *n.* a kind of bed, made of canvas or other cloth, and hung from cords at both ends. *In the days of sailing ships, sailors usually slept in hammocks.*

hamper *vb.* hinder or obstruct. *n.* a case made from woven cane, usually packed with food and drink.

hamster *n.* a small, roundish rodent, often kept as a pet.

hamstring *n.* a tendon behind the knee.

hand 1. *n.* the part of the arm beyond the wrist with five fingers (one of which is the thumb). 2. *n.* a measure of the height of horses or ponies equal to 10 cm. 3. *vb.* give something with the hand. *Please hand me a glass of milk.*

handbag *n.* a small bag or purse, usually carried by women.

handcuffs *pl. n.* a pair of bracelets for locking a prisoner's hands together.

handicap *n.* anything that makes it more difficult to do things.

handicapped *adj.* having a physical or mental disability, such as blindness, weak-mindedness or deformity.

handicraft *n.* a craft, skill or trade; a piece of work made by a craftsman or craftswoman.

handiwork *n.* work done by the hands.

handkerchief (**hang**-*ker-chief*) *n.* (plural **-chieves**) a piece of cloth or paper, carried in a pocket or handbag, used for wiping the nose.

handle 1. *n.* part of an object by

which it is held. 2. *vb*. feel something with the hands.

handlebar *n*. the bar with which a bicycle or motor cycle is steered.

hand over *vb*. give something to someone else, often when you do not want to. *The thief made us hand over the money*.

handsome *adj*. good looking, usually applied to men.

handwriting *n*. writing done with a pen or pencil, but not typed or printed. *She has very clear handwriting*. **handwritten** *adj*.

handy *adj*. within reach, nearby. *The shops are handy*.

hang *vb*. 1. (past **hung**) hold from above so that the lower part is free. *Ripe cherries hang from that tree*. 2. (past **hanged**) execute a person by hanging from the neck.

hang around *vb*. wait.

hangar *n*. a large building where aircraft are kept.

hanger *n*. a device on which to place clothes so that they can be put away in a wardrobe.

hang-glider *n*. frame on which a person can glide through the air. Hang-gliding is a popular sport in many countries.

hangover *n*. the unpleasant feeling after having drunk too much alcohol.

happen *vb*. take place. *The sales happen every year in January*. take place by chance. *My friend and I happen to share the same birthday*.

happening *n*. something that happens; an event.

happiness *n*. the state of being happy or contented.

happy *adj*. contented; cheerful; pleased.

harangue *n*. a ranting, rousing speech given to a large crowd or person. *vb*.

harass *vb*. worry, trouble or confuse by repeated attacks. **harassment** *n*.

harbour *n*. a shelter for ships. *vb*. give shelter.

hard 1. *adj*. solid or firm; not soft. *The ground was too hard to dig*. *adj*. difficult. *This sum is too hard for me to do*. 3. *adv*. taking trouble. *She tried hard to win the match*. 4. *adj*. tough. *You're a hard man*.

hardback *n*. book bound in a hard, long-lasting cover.

hardly *adj*. only just. *She had hardly reached home when the telephone rang*.

Hang-gliding is a popular sport in many countries.

hardware *n.* electronic parts of a computer; ironmongery.
hardy *adj.* strong, able to face difficulties.
hare *n.* an animal like a large rabbit with long ears and a short tail.
harm *vb.* & *n.* hurt, damage.
harmless *adj.* safe; not dangerous.
harmonica *n.* a mouth organ.
harmony *n.* 1. an agreeable musical sound. 2. a secondary tune that blends with the main melody. **harmonize** *vb.*
harness *n.* all the leather straps and other equipment by which a horse is controlled.
harp *n.* a large musical instrument played by plucking strings with the fingers of both hands.
harpoon *n.* a spear on a rope for catching whales and large fish. *A harpoon is thrown or fired and can then be pulled back.* *vb.* strike with a harpoon.
harpsichord *n.* a stringed instrument with a keyboard similar to a piano.
harpy *n.* a monster from Greek and Roman myth with a woman's head and body and a bird's wings and claws.
harridan *n.* a bad-tempered woman.
harrier *n.* 1. a hound used for hunting hares. 2. a type of falcon.
harrow *n.* a device to break up the soil after ploughing. Disc harrows contain sharp rotating discs mounted on a shaft. *vb.* 1. draw a harrow over. 2. distress.
harsh *adj.* rough, unkind; hard to the feelings; coarse to touch.
harvest *n.* the time for cutting and bringing in grain and other crops; the crops brought in at harvest time. *vb.* gather in the harvest.
hassle 1. *n.* disagreement. 2. *vb.* harass.
haste *n.* hurry, quickness of movement. **hasten** *vb.*
hat *n.* a covering worn on the head, usually with a brim.
hatch 1. *vb.* come out of an egg. 2. *n.* movable covering over an opening.
hatchback *n.* car with a back door hinged at the top.
hatchet *n.* a chopper; a small axe. *'To bury the hatchet' was an American Indian expression meaning 'to make peace'.*
hate *vb.* & *n.* loathe; dislike someone or something very much. **hatred** *n.* active dislike, intense loathing.
haul (rhymes with *ball*) *vb.* pull a heavy load.
haunt *vb.* (of a ghost) to visit a place often.
have *vb.* own or possess something.
havoc *n.* ruin, chaos, destruction.
hawk *n.* 1. a bird of prey. 2. someone who supports a warlike policy.
hawthorn *n.* a small tree related to the rose and often found in hedges.

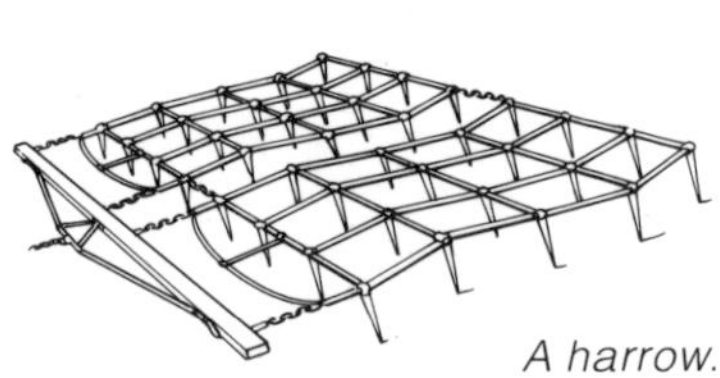

A harrow.

hay *n.* dried grass used to feed animals.
hay fever *n.* an allergy; people who suffer from hay fever react to the pollen in the air by sneezing.
haystack (or **hayrick**) *n.* a large pile of hay.
hazard *vb.* risk, venture on. *Hazard a guess.*
hazel 1. *n.* a small nut tree. 2. *n.* & *adj.* the brownish-green colour of some people's eyes.
H-bomb *n.* hydrogen bomb.
head *n.* 1. the top part of the body, above the neck. 2. the chief person, e.g. the head teacher in a school. *vb.* lead (a strike etc.).
headache (rhymes with **bake**) *n.* a pain in the head.
headlight *n.* one of the main lights at the front of a vehicle.
headline *n.* a few words in larger print at the top of a story in a newspaper.
headquarters *n.* the main office of an organization; an army base.
headway *n.* progress.
headwind *n.* blowing directly from in front.
heal *vb.* make better, particularly of a wound.
health (*helth*) *n.* how well or ill the body or mind are.
healthy *adj.* well and strong.
heap *n.* a pile of things. *vb.* pile things on, load.
hear *vb.* listen; notice a sound or noise. **hearing** *n.*
hearing aid *n.* a device worn by a person with poor hearing to amplify (make louder) sound.
hearse *n.* vehicle for carrying a coffin to the grave.

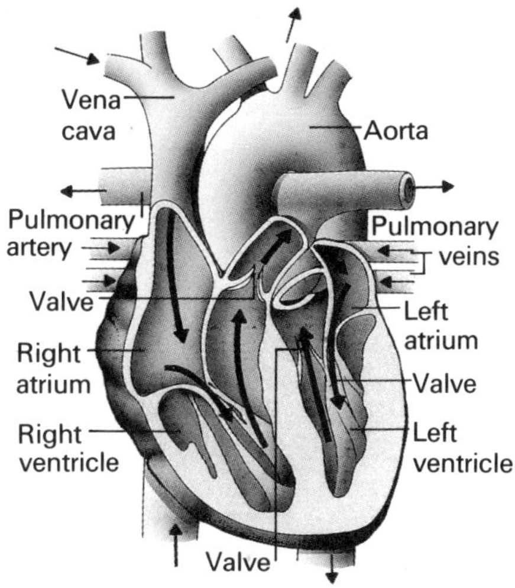

heart *n.* the organ or part of the body which pumps blood around the body.
heartless *adj.* without feeling or pity.
heart-break *n.* great sorrow. **heart-breaking** *adj.*
hearth *n.* the floor or surroundings of a fireplace.
heat 1. *n.* hotness. 2. *vb.* make hot. *We heated the milk.*
heater *n.* something that produces heat. *The heater in my car takes a long time to warm up.*
heath *n.* a piece of unused land, usually covered with shrubs and a few trees.
heather *n.* small evergreen shrub of moors and heaths.
heave *vb.* shift, raise up with effort.
heaven (**he**-*ven*) *n.* the home of God.
heavy *adj.* having considerable weight; dull, boring.
hectare *n.* a measure of area. *A football field is about $\frac{2}{3}$ of a hectare.*

hedge *n*. a row of bushes making a fence around a field or garden. *vb*. surround with a fence; give an evasive answer.
hedgehog *n*. a small animal that is covered in prickles. It defends itself by rolling into a ball.
heed *vb*. take notice of. *He heeded the warning signs*.
heel *n*. the back part of the foot. Part of sock etc. that covers or supports the heel.
hefty *adj*. big and powerful.
Hegira *n*. the flight of Muhammed from Mecca to Medina in AD 622.
heifer (rhymes with *deafer*) *n*. a young cow that has not had a calf.
height (rhymes with *bite*) *n*. the measurement from the bottom to the top of something. *vb*. **heighten** raise, make higher.
heir/heiress (*air*/**air**-*ess*) *n*. the person who will inherit somebody's property or position. *Prince Charles is heir to the British throne*.
helicopter *n*. an aircraft with a horizontal rotor which acts as both propeller and wings.
helium *n*. a very light gas (symbol He).
hell *n*. the home of the devil, place of punishment.
helm *n*. tiller, wheel, steering gear of a ship.
helmet *n*. a strong covering that protects the head. *The motor-cyclist wore a crash helmet*.
help *vb*. & *n*. aid someone; come to their assistance.
helpful *adj*. useful; providing help. *Thank you for being so helpful*.
helping 1. *adj*. giving help or assistance. *Can I give you a helping hand with the washing up?* 2. *n*. a portion of food.
helpless *adj*. not able to look after yourself. *A baby bird is helpless if it falls out of the nest*.
hem *n*. the edge of cloth or clothing that is turned over and sewn.
hemisphere *n*. half a sphere; half the Earth. *America is in the western hemisphere*.
hemlock *n*. poisonous plant.
hen *n*. any female bird, but especially a farmyard chicken.
henna *n*. a reddish dye from a tropical plant, used on the hair.
her *pron*. the female possessive pronoun. *It is her birthday today*.
heraldry *n*. the study of coats of arms.
herb *n*. plants with leaves that

The designs used in heraldry were displayed on the shields and banners of medieval kings and knights. Similar patterns are seen on flags today.

Tierced in Pale — Checky — Per Bend Sinister — Gyronny

are used for flavouring food or for scent.

herbivore *n.* an animal that eats plants, especially grass. **herbivorous** *adj.*

herd *n.* a group of animals grazing or moving together.

here *adv.* in or at this place. *Come here.*

heredity *n.* the passing on of physical characteristics from parents to offspring.

heresy *n.* opinion against what is generally accepted or officially declared. **heretic** *n.* person who supports heresy.

hermit *n.* a person who chooses to live alone, usually for religious reasons.

hero (plural **heroes**) *n.* 1. a man admired for his bravery. 2. the most important male character in a play, film or story. **heroic** *adj.* **heroism** *n.* heroic conduct, behaviour worthy of a hero or heroine.

heroin *n.* a powerful, pain-killing but dangerous drug made from morphine.

heroine *n.* 1. a woman admired for her bravery. *n.* the most important female character in a play, film or story.

heron *n.* a long-legged wading bird.

herring *n.* a small sea fish. When smoked it is called a kipper.

hesitate *vb.* stop briefly; show indecision. **hesitation** *n.* **hesitant** *adj.*

hexagon *n.* a figure with six equal sides.

heyday *n.* peak, bloom (of youth, success etc).

hibernate *vb.* spend the winter asleep. **hibernation** *n.*

hiccough (*hiccup*) *n.* a sound like a sudden, sharp cough.

hidden *vb.* past of **hide**.

hide 1. *vb.* put something where others cannot find it; go into a place where you cannot be seen. 2. *n.* the skin of a large animal.

hideous *adj.* dreadfully ugly.

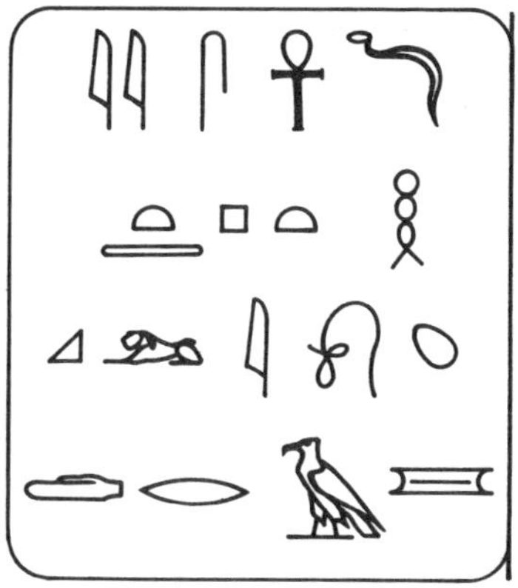

The Egyptians first used symbols or hieroglyphics as a form of writing.

hieroglyphics *pl. n.* an ancient form of picture writing.

hi-fi *n.* & *adj.* short for high-fidelity; apparatus to give good quality reproduction of recorded sound.

high *adj.* tall. *The mountain is 2000 metres high.*

highbrow *n.* & *adj.* (person) of very intellectual interests.

highway *n.* a main road.

highwayman *n.* a robber on horseback.

hijack *vb.* & *n.* (seize) control of a vehicle or aircraft during a journey by threat of violence.

hike *vb.* go for a long country walk. (To **hitch-hike** is to thumb lifts from passing cars.)

hill *n.* a steep place; a slope; a small mountain. **hilly** *adj.*
hilt *n.* the handle of a sword.
hind (hynd) *n.* female deer.
hinder *vb.* prevent, delay.
Hindu *n.* someone from India; a follower of the religion Hinduism.
hinge *n.* a joint on which a door or gate swings when opened or shut.
hint *vb.* suggest something without really saying it. *Carol hinted that she would like a new dress for her birthday. n.* disguised suggestion.
hip *n.* the joint where the leg joins the trunk of the body.
hippodrome *n.* circus, arena for horse races and chariot races in ancient Rome.
hippopotamus *n.* a large African animal that lives in and near lakes and rivers.
hire *vb.* rent; pay for the use of something. *We hired a car for a week when we went to Florida.*
hire-purchase *n.* a way of buying things by which you pay for them a bit at a time, by instalments.
hiss *vb.* & *n.* (make) a long S sound like a snake; to express anger, disapproval etc.
history *n.* the study and written account of past events. **historian** *n.* a person who studies and writes about the past. **historic** *adj.* famous in history. *The battle of Gettysburg was an historic event.*
hit 1. *vb.* & *n.* stick or knock something; a blow. 2. *n.* a success – especially record or show.
hitch 1. *n.* a setback, hold-up. 2. *vb.* fasten with a loop. 3. *vb.* thumb a lift (hitch-hike).
hive *n.* (or bee-hive) a place for bees to live in.
hoard (*hawd*) *n.* & *vb.* store away secretly, especially money.
hoarding *n.* temporary fence of boards around a building and often covered with posters.
hoarse *adj.* of the voice, rough or croaking.
hoax *n.* a trick or practical joke. *vb. The bomb warning turned out to be a hoax.*
hobble *vb.* limp, stumble along.
hobby *n.* something a person likes doing when not working. *Nick's hobby is collecting stamps.*
hock *n.* 1. joint in hind leg of horse etc. 2. a German white wine.
hockey *n.* a game played with curved wooden sticks and a ball between two teams of eleven players (also **ice hockey**).
hoe *n.* a tool for loosening the earth and digging out weeds. *vb.* use a hoe.

A Dutch hoe (above) *and a draw hoe* (below).

hog *n.* pig.
Hogmanay *n.* (*Sc.*) New Year's Eve.
hold 1. *vb.* keep firmly in the

hand. 2. *n.* part of the hull of a ship where cargo is stored. 3. *vb.* contain. *This can holds a gallon.*

hold on *vb.* wait (especially on the telephone).

hold up *vb.* delay. *I hope I haven't held you up.*

hole *n.* a hollow place; a pit, space or burrow.

holiday *n.* a day off work or school; a vacation, usually taken away from home, and often abroad. *We're going to France for our holiday this year.*

holler *vb.* shout, make a loud noise.

hollow 1. *adj.* not solid; empty inside. *The squirrels lived in a hollow tree.* 2. *n.* a hollow place or small valley. *vb.* to make hollow.

holly *n.* an evergreen tree with glossy prickly leaves and red berries.

hollyhock *n.* tall flowering plant.

holography *n.* a way of producing 3-dimensional images.

holster *n.* a case for a gun, worn on a belt or under the arm.

holy *adj.* having religious significance; connected with God. *The New Testament is the holy book of Christianity.*

home *n.* the place where you live.

homesick *adj.* sad at being away from your home.

homework *n.* school work that is done at home.

homicide (*homee-side*) *n.* killing of a human being.

homo- *prefix* meaning same, e.g. **homosexual** *n.* & *adj.* sexually attracted to one's own sex.

honest (**on**-*est*) *adj.* truthful, not likely to cheat. **honesty** *n.*

honey *n.* the sweet substance made by bees from the nectar of flowers.

honeycomb *n.* the wax container made by bees in which to store their honey.

honeymoon *n.* a holiday for a newly married couple. *vb.* spend honeymoon.

honeysuckle *n.* climbing plant with sweet-smelling flowers; woodbine.

honk *n.* & *vb.* the call of a wild goose.

honour *n.* respect, high regard, esteem.

hood *n.* a covering for the head and neck. (*U.S.* a car's bonnet.)

hoodwink *vb.* trick or mislead.

hoof (plural **hoofs** or **hooves**) *n.* the hard part of the foot of a horse, and of some other animals.

hook *n.* a bent piece of metal, such as a fish-hook. *vb.* catch or fasten with a hook. **hooked** *adj.*

hooligan *n.* ruffian, member of a gang of ruffians.

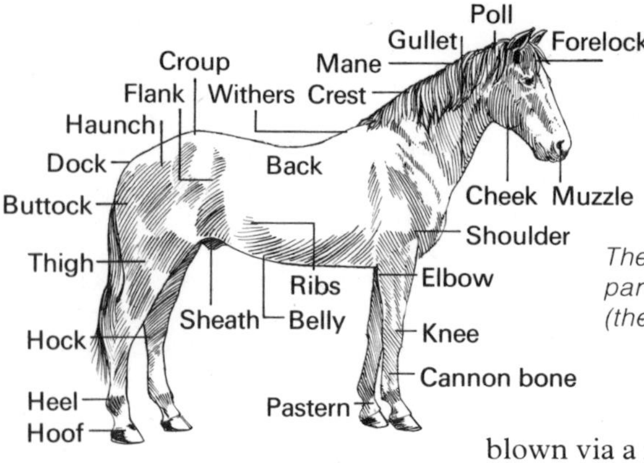

The names of the different parts of a horse's body (the points of a horse).

hoop *n.* ring of metal or wood for binding casks; a child's plaything; a metal arch used in the game of croquet.

hoot *vb.* & *n.* (make) a sound of mockery; sound of a motor horn etc; sound of an owl.

hop 1. *vb.* & *n.* jump on one leg, or (of a bird) with both feet together. 2. *n.* a plant belonging to the nettle family used to make beer.

hope *vb.* & *n.* wish for something pleasant to happen. *I hope I pass the exam.*

hopeful *adj.* having hope.

hopefully 1. *adv.* in a hopeful way. 2. (*casual*) it is hoped. *Hopefully the weather will be warm.*

hopeless *adj.* without hope.

horizon *n.* the line where the land and the sky seem to meet.

horizontal *adj.* flat; level with the horizon.

hormone (**hoar**-*mone*) *n.* chemical substance which regulates the body's activities.

horn 1. *n.* one of the long, pointed growths on the head of some animals. 2. *n.* a brass musical instrument that is blown via a mouthpiece.

hornet *n.* large insect of wasp family.

horoscope *n.* a prediction about someone's future, based on the sign of the zodiac under which they were born; fortune-telling.

horrible *adj.* unpleasant, frightening or ugly.

horror *n.* fright. *He watched in horror as his boat drifted out to sea.*

horse *n.* a four legged-animal with hooves, long mane and tail used for riding and pulling carts and carriages.

horsepower *n.* a unit for measuring the power of engines.

horseshoe *n.* a U-shaped piece of iron used to protect a horse's hoof.

horticulture *n.* the art of gardening.

hose *n.* a long flexible tube through which water and other liquids can pass. *vb.* wash down with a hose.

hospital *n.* a building where sick or injured people are taken care of. **hospitalize** *vb.*

hospitality *n.* generous, friendly welcome and

entertainment of guests.

host *n.* 1. a person who has guests in his house. 2. a huge crowd. 3. bread used in the Holy Communion or Mass.

hostage (**hoss**-*tij*) *n.* a person who is held prisoner and threatened until certain demands are agreed to.

hostel *n.* lodging for students etc.

hostess *n.* 1. a women who has guests in her house. 2. women who looks after travellers on an aircraft.

hostile *adj.* unfriendly.

hot *adj.* possessing heat. *It was so hot that we all got sunburned.*

hot dog *n.* a US snack, consisting of a hot frankfurter (sausage) in a bread roll.

hotel *n.* a building where travellers pay to stay and have meals.

hotfoot *adv.* in great haste.

hound *n.* a name for various kinds of dog, especially those used in hunting. *vb.* hunt with hounds.

hour *n.* a period of 60 minutes. *There are 24 hours in a day.* **hourly** *adj.* & *adv.* occurring once every hour.

house *n.* a building in which people live, a home.

houseboat *n.* a boat on which people live.

household *n.* all the people who live together in a house. *Our household consists of my mother, brother and me.* **householder** *n.* head of a household.

housekeeper *n.* a person who is paid to look after a home.

housewife *n.* a married woman who looks after a home.

housework *n.* work such as cleaning and washing done in the house.

hovel *n.* a small, very poor house or cottage.

hover *n.* stay in the air in one place. *A dragonfly hovers over the water.*

hovercraft *n.* an air cushion vehicle designed to skim over the surface of water or land.

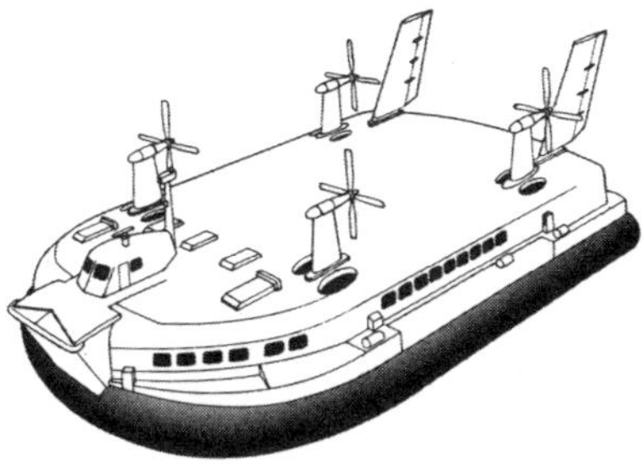

Powerful fans inside a hovercraft produce a cushion of air which enables the craft to glide quickly over water or flat land.

how *adv.* in what way? *How do you spell this word?*

howdah *n.* a seat, often with a canopy, on an elephant's back.

however *adv.* & *conj.* by whatever means. *However hard you try*; nevertheless. *I'd like to go. However I can't afford it.*

howl *vb.* & *n.* (make) a long, sad noise like a dog makes when it is hurt.

hub *n.* central part of a wheel from which spokes radiate.

hue *n.* colour, tint.

huff 1. *n.* fit or crossness. 2. *vb.* capture a piece in the game of draughts.

hug *vb.* embrace someone by clasping them tightly with your arms. *n.* a tight embrace.

Hummingbirds are found in the Americas.

huge *adj*. vast; enormous.
Huguenot (**hew**-*ge-no*) *n*. French Protestant in the 1700s.
hull *n*. the body of a ship.
hum 1. *n*. a low murmuring noise. 2. *vb*. sing with the mouth closed. *He always hums while he is working*.
human *adj*. & *n*. behaving or looking like people. *n*. human being. **humankind** *n*.
humane *adj*. kind, gentle; merciful. *n*. **humanity** showing kindness.
humanity *n*. the human race as a whole.
humble *adj*. 1. not vain or proud. *He was always very humble*. 2. of poor quality or little importance. *Be it ever so humble, there's no place like home*.
humbug *n*. 1. fraud, nonsense. *The speech was a lot of humbug*. 2. hard boiled sweet.
humdrum *adj*. dull, uneventful.
humidity *n*. the amount of moisture in the atmosphere. This moisture consists of tiny water particles moving about freely in the air. **humid** *adj*.
humiliate *vb*. offend, make a person look ridiculous or ashamed.
hummingbird *n*. a small brightly coloured bird whose wings flap so quickly that they make a humming sound.
humour *n*. a mood. *She is in a bad humour*; an ability to be amused by or to laugh at funny sayings, drawings or stories. *Dominic has a very good sense of humour*. **humorous** *adj*.
hump *n*. a round lump like that on a camel's back.
hundred *n*. the figure 100; 10 times 10.
hung *vb*. past of **hang**.
hunger *n*. the feeling of needing food. **hungry** *adj*.
hunk *n*. a large slice (of bread etc).
hunt *vb*. 1. go after, and often kill, animals for sport or food. *n*. people hunting with a pack. 2. look for something.
hunter *n*. a person who hunts animals.
hurdling *n*. a foot race in which barriers called hurdles have to be jumped.
hurl *vb*. throw with great force. *n*. a violent throw.
hurricane *n*. a violent storm.
hurry *vb*. move quickly. *You'll be late if you don't hurry*. *n*.

great haste; eagerness.

hurt *vb.* cause pain. *He's hurt his leg.*

husband *n.* a married man. *Her husband is a lot older than she is.*

hush *vb.* make or become silent. **hush up** keep secret. **hush-hush** *adj.* very secret.

husky 1. *adj.* having a hoarse, whispering voice. 2. *n.* a kind of dog, bred to pull sledges in the far north of America.

hut *n.* a small building, often made of wood and used as a temporary shelter. *The children made a hut out of branches.*

hutch *n.* a cage or box for rabbits or other small animals.

hyacinth *n.* a garden flower, often blue or purple in colour.

hybrid *n.* plant or animal produced by parents of different species, e.g. a mule (male donkey and female horse).

hydrant *n.* water pipe in a street.

hydraulic power *n.* a form of power based on the pressure of water or other liquids which are forced through pipes.

hydro *prefix* meaning water.

hydroelectric *adj.* producing electricity from the power of falling water.

hydrofoil *n.* a boat which, at speed, rises out of the water supported on wing-like struts, or *foils*, that project from the lower hull.

hydrogen *n.* a colourless, odourless, tasteless gas that is lighter than air (symbol H).

hyena *n.* a savage dog-like creature that hunts in packs at night and feeds mostly on dead animals. Found mostly in India and part of Africa.

hygiene *n.* the science of health and cleanliness. **hygienic** *adj.*

hymn (rhymes with *rim*) *n.* a religious song praising God.

hyphen *n.* a mark like this - showing where a word has been divided at the end of a line, or where two words have been joined to make one, as self-respect. **hyphenate** *vb.*

hypnosis *n.* a condition like deep sleep in which someone's actions can be controlled by another person. **hypnotize** *vb.*

hypochondria (*high-po-***kon***-dree-a*) *n.* a fear of becoming ill. **hypochondriac** *n.* & *adj.*

hypocrisy (*hip-***pok***-kra-see*) *n.* pretending to be good.

hypodermic syringe (*high-po-***dur***-mik*) *n.* an instrument for injecting drugs under the skin; a hollow needle.

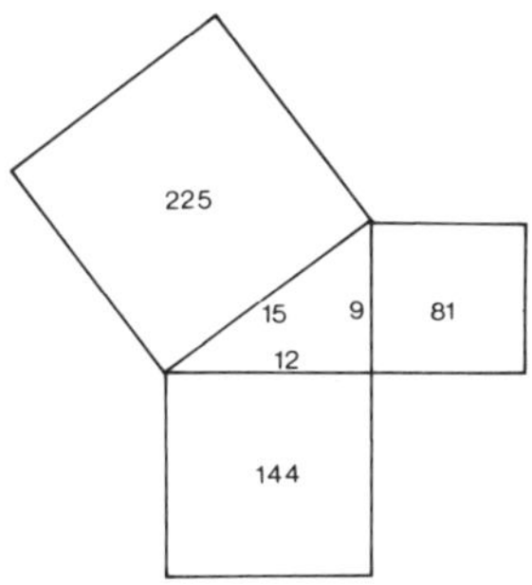

The square on the hypotenuse of a right-angle triangle is equal to the sum of the squares on the other two sides.

hypotenuse (*high-***pot***-i-neus*) *n.* side of right-angle triangle opposite the right angle.

hysterical *adj.* in a state of wild excitement. **hysteria** *n.*

I

I *pron.* first person singular; the speaker or writer.

Iberian *adj.* of Spain and Portugal (ancient Iberia).

ibex *n.* (plural. **ibexes**) a species of wild goat living in the mountains of Europe, Asia and Africa. It has broader horns than the true wild goat.

ibis *n.* stork-like bird with a long curved beak, found world-wide in warm regions, usually near water.

ice *n.* frozen water. *vb.* freeze; cover with icing sugar.

iceberg *n.* a floating mass of ice.

ice-cream *n.* a kind of soft, frozen sweet, sometimes eaten in cornets or wafer-biscuits.

ice hockey *n.* a game played on ice between two teams, using hockey sticks to hit a rubber puck with the aim of scoring goals. Each team is of six players and a goalkeeper.

ice skate *n.* a boot with a blade underneath for skating (sliding rapidly) on ice.

icicle *n.* a pointed piece of ice. *An icicle is made of dripping water that freezes.*

icing *n.* 1. a sweet covering for cakes. 2. formation of ice on an aircraft's wings.

icon *n.* the name in the Eastern Orthodox Church for any picture or image of Christ, the Virgin Mary, an angel or a saint. Usually it is a painting on wood showing the human form in a flat, stylized way.

idea *n.* a thought, a plan in the mind.

ideal *adj.* perfect, just what you want. *We thought that the plans for the holiday were ideal. n.* a model of perfection.

identical *adj.* exactly the same.

identify *vb.* establish identity of. *He identified the pop star at once.*

identity *n.* individuality; distinguishing character.

idiot *n.* a person who is so weak-minded that others have to look after him or her. **idiotic** *adj.* foolish.

idle 1. *adj.* lazy; unoccupied. 2. *vb.* turn round slowly (of a car engine).

Ice hockey is a very fast game where the players wear special padded clothing, helmets and face masks, to protect them from injury.

idol *n.* object of worship; fake god. **idolize** *vb.* worship, love greatly.
if *conj.* in the event that; on condition that; whether.
igloo *n.* an Eskimo hut made of blocks of snow.
igneous *adj.* formed by great heat or volcanic action.
ignite *vb.* set fire to.
ignorant *adj.* knowing very little; uneducated. **ignorance** *n.*
ignore *vb.* take no notice of something or somebody. *The man ignored us and walked straight past.*
iguana *n.* large lizard found in tropical America, Madagascar and Polynesia.

The iguana is one of the largest of all the lizards, and has a row of spines along its back.

il- *prefix* before l indicates negation, against, e.g. **illegal** *adj.* against the law. **illogical** *adj.* not logical.
ill *adj.* unwell, sick. **illness** *n.*
illegal *adj.* against the law.
illegible *adj.* unclear, impossible to read.
illiterate *adj.* unable to read. **illiteracy** *n.*
illogical *adj.* without logic.
illuminate *vb.* light up; make clear. **illumination** *n.*
illustrate *vb.* explain with pictures. **illustration** *n.* a picture in a book or magazine.
im- *prefix* form of **in-** used before words beginning with b, m and p. meaning against, without or negative, e.g. **immature** *adj.* not mature. **immoderate** not moderate. **immoral** without morals etc.
imaginary *adj.* not real; existing only in a person's mind. *David has made up an imaginary friend called Little David.*
imagine *vb.* make up a picture in the mind. **imaginative** *adj.* using imagination. **imagination** *n.* fancy; creative power in the mind.
imbecile *n.* an idiot.
imbibe *vb.* take in, especially used of drink.
imitate *vb.* copy another person. **imitation** *n.*
immediately *adv.* now; without losing time. *I must run down to the shops immediately before they close.*
immense *adj.* vast, huge, enormous.
immigrant *n.* someone who comes to live in a country that is not their own.
immigrate *vb.* come to live in a country.
imminent *adj.* about to happen. *Disaster is imminent.*
immunize *vb.* make safe from an illness. **immunization** *n.*
imp *n.* (in stories) a little devil.
impair *vb.* weaken. *The climate impaired his health.*
impala *n.* reddish-brown African antelope living in great herds.

impatient *adj*. not patient; not wanting to wait for others. **impatience** *n*.
impede *vb*. get in the way of, hinder.
impersonate *vb*. pretend to be someone else.
impertinent *adj*. cheeky; irreverent.
implement 1. *n*. a tool or instrument. 2. *vb*. carry out, do.
impolite *adj*. not polite, rude.
import *vb*. (**im**-*port*) bring goods into your country.
important *adj*. something that matters a great deal. **importance** *n*.
impose *vb*. inflict on.
impossible *adj*. not possible; something that cannot be done.
impresario *n*. manager of a musical company etc.
impress *vb*. fix firmly in the mind; affect strongly. *His work impressed me*. **impressive** *adj*. creating a deep impression on the mind.
imprison *vb*. put into prison.
impromptu *adv*. & *adj*. without preparation.
improve *vb*. make something (or become) better. **improvement** *n*.
in- *prefix* meaning negation, e.g. **inaccurate** *adj*. not accurate. **inactive** *adj*. not active etc. In most cases words beginning with this are the exact opposite of the main word so it is generally only necessary to look up this definition to discover the contrary meaning, e.g. **adequate, inadequate**.
incense *n*. a substance, used in religious ceremonies, that gives off a sweet smell when burned.
incentive *n*. & *adj*. stimulus, something that encourages. *A carrot is an incentive to a donkey*.
incessant *adj*. continual, unceasing.
inch *n*. a unit of measurement equal to 2.54 cm. *There are 12 inches in 1 foot*.
incident *n*. an event, a minor happening. *It was only an incident in the story*.
incite *vb*. stir up, rouse, urge on.
incline *vb*. lean, slope towards. **inclination** *n*. leaning; preference.
include *vb*. contain as part of the whole; take into account.
incognito *adj*., *n*. & *adv*. (passing under) an assumed or false name. *Travelling incognito*.
income *n*. pay; money received for work and from other sources during a period. *Income tax*.
incorporate *vb*. include and make part of.
increase *vb*. (*in*-**crease**) make greater in size or amount. The number of pupils in our class

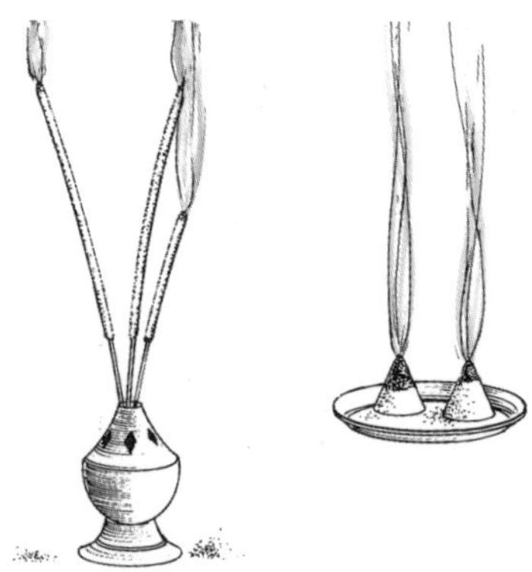

Incense burners.

has greatly increased. *n.* (**in-***crease*) growth, enlargement.
incredible *adj.* something that cannot be believed.
incubate *vb.* keep eggs warm in order to hatch them.
incur *vb.* (past **incurred**) bring upon oneself.
indeed *adv.* really; in truth. *It was a very big dog indeed.*
independent *adj.* free; not controlled by others. **independence** *n.*
index *n.* a list at the end of a book, giving all the subjects of the book in alphabetical order and the pages on which they appear.
Indian *n.* a person from India; one of the original people of America.
indicate *vb.* point to; sign of. **indication** *n.*
indifference *n.* lack of concern, absence of feeling.
indifferent *adj. He was indifferent to the feelings of others.*
indigenous *adj.* native, belonging from the beginning. *Kangaroos are indigenous to Australia.*
indigestion *n.* difficulty in digesting food. **indigestible** *adj.*
indignant *adj.* angry, scornful especially at injustices, cruelty etc.
individual 1. *adj.* of or for one person only. *We each had an individual parcel of food.* 2. *n.* a person. *He's a strange individual.*
indoors *adv.* inside a building.
indulge *vb.* take pleasure in, gratify, desire. **indulgent** *adj.* too lenient.
industry *n.* 1. work done in factories. 2. a trade or business. *Steel-making is an important industry.* **industrial** *adj.* to do with manufacturing. **industrious** *adj.* hard working.
inertia *n.* lack of energy; (in physics) property of an object that causes it to resist being moved or to change its motion.
infant *n.* a baby or child under about two years old. **infantile** *adj.* childish.
infantry *n.* soldiers who fight on foot – the main combat forces in most armies.

An infantry soldier in combat uniform.

infection *n.* an illness that can be spread by harmful germs.
inferior *adj.* lower in rank or quality.
infinity *n.* a time or space without end; too big to be imagined.

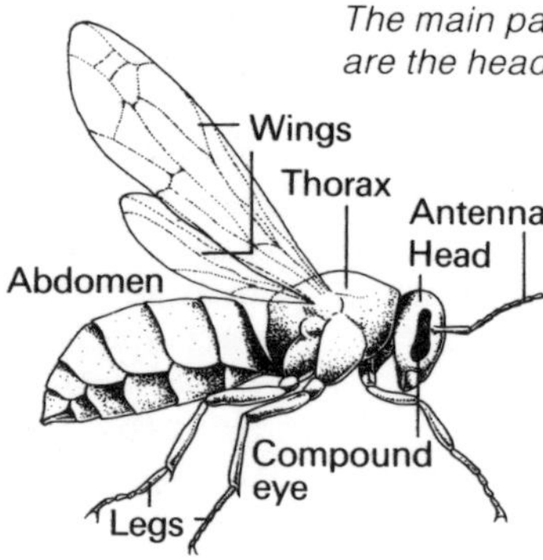

The main parts of an insect's body are the head, thorax and abdomen.

infirmary *n.* a hospital (especially in schools).
inhabitant *n.* a person who lives in or inhabits a place or country. *The American Indians were the first inhabitants of that continent.*
inhale *vb.* breathe in.
inherit *vb.* receive money or property from someone who has died. **inheritance** *n.* that which is received.
initial (*in*-**ish**-*al*) 1. *adj.* at the beginning. 2. *n.* the first letter in a name. *Simon Powell's initials are S.P. vb.* sign with initials.
injection *n.* medicine given with a hypodermic syringe. **inject** *vb.*
injure *vb.* hurt or damage. **injury** *n.* damage or harm, particularly to the body. *The unfortunate man died of his injuries.*
ink *n.* a coloured fluid used for writing, drawing or printing.
inkling *n.* hint, suspicion. *She had no inkling I would turn up today.*
inland *adj.* away from the sea. *Chicago is an inland city.*
inn *n.* a public house where food and drink are sold and people can stay.
innings *pl. n.* a team's turn at batting in cricket.
innocent *adj.* not guilty; doing no harm. **innocence** *n.*
inoculate *vb.* give a mild form of a disease in order to protect a person from the disease. **inoculation** *n.*
inquest *n.* (*in-kwest*) official inquiry, especially into cause of death.
inquire *vb.* ask about something or someone. **inquiry** *n.* investigation. (also **enquire**, **enquiry**).
inquisitive *adj.* wanting to find out about things, curious.
insanity *n.* mad, senseless. **insane** *adj.*
insect *n.* a small animal with six legs and no backbone.
insecticide *n.* a mixture used to kill insects.
insert *vb.* put in, place in between. *n.* thing inserted.
inside *adj.* within. *The heart is inside the body.*
insignia *n.* badges of office, authority etc.

insipid *adj*. without flavour; dull. **insist** *vb*. press for, speak emphatically, demand.

insomnia *vb*. inability to sleep.

inspect *vb*. examine carefully. **inspection** *n*.

inspire *vb*. encourage someone to do something, influence. **inspiration** *n*. creative influence, a sudden idea.

instalment *n*. a part of something, especially a story or payment.

instant *n*. a moment; a very short time. **instantly** *adv*. at once.

instead *adv*. in place of. *She is taking the class instead of our usual teacher, who is ill.*

instinct *n*. something that makes animals do things that they have not learned to do, inborn behaviour.

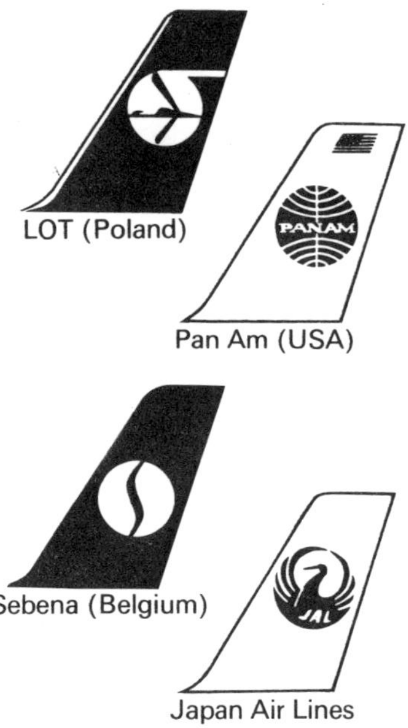

Insignia of some of the world's airlines. They usually appear on the tail fin of planes and in advertisements.

institute *vb*. set up, establish. *n*. organization or establishment for a special purpose.

instruct *vb*. teach, direct. **instruction** *n*. teaching, order.

instrument *n*. 1. delicate tool or implement for a special purpose. 2. something used for making musical sounds. *A musical instrument*.

insulate *vb*. isolate, prevent passage of electricity etc. **insulator** *n*.

insulin *n*. a hormone secreted by the pancreas used in treating diabetes.

insult (*in*-**sult**) *vb*. be rude to someone. (**in**-*sult*) *n*. a rude remark. *It was an insult to call Bill a stupid lazy fellow.*

insurance *n*. a method of protecting against loss through such risks as fire or theft, accident or death. **insure** *vb*.

integrate *vb*. combine into one.

integrity *n*. honesty, purity, soundness.

intelligent *adj*. clever and able to understand easily.

intelligence *n*. the ability to reason and understand.

intend *vb*. mean to, have in mind to. *I intend to finish the weeding*. **intention** *n*. purpose, object.

intense *adj*. earnest; very strong. **intensity** *n*. **intensive** *adj*. concentrated. *The intensive care ward*.

inter- *prefix* meaning among, between etc, e.g. **inter-continental**.

interest *n.* 1. enthusiasm, being keen on something. *He takes a great interest in my work.* 2. money paid (by or to a bank etc,) on a loan. *I have just been paid the interest on my account.*

interested *adj.* wanting to know and learn about. *Robert is very interested in ships and borrowed three books about them.*

interfere *vb.* 1. meddle in other people's affairs. 2. get in the way of something.

interior *adj.* inside, inland. *n.* the inside of anything.

internal combustion engine *n.* type of engine that works by the combustion (burning) of a fuel-air mixture within the cylinders of the engine.

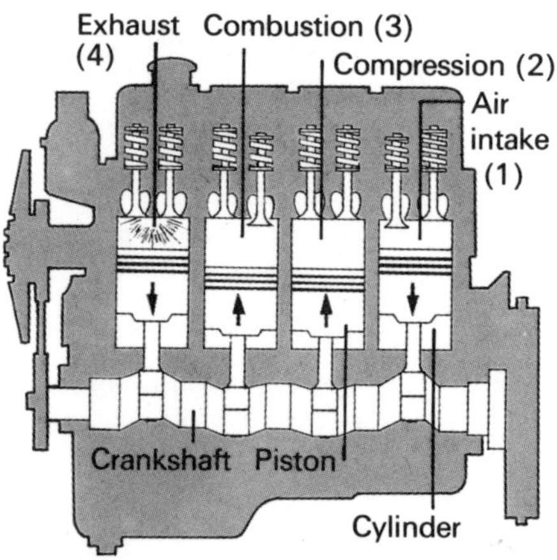

international *adj.* affecting two or more nations. *The United Nations is an international organization.*

interpret *vb.* 1. show the meaning of. *He interpreted the signs as meaning that it would rain.* 2. translate from one language to another.

interrupt *vb.* disturb someone who is doing something. **interruption** *n.*

interview *vb.* question to find information or discover suitability of a person for a job etc. *n.*

intestines *pl. n.* the tubes through which our food passes after it has been through the stomach.

intimate *adj.* close, familiar. *An intimate friend.*

into *prep.* put or go inside something. *Come into the kitchen.*

intolerance *n.* inability to accept or consider the ideas or opinions of others. **intolerant** *adj.*

intoxicate *vb.* make drunk.

intricate *adj.* complicated and involved.

introduce *vb.* 1. make people known to each other. *Edward introduced me to his mother.* 2. bring into use, *Decimal coins were introduced in 1971.*

introduction *n.* introducing; the first part of the book which tells you what the book is about.

invade *vb.* go into another country or place to fight against the people. **invasion** *n.*

invalid *n.* an ill or weak person. 2. *adj.* not legally acceptable.

invent *vb.* make something for the first time, devise, fabricate (a false story). **invention** (*in-***ven***-shun*) *n.* something that has been invented.

inventor *n.* someone who invents things.

invertebrate *n.* an animal with

no backbone, such as an insect, a worm or snail. *adj*.

invisible *adj*. unseen; cannot be seen. *The hem was sewn so neatly that it was invisible*. **invisibility** *n*.

invite *vb*. ask someone to come somewhere. *Susan's aunt may invite her to go to India next year*. **invitation** *n*. spoken or written words that ask you, or invite you, to come.

invoice *n*. a list of goods sent with their prices.

iodine *n*. a grey-black crystal element which when heated gives off a violet vapour. Iodine is found in seaweed and is essential for the proper working of the thyroid gland. (Symbol I.)

ion *n*. an atom or group of atoms that is electrically charged because it has gained or lost electrons.

ionosphere *n*. a layer of the Earth's atmosphere starting at about 80 km (50 miles) up and ending about 500 km (300 miles) above sea level.

IOU (I owe you) *n*. a piece of paper signed by a borrower of money and given to the lender acknowledging the debt.

iris 1. *n*. a flower with pointed leaves. 2. *n*. the coloured part of the eye.

irk *vb*. trouble, bother.

iron 1. *n*. a heavy, common metal (symbol Fe). 2. *n*. a tool for pressing clothes. 3. *vb*. press clothes.

iron lung *n*. a respirator or machine to aid breathing and used when the chest muscles are paralysed.

ironmonger *n*. a person who sells tools, nails and other things.

irrigate *vb*. take water to dry land in order to help crops to grow. **irrigation** *n*.

irritate *vb*. make angry, annoy. **irritable** *adj*. easily annoyed.

Islam *n*. the religion revealed through the prophet Muhammed. **Islamic** *adj*.

island *n*. land area surrounded by water. **islander** *n*. someone who lives on an island.

isobar *n*. line on a weather map which joins places with the same atmospheric pressure.

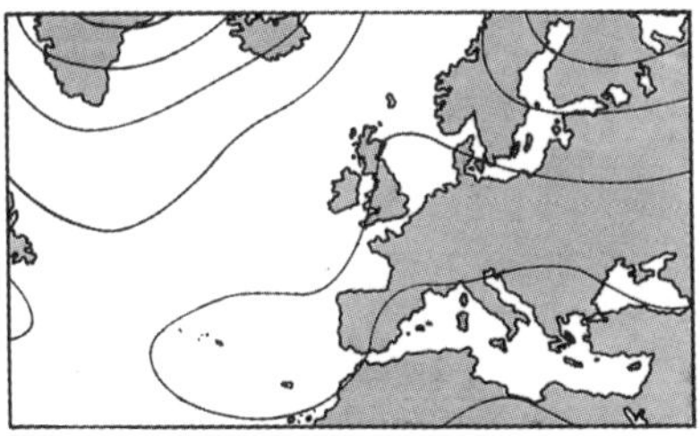

isolate *vb*. place alone, set apart.

isotope *n*. the form of an element that has neutrons added to or taken away from the nucleus of its atoms.

The iris is a popular garden flower.

issue *n.* going or flowing out; offspring (children); putting into circulation money, books etc. *vb.*

isthmus *n.* a strip of land joining two larger pieces of land.

italics *pl. n.* words that are printed at a slope *like this.*

itch *n.* an uncomfortable feeling in the skin, which makes you want to scratch. **itchy** *adj.*

item *n.* a single unit on a list. *How many items of furniture should there be?*

itinerary *n.* plan or record of a journey.

it's short for it is. *It's me.*

its *pron.* the possessive form of it. *The cat was washing its face.*

ivory *n.* the white bone-like material from which elephant's tusks are made.

ivy *n.* a climbing evergreen plant with shiny, dark-green leaves.

J

jab *vb.* & *n.* poke, stab. *He accidentally jabbed me with the end of his umbrella.*

jack *n.* 1. a tool for raising heavy weights off the ground. 2. a knave in a pack of cards.

jackal *n.* a kind of wild dog.

jackboot *n.* long boot reaching over the knee.

jackdaw *n.* a bird of the crow family.

jacket *n.* a short coat, which may be part of a suit.

jackpot *n.* top prize in a slot machine lottery.

Jacobean *adj.* belonging to the reign of James I (VI of Scotland).

Jacobite *n.* & *adj.* a follower of the exiled Stuart royal family during the late 17th and 18th centuries in England and Scotland.

jade *n.* a hard green, blackish green or white stone, used in jewellery, ornaments etc.

jagged *adj.* rough with sharp edges. *The ship was wrecked on the jagged rocks.*

jaguar *n.* a large American wild cat with yellow and black spots like a leopard.

jail *n.* see **gaol**.

jam 1. *vb.* push things together tightly. *He jammed his clothes into his suitcase.* 2. *vb.* cause interference on the radio. 3. *n.*

food made by boiling fruit and sugar together.
jamboree (*jam-bu-***ree**) *n.* rally of scouts; a large festive gathering.
jangle *vb.* sound harshly; out of tune. *n.*
January *n.* the first month of the year.
jar 1. *n.* pot, often made of glass, for jam and other things. 2. *vb.* make a harsh, grating noise. **jarring** *adj.*
jargon *n.* the special or technical language of a group of people.
jasmine *n.* a shrub with white or yellow flowers and which yields oils that are used in perfume.
jaundice *n.* a disease in which there is a yellowing of the skin caused by too much yellow bile pigment in the blood.
jaunt *n.* short trip, especially for pleasure.
javelin *n.* a short, light throwing spear.
jaw *n.* the bones of the mouth. *Your teeth are set in your jaw.*
jazz *n.* a type of popular music first played by American negroes.
jealous (**jel**-us) *adj.* being unhappy because you want what others have. **jealousy** *n.*

jeans *pl. n.* tight-fitting, casual trousers made of tough, blue material called denim.
jeep *n.* a kind of motor car originally used by the US Army for going over rough ground.
jeer *vb.* mock, make fun of, scoff. *n.*
jelly *n.* a soft, wobbly kind of food, usually brightly coloured and flavoured with fruit.
jellyfish *n.* an invertebrate sea animal with a round, semi-transparent soft body fringed with stinging tentacles.
jenny *n.* female donkey, a she-ass.
jeopardy (**jep**-*ur-dee*) *n.* danger, peril. **jeopardize** *vb.* put in danger.
jerboa *n.* jumping rodent of Africa with long back legs.
jerk 1. *n.* a sudden rush or movement. 2. *vb.* move abruptly.
jersey (plural **jerseys**) *n.* a knitted woollen upper garment.
jet *n.* 1. a fast stream of liquid or gas. 2. an aircraft with an engine that sucks in air and pushes it out at the back, so pushing the aircraft forward. 3. hard, black mineral often used in jewellery.
jetsam *n.* cargo from a ship thrown overboard and then washed ashore.

A jet engine drives an aircraft forward by pushing hot gases backwards.

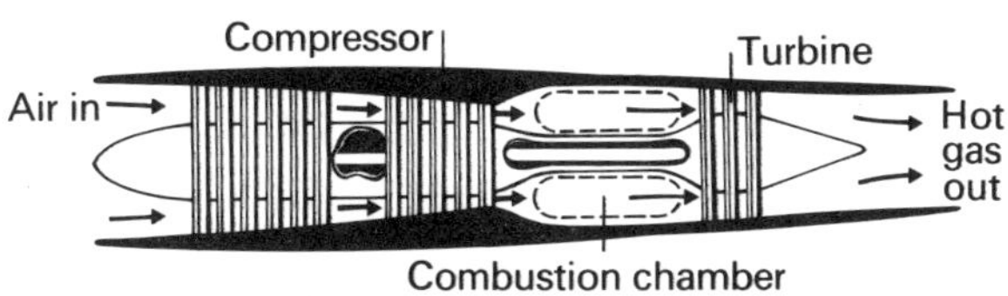

jettison *vb.* throw overboard.
jetty *n.* a pier; a landing stage.
Jew *n.* a person belonging to the Hebrew race or religion (Judaism). **Jewish** *adj.* **Jewry** *n.* Jews collectively.
jewel *n.* a precious stone.
jeweller *n.* a person who makes or sells jewellery.
jewellery *n.* ornaments with jewels or other decorations.
jiffy *n.* a moment. *I'll be there in a jiffy.*
jig *n.* & *vb.* a lively dance.
jigsaw *n.* a special kind of saw for cutting small pieces of wood very accurately. *A jigsaw puzzle is a picture, mounted on wood or cardboard, which has been cut up by a jigsaw.*
jingle *vb.* & *n.* (make) a tinkling noise; a clinking sound; a catchy tune or rhyme. *Many TV ads have clever jingles.*
jittery *adj.* nervous.
job 1. *n.* a person's work. 2. *adj. phrase* with verb *be. It's a good job you brought your raincoat.*
jockey *n.* a person who rides in horse-races, usually for wages.
jodhpurs (**jod**-*purrs*) *pl. n.* riding breeches that are loose-fitting round the hips but close-fitting from knee to ankle.
joey *n.* (*Aust.*) a young animal, especially a kangaroo.
jog *vb.* 1. run at a slow, steady pace. *n.* 2. nudge (memory).
John Bull *n.* a character who is a personification or caricature of the English nation.
join *vb.* put together, unite; take part in; become a member of.
joiner *n.* a person who works with wood; a carpenter.
joint 1. *n.* a point where two parts join. *The knee is the joint between the upper and lower bones of the leg.* 2. *adj.* shared, common. *They have a joint bank account.*
join up *vb.* join the army, navy or air force; enlist.
joist *n.* a beam supporting a floor or ceiling in a building.
joke *n.* a funny story or remark. *vb.* tell a joke or do something to amuse.
joker *n.* 1. a person who jokes. 2. a fifty-third card in a pack of cards, used in some games.
jolly *adj.* cheerful; merry. *Father Christmas is usually portrayed as a jolly old gentleman with a white beard.*
jolt *vb.* move or shake with

Joints of the human knee and of the hip.

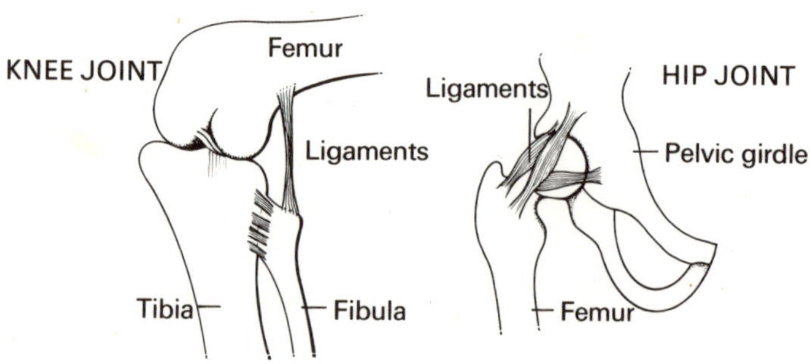

In the Middle Ages, jousting was a popular sport. Jousts took place between knights on horseback. They wore heavy armour and carried lances.

sudden jerks. *n.* a shock or sudden jerk. *The train came to a stop with a jolt.*

jostle *vb.* shove; push against.

jot *vb.* make a note; write down briefly. *Let me jot down your telephone number.*

journalist *n.* a person who writes about or edits the news in magazines and newspapers.

journey 1. *n.* a distance travelled. 2. *vb.* travel.

joust *n.* & *vb.* a combat between mounted knights in a tournament; to fight in a tournament.

joy *n.* happiness.

jubilee *n.* a festival or celebration usually of an anniversary. *Queen Victoria celebrated her Diamond Jubilee after she had reigned for 60 years.*

judge 1. *vb.* decide what is right or best out of number of people or things. 2. *n.* a person who judges, particularly in a law court or competition. **judgement** *n.* decision of a court, opinion; estimate.

judo *n.* a fighting sport, developed in Japan as a form of self defence.

jug *n.* an object for holding liquids, with a handle and a lip for pouring.

juggernaut *n.* a massive lorry.

juggler *n.* an entertainer who tosses things in the air, catches and throws them up again. **juggle** *vb.*

juice (rhymes with *loose*) *n.* the liquid part of fruit or other food. **juicy** *adj.*

July *n.* the seventh month of the year.

jumble *n.* a muddle; a disorder. *A jumble sale. vb. She jumbled the papers together.*

jumbo *adj.* (originally the name of a circus elephant) a massive person, animal or thing. e.g. jumbo jet.

jump *vb.* & *n.* leap, spring. **jumpy** *adj.* nervous.

jump at *vb.* accept enthusiastically. *Jane jumped at the chance of a lift to the horse show.*

jumper *n.* a sweater; a pullover (usually worn by children).

junction *n.* a join or joining place, especially where several roads or railway lines meet.

June *n.* the sixth month of the year.

jungle *n.* thick forest in hot countries.
junior *adj.* younger or less high in rank. *John is the office junior and reports to the manager.*
juniper *n.* evergreen shrub with purple berries.
junk *n.* 1. rubbish. 2. a Chinese sailing boat.
junket *n.* 1. a sweet dish of milk curds. 2. a feast or picnic.
juror *n.* a member of a jury.
jury *n.* people who are chosen to decide whether an accused person is guilty or not guilty in a law court.

A three-masted Chinese sailing junk. It has a flat bottom for shallow seas.

just 1. *adv.* exactly. *That colour is just right.* 2. *adv.* a moment ago. *I have only just arrived.* 3. *adj.* fair, honest. *That is a just law.*
justice *n.* 1. the law; fairness. 2. a judge. *A Justice of the Peace is a local magistrate.*
justify *vb.* show or prove to be right.
jut *vb.* stick out, project.
jute *n.* a coarse fibre used to make sacks.
juvenile *n.* a young person.

K

kaleidoscope *n.* a device made with mirrors which creates repeated colours and patterns.
kangaroo *n.* an Australian animal with strong back legs. The female has a pouch in which she carries her baby called a joey.
kaolin *n.* white clay used to make porcelain.
karate (*ka*-**raht**-*tay*) *n.* an oriental style of unarmed combat, using kicks and punches. As a sport, it involves both mock fights and formal examinations for the various grades of skill.
kayak (**kye**-*ack*) *n.* an Eskimo canoe made of sealskin.

Karate is one of the so-called martial arts – various kinds of combat which come from the Far East. The others include judo, aikido and kung-fu.

kazoo *n.* a small musical instrument played with the mouth.
keel *n.* the heavy strip of metal or wood running along the bottom of a ship. *vb.* (over) capsize.
keen *adj.* eager; enthusiastic.
keep 1. *vb.* have something and not give it to anyone else. 2. *vb.* look after something for somebody. *Keep the book until I see you again.* 3. *n.* a strong tower in a castle.
keeper *n.* one who looks after people or things, particularly animals in a zoo. *He had been the elephant keeper for 20 years.*
keep on *vb.* continue doing something. *Stan keeps on talking, even when the teacher tells him not to.*
keepsake *n.* memento; something treasured because of the giver.
keep up with *vb.* not to lag behind. *He managed to keep up with the others in the race.*
keg *n.* a small barrel.
kelp *n.* kind of seaweed.
kennel *n.* a shelter for a dog. *vb.* keep a dog in a kennel.
kept *vb.* past of **keep**.
kerb *n.* the stone edge of a pavement.
kernel *n.* the soft inner part of a nut, which we can eat.
kerosene see **paraffin**.
kestrel *n.* a kind of small hawk.
ketchup *n.* a sauce made from tomatoes and other things. (Catsup in the USA.)
kettle *n.* a kind of pot with a lid, handle and spout, used for boiling water in.
key (rhymes with *me*). 1. *n.* a metal device to undo a lock or wind a clock. 2. *n.* solution, explanation, code. 3. *n.* part of a machine or instrument pressed with the fingers. *The piano keys were made of ivory.* 4. *n.* one of the systems of notes in music. 5. *adj.* of vital importance.
keystone *n.* central stone supporting arch.
khaki *adj.* a dull yellow-green colour.
kibbutz *n.* (plural **kibbutzim**) agricultural centre in Israel.
kick *vb.* hit something, such as a ball, with your foot. **kick-off** *n.* kick of a ball which starts a game.
kid 1. *n.* a young goat. 2. *n.* (casual) a child. 3. *vb.* tease, hoax.
kidnap *vb.* steal someone, often to get money as a ransom. **kidnapper** *n.*
kidney *n.* (plural. **kidneys**) one of a pair of bean shaped organs of the body that remove the waste matter from the blood.
kill *vb.* put to death; take the life of someone or something.
kiln *n.* an oven or furnace for baking bricks or pottery to make them hard.

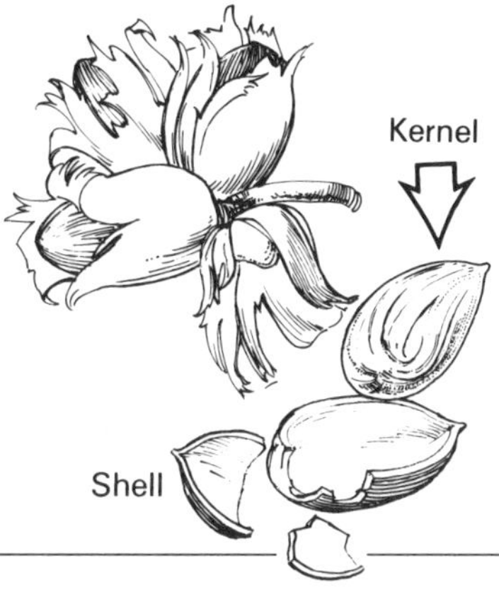

kilo- *prefix* a Greek word for one thousand. *Kilowatt; kilogramme* etc.
kilogramme (or **kilogram**) *n.* a measure of weight, often shortened to kg. *There are 1000 grammes in one kilogramme.*
kilometre *n.* a measure of length, often shortened to km. *There are 1000 metres in a kilometre.*
kilt *n.* a skirt often made of tartan cloth. *Kilts are worn by men and women in Scotland and some other countries.*
kimono (*ki*-**moan**-*oh*) *n.* a loose gown with wide sleeves worn in Japan.
kin *n.* relatives.

The kimono is the traditional costume of Japan for both men and women.

kind 1. *adj.* pleasant or gentle. 2. *n.* type or sort. *What kind of tree is that?* **kindness** *n.* the act of being kind, or treating someone well. *Thank you for all your kindness to me.*
kindergarten *n.* a school for very young children.
king *n.* a male ruler; a monarch.
kingdom *n.* a country ruled by a king or a queen.
kingfisher *n.* a small, brightly coloured bird with a large head and a beak like a dagger.
kiosk (**key**-*ossk*) *n.* a small hut or stall, used for selling newspapers, sweets etc. *A telephone box is sometimes called a telephone kiosk.*
kipper *n.* a smoked herring, sometimes eaten for breakfast in Britain.
kirk *n.* a Scottish word for church.
kirsch *n.* a strong alcoholic drink distilled from cherries.
kismet *n.* an Arabic word for fate or destiny.
kiss *vb.* & *n.* touch with the lips as a sign of love or friendship.
kit *n.* equipment.
kitchen *n.* a room in a house where the cooking is done. **kitchenette** *n.* a small kitchen.
kite *n.* 1. a bird of prey related to the falcon family, noted for its long wings, deeply forked tail and graceful flight. 2. a frame of wood covered with light material which can be made to fly.
kitten *n.* a young cat. **kittenish** *adj.*
kittiwake *n.* kind of seagull.
kiwi (*kee-we*) *n.* a New Zealand bird that cannot fly.

Knitting by hand is a way of making a fabric stitch by stitch and row by row. Wool or yarns are looped around each other using a pair of knitting needles. Here the first row of knitting is being 'cast on' to the needles.

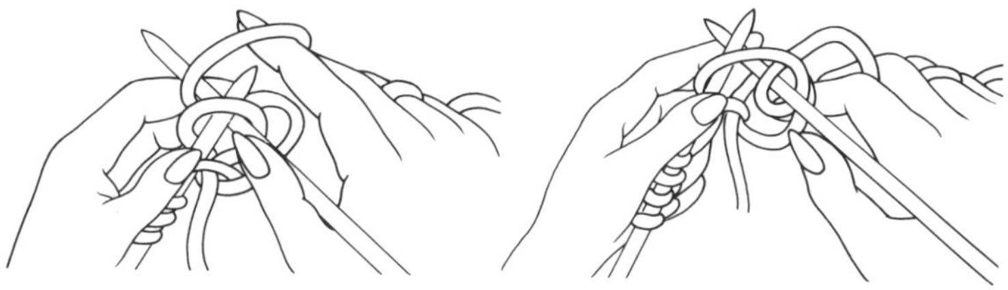

klaxon *n.* a loud horn or hooter.
knack (*nack*) *n.* skill or ability.
knapsack (*napsack*) *n.* a canvas bag carried on the back.
knave (*nave*) *n.* 1. rascal, cheat. 2. the jack in a pack of cards.
knead (*need*) *vb.* work dough, or clay with the hands.
knee (*nee*) *n.* the hinged joint in the middle of the leg. **kneecap** *n.* the bone at the front of the knee, the patella.
kneel (*neel*) *vb.* go down on your knees, especially in prayer.
knell (*nell*) *n.* the sound of a bell rung to announce a death.
knew (*new*) *vb.* past of **know**.
knickers (*nickers*) *pl. n.* woman's two-legged undergarment.
knicknack (*nicknack*) *n.* a trinket or useless ornament.
knife (*nife*) *n.* a sharp bladed cutting tool with a handle. *vb.* (past **knifed**) stab with knife.
knight (*nite*) *n.* in the Middle Ages a mounted nobleman who served his king; today, the lowest rank of titled person with the title 'Sir'; a chesspiece.
knit (*nit*) *vb.* make clothing out of wool or other fibre, using knitting needles.
knob (*nob*) *n.* a round handle.
knock (*nock*) *vb.* hit or strike something. *n. Was that a knock at the door?*
knock down *vb.* force to the ground with a blow.
knocker *n.* an ornamental hammer on a door.
knock off *vb.* (casual) stop work for the day; steal.
knoll (*noll*) *n.* a small hill.
knot (*not*) *n.* 1. string or rope tied in such a way that it cannot come undone. *vb.* form knots. 2. hard mass in wood where a branch joins the trunk. 3. a unit of speed (nautical miles per hour) used for ships. A nautical mile is 1.85 km (6000 ft). **knotty** *adj.* full of knots; puzzling.

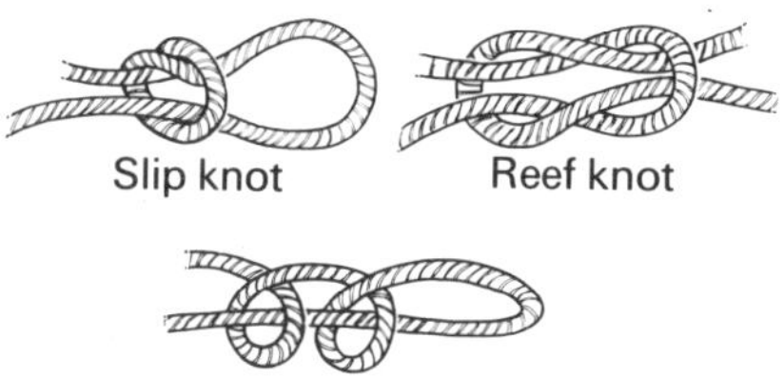

There are many ways of tying knots. Knots are especially important in sailing ships.

know (past **knew**) *vb.* 1. be sure of something; be in possession of the facts. *Do you know which is the longest river in the world?* 2. be familiar with, or recognize someone or something. *I'll know him when I see him.*

know-how *n.* practical knowledge.

knowledge (*noll-edge*) *n.* understanding; information in the mind. **knowledgeable** *adj.*

knuckle (*nuckle*) *n.* the bones at the finger joint, especially at the root of the fingers.

The koala is a marsupial.

koala *n.* a small furry Australian animal that lives in trees.

kookaburra *n.* an Australian bird related to the kingfisher. It is also known as the 'laughing jackass', because of its laughter-like call.

Koran *n.* the sacred book of Islam.

kosher *adj.* food that has been prepared in accordance with Jewish law.

L

label *n.* a piece of paper or card with writing on it attached to something. The label may say what the thing is or where it is going. *vb.* attach a label.

laboratory *n.* a place used for scientific experiments.

labour *n.* work; people who work. *vb.* work hard.

labour exchange *n.* (now job centre) a place which finds work for the unemployed and pays out unemployment benefit.

Labrador dog *n.* a sporting dog (retriever) originally from Newfoundland and with a black or golden coat, now popular as a pet.

labyrinth *n.* a maze, a tangle of intricate ways and connections.

lace 1. *n.* a delicate fabric made with patterns of thread. 2. *n.* cord for fastening a shoe, dress etc. *vb.* fasten with laces. 3. *vb.* add alcohol to other drinks.

lack *n.* & *vb.* need, be without, be missing. **lacking** *adj.*

lacquer *n.* a hard shiny varnish; a substance sprayed on the hair to keep it in place. *vb.* coat with lacquer.

lacrosse *n.* a team game played with a racket that has a net to catch and throw the ball with.

lame *adj.* not able to walk properly.

lament *vb.* mourn; express sorrow. *n.* elegy, sorrowful song. **lamentable** *adj.* sad; pitiful; worthless.

lamp *n.* a light, often portable.

lamp-post *n.* the post or pillar that supports a street light.

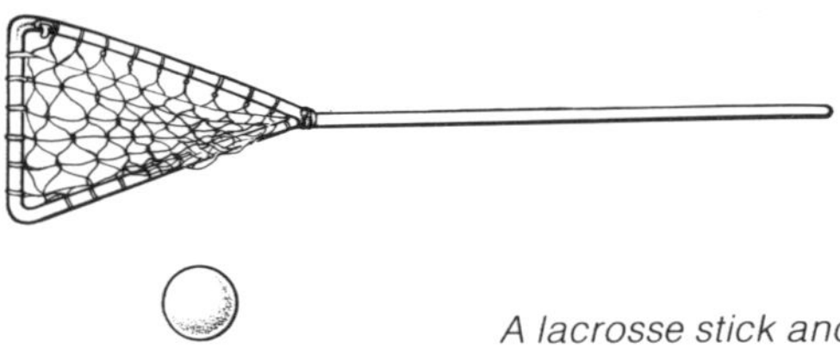

A lacrosse stick and ball.

lad *n.* a boy.

ladder *n.* two lengths of wood or other material fastened with cross-bars (called rungs). *A ladder is used for climbing up and down walls.*

ladle *n.* a large deep spoon used for serving soup. *vb.* transfer with a ladle.

lady *n.* 1. a female person; the feminine of 'gentleman'. 2. a woman's title. *Lady Smith is the wife of Sir John Smith.*

ladybird *n.* a small flying beetle with bright spots.

lager *n.* a light-coloured beer.

lagoon *n.* a shallow salt-water lake separated from the sea by a sand bank.

laid *vb.* past and past part. of **lay**.

lair *n.* a wild animal's den.

laird *n.* (*Sc.*) a lord; landowner.

lake *n.* a large area of water surrounded by land.

lamb *n.* a young sheep, the meat of a young sheep. *vb.* give birth (to lambs).

lance 1. *n.* a kind of spear formerly used by knights and cavalry. 2. *vb.* (in surgery) to pierce or cut open.

land 1. *n.* all those parts of the Earth's surface which are not sea. 2. *n.* the area owned by someone. *Farmer Green's land goes as far as the river.* 3. *vb.* come to land from the sea or the air. *Our plane should land early.* **landing** *n.*

landing *n.* 1. bringing into ground; bringing in to shore. 2. level part at the top of a flight of stairs.

landlady, landlord *n.* a person who owns a house or other property and lets it out to others; keeper of an inn. *I must pay the rent to my landlady tomorrow.*

landmark *n.* something that can be seen from a distance and which helps you find the way. *A church steeple is often used as a landmark by ramblers and other map-readers.*

The lapwing is also called the peewit, after the sound of its shrill cry.

landscape *n.* what you see when you look across a large area of land; a picture of a landscape.

lane *n.* 1. a narrow road, usually in the country. 2. one of the divisions of a highway, especially a motorway. *He drove all the way in the inside lane.*

language *n.* the words we use to talk or write to each other. *Many different languages are spoken in Africa.*

lank *adj.* drooping, limp, thin. **lanky** *adj.*

lanolin *n.* the oily substance found in sheep's wool.

lantern *n.* a case with glass sides for holding a light so that is does not blow out.

lap 1. *n.* your upper legs when you are sitting. 2. *vb.* drink with the tongue like an animal. 3. *n.* one circuit of a race track.

lapel *n.* folded back part of a coat collar.

lapse *n.* falling back, fall into disuse; a mistake. *vb.*

lapwing *n.* bird of the plover family.

larceny *n.* theft.

larch *n.* a cone-bearing tree that, unusually, loses its leaves in winter.

lard *n.* fat of a pig prepared for cooking.

larder *n.* a room where food is kept cool.

large *adj.* big, broad or wide.

lark *n.* 1. a small brown bird famous for its beautiful song. 2. a frolic, mischief. *vb.*

larva (plural **larvae**) *n.* an insect in the first stage when it comes from its egg.

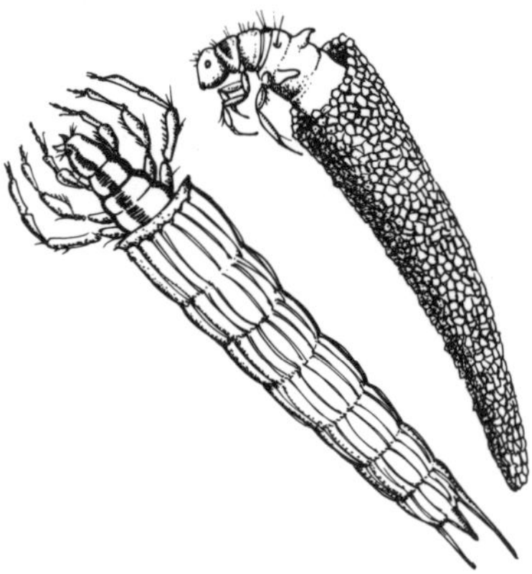

larynx *n.* the cavity in the upper windpipe (air passage in the throat) where sounds are produced; also called the voice box.

laser *n.* a device for sending out enormously strong light waves.

lash *vb.* make rapid movements (of tail etc.); thrash or fasten with a rope. *n.* whip.

lass *n.* a girl.

lasso (*lass*-**oo**) *n.* a long rope with a loop used by cowboys to catch cattle and horses; *vb.* use a lasso.

last 1. *adj*. coming at the end. *I came last in the race*. 2. *vb*. stay or continue. *Have we enough food to last the week?* 3. *n*. a wooden model of a foot used by shoemakers.

latch *n*. the fastening of a door or gate.

late *adj*. 1. not early; past the correct time. *They were late for the class*. 2. previous; no longer alive. *He knew the late king*.

lately *adv*. not long ago.

latex *n*. milky juice of some trees, especially rubber trees.

lathe *n*. a machine for holding and turning wood or metal while it is being shaped.

lather (rhymes with *rather*) *n*. froth that is formed by mixing soap with water. *vb*.

Latin *n*. language of ancient Rome; *adj*. concerning countries where languages are descended from Latin.

latitude *n*. 1. a distance measured in degrees north or south of the equator.
2. freedom of movement, scope.

latter *adj*. & *n*. the more recent, the second one mentioned of two. *Romulus and Remus were brothers: the latter* (*Remus*) *was younger than the former* (*Romulus*).

laugh *vb*. the sound you make when you think something is funny. **laughter**. (*n*.).

launch (*lawnch*) 1. *n*. a sort of power-boat. 2. *vb*. put a boat into water. 3. *vb*. start something off. *The rocket was launched from Cape Canaveral*.

laundrette *n*. a shop with washing machines where people pay to do their washing.

laundry *n*. a place where clothes are washed; the clothes that have to be washed.

Lines of latitude are measured in degrees.

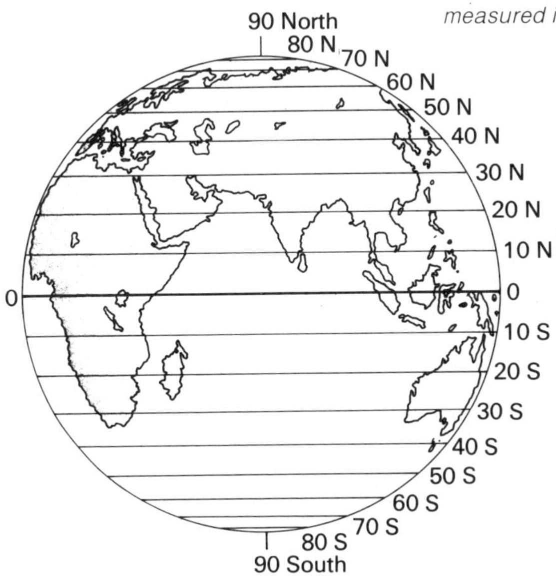

laurel *n.* sweet bay tree, whose leaves the ancient Greeks and Romans made into wreaths, emblems of victory.

lava *n.* hot liquid rock that flows from an active volcano.

lavatory *n.* a toilet; a room with a toilet in it.

lavender *n.* a small Mediterranean shrub with fragrant narrow leaves and pale purple flowers; cultivated on a large scale for use in the perfume industry.

law *n.* a set of rules, usually made by a government, that people have to obey. **lawful** *adj.* permitted by law.

lawn *n.* 1. an area of short cut grass. 2. a fine material used for nightdresses, blouses and other clothes.

lawnmower *n.* a machine for cutting grass.

lawyer *n.* a person who works in the law; a solicitor, barrister or advocate.

lax *adj.* careless, not strict.

lay 1. *vb.* past of **lie**. *We lay down on the lawn.* 2. *vb.* (past **laid**) of a bird, lay (produce) eggs; 3. *vb.* (past **laid**) put down; prepare a table; 4. *n.* as distinct from clergy; non-professional.

layabout *n.* lazy person.

layby *n.* a place at the side of the road where vehicles can pull off and stop.

layer *n.* something that is spread over a surface of something else. *A thick layer of clay had washed over the river bank.*

lazy *adj.* not wanting to do much work; idle. **laze** *vb.* relax.

A sprig of laurel.

lead (rhymes with *bed*) *n.* a soft, heavy, blue-grey metal (symbol Pb).

lead (rhymes with *reed*) 1. *vb.* go in front to guide others. 2. *n.* the first place. *Chris had a lead of about a metre in the race.* 3. *n.* a leather strap etc. for leading a dog.

leader *n.* a person who leads.

leaf (plural **leaves**) *n.* 1. one of the flat green parts of a plant growing from the stems of a branch. 2. a sheet of paper.

league (*leeg*) *n.* 1. a group of sports clubs that play matches against each other. 2. an alliance; nations that agree to help each other.

leak *n.* a hole through which liquid or gas can escape. *vb.*

lean 1. *vb.* be or put in a sloping position. *The ladder is leaning against the house.* 2. *adj.* thin, having little fat.

leap *vb.* & *n.* jump high or far. **leapt** or **leaped** *vb.* past of **leap**.

learn *vb*. (past **learnt** or **learned**) get knowledge or information, find out. *Did you learn French at school?*

learned (**lern**-*id*) *adj*. having much knowledge. **learner** *n*. a person learning.

lease *n*. legal document letting land, a house etc. for a stated period and on certain conditions. *vb*. grant or take on a lease. **leaseholder** *n*.

least *adj*. the smallest in size or quantity.

leather (**leth**-*er*) *n*. material made from the skin or hide of animals. *Shoes are made of leather*.

leave 1. *vb*. (past **left**) go away. *I leave for Paris tomorrow*. 2. *vb*. part with something; to lose it. *Did you leave your case at home?* 3. *vb*. not to use something. *Do you always leave so much of your food?* 4. *n*. permission to be absent; a holiday. *He was given a month's leave from his job*.

leaves *pl. n*. more than one **leaf**.

lectern *n*. a desk, especially in church, from which readings are given.

lecture *n*. a lesson or period of instruction. *vb*. deliver a lecture; tell off, reprimand. **lecturer** *n*.

led *vb*. past of **lead**.

ledge *n*. a narrow shelf on a wall or cliff.

ledger *n*. a (large) book, particularly one used for keeping accounts.

lee *n*. the side of something away from the wind.

leech *n*. a kind of worm which lives in damp places and sucks the blood of animals and people.

leek *n*. a vegetable with a thick white stem and broad flat leaves related to the onion.

left 1. *vb*. past of **leave**. 2. *n*. & *adj*. the side opposite to right. *In Britain, people drive on the left*.

leg *n*. one of the lower limbs used in walking, running and standing. *Most animals have four or more legs*.

legal (*lee-gal*) *adj*. to do with the law; correct by the law. *Is it legal to ride a bicycle on the pavement?* **legalize** *vb*. make lawful.

legend (**ledge**-*end*) *n*. an old story. **legendary** *adj*. told about in old stories.

legion *n*. a division of the Roman army of between 3000 and 6000 men; any large force; an association.

legislate *vb*. make laws.

leisure (rhymes with *measure*) *n*. rest, time free from work. **leisured** *adj*. having plenty of free time.

lemming *n*. a small Arctic rodent.

lemon *n*. a small oval citrus fruit with a yellow skin and acid juice. Lemon trees are widely cultivated in southern Europe and the Middle East.

lemonade *n*. a lemon-flavoured drink.

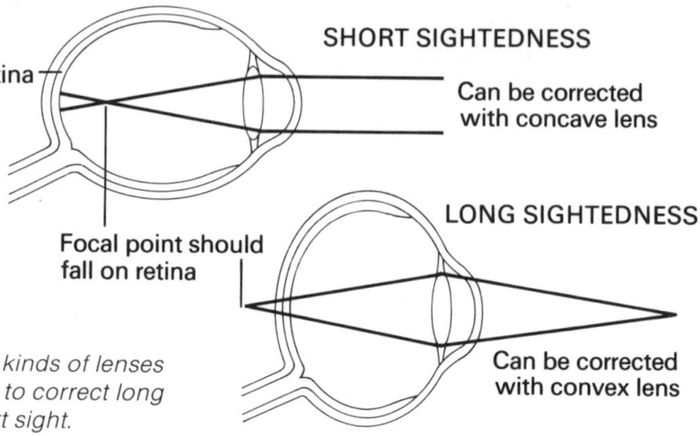

Different kinds of lenses are used to correct long and short sight.

lend *vb.* give something to someone for a time, expecting to get it back. The other person borrows it.
length *n.* from one end to the other in distance or time. **lengthen** *vb.* make or become longer.
lens *n.* (plural **lenses**) a piece of glass with one or two curved surfaces, used in cameras, spectacles, telescopes and microscopes.
Lent *n.* the 40 days that Christians observe as a preparation for Easter. It begins on Ash Wednesday.
lent *vb.* past of **lend**.
lentils *pl. n.* the seeds of a food plant of the pea family that grows in hot countries.
leopard (**lep**-*ard*) *n.* large African animal belonging to the cat family with black spots on a yellowish coat. In India leopards are called panthers.
leotard (**lee**-*o-tard*) *n.* a one-piece garment worn for gymnastics and other sports.
leprechaun (**lep**-ri-cawn) *n.* an Irish fairy.
leprosy *n.* a disease mainly of the skin causing loss of feeling and a gradual eating away of the skin.
less *adj.* a smaller amount. **lessen** *vb.* make less; reduce.
lesser *adj.* not so great as, smaller of two. *'The lesser of two evils'.*

Leotards are worn by gymnasts.

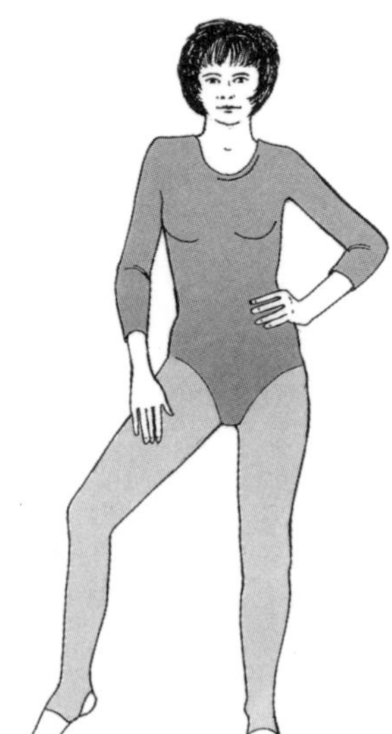

lesson *n.* 1. a period in class, usually when only one subject is taught; a warning, an example. 2. a reading from the Bible during a church service.

lest *conj.* for fear that, in order to avoid.

let *vb.* 1. allow someone to do something. *Bob let us see his scar.* 2. rent property to someone. *Mrs Small lets one floor of her house.*

let down *vb.* fail to do something that somebody expected you to do. *The workmen promised to mend our roof, but they let us down, and the rain came in.*

lethal *adj.* causing death.

let off *vb.* 1. free someone who has done wrong. *Our teacher let us off the punishment because it was half-term.* 2. cause a firework to explode.

letter *n.* 1. a part of the alphabet. *Our alphabet contains 26 letters.* 2. a written message, usually sent by post.

letterbox *n.* 1. an opening in a door for receiving post. 2. a postbox; a place for delivering letters for collection.

lettering *n.* the style of letters used in an inscription etc.

lettuce *n.* a salad vegetable that grows close to the ground on a very short stem; it has large green leaves.

level 1. *adj.* flat; even. *The surface of the snooker table is perfectly level.* *vb.* make flat. 2. *n.* the base from which a height is measured. *The height of mountains is measured from sea level.* 3. *n.* the height to which a liquid rises in a container. *Please check the water level in the radiator.*

level crossing *n.* a place where a road crosses a railway line without using a bridge or tunnel.

lever *n.* a tool used to lift something heavy or to force it open. *vb.* use a lever; raise with a lever.

leveret *n.* a young hare.

levy *vb.* raise or collect taxes. *n.* the tax raised.

lexicon *n.* a dictionary.

liar *n.* someone who does not tell the truth.

liberal *adj.* free, generous; tolerant.

liberate *vb.* set free, release.

liberty *n.* freedom.

library *n.* a building or room where books are kept and, usually, borrowed from. **librarian** *n.* a trained person who works in a library.

lice *pl. n.* more than one louse.

licence *n.* a permit to do something. *He has a licence to drive a car.*

license *vb.* to give a licence; authorize.

lichen (**lie**-*ken*, **lich**-*en*) *n.* a small dry looking plant that grows on rocks or trees.

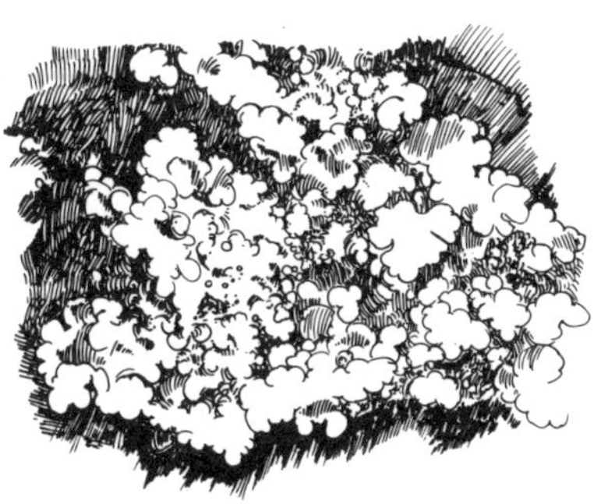

lick *vb.* & *n.* touch something with the tongue; the act of licking.

lid *n.* the top covering of something, such as a saucepan.

lie 1. *vb.* & *n.* (say) something that is not true. 2. *vb.* put yourself down flat. *If you lie on the floor, you can see the crack.* 3. *vb.* (of places) be in a certain place. *The small islands lie just off the coast.*

life *n.* (plural **lives**) 1. all living things. *When did life begin on earth?* 2. the time between birth and death. 3. liveliness; energy. *The young children were full of life.*

lifeboat *n.* a boat for rescuing people at sea.

lift 1. *vb.* raise up; take up. 2. *n.* an apparatus for carrying people or goods up and down a building. 3. *n.* a ride in a vehicle given to a walker.

lift-off *n.* the take-off of a rocket.

light 1. *n.* something that shines brightly so that we can see things; illumination. 2. *vb.* set on fire. 3. *adj.* not heavy. 4. *adj.* not dark in colour. *A light blue suit.*

lighten *vb.* 1. make or become lighter; make easier to bear. 2. make or grow bright.

lighter 1. *n.* device for lighting cigarettes etc. 2. *n.* flat-bottomed boat used for unloading goods from a ship. 3. *adj.* comparative of light. not so heavy; not so dark.

lighthouse *n.* a tower with a flashing light in it that warns ships away from dangerous rocks.

lighting *n.* artificial light such as candles or gas lamps.

lightning *n.* a flash of light in the sky during a thunderstorm.

like 1. *vb.* think well of someone or something. 2. *vb.* enjoy doing something. 3. *adj.* similar to. *She looks like her sister.*

likely *adv.* expected to happen. *It is likely to rain today.*

lilac *n.* a shrub grown in many parts of the world for its fragrant white or purple flowers.

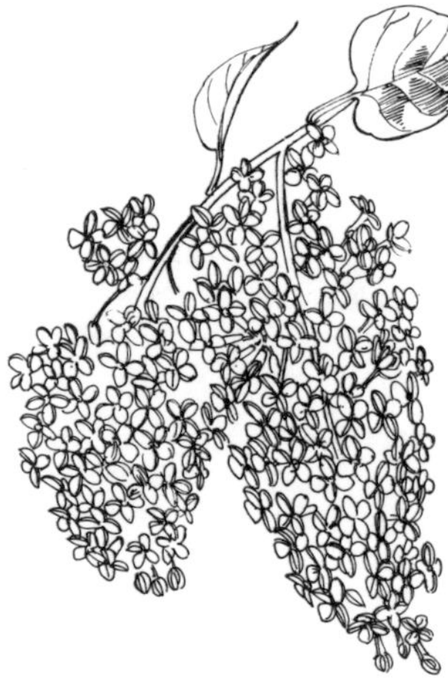

Hanging lilac flowers are a common garden shrub.

lily *n.* a plant growing from a bulb, with white, yellow or red flowers. The lily family includes onions, asparagus and tulips.

limb *n.* a leg or an arm.

lime *n.* 1. a substance obtained from heating limestone, and used in making cement. 2. the small, green, lemon-like fruit of a tropical tree. 3. a deciduous tree also called the linden.

limerick *n.* a funny five-line poem with this form:

There was a young man from Nepal
Who went to a fancy dress ball;
He thought he would risk it
And go as a biscuit,
But a dog ate him up in the hall.

limestone *n.* a rock containing the chemical substance calcium carbonate.

limit 1. *n.* a line or point that you cannot or should not go beyond. *The speed limit in the town is 30 miles an hour.* 2. *vb.* restrict something. *You should limit her to three sweets before tea.*

limousine *n.* a large and luxurious motor car.

limp 1. *adj.* not stiff. *The skirt became very limp after she washed it.* 2. *vb.* walk unevenly.

limpet *n.* a kind of shellfish that clings to rocks.

linctus *n.* a soothing syrup, often prescribed for a cough.

line 1. *n.* a long thin mark. 2. *n.* a piece of rope or string. 3. *n.* a row of people or things. *We stand in line for dinner.* 4. *n.* a transport system. *There goes a Green Line bus.* 5. *vb.* put a lining into something.

linen *n.* cloth made from the fibres of the flax plant.

liner *n.* a big passenger ship.

linger *vb.* wait about, be slow to go.

linguist *n.* 1. a person who speaks several languages. 2. a person who makes a scientific study of how language works.

lining *n.* a layer of material inside something.

link 1. *n.* one loop of a chain. 2. *vb.* join things together.

Limestone rock is easily worn away by the action of water, creating caves. The water seeps through cracks in the rock, and the acid in the water gradually eats away at the rock, widening the cracks into passageways and caverns. Underground streams form, which further widen the caverns, and over the years dripping water forms stalactites and stalagmites on the cave roofs and floors.

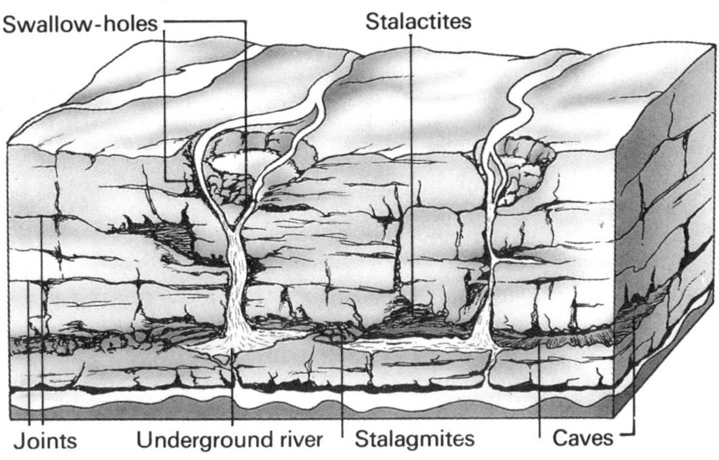

linnet *adj*. a small brownish bird of the finch family.
linoleum (*abbr*. **lino**) *n*. a floor covering.
linseed *n*. seed of flax.
lion *n*. a large member of the cat family.
lioness *n*. a female lion. **lionize** *vb*. treat as a celebrity.
lip *n*. 1. one of the top or bottom edges of the mouth. 2. the specially shaped part of a jug from which the liquid is poured.
liquid *n*. a substance like water that flows. *A liquid is not a gas or a solid. adj*. in a fluid state. **liquefy** *vb*. make or become liquid.
liquorice (*lik-er-iss*) *n*. a black sweet made from the root of the liquorice plant.
lisp *vb*. speak using a 'th' sound for 's'.
list 1. *n*. a number of names or things written down one above the other. *Did you put bread on the shopping list? vb*. enter on list. 2. leaning of ship to one side *vb*.
listen *vb*. hear something. *Listen to this*.
lit *vb*. past and past part. of **light**.
literate *adj*. able to read and write; educated.
literature *n*. books and writing, in general of a high quality.
litre (rhymes with *heater*) *n*. a measure of liquids; 1000 cubic centimetres.
litter *n*. 1. rubbish thrown away in a public place. *vb*. 2. all the newly born offspring of an animal. *Our cat had a litter of four kittens*.
little *adj*. not much; small or tiny.
liturgy *n*. the form of service or ritual of a church.
live (rhymes with *hive*) *adj*. living. **lively** *adj*. full of life and energy.
live (rhymes with *give*) *vb*. 1. exist; be alive. *He lived 100 years ago*. 2. inhabit. *They live in London*.
liver *n*. an organ of the body that does many jobs, including getting rid of things the body does not want and making things it needs.

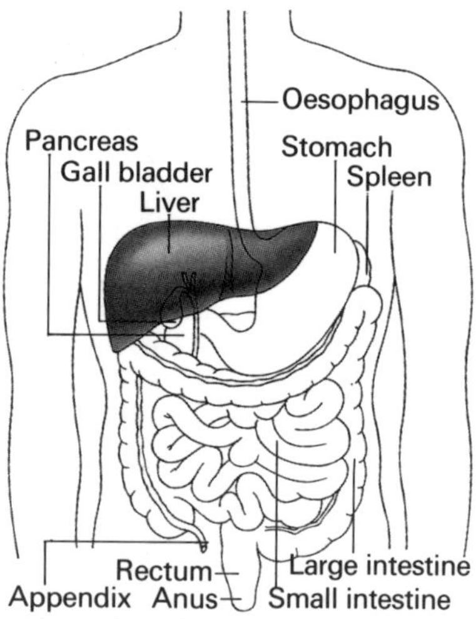

livery *n*. 1. distinctive uniform worn by servants of a great household or city company. 2. a stable for boarding or hiring horses.
livestock *n*. farm animals.
livid *adj*. 1. very angry. 2. discoloured, like a bruise.
living *adj*. alive.
living-room *n*. a sitting room; the main room in a house.

A llama.

lizard *n.* a four-legged reptile with a tail.
llama *n.* an animal of South America related to the camel family, but without a hump.
load (rhymes with *code*) 1. *n.* something that has to be carried. *She took a load of washing to the laundrette.* 2. *vb.* put something on to something. *They loaded the cart with hay.*
loaf 1. *n.* a complete piece of bread. *I bought two loaves from the baker.* 2. *vb.* laze about.
loafer *n.* 1. a lazy person, someone who loafs. 2. a flat casual shoe.
loam *n.* fertile, easily cultivated soil.
loan *n.* something that has been lent to you, usually money.
loathe (rhymes with *clothe*) *vb.* detest, dislike very much.
loathsome *adj.* causing loathing and disgust.
lob *vb.* toss a ball high into the air. *She lobbed the tennis ball over the net.*
lobby *n.* entrance hall to hotel, theatre etc. (especially USA).
lobelia *n.* a common garden plant with white, blue or red flowers.
lobster *n.* a shellfish with a hard shell and ten legs, two of which carry large claws.
local *adj.* belonging to a fairly small area. *This newspaper gives local news about our town.*
localize *vb.* restrict to a particular place.
locate *vb.* find exact position; establish in a particular place.
location *n.* the place where something is.
loch *n.* a Scottish lake.
lock 1. *vb.* fasten something. *n.* a fastening for a door or a box that needs a key to open it. 2. *n.* a piece of hair. 3. *n.* a section of a canal or river where the water levels can be changed by opening and shutting large gates.

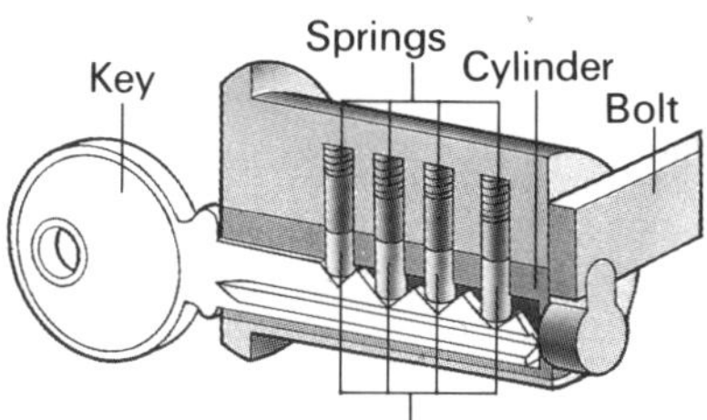

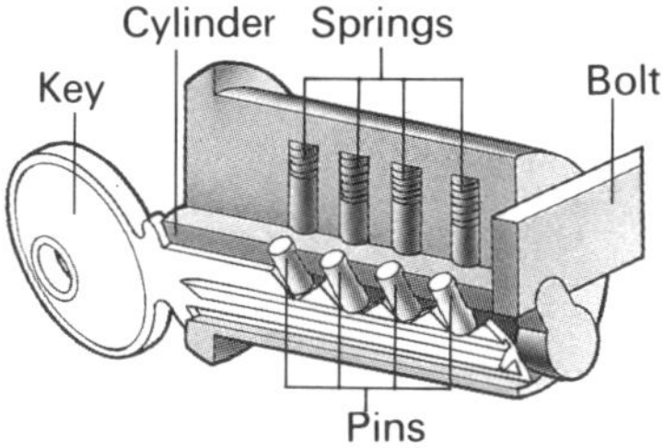

locker *n.* a cupboard that can be locked.
locket *n.* a small case worn on a chain around the neck. *A locket may contain a picture.*
locomotive *n.* a machine on wheels that pulls trains.
locust *n.* an insect like a grasshopper.
I long to see you.
longitude *n.* a distance measured in degrees east or west from a line on the map joining Greenwich and the North and South Poles.
loo *n.* (*casual*) lavatory.
look *vb.* use one's eyes to see something.

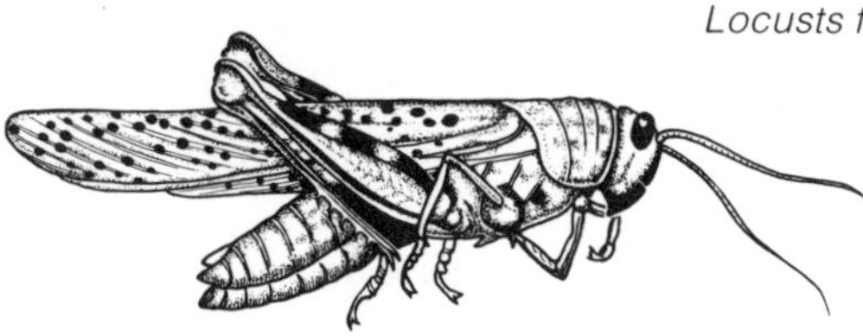
Locusts fly in huge swarms.

lodge 1. *n.* a small house at the gates of a large house. 2. *vb.* stay in someone's house and pay to stay there. 3. *n.* a beaver's home.
loft *n.* a room at the top of a house used for storing things; an attic.
log *n.* 1. a length of tree that has been cut down. 2. a written record of happenings, especially in a ship.
logic *n.* the science of or particular method of reasoning. **logical** *adj.* in accordance with the principles of logic.
loiter *vb.* go along very slowly; dawdle.
lollipop *n.* a sweet, often frozen, on a stick.
lonely *adj.* 1. without friends. 2. away from other people. *They had a lonely house on a moor.*
long 1. *adj.* in length. *How long is that table? adj.* of unusually great length. *He has very long legs.* 3. *vb.* wish for very much.
look after *vb.* take care of. *Can you look after our cat while we are away?*
look forward to *vb.* think with pleasure about something that is going to happen.
looking glass *n.* a mirror.
look into *vb.* investigate.
look out 1. *vb.* watch to see whether anyone is coming, or whether something will happen. 2. *n.* a sentry.
look up *vb.* search for a word or item in a dictionary, encyclopedia or other reference book. 2. improve. *The weather is looking up.*
look up to *vb.* admire someone. *I always looked up to my brother because he was so good at football.*
loom 1. *n.* a machine for weaving cloth. 2. *vb.* appear in a vague or misty way; get larger. *The house loomed through the fog.*
loop *n.* a circle or part circle of wire, string or other material.

loose (*loos*) *adj*. not tight or firm. *One of my teeth is loose.* **loosen** *vb*. make or become loose.
loot *n*. & *vb*. plunder.
lop *vb*. cut off the ends of (especially a tree).
lord *n*. a nobleman.
lorry *n*. a big, open vehicle that carries heavy loads.
lose (*looz*) *vb*. (past **lost**) 1. no longer to have. 2. go astray. 3. be beaten in a game.
lost *vb*. past part. of **lose**.
lotion (**low**-*shun*) *n*. a liquid applied to the skin for cosmetic or medicinal reasons.
loud *adj*. noisy; not quiet.
loudspeaker *n*. part of a radio or record player that makes electric waves into sound.
lough (*lock*) *n*. Irish word for lake.
lounge 1. *vb*. sit or stand in a lazy way. 2. *n*. a sitting-room.
louse *n*. (plural **lice**) a small blood-sucking insect that feeds on animals or humans.
love *vb*. & *n*. be very fond of someone or something.
lovely *adj*. attractive; pretty. *What a lovely room.*
low *adj*. not tall; near the ground. *A low table.*

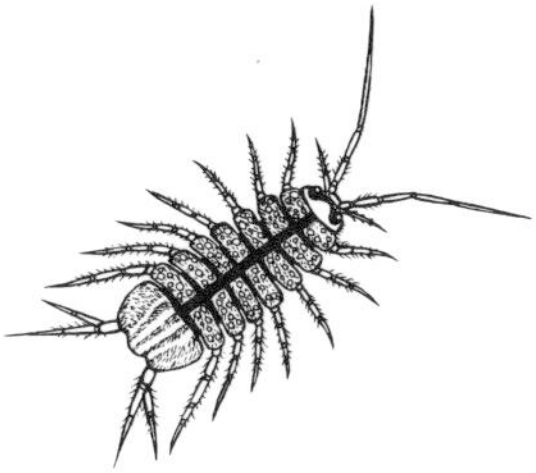

Tiny lice live on people and animals.

lower 1. *adj*. not as high as. 2. *vb*. make something less high.
loyal *adj*. true to others.
lubricate *vb*. use oil or grease to make a machine work smoothly by cutting down the friction between two surfaces.
lucid *adj*. clear, easy to understand.
luck *n*. chance; good fortune. *Wish me luck.*
lucky *adj*. fortunate. *How lucky you were passing by.*
ludo *n*. a game in which coloured counters are moved about a board according to the fall of a dice.
luggage *n*. the cases, bags and other containers that are taken on a journey.

Cloth has been woven on hand looms for thousands of years.

lugworm *n*. a large worm used by fishermen as bait.
lukewarm *adj*. tepid, slightly warm; half-hearted.
lullaby *n*. a song that is sung to send a baby to sleep. **lull** *vb*. send to sleep.
lumbago *n*. inflammation of the muscles of the back.
lumber *n*. rough timber.
lumberjack *n*. a person who cuts down trees, especially in North America.
lump *n*. a bump, a swelling.
lunacy *n*. foolishness; insanity. **lunatic** *n*. person who is insane.
lunar *adj*. of or about the Moon. *There will be a lunar eclipse this week*.

Lupin flowers.

lunch *n*. the midday meal (from **luncheon**, now rare). *vb*. eat lunch.
lung *n*. your body has two lungs inside your chest, forming a single organ by which you breathe.

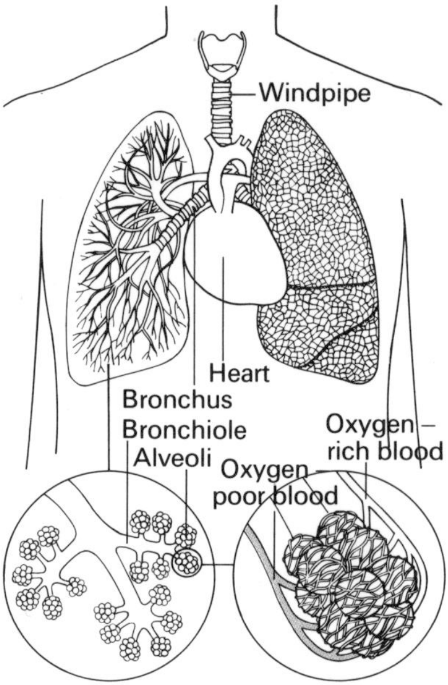

lunge *vb*. & *n*. thrust at or attack suddenly.
lupin *n*. plant with flowers on a long spike.
lurk *vb*. wait unseen. *Strange creatures lurk in these woods*.
lust *n*. great desire.
lute *n*. plucked string instrument similar to a guitar.
luxury *n*. an expensive thing that is not really needed. *Most people think that a fur coat is a luxury*. **luxurious** *adj*. very comfortable.
lynx *n*. a wild cat with a short tail and tufted ears.
lyre *n*. a harp-like instrument.

M

mace *n.* 1. symbolic staff of authority. 2. spice made from outer skin of nutmeg.
machete (*ma*-**chet**-*ee*) *n.* heavy knife used as a weapon in Central America.

macabre *adj.* horrifying, gruesome.
macaroni *n.* long tubes of flour paste that are cooked and eaten. *Macaroni and spaghetti are Italian dishes.*
macaroon *n.* sweet biscuit made of almonds.
macaw *n.* a large brightly coloured parrot found in the tropical rainforests of Central and South America. Many species have gaudy green, blue, red or yellow feathers.

machine *n.* a tool that has movable parts working together to do something.
machine gun *n.* a gun that can fire many bullets very quickly without being reloaded.
machinery *n.* machines; the moving parts of machines.
mackerel *n.* slender, streamlined fish with a wide-forked tail, found in all the world's seas.
mackintosh *n.* a waterproof coat.
mad *adj.* insane, crazy; angry. **madden** *vb.* irritate; make mad.
madam (**mad**-*um*) *n.* polite form of addressing a woman.
madame (*ma*-**darm**) *n.* the French for Mrs or madam.
made *vb.* past of **make.**
magazine *n.* 1. a paper-covered book of text and advertisements that comes out weekly or monthly. 2. the part of a gun that holds the bullets.

maggot *n.* larva, grub of a fly.
magic *n.* the belief that by doing or saying certain things, nature can be controlled and people can be influenced supernaturally. *adj.*
magician (*ma*-**ji**-*shun*) *n.* a person who does magic tricks.
magistrate *n.* a minor judge; a person who has the power to put the law into force.
magma *n.* molten rock which, when it solidifies, becomes igneous rock.
magnet *n.* a piece of iron or steel that can pull other pieces of iron and steel towards it. **magnetic** *adj.* acting like a magnet.

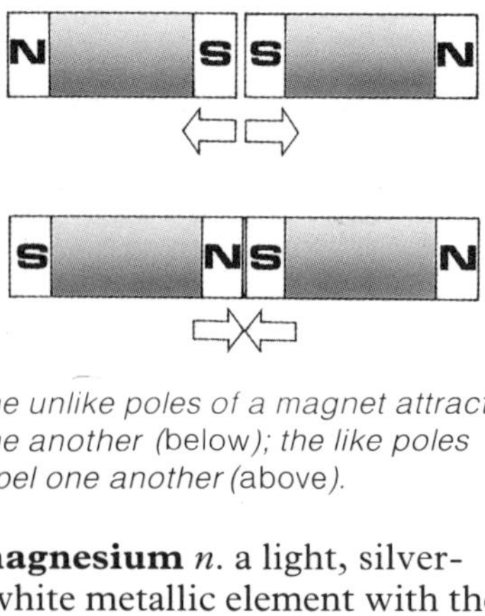

*The unlike poles of a magnet attract one another (*below*); the like poles repel one another (*above*).*

magnesium *n.* a light, silver-white metallic element with the chemical symbol Mg.
magnificent *adj.* marvellous; very impressive.
magnify *vb.* make something appear bigger. *If you look through a drop of water, it will magnify things.* **magnification** *n.*
magnifying glass *n.* a lens that magnifies things.
magnolia *n.* a tree or shrub

famous for its large, pale, fragrant flowers which bloom early in spring.
magpie *n.* black and white bird related to the crow.
Magyar *n.* & *adj.* language and person of Hungary.
mahogany *n.* a tall tree growing in tropical Africa and America the hard red wood of which is used for making furniture.
maid *n.* a girl; a female servant.
mail *n.* 1. letters and parcels sent by post. *vb.* send by post. 2. armour made of metal rings.
maim *n.* injure, cripple.
main *adj.* the most important; the largest. *The main road runs near our house.*
mainland *n.* principal or larger land mass, without nearby islands.
mainly *adv.* for the most part, chiefly.
maintain *vb.* 1. keep in good order. 2. support. 3. assert as true. 4. carry on.
maize *n.* a cereal crop, also called sweetcorn and Indian corn.
majesty *n.* having impressive or royal appearance; a title given

to kings and queens, who are addressed as 'Your Majesty'. **majestic** *adj*.

major 1. *n*. an army officer between captain and lieutenant colonel. 2. *adj*. important. *The scientist made a major new discovery*.

majority *n*. the greater part of a number. *The majority of the class voted to go swimming*.

make 1. *vb*. (past **made**) create or invent something; prepare; gain. 2. *n*. the maker's name. *What make is your car?*

make for *vb*. go towards.

make off *vb*. run away.

make out *vb*. understand.

make-shift *adj*. temporary substitute.

make-up *n*. the cosmetics (paints and powders) people put on their faces.

make up for *vb*. do something good after you have done something bad. *I was nasty to my sister, but I made up for it by helping her this afternoon.*

mal- *prefix* meaning bad or not, e.g. **malformed** *adj*. badly formed, **maltreat** *vb*. treat badly etc.

malaria *n*. a disease which occurs mostly in tropical and subtropical areas. It is transmitted from infected to healthy people by the female *Anopheles* mosquito.

male 1. *n*. & *adj*. (of) a boy or man 2. *n*. any creature of the sex that does not lay eggs or give birth.

mallet *n*. wooden hammer; implement for hitting croquet ball.

malt *n*. barley prepared for brewing.

mammal *n*. any of the animals of which the females feed their young with milk from their bodies.

mammoth *n*. a large animal like an elephant, but now extinct.

Mammoths died out after the Ice Ages.

man *n.* (plural **men**) a grown up male human; sometimes also used to mean all people, men and women. (**mankind**). *vb.* supply with men; guard.

manage *vb.* 1. take charge of some thing. *She manages a supermarket*. 2. succeed in doing something even if it is not easy. *I can just manage to keep up with you.*

manager *n.* a person whose job is to take charge of other people at work.

mane *n.* the long hair on the neck of a horse or lion.

manger *n.* a box for horses or cattle to eat from in a stable.

mania *n.* a mental illness; a craze.

manicure *n.* & *vb.* care of the hands and nails. **manicurist** *n.*

manifesto *n.* statement of policy.

mankind *n.* all people – men, women and children – everywhere.

manner *n.* the way a thing is done or happens. **manners** *pl. n.* how you behave towards others. *She has very good manners.*

manoeuvre (*man*-**oo**-*ver*) *n.* planned movement of troops, skilful plan. *vb.* guide, manipulate.

manor *n.* in the Middle Ages, a lord's house and the land he owned.

manse *n.* (Sc.) a vicarage.

mansion (**man**-*shun*) *n.* a large, grand house.

manslaughter *n.* killing a person without planning to do so.

manu- *prefix* meaning hand, e.g. **manuscript** written by hand.

manual 1. *adj.* of or done with the hands. *Has your car got manual or automatic gears?* 2. *n.* handbook, textbook.

manufacture *vb.* make things in a factory.

many *adj.* a lot; several; a large number. *A millipede has many legs.*

map *n.* & *vb.* a drawing of the Earth's surface or part of it, often showing things such as rivers, mountains, countries and towns; to make a map.

A map of the Earth.

maple *n.* a deciduous tree native to the northern hemisphere. In autumn, its leaves turn spectacular shades of yellow, orange and red. One species, the sugar maple, is tapped for its sweet syrup. The maple leaf is the emblem of Canada.

Maples have winged seeds which spiral away from the tree in autumn. This common maple is a sycamore.

marathon *n.* a long-distance race of 42.19 km (26 miles 385 yards). It has been run in the Olympic games since 1896.

marble *n.* 1. a hard stone that can be carved and polished. 2. a small glass or china ball used in games.

march *vb.* walk with a regular pace like a soldier; a piece of music to which people can march.

March *n.* the third month of the year.

mare *n.* a femal horse.

margarine *n.* a fat used instead of butter.

margin *n.* the blank space around the edge of a page of printing or writing; border.

marigold *n.* a garden plant belonging to the daisy family, with bright yellow or orange flowers.

marina *n.* a dock for yachts with every facility for a yachting holiday.

marine (*mareen*) *adj.* to do with the sea. *A whale is a marine animal. n.* a soldier serving on board ship.

mariner *n.* an old-fashioned word for a sailor.

marionette *n.* a puppet moved by strings.

Marionettes like this are often used in puppet shows.

mark 1. *n.* & *vb.* a spot or pattern on something. *There is a dirty mark on your shirt.* 2. *vb.* judge quality of and correct. *The teacher will mark our homework.* 3. *n.* unit of money in Germany.

market *n.* a group of open-air shops or stalls; anywhere that goods are sold. *vb.* sell goods in a market.

marmalade *n.* a jam made from oranges and lemons.

marquis, marquess (**mar**-*kwiss*) *n.* nobleman ranking below a duke but above an earl.

marriage (**mar**-*idge*) *n.* a wedding.

Marrows are related to pumpkins.

marrow *n.* 1. soft tissue containing blood vessels in the cavities of bones. 2. large fleshy vegetable of the gourd family.

marry *vb.* become husband and wife, unite in **marriage** (*n.*).

marsh *n.* low-lying, wet land.

marsupial *n.* one of a group of mammals in which the females carry their young in a pouch on their bodies, e.g. a kangaroo.

martial *adj.* warlike.

martin *n.* small bird related to the swallow.

martyr *n.* someone who suffers or dies for their beliefs. *There were many martyrs among the early Christians.*

marvellous *adj.* splendid; excellent. *What a marvellous view.* **marvel** *n.* wonderful happening. *vb.* be astonished.

Marxist *n.* & *adj.* of or a supporter of the thinking of Karl Marx (1818–83). **Marxism** *n.*

marzipan *n.* sweet paste made from almonds.

mascara *n.* colouring used on eye-lashes.

mascot *n.* a person, animal or thing thought to bring good luck. *The regiment's mascot is a goat.*

masculine *adj.* male, manly.

mash *vb.* & *n.* pulp.

mask *n.* a covering for the face; a disguise; face of a fox. *vb.* cover with a mask; disguise.

The kangaroo is a marsupial.

mason *n.* a person who works in stone; a builder.
Mass *n.* Eucharist or Holy Communion service.
mass *n.* 1. a large amount. 2. the amount of material in something.
massacre *n.* brutal killing of large numbers of people. *vb.*
massage *n.* treatment of body by rubbing and pressing with the hands. *vb.*
massive *adj.* huge and solid.
mast *n.* 1. the pole that holds a ship's sails. 2. fruit of beech and oak used as pig food.
master *n.* a man who has other people working for him; the captain of a merchant's ship; a male schoolteacher. **masterly** *adj.* skilful. **mastery** *n.* control, authority.
masterpiece *n.* a work of art done with great skill.
mastiff *n.* large thick-set dog.
mat *n.* a floor or table covering.
match 1. *n.* a game or contest. *A football match.* 2. *n.* a small thin piece of wood, with the end coated with an inflammable substance, used for lighting fires etc. 3. *n.* equal to. *The champion wrestler was more than a match for the challenger.* 4. *vb.* go with something. *Does this handbag match my shoes?*
mate *n.* 1. a companion; (usually of animals) each parent of a young one is the mate of the other parent. 2. *vb.* produce young. 3. an officer of a merchant ship, under a captain.
material *n.* any substance from which something is or can be made. *Bricks, wood and cement are all building materials.*
maternal *adj.* of or concerning a mother; motherly.
matriarch *n.* the mother or woman head of a family or tribe.
mathematics *pl. n.* (*abbrev.* **maths**) the science of numbers and shapes.
matinée (**mat**-*in-ay*) *n.* afternoon performance in a theatre.
matrimony *n.* marriage.
matron *n.* a person (usually female) in charge of the nurses in a hospital; a married woman of mature age (now old-fashioned).

The mastiff is one of the largest breeds of dog.

One of the most famous mazes in Britain is at Hampton Court Palace.

matt *adj*. dull, without shine. *matt paint*.

matter 1. *n*. the stuff of which things are made. 2. *vb*. be important. *We think it matters that you are late*.

mattress *n*. a cloth case stuffed with hair, feathers or other material, often supported with springs, and placed on top of a bed for lying on.

mature *adj*. ripe, completely developed. *vb*. **maturity** *n*.

mauve (rhymes with *rove*) *n*. & *adj*. a pale purple colour.

maximum *adj*. & *n*. the greatest possible. *The maximum speed limit in the USA is 55 miles per hour*.

may 1. *vb*. about something that could possibly happen. *I may be able to help you*. 2. *n*. Hawthorn blossom.

May *n*. the fifth month of the year.

maybe *adv*. perhaps.

mayonnaise *n*. a cold sauce made with oil, vinegar and eggs.

mayor (rhymes with *mare*) *n*. the head of a town or city.

maze *n*. network of winding paths from which it is difficult to find a way out.

meadow *n*. a grassy field, particularly near a river.

meagre (**me**-*gur*) *adj*. lean, poor.

meal *n*. 1. food eaten at a particular time, e.g. breakfast, lunch and dinner. *When do you have your main meal?* 2. grain ground to powder; flour.

mean 1. *vb*. stand for; show. *A red flag means danger*. 2. *vb*. plan to do something. *We always mean to be good, but often we aren't*. 3. *adj*. miserly; unwilling to share with others. 4. *adj*. average.

meander *vb*. wander about.

meaning *n*. what something means. *The English meaning of the French word 'chat' is 'cat'*.

means *pl. n*. 1. method by which something is done. 2. money.

meant *vb*. past of **mean**.

meanwhile *adv*. (or **meantime**) during the same time. *We were in the garden. Meanwhile the thieves entered the house by a front window*.

measles *n*. an infectious disease which cause red spots on the body and a fever.

measure *vb*. find the size or amount of a thing; *n*. something in which size, weight, length etc. can be stated. *A metre is a measure of length*.

measurement *n*. the size, height or amount of something.

meat *n*. the flesh of cows, sheep and other animals eaten as food.

mechanic *n.* a person who works with machines.
mechanical *adj.* to do with machines; worked by machinery.
mechanics *pl. n.* the branch of physics that deals with the effect of forces acting on bodies.

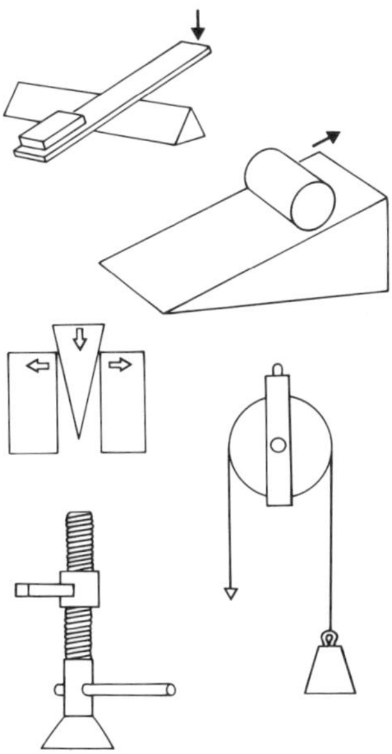

Simple machines like these were amongst man's earliest inventions. They make it easier for us to do work. When we operate them, we do a little work over a long distance so that the machines can do a lot of work over a short distance.

medal *n.* a flat piece of metal, often like a coin, with words or a picture on it, given as recognition for excellence or achievement.
meddle *vb.* interfere in.
medicine (**med**-*sin*) *n.* 1. the science of healing. 2. something taken to make you better when you are ill.
medieval (**med**-*ee*-**ee**-*val*) *adj.* of the Middle Ages.
mediocre (*meed-ee*-**oh**-*kur*) *adj.* average quality, second rate.
meditate *vb.* think deeply about. **meditation** *n.*
medium (**mee**-*dium*) *adj.* middle size. *The robber was of medium height with fair hair.*
medlar *n.* a low-growing, ornamental tree whose fruit is made into jelly.
meet *vb.* (past **met**) join or come face to face with someone. *When shall we meet again?*
meeting *n.* a coming together of two or more people.
megalith *n.* large prehistoric stone.

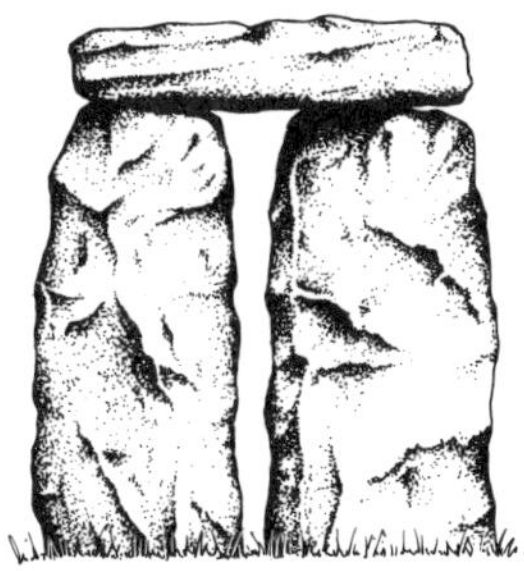

melancholy (**mel**-*an-kolee*) *adj.* sad, gloomy *n.*
mellow *adj.* soft and ripe. *vb.* soften (with age or experience).
melody *n.* tune; principal part in harmonized music. **melodic** *adj.*
melon *n.* a creeping or climbing plant grown in warm climates for its large juicy fruit.
melt *vb.* turn a solid into a liquid by heating it. *The ice cream melted in the sun.*

member *n.* 1. a person who belongs to a group or team of people. *Winston is a member of the football team.* 2. a limb, an arm or leg.
memory *n.* the ability to remember things; what is remembered. *I have a very clear memory of being in hospital.* **memorize** *vb.* learn by heart. **memorable** *adj.*
men *n.* plural of **man**.
menace *n.* & *vb.* threat(en).
menagerie *n.* collection of wild animals.
mend *vb.* & *n.* repair. *on the mend* getting better.
menorah *n.* the seven-branched candlestick used in Jewish worship. The seven branches are supposed to represent the Sun, Moon and five planets know to antiquity.

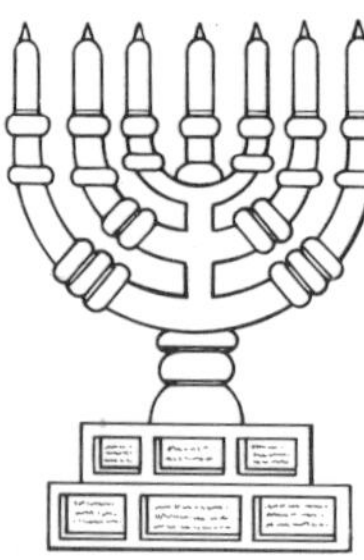

In Jewish households, the menorah is lit on the Sabbath.

menstruation *n.* the discharge of blood from the uterus.
mental *adj.* concerning the mind; (*casual*) daft.
mention *vb.* refer to, remark. *n.* brief note.
menu *n.* a list of the food you can have at a meal in a restaurant.
merchant *n.* a person who makes a living by buying and selling things.
mercury *n.* a heavy, silver-coloured liquid metal; quicksilver.
mercy *n.* readiness to forgive, compassion; a fortunate happening.
merge *vb.* blend, combine with. **merger** *n.*

Meridians are an aid to navigation.

meridian *n.* any line of longitude. The prime meridian (0° longitude) passes through Greenwich Observatory.
merit *vb.* deserve, be worthy of. *You merit full marks for your work.*
mermaid *n.* a legendary creature with a woman's body and a fish's tail.
merry *adj.* happy and cheerful.
merry-go-round *n.* a fairground machine with toy animals and vehicles that you ride on as it goes round.
mesmerize *vb.* hypnotize.
mess *n.* 1. untidiness and dirt. 2. a place where soldiers and sailors take their meals.

message *n.* a piece of information sent to somebody.
messenger *n.* a person who carries a message.
messrs (**mess**-*erz*) abbreviated plural of Mr used in the title of a company (*Messrs Jones, Smith & Sons*) or in a list of men's names.
met *vb.* past of **meet**.
metal *n.* any sort of material like iron, steel, tin, or copper.
metaphor *n.* word or phrase taken from one field of experience and used to say something in another field. e.g. *All the world's a stage, 'Did you land a job today?' 'No, not a bite'.*
meteor *n.* a small solid body that rushes from outer space into the Earth's atmosphere.
meteorite *n.* a meteor that reaches the Earth without burning up.
meteorology *n.* the study of the changing conditions in the atmosphere and the causes of weather.

As a meteor enters the Earth's atmosphere, friction heats it and makes it glow.

meter *n.* an instrument for measuring or recording quantities, speed, etc. *The gas meter shows how much gas we use in our house.*
method *n.* a way of doing something; a system.
metre (rhymes with *beater*) *n.* 1. a measure of length. *There are 100 centimetres in a metre.* 2. the rhythm of a line or verse.
metric *adj.* the system of measuring based on the metre, the kilogramme and the litre.
metropolis *n.* the capital or main city of a country or area.
mice *n.* plural of **mouse**.
micky *n.* (take the ---- out of) tease, annoy.
micro- *prefix* meaning small minute; a millionth part of, e.g. **microfilm, microwave**.
microbe *n.* a tiny creature that can be seen only through a microscope.
microphone *n.* an instrument that picks up sound waves and turns them into electric waves for broadcasting or recording.

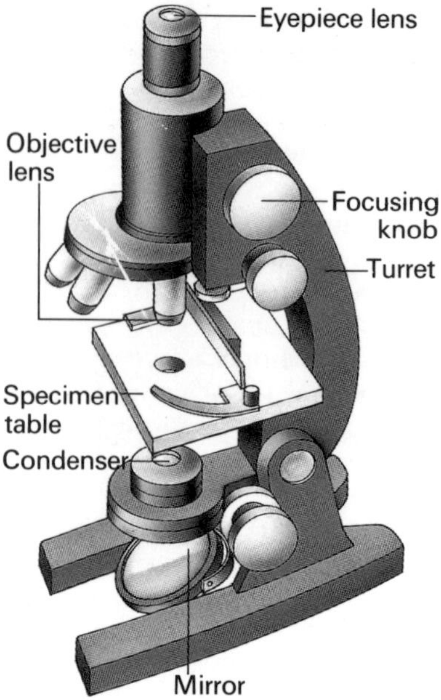

microscope *n.* an instrument for making very small things big enough to see; it magnifies them.
middle *n.* the centre part of something; a person's waist.
midge *n.* small insect; gnat.
midget *n.* a very small person.
midnight *n.* twelve o'clock at night.
midwife *n.* a person who helps at the birth of a child. **midwifery** *n.*
might 1. *vb.* past of **may**. *You might have told me earlier*. 2. *n.* power; strength.
mighty *adj.* very strong.
migraine *n.* a throbbing headache accompanied with a feeling of wanting to be sick.
migrate *vb.* move from one place to another to live, as birds do in the autumn and spring. **migration** *n.*
mild *adj.* soft, gentle; (of weather) quite warm.
mildew *n.* tiny fungus on plants or growing decaying matter.
mile *n.* a measure of distance; 1760 yards; 1.6 kilometres.
militant *adj.* aggressive, warlike.
military *adj.* to do with soldiers and war.
milk *n.* a food that all baby mammals live on. It comes from the breasts, or mammaries, of the baby's mother. The baby sucks the milk from its mother's nipple. *vb.* draw milk from.
mill *n.* 1. a factory. *A steel mill.* 2. a building or machine for grinding grain.
millennium *n.* a thousand years.
millepede *n.* see **millipede**.
millet *n.* important cereal crop, cultivated as a basic food in the drier regions of Africa and Asia – especially in India and China.
milligram (-me) *n.* a very small measure of weight; one thousandth of a gram(me).
millimetre *n.* a small measure of length, shortened to *mm.* (10 mm = 1 centimetre.
milliner *n.* person who sells women's hats.
million *n.* one thousand thousand (1,000,000).
millionaire *n.* a rich person who owns a million dollars or pounds.
millipede *n.* small worm-like animal with a tough outer skeleton, segmented body and two pairs of legs on almost every segment.
mime *vb.* & *n.* act without using words.

mimic *vb*. imitate someone. *n*. a person who mimics.

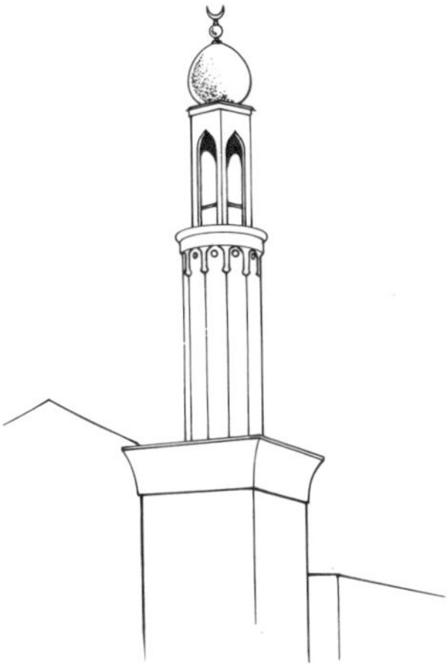

minaret *n*. a tall tower by a mosque from the top of which Muslims are called to pray.
mince *vb*. cut into tiny pieces. *n*. meat that is chopped up finely.
mincemeat *n*. mixture of dried fruits and fat that is cooked in pies and tarts, especially at Christmas.
mind 1. *n*. that part of a person which thinks, has ideas, and remembers; the brain. 2. *vb*. look after. *Our dog minds the house when we are out*. 3. *vb*. object to something. *I do mind being left alone*.
mine 1. *pron*. belonging to me. 2. *n*. a deep hole in the ground from which coal or other minerals are taken. *vb*. take minerals from the ground. **miner** *n*. a mine worker.
mineral *n*. a natural material that comes from the ground. Coal, salt and diamonds are all minerals. *adj*. of or belonging to minerals.
minestrone *n*. a thick soup of Italian origin containing pasta and vegetables.
mingle *vb*. blend, mix (with).
miniature *adj*. very small in scale.
minimize *vb*. reduce to smallest possible amount.
minimum *adj*. the least possible amount. *The minimum price of a seat was £2.*
minister *n*. 1. a clergyman; a parson. 2. the head of a government department. **ministry** *n*.
mink *n*. cat-sized amphibious mammal with a brown coat and bushy tail.

Mink are bred for their fur. In the wild, they are fierce hunters.

minnow *n*. small freshwater fish belonging to the carp family. Most species are under 15 cm (6 in) long.
minor *adj*. lesser or smaller; unimportant. *His car was involved in a minor accident, and was only slightly damaged.*
Minotaur *n*. a bull-headed monster of Greek myth, which lived in the labyrinth of Crete. It was killed by Theseus.
minstrel *n*. a singer or musician of the Middle Ages.
mint *n*. 1. a green, leafy herb used for flavouring food. 2. a place where coins are made.

minus *prep*. the mathematical sign '−' meaning take away or less than. (6−4=2).
minute (**min**-*it*) *n*. a short period of time. *There are 60 minutes in one hour.*
minute (*my*-**nute**) *adj*. very tiny.
miracle *n*. a remarkable event that cannot be explained.
mirage *n*. an image of something caused by atmospheric conditions, a visual illusion.
mire *n*. boggy ground.
mirror *n*. a shiny surface that reflects things; a looking-glass. *vb*. reflect as a mirror.
mis- *prefix* meaning bad or wrongly. The meaning of such words can be found by referring to the main word. e.g. **misbehave, misprint, mispronouce** etc.
mischief *n*. naughtiness. **mischievous** *adj*.
miser *n*. a person who loves money for itself; a mean person.
miserable *adj*. very unhappy.
misery *n*. great unhappiness.
miss *vb*. 1. fail to hit, catch or see something that you want to. *If Sally does not hurry she will miss the train.* 2. be sad because someone is not with you. *When mother was in hospital we all missed her very much.*
Miss *n*. the title that goes before the name of an umarried woman. *Miss Moody is the head teacher of our school.*
misshapen *adj*. out of shape, deformed.
missile *n*. an object or weapon that is thrown or sent through the air, often by a rocket.
missing *adj*. not present; not found.
mission (**mi**-*shun*) *n*. people sent to do some special work; an errand.
missionary *n*. a person who goes to another country to tell people about his or her religion and to do helpful work. *adj*.
mist *n*. a thin fog; water vapour in the air.
mistake *vb*. & *n*. (past **mistook**, past part; **mistaken**) something you do without intending to. *I made a mistake in my arithmetic.*

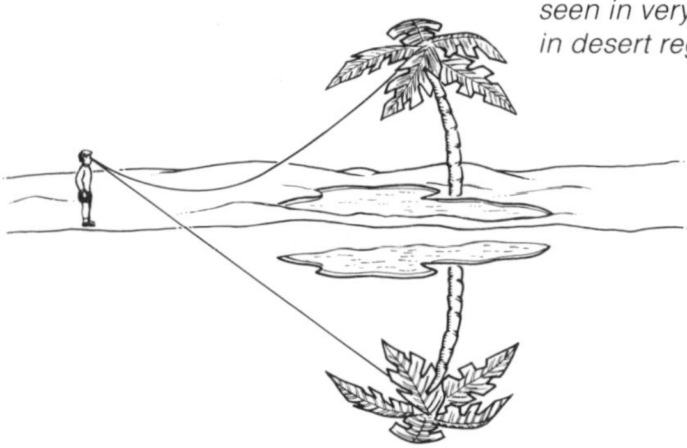

A mirage is caused by light rays that are bent by layers of air at different temperatures. Mirages are usually seen in very hot weather, especially in desert regions.

mistook *vb.* past of **mistake**.
mister *n.* (written as Mr) the title that goes before a man's surname. *Our teacher is called Mr Todd.*
mistletoe *n.* an evergreen plant with shiny white berries which grows as a parasite on trees, especially apple trees; widely used as a Christmas decoration.

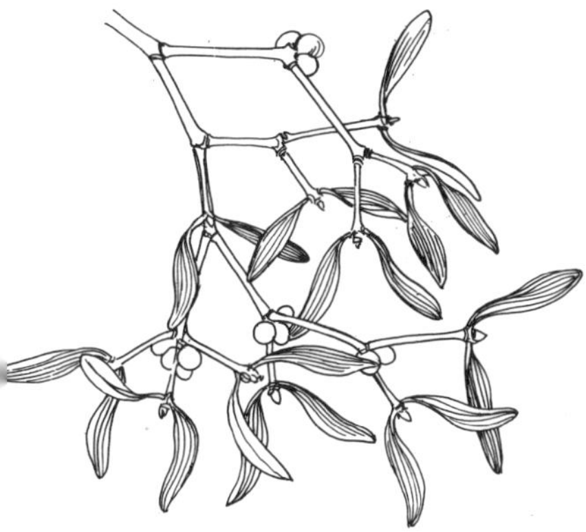

mistral *n.* a cold north wind which blows during the winter in southern France.
mitre *n.* 1. head-dress worn by a bishop. 2. special joint at corner of picture frame etc.
mitten *n.* a kind of glove with one place for four fingers together and another for the thumb separately.
mix *vb.* mingle or join together. **mixer** *n.* a machine for mixing things.
mixture *n.* anything made by mixing things together.
moan *vb.* groan, especially with pain or unhappiness; grumble. *vb.* a groan.
moat *n.* a deep ditch around a castle.
mob *n.* noisy crowd, gang. *vb.* crowd around.
mobile *adj.* moving, movable. **mobility** *n.*
moccasin *n.* shoe made of deerskin or soft leather.
mock *vb.* make fun of, scoff at. **mockery** *n.*
model *n.* 1. a copy of something usually smaller. *The architect showed us the model he had made of the new building. vb.* make a model. 2. someone who sits while an artist or photographer paints or photographs them; someone whose job is to wear and show new clothes.
moderate (**mod**-*er-at*) *adj.* not extreme; quite good.
modern *adj.* of present or recent times. *My mother likes living in a modern house, but my father would like to move to an older one.* **modernize** *vb.* (make modern) bring up to date.
modest *adj.* not boastful, not excessive. **modesty** *n.*
mohair *n.* hair of the Angora goat used to produce a soft, fluffy yarn.

A bishop wears a mitre as a sign of his rank.

moist *adj*. slightly wet.
moisten *vb*. to make moist.
moisture *n*.

mole *n*. 1. a small furry animal that lives in a tunnel underground. 2. a small dark mark on the skin. 3. a spy who has been accepted into another country's secret service, government, etc.

molecule *n*. a number of atoms joined together to form a stable and definite structure.

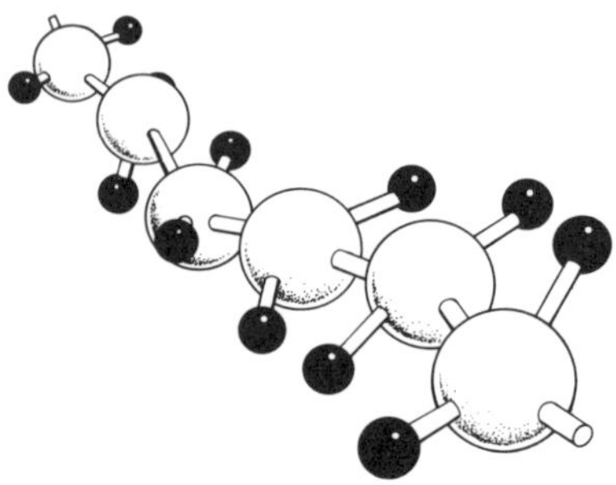

molest (*mo*-**lest**) *vb*. annoy, pester.

mollusc *n*. one of a group of animals with soft bodies. Most molluscs, like snails, limpets and oysters, have hard shells.

moment *n*. a very short period of time. *Wait a moment*.

monarch ('ch' like 'k') *n*. king or queen.

monastery *n*. a place where monks live and work.
monastic *adj*.

Monday *n*. the second day of the week, between Sunday and Tuesday, named after the Moon.

money *n*. coins or bank notes used to buy things.

mongoose *n*. (plural **mongooses**) a small mammal of Africa and southern Asia, a relative of the weasel. It has a low body, a bushy tail and short legs. An adult mongoose is about half a metre ($1\frac{1}{2}$ ft) long.

mongrel *n*. a dog that is a mixture of different types of dog. *adj*.

monk (rhymes with *bunk*) *n*. a member of a religious group of men who live, work and pray together in a monastery.

monkey (*munky*) *n*. a furry animal that belongs to the same group as apes and people. *Monkeys are primates*.

mono- *prefix* meaning one, alone, e.g. **monochrome** painting in one colour,

Mongooses are quick and fierce. They can catch and kill quite large snakes, as well as rats, mice and birds.

monosyllable word with one syllable, e.g. me.
monopoly *n.* sole control of something.
monorail *n.* a railway which runs on one rail.
monsieur (*mus*-**yer**) *n.* (plural **messieurs** pronounced **may**-*s-yer*) the French for mister or sir.
monsoon *n.* a wind system in which prevailing winds blow in opposite directions in winter and summer. In India, the well-known summer monsoon brings heavy rainfall.
monster *n.* a large and frightening creature. *adj.* very large.
month *n.* one of the twelve parts into which the year is divided. **monthly** *adv.* once a month.
monument *n.* something that reminds us of a person or event. *The column in Trafalgar Square in London is a monument to Nelson.*
mood *n.* the way you feel. **moody** *adj.* subject to changes of mood; gloomy.
Moon *n.* the Earth's only natural satellite and our nearest neighbour in space.
moonlight *n.* the light from the Moon.
moor 1. *n.* an open area often covered with heather. 2. *vb.* tie up a boat.
moose *adj.* a large, dark brown deer found in the cold northern forests of Alaska and Canada. The male carries huge, flattened antlers. Moose are similar to the European and Asian elk.
mop *n.* a bundle of fibres on the end of a stick, used for cleaning floors etc.
moped (*mo-ped*) *n.* a kind of small motor bicycle.
morale (*more*-**ahl**) *n.* condition of the state of mind and confidence of people. *Morale is high! We're going to win!*
morals 1. *pl. n.* rules or system of good behaviour. **moral** *adj.* concerned with what is right or wrong. 2. *n.* (**moral**) the point taught by a story. *He's in hospital. The moral of that is, don't ride on the wrong side of the road.*

The Moon is 384,400 km from the Earth. It has no light of its own, but reflects light from the Sun.

A motorcycle.

more *adj*. a greater amount or number. *May I have some more pudding?*

morning *n*. the early part of the day, between night and afternoon.

Morse code *n*. a system of sending messages with a series of dots and dashes for letters.

mortal *adj*. that which must die; causing death. *A mortal wound*. *n*. a human being.

mortar *n*. 1. a mixture of cement, lime, sand and water. *Mortar is used to hold bricks together*. 2. *n*. a vessel for grinding substances in (with a **pestle**).

mortgage (**more**-*gage*) *n*. transferring property as security for a sum of money borrowed. *vb*. make over by mortgage.

mosaic *n*. a picture made from little bits of coloured stone or glass set into cement. *adj*.

Moslem see **Muslim**.

mosque (*mosk*) *n*. a building in which Muslims worship.

mosquito (*mos*-**kee**-*to*) *n*. (plural **mosquitoes**) small insects that suck blood. Some mosquitoes carry malaria and other diseases.

moss *n*. small green or yellow plants that grow on damp surfaces in low, closely packed clusters.

most *adj*. *pron*. & *adv*. the greatest; the largest number.

motel *n*. a roadside hotel for people who arrive by car.

moth *n*. a winged insect, like a butterfly, that usually flies at night.

mother *n*. a female parent; a woman who has children. *vb*. act like a mother.

motion *n*. 1. moving. 2. gesture. 3. formal proposition.

motive *n*. something that causes a person to take action.

motor *n*. an engine that uses electricity, petrol or oil to produce a movement.

motor car *n*. a motor-driven,

usually four-wheeled, vehicle.
motor cycle *n*. a two-wheeled vehicle propelled by an internal combustion engine.
motorway *n*. a wide road with separate carriageways built for fast traffic.
mottled *adj*. marked with spots of different colours.
mould (rhymes with *sold*) 1. *n*. a hollow container. When a hot substance is poured into a mould it cools into the shape of the container. 2. *vb*. to shape. 3. *n*. a small fungus that grows on damp decaying things.
moult (rhymes with *colt*) *vb*. change old feathers or an old skin for new ones. *Snakes moult and have new skin under the old one*.
mount 1. *vb*. go up something; get on to a horse to ride it; rise sharply, rise in price. *The cost of sweets will mount after the budget*. 2. *n*. a horse; small hill.
mountain *n*. a very high hill.
mountaineer *n*. a person who climbs mountains.
mourning *n*. grief, great sadness after someone dies. **mourn** *vb*.
mouse *n*. (plural **mice**) a very small rodent.
moustache *n*. hair grown on the upper lip.
mousy *adj*. 1. looking like a mouse, i.e. having light brown or grey hair. 2. shy.
mouth *n*. the opening in the face into which you put food and through which your voice comes; that part of a river where it flows into the sea.
mouth-organ *n*. a small musical instrument played by blowing and sucking.
move *vb*. change position of something, residence etc.; stir; affect with emotion. *n*. e.g. a chess move. **movable** *adj*. that can be moved. **moving** *adj*. affecting the emotions. *It was a moving play*.
movement *n*. 1. activity; the act of moving. 2. section of a piece of music.
movie *n*. motion picture.
mow (rhymes with *toe*) *vb*. cut grass or hay. **mower** *n*. mowing machine.

Fold mountains are formed by rocks being forced together.

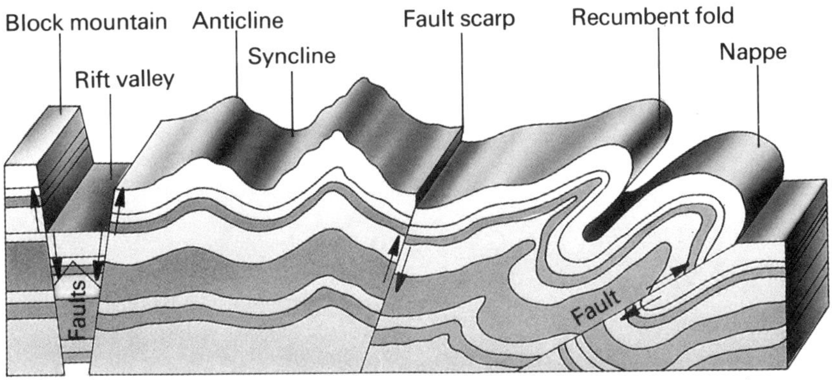

MP *abbrev*. Member of Parliament.
Mr *abbrev*. The polite title given to a man (short for Mister) e.g. *Mr Smith*.
Mrs *abbrev*. the title that goes before the surname of a married woman.
Ms (*miz*) *n*. a title used before the surname of a woman. It does not show whether or not she is married.

A mule is a cross between a donkey and a horse.

much *adj*. & *adv*. a great deal; a considerable amount. *You are making too much noise*.
muck *n*. manure, filth.
mud *n*. wet soft earth. **muddy** *adj*. covered with mud.
muddle *n*. an untidy mess. *vb*. confuse.
muesli (**mooz**-*lee*) *n*. a mixture of cereal, nuts and dried fruit etc.
muezzin *n*. person in a mosque who calls people to prayer from a minaret.
mug 1. *n*. a tall kind of cup without a saucer. 2. *n*. a fool. 3. *vb*. attack someone from behind and steal their money. *n*. mugger.
mugger *n*. someone who attacks and robs people in a public place.
muff *n*. a cylindrical object made of fur or fabric, with a hole in the centre. Once carried by women to keep their hands warm.
muffin *n*. a round, flat bun made with flour and yeast, which is eaten toasted, split and buttered.
muffle *vb*. to wrap up for warmth or to deaden sound.
mulberry *n*. a tree with juicy purple or white fruit. Its leaves are used for feeding silk worms.
mule *n*. 1. a horse-like animal that is the foal of a male ass and a female horse or pony (a mare). 2. kind of slipper without a back.
multi- *prefix* meaning many, e.g. **multilateral** many sided.
multiply *vb*. make something a number of times bigger. *When you multiply by 3, the answer is 3 times bigger*. **multiplication** *n*.
mumble *vb*. mutter; talk indistinctly.
mummy *n*. the preserved body of a human or animal.
mumps *n*. an illness that makes the neck and sides of the face swell.
mural *n*. a picture painted on a wall.
murder *n*. & *vb*. criminal killing of someone. **murderer, murderess.**
murmur *vb*. & *n*. make a low sound; mutter. *All he could hear*

was the gentle murmur of the river.

muscle (**mus**-*sel*) *n.* one of the fleshy parts of the body that make you move. *You make movement by tightening the right muscles.* **muscular** *adj.*

museum (*mu-zee-um*) *n.* a building where interesting things from other times and places are kept and shown to the public.

mushroom *n.* a kind of fungus that is safe to eat.

music *n.* the sound made by someone who sings or who plays a musical instrument. **musical** *adj.* **musical** *n.* a play or film in which music is an essential part.

musician (*mu*-**zish**-*un*) *n.* a person who makes music.

musk *n.* a strongly scented substance found in the glands of some male animals. The musk of the musk deer is used as a basis for perfumes.

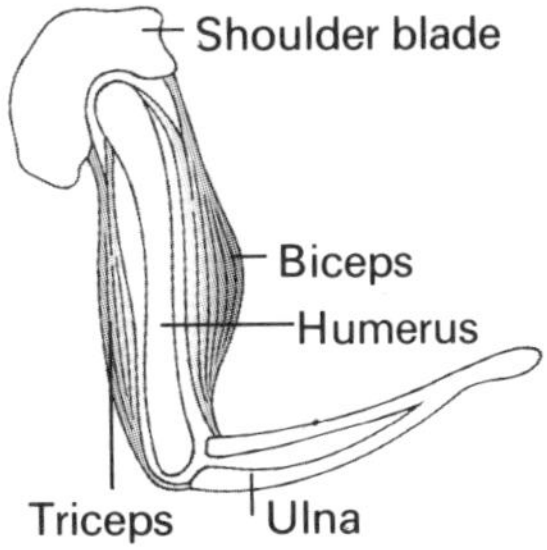

Bicep muscle contracts, elbow bends

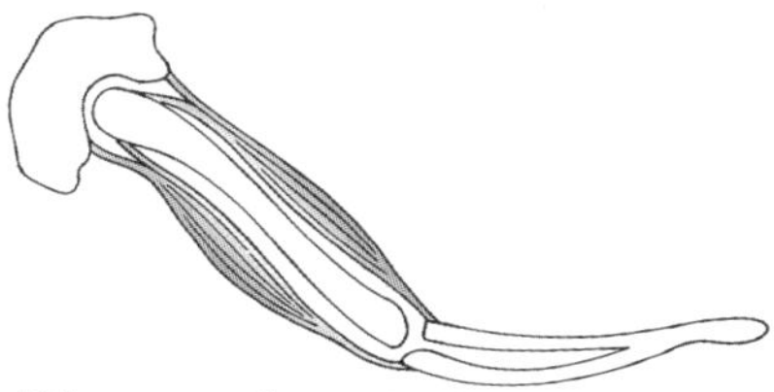
Tricep muscle contracts, arm straightens

To bend your forearm, the biceps muscles contract.

Some musical instruments.

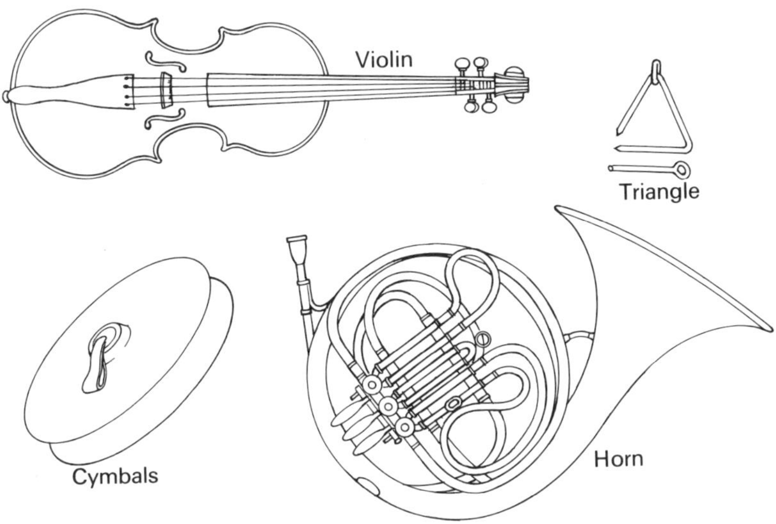

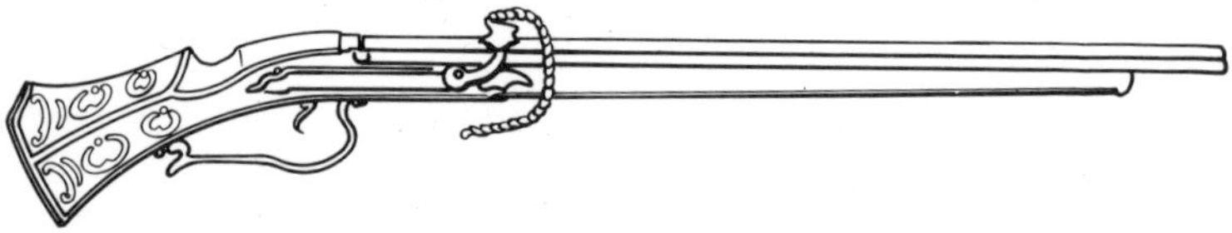

The heavy musket was a military weapon used by infantry soldiers before the rifle.

musket *n.* a firearm, in use from about 1540 to about 1840. It was muzzle-loading and smooth-bore. Matchlocks, wheellocks and flintlocks were all different versions of it, as the firing mechanism was improved.
Muslim *n.* a follower of the Islamic religion.
muslin *n.* a fine cotton cloth.
mussel *n.* a small mollusc found mainly in the sea.
must *auxiliary verb* (a verb which goes with and helps another verb). expressing command. *You must not walk on the grass.* expressing obligation. *I must finish this letter today*. expressing a result or deduction. *She left two hours ago. She must be nearly home by now*. expressing the obvious. *You must have heard of Henry VIII.*
mustang *n.* the wild horse of North America.
mustard *n.* a hot-tasting condiment made from the mustard plant and used to flavour food; dark yellow colour.
muster *vb.* collect together (originally used of soldiers).
mute *adj.* 1. silent. 2. dumb; unable to speak. *n.* someone who cannot speak.
mutilate *vb.* injure, damage, disfigure.
mutiny *n.* uprising, revolt, especially by members of armed forces.
mutter *vb.* speak in a low tone, under your breath; murmur.
mutton *n.* the meat of a sheep.
muzzle *n.* 1. open end of a gun barrel. 2. animal's snout. 3. a device put over an animal's mouth and nose to stop it biting. *vb.*
mystery *n.* something that is difficult to explain. **mysterious** *adj.*

Muzzles are put on greyhounds when they are racing to stop them biting the other dogs in the race.

mystify *vb.* bewilder.
myth *n.* an old story about imaginary people.
mythology *n.* the study of myths; a collection of myths.
myxomatosis *n.* a disease of rabbits.

N

nag 1. a horse, usually small and of poor quality. 2. *vb.* worry and find fault with constantly; scold. **nagging** *adj.*

nail *n.* 1. a thin piece of metal with a point at one end and a flat head at the other, used to fasten things together. *vb.* fasten with nails. 2. the hard layer over the outer tip of a finger or toe.

naked *adj.* bare, without any clothes on; unprotected, unaided (eye).

name *n.* the word which we use for a person, animal or thing. *vb.* give a name to.

namely *adv.* that is to say.

namesake *n.* a person of the same name.

nanny *n.* a child's nurse.

nanny-goat *n.* a female goat.

Like the horns of animals, nails are made of hard skin.

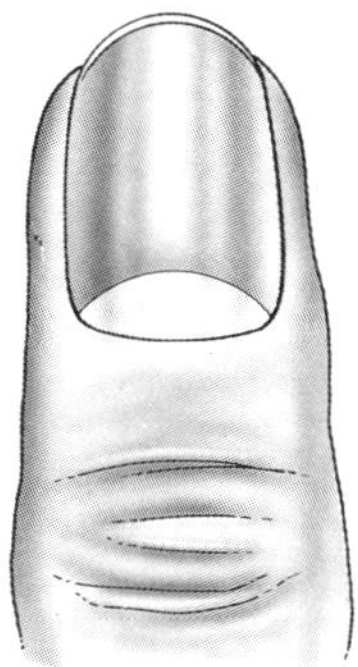

nap *n.* & *vb.* (take) a short sleep.

naphtha *n.* a highly inflammable oil.

napkin *n.* a cloth for wiping fingers and lips and for protecting clothes at meals.

nappy *n.* a cloth used like pants for a baby.

narcissus *n.* plant similar to a daffodil; name of a mythological Greek youth who fell in love with his own reflected image and was turned into a flower.

The narcissus blooms in spring. Its flowers are usually yellow or white.

narrate (*na*-**rate**) *vb.* relate, give an account of. **narrative** *n.* story. **narrator** *n.* person who tells a story.

narrow *adj.* not wide, small in width; intolerant (narrow-minded).

narwhal *n.* a small whale, about 5 metres (17 ft) long, found in the Arctic Ocean. Narwhals swim together in great schools and feed mainly on cuttlefish and squid.

nasal *adj*. of the nose.
nasturtium (na-**stir**-*shum*) *n*. garden climbing plant with orange or yellow flowers.
nasty *adj*. unpleasant; not nice; spiteful.
natal *adj*. of one's birth.
nation (**nay**-*shun*) *n*. a country and the people who live in it.
national (**nash**-*unal*) *adj*. belonging to one country. *The national flag of the United States is the Stars and Stripes.* **nationality** *n*. *He has British nationality.*
national anthem *n*. official hymn or song of a nation.
nationalist *n*. a person who wants independence for his or her country or province.
nationalize *vb*. transfer industry etc. from private ownership to control by the state.
national parks *pl. n*. special areas of land that are set aside and protected by governments.
native *n*. a person who was born in a particular place.
nativity *n*. being born; a birthday. *A nativity play is about the birth of Jesus.*
natterjack *n*. a small European toad with a yellow stripe down its back. It runs rather than hops like most toads.
natural *adj*. made by nature, not by people or machines.
natural gas *n*. a gas which occurs naturally underground and does not have to be manufactured.
naturalist *n*. student of nature.
naturally *adv*. of course; as might be expected; without putting on airs; plain.
nature *n*. 1. the whole universe and all its life. *Nature includes everything that is not made by people or machines.* 2. essential character or quality of a person. *It was not in her nature to be unkind.*
naught *n*. nothing.
naughty *adj*. badly-behaved, wicked (usually used of children).
nausea (**naw**-*zee-ah*) *n*. feeling like being sick; extreme disgust.

Natural gas is found deep underground and below the sea bed. The gas, which is mostly methane, comes from decayed plants and animals buried between layers of rock.

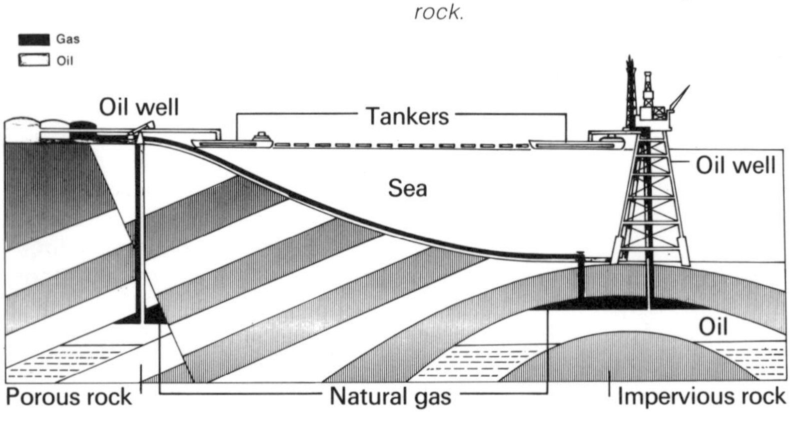

nauseate *vb.* to make sick, disgust.

nautical *adj.* concerned with ships, sailors and navigation.

nautilus *n.* a sea animal with a soft body inside a hard, spiral shell. The shell is lined with a shiny substance called mother of pearl.

nave *n.* the main part of the church from the front porch to the altar.

navel *n.* the 'belly button', a depression in the stomach left after the umbilical cord is cut.

navigate *vb.* find the way for a ship or aircraft.

navigation *n.* working out the correct route for a ship, aircraft etc.

navy *n.* a country's warships and all the people who sail in them. **naval** *adj.* concerning the navy and ships.

near *adv.* & *prep.* close at hand. *Tom was standing near the door.*

nearly *adv.* almost. *You nearly missed the bus.*

neat *adj.* tidy, everything in the right place.

nebula *n.* a bright cloud of dust or gas in outer space.

necessary *adv.* that which has to be done. *It is necessary to have a licence to drive a car.* **necessity** *n.* something that is needed, indispensable thing.

neck *n.* the narrow part of the body between the head and shoulders.

necklace (**neck**-*less*) *n.* a string of beads or other ornaments worn around the neck.

nectar *n.* a sweet liquid in flowers that is collected by bees.

nectarine *n.* a type of peach. Nectarines taste like peaches but they are smaller and have a smooth skin instead of a fuzzy one.

need *vb.* require; want something urgently. *She's been working very hard and needs a holiday. n.* a want or requirement.

needle *n.* 1. a pointed instrument used for sewing or knitting. 2. a pointer in a meter or a compass. 3. leaf of fir or pine.

needlework *n.* sewing, embroidery, etc.
needy *adj.* poor, without money.
negative 1. *adj.* expressing denial or refusal. *He gave a negative answer by which he means no.* the opposite of positive. 2. *n.* photographic image in which light areas are dark and dark areas are light.
neglect *vb.* give little care to. *If you neglect your garden, it will become full of weeds.* **negligence** *n.*
negotiate *vb.* discuss so as to reach an agreement. *The union is negotiating with the management over new working hours.* deal in. **negotiation** *n.*
Negress *n.* a Negro woman or girl.
Negro *n.* a person who belongs to the black-skinned people of Africa or originating from there.
neigh *n.* & *vb.* a noise made by a horse.
neighbour (**nay**-*ber*) *n.* someone who lives near you.
neighbourhood *n.* the area around the place where you live. **neighbourly** *adj.* like a good neighbour, friendly.
neither *adj.* & *pron.* not one nor the other.
neolithic *adj.* of the last part of the Stone Age, when men were beginning to cultivate the land and domesticate animals.
neon *n.* a colourless gas used in light tubes (symbol Ne).
nephew *n.* the son of your brother or sister.
nereid *n.* a sea nymph in Greek mythology.
nerve *n.* 1. a fibre that carries feelings and messages between the body and the brain. 2. boldness and self-assurance.
nervous *adj.* easily frightened, excitable, tense; also **nervy**.
nest *n.* a home a bird or other animal makes out of twigs, grass and feathers etc, generally as a shelter for its young. *vb.* make or have a nest.
nestle *vb.* to settle down comfortably; snuggle up to someone or something.
nestling *n.* a bird too young to leave the nest.
net *n.* 1. a material made of loosely woven string, thread or wire, so there are many holes between the threads. *vb.* catch or cover with a net. 2. *adj.* the price of something after discount, postal charges etc. have been taken off. Similarly for net weight.
netball *n.* a team game in which a ball is thrown into a net.
nether *adj.* lower.
Netherlands *n.* another name for Holland. In history, used to describe the Low Countries (Holland and Belgium).
netsuke (**net**-*ski*) *n.* carved Japanese ornaments.

The South American oven bird builds a mud nest shaped like an old-fashioned oven.

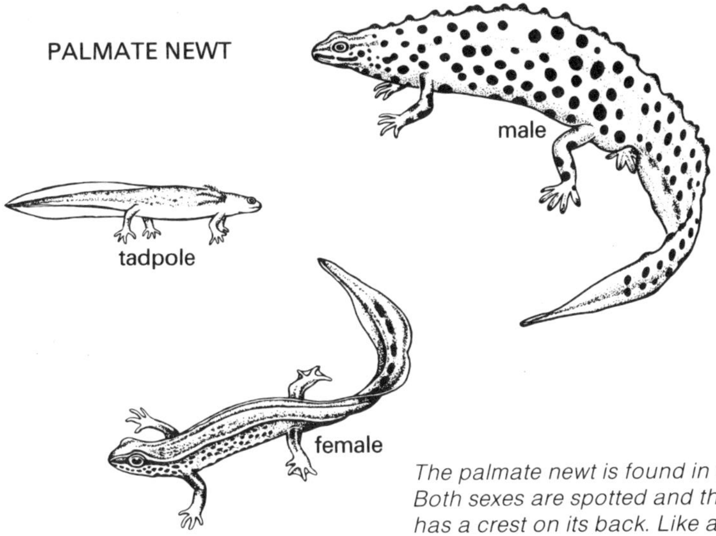

The palmate newt is found in Europe. Both sexes are spotted and the male has a crest on its back. Like all amphibians, newts must return to the water to breed.

nettle 1. *n.* a common weed with stinging hairs on its leaves. 2. *vb.* irritate, provoke.
neural *adj.* of the nerves.
neuter (*new-ter*) *adj.* neither male nor female.
neutral *adj.* not taking sides, especially in a war or dispute; vague (of colours etc.).
neutron *n.* an electrically neutral atomic particle.
never *adv.* not ever; at no time. *I have never seen him before.*
new *adj.* made or used for the first time; not old.
Newfoundland *n.* large breed of dog, a good swimmer with a long, thick coat.
news *n.* recent or up-to-date information; a programme about recent events on TV or radio; the contents of a newspaper.
newspaper *n.* a set of printed sheets of paper containing news, usually published either daily or weekly.
newt *n.* a lizard-like amphibian.
next 1. *adj.* nearby. *They live next door to us.* 2. *adv.* following. *What would you like to do next?*
nib *n.* the point of a pen.
nibble *vb.* eat in very small bites. *n.* a small bite.
nice *adj.* good or pleasant. *Have a nice time.*
nick 1. *n.* notch 2. *adv.* only just (of time). *In the nick of time.* 3. *vb.* (*slang*) steal. 4. *n.* (*slang*) health. *In good nick.* 5. *n.* prison. *He is doing time in nick.*
nickel 1. *n.* a tough, hard, silvery-white metal element (symbol Ni) widely used in the form of plating and in alloys. It is electroplated on to metals such as steel to protect them from corrosion, and is added, with chromium, to steel to make it stainless. 2. *n.* a US coin worth five cents.

nickname *n.* an extra name given to someone, usually as a joke. *We call Mr Baker by his nickname, Floury.*
niece (rhymes with *fleece*) *n.* the daughter of your brother or sister.
night *n.* the time between evening and morning, when it is dark. **nightly** *adj.* happening every night.

nightingale *n.* a bird famous for its beautiful song which is usually heard in the late evening or early morning.

The Norse people came from Norway. They sailed to many lands in their longboats.

nightmare *n.* a frightening dream.
nil *n.* nothing, zero, nought.
nimble *adj.* quick moving; agile.
nip *vb.* pinch like a crab.
nit *n.* the egg of the louse found in the hair.
nitrogen *n.* a colourless, tasteless gas. It is an element with the symbol N.
noble *adj.* of high rank or birth; of high character or ideals. *n.* Also **nobleman** *n.* **noblewoman** *n.*
nobody *n.* no one; no person. *There's nobody here.*
nocturnal *adj.* belong to, or active in, the night.
nod *vb.* & *n.* bow the head slightly; be drowsy.
noise *n.* a sound (usually loud). *Don't make so much noise.* **noisy** *adj.* making a lot of noise.
nomad *n.* a member of a group of people who wander from place to place.
non- *prefix* meaning not. The sense of words with the prefix

Notes in music, like these crotchets (single notes) and quavers (double notes), are played from a music score.

should be clear when the meaning of the main word is known. e.g. **non-smoker** a person who does not smoke, **non-stop** without stopping, etc.

nonsense *n*. foolish talk or behaviour.

noon *n*. midday; twelve o'clock in the daytime.

noose *n*. a loop of rope. *The noose becomes tighter when one end of the rope is pulled. vb.* catch with a noose.

nor *conj*. and not, not either.

Nordic *adj*. of or relating to tall, blond Germanic people of northern Europe.

norm *n*. standard of quality, etc.

normal *adj*. usual, as expected. *The normal buses will run during the holiday*.

Norse *n*. & adj. (language) of ancient Scandinavia, especially Norway.

north *n*. one of the points of the compass. *When you face the sunrise, north is on your left*.

nose *n*. the organ in the middle of the face used by people and many animals for breathing and smelling.

nostalgia *n*. homesickness; a wish to return to some past period.

nostril *n*. either of the openings in the nose through which you breathe and smell.

nosy *adj*. inquisitive.

not *adv*. a word that gives a negative statement. *I do not know what you are talking about*.

note 1. *vb*. write down a few words to remind yourself or someone else about something. Notebook. 2. *n*. a short letter. 3. *n*. a single musical sound. *Catherine played one note on the piano*. 4. *n*. paper money.

noted *adj*. famous, well known *for*.

nothing *n*. not anything. *Have you nothing to say?*

notice (**no**-*tiss*) 1. *n*. something written down or shown to people to tell them something. *The notice on the door said 'KEEP OUT'*. 2. *vb*. see something. *I noticed that she had a new hat*.

notify *vb*. inform, make known. **notification** *n*.

nougat (**noo**-*ga*) *n*. sweet made from nuts, sugar and egg whites.

nought (*naut*) *n*. nothing, zero, the figure 0.

noun *n*. the name of a person, place or thing. *John, Paris and cat are all nouns*.

novel 1. *n.* a long written story. **novelist** *n.* writer of novels. 2. *adj.* new, strange, unknown.
novella *n.* a short novel.
novelty *n.* 1. a new experience. *Riding a motorbike was a novelty for me.* 2. a cheap trinket.
November *n.* the eleventh month of the year.
novice (**nov**-*iss*) *n.* beginner; a person who enters a convent or monastery on a trial basis.
now *adv.* at the present time. *You may go home now.*
nowadays *adv.* at the present time.
nowhere *adv.* not anywhere.
nozzle *n.* spout of a waterhose etc.
nuclear *adj.* 1. to do with atomic energy. *When the nucleus of an atom is split it produces nuclear energy.* 2. (in other sciences) to do with the central parts of larger things.
nucleus *n.* a central part of something, such as an atom or a cell (in biology).
nude *adj.* naked; bare; having no clothes.
nudge *vb.* & *n.* (a) push gently with the elbow to attract attention.
nugget *n.* solid lump, especially of precious metal, e.g. gold.
nuisance *n.* something or somebody that causes trouble.
numb (rhymes with *gum*) *adj.* not able to feel. *vb.* make numb.
number *n.* 1. a word or figure showing how many. *5, 37 and 6 are all numbers.* 2. a quantity or amount. *There were a large number of books left on the shelf.*
numerous *adj.* great numbers of, many.
numismatic *adj.* to do with coins and medals.
nun *n.* a woman who has taken vows to live a religious life.
nurse *n.* a person who is trained to look after people who are ill, very young or very old. *vb.* act as a nurse; cherish.
nursery *n.* 1. a room for a baby or small child. *A nursery school is for very young children.* 2. a place where young plants are grown for sale.
nut *n.* 1. the fruit of certain plants with a hard shell. 2. a piece of metal with a hole in the centre that screws on to a bolt to fasten it.

The nutmeg is grated before it is used in cooking.

nutmeg *n.* the hard seed of a tropical fruit used as a spice; another spice, mace, comes from the outer part of the nutmeg fruit.
nylon *n.* an artificial fibre.
nymph *n.* 1. minor goddess of nature in ancient mythology. 2. larva of certain insects such as dragonflies.

O

oak *n.* a large tree on which acorns grow.

oar (rhymes with *sore*) *n.* a pole with a flat end for making a rowing boat move through water. *Most rowing boats have two oars.*

oasis (*o*-**ay**-*sis*) *n.* a fertile place in the desert.

oast *n.* kiln for drying hops.

oats *pl. n.* grain from a cereal. *Ground oats are called oatmeal and are used to make porridge.*

obedient *adj.* doing what you are told. *Our dog was very naughty as a puppy, but now he is quite obedient.*

obelisk *n.* a stone monument, in the shape of a tall pillar: four-sided narrowing upwards, and topped by a small pyramid shape. *Cleopatra's Needle in London is an example of an obelisk.*

obey (*o*-**bay**) *vb.* do what you are told.

obituary *n.* an announcement of a person's death.

object (**ob**-*ject*) 1. *n.* anything that can be touched or seen. 2. *vb.* (*ob*-**ject**) say that you do not agree with something. *She objected to the way the people were chosen.* **objection** *n.* expression of disapproval. **objectionable** *adj.* disagreeable.

oblige *vb.* 1. make someone do something. 2. do a favour. 3. be bound to someone by gratitude. **obligation** *n.* duty.

oblique *adj.* slanting; roundabout; indirect.

obliterate *vb.* destroy completely. *The bombs obliterated the centre of the city.* **obliteration** *n.*

oblong *n.* a rectangle; a flat figure with two parallel pairs of straight sides, two longer than the others, and four right angles.

oboe *n.* a musical instrument made of wood and played by blowing.

obscure *adj.* dim, vague, indistinct. *vb.* hide. *The tree is obscuring the tower.*

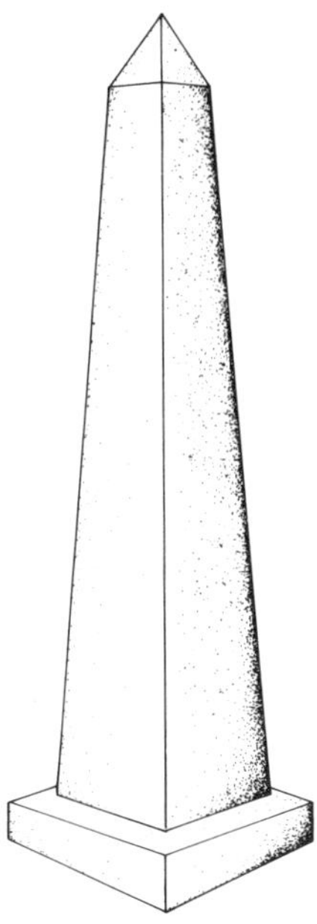

Stone obelisks were first erected by the ancient Egyptians.

About 70 per cent of the Earth's surface is covered by the oceans.

The largest ocean is the Pacific.

observatory *n.* a place from which observations are made, usually of heavenly bodies.
observe *vb.* notice; watch carefully; follow orders, instructions. **observation** *n.* observing; comment.
obsession *n.* an idea which takes control of a person to an unreasonable degree.
obsolete *adj.* no longer used, discarded.
obstacle *n.* something that gets in the way; a hindrance.
obstinate *adj.* not easily made to agree to do something. *A donkey can be very obstinate if it does not want to work.*
obstreperous *adj.* unruly and noisy; hard to control.
obstruct *vb.* block; get in the way. **obstruction** *n.*
obtain *vb.* get possession of something.
obtuse *adj.* 1. an angle which is more than one right angle and less than two right angles. 2. stupid and slow to understand.
obverse *n.* front surface of a coin or medal bearing the head ('heads') or main design.
obvious *adj.* easily seen or understood. *The solution is not obvious to me.*
occasion *n.* a special time or event. **occasional** *adj.*
occident *n.* the west or western part of the world. **occidental** *adj.*
occult *adj.* secret and mysterious; not known to most people.
occupation *n.* what you do or are doing; your job.
occupy *vb.* live in or be in. *Sam will occupy the second floor of the building*. **occupant** *n.* person living in a property.
occur *vb.* (past **occurred**) happen; take place. **occurrence** *n.* happening; incident.
ocean (**o**-*shun*) *n.* one of the great bodies of sea water that surround the continents.
o'clock *n.* the hour of the day. *We start school at 9 o'clock.*
octagon *n.* flat figure with eight equal sides. **octagonal** *adj.*
octave *n.* (in music) eight notes of a scale (e.g. ***C, D, E, F, G, A, B, C***).
October *n.* the tenth month of the year.

octopus *n.* a sea animal with a soft body and eight arms.

odd *adj.* 1. peculiar, strange. 2. a number that cannot be divided exactly by two. *3, 27 and 101 are odd numbers.*

oddments *n. pl.* odds and ends; scraps; bits and pieces.

odour *n.* smell.

off *prep.* from; away from. *Stephen fell off his bicycle.*

offend *vb.* annoy, displease. *I am sorry if I have offended you.* **offence** *n.*

offer *vb.* 1. say that you will do something for someone. *I thanked him for offering to help me clean the room.* 2. hold out something to someone. *Sean offered me a bag of sweets. n.* a price proposed.

office *n.* a place where people work whose business needs writing and recording.

officer *n.* a senior person in the army, air force or navy; president or treasurer etc. of a society.

offspring *n.* the child or children of a family; young animals.

often *adv.* many times; frequently.

ogre (**o**-*ger*) *n.* a cruel giant in stories.

How oil is refined.

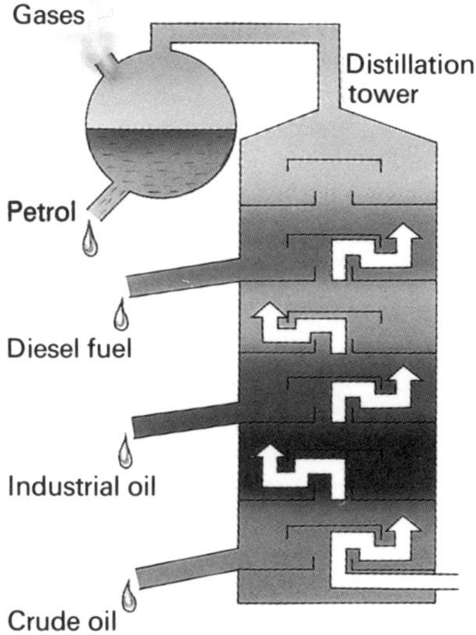

oil *n.* kinds of liquid that do not mix with water and usually burn easily. *vb.* apply oil, lubricate.

ointment *n.* a medicine made in a paste or cream.

The octopus is the most intelligent of all animals without backbones. It can be trained to solve simple problems.

old *adj*. having lived for a long time; out-of-date.

old-fashioned *adj*. out-of-date, not worn or used nowadays.

olive *n*. a small oval fruit with a hard stone and bitter, oily flesh. *adj*. dullish green colour (colour of an olive).

omelet, omelette *n*. a kind of pancake made of fried beaten eggs, often with a meat or vegetable filling.

omen *n*. sign of good or evil to come. **ominous** *adj*. threatening.

omit *vb*. leave out; fail to put in. **omission** *n*.

omni- *prefix* meaning all, e.g. **omnipotent** all powerful, **omnivorous** feeding on all kinds of food.

once 1. *adv*. at one time only. *I have only been to Venice once.* 2. *adv*. at a time in the past. *She once lived in Africa.*

onion *n*. a strong-tasting bulb eaten as a vegetable or to add flavour to other foods.

onlooker *n*. spectator.

only *adv*. & *adj*. a single one; no one or nothing else. *He was the only person to give the right answer to the problem.*

onrush *n*. forward rush or flow.

onset *n*. 1. attack 2. start; beginning.

onyx (**on**-*iks*) *n*. semi-precious stone with layers of different colours.

ooze *vb*. flow or leak out slowly.

opal *n*. a precious stone, a form of quartz much prized for its rainbow play of colours.

opaque (*o*-**pake**) *adj*. not letting the light through; dull.

open *adj*. & *adv*. not closed. *Leave the door open. vb*. make or become open.

openly *adv*. in public; frankly.

opera *n*. a play in which the words are sung.

operate *vb*. 1. work. *Do you know how to operate the machine?* 2. carry out a surgical operation.

operation (*opper*-**ay**-*shun*) *n*. 1. a treatment by a doctor in which the patient's body is cut. 2. a carefully planned action.

operator *n*. a person who works a machine – e.g. a telephone switchboard.

opinion *n*. what someone thinks; an idea with which not everyone agrees. **opinionated** *adj*. stubborn in one's opinions.

opossum *n*. a marsupial mammal that lives in North and South America.

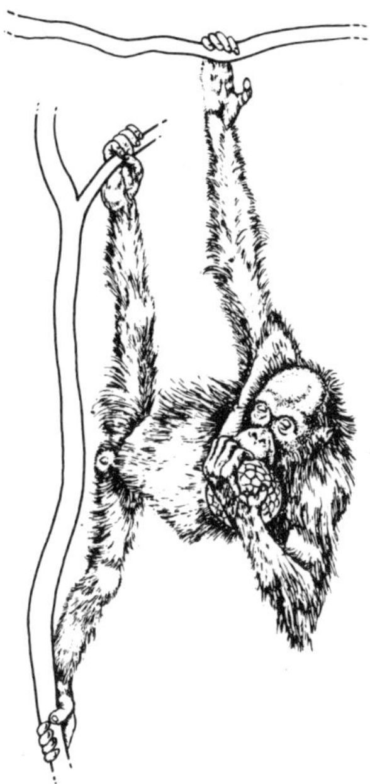

Orang-utans live alone or in small family groups. They could become extinct soon.

opponent *n.* someone who opposes something; a foe.
opportune *adj.* suitable, convenient.
opportunity *n.* a good chance to do something. *While the children were out, their mother took the opportunity to clean their rooms.*
oppose *vb.* resist; be against. *I oppose the plan to rebuild the bus station.*
opposite 1. *n.* entirely different. *Fat is the opposite of thin.* 2. *adj.* on the other side. *The house opposite is painted blue.*
oppress *vb.* to govern cruelly and harshly. *Tyrants oppress their subjects.*
opt *vb.* make a choice.
optician (*op*-**tish**-*un*) *n.* a person who tests eyes and sells spectacles. **optic** *adj.* concerning the eyes or sight.
optimism *n.* belief that the best will happen. **optimist** *n.*
or *conj.* a connecting word introducing the second of two choices. *Coffee or tea?*
oral *adj.* spoken; concerning the mouth.
orange 1. *n.* round juicy fruit with a thick skin. 2. *n.* & *adj.* a colour like an orange.
orang-utan *n.* a reddish-brown ape that lives in the forests of Indonesia.
orator *n.* an eloquent public speaker.
oratorio *n.* musical work for choir and orchestra often on a Biblical subject and without action or scenery.
orb *n.* sphere or globe.
orbit *n.* the path followed by any body in space around another body. *vb.* travel in an orbit.
orchard *n.* a piece of ground where fruit trees are grown.
orchestra (**ork**-*estra*) *n.* a group of musicians who play together. **orchestral** *adj.*
orchid *n.* one of a family of attractive flowering plants.
order 1. *vb.* command somebody to do something. *The officer ordered the troops to advance.* 2. *n.* a list of things that you want. *The waiter took our order for lunch.* 3. *n.* a succession of events. 4. *n.* tidiness. 5. *n.* religious community. *These monks belong to the Order of Saint Benedict.*

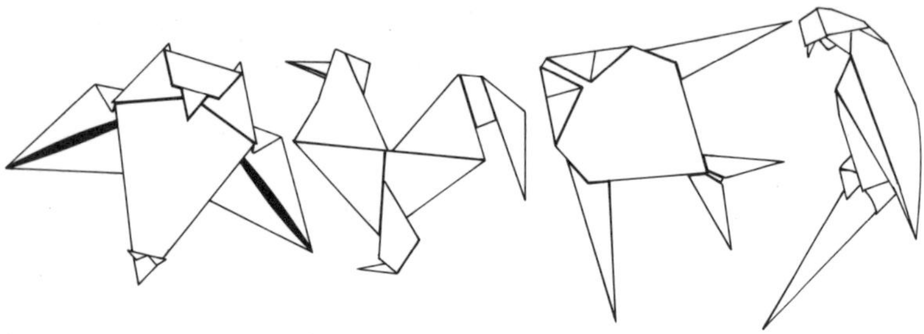

These origami birds are made simply by folding paper.

orderly 1. *adj*. tidy. 2. *n*. a soldier who looks after an officer; hospital employee who does routine work.
ordinary *adj*. normal; usual; not strange or interesting.
ore *n*. rock or earth from which metal can be taken.
organ *n*. 1. any part of an animal's body that has a particular job to do. *The heart is the organ that pumps blood round the body*. 2. a musical instrument with a keyboard and pipes. **organist** *n*. organ player.

An 18th-century church organ.

organism *n*. a living animal or plant.
organization *n*. an organized group of people.
organize *vb*. make arrangements for something to happen; give orderly structure to.
origami *n*. Japanese art of folding paper into intricate and beautiful shapes.
origin *n*. beginning, source; starting point. **originate** *vb*. create, come into being; spring from.
original *adj*. the earliest or first; new, not copied. *n*. thing from which another is copied.
ornament *n*. something which is used as a decoration. *vb*. adorn. **ornamental** *adj*.
ornate *adj*. ornamented, adorned.
ornithology *n*. study of birds. **ornithologist** *n*.
orphan *n*. a person whose parents are dead. *adj*. **orphanage** *n*. an institution for orphans.
orthodox *adj*. holding correct or acceptable opinions; not heretical; conventional. **orthodoxy** *n*.

osmosis *n.* the process by which liquids pass through a porous membrane (skin) until the fluids on both sides of the membrane have been equalized in some way.

osprey *n.* a large fish-eating bird of prey found in most parts of the world. It is brown with a white head and underparts.

ostrich *n.* a very large bird that lives in southern Africa. Ostriches cannot fly but are very fast runners.

other *adj.* one of two; different; alternative.

otherwise *adv.* 1. in another way. 2. if not, or else. *You'd better hurry, otherwise we'll go without you.*

otter *n.* a flesh-eating water animal that lives in many parts of the world.

ought auxiliary or helping *vb.* expressing duty, probability etc. *We ought to help those in need. She ought to have got home by now.*

ouija (**wee**-*jah*) *n.* a board with the letters of the alphabet, used by spiritualists to transmit messages during seances.

ounce *n.* small measure of weight. *There are 16 ounces (oz) in one pound (lb.). An ounce equals 28.35 grammes.*

our *pron.* & *adj.* belonging to us. *Come to our house.*

oust *vb.* drive away, get rid of.

out- *prefix* meaning more, longer outside, beyond.

outback *n.* the interior of Australia; the bush.

outboard motor *n.* a motor for driving a small boat. It is hung over the stern (back) of the craft.

outbreak *n.* a start; a breaking out; an epidemic.

outcast *n.* a person who has no home or friends.

outdoors *adv.* outside a house or other building.

outfit *n.* all the clothes needed for a special purpose.

outgrew past of **outgrow**.

outgrow *vb.* become too large for something. *Robert will soon outgrow his grey trousers.*

outing *n.* a day's holiday.

The ostrich is the largest of all birds alive today.

outlaw *n.* a person who has broken the law; a bandit. *vb.* declare a person an outlaw.
outlay *n.* money spent on something.
outline *n.* the outside shape of something, a drawing that shows only the shape of something; the main facts about something.
outright *adv.* all at once; completely.
outside *n.* & *adv.* the opposite of inside; the outer surface of something; the outdoors.
outskirts *n.* the edges of a town.
outspoken *adj.* frank, plain, factual.
outwit *vb.* be too clever for.
oval *n.* & *adj.* an egg-shaped figure.
ovary *n.* part of female animal that produces eggs.
ovation *n.* warm applause.
oven *n.* the enclosed part of a stove where food is baked or roasted.
over 1. *adj.* above. 2. *adv.* finished. 3. *n.* a number of balls, usually six, bowled by one person in a cricket match. 4. *prefix* (**over-**) excessive, beyond, further than. Words prefixed with over- are usually self explanatory, if the main word is known.
overalls *n.* a piece of clothing worn over others to keep them clean.
overboard *adv.* having fallen into the water from a ship or boat. *'Man overboard'*.
overcome *vb.* conquer.
overdraft *n.* a bank loan in which a customer's account shows that there are insufficient funds to meet cheques. The bank charges interest on the amount outstanding ('in the red').

The long-eared owl's 'ears' are really tufts of feathers.

overflow *vb.* flood, spill out. *I left my bath running and it overflowed all over the floor.*
overhang *n.* & *vb.* hang out over something.
overhaul *vb.* 1. examine thoroughly and repair if necessary. 2. overtake.
overheads *pl. n.* the running costs of a business such as administrative and advertising costs not directly related to production.
overlap *vb.* cover one thing partly with another; partly coincide.
oversee *vb.* supervise, superintend.

oversight *n.* a careless mistake.
overtake *vb.* pass another moving thing, particularly a vehicle.
overtime *n.* time spent working after usual hours; extra wages paid for such work.
overture *n.* 1. musical introduction. 2. opening of negotiations.
owe (rhymes with *low*) *vb.* need to pay money back to someone.
owl *n.* a bird of prey that hunts by night.
own *vb.* possess or have. *Father owns that field.* **owner** *n.* someone who owns something. *My father is the owner of that field.*
ox *n.* (plural **oxen**) a male animal of the cattle family.
oxygen *n.* one of the gases of the air (symbol O).
oyster *n.* a shellfish that is highly prized as a table delicacy.
ozone *n.* a form of oxygen in which each molecule contains three atoms instead of two.

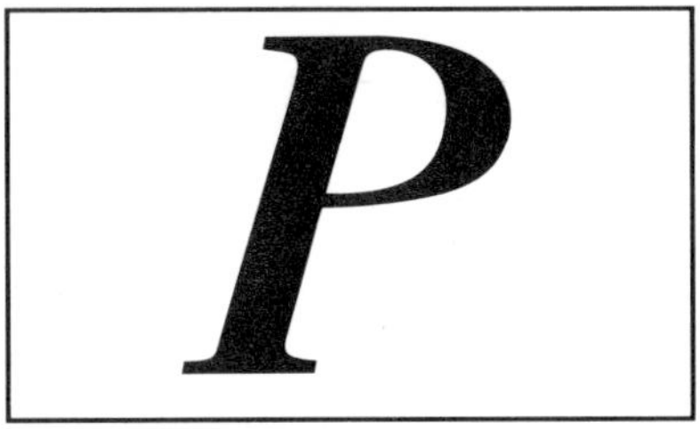

pace *n.* a single step; speed or way of walking. *vb.* walk slowly and regularly. *He paced up and down the room.*
pacify *vb.* make calm, peaceful.
pack 1. *vb.* put things into a bag or other container ready for a journey. *n.* a holder for carrying things on a journey. 2. *n.* a group of animals that hunt together.
package *n.* a parcel or bundle of things packed together.
packet *n.* a small parcel.
pack-ice *n.* large pieces of floating ice in the ocean.

A large cargo-carrying tanker cutting a path across a field of pack-ice in the Arctic Ocean.

pact *n.* an agreement.
pad 1. *vb.* walk along softly. 2. *n.* a kind of small cushion used to protect something from rubbing. 3. *n.* sheets of paper joined together at one edge.
paddle 1. *n.* a short oar for making a canoe move through water. *vb.* propel with paddle. 2. *vb.* walk in water with bare feet.
paddock *n.* small enclosed field for horses.
paddy *n.* 1. field where rice is grown. 2. the growing rice itself.
padlock *n.* a removable lock.
pagan *n.* & *adj.* (obsolete) a person who is not a member of one of the world's religions; a heathen; a person of no religion.
page *n.* 1. a leaf or sheet of paper, particularly in a book. 2. a boy working in a hotel, or attending the bride at a wedding.
pageant *n.* an open-air show or display, often celebrating an historical event.
pagoda *n.* an Asian temple, usually in the form of a tower with many storeys.
paid *vb.* past of **pay**.
pail *n.* an old-fashioned word for a bucket.
pain *n.* an unpleasant feeling in the body; suffering.
painful *adj.* something that causes pain. **painstaking** *adj.* careful.
paint *n.* coloured liquid, which can be used for decorating and protecting walls or other surfaces, or for making pictures. *vb.* cover with paint; create a picture with paint.
painting *n.* a painted picture.
pair *n.* two of the same kind. *Look at that pair of doves sitting on my windowsill.*
pal *n.* a friend.
palace *n.* the home of a ruler, such as a king, queen, bishop.
palate *n.* the roof of the mouth.
pale *adj.* not having much colour. **pallor** *n.* lack of colour.
palette *n.* board with a thumb-hole on which an artist mixes paints.
palfrey *n.* a lady's riding horse in the Middle Ages.
palindrome *n.* word or sentence etc. that can be read backwards or forwards and has the same meaning. *Able was I ere I saw Elba.*
palisade *n.* a fence made of stakes.

The roof of each storey of a pagoda curves upwards.

An artist mixes his colours on a wooden palette.

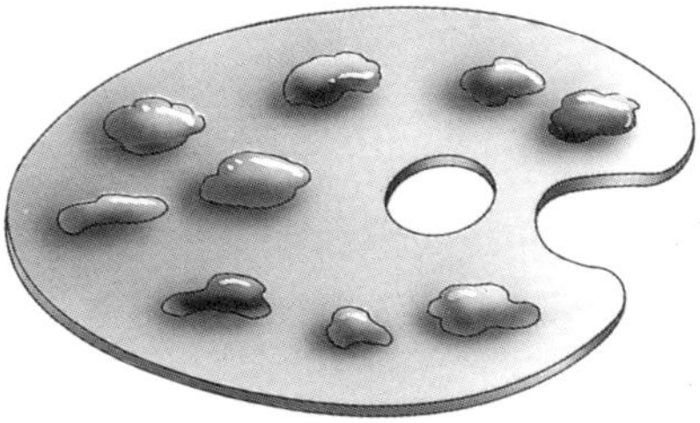

pall (*pawl*) *n.* a dark cloth spread over a coffin. *vb.* to cease to be interesting or attractive.
pallet *n.* a bed or mattress made of straw.
pallid *adj.* pale in colour.
palm *n.* 1. the inner surface of the hand. 2. a tree with no branches but many large leaves near the top.
palomino *n.* a golden-coloured horse with a cream or white mane and tail.
paltry *adj.* of little worth, small and insignificant.
pampas *n.* vast grass-covered plain of South America.
pamper *vb.* spoil.
pamphlet (**pamf**-*let*) *n.* a leaflet.
pan 1. *n.* a wide, flat vessel or saucepan, especially one used for frying food. 2. *prefix* meaning of or all. *Pan-American means all states of North and South America.*
panama *n.* a type of straw hat.
pancake *n.* a flat cake made from batter cooked in a frying pan.
pancreas *n* a gland near the stomach which helps the digestion.
panda *n.* bear-like animals from China and Nepal. There are two species – the Giant panda and the Red Panda.
pane *n.* a single sheet of glass in a window.
panel *n.* 1. a division of a surface such as in a door. 2. a group of experts, entertainers etc.
panic *n.* a sudden fear or terror which may lead people to behave foolishly. *vb.* be affected by panic. **panicky** *adj.*
panorama *n.* a wide, all round view. **panoramic** *adj.*
pansy *n.* a garden flower of the violet family, usually purple, yellow or white in colour.
pant *vb.* breathe in and out quickly.
panther *n.* a leopard, especially a black one.
pantomime *n.* a kind of play with music and dancing, often performed at Christmas time.
pantry *n.* a room or large cupboard where food, cutlery, crockery etc. are kept.

The panda is a black and white herbivorous animal.

pants *n*. underclothes for the lower part of the body; trousers are also called pants, especially in USA.

papal *adj*. of or relating to the Pope.

paper *n*. thin flat sheets of material for writing or printing on. *vb*. stick paper on walls.

paperback *n*. book bound in a paper cover.

papier-mâché (**pap**-*yeh*-**mash**-*eh*) *n*. pulped paper used for modelling.

papoose *n*. North American Indian baby.

paprika *n*. hot red pepper.

papyrus (*pap-i-rus*) *n*. a kind of paper made from the papyrus reed in ancient Egypt.

par *n*. equality, normal amount.

parable *n*. a story that teaches a simple lesson.

parachute *n*. an umbrella-like apparatus used for floating down from an aircraft. *vb*. descend by parachute.

parade *n*. 1. a procession. 2. soldiers gathered for inspection. *vb*. assemble; display.

paradox *n*. a statement which seems contradictory but is nonetheless true.

paraffin *n*. an oil used for burning in jet engines, heaters and lamps (also called kerosene).

paragraph *n*. several sentences grouped together because they deal with one main idea.

parakeet *n*. small, long-tailed parrot.

parallel *adj*. lines that are the same distance from each other along their full length. *The*

When a parachute opens a large canopy fills with air. This causes air resistance which slows down the speed the parachutist falls to the ground.

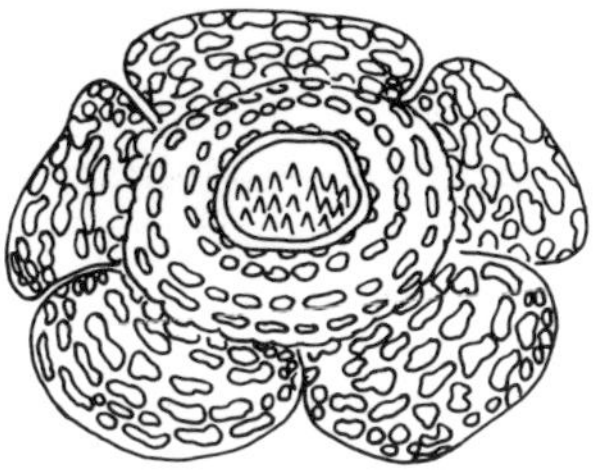

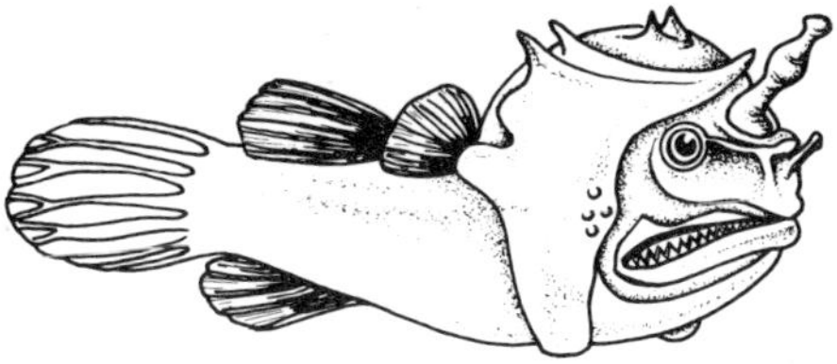

Examples of parasites. Rafflesia is a parasitic plant that produces the largest flower in the world – up to a metre across. The tiny male deep-sea fish Photocorynus spiniceps *lives by attaching itself to the much larger female and sucking her blood.*

railway tracks are parallel. vb.

paralysed *adj*. unable to move or feel. **paralysis** *n*. **paralyse** *vb*. make helpless.

paramount *adj*. supreme.

parapet *n*. low wall along edge of roof etc.

paraplegia *n*. paralysis of the legs and lower part of the body.

paraquat *n*. a poisonous chemical used to kill weeds.

parasite *n*. an animal or plant that gets its food from another living animal or plant. **parasitic** *adj*.

parasol *n*. a sunshade similar to an umbrella.

paratroops *n*. soldiers trained to jump by parachute into a battle zone.

parcel *n*. a package that has been wrapped up in paper, usually for sending through the post.

parchment *n*. the skin of a sheep or goat, specially dried and prepared, and used in former times for writing on. *Parchment was used for books and documents before the introduction of paper.*

pardon *vb*. forgive someone. *n*. forgiveness.

parent *n*. a mother or father.

parish *n*. 1. the district around a church which is attached to that church. 2. smallest unit in local government.

park *n*. 1. a public garden. 2. a place where people can leave their cars (car park). *vb*. stop one's car in a parking place.

parka *n*. originally a hooded skin jacket worn by eskimos. Now a kind of anorak.

parliament *n*. the group of people who are elected to make the laws of a country.

Parmesan *n*. a kind of hard cheese from Italy, usually grated on pasta dishes.

parody *n*. piece of music or literature in which an artist's style is imitated in order to amuse or ridicule; satirical imitation.

parole *n*. a release of a prisoner before his or her prison sentence is finished.

parrot *n*. a brightly coloured tropical bird with a hooked beak.

parry *vb*. to block or turn aside, especially when fighting with weapons.

parsimony *n*. meanness with money. *adj*. **parsimonious**.

parsley *n*. a herb grown in temperate lands. Its fine, curly leaves are either used fresh to decorate foods, or fresh or dried as a flavouring.

Parsley is a herb which can be easily grown in most gardens.

parsnip *n*. a sweet root vegetable.
parson *n*. a vicar or rector of the Church of England.
part 1. *n*. a piece of something; not the whole thing; a role in a play. 2. *vb*. divide into parts; leave one another's company.
partake *vb*. share in something.
participate *vb*. take part in; share.
participle *n*. an adjective formed from a verb. e.g. a going concern.
particle *n*. a very small part of something.
particular *adj*. one rather than another. *This particular book is very interesting*. **particularly** *adv*. *I particularly like this book*.
partition 1. *n*. a temporary wall or screen. 2. *vb*. separate into parts. *India was partitioned into two countries – India and Pakistan*.
partly *adj*. to some extent; not all. *The pedestrian was partly to blame for the accident*.
partner *n*. & *vb*. a person who does something with someone else. *Alice is my tennis partner*. **partnership** *n*.
partridge *n*. common game bird, related to the pheasant, and found in Europe, Africa and Asia. Most species live on the ground.

Partridges live in open fields and nest on the ground.

party *n*. a group of people who come together to enjoy themselves; an organized group who try to get certain people elected to parliament.
pasha *n*. a high-ranking officer of the Turkish Empire.
pass 1. *vb*. go by. *You have to pass the school to reach the park*. 2. *vb*. give something to someone who cannot reach it. *Please will you pass me the butter*. 3. *vb*. satisfy examiners. *I passed all my exams*. 4. *n*. a piece of paper that allows you to go somewhere or do something. *My grandma has a pass that allows her to go free on*

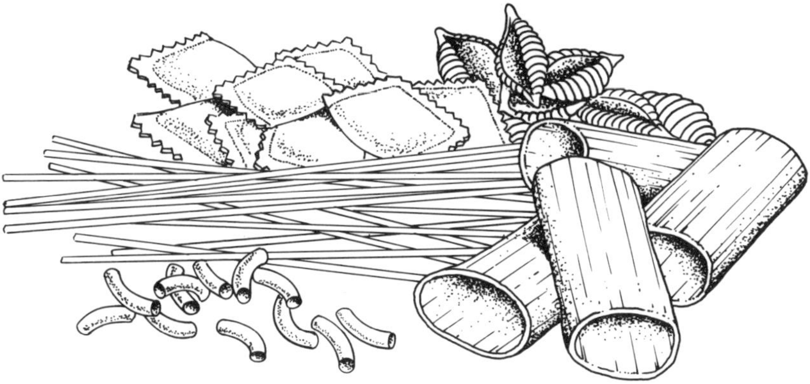

the buses. 5. *n*. a narrow passage through mountains.

passage *n*. a narrow way between buildings or through a building.

passenger *n*. a person being taken in a motor vehicle, ship or aircraft.

passerine *n*. & *adj*. (in zoology) order of perching birds.

passion *n*. strong emotion; enthusiasm.

Passover *n*. an important Jewish religious festival, lasting eight days and held in springtime. It commemorates the escape from Egypt under Moses. There is a ritual meal in the home on the first evening.

passport *n*. a document that travellers show when going from one country to another.

password *n*. a secret word that helps someone to be recognized by a sentry.

past 1. *n*. the time before the present time. *The Sumerians lived in the distant past*. 2. *adv*. up to and farther than something. *You go past the school to get to the hospital*.

Pasta comes in many different shapes, but long thin spaghetti is the commonest.

pasta *n*. Italian dish made from cooked flour paste in various shapes (e.g. macaroni, spaghetti etc.).

paste *n*. any thick semi-liquid substance, such as toothpaste; a kind of glue used for sticking paper. *vb*. stick things together with paste.

pastel *n*. a crayon. *adj*. soft, pale (colour).

pastern *n*. part of a horse's foot between fetlock and hoof – the 'ankle'.

pasteurize *vb*. kill germs by heating, especially milk. How to do this was discovered by Louis Pasteur.

pastime *n*. a game, a hobby; anything done to pass the time in a pleasant way.

pastor *n*. a clergyman.

pastry *n*. a mixture of flour, fat and water, cooked to make pie-crusts.

pasture *n*. a field or piece of land for grazing cattle or sheep.

pat *vb.* & *n.* tap with the flat of the hand. *She patted the dog, which wagged its tail.*

patch 1. *n.* a small piece of ground or colour. *There was a small patch of grass in the playground.* 2. *n.* a small piece of material sewn on to clothing to cover a hole. *vb.* mend with a patch.

patchwork *n.* bits of material sewn together in a pattern.

patella *n.* the kneecap.

patent 1. *n.* document giving an inventor the exclusive right to make and profit from his or her invention for (in England) 16 years. The inventor may choose to sell this right to others. 2. *adj.* obvious; unconcealed.

paternal *adj.* of or relating to a father, fatherly.

path *n.* a narrow track or footway.

pathetic *adj.* moving one to pity or contempt.

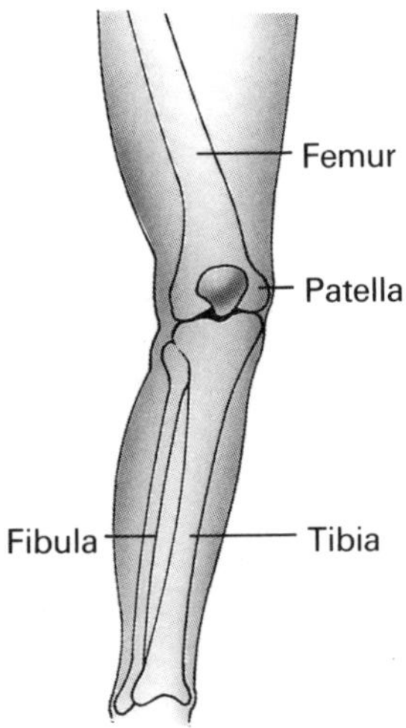

The patella is between the two long bones of the leg.

patience (**pay**-*shunce*) *n.* be able to wait calmly without complaining.

patient (**pay**-*shent*) 1. *n.* someone who is looked after by a doctor. 2. *adj.* able to wait a long time without getting cross.

patio *n.* courtyard near a house.

A patio is a paved or concreted area beside a house.

patriarch *n.* father or founder of a tribe. *Abraham was a patriarch of Old Testament times.*

patriot *n.* a person who loves his or her country and all it stands for. **patriotism.** *n.*

patrol *vb.* & *n.* 1. go around a place to see that everything is correct. *His job is to patrol the factory at night.* 2. a small group of soldiers, aircraft or ships carrying out a special task in wartime. 3. *n.* a small group in the Scout movement.

pattern *n.* 1. a design that is repeated on something to make

The peacock has a beautiful spreading tail, which he uses for display. The female peafowl is the peahen.

it look pretty. *I have a dress with a pattern of flowers on it.* 2. anything that is copied to make something else. *Mother used my dress as a pattern to make a dress for my sister.* 3. a repeating feature in mathematics.

pause (*paws*) *n.* stopping for a short time. *vb.* wait.

pave *vb.* cover the ground with flat stones.

pavement *n.* a hard path at the side of a road.

paw *n.* the foot of some kinds of animal, such as dogs and cats.

pawn 1. *n.* a chesspiece of least value. 2. *vb.* hand over something of value as security for money borrowed.

pay 1. *n.* money for doing a job, particularly when given weekly or monthly. 2. *vb.* hand over money in exchange for something.

pea *n.* climbing plant cultivated for its seeds which are eaten as a vegetable. The round seeds – peas – are contained in a long pod and picked when they are unripe and green.

peace *n.* freedom from war or violence; calmness.

peach *n.* a sweet, roundish juicy fruit with a hard stone and yellow-red fuzzy skin.

peacock *n.* a large ornamental bird, the male peafowl.

peak *n.* the top of a mountain; highest point on a graph.

peal *n.* a loud ringing of bells.

peanut *n.* a groundnut; a nut that grows in a pod under the ground.

pear *n.* a sweet, juicy fruit that is narrow at one end.

pearl *n.* a silver-white gem found in some oysters (a kind of shellfish).

peasant *n.* a person who works on the land.

peat *n.* a kind of turf which can be used as a fuel instead of coal.

pebble *n.* a small rounded stone.

peccary *n.* a wild pig of Central and South America.

peck *vb.* use the beak to pick up food or cut something.

peckish (*casual*) *adj*. hungry.
peculiar *adj*. very strange or unusual. *The man was wearing a peculiar hat with green feathers all over it*.
pedal *n*. a part that is pressed by the foot to make something work. *The pedals of a bicycle turn the wheel*. *vb*. press pedals.
pedestal *n*. base of a column.
pedestrian *n*. a person walking in the street. *adj*. of walking; dull, uninspired.
pedigree *n*. & *adj*. a record of the members of a family who have lived up to now. *Our dog has a pedigree that shows even her great grandparents*.
peek *vb*. glance quickly.
peel *vb*. remove the skin of a fruit or vegetable. *n*. a piece of fruit or vegetable skin. *Don't throw orange peel onto the pavement*.
peep *vb*. look at something quickly, or through a small hole or space. *n*. a glance.
peer 1. *vb*. look at closely, as if unable to see properly. 2. *n*. an equal. 3. *n*. a lord (fem. **peeress**).
peg *n*. 1. a small piece of wood or other material, used for hanging things on. *Hang your coat on that peg*. 2. a clip for fastening clothes to a line. *vb*.
Pekinese *vb*. small breed of dog with a snub-nose and long silky hair.
pelican *n*. a large brown or white water bird.
pellet *n*. small, round, compressed ball.
pelt 1. *vb*. hurl or strike repeatedly. 2. *n*. an animal's skin or fur.
pen *n*. 1. a small fenced place for animals. 2. a tool for writing that uses ink. 3. a female swan.
pen name *n*. false name used by a writer.
penalty *n*. fine or punishment.
pencil *n*. writing instrument consisting of graphite ('lead') encased in wood. *You can usually rub out marks made with a pencil*.
pendant *n*. an ornament that hangs down on a chain.

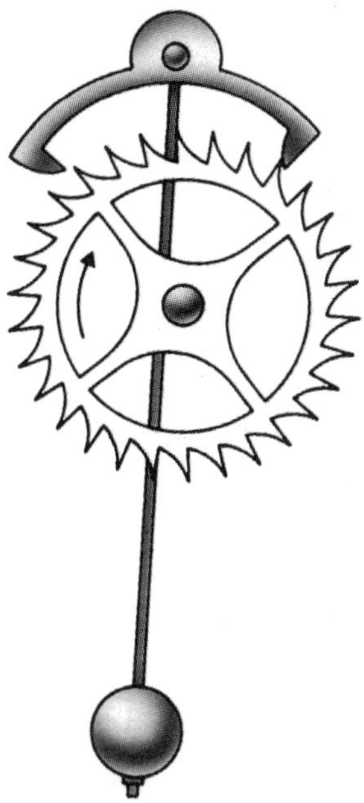

A swinging pendulum makes a clock keep time.

pendulum *n*. weighted rod that is hung so that it can swing back and forth, as on some clocks.
penetrate *vb*. pierce, pass into. *The arrow penetrated his skin*. **penetrating** *adj*. discerning.

Emperor penguins live and breed in the Antarctic.

pen-friend *n.* someone who writes to you and to whom you write although you have not met. *My pen-friend Ali lives in Nigeria.*

penguin *n.* a flightless, fish-eating sea bird, found in the southern hemisphere, especially the Antarctic.

penicillin *n.* a substance used in medicine to kill bacteria.

peninsula *n.* a piece of land almost surrounded by sea. *Italy is a peninsula.* **peninsular** *adj.*

penis *n.* male organ of reproduction in mammals.

penknife (**pen**-*nife*) *n.* a small knife that shuts into itself.

penny *n.* (plural **pence, pennies**) a small British and Irish coin. *There are 100 pence in one pound or punt.*

penny-farthing *n.* early bicycle with a large front wheel and a small back wheel invented in the 1870s.

pension (**pen**-*shun*) *n.* money paid regularly to someone who has retired from work etc. *vb.* give a pension.

pensive *adj.* thoughtful.

penta- *prefix* meaning five, e.g. **pentagon** *n.* a five-sided figure.

pentathlon *n.* athletic contest of five different events.

Pentecost *n.* Jewish harvest festival. Christian Whitsun.

penultimate *adj.* next to last.

people (*peeple*) *n.* men, women and children; human beings; race. *All the people in our street came to the party. vb.* populate.

pepper *n.* a hot-tasting powder made from dried berries of various tropical plants. *Pepper is used to flavour food.*

peppermint *n.* kind of mint grown for its oils.

per *prep.* by, through, by means of, for each, e.g. **per cent**; for each hundred, a fraction written as part of 100. *50 per cent is 50 parts in 100 or $\frac{1}{2}$; 10 per cent is 10 parts in 100 or $\frac{1}{10}$. Per cent is usually written %.*

perceive (*pur*-**seeve**) *vb.* become aware of. **perception** *n.* understanding; acute awareness.
perch *n.* 1. resting place for a bird. *vb.* rest on a perch. 2. a common European freshwater fish.
percussion instrument *n.* a musical instrument that is struck or shaken. *Drums, tambourines and triangles are percussion instruments.*
perennial *n.* & *adj.* lasting for a long time; for more than a year. *Roses and lilies-of-the-valley are perennial flowers.*
perfect *adj.* so good that it cannot be made better. *vb.* make perfect.
perforate *vb.* make holes in.
perform *vb.* do something in front of other people. *We performed our play in front of the whole school*; do something; carry out. *I am sure that he will perform the task perfectly.* **performer** *n.*
performance *n.* something that is done so that other people can see or hear it.
perfume (**purr**-*fyoom*) 1. *n.* a scent, a sweet-smelling liquid. 2. *vb.* (*purr*-**fyoom**) spread a sweet scent around.
perhaps *adv.* maybe; possibly. *Perhaps they have forgotten to come.*
peril *n.* danger, risk of danger.
perimeter (*per*-**rim**-*e-ter*) *n.* the distance around the outside of an area.
period *n.* 1. a length of time. 2. occurrence of menstruation. **periodic** *adj.*
periodical *n.* publication which appears at regular intervals.
periscope *n.* an instrument like a tube with mirrors in it that lets someone see over something. *We used a periscope to see over the heads of the crowd.*

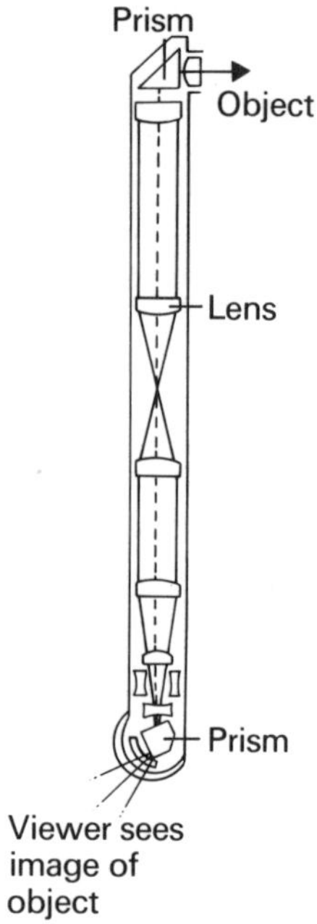

Objects not in a direct line of vision can be seen with a periscope.

perish *vb.* become destroyed, come to an end, die. **perishable** *adj.* not long lasting. *Salads are highly perishable.*
periwinkle *n.* a trailing plant with evergreen leaves and blue or white flowers.
perky *adj.* bright and lively.
permafrost *n.* a term used for layers of soil or rock that are permanently frozen.

The rules of perspective enable you to draw things in a realistic way.

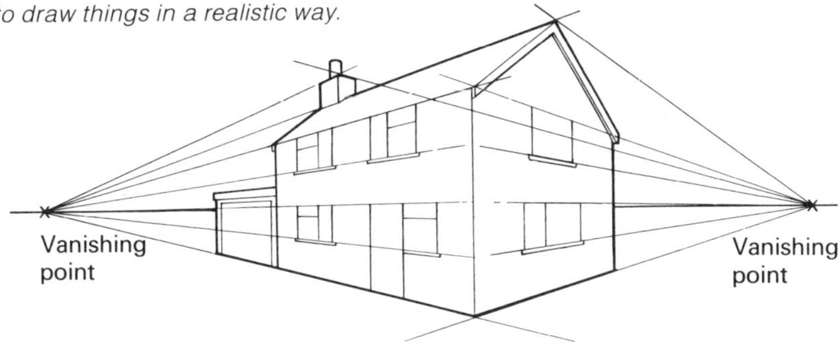

permanent *adj*. unchanging; not expected to change. *This is now our permanent address.* **permanence** *n*.

permission *n*. being allowed to do something. *The teacher gave us permission to go home early.*

permit (**perr**-*mit*) *n*. something to say that a certain thing can be done.

permit (*pur*-**mit**) *vb*. allow.

perpendicular *adj*. upright, at right angles to the horizon.

perpetual *adj*. lasting for ever.

persecute *vb*. illtreat or harass someone. *Naomi was persecuted because of her religion.*

persist *vb*. go on resolutely, stubbornly; take a firm stand.

person *n*. any man, woman or child. *Did a person in a brown hat come in here?*

personality *n*. special characteristics that distinguish a person; a character; a well known personality.

perspective *n*. a method of representing in two dimensions the optical effect of distance in three dimensions.

persuade (*per*-**swade**) *vb*. make or try to make someone change their mind, influence, convince. **persuasion** *n*.

pessimism *n*. a belief that everything will turn out badly; the opposite of optimism. **pessimist** *n*.

pest *n*. an animal that is harmful or causes trouble. *Rats are pests on a farm because they eat grain.*

pester *vb*. annoy continually; keep asking questions.

pestle *n*. implement for pounding substances (in a **mortar**).

pet *n*. a tame animal kept for fun. *vb*. treat as a pet; fondle.

petal *n*. one of the leaf-like parts of the flower of a plant.

peter out *vb*. come gradually to an end.

petrify *vb*. (literally) turn into stone; terrify.

petrol *n*. a liquid fuel made from oil and used to power motor vehicles. *Petrol is short for petroleum.*

petty *adj*. small, unimportant, trivial. **petty-cash** *n*. cash kept for small items.

pew (*pyou*) *n*. a bench in a church.

pewter (**pyou**-*ter*) *n*. a dull grey metal which is an alloy (mixture) of lead and tin.

A pharaoh in kilt and cloak. His double crown showed that he ruled both the north and the south of Egypt.

pharaoh (**fair**-*oh*) *n.* a king of ancient Egypt.
pharmacy *n.* a place where medicines are prepared and dispensed. A chemist's shop.
phase *n.* a stage in the development of something; one of the various stages of the Moon's monthly journey around the Earth. *vb.* carry out by phases.
pheasant *n.* a long-tailed game bird common in many parts of the world.
phenomenon (*fee*-**nom**-*enon*) *n.* a remarkable person, happening or thing. **phenomenal** *adj.* amazing.
phi (*fie*) *n.* the 21st letter of the Greek alphabet Φ which is shown in English spelling as *ph*. All words beginning with *ph* in English come from a Greek word and are pronounced with the sound of f. e.g. **phone** (*fone*).
phial *n.* a small bottle for storing liquids.
philanthropist *n.* someone who loves their fellow men and does good to them.
philo (**feel**-*oh*), but pronounced like 'fill' in other words. *prefix* meaning love of, e.g. **philosophy** love of wisdom.
philosophy *n.* the search for knowledge; the study of ideas. **philosopher** *n.*
phobia *n.* strong fear, dislike of.
phoenix *n.* a mythical Arabian bird which was supposed to burn itself to death every 500 years, and was then miraculously reborn from its own ashes.

phone *n.* & *vb.* short for **telephone**.
phonetics *pl. n.* the branch of the study of languages that deals with pronunciation and which uses special *phonetic alphabets* to cover all the different sounds that languages use. **phonetic** *adj.*
phoney (**fo**-*ney*) *adj.* sham, not genuine.

How photosynthesis works.

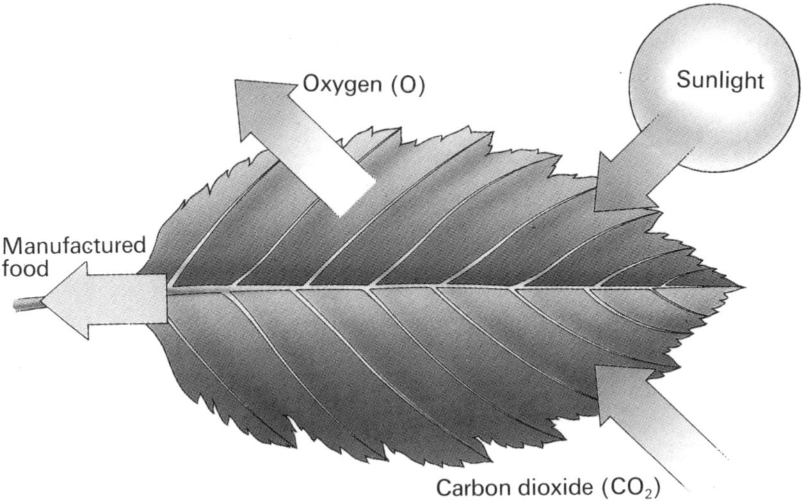

phosphorous *n.* a non-metallic element that occurs in various different physical forms (symbol P).

photography *n.* the process or art of taking pictures with a camera.

photostat *n.* a copy of writing or pictures made by a special machine. *vb.*

photosynthesis *n.* a process by which green plants turn carbon dioxide and water into sugar, with the release of oxygen.

phrase *n.* a group of words linked together to form part of a sentence. *'Part of a sentence' is a phrase in the last sentence.*

physical *adj.* 1. having to do with the body. 2. of map, showing features like high and low ground and rivers.

physics *n.* the study of light, heat, sound and energy.

piano *n.* a musical instrument with a keyboard. **pianist** *n.* a person who plays the piano.

piccolo *n.* a small musical wind instrument, played like a flute, which makes very high notes.

pick 1. *vb.* select or choose something. 2. *vb.* dig at something (with your fingers). 3. *n.* a sharp tool for digging.

picket *n.* 1. a person or group of people who, during a strike, try to prevent from working those who want to work. 2. a stake dug into the ground.

pickle *vb.* preserve vegetables or other food in vinegar, brine etc.

pick up *vb.* 1. lift something up with your hand. *Pick up your pencils when I say 'Now'.* 2. give someone a ride in your car. *I picked up old Mr Brown and took him to the library.*

picnic *n.* a meal eaten out of doors in the countryside. *This field will be just right for our picnic. vb.* (past **picknicked**).

picture *n.* drawing, painting, photograph or other illustration. *vb.* describe; imagine.
pie *n.* food in a pastry case.
piebald *adj.* & *n.* (colour of) horse with patches of black and white.
piece *n.* a part of something; a fragment; a musical or literary composition. *vb.* put together, mend.
pier (*peer*) *n.* a structure built out over water. *A pier is a place for ships to stop at.*
pierce *vb.* bore through, make a hole in, perforate.
pig *n.* a farm animal the meat of which provides pork and bacon.
pigeon (**pid**-*jun*) *n.* a medium-sized bird found all over the world. *Many pigeons live in towns and cities.*
piglet *n.* a young pig.
pigment *n.* anything used to give colour, e.g. to paints, plastics etc.
pigsty *n.* a building for pigs.
pigmy see **pygmy**.
pigtail *n.* a plait of hair worn down the back of the neck.
pike *n.* 1. a kind of spear used in former times. 2. a fierce freshwater fish.
pilchard *n.* small fish of the herring family.
pile 1. *n.* a heap of things on top of each other. *vb.* throw in a pile. 2. *n.* (atomic pile) nuclear reactor.
pilgrim *n.* a person who travels to visit a holy place.
pilgrimage *n.* a pilgrim's journey.
pill *n.* a small ball of medicine.
pillar *n.* a post, often made of stone, for supporting a building.

A pigtail.

pillar-box *n.* a collecting box for letters in the street.
pillion *n.* a saddle for a passenger on a motor bike.
pillow *n.* a kind of cushion on a bed for supporting the head.
pillowcase *n.* washable cover for a pillow.
pilot *n.* a person qualified to fly an aircraft; a person who is trained to take a ship through difficult waters. *vb.* guide. *adj.* experimental; small scale.
pimple *n.* small inflamed swelling on the skin.
pin *n.* a small, thin piece of metal like a tiny nail, sharp at one end, and used for fastening things together. *vb.* fasten with pins.
pinafore *n.* a kind of apron worn over a dress. *She wears a pinafore to keep her dress clean.*
pincer *n.* 1. claw of crab, lobster etc. 2. (**pincers.** *pl.*) a tool for

gripping things, especially for pulling out nails.

pinch *vb.* 1. grip between a finger and a thumb; hurt by squeezing. 2. (*slang*) steal.

pine *n.* an evergreen coniferous (cone-bearing) tree with needle-like leaves. **pine-cone** *n.* fruit of the pine.

pineapple *n.* a large, sweet, juicy tropical fruit with a prickly covering.

pinion *n.* bird's wing and more especially the outer joint.

pink 1. *n.* & *adj.* a pale red colour. 2. a kind of garden flower.

pint *n.* a measure for liquids etc. *There are eight pints in one gallon.*

pioneer *n.* a person who goes to a new place or country to settle; someone who is the first to do something.

pious *adj.* holy, devout.

A pineapple.

pip *n.* the seed of a fruit.

pipe *n.* 1. a tube along which water etc. can flow. 2. a device, usually wooden, for smoking tobacco.

pipe-dream *n.* a fantastic plan or hope.

pipe-line *n.* a line of pipes for conveying gases, liquids etc.

An overland pipeline used for transporting oil from wells in southern Iran.

piranha *n.* savage freshwater fish from tropical South America.
pirate *n.* a sea robber.
pirouette *n.* & *vb.* (in ballet) a spin round on one leg.
pistil *n.* the seed-producing part of a flower.
pistol *n.* a small gun that is held in one hand.
pit 1. *n.* a deep hole with steep sides. 2. *n.* a coal mine.
pitch 1. *n.* a ground marked out for games like football and cricket. 2. *vb.* throw something. 3. *n.* a sticky black material like tar. 4. *vb.* put up a tent. *They will pitch the tent out of the wind.* 5. *n.* the sound of a musical note – i.e. whether it is higher or lower than another.
pitcher *n.* 1. a large jug. 2. a person who throws (pitches) the ball in baseball.
pitchfork *n.* a long-handled fork used for lifting hay.
pitfall *n.* a covered pit acting as an animal trap; an unknown danger.
pity *n.* a feeling of sadness for someone's troubles. *vb.*
placard *n.* a board or poster in a public place.
place *n.* a particular area or location. *vb.* put something in position.
placid *adj.* calm; not easily upset.
plagiarize *vb.* use someone else's ideas or writings etc. and pass them off as one's own.
plague (*playg*) *n.* a dangerous illness which is very quick to spread. *vb.* pester, bother.
plaice *n.* a kind of flatfish, often eaten as food.
plain 1. *adj.* simple; ordinary; with no pattern on it. *Her dress was plain blue with a lace collar.* 2. *n.* a large flat area of country.
plaintiff *n.* person who brings a suit or action in a court of law.
plait (rhymes with *flat*) *vb.* twist three or more strips together. *n.*

A pirate.

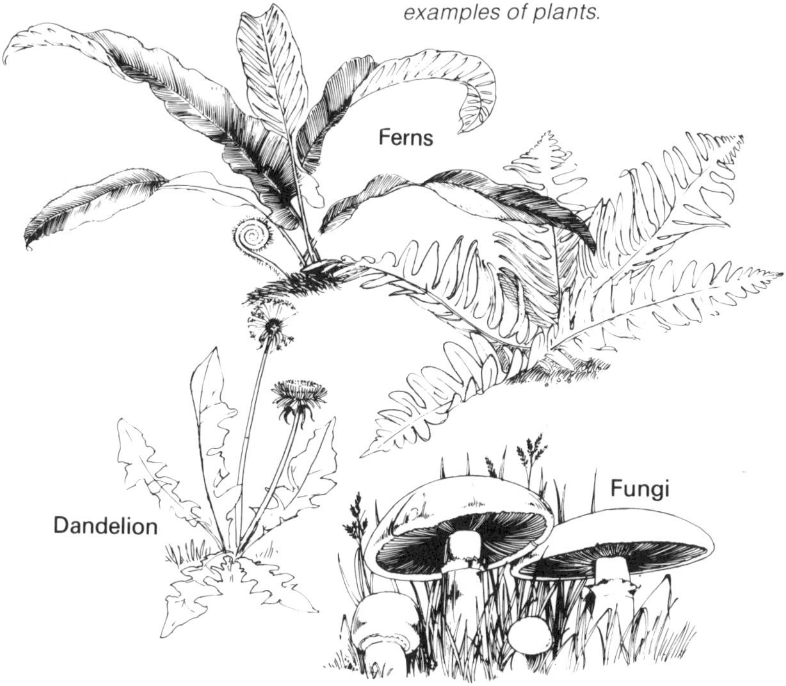

Ferns, dandelions and fungi are all examples of plants.

plan 1. *n.* a drawing that shows where things are. 2. *vb.* decide what you are going to do. *Shall we plan a walk at the weekend?*

plane *n.* 1. short for aeroplane. 2. a tool for making wood smooth. *vb.* 3. a tall tree with large leaves and bark that peels.

planet *n.* one of the bodies that move around a star.

planetarium *n.* a big room or building, with a domed ceiling, for reproducing the movement of planets and other heavenly bodies.

plank *n.* a long flat piece of wood.

plankton *n.* tiny plants and animals that drift in the sea.

plant *n.* 1. any living thing (particularly a flower) that is not an animal. *vb.* put a plant in the ground. *We have just planted several trees.* 2. a factory or any other industrial buildings or machinery.

plaster *n.* a coating put on walls and ceiling, to give a surface for decoration. It is made from certain cement powders, mixed with water and sand. *vb.* smear with plaster. *The walls of the house need plastering.*

plastic *n.* & *adj.* a light, strong material that is manufactured; made of plastic.

plate *n.* a flat, round piece of crockery, from which food is eaten.

plateau (*plat*-**oh**) *n.* (plural **plateaus, plateaux**) level land higher than the land around it.

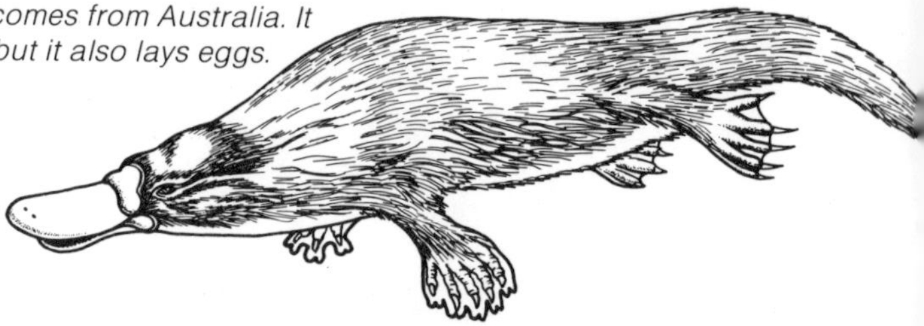

The platypus comes from Australia. It is a mammal, but it also lays eggs.

platform *n.* a small raised stage; the raised place beside the railway lines where people wait at a station.

platinum *n.* silvery valuable metal.

platitude *n.* a dull, stale, commonplace remark. e.g. *Long time no see.*

platypus *n.* an odd-looking dark-brown furry animal with a bill (beak).

play 1. *vb.* have fun and not work; perform on a musical instrument; take part in or play a game. 2. *n.* a story that is told by people acting and talking to each other, usually on a stage; a dramatic piece.

playground *n.* an area for children to play in.

playtime *n.* a period when children can stop working and amuse themselves; break-time.

playwright *n.* a person who writes plays; a dramatist.

plead *vb.* present a case in a law court; urge.

pleasant *adj.* nice; good or agreeable.

please 1. *vb.* make someone happy. 2. *imperative.* with your permission. *Please shut the door.*

pleasure *n.* the feeling of being happy.

pleat *n.* a fold in cloth or paper. *vb.* make a pleat.

plebiscite (**pleb**-*iss-ite*) *n.* direct voting by all electors on a particular question or issue.

plectrum *n.* an implement made of horn, plastic or metal for plucking the strings of guitar, zither etc.

pledge *n.* security; something pawned; word of honour. *vb.* promise, give one's word.

plenty *n.* much; a lot. *We have plenty of time.* **plentiful** *adj.* in large numbers or quantities.

plesiosaur *n.* an extinct long-necked marine reptile.

pleurisy *n.* painful inflammation of the delicate surface (pleura) of the lung.

plod *vb.* trudge; walk or work with effort.

plot *n.* 1. a secret agreement to do something, usually bad. *The police discovered a plot to rob the bank. vb.* scheme. 2. a small piece of ground. 3. the main things that happen in a story.

plough (rhymes with *how*) *n.* a machine used to cut and turn over land to prepare it for planting. *n.*

pluck 1. *vb.* pull feathers off a bird; gather; make sound on a guitar. 2. *n.* courage. **plucky** *adj.*

plug *n.* 1. a piece of wood, rubber or other material used to fill a hole. 2. a device for joining electrical equipment to the electricity supply. *vb.* stop with plug.

plum *n.* a sweet fruit with juicy flesh and a hard central stone.

plumage *n.* all the feathers of a bird.

plumber (*plum-mer*) *n.* a person who fits and repairs water pipes in a building.

plump *adj.* rounded. *vb.* make plump. *She plumped up the cushions.*

plunder *vb.* rob violently especially in war. *n.* things stolen by force; loot.

plunge *vb.* jump or fall into. *The man plunged into the canal after the drowning child.*

plural *adj.* a word which shows that there are more than one. *Cats, kittens and children are all plural nouns.*

plus *prep.* & *adj.* and, added to. *Four plus six equals ten.*

p.m. *abbrev.* after mid-day; (from the Latin words *post meridiem*).

pneumatic (*new*-**matt**-*ik*) *adj.* worked by air under pressure; filled with air.

A plough is attached to a tractor for cutting furrows.

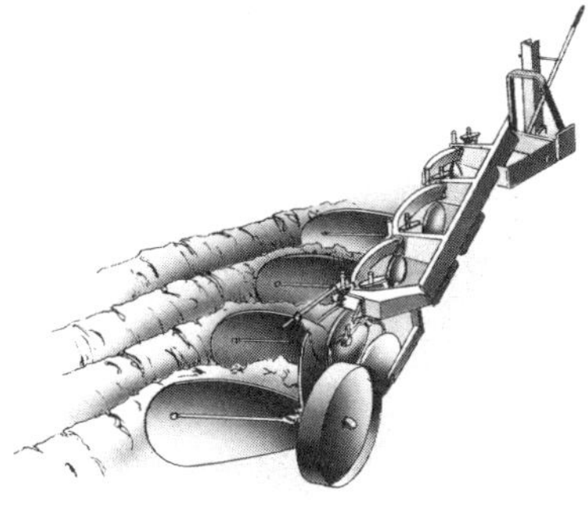

pneumonia (*new*-**moan**-*ya*) *n.* a serious illness of the lungs.

poach vb. 1. cook by simmering in water. e.g. poached eggs. 2. take game or fish illegally. **poacher** *n.*

pocket *n.* a bag sewn into a garment for carrying things; receptacle for balls in snooker etc.; a cavity for deposit (of gold etc.). *vb.* put into one's pocket; take illegally.

pod *n.* a long seed holder on some plants. *Peas grow in a pod.*

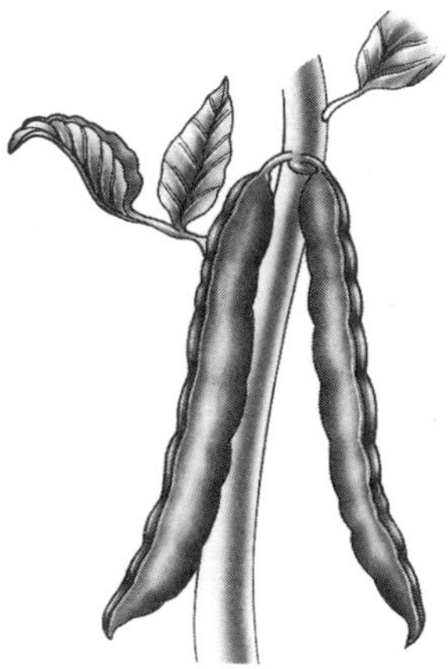

poem (*po-em*) *n.* a piece of writing with a special rhythm. *Poems are often written in short lines with the last word in one line rhyming with the last word of another line.*

poet (**po**-*et*) *n.* a person who writes poems.

poetry (**po**-*etry*) *n.* poems.

point 1. *n.* the sharp end of something, such as a needle or pencil. 2. *vb.* stick out a finger in the direction of something. 3. *n.* the main idea. *Do you see the point of what has just been said?*

poison *n.* & *vb.* a substance that makes people ill or die. **poisonous** *adj.*

poke *vb.* push with a stick, finger etc. **poker** *n.* instrument for stirring a fire.

poker *n.* a card game in which the player bets that the value of his hand is higher than those of the other players.

polar *adj.* of or near the North or South Poles. *Polar bears live near the North Pole.*

pole *n.* 1. either the most northerly point of the Earth (the North Pole) or the most southerly point (the South Pole). 2. one of the ends of a magnet. 3. a tall, thin piece of wood or metal; a post.

police *n.* the people who help to keep the law and catch criminals. *vb.* control, provide with police.

policy *n.* a considered method of action carried out by a government etc.

polish *vb.* make something smooth and shiny. *n.* smoothness; substance used to polish a surface.

polite *adj.* well-mannered.

politics *pl. n.* the science or art of government. **politician** *n.* a person taking part in politics.

poll (rhymes with *coal*) *n.* voting, number of votes. (*opinion poll*).

pollen *n.* a fine powder on flowers which fertilizes other flowers. **pollinate** *vb.* fertilize with pollen.

pollution *n.* the spoiling of air, soil, water or the countryside by poisonous wastes. **pollute** *vb.*

polo *n.* a game similar to hockey and played on horseback.

poly- *prefix* meaning many as in **polyandry** having more than one husband, **polysyllable** a word with more than one syllable.

The North Pole is the northernmost point on the Earth's surface.

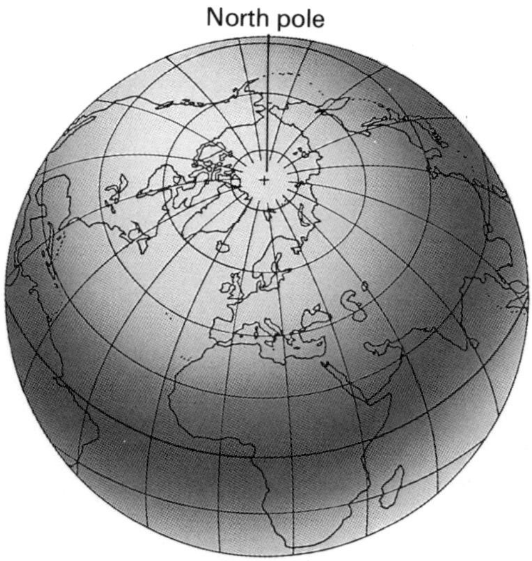

polytechnic (*poll-i-***tek***-nik*) *n.* a school giving instruction in many technical subjects.
polythene *n.* a plastic material used for making wrappings and bags.
pomegranate *n.* a fruit with a red rind and flesh full of seeds.

pomp *n.* splendour and ceremony.
pond *n.* a small area of water; a tiny lake, which may be natural or artificial.
pony *n.* (plural **ponies**) a small horse.
poodle *n.* small lively dog with a black or white curly coat; the coat is often clipped. Poodles were originally Russian gundogs.
pool *n.* 1. a very small area of water; a pond. 2. a game like billiards.
poor 1. *adj. & n.* having little or no money. 2. *adj.* deserving pity. *The poor old lady has been ill for many years.* 3. *adj.* not good. *Tom's exam results were very poor.*
pop 1. *n.* a small bang. 2. *abbr.* short for popular, as in pop music and pop art.
Pope *n.* the head of the Roman Catholic Church.
poplar *n.* slender, quick growing tree of the willow family.
pop music *n.* short for popular music.
popular *adj.* liked by a lot of people. *I think Andrew is the most popular boy in our class.* **popularity** *n.* being generally liked. **popularize** *vb.* make popular.
population *n.* all the people living in a place, city, country or the world. **populate** *vb.* fill with people.
porcelain *n.* fine china.
porch *n.* a covered entrance to a building.
porcupine *n.* a rat-like animal covered with pointed spines.
pore *n.* a tiny opening in the skin. **porous** *adj.* having pores and so allowing liquid through.
pork *n.* the flesh of a pig.
porpoise *n.* a small sea animal of the whale family.
porridge *n.* a soft food made of oatmeal.
port 1. *n.* a harbour; a town by the sea with a harbour. 2. *n. & adj.* the left side of the ship or aircraft as you are facing forward. 3. *n.* the name of a Portuguese wine.
portable *adj.* capable of being carried, especially by hand. *A portable typewriter.*
portcullis *n.* a grating lowered to protect a gateway in a castle.

porter *n.* a person who is employed to carry things; doorkeeper especially of large buildings.

porthole *n.* a round window in a ship.

portray *vb.* make a picture of. **portrait** *n.* a picture of a person.

Portuguese man-of-war *n.* a kind of jellyfish.

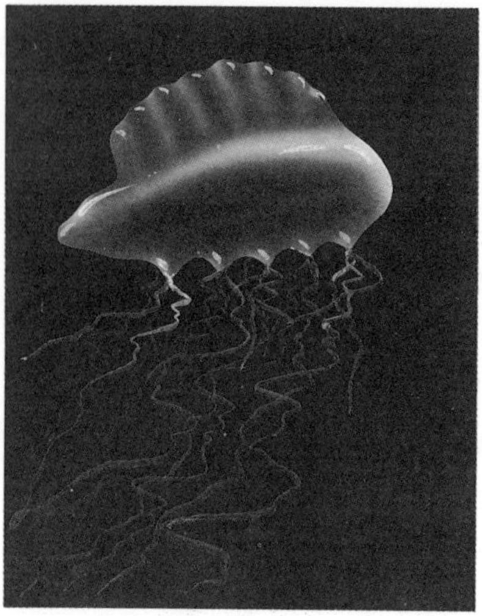

pose *vb.* 1. arrange or place. 2. behave in an affected way; show off. 3. put (a question or problem).

position *n.* the place taken by somebody or something. *When you are all in position, the race will begin.* *vb.* place in position.

positive 1. *adj.* not negative; clear, confident, undoubted. 2. *n.* photographic print.

possess *vb.* have or own. *Do you possess any money?* **possession** *n.* thing owned. **possessive** *adj.* unwilling to share.

possible *adj.* & *n.* that which can happen, exist or be achieved etc.

possum *n.* (phalanger) the name given to a group of Australian marsupials.

post- *prefix* meaning behind or after. e.g. **post-mortem** examination after death.

post *n.* 1. the mail. *vb.* send a letter. 2. a thick upright pole, such as a goalpost. 3. a job or position.

postcard *n.* a card, often with a picture on one side, which you can write a message on and send through the post. *A postcard does not need an envelope.*

poster *n.* a picture, usually with writing, which goes on a wall to advertise something.

post office *n.* a building or room in which postal business is carried out.

postpone *vb.* put off until a later time, defer. **postponement** *n.*

pot *n.* round vessel for holding liquids etc. *vb.* plant in a flower pot.

potassium *n.* an extremely reactive metallic element (symbol K).

potato *n.* (plural **potatoes**) the edible tuber of the potato plant, widely eaten as a vegetable.

potion *n.* a drug or poison.

potter *n.* a person who makes pots.

pottery *n.* pots and other things made of baked clay; a place where pottery is made.

pouch *n.* small bag; the receptacle in which marsupials – kangaroos etc. – carry their young.

poultry *n.* hens, ducks, geese,

turkeys and any other domestic fowl.

pounce *vb.* make a sudden attack. *The cat pounced on the mouse. n.* sudden swoop.

pound 1. *n.* a measure of weight. *There are 16 ounces in one pound (1 lb.).* 2. *n.* a British unit of money. *There are 100 pence in a pound (£1).* 3. *vb.* hit heavily and often.

pour *vb.* let liquid flow from a jug or other container.

poverty *n.* being poor.

powder *n.* fine dry particles; cosmetics or medicine in this form. *vb.* sprinkle with powder.

power *n.* the strength or ability to do something; a country with great influence.

powerful *adj.* very strong or important.

power station *n.* a building for generating and distributing electricity.

practicable *adj.* capable of being done or used.

practical *adj.* able to do useful things.

practice *n.* 1. something you do often to get better at it. *My piano practice lasts for an hour every day.* 2. Action not theory.

Pottery.

3. professional business of doctor, lawyer etc.

practise *vb.* 1. do something often so that you can do it well. *I practise the piano every day.* 2. work at as a profession. *She practises medicine.*

prairie *n.* a wide plain with very few trees, especially in North America.

praise *vb.* say good things about someone. *n.*

pram *n.* a carriage for a child pushed by a person on foot.

prance *vb.* move in a light-footed way.

prank *n.* practical or mischievous joke.

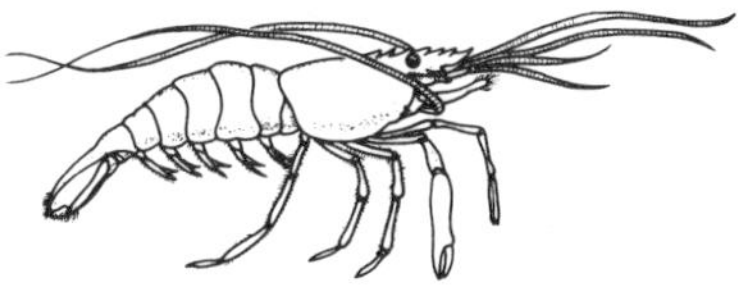

prawn *n.* a small sea animal with a thin shell and five pairs of legs. *Prawns look like large shrimps and can be eaten as food.*

pray *vb.* talk to God.

prayer *n.* what is said when talking to God.

pre- *prefix* meaning beforehand, e.g. **prehistoric** before history was written.

preach *vb.* give a sermon; give advice. **preacher** *n.*

precaution *n.* care or action taken beforehand to prevent harm or to bring about good results.

precede *vb.* go before in rank or importance.

precious (**pre**-*shuss*) *adj.* very valuable.

precipice *n.* the steep side of a mountain or high cliff.

précis (**pray**-*see*) *n.* summary of essential facts.
precise *adj.* exact, very accurate. *Give me the precise details of what happened.*
predator *n.* an animal that hunts other animals. *A tiger is a predator in the jungle.*
predict *vb.* say what is likely to happen in the future; forecast.
preen *vb.* (of birds) cleaning feathers with the beak; groom oneself.

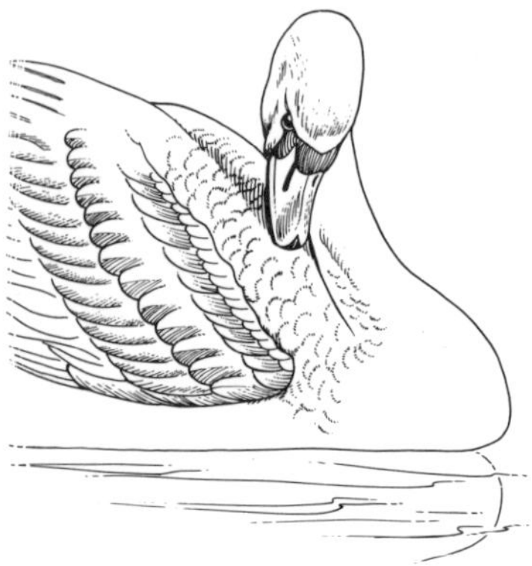

Swans and ducks preen their feathers to keep them clean.

preface *n.* an introduction to a book.
prefer *vb.* like one thing rather than another. *I prefer rugby to soccer.*
pregnant *adj.* to be going to have a baby.
prehistoric *adj.* things that happened before the time when people could write.
prejudice *n.* biased or one sided opinion.
preliminary *adj.* introductory; before the main business.
premiere (*prem-ee*-**air**) *n.* first performance of a film or play.
premium *n.* the regular payment for an insurance policy; a bonus.
prepare *vb.* get ready. **preparation** *n.*
Presbyterian *n.* a member of the Presbyterian Church.
prescription *n.* a doctor's order for medicine. **prescribe** *vb.* advise use of.
presence *n.* being in a place; the bearing or appearance of a person.
present (**prez**-*ent*) 1. *n.* something that is given to somebody, a gift. 2. *n.* this time; now. *At present there are 20 children in my class.* 3. *adv.* being in the place spoken about. *Who was present at the meeting?*
present (*pree*-**zent**) *vb.* 1 give someone something in public. *The mayor presented prizes at our school open day.* 2. show or perform. *Our class presented a play.* **presentable** *adj.* fit to be shown.
presently *adv.* soon; (*Sc* & *US*) now.
preserve *vb.* keep safe from harm; make something last a long time. *The ancient Egyptians preserved their dead pharaohs as mummies.*
president *n.* the (usually) elected head of a country or organization.
press 1. *vb.* push on something. *The boys pressed their noses against the window of the cake shop.* 2. *vb.* press something flat by pushing hard on it. *Father presses his trousers.* 3. *n.* a printing machine. 4. *n.* newspapers.

pressure (rhymes with *thresher*) *n.* how much one thing is pressing on another or against the walls of a container; urgency.
prestige *n.* having a good reputation; having influence.
presume *vb.* take for granted; suppose to be true. **presumption** *n.* having reason to think something probable; impudence.
pretend *vb.* give the impression that something is the case when it is not. *Let's pretend we're asleep.*
pretext *n.* false excuse.
pretty *adj.* attractive; nice-looking. *Victoria wore a pretty dress to the party.* *adv.* fairly, moderately.
prevail *vb.* triumph over; get one's own way.
prevalent *adj.* common, widespread.
prevent *vb.* stop something happening. *The rain prevented us from going out yesterday.* **prevention** *n.*
preview *n.* an advance showing or performance of a film, play etc. before it is seen by the public.
previous *adj.* former, coming before. **previously** *adv.*
prey (rhymes with *ray*) *n.* an animal that is hunted by another animal. *A bird of prey is a bird that hunts animals and other birds.*
price *n.* the sum of money that is paid for something. *vb.* fix a price; ask the price of.
priceless *adj.* 1. too valuable to have a price. 2. funny.
prick *vb.* make a mark with a small sharp point.
prickle *n.* a sharp point in the stem of a plant, a fine thorn.
pride *n.* the feeling of being proud; sense of one's own worth. *vb.* be proud of; flatter oneself.
priest (rhymes with *least*) *n.* a person who is trained to perform religious acts.
prim *adj.* precise, prudish, stiff.
prima donna *n.* principal female singer in an opera etc; a vain person.
primary *adj.* first in time or importance. *The primary colours are blue, red and yellow.*
primate *n.* 1. (biology) member of the highest order of mammals that includes lemurs, monkeys, apes and humans. 2. (ecclesiastical) an archbishop.

Primates are the most advanced living mammals. They range from small monkeys to the great apes, and human beings.

A modern printing press is able to print in four colours; red, blue, yellow and black.

prime minister *n.* a head of government (especially in the Commonwealth).

primitive *adj.* undeveloped, simple, rough; old fashioned.

primrose *n.* a spring flower with yellow petals.

prince *n.* the son of a king or queen.

princess *n.* the daughter of a king or queen.

principal *adj.* the most important. *n.* head of a college etc.

principle *n.* an important rule; law of nature. *Always telling the truth is a good principle to follow.*

print 1. *n.* letters that you do not join together. 2. *vb.* use a machine to put letters or pictures on to paper. *This book has been printed.*

printer *n.* a person or company that prints books, newspapers etc.

printing *n.* a way of reproducing words and pictures by pressing an inked pattern onto paper, fabric etc.

print-out *n.* printed sheets produced by a computer.

prior 1. *adj.* earlier. *A prior engagement.* 2. *adj.* before. *We ate prior to your arrival.* 3. *n.* head of a religious house called a **priory** (*n.*).

prism *n.* a solid block of transparent material used in various instruments to disperse (split up) or reflect light or other rays.

prison *n.* a secure building in which people who break the law may be kept.

prisoner *n.* a person who is kept in prison.

private *adj.* not open to the public; belonging to only one person or to a few people.

privilege *n.* special advantage, favour.
prize *n.* something that is given to someone as a reward. *I won a prize in the poetry competition.* *vb.* value highly.
probably *adj.* likely to happen, but not certain. *We will probably go to the country next week.*
probation *n.* 1. period of testing a person's suitability. 2. suspending a prisoner's sentence and allowing him or her freedom under supervision.
probe *vb.* explore or examine closely.
problem *n.* a question for which an answer is needed; a difficulty that needs to be solved. *We are having a problem with our roof.*
procedure *n.* method of doing things.
process *n.* a way of making something. *The process of making paper is a complicated one.*
procession *n.* a number of people and vehicles moving along together; a parade. **proceed** *vb.* go forward; continue; resume.
proclaim *vb.* announce publicly; declare. **proclamation** *n.*
procrastinate *vb.* delay, put off.
prodigal *adj.* wasteful, extravagant. *n.* person who spend recklessly. *Jesus told the parable of the prodigal son.*
produce (**prod**-*yous*) *n.* things that are made or grown.
produce (*pro*-**dyous**) *vb.* 1. make. 2. bring something out to show it. *The magician produced a rabbit from his hat.*
producer *n.* 1. someone who makes or grows something. 2. person who directs production of a play etc.
product *n.* something that is produced. *The product of that factory is ice cream.*
profess *vb.* declare, admit openly (beliefs etc.); have as a **profession** or occupation. **professional** *n.* & *adj.*
profit *n.* the difference between the cost of making something and the price it is sold at.

A prism splits white light into a spectrum of colours: the seven colours of the rainbow.

profound *adj.* deep; having great depth of knowledge; difficult to understand.
program *n.* (US spelling of programme) a set of instructions to a computer.
programme *n.* 1. a list of events or things that are going to happen. 2. a printed leaflet giving details of a theatre show, football match, etc. 3. an entertainment on radio or television.
progress (**proh**-*gress*) *n.* advance, improvement. *vb.* (*proh*-**gress**) improve; move on.
progressive *adj.* moving forward, advancing. *n.* a person who favours social advances and reforms.
prohibit *vb.* forbid.
project (**proj**-*ekt*, 'o' as in 'not', or as in 'go') *n.* a plan to be worked on. *Our class is working on a project to start a vegetable garden. vb.* (*proh*-**jekt**) make plans for; throw; jut out.
projectile *n.* a rocket.
projector *n.* machine for showing (projecting) motion or still pictures on a screen.
prologue *n.* 1. the opening lines of a play or speech. 2. a preliminary event.
prolong *vb.* cause to continue, make longer.
prom *n.* 1. short for promenade. 2. musical concerts where some of the audience can walk about are called *proms* (promenade concerts).
promenade *n.* place made for leisurely walking.
prominent *adj.* outstanding, noticeable, distinguished. *He is a prominent member of the club.*

The Parade, an old English sea-side promenade.

promise *vb.* say that you will do something. *n.* What you have promised to do. *I promised to tidy my room, but I did not keep my promise.* **promising** *adj.* likely to turn out well.

promote *vb.* raise to a higher position or office; encourage. *We should like to promote a good atmosphere in the school.*

prompt 1. *adj.* on time; without delay. 2. *vb.* urge; incite; help actor by saying words he or she has forgotten.

prone *adj.* 1. lying flat. 2. liable, disposed to. *He was prone to lie.*

prong *n.* one of the sharp ends of a fork.

pronghorn *n.* shy antelope-like animal of North America. It is about 90 cm (3 ft) tall.

pronoun *n.* a word used for a noun, like he, she, it, they, him, our.

pronounce *vb.* make the sound of a word. **pronunciation** *n.*

proof *n.* 1. something that shows that what is said is true, evidence. *I need some proof before I will believe it.* 2. impression of type that can be corrected before final printing. **proof-reader** *n.* a person who corrects printers' proofs.

prop *n.* & *vb.* support, or lean against something. *The ladder was propped against the wall.*

propaganda *n.* spreading of ideas or information and the information so spread.

propel *vb.* send forward.

propeller *n.* two or more blades that spin round.

proper *adj.* right, suitable. *She was not wearing the proper clothes for a party.*

properly *adj.* correctly. *Can your little brother read properly yet?*

property *n.* things owned.

prophet *n.* 1. a person who tells what is going to happen in the future. 2. in the Bible, a person who speaks for God. **prophesy** *vb.* speak as a prophet; foretell. **prophecy** *n.* something foretold by a prophet, a prediction.

proportion *n.* part of; a ratio. *The proportion of people who use hearing-aids has increased.*

propose *vb.* suggest, put forward an idea; intend to; offer marriage. **proposal** *n.*

proprietor *n.* owner of a business.

prosaic *adj.* ordinary, uninteresting.

prose *n.* written language without metre; not poetry.

prosecute *vb.* bring before a law court; start legal action. **prosecution** *n.*

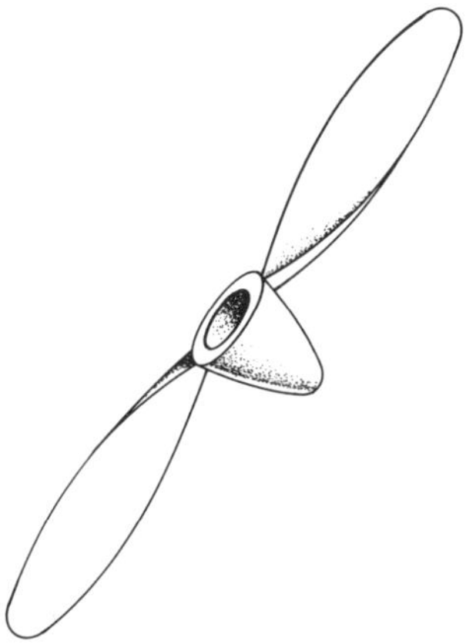

A propeller provides the force to drive a boat or an aircraft.

prosper *vb.* flourish, grow rich, be successful. **prosperity** *n.* **prosperous** *adj.*
protagonist *n.* the chief person in a story or drama.
protect *vb.* keep safe from danger, guard. **protection** *n.* that which protects.
protein (**pro**-*teen*) *n.* a body-building material in some foods, like eggs, meat and milk.
protest (*proh*-**test**) *vb.* say or show how you think something is wrong; object to. *We had to protest about the new school rules. n.* (**proh**-*test*) an objection.
Protestant *n.* a member of any Christian Church which resulted from the protest against and separation from the Roman Catholic Church.
proto- *prefix* meaning first. e.g. **prototype** the first model of something before general production.
protrude *vb.* extend beyond a surrounding surface.
proud *adj.* 1. thinking that you are better than others. 2. pleased that someone else has done well.
prove *vb.* show that something is true. *Can you prove that you saw a ghost?*
proverb *n.* a short saying that gives a warning or advice.
provide *vb.* give something that is needed. *Our teacher provided us with new pencils.*
province 1. *n.* a large area of a country with its own government. 2. *pl. n.* the whole country outside the capital. **provincial** *adj.*
provision *n.* what is provided. (*pl.*) food and drink. **provisional** *adj.* temporary.
provoke *vb.* stir up feeling; irritate. **provocative** *adj.* to cause irritation or anger. **provocation** *n.*
prow *n.* the bows of a ship; the forepart.
prowess *n.* valour; expertness.
prowl *vb.* go about silently and secretly.
proximity *n.* nearness in distance or time.
prudent *adj.* careful to avoid unwanted situations.
prudish *adj.* prim, affected modesty. **prude** *n.*
prune 1. *n.* a dried plum. 2. *vb.* cut away parts of a plant to control the way it grows.
pry *vb.* look into; interfere inquisitively.
psalm (*sahm*) *n.* a sacred song in the Book of Psalms in the Old Testament in the Bible.
psycho- (**sye**-*co*) *prefix* meaning of the mind.
psychology (*sye*-**koll**-*o-jee*) *n.* the study of the mind and how it works.
psychopath (**sye**-*kuh-path*) *n.* mentally ill or unstable person.

ptarmigan (**tar**-*mig-an*) *n.* a bird of the grouse family whose plumage changes from brown and white in summer to grey and white in winter.

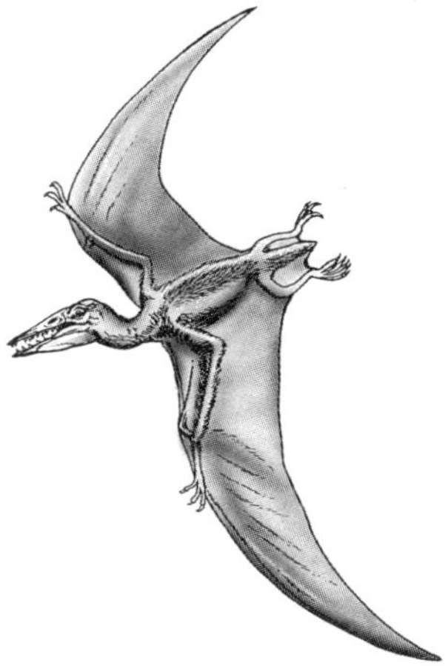

pterodactyl (*tero*-**dack**-*til*) *n.* prehistoric flying reptile.
P.T.O. *abbrev.* please turn over.
pub *n.* short for public house, inn.
puberty *n.* period when boys and girls mature and become men and women capable of producing children.
public 1. *adj.* known to everyone; belonging to everyone. 2. *n.* the people; the community as a whole.
publican *n.* keeper of a public house.
publication *n.* issuing of a book or written material.
publicity *n.* making known publicly by means of advertisements etc.
publicize *vb.* advertise or make publically known.
publish *vb.* have a book, newspaper or magazine printed for sale or to be given away; make known generally. **publisher** *n.*
pudding *n.* a food made with flour, often boiled; the sweet course of a meal.
puddle *n.* a small hole in the ground full of water.
pudgy *adj.* overweight; fat.
puff 1. *n.* a short blast of wind or smoke. 2. *vb.* to breathe hard or pant.
puffin *n.* a bird of the auk family.
pug *n.* small breed of dog with a snub-nose and tightly curled tail.
pull *vb.* heave something towards yourself.
pull down *vb.* (of buildings) take them down on purpose.
pullet *n.* a young hen.
pulley *n.* a wheel with a rope round it, used to lift or move heavy things more easily.
pull-off *vb.* succeed with something.
pullover *n.* a jersey or sweater.
pulmonary *adj.* related to the lungs.
pulp *n.* 1. soft part of a fruit. 2. soft mass of other material, especially wood, for making paper. *vb.* destroy shape and hardness by beating something, often with water.
pulpit *n.* a raised structure in a church from which the priest or minister talks.
pulse *n.* the throbbing of your heart that you can feel in your wrist; rhythmical beat. *vb.* **pulsate.**
pulverize *vb.* crush or crumble to dust.
puma *n.* large member of the cat family from America. Also known as cougar and mountain lion.
pumice *n.* a light, porous volcanic stone used for scrubbing.

pump *vb.* push liquid or air through pipes. *The heart pumps blood around our bodies through tiny tubes.* *n.* a machine or apparatus that does this.

pumpkin *n.* a large usually round orange-coloured vegetable which grows on the ground.

punch 1. *vb.* hit someone with the fist. *n.* a blow with the fist. 2. *n.* a tool for cutting holes. 3. *n.* a mixture of wine, lemon, hot water, spices etc.

punctual *adj.* on time.

punctuation *n.* the marks used in writing like the full stop (.), the comma (,), the semicolon (;), the colon (:), the question mark (?) and the exclamation mark (!). **punctuate** *vb.*

puncture *vb.* & *n.* pierce; make a hole in something; a hole.

punish *vb.* do something to someone who has done wrong so that they will not want to do it again. **punishment** *n.*

punt *n.* 1. long flat-bottomed boat propelled by a pole. 2. Irish unit of money.

puny *adj.* small.

pupa *n.* (plural **pupae**) the chrysalis stage in an insect's development.

pupil *n.* 1. a person who is learning from a teacher, a student. 2. the round dark opening in the coloured part (the iris) of the eye.

puppet *n.* a kind of doll that can be made to move by pulling strings or by some other method.

puppy *n.* a young dog.

purchase *vb.* & *n.* buy, or something that is bought.

pure *adj.* clean; not mixed with anything.

purple *adj.* & *n.* a dark, red-blue colour.

purpose *n.* intention, object.

purr *vb.* the low vibrating noise made by a contented cat.

purse 1. *n.* an object used for carrying money. 2. *vb.* screw up your lips.

pursue *vb.* chase after. *The crowd pursued the thief.* **pursuit** *n.*

pus *n.* yellowish fluid around an inflamed part of the skin, e.g. a pimple.

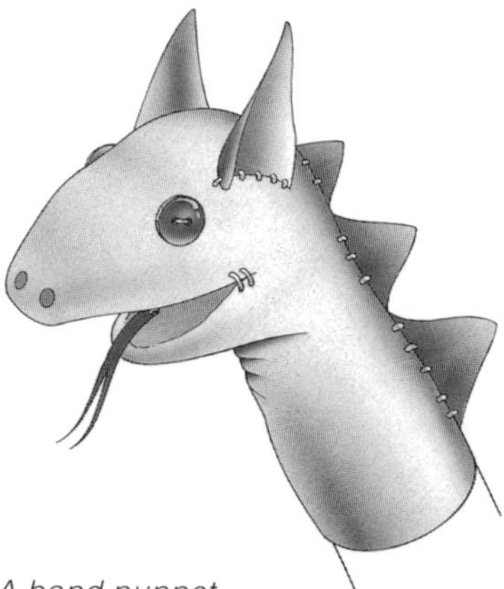

A hand puppet.

push *vb.* press on something; shove.
pusher *n.* a person who sells illegal drugs.
put *vb.* place something somewhere.
put by *vb.* keep something to use it later; save. *I put by some of my money every week for my holiday.*
put off *vb.* 1. decide to do something later than planned. *We had flu so we put off the party until next week.* 2. feel badly about something you dislike. *I was quite put off by the way she spoke to me.*
putrefy *vb.* go bad, rot.
putter *n.* a type of golf club used on the green, which is the area of short grass round a hole.
putty *n.* a greyish paste which hardens when dry and is used for fixing glass into window frames.
put up *vb.* accommodate for a short time. *I can put you up for the night.*
put up with *vb.* not to complain about something even though you do not like it; tolerate. *It's not a very nice place, but my brother likes it, so I will just have to put up with it.*
puzzle *n.* a difficult problem. *vb.* be perplexed.
Pygmy *n.* small, dark-skinned people who live in the hot equatorial forests of Africa. The men are seldom taller than 1.5 metres (5 ft) and the women are even smaller.
pyjamas *n.* a loose jacket and trousers worn in bed.
pylon *n.* tall metal tower supporting electric cables.
pyramid *n.* a structure with a square (or other) base and sloping sides that meet at the top.
python *n.* a large kind of snake.

quack 1. *vb.* make a noise like a duck. 2. *n.* a person who pretends to be a doctor, but is not properly qualified.
quadrangle *n.* a four-sided courtyard.
quadrant *n.* 1. an instrument for measuring vertical angles. 2. quarter of a circle.
quadruped *n.* a four-footed animal. *A horse is a quadruped.*
quadruple *adj.* in four parts.
quadruplet *n.* one of four babies born at the same time to the same mother.
quail *n.* a small game bird, related to the partridge, and found in most parts of the world.

quaint *adj*. odd but pleasant; old-fashioned. *We spent our holiday in a quaint little fishing village in Cornwall.*
quake *vb*. tremble with fear.
qualification *n*. 1. knowledge or skill making person fit for a post. 2. modification.
qualify *vb*. 1. become fit for a post. 2. limit the meaning of a statement so that it is less general.
quality *n*. how good or bad a thing is. *We want the best quality of carpet.*
qualm 1. *n*. sudden feeling of sickness. 2. sudden doubt.
quantity *n*. how much; the size, weight or number of anything. *What quantity of cement do you need?*
quarantine (**kwar**-*ant-een*) *n*. a period when someone who has a disease is kept away from other people so that they cannot catch it.
quarrel *vb*. & *n*. argue angrily. **quarrelsome** *adj*.
quarry *n*. 1. a place where stone for building and other purposes is taken out of the ground. 2. an animal that is hunted.
quart (*kwort*) *n*. a measure of liquids (1.14 litres). *There are two pints in a quart.*
quarter *n*. 1. a fourth part of a whole; $\frac{1}{4}$. 2. a district. *The Latin Quarter of Paris.*
quarterly *adj*. due every quarter of the year i.e. every three months. *n*. publication issued every quarter.
quartet *n*. four people doing something together, especially making music.
quartz *n*. a common, hard mineral.
quash *vb*. set aside, declare as not valid.
quasi- *prefix* meaning seemingly or almost.
quaver 1. *vb*. tremble, trill (of singing voice). 2. *n*. a very short note in music.

A ship loading at a quay.

quay (*key*) *n.* a landing place for ships.
queasy *adj.* feeling sick; nauseous.
queen *n.* 1. the female ruler of a country or the wife of a king. 2. the most powerful piece in chess.
queer *adj.* strange and peculiar. *This soup tastes very queer.*
quell *vb.* overcome, subdue, crush.
quench *vb.* satisfy thirst; put out fire.
querelous *adj.* complaining.
query *n.* a question. *vb.* ask a question.
quest *n.* a search.
question *n.* something that you ask when you want to find out something and get an answer; subject being discussed. *vb.*
question mark *n.* a punctuation mark, like this ?. It goes at the end of written questions.
question master *n.* chairman of a quiz game.
questionnaire *n.* set of questions.
queue (rhymes with *dew*) *n.* a line of people waiting for something.
quibble *vb.* object to; argue.
quiche (*keesh*) *n.* a pastry shell filled with beaten egg and milk and savoury ingredients and then cooked.
quick *adv.* fast; speedy.
quickly *adj.* to do something fast.
quicksand *n.* a kind of swamp consisting of sand and water which will suck down a person or animal that tries to walk on it.
quick-silver *n.* another name for the metal mercury.
quid *n.* (*slang*) of money, a pound. *Can you lend me a quid please?*
quiet *adj.* not noisy; silent.
quiff *n.* prominent tuft of hair.
quill *n.* large feather used as a pen or plectrum.
quilt *n.* a padded bed covering.
quince *n.* a tree and its acid pear-shaped fruit.
quinine *n.* a strong, bitter-tasting substance made from the bark of the cinchona tree, used as a medicine to treat malaria.
quintuplet *n.* one of five babies born on the same day to the same mother.
quirk *n.* individual mannerism.
quit *vb.* leave; give up.
quite *adv.* 1. completely, wholly, entirely. *You are quite right.* 2. more or less, to some extent. *He dives quite well, but he's a poor swimmer.*
quiver *vb.* shake rapidly from side to side; shiver.
quiz *n.* a set of questions asked to find out how much people know, usually as a competition.
quoits ('Qu' like 'k') *pl. n.* a game that involves trying to throw rings on to pegs.
quotation *n.* 1. phrase or passage from a book, poem or play. 2. estimate of how much a thing will cost.
quotation marks *pl. n.* punctuation marks like this "....." or this '.....'. They are mainly used in writing to show spoken words.
quote *vb.* repeat someone else's words.

R

rabbi *n.* a teacher of Jewish law, the leader of a synagogue.
rabbit *n.* a small brownish-grey mammal with long ears and a very short tail.
rabble *n.* a mob, disorganized crowd of people.
rabies *n.* a usually fatal disease of the nervous system which is caught by being bitten by a rabid animal.
raccoon *n.* an American mammal with long greyish fur.

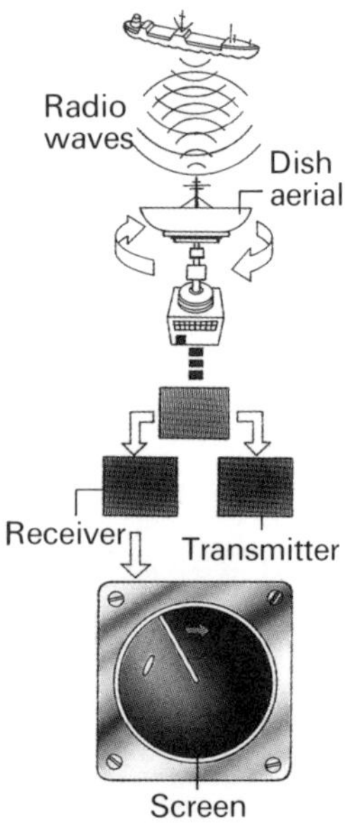

Radar works by sending out a high-powered beam, which bounces off solid objects.

race 1. *n.* a group of people of common ancestry who are alike and have the same coloured skin. 2. *vb.* compete with others to find out who is fastest. *n.* a contest of speed. **racial** *adj.*
racialist *n.* 1. a person who believes that the races are fundamentally different. 2. someone who supports or stirs up racist conflicts.

rack *n.* 1. framework or stand for holding objects. 2. a medieval instrument of torture.
racket *n.* 1. a lot of noise, a din. 2. (also **racquet**) a light bat used to hit balls in tennis, badminton or squash. 3. an unlawful means of making a living.
radar *n.* an instrument that sends out radio waves. These waves are reflected back off objects like aircraft or ships, and the reflection shows where the object is.
radiate *vb.* 1. give out heat and light. 2. be arranged like spokes.
radiator *n.* 1. a piece of equipment that sends out heat. 2. the part of a car that keeps

A raft is used to rescue possessions in a flooded Amazon region in Peru.

the cooling water at the correct temperature.

radical *adj*. fundamental, going to the root; (in politics) in favour of reforms and social change.

radio *n*. an instrument that receives radio waves and uses them to produce sounds. *vb*. transmit by radio.

radio waves *pl. n*. invisibile waves sent out by a transmitter and travelling very fast.

radish *n*. a small roundish root with a strong peppery taste.

radium *n*. a rare, radioactive metal.

radius *n*. (plural **radii**) a straight line from the centre of a circle to its edge or circumference.

raffia *n*. a fibre from an African palm tree, used for weaving matting etc.

raffle *n*. & *vb*. a lottery; dispose of by lottery.

raft *n*. logs fastened together to make a sort of boat.

rafter *n*. one of the cross-bars of wood in a roof.

rag *n*. a piece of torn clothing or cloth.

rage *n*. great anger. *vb*. rave, be violent.

raid *n*. & *vb*. a surprise attack.

rail *n*. 1. a long bar or rod. 2. one of the long metal strips that form a railway line.

railings *pl. n*. a fence made of metal bars.

railway *n*. the organization that controls a system of tracks, and the trains that run of them. *US* **railroad**.

rain *n*. drops of water falling from the sky. *vb*. fall or send down as rain.

rainbow *n*. an arch of colour in the sky. *A rainbow is caused by sun shining on rain or mist*.

raincoat *n*. a waterproof overcoat.

rainfall *n*. the amount of rain that falls in a period of time.

raise *vb*. lift up; make higher.

raisin *n*. a dried grape.

rajah *n*. an Indian king or ruler.

rake *n*. a tool like a comb on a long handle. *vb*. use a rake.

rally *vb.* come together, arouse, recover from illness. *n.* meeting, competitive event.
ram *n.* a male sheep. 2. *vb.* hit and push hard. *The ship rammed the submarine.*
Ramadan *n.* the ninth month of the Muslim year. During it, all Muslims must fast from dawn to dusk.
ramble 1. *vb.* wander about without purpose. 2. *vb.* talk in a disconnected way. 3. *n.* a walk for pleasure.
ramp *n.* a sloping floor, path etc, leading from one level to another.
rampage *vb.* to behave in a violent manner, run riot. *n.* uncontrolled, violent behaviour as in *on the rampage.*
rampart *n.* fortified mound of earth.
ramshackle *adj.* broken down; derelict.
ran *vb.* past of **run**.
ranch *n.* a large farm in North America with a lot of land for grazing.
rancid *adj.* smelling and tasting stale, especially fats. *The butter was rancid.*
random *adj.* (at random) without purpose; haphazard.
rang *vb.* past of **ring**.
range 1. *n.* a row of mountains. 2. *n.* the distance over which a gun has to fire a bullet. 3. *n.* a large area of open country (USA). 4. *n.* an old-fashioned kind of oven. 5. *vb.* place in rows.
ranger *n.* 1. keeper of a forest or national park. 2. (USA) specially trained soldier. 3. (in colonial times) mounted policeman. 4. senior guide or scout.
rani *n.* the wife of a rajah; an Indian queen.
rank *n.* 1. a title or place that shows how important someone is. *General is a very high rank in the army.* 2. row, a line.
ransack *vb.* search thoroughly; plunder.
ransom *n.* money paid to a kidnapper to make him or her release a prisoner. *vb.* buy freedom.
rap *n.* & *vb.* the sound of knocking.
rape *n.* 1. forcing a person (especially a woman) to have sexual intercourse without consent. *vb.* commit rape on. 2. plant grown as animal fodder.
rapid 1. *adj.* swift; fast. 2. *n.* a sudden steep slope in a river.
rapier *n.* a kind of sword with a slim blade, used for thrusting.
raptor *n.* a bird of prey such as an eagle or a hawk.
rapture *n.* extreme delight.
rare *adj.* unusual; not often found.

A rapier is a long sword, used in France in the 18th century.

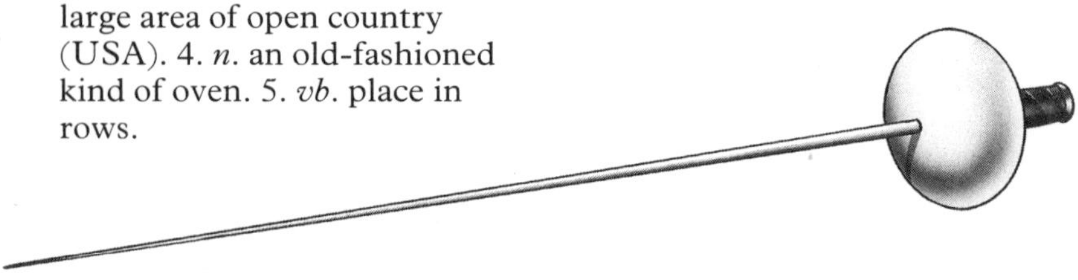

rascal *n.* a worthless fellow; a mischievous child.
rash 1. *n.* lots of red spots on the skin. 2. *adj.* reckless, hasty.
rasher *n.* a thin slice of bacon.
rasp *vb.* to scrape or scratch roughly. *n.* a type of file.
raspberry *n.* a small red berry which is good to eat.
rat *n.* a rodent (gnawing animal) found in large numbers all over the world. *vb.* **rat on** (slang) betray friends.
rate 1. *n.* charge or payment, according to some standard. *My rate for cleaning windows is £4 an hour.* 2. *n.* speed over a given distance. 3. *pl. n.* local government tax. 4. *vb.* estimate, regard. *How do you rate her chances of winning?*
rather 1. *adj.* somewhat. *Our friend is rather late.* 2. *adv.* preferably. *I would rather stay at home than go out.*
ratify *vb.* to formally approve or confirm something: used of treaties and legal agreements.
ratio *n.* the relationship in amount or size between two or more things. *The ratio of text to pictures in this book is about 2 columns (of text) to 1 (of pictures).*
ration *n.* a fixed portion, expecially of food. *In the war the tea ration was 4 ounces a week.*
rational *adj.* 1. based on reason; sensible. *Tom's argument sounded very rational.* 2. able to think clearly.
rattle 1. *vb.* make a clattering noise. 2. *n.* a baby's toy which makes a rattling noise when shaken.

The rattlesnake lives in the deserts of the Americas. It rattles its tail in warning before it strikes.

rattlesnake *n.* a poisonous snake from America.
ratty *adj.* irritable, easily annoyed.
raucous *adj.* harsh and unpleasant sounding.
rave *vb.* talk wildly without making sense; speak with great enthusiasm. *She raved about his bushy beard.*
ravel *vb.* tangle up: the opposite of **unravel**.
raven *n.* a large black bird of the crow family.
ravine *n.* a deep valley or gorge.
ravioli *n.* squares of pasta with a meat or cheese filling.
raw *adj.* 1. uncooked. *It can be dangerous to eat raw meat.* 2. without experience. *Many of the soldiers were raw recruits.* 3. sensitive to touch.
ray *n.* 1. line or beam of light, heat or some kind of energy. 2. a flat fish.
rayon *n.* the name given to various artificial textile fibres containing cellulose, a substance found in the walls of plant cells.
razor *n.* an instrument for shaving hair from the skin.

A reactor.

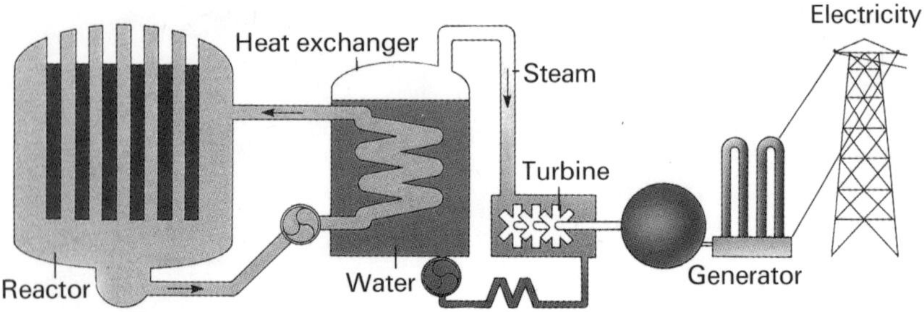

re- 1. *prep.* concerning, '*Re the book you lent me...*'. 2. *prefix* meaning again, repeated. By knowing the meaning of the main word the sense of the prefixed word should, in most cases, be obvious, e.g. reintroduce, rethink etc.

reach *vb.* get or grab hold of something; arrive at.

react *vb.* respond to; change chemically.

reactor *n.* an apparatus in which atomic energy is produced.

read *vb.* look at, and understand, writing or printing.

ready *adv.* prepared. *Are you ready yet?* In a fit state; willing.

real *adj.* actual; alive; correct; genuine.

realize *vb.* come to understand. *Judy realized that she must have seen a ghost.*

really *adv.* truly; correctly. *Do you really mean that?*

realm (*relm*) *n.* another word for kingdom.

reap *vb.* cut and collect a cereal crop, such as wheat.

rear 1. *n.* & *adj.* the back part; at the back. *I like to sit at the rear of the classroom.* 2. *vb.* look after animals as they grow up. 3. *vb.* (of a horse) stand up on the back legs.

reason *n.* anything that explains why or how something has happened; power of mind to think. *vb.* try to reach conclusions by thinking. **reasonable** *adj.* having good judgement; moderate; fair.

rebate *n.* discount, reduction.

rebel (**rebb**-*l*) *n.* someone who revolts against a government; someone who refuses to obey orders. *vb.* (*re*-**bell**) revolt, organize a rebellion. *n.*

rebuke *vb.* speak severely to, reprimand. *n.*

recall *vb.* 1. remember; bring back to mind. 2. call someone back.

recede *vb.* move back, withdraw. **recession** *n.* decline in activity or prosperity.

receipt (*re*-**seet**) *n.* an official piece of paper stating that a bill has been paid.

receive (*re*-**seeve**) *vb.* get something that has been given to you or sent to you; accept.

recent *adj.* not long ago.

receptacle *n.* container.

recital *n.* a performance, usually of music. *A piano recital.*

recite *vb.* say aloud from

memory. *Paul can recite a poem by heart.*

reckless *adj.* careless, rash, wild.

reckon *vb.* calculate, count; estimate; suppose, think. *I reckon it's time to go.*

reclaim *vb.* 1. restore poor or abandoned land to agricultural use. 2. get back something you are entitled to.

recline *vb.* lean; lie.

recognize *vb.* know that you have seen somebody or something before. *I wonder if she will recognize me after all those years?* To acknowledge.

recommend *vb.* advise; speak or write well of. *I recommend this book.*

reconcile *vb.* 1. make friends after a quarrel. 2. resign oneself to.

record (**reck**-*ord*) 1. *n.* a flat disc which makes sounds when it is turned on a record-player. 2. *n.* & *adj.* the best performance known. *She scored a record number of goals.*

record (*ree*-**kord**) *vb.* 1. write something down so that it will be remembered. 2. put sounds on a record or tape.

recorder *n.* a musical instrument made of wood or plastic, played by blowing into one end.

recording see **record**.

record-player *n.* a machine for playing records.

recover *vb.* 1. get something back. *He recovered his boot from the mud.* 2. get better. *I am glad you have recovered from your fall.* **recovery** *n.*

recruit *n.* a newly enlisted or drafted member of the armed forces. *vb.* enlist.

rectangle *n.* a four-sided figure in which the opposite sides are equal to each other and all four angles are right angles.

recuperate *vb.* get better after an illness; restore, recover.

recur *vb.* (past **recurred**) occur again. **recurrence** *n.*

red *n.* & *adj.* the colour of blood. *Red is one of the primary colours.*

reduce *vb.* make less.

redundant *adj.* exceeding what is needed (of workers and so dismissed). **redundancy** *n.*

reed *n.* tall, firm-stemmed grass that grows near water.

reef *n.* a ridge of rock near the surface of the sea.

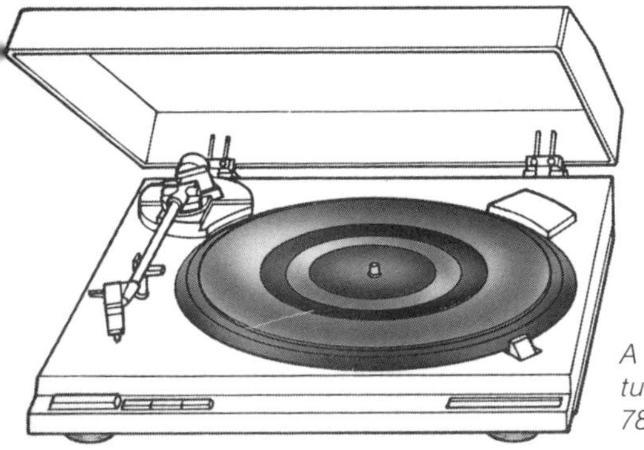

A modern record player has a turntable which rotates 33, 45 or 78 times a minute.

An example of refraction.

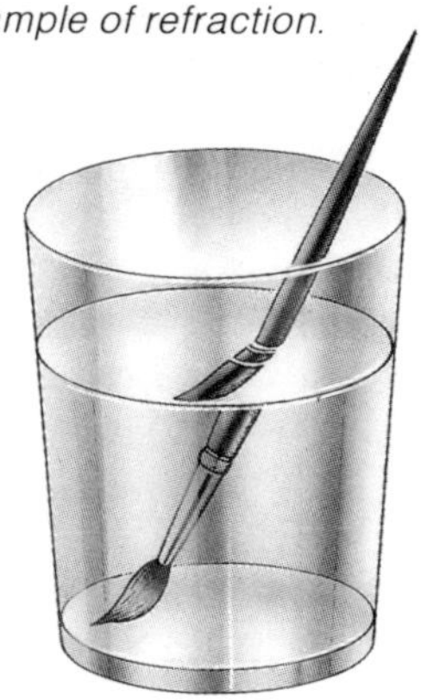

reel 1. *n.* device for winding, e.g. fishing line; length of film on a spool. 2. *n.* Scottish dance. 3. *vb.* sway, be giddy.
refectory *n.* a dining room in a convent, monastery or some schools.
referee *n.* a person who controls a football or boxing match. **ref** (*abbrev.*). *vb.*
reference book *n.* a book that is used to find particular pieces of information. You do not usually read through the whole book. *Dictionaries and encyclopedias are reference books.*
referendum *n.* voting on a particular issue by all voters; a plebiscite.
refine *vb.* remove impurities. **refinery** *n.* a place where oil or sugar etc is refined.
reflect *vb.* send back light, heat, sound or radio waves from any object.
reflection *n.* the picture you see in a mirror or in calm water.
reform *vb.* make a great political or social change; improve. **reformation** *n.*
refraction *n.* the bending of light when it passes from one medium to another.
refrain 1. *vb.* curb, restrain, keep oneself from doing. 2. *n.* regularly recurring phrase or verse at the end of stanzas of a poem.
refresh *vb.* give new energy to.
refrigerator *n.* a sort of cupboard in which food is kept very cold so that it does not go bad.
refuge *n.* a shelter from danger. **refugee** *n.* person escaping danger and seeking shelter.
refund *vb.* return money. *n.*
refuse (*re*-**fyuse**) *vb.* say that you will not do something that you are asked to do. **refusal** *n.*
refuse (**ref**-*yuse*) *n.* rubbish, things that are thrown away.
regal *adj.* concerning kings and queens, royal; magnificent.
regalia *n.* emblems and symbols of royalty (crown, sceptre etc).
regard *vb.* look at; take into consideration; hold in high esteem. *n.* look, concern; (*pl*) friendly feelings. *I send you my regards.*
regarding *prep.* concerning.
regatta *n.* a race meeting for boats and yachts.
regent *n.* a person who takes the place of a monarch if the monarch is too young or too ill to rule.
reggae (**reg**-*ay*) *n.* West Indian music with a strong beat.
regime (ray-**jeem**) *n.* a system of government; a set of rules for diet etc.
regiment *n.* a large army unit.
region (**ree**-*jun*) *n.* an area of the world or of a country with

Reindeer are bred for their milk, meat and skins. They also pull sledges.

no particular border. *Evergreens grow mainly in the colder regions of the world.* **regional** *adj*.

register 1. *n*. a book in which lists of things or other information is kept. 2. *vb*. record; put in writing. *I wish to register a complaint.*

regress *vb*. move backwards. *n*. **regression**.

regret *vb*. be sorry for something that has been done. *n*.

regular *adj*. happening in the same way or at the same time again and again. *There is a regular bus service between most big cities.*

regulate *vb*. 1. govern or control according to rules. 2. adjust (a watch etc).

regulation *n*. a rule or order. *adj*. according to the rules, standard or normal.

rehearse *vb*. practise, particularly for a play or concert. **rehearsal** *n*. a practice performance of a play.

reign (rhymes with *pain*) *vb*. & *n*. rule as a king or queen; period of rule.

reindeer *n*. a kind of large deer that lives in cold regions.

reinforce *vb*. strengthen, give additional support.

reins (rhymes with *canes*) *pl. n*. straps fastened to a bridle to control a horse.

reject *vb*. refuse to accept or keep something because it is not good enough. *n*.

rejoice *vb*. an old-fashioned word meaning 'to be happy'.

relapse *vb*. slip or fall back into a former worse state. *n*. *He was getting better; then he had a relapse.*

relative *n*. someone who belongs to the same family as you. *Your aunt and uncle are your relatives.*

relax *vb*. become less tight; loosen. *If you relax your muscles you will feel better.*

relay race *n*. a race in which each person in a team goes part of the distance.

release *vb*. set free, liberate; put into circulation.

relegate *vb*. send to or put in a lower position. *At the end of the season, the football team was relegated to the second division.*

relevant *adj*. relating to or connected with the subject being discussed etc.

reliable *adj*. can be trusted and depended upon.

relic *n*. something that survives destruction; something belonging to a holy person kept as an object of reverence.

relief (*re*-**leaf**) *n.* 1. removal or lessening of pain etc. 2. help given to refugees etc. 3. carving etc. in which the designs stand out from the surface.

relief map *n.* a map that shows where high and low areas of land are.

relieve *vb.* free; give aid to.

religion *n.* a belief that there is a god who created and controls the universe. **religious** *adj.*

relish 1. *n.* enjoyment of food etc. 2. *n.* a sauce. 3. *vb.* get pleasure from.

reluctant *adj.* unwilling, hesitating. *He was reluctant to help.* **reluctance** *n.*

rely *vb.* depend on. *I rely on you to give me a lift tomorrow.*

remain 1. *vb.* stay after others. *Sue remained in the house when the others went out.* 2. *vb.* be left over after some has been taken away. *You can have the few sweets that remain.* 3. *pl. n.* what is left after some amount has been taken away; a dead body.

remainder *n.* what is left over when a part has gone or been taken away.

remark *vb.* & *n.* comment, observe. **remarkable** *adj.* worth noticing; extraordinary.

remedy *n.* medicine or treatment for a disease. *vb.* put right.

remember *vb.* keep something in mind; recall, or bring something to mind; not to forget. *Remember to telephone me when you arrive.*

remind *vb.* make or help someone remember. *Sarah reminded everyone about her birthday.*

remiss *adj.* careless, neglectful of duty or responsibility.

remote *adj.* far away from other places. *We spent our honeymoon on a remote island.*

remove *vb.* take away.

Renaissance *n.* a French word meaning 'rebirth' and describing the great revival in learning, art etc. that took place in Europe from the 14th to 16th century.

rendezvous (**ron**-*day-voo*) *n.* an appointed meeting place. *vb.* meet at an appointed place.

rent 1. *n.* a regular payment made for the use of a house or other place or thing. 2. *vb.* have the use of something you pay a rent for.

repair *vb.* make something that is broken whole again; mend.

A famous Renaissance dome in Florence, Italy.

repeat *vb.* say or do again.
repeatedly *adj.* again and again.
repel *vb.* drive back, turn away.
repellent *adj.* unattractive.
repent *vb.* feel sorrow or regret for the wrong one has done.
replace *vb.* put back where it came from. *Please replace the book on the right shelf.*
replica *n.* an exact copy of something.
reply *vb.* answer someone. *n.* an answer.
report 1. *vb.* tell of something; give an account of (for publication); the account itself, spoken or written. 2. *n.* a bang.
reporter *n.* a person who obtains and writes about news for a newspaper, TV etc.

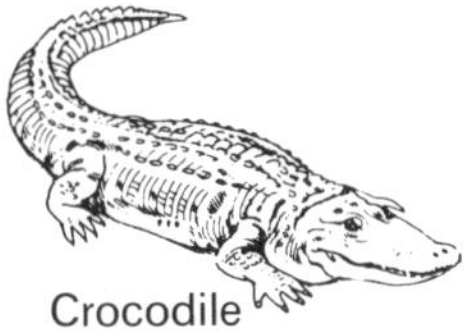
Crocodile

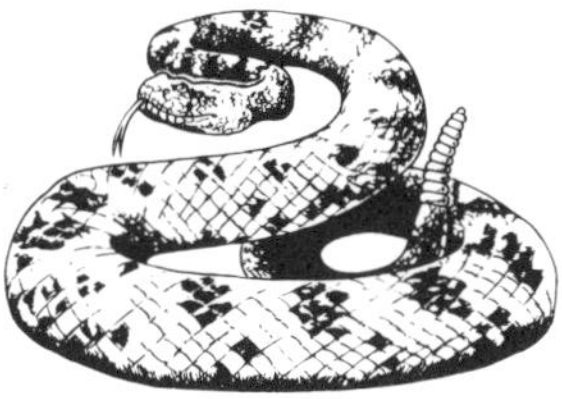
Rattlesnake

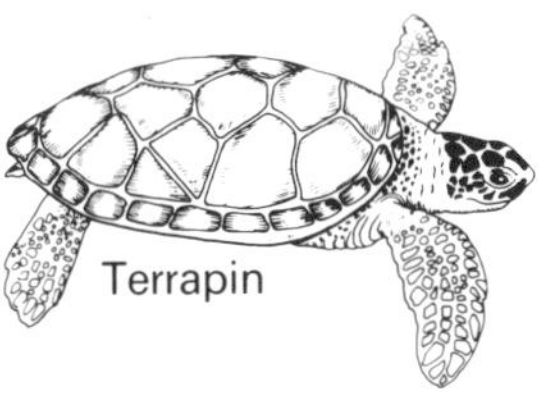
Terrapin

Reptiles are the most advanced cold-blooded animals.

represent *vb.* act or speak for other people. *Your MP represents you in Parliament.*
reprimand *vb.* speak sharply to, scold. *n.* official rebuke.
reproduce *vb.* 1. make something happen again; copy. *The concert was recorded on tape and reproduced the next day.* 2. give birth. **reproduction** *n.*
reptile *n.* a cold-blooded vertebrate animal that creeps or crawls. *Crocodiles, snakes and tortoises are all reptiles.*
republic *n.* a country that elects a president as head of state and does not have a king or queen.
reputation *n.* a person's qualities or character as seen and judged by others.
request *vb.* & *n.* ask for something. *He requested this tape.*
require *vb.* 1. need. *She requires some help with the costumes.* 2. insist on.
rescue *vb.* take from danger; set free. *The knight will rescue the princess from the dragon. n.* being rescued.
research (*re*-**surch**) *vb.* investigate, look into carefully. *n.* inquiry, scientific study.
resemble *vb.* be or look like something or somebody else. *Alan resembles his grandfather.* **resemblance** *n.*
reserve 1. *vb.* keep back to use later. *Shall I reserve a chair for you if you are late? n.* a place kept for a special purpose. *You can see some very rare birds at the bird reserve.* 2. *n.* a player who will not play for the team unless someone else is unable to play. **reserved** *adj.* shy.

A human eyeball. The retina receives images, enabling us to see.

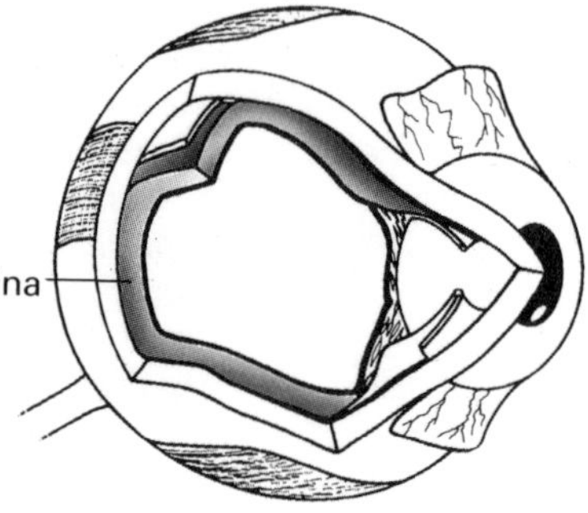

reservoir *n.* a place where a large amount of water is stored, often in an artificial lake.

resident *n.* someone who lives in a particular place, a permanent inhabitant. *Lee is now resident in Wales.* **reside** *vb.*

resign (*re*-**zine**) *vb.* give up, especially to give up a job. **resignation** *n.*

resin *n.* a sticky gum that oozes (leaks slowly) from trees; rosin, the best known, comes from pines.

resist *vb.* oppose; go against. **resistance** *n.*

resources *pl. n.* the useful things that a person or country has. *Oil is one of our country's greatest resources.*

respect *vb.* & *n.* (have) a high opinion of; esteem. **respectable** *adj.* decent, of good solid behaviour.

resort 1. *vb.* turn to. *He was so unhappy he resorted to overeating.* 2. *n.* holiday centre.

re-sort *vb.* sort again.

resolve *vb.* decide, be determined to. *I resolve to get to work on time in the future.*

responsible *adj.* in charge of something. *I am responsible for the paint cupboard.*

rest 1. *vb.* lie down; relax. 2. *n.* the remainder. *What has happened to the rest of our group?* **restful** *adj.* quiet, soothing.

restaurant *n.* a place where you can buy and eat food.

restore *vb.* put back as it was before; repair. *Sue restores old furniture.*

restrict *vb.* keep within bounds, limit. **restriction** *n.*

result 1. *n.* & *vb.* something that happens because of some action or happening. *Joe's injury was the result of a kick at football.* 2. *n.* the final score in a game.

resume *vb.* begin again, take back. *After the interval the concert resumed.*

resurrect *vb.* bring back to life. **Resurrection** the rising of Jesus Christ from the tomb.

retail *vb.* sell goods in a shop. (*see also* **wholesale**)

retain *vb.* hold back, keep.

retina *n.* coating at the back of the eyeball which is sensitive to light.

retire *vb*. 1. give up work, usually because one is old. 2. go back; withdraw. *The rain was so heavy, we had to retire to the pavilion.*
retreat *vb*. go back from.
return *vb*. 1. give something back. *Could you please return my pen.* 2. go back. *When do you return from your holiday?*
reunion *n*. being re-united, a coming together again.
reveal *vb*. uncover; make known. *I can now reveal the secret.*
revenue *n*. the money that a government receives from taxation etc.
revere *vb*. show respect, honour for.
reverse 1. *vb*. go backwards, particularly in a vehicle. 2. *n*. the opposite of something. **reversible** *adj*. able to be reversed.
review 1. *n*. published opinion of a book, play etc. *vb*. examine, criticize. 2. *vb*. & *n*. inspect troops. *n*.
revise *vb*. look over again in order to correct or improve. **revision** *n*.
revive *vb*. bring back to life or consciousness; make active again. *The Olympic Games were revived in modern times.*
revolt *vb*. rebel, turn away from or feel disgust at.
revolution *n*. 1. a time when a government is changed by force, not by an election; a time when ideas and the way people live are changed by new ideas or actions, as in the *Industrial Revolution*. 2. a full turn of a wheel. **revolve** *vb*.
revolver *n*. a hand gun with its ammunition held in a revolving cylinder.
reward *n*. a present given to someone for what they have done. *We were given a reward for helping to catch the thief*. *vb*. give reward.
rheumatism *n*. the name given to a group of diseases which cause pain in the muscles and joints and makes them stiff and hard to move.
rhinoceros *n*. a large African or Asian animal with a very thick skin and one or two horns.

Rhubarb stalks.

rhubarb *n*. the stalks of the rhubarb plant cooked and eaten.
rhyme (sounds like *time*) *vb*. use a word that sounds like another word. *'Egg' and 'beg' rhyme with each other*. *n*.
rhythm (**rith**-*em*) *n*. the pattern of beats in music and poetry.
rib *n*. one of the curved bones of the chest.

ribcage *n.* bone structure protecting organs in the chest.
ribbon *n.* a narrow piece of material used as an ornament or for tying things, as well as in typewriters.
rice *n.* a grain that is used as food. *Rice grows in wet parts of India and China.*
rich *adj.* 1. having a great deal of money, wealthy. 2. (of food) containing a great deal of fat, cream etc.
rickshaw *n.* small oriental two-wheeled vehicle drawn by a man on foot or on a bicycle.

rid (get rid of) *vb.* throw away something that is not wanted.
riddle *n.* a puzzling question. *'What goes up when the rain comes down?' is a riddle. (The answer is an umbrella.)*
ride *vb.* (past **rode** past part. **ridden**) travel on something, particularly a horse or bicycle.
rider *n.* a person who rides, particularly on horseback.
ridge *n.* a long narrow part higher than what is on either side.
ridiculous *adj.* silly enough to be laughed at. **ridicule** *vb.* make fun of.
rifle *n.* a gun that is held against the shoulder when it is fired.
rift *n.* a split, opening; chasm.
rig 1. *n.* arrangement of ships' sails. 2. *n.* equipment for drilling oil wells.
rigid *adj.* stiff; unbending; strict.
right 1. *n.* & *adj.* the opposite of left. 2. *adj.* correct; accurate; good. *Do you have the right time?*
rim 1. *n.* the edge of a container. 2. *n.* the outside edge of a circle.
rind *n.* the skin of some fruits and vegetables, and of cheese and bacon.
ring 1. *n.* a circle, such as the ring in a circus. 2. *n.* a circular band of gold or other material worn on a finger as an ornament. 3. *n.* the sound made by a bell. 4. *vb.* telephone someone. *Ring me in the morning.*
ring off *vb.* end a telephone call.
ring up *vb.* telephone.
rink *n.* a place for skating.
rinse *vb.* wash out in clean water.
riot *n.* a noisy and violent disturbance by a crowd. *vb.* take part in a riot.
rip *vb.* tear something.
ripe *adj.* (of fruit) ready to be eaten. **ripen** *vb.* grow ripe.
ripple *n.* small movement on the surface of water.
rise *vb.* come or go up; get up.
risk *n.* the chance of danger or

loss. *vb.* expose to risk. **risky** *adj.*

rite *n.* the set words and actions of a (religious) ceremony. **ritual** *adj.* & *n.* concerned with rites; the rite itself.

rival *n.* a competitor; an opponent. *vb.* compete with.

river *n.* a large stream of water that flows from higher to lower ground and into another river, a lake or sea.

rivet *n.* a bolt for joining metal plates together. *vb.* join with rivets; hold the attention.

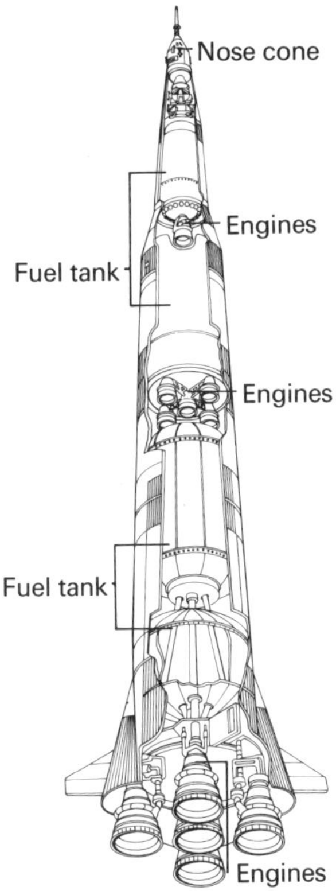

A space rocket consists of several stages which are each fired in turn.

road *n.* a wide path or highway for cars and other vehicles.

roam *vb.* wander; go here and there.

roar *n.* & *vb.* loud deep sound like the noise a lion makes.

roast *vb.* cook food in an oven.

rob *vb.* take or steal things. **robber** *n.* a person who steals; a thief. **robbery** *n.* theft.

robe *n.* a long dress or gown, sometimes worn as part of a national or ceremonial costume. *vb.* put on robes.

robin *n.* a small bird of the thrush family with rusty-orange feathers on its throat and breast. *Robins often make their homes in town gardens.*

robot *n.* a machine that can be made to do things that people do.

rock 1. *n.* a large stone. 2. *n.* a type of popular music with a strong beat. 3. *vb.* move from side to side.

rocket *n.* 1. a firework that shoots up into the sky. 2. a device for sending missiles and spacecraft into space.

rod *n.* a long, straight stick.

rode *vb.* past of **ride.**

rodent *n.* one of a group of mammals that gnaw things. *Rats, mice and squirrels are all rodents.*

rodeo *n.* performance by American cowboys and cowgirls of riding and other skills.

rogue *n.* a bad man; a rascal.

roll 1. *vb.* turn over and over. 2. *n.* make something into a shape like a tube. 3. *vb.* flatten with roller. 4. *n.* a small loaf of bread.

roller-skates *pl. n.* set of wheels attached to a boot for skating or gliding on the ground.
rolling-pin *n.* a long tube used for rolling out pastry to flatten it.
Roman Catholic *n.* a Christian who accepts the Pope as the head of the Church.
romance *n.* medieval tale of chivalry; a love story. *vb.* exaggerate. **Romance** *adj.* languages based on Latin. **romantic** *adj.* imaginative, remote, mysterious.
Romanticism *n.* a late 18th- and early 19th-century artistic movement.
roof *n.* the top covering of a building. *vb.* cover with a roof.
rook 1. *n.* a bird belonging to the crow family. 2. *n.* castle-shaped chess piece. 3. *vb.* defraud.
room *n.* a space; a compartment in a building, such as a living room or bedroom.
roost *n.* & *vb.* a resting place for birds; a perch.
root *n.* the part of a plant that grows under the ground.
rope *n.* thick strong cord. **ropy** *adj.* 1. like rope. 2. poor quality.
rose *vb.* past of **rise.**
rose *n.* a beautiful kind of garden flower; *adj.* deep pink.
rosemary *n.* an evergreen shrub used in cooking and making perfume.
Rosh Hashanah *n.* the festival of the Jewish New Year.
rot *vb.* go bad; decay.
rotate *vb.* go around and around. **rotation** *n.*
rotor *n.* the rotating blades on top of a helicopter which serve as both the propellers and wings of a fixed wing aircraft. They provide both 'thrust' and 'lift'.
rotten *adj.* to be soft or bad. *Wasps like to eat rotten apples.*
rouble *n.* Russian unit of money.
rough (rhymes with *cuff*) *adj.* 1. not smooth. *My dog has a rough coat.* 2. not gentle. 3. done quickly and not meant to be exact. *Can you draw me a rough plan of the town?*
round *adj.* shaped like a circle or a ball.
roundabout 1. *n.* a merry-go-round; a fairground ride on which people sit and go round and round. 2. *n.* a place where a number of roads meet and the traffic goes round in a circle.
rouse *vb.* wake up, stir; excite.
route (rhymes with *boot*) *n.* the road or direction taken to get somewhere.

Rosemary is a common herb.

routine (root-**een**) *n.* set way of doing things.
row (rhymes with *cow*) *n.* & *vb.* noise, quarrel.
row (rhymes with *go*) 1. *vb.* use oars to make a boat move through water. 2. *n.* a line. *She planted a row of beans in her garden.*
rowdy *adj.* noisy and disorderly.
royal *adj.* to do with kings and queens. *When a king is married he has a royal wedding.* **royalty** *n.* being royal; a percentage paid to an author etc, according to sales.
rub *vb.* 1. slide or press something against something else; polish; 2. rub out, remove marks etc on paper, blackboard etc.
rubber *n.* 1. a strong, elastic material made from the sap of a rubber tree. 2. a piece of rubber, or plastic, used for wiping out pencil marks.

Both elastic bands and erasers are made of rubber.

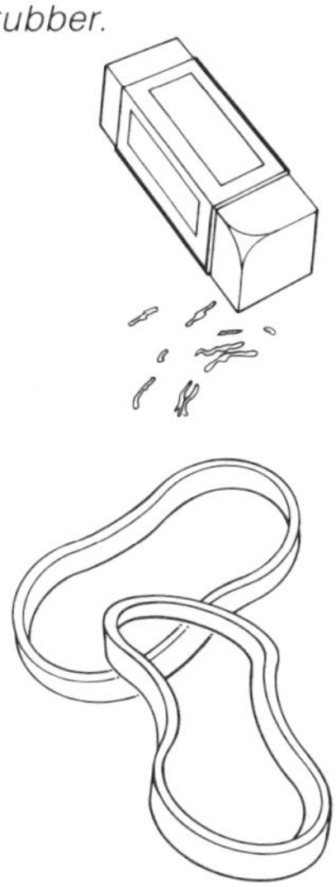

rubbish *n.* waste matter that is thrown away.
rubble *n.* debris – pieces of stone, brick etc. from a building.
ruby *n.* a precious red stone.
rucksack *n.* a bag that can be strapped on your back for carrying.

The rudder on the helicopter's tail controls the aircraft as it turns.

rudder *n.* a flat, upright, moveable part at the back of a boat or aircraft used for steering.
rude *adj.* 1. bad-mannered; impolite. 2. crude or simple (now old-fashioned).
ruffian *n.* a violent, lawless person.
rug *n.* a mat or small carpet or bed cover.
rugby *n.* a kind of football played by two teams with a oval-shaped ball which can be kicked, carried or passed from hand to hand.
ruin (**roo**-*in*) 1. *vb.* spoil completely. 2. *n.* the remains of an old building. *We visited the ruins of an abbey.*

rule 1. *n.* a law; something that must be obeyed. 2. *vb.* be in charge of a country, keep under control, govern. *William the Conqueror ruled England after 1066.*
ruler 1. *n.* a straight piece of wood, plastic or metal used for drawing lines or measuring. 2. *n.* a person who rules a country.
rum 1. *n.* an alcoholic liquor distilled from the fermented products of the sugar cane. 2. *adj.* odd.
rumble *vb.* & *n.* deep sound of distant thunder.
ruminant *n.* animal such as cow and deer which chews the cud.
rummage *vb.* search through a confused pile of things.
rumour *n.* a story that is passed around, but may not be true; hearsay. *There is a rumour that a spacecraft has landed in China.*
rump *n.* buttocks; back part of an animal.
rumple *vb.* wrinkle, crease.
run *vb.* (past **ran**) go very fast (of a person or animal); go smoothly; control. *She runs the office. n.* the act of running; (in cricket) a score made by running between the wickets.
run across *vb.* meet someone by chance. also **run into.**
rung *vb.* past of **ring**.
rung *n.* one step of a ladder.
runner *n.* messenger; person who runs in a race; the keel on which a sledge slides.
runway *n.* the hard surface on which an aircraft takes off and lands.
rural *adj.* of or about the countryside.
rush 1. *vb.* go very fast. 2. *n.* a kind of strong grass that grows near water.
rusk *n.* piece of bread rebaked until it is crisp.
rust *n.* the reddish-brown crust that forms on iron and some other metals when they become damp. *vb.* become covered with rust. **rusty** *adj.* rusted; out of practice. *My piano playing is rusty.*
rustic *adj.* to do with the country.
rustle 1. *n.* & *vb.* crisp sound of dry leaves. 2. *vb.* steal livestock.
rut *n.* a furrow in a road made by wheels. *The cart track was full of ruts and potholes.*
ruthless *adj.* having no pity.
rye *n.* a cereal grain that, with barley, is one of the hardiest grown. It is used to make flour as well as alcoholic drinks such as whisky, gin, vodka and kvass.

Rye is widely grown in the cooler regions of the world. When the grain is milled, it produces a dark-coloured flour.

S

sabbath *n.* a weekly religious day of rest. The sabbath is Saturday for Jews, and Sunday for Christians.

sable *n.* a small carnivorous mammal of the Arctic regions, prized for its fur. *adj.* a poetic word for black.

sabotage (**sabb**-*oh-tazh*) *vb.* & *n.* damage something on purpose.

sabre (**say**-*ber*) *n.* a sword with a curved blade.

sabre-toothed tiger *n.* prehistoric carnivorous mammal. In its largest form it was bigger than a modern lion, and had two canine teeth 20 cm (8 in) long in its upper jaw, for slashing at its prey.

saccharin (**sack**-*er-in*) *n.* white crystalline substance, 300 times as sweet as sugar, discovered in 1879. It is used in the diets of diabetics and slimmers.

sachet *n.* a small packet.

sack 1. *n.* a large bag made of strong material. 2. *vb.* dismiss someone from their job. 3. *vb.* destroy a town captured in war.

sacred *adj.* to do with religion and worship. *The Bible and the Koran are sacred books.*

sacrifice *vb.* give away something precious, often to God. *n.* the thing that is given away.

sad *adj.* unhappy; sorrowful. **sadden** *vb.*

saddle *n.* the rider's seat used on a bicycle or a horse. *vb.* put saddle on; burden someone with a task or person.

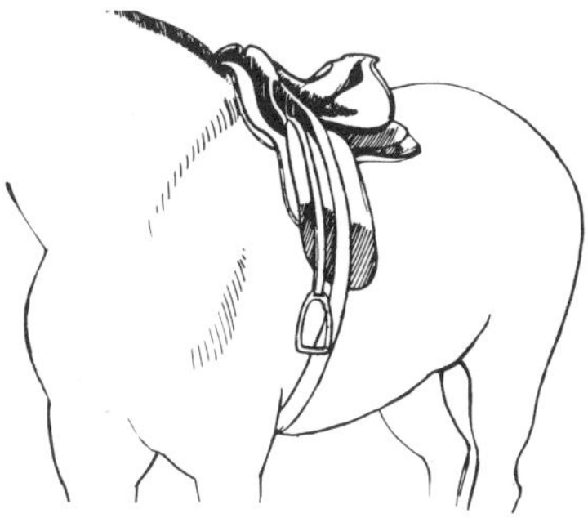

A horse's saddle.

saddlebag *n.* a small bag attached to a saddle.

safari (*sa*-**far**-*ee*) *n.* an expedition, usually in a hot country, at one time for the purpose of hunting animals, but today for observing and photographing them.

safe 1. *adj.* protected from danger. 2. *n.* a special strong, locked cupboard where money and other valuable things can be kept.

Salamanders look like lizards, but they are amphibians, not reptiles.

safeguard *vb.* protect. *n.* something that protects.

safety *n.* being safe from fear or danger. *The cattle were moved from the flooded fields to a place of safety.*

safety-pin *n.* a pin that locks its sharp point into itself, and so cannot prick anyone.

saffron *n.* a type of crocus, the stigmas of whose flowers give us the powder called saffron which is used as a flavouring in food and as a yellow dye.

sag *vb.* droop, bend, hang down (especially in the middle).

saga (**sah**-*gah*) *n.* an old story, especially one that tells of the ancient Norse heroes of Scandinavia.

sage 1. *n.* perennial herb belonging to the mint family, the leaves of which are used in cooking as a seasoning. 2. *adj.* & *n.* wise; a wise person.

said *vb.* past of **say**.

sail 1. *vb.* travel across water in a ship or boat, especially when the travel is powered by wind.

sailor *n.* a person who goes to sea in a ship, or who sails a boat; a member of a ship's crew.

saint *n.* an extremely good person, particularly one who has been recognized as holy by the Church.

sake *n.* used in expressions like *for my sake, for the sake of ...* because of, out of consideration for.

salaam *n.* an Arabic word meaning peace and a form of greeting in the East.

salad *n.* a mixture of uncooked vegetables such as lettuce, tomato and cucumber.

salamander *n.* a small amphibian with a lizard-like body.

salary *n.* the money paid to someone for their work, usually paid monthly.

sale *n.* 1. the act of selling. 2. a time when a shop sells off goods cheaply.

salesperson *n.* somebody whose job is selling things.

saliva (*sal*-**eye**-*va*) *n.* spit; the liquid in your mouth. It helps in chewing and starts digestion.

salmon *n.* (plural same) a kind of fish that is highly prized as food.

salt *n.* a chemical compound formed, with water, when a metal or other substance reacts with an acid; common table salt, or sodium chloride. *You add salt to bring out the flavour of food. adj.* having a **salty** taste. *adj.* containing salt. *It is easier to float in salt water than in fresh water.*

Saluki *n.* a breed of hunting dog with long hairs on its ears and tail.
salute *vb.* & *n.* raise your stiffened hand to your forehead or hat as a greeting, as soldiers do.
salvage *vb.* save from loss or destruction.
salvation *n.* rescue; saving the soul.
salver *n.* a silver tray.
salvo *n.* the firing of several guns at the same time.
samba *n.* Brazilian dance.
same *adj.* similar to, or identical with something. *Sally and I go to the same school.*
samovar *n.* a Russian tea urn.

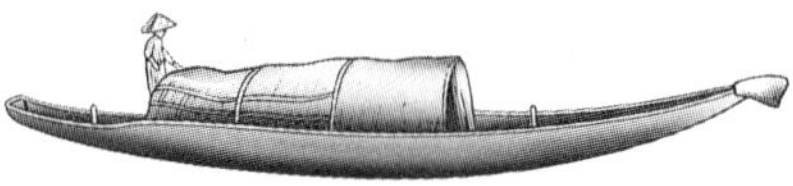

sampan *n.* a kind of Chinese boat.
sample *n.* an example of something, which can be used to show what the others are like. *vb.* try qualities of.
samurai *n.* a Japanese warrior of former times.
sanction *vb.* allow, authorize. *n.*
sanctuary *n.* a safe place for people, or for birds and animals. *In a bird sanctuary it is against the law to hunt or kill the birds.*
sand *n.* tiny grains of minerals, mainly quartz, formed by the erosion of rocks, and often forming beaches.
sandal *n.* a kind of open shoe, attached to the foot by straps.
sandbag *n.* sack filled with sand used for protection against explosions, flooding and other damage.
sandpaper *n.* paper coated with sand used for smoothing.
sandstone *n.* a rock consisting of grains of sand, mostly quartz, which have been compressed together.
sandwich *n.* a kind of food, consisting of meat or other filling between two slices of bread.
sane *adj.* sensible, normal, sound in mind. **sanity** *n.*
sang *vb.* past of **sing**.
sanitary *adj.* of or concerning health especially relating to cleanliness.
sank *vb.* past of **sink**.
Sanskrit *n.* & *adj.* a language of ancient India.
sap *n.* the juice in the stems of plants.
sapling *n.* a young tree.

The Japanese samurai were fierce warriors, from the 11th century to the 19th century.

sapphire *n.* transparent blue stone, valued as a gem; the hardest mineral known apart from diamond.
sarcasm *n.* a bitter remark of contempt or scorn, often ironical. **sarcastic** *adj.*
sarcophagus (*sa*-**kof**-*a*-*gus*) *n.* a stone coffin.
sardine *n.* a small fish of the herring family.
sari *n.* a length of cloth draped around the body as a dress, and worn mainly by Indian women.

sash *n.* 1. a band or scarf, worn across the shoulder or around the waist. 2. the frame of a sliding window.
Sassenach (**sass**-*en*-*ak*) *n.* a Scottish word meaning Saxon and so the English.
sat *vb.* past of **sit**.
Satan *n.* the devil; the evil one in many religions.
satchel *n.* a shoulder bag used to carry books.

The Pioneer Spacecraft, in 1983, was the first satellite to be launched from Earth into the solar system.

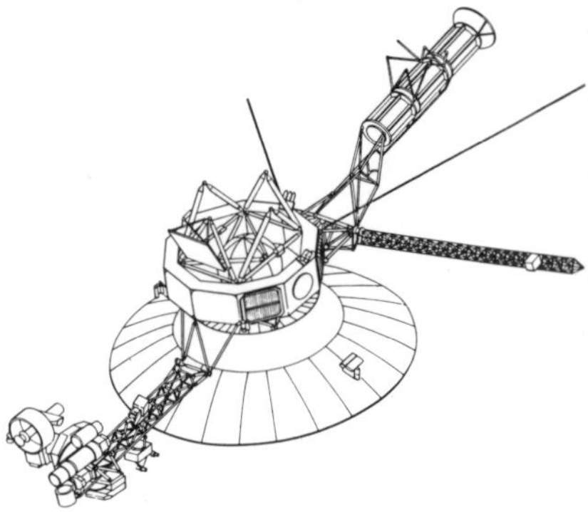

satellite *n.* 1. a moon. 2. an artificial object put into orbit around the Earth.
satire *n.* a form of comedy in which sarcasm and wit are used to ridicule people's follies.
satisfactory *adj.* all right, or good enough.
satisfied *vb.* past of **satisfy**.
satisfy *vb.* please, make someone contented. *He wanted to satisfy his teacher, so he did his homework carefully.* fulfill; comply with.
saturate *vb.* fill something (e.g. a sponge) so completely that no more can be absorbed.
Saturday *n.* the seventh day of the week, between Friday and Sunday; named after Saturn, Roman god of harvests.
sauce *n.* a liquid mixture served with some foods for added flavour.
saucepan *n.* a metal cooking pot with a handle and sometimes a lid.
saucer *n.* a small curved plate on which a cup stands.

Sable antelope and impala at a savanna watering hole.

saucy *adj*. cheeky, impudent. **sauciness** *n*.
sauna (**saw**-*na*) *n*. a kind of hot steam bath, of Finnish origin.
saunter *vb*. stroll, walk in a leisurely way.
sausage *n*. a chopped meat mixture which is made into a tube-shape inside a skin.
savage *adj*. wild and fierce; uncivilized. *vb*. attack and bite (of animals).
savanna *n*. & *adj*. large areas of grassy African plains. The *llanos* and *campos* of South America are other examples of savanna vegetation.
save *vb*. 1. rescue. *The crew of the sinking ship were all saved.* 2. build up a reserve of money. *We are saving up for our summer holiday*. 3. keep for future use. 4. bring about spiritual salvation.
savings *pl. n*. the money someone has saved, often kept in a bank.
savoury *adj*. salty and spiced, not sweet.
saw 1. *n*. a sharp tool with teeth for cutting wood. 2. *vb*. cut something with a saw. *How long will it take to saw those planks in half*? 3. *vb*. past of **see**.
sawdust *n*. dust of tiny pieces of wood, made by sawing.
saxophone *n*. a metal musical instrument, played by blowing into it, used mainly in jazz bands.
say *vb*. speak; announce something.
saying *n*. a well-known phrase or proverb. *'Too many cooks spoil the broth' is a saying.*
scab *n*. the dry protective crust that grows over a wound.
scaffolding *n*. a structure of tubes and planks used when a building is being put up or repaired.

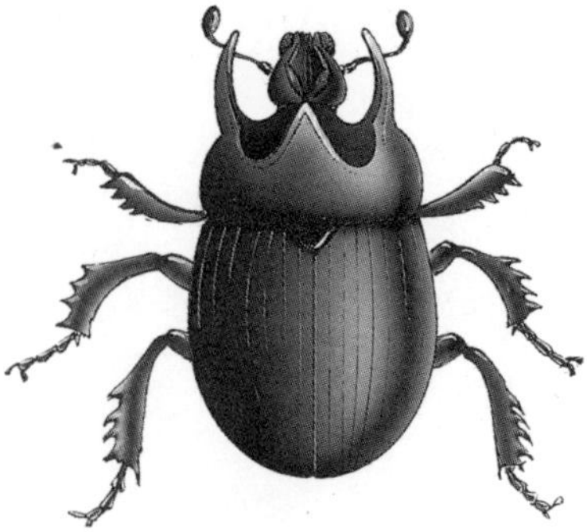

The scarab is a type of beetle. It was sacred to the ancient Egyptians, who believed that a giant scarab rolled the sun through the sky each day.

scald *vb.* & *n.* burn with hot liquid or steam.

scale 1. *n.* one of the thin pieces of hard skin that covers the bodies of fish and reptiles. 2. *n.* a series of measuring marks on an instrument such as a ruler or thermometer. 3. *n.* a set of musical tones arranged in order. 4. *vb.* climb something.

scalene *n.* a triangle with three unequal sides.

scales *n.* an instrument for measuring how much things weigh.

scalp *n.* the skin on your head.

scalpel *n.* a small knife used by surgeons.

scan *vb.* 1. read over quickly. 2. pass a beam of light over (in television and radar). 3. (in poetry) have the correct rhythm.

scandal *n.* a disgraceful fact or event which causes outrage. **scandalize** *vb.* shock.

Scandinavia *n.* term used to include Denmark, Finland, Iceland, Norway and Sweden.

scar *n.* the mark left on skin from a wound, after it has healed. *vb.* mark with scars.

scarab *n.* a type of dung beetle, considered sacred by the ancient Egyptians.

scarce *adj.* rare, uncommon, in short supply. *Because of the fuel shortage, oil is very scarce.* **scarcity** *n.* being scarce, in short supply.

scare *vb.* frighten.

scarecrow *n.* figure of person dressed in old clothes set up in a wheatfield etc. to frighten away birds.

scarf *n.* (plural **scarves**) a piece of cloth, generally used to cover the head or shoulders.

scarlet *n.* & *adj.* bright red.

scatter *vb.* go off in different directions, to throw something so that it spreads out. *Jilly scattered crumbs on the bird table.*

scavenge *vb.* feed on carrion or garbage. **scavenger** *n.* *Dogs are terrible scavengers.*

scene (*seen*) *n.* 1. the place where something happens. *Luckily, there was a policeman at the scene of the accident.* 2. a section of a stage play; place represented on the stage.

scenery (**seen**-*ery*) 1. *n.* the natural features of a place, such as hills, fields and trees. 2. *n.* the painted curtains and screen used to make a theatre stage look like a real place.

scent (*sent*) *n.* a smell, usually a pleasant one; a perfume; odour of an animal. *vb.* detect.

sceptic (**skep**-*tic*) *n.* a person who doubts the truth (of religion etc.) **sceptical** *adj.*

schedule (**shed**-*ule* or **sked**-*ule*) *n.* a timetable, a plan, a scheme. *vb.*
scheme (*skeem*) *n.* a plan. *vb.* plot, plan.
schism (**siz**-*um*) *n.* a break or split in a political party or religious group.
scholar *n.* a student; a clever person who has studied hard and knows a great deal; a person who has won a scholarship (prize) at a school or college. **scholarly** *adj.* learned.
scholarship *n.* money won by someone in an exam to pay school or university fees.
school *n.* 1. a place where children are educated; its building. 2. a group or shoal of fish swimming together.
schooner *n.* a fast sailing ship, generally with two masts.
science *n.* 1. knowledge got by studying, watching and testing. 2. a special branch of study like physics, biology or astronomy. **scientific** *adj.*
science fiction *n.* stories that are based on imagined scientific events.
scientist *n.* a person who studies a scientific subject.
sci-fi *abbrev.* science fiction.
scissors *pl. n.* a tool with two blades joined together, which cut when they meet.
scoff 1. *vb.* mock; make fun of. 2. eat greedily.
scold *vb.* speak crossly to someone about what they have done or not done. *The teachers scolded them for being late for school.*
scone (*skon*) *n.* a small, flat round cake.
scoop *n.* 1. a ladle or large spoon; *vb.* to spoon. 2. an important news story found in only one newspaper.
scooter *n.* 1. a child's toy with two wheels, a base and a handlebar. 2. a **motor-scooter** is a light kind of motor-bike with a small engine.

A schooner.

scorch *vb.* darken the suface of something by burning it slightly. *n.* a slight burn.
score 1. *n.* a result in a game. *At the final whistle the score was two goals to nil. vb.* gain points in a game. 2. *vb.* scratch or mark something. 3. *n.* an old-fashioned word for twenty. 4. *n.* copy of music showing all vocal and instrumental parts. *vb.*
scorn *vb.* feel or show contempt; despise *n.*
scorpion *n.* a small creature of the spider family, with a poisonous sting in its tail.
Scotch *n.* & *adj.* whisky from Scotland; made in or from Scotland.
scot-free *adj.* without punishment.
scoundrel *n.* rogue, a person without principles.
scour *vb.* 1. clean thoroughly. 2. rush about looking for something.
scout *n.* 1. someone who is sent out ahead of his or her group to look for difficulties or dangers. 2. a member of the Scout Association.
scowl *n.* a cross look, when someone wrinkles up their forehead in anger. *vb.* frown at.
scramble *vb.* 1. climb or crawl up. *We managed to scramble to the top of the hill.* 2. mix up, as in *scrambled eggs.*
scrap 1. *n.* a small piece of something, a fragment. 2. *vb.* get rid of something. 3. *n.* old cars or other metal objects that have been thrown away. 4. *n.* a fight.
scrapbook *n.* a book in which to stick cut-out pictures or papers.

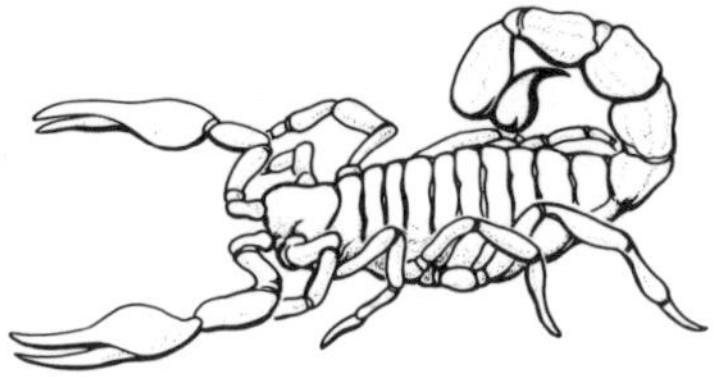

Scorpions live in warm, dry places. Their long pincers are used to catch insects and spiders. The scorpion's sting is poisonous, and can be fatal.

scrape *vb.* 1. scratch; slide along. *Our dad scraped his car on the gate-post.* 2. only just succeed. *Bill only just scraped through his exam.*
scratch *vb.* drag a sharp point, such as a needle or fingernail, over something; rub with nails to relieve itching.
scrawl *vb.* & *n.* scribble; hasty or bad handwriting.
scream *n.* a high-pitched yell, usually of pain or fright. *vb.* make a cry.
screech *n.* a shrill cry. *vb.*
screen 1. *n.* a partition; a frame covered with wood or cloth, and used to hide something. *They put a screen around my bed in hospital when the doctor came.* 2. *n.* upright surface on which films etc. are projected; part of television or radar on which picture appears. 3. *vb.* protect someone. 4. *vb.* show on screen. 5. *vb.* investigate a person's life and character for reliability.
screw *n.* a nail with a spiral groove called the thread which pulls the screw into the wood. *vb.* fasten with a screw.
screwdriver *n.* a tool for driving screws into walls and other things.

A scythe.

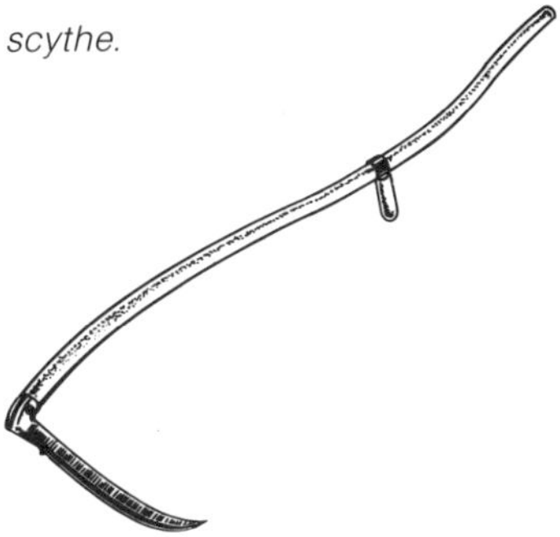

scribble *vb.* scrawl, write carelessly; make untidy patterns with a pen or pencil. *Our teacher scolded me for scribbling in my book.*
scripture *n.* holy writings, especially the Bible.
scroll (rhymes with *hole*) *n.* a roll of paper with writing or pictures on it.
scrounge *vb.* cadge.
scrub 1. *vb.* clean by rubbing with a wet brush. 2. *n.* ground covered with shrubs, brushwood etc.
scruff *n.* the back of the neck.
scruffy *adj.* shabby and untidy.
scrump *vb.* steal fruit from a tree, especially apples.
scruple *n.* a doubt because of what one's conscience says.
scull *vb.* row with small light oars. **sculls** *n.*
sculptor *n.* a person who makes statues or carvings.
sculpture *n.* the art of making things from wood, stone or other hard materials; something made by a sculptor.
scum *n.* impurities that float to the surface of a liquid.
scurf *n.* flakes of dead skin on the scalp.
scurry *vb.* move quickly with short, fast steps.
scythe ('sc' like 's') *n.* a tool with a curved blade for cutting grass or corn.
sea *n.* the big areas of salt water which cover most of the Earth; the oceans.
sea-anemone *n.* a soft-bodied, tube-like sea animal.

seagull *n.* a bird that lives near the sea and eats fish.
sea-horse *n.* a small fish with a horse-shaped head.
seal 1. *n.* a smoothly furred animal that lives in or near the sea. 2. *vb.* close something by sticking its edges together. *We sealed the letter with glue.* 3. *n.* an impression stamped on to something to show that it is genuine. *The letter was stamped with the king's seal.*
sea-level *n.* land that is at the same level as the sea, and used to measure the height of all other land. *The hill was 40 metres above sea-level.*
sea-lion *n.* a sea mammal that is very similar to the seal but which has small ears on the outside.
seam *n.* the line where two pieces of cloth are sewn together.

search *vb.* look for thoroughly. *n.* the act of searching, an investigation.
seashell *n.* the hard covering of a sea-creature.
sea-shore *n.* the seaside; the land closest to the sea.
seaside *n.* the sea-shore; the beach. *We are spending a week by the seaside.*
season *n.* a time or part, one of the four divisions of the year called spring, summer, autumn and winter.
seasoning *n.* flavouring added to food. **season** *vb. salt, pepper and herbs are seasonings.*
seat *n.* a piece of furniture for sitting on; the right to sit as a member of parliament etc.
sea-urchin *n.* a small spiny creature that lives on the sea-bed.

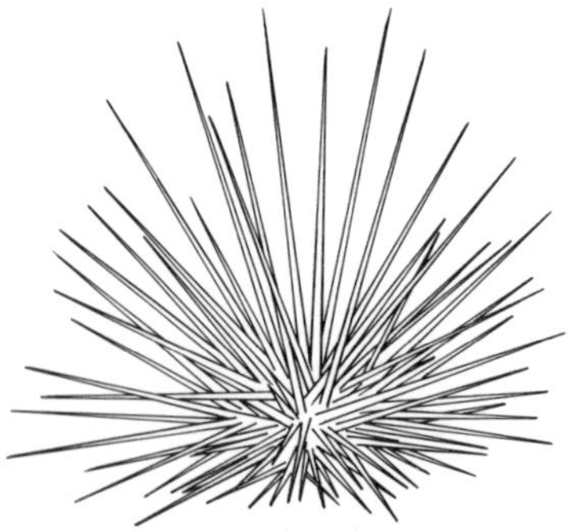

seaweed *n.* a large group of plants that grow in or near the sea.
seaworthy *adj.* a ship that is in a fit state to go to sea.
secateurs *pl. n.* pruning clippers.
second 1. *adj.* the one after the first. *He came second in the race.* 2. *n.* one-sixtieth of a minute. 3. *n.* the assistant to a boxer or duellist. 4. *vb.* give one's support to. *I second that idea.*
second-hand *adj.* already used, not new. *We bought my bike second-hand from a neighbour.*
secret *n.* a piece of information that is kept hidden, confidential. *adj.*
secretary *n.* 1. an office worker who types letters and makes arrangements for other people. 2. the person who looks after the financial affairs of a company.
sect *n.* a group of people who have beliefs (especially religious) in common.
section *n.* one of the parts into which something can be divided. *The apple was cut up and I got a section of it.*
sector *n.* any part of a circle between two radii and the circumference.
secure 1. *adj.* safe, out of danger. 2. *vb.* fix something so that it is safe. *The guard made sure the door lock was secure.*
sedate *adj.* calm and settled in manner; not lively.
sedative *n.* a calming drug.
seduce *vb.* tempt or lead astray. **seduction** *n.* **seductive** *adj.*
see *vb.* (past **saw**, past part. **seen**) 1. observe with the eyes. *Can you see that star?* 2. understand. *Now I see what you mean.*
see about *vb.* make arrangements for something to happen. *I'll see about ordering a Christmas tree.*
seed *n.* a tiny part of a plant, from which a new plant may grow.

seek *vb.* (past **sought**) look for; try to obtain.
seem *vb.* appear to be. *He seems honest enough, but you can never be sure.* **seeming** *adj.* apparent but not real.
see off *vb.* go with someone to the place where they start a journey.
see-saw *n.* a long plank balanced on a central support, which rocks up and down when people sit on the ends.
seethe *vb.* boil (with anger etc.).
segment *n.* one separate part of something. *Oranges can be divided into separate segments with your fingers.*
segregate *vb.* keep apart or set away from others. **segregation** *n.*
seize (rhymes with *sneeze*) *vb.* grab something firmly, or by force; snatch. *The mugger seized the woman's handbag.*
seldom *adj.* not often.
select *vb.* choose from a group as best or most suitable. *Ben was selected from his class for the team.* **selection** *n.* what is selected.
self- *prefix* meaning by oneself or itself, automatic, independent.
self *n.* (plural **selves**) a person's individuality, most often used in pronouns such as myself, yourself etc.
self-defence *n.* protecting yourself against attack.
selfish *adj.* caring too much about yourself and what you want, rather than about other people.
self-service *n.* a restaurant or shop set out so that the customers can serve themselves.
sell *vb.* (past **sold**) exchange something for money.
semaphore *n.* a system of sending messages with flags which you hold in the air.

Semaphore is a way of signalling an alphabetic code.

semi- *prefix* meaning half: **semi-circle; semi-detached** house.
send *vb*. (past **sent**) cause something or someone to go to a particular place; dispatch.
send off for *vb*. write asking for something you want to be sent to you. *I am going to send off for that record.*
senile *adj*. old and feeble.
senior *adj*. older in years, or more important that others.
señor *n*. the Spanish word for Mister or Sir.
señora *n*. the Spanish word for Mrs or Madam.
señorita *n*. the Spanish word for Miss.
sensation *n*. being aware through the senses; feeling; a thrilling event. *The first space flight was a great sensation.* **sensational** *adj*.
sense 1. *n*. one of the ways your body has to tell you what is happening around you: sight, hearing, touch, smell and taste. 2. *n*. the meaning of something. *I can't make sense of what he is saying because he is talking too fast.*
sensible *adj*. behaving in an intelligent way. **sense** *n*. such behaviour.
sensitive *adj*. affected by external stimulation (e.g. light). *The film is very sensitive to colour*. easily hurt; delicate.
sent *vb*. past of **send**.
sentence *n*. 1. a group of words that make sense together and include a verb. 2. a punishment given to a criminal by a law court. *The burglar got a sentence of two years in prison. vb.* pronounce sentence on.
sentimental *adj*. full of feelings (sentiments) especially soft, romantic ones; over-emotional.
sentry *n*. someone whose job is to guard something and warn others of danger.
sepal *n*. a kind of leaf that forms the outside part of a flower.

separate 1. *adj*. divided, not joined together. *The jigsaw came in 100 separate pieces.* 2. *vb*. divide something up. *She asked me to separate the peas from the beans.* **separation** *n*.
September *n*. the ninth month of the year.
sequel *n*. the next part, continuation or instalment of a story etc.
sequence *n*. order of things coming after one another. *A sequence of events.*
sequoia *n*. one of a family of North American *conifers* (cone-bearing trees).
serene *adj*. calm, unruffled.
serf *n*. a person in history who belonged to the place where he

or she lived, and to the lord who owned the land. A serf was a kind of slave.

sergeant *n.* a non-commissioned rank in the army, air force or police.

serial *n.* a story that is told in parts, instead of all at one time. *We watch the serial on TV every Sunday night.*

series *n.* a number of things that happen one after the other, and which belong together in some way. *Peter had a series of colds last winter.*

serious *adj.* thoughtful, not funny; important because of possible danger.

sermon *n.* a religious speech; lecture delivered from a pulpit.

The giant sequoia of California is the world's largest tree.

serpent *n.* an old-fashioned word for a snake.

serrated *adj.* having teeth or notches on the edge. *A serrated knife.*

servant *n.* a person who is paid to work in the house of another person.

serve *vb.* 1. work for someone. 2. sell things in a shop. 3. give out the food at a meal.

service 1. *n.* occupation of a servant. 2. *pl. n.* the armed forces. 3. *n.* a set of utensils, etc. *A dinner service containing twelve plates etc.* 4. *n.* supplying what is necessary. *Water, gas and electricity are essential services.* 5. *n.* a religious ceremony. 6. *n.* (in tennis etc.) the act of serving a ball. 7. *n.* maintenance (of a car etc.) *vb.*

serviette *n.* a piece of cloth or paper used at meals to stop food getting on to your clothes, and to wipe your mouth on. Also called a **napkin**.

session *n.* a meeting or series of meetings or 'sittings' of lawcourts to carry out business.

set 1. *n.* a group of people or things that belong together, especially in mathematics. *We bought a set of table mats for our brother.* 2. *vb.* become hard. *The jelly was left to set overnight.* 3. *vb.* arrange things in a certain way. *Will you set the table for dinner, please?*

set about *vb.* begin to do something.

set eyes on *vb.* catch sight of something.

set in motion *vb.* start something off.

set off *vb.* start out on a journey.

set sail *vb.* begin a voyage.
settee *n.* a sofa, a long soft seat.
settle *vb.* 1. go to a place and stay there. *My uncle went to Canada to settle.* 2. decide something. *We couldn't agree which of us should eat the cake, so we asked Dad to settle the argument for us.* 3. pay a bill.
settlement *n.* 1. a place to where people have moved, built houses and decided to live. 2. terms of an agreement.
set upon *vb.* attack someone.
sever *vb.* cut or break; separate.
several *adj.* some, usually three or more, but not many. *There were several coats left in the hall.*
severe *adj.* strict or harsh, not gentle. *The weather was very severe.*
sew *vb.* (past **sewed**, past part. **sewn**) join pieces of material together with a needle and thread. **sewing** *n.*
sewage *n.* human waste, carried through drains by water.
sewer *n.* large drain for taking away waste water.
sewing machine *n.* a machine for sewing cloth, leather etc.
sex *n.* being male or female; **sexual** (*adj*) desires.
sextant *n.* a scientific instrument used in navigation.
shabby *adj.* worn-out; old and dusty. *He always wore a shabby old suit to the office.*
shack *n.* a hut, especially a roughly built one.
shade *n.* 1 out of direct sunlight. *The dog sat in the shade where it was cool.* 2. something which protects against strong light or heat. *The lampshade was made from paper.* *vb.* screen from light. 3. how dark or light a colour is. *My shirt is a darker shade of green than yours.*
shadow 1.*n.* the dark shape made by an object when it is in a strong light. 2. *vb.* follow someone closely, as their shadow does.
shady *adj.* in the shade; uncertain; dishonest.
shaft *n.* 1. a long handle, such as the one on a spear. 2. a narrow, deep hole that leads to a mine or pit.
shaggy *adj.* having tangled hair.
shake *vb.* (past **shook**; past part. **shaken**) move vigorously from side to side, or up and down. *In some countries, people shake hands with friends every time they meet.* tremble, vibrate. **shaky** *adj.* unsteady, trembling.
shale *n.* a type of soft, light rock, similar to slate.
shall *auxiliary vb.* a word that indicates determination, or that something will happen in the future. *I shall get up early tomorrow.*

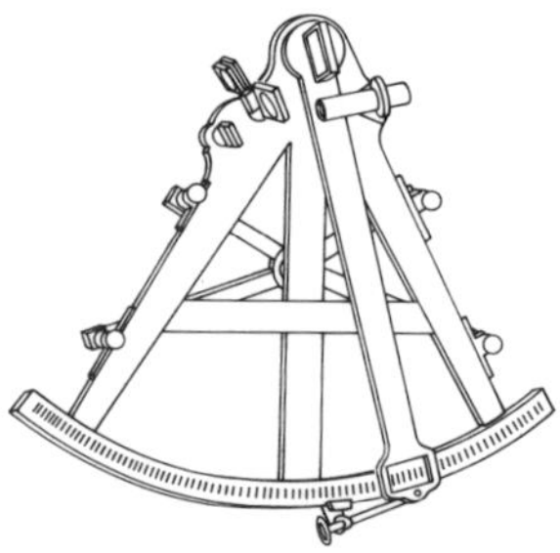

A sextant is used in navigation. Ships can find their position at sea by calculating the angle of the celestial body (the Sun, a star or planet) to the horizon.

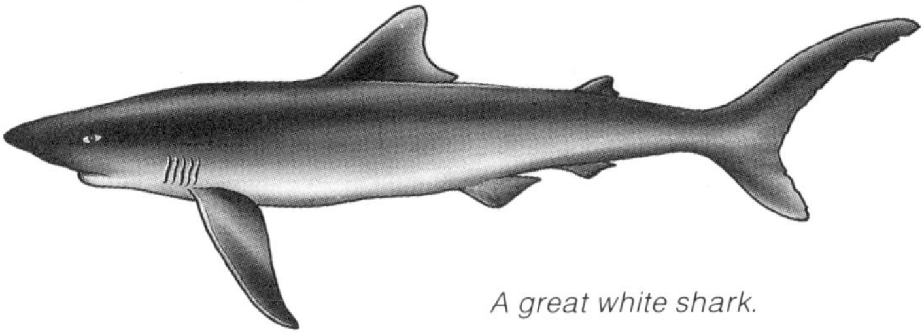
A great white shark.

shallow *adj*. not deep. *The water was shallow and only covered my feet.*
shalom *interj*. a Jewish greeting.
shame 1. *n*. feeling sorry and regretful for having done something wrong; guilty feeling. 2. *n*. (*casual*) a regrettable thing. *What a shame you couldn't come*. 3. *vb*. make ashamed.
shampoo *n*. liquid for washing your hair. *vb*.
shamrock *n*. the name for some kinds of clover.
shandy *n*. a drink made from beer and lemonade or ginger beer.
shan't *vb*. abbrev. for **shall not**.
shanty *n*. 1. crudely built hut or dwelling. *A shanty town*. 2. sailor's song.
shape *n*. the outline of something; what appearance it has. *The soap was made in the shape of a bear*. *vb*. give shape to. **shapely, shapeless** *adjs*.
share *vb*. divide and distribute something among a group. *Annie shared her sweets with us*.
shark *n*. a family of large and fierce sea fish.
sharp 1. *adj*. having a pointed edge or end that cuts things easily. 2. *adj*. sudden or quick. *There was a sharp bend in the road*. 3. *n*. a musical note raised by a semitone. **sharpen** *vb*. make sharp.
shatter *vb*. break into small pieces.
shave *vb*. cut hair close to the skin. *Most men shave their chin every day*. *n*. **shaving**.
shawl *n*. a cloth worn around your shoulders for warmth or for decoration.
sheaf *n*. (plural **sheaves**) a bundle of grain stalks tied together after they have been harvested.

A sheaf of corn.

shear *vb*. cut the wool from a sheep.
shears *pl. n*. a pair of scissors like large blades, used for cutting plants or shearing sheep.

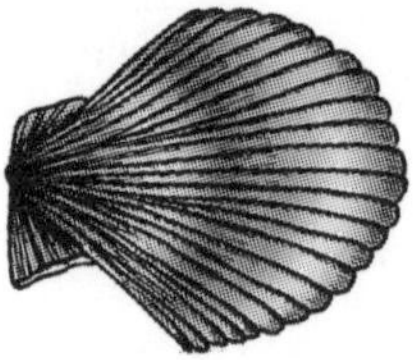
Queen scallop

Tower shell

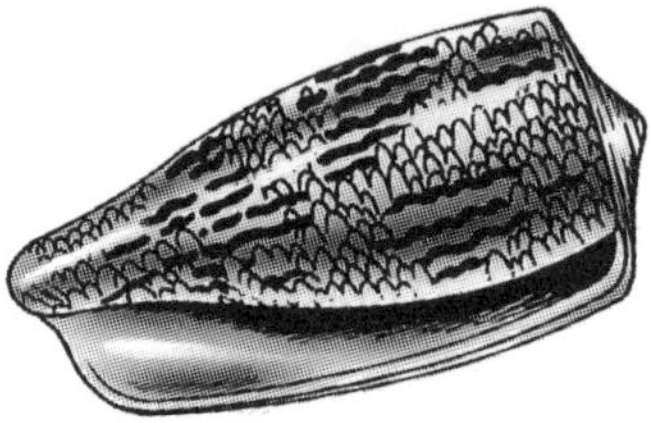
Cone shell

Seashells like these are the protective coverings of soft-bodied marine animals.

sheath *n.* a close-fitting cover, especially for a sword or a knife. **sheathe** *vb.*
shed 1. *n.* a small hut. 2. *vb.* let things fall off or drop away. *Some trees shed their leaves in the autumn.*
sheen *n.* glossiness, brightness.
sheep *n.* (plural **sheep**) a common farm animal with a woolly coat.
sheepdog *n.* a dog that herds sheep together for a farmer.
sheer 1. *adj.* very steep, like the side of a cliff. 2. *adj.* of fine material, can be seen through.
sheet *n.* a thin flat piece of metal, paper or material; a bed-covering made of linen, cotton, nylon etc.
sheikh (*shake*) *n.* an Arab chief.
shekel *n.* the unit of currency of Israel.
sheldrake *n.* a species of wild duck.
shelf *n.* (plural **shelves**) a plank fixed to a wall etc. on which to keep books or other articles.
shell 1. *n.* a thin hard outer covering. 2. *n.* explosive artillery projectile. 3. *vb.* remove shell from.
shellfish *n.* a soft-bodied water animal that lives inside a shell for protection.
shelter *n.* a place that protects you from unpleasant weather. *vb.* serve as a shelter; take shelter.
shepherd *n.* a person who looks after sheep for a living. *vb.* **shepherdess** *n. fem.*
sheriff *n.* a law officer, particularly in the USA.
sherry *n.* a wine fortified with brandy originally from the Cadiz region of Spain.
shield 1. *n.* a large piece of metal, wood or leather used to protect the person who carries it against attack. 2. *vb.* cover or protect something. *He used his*

hand to shield his eyes from the glare.

shift *vb.* change the postion of something. *Graham wants to shift the table into the corner of the room.*

shilling *n.* a coin used in several countries before decimal currency. A British shilling was worth 5 new pence, and there were 20 shillings in a pound (£1).

shin *n.* the front of the leg between the knee and the ankle.

shine *vb.* (past **shone**) give out a steady beam of light. **shiny** *adj.*

shingle *n.* pebbles, particularly on a beach.

ship *n.* a large boat. *vb.* take, send by ship.

shipwreck *n.* an accident in which a ship is sunk or badly damaged at sea; a wrecked ship.

shipyard *n.* a place where ships are built or repaired out of the water.

shire *n.* 1. a county. 2. large horse once used for pulling heavy loads.

shirk *vb.* run away from, avoid doing. *She shirked her responsibilities.*

shirt *n.* an article of clothing for the top half of the body, with sleeves and a collar, usually worn by men.

shiver *vb.* shake with cold or fear.

shoal *n.* a group of fish swimming together.

shock *n.* an unpleasant surprise. **shocking** *adj.* scandalous, very bad.

shoe *n.* a protective covering for the foot.

shone *vb.* past of **shine**.

shook *vb.* past of **shake**.

shoot 1. *vb.* use a gun, or a bow and arrow; wound with gun. 2. *vb.* go quickly. 3. *vb.* photograph with a cine-camera. 4. *n.* the tip of a young growing plant. 5. *vb.* aim for goal at soccer, hockey, netball etc.

shop 1. *n.* a room or building where goods are sold. 2. *vb.* buy things from a shop. **shopper** *n.*

shopkeeper *n.* a person who owns or looks after a shop.

shop-lifter *n.* a person who steals from a shop.

shop steward *n.* a spokesperson elected by workers.

shore *n.* the land along the edge of a sea or lake.

The giant shire horse.

short 1. *adj.* the opposite of long or tall. *Both his parents are very short.* **shorten** *vb.* make or become short in length or time. 2. *adv.* to be lacking in something. *I am running short of envelopes.* **shortage** *n.*

shortbread *n.* a crumbly cake made of flour and butter.

shortcoming *n.* a failing, defect.

shorthand *n.* a way of writing quickly by means of symbols.

A shot-putter in action during a competition.

shortly *adv.* soon, before long.
shorts *n.* short trousers that come to just above your knees.
short-sighted *adj.* condition of someone who can see clearly when things are close, but cannot see things that are farther away.
shot *vb.* past of **shoot**.
shot *n.* 1. the firing of a gun. *We heard a shot in the distance.* 2. an attempt to do something. 3. injection of a drug. 4. lead pellets in the cartridge of a shotgun.
shot put *n.* an athletic event which involves throwing a heavy metal ball as far as possible with one hand. The ball weighs 7.3 kg (16 lb) for men, 4 kg (8 lb 13 oz) for women.
should *vb.* a word meaning 'ought to'. *I should apologize to her because I broke her cup.*
shoulder *n.* the part of your body from your neck to your arm. *vb.* push with shoulder; assume responsibility. *She shouldered the job of bringing up her brother's children.*
shout *vb.* & *n.* call out or speak loudly; a loud cry. *My grandfather is a bit deaf, so you'll need to shout.*
shove *vb.* & *n.* push.
shovel *n.* a large spade with a curved blade for shifting coal etc. *vb.* use a shovel.
show 1. *vb.* (past part. **shown**) let something be seen. *Show me what you have written.* 2. *n.* a play or other entertainment. *The artist arranged a show of his paintings.*
shower *n.* 1. a short period of light rain. 2. a special device for sprinkling water over oneself, as a form of bath.
show off *vb.* display something, or try to make people think you do something very well.
show up *vb.* 1. expose. 2. arrive.
shrank *vb.* past of **shrink**.
shrapnel *n.* fragments from a

bomb etc.
shred *vb.* tear or cut into pieces. *n.* a narrow torn off piece.
shriek *n.* & *vb.* a high-pitched scream.
shrill *adj.* high and loud (of a sound).
shrimp *n.* a small edible shellfish with a long tail.
shrine *n.* the tomb or chapel of a saint.
shrink *vb.* (past **shrank**) get or make smaller. *Wool often shrinks in hot water.*
shrub *n.* a bushy plant, like a small tree.
shrug *vb.* raise or lift the shoulders. *n.* a symbol of indifference.
shrug off *vb.* brush aside; take no notice of.
shrunk *vb.* past part. of **shrink**.
shudder *vb.* & *n.* shake suddenly with cold or fear.
shuffle 1. *vb.* mix cards etc. so that they are not in any special order.
shun *vb.* avoid, keep away from.
shut *vb.* close. *Shut that door.*
shutter *n.* 1. a cover for a window. 2. part of a camera.
shuttle *n.* an instrument used in weaving for carrying thread backwards and forwards.
shuttlecock *n.* a cork filled with feathers that is hit back and forth in the game of badminton.

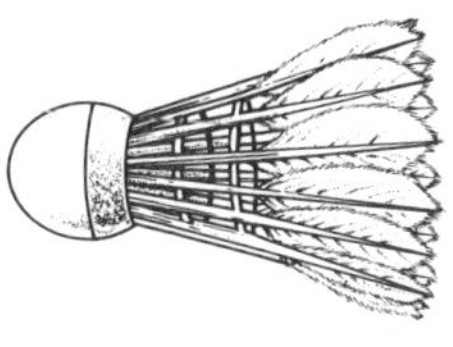

A shuttlecock.

shuttle service *n.* an aircraft or train that travels regularly between two places.
shy 1. *adj.* not liking to meet other people. 2. *vb.* turn away in sudden fear. *Horses sometimes shy away from strange objects.*
sick 1. *adj.* ill, not well. 2. *vb.* to be sick is to vomit, or to bring food back through your mouth from your stomach. **sicken** *vb.* begin to feel ill; feel loathing. **sickening** *adj.* annoying. **sickness** *n.* being ill.
sickle *n.* a reaping tool with a curved blade.
side *n.* 1. the edge, wall or boundary of something. 2. the part of your body between the armpit and the hip. 3. a team in a game, or a country in wartime.
sideways *adj.* with one side first. *Crabs move sideways along the ground.*
siege ('ie' as in 'ee') *n.* a time when an army surrounds (besieges) a town or building so that people cannot get in or out.
siesta (**see**-*yes-ta*) *n.* an afternoon nap.
sieve (rhymes with *give*) *n.* a frame with a stiff net, used to separate small things from larger ones, or to drain liquid off. *vb.* use a sieve.
sift *vb.* put through a sieve.
sigh (rhymes with *die*) *vb.* breathe out loudly, usually to show that you are tired or bored. *n.*
sight *n.* 1. the ability to see. *Sight is one of the five senses.* 2. something that is seen by someone. *We saw a very strange sight on the beach.*

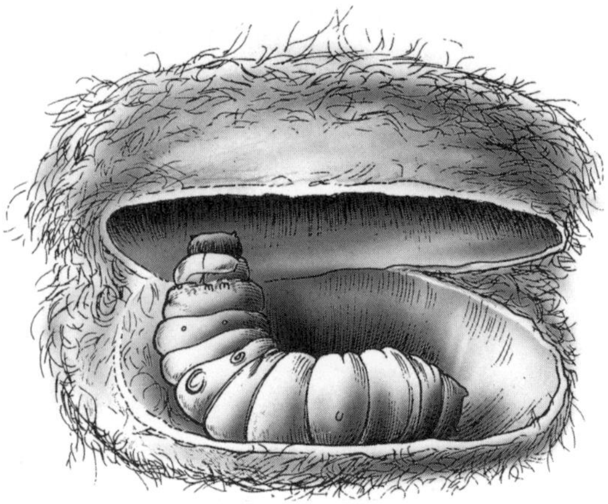

The silkworm moth caterpillar spins a cocoon of silk.

sign 1. *n.* board with words or pictures to give information to people. *The sign said 'danger'.* 2. *vb.* write your own name on something. 3. *n.* a mark or clue that has a special meaning. *The footprints were a sign that someone had been to the house.*

signal 1. *n.* a sound or movement that has a special meaning, especially from a distance. *Car drivers have to signal before they turn.* 2. *vb.* send a message. *He used semaphore to signal the news.*

signature *n.* someone's name written in their own writing.

significance *n.* the importance of; the meaning of. *What is the significance of a dog wagging its tail?*

signor *n.* (*pl.* **signori**) the Italian word for Mister or Sir.

signora *n.* (*pl.* **signore**) the Italian word for Mrs or Madam.

signorina *n.* the Italian word for Miss.

signpost *n.* a sign, fixed to a post, that tells you the direction and distance of places.

silage ('i' rhymes with 'eye') *n.* animal fodder made from green crops and preserved in a silo.

silence *n.* a time when there is complete quiet. *vb.* make silent.

silent *adj.* without any sound.

silhouette *n.* the outline or shape of something.

silicon *n.* after oxygen the most common element in the Earth's crust (symbol Si). It is found in quartz.

silk *n.* a natural fibre from the cocoon of the silkworm moth. **silky** *adj.* like silk.

sill *n.* the ledge along the bottom of a window.

silly *adj.* stupid; foolish.

silt *n.* deposit of fine soil left by a river. *vb.* become choked with silt.

silver 1. *n.* a valuable whitish shiny metal (symbol Ag), or coins made from metal of the same colour. 2. *n.* & *adj.* a colour that looks like the metal.

silver wedding *n.* 25th wedding anniversary.

similar *adj*. like something else, but not exactly the same; of the same kind. *Robyn has a similar dress to mine, but hers has red bows instead of blue ones.*
simmer *vb*. cook in a liquid just below boiling point.
simper *n*. & *vb*. smile or grin in a self-conscious way.
simple *adj*. 1. easy; not difficult. *This game is simple*. 2. basic; not complicated. *A screw is a simple machine*. **simplify** *vb*. make simple.
simpleton *n*. a stupid person.
sin *n*. breaking a religious law, or doing something that is known to be wrong. *vb*. commit a sin.
since 1. *prep*. from that time. *We haven't met since we were little*. 2. *adv*. because. *I often meet John, since we live in the same street*.
sincere *adj*. honest, true.
sing *vb*. (past **sang**, past part. **sung**) use the voice to make musical sounds.
singe *vb*. burn something slightly at the edges.
singer *n*. a person who is good at singing.
single *adj*. 1. just one. *You have only a single chance in this game*. 2. *adj*. unmarried.
singular *n*. & *adj*. one person or thing, not plural.
sinister *adj*. frightening, something that seems evil.
sink 1. *vb*. (past **sank,** past part. **sunk**) drop down through liquid; decline. *A stone will sink to the bottom of a pool*. 2. *n*. a basin for washing clothes or dishes in.
sip *vb*. drink small mouthfuls.
siphon *n*. tube for transferring liquid from one vessel to a lower one – once it is full of liquid, the difference in pressure at the ends of the tube ensures a continuous flow. *vb*. draw through a siphon.

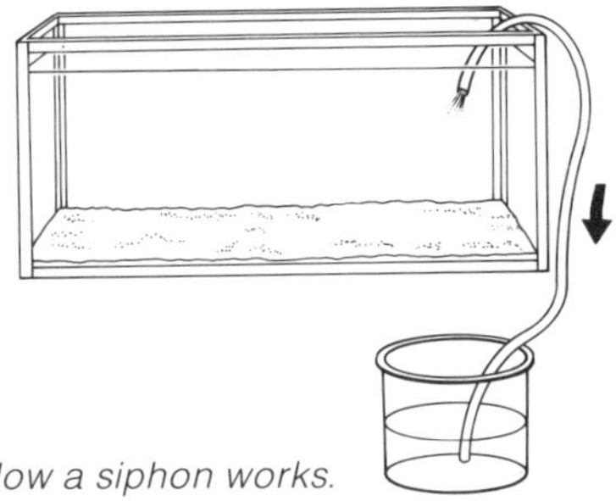

How a siphon works.

Sir *n*. the title placed before the name of a knight or baronet. *Sir John Smith;* a polite way of addressing a man.
siren *n*. an instrument for making a loud warning signal, like a police siren.
sister *n*. a daughter of the same parents as someone; a nun; a hospital nurse with authority over others.
sit *vb*. (past **sat**) rest on your bottom; take (exams).
site *n*. a place for buildings. *There was a bulldozer on the building site*. *vb*. locate or place.
situate *vb*. place, locate.
situation *n*. a place or position; a temporary state or condition. *The situation is serious*. a set of circumstances.
size *n*. measurement, showing how large or small something is.
skate *n*. a steel blade fixed to a boot for fast movement on ice. *vb*. glide on skates.

skeleton *n.* the framework of bones in the body of an animal.
sketch *vb.* & *n.* draw quickly and roughly; an outline.
skewbald *n.* & *adj.* (a horse) marked in white and patches of another colour, except black.
ski *n.* long strips of wood or other material fixed to boots for fast movement over snow. *vb.* go on skis.
skid *vb.* slip out of control. *Cars often skid on icy roads.*
skill *n.* the ability to do something very well. **skilful** *adj.*
skim *vb.* 1. remove scum from the surface of a liquid. 2. pass lightly over.
skin 1. *n.* the covering on the outside of the body. 2. *vb.* remove the skin of an animal; peel.
skin-diving *vb.* going underwater while breathing from tanks of oxygen.
skinhead *n.* teenager with closely cropped hair.
skip *vb.* 1. hop or jump, as over a skipping rope. 2. *n.* a large metal container for rubbish.

When the skunk is threatened or annoyed it raises its tail and shoots out a foul-smelling liquid. The smell is so disgusting that it puts off would-be predators immediately.

skipper *n.* the captain of a ship or boat.
skirt *n.* a piece of clothing worn by women around the lower half of the body, and not divided like trousers. *vb.* go round edge or border of.
skull *n.* the bony frame of the head.
skunk *n.* a North American mammal, related to the weasel and the badger.
sky *n.* the dome of the heavens overhead.
sky-diving *n.* a form of parachute jumping.

A skin-diver with an underwater camera.

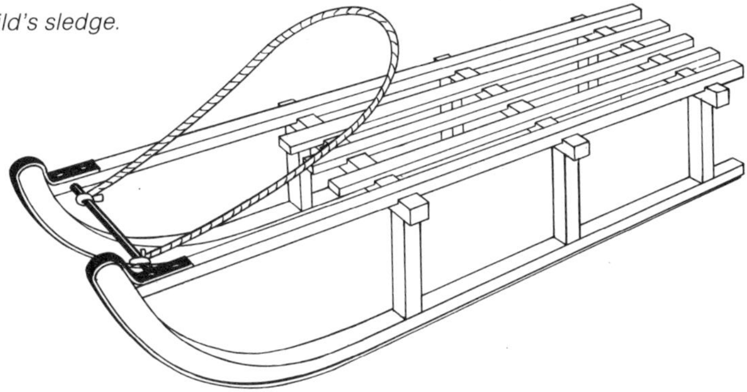
A child's sledge.

skylight *n.* a window in the roof of a building.
skyline *n.* the silhouette or outline of things against the sky.
skyscraper *n.* a very tall building with many floors.
slab *n.* a thick slice. *This slab of marble is too heavy to carry.*
slack *adj.* 1. loose. *That rope is too slack.* 2. careless; lazy. **slacken** *vb.* make or become slack.
slain *vb.* past of **slay**.
slam *vb.* & *n.* shut (a door) very hard and noisily; the noise made by slamming.
slander *vb.* damage a person's character by spreading lies. *n.* **slanderous** *adj.*
slang *n.* a way of using words that is thought to be less correct than other ways. *'Copper' is slang for 'police officer'.*
slant *n.* a slope, like the one a ladder makes when it is up against a wall; attitude; bias. *vb.*
slap *vb.* hit something with the flat of the hand. *n.* a blow.
slash *vb.* make long cuts in something. *n.* a slashing cut.
slate 1. *n.* a greyish kind of rock, which can be split into thin sheets for use as a roofing material. 2. *n.* a writing tablet, made of slate, formerly used in schools. 3. *vb.* criticize; condemn. *The newspapers all slated the new play.*
slaughter *vb.* kill, usually when many animals or people are killed at once. *n.* killing of animals for food.
slave *n.* a person who is owned by someone else, and has to work without pay, doing exactly what their owner wants. **slavery** *n.*
slay *vb.* kill.
sled or **sledge** *n.* a small vehicle used for travelling over snow or ice. A sledge has runners made from strips of wood or metal instead of wheels. Also used on grass or snowy slopes by children.
sleep *n.* the time when you are unconscious and resting. *I average eight hours' sleep a night. vb.* be or fall asleep.
sleeping-bag *n.* a padded bag for sleeping in, often used when camping.
sleepless *adj.* unable to sleep.
sleepy *adj.* tired; full of sleep; ready for bed.

sleet *n.* & *vb.* a mixture of rain and snow.
sleeve *n.* 1. the part of an article of clothing that covers the arm. 2. a cover for something, particularly a disc.
sleigh (rhymes with *ray*) *n.* a large vehicle used for travelling over snow or ice. Some sleighs have engines, others are pulled by animals.
slender *adj.* thin, narrow.
slept *vb.* past of **sleep**.
slew *vb.* past of **slay**.
slice *n.* a thin piece cut from something, such as a loaf of bread. *vb.* cut something into slices.
slick *n.* patch of oil on water.
slide 1. *vb.* move smoothly over something. *It's fun to slide on the ice in winter.* 2. *n.* a structure in a playground or park, on which children climb and slide. 3. *n.* a piece of glass etc. for use in a microscope or projector.
slight 1. *adj.* small, not important. *Belinda made a slight mistake.* 2. *vb.* ignore; treat with contempt.
slim *adj.* thin, slender. *vb.* eat less and try to lose weight.
slime *n.* unpleasantly wet, slippery stuff. **slimy** *adj.*
sling 1. *n.* piece of cloth used to support an injured arm. 2. a loop of leather used for throwing stones, sometimes also called a slingshot. 3. *vb.* hurl. 4. *vb.* hang or suspend from something.
slink *vb.* move away slowly (in fear or shame).
slip *vb.* miss your footing; slide.
slipper *n.* a soft shoe worn in the house.
slippery *adj.* easy to slip or slide on, such as an icy or oily surface.
slit 1. *n.* a long narrow hole. 2. *vb.* make a cut in something.
slither *vb.* slide unsteadily; slip.
sliver *n.* a long thin piece; a slice.
slogan *n.* a motto; catchy phrase used in advertising.
slope *n.* a slanting place, especially on a hill. *vb.*
sloppy *adj.* messy, untidy; over-sentimental.
slot *n.* a narrow opening in something that smaller things can be pushed through. *Some front doors have slots for letters.*
sloth (rhymes with *both*) 1. *n.* a slow-moving, tree-dwelling mammal found in tropical America. 2. *n.* laziness.

slow *adj.* moving at a sluggish pace; not fast; taking a long time to do; (of clocks) behind correct time.
slug *n.* a crawling land mollusc, related to the snail, but with little or no shell.
slum *n.* an overcrowded area with old, poor quality houses in which too many people have to live.
slump *vb.* & *n.* fall suddenly or heavily; a decline in trade.
sly *adj.* clever at tricking people

A blacksmith at work.

in secret; cunning.

smack *vb*. hit hard with the flat part of your hand. *n*. a slap; the sound of a smack.

small *adj*. little; tiny; not large.

smallpox *n*. a very dangerous disease with fever and spots.

smart 1. *adj*. clever. 2. *adj*. well-dressed, neat. 3. *n*. a sharp stinging pain.

smash *vb*. break something to pieces.

smear *vb*. spread grease or paint roughly over a surface; daub. *n*.

smell 1. *n*. the sense which tells you what scent something has. 2. *vb*. use your sense of smell; to sniff. 3. *n*. a scent, often unpleasant.

smelt *vb*. separate a metal from its ore by heating to a high temperature.

smile *vb*. turn up the corners of the mouth as a sign of pleasure or amusement; grin. *n*.

smith *n*. someone who makes things from metal. *A goldsmith makes jewellery and ornaments from gold*.

smog *n*. heavily-polluted, smoky air. *The word 'smog' is made up from 'smoke' and 'fog'*.

smoke 1. *n*. the greyish vapour given off by a fire. 2. *vb*. smoke cigarettes or other kinds of tobacco; emit smoke. *The chimney smokes*. **smoker** *n*. a person who smokes tobacco.

smooth *adj*. even or slippery; gentle to the touch. *That floor has a very smooth surface now that it has been sanded and polished*. *vb*. make smooth.

smother *vb*. deprive of air, stifle by covering with a blanket etc.

smoulder *vb*. burn very slowly, without a flame.

smudge *n*. dirty mark, blur, stain.

smug *adj*. self-satisfied.

smuggle *vb.* take things into a country secretly, by hiding them. *Smuggling is against the law.*
snack *n.* a small quick meal.
snaffle *n.* a kind of bit in the harness of a horse.
snag *n.* a small difficulty.
snail *n.* a small animal with a soft body and a hard protective shell.
snake *n.* a long, thin reptile without legs or eyelids. *Some snakes are poisonous.*
snap 1. *vb.* break suddenly. 2. *vb.* bite at someone suddenly. *Dogs sometimes snap at unfriendly people.* 3. *n.* **snap**(**shot**) a photograph. 4. *n.* a simple card game.
snare *n.* & *vb.* a trap for animals.
snarl *vb.* growl like a dog does when it is angry or frightened.
snatch *vb.* take away quickly. *The cat tried to snatch the fish from the plate. n.* a sudden grab.
sneak *vb.* to move stealthily, quietly, furtively. *He sneaked away. n.* an underhanded person.
sneer *vb.* (at) scoff, show contempt *n.* a scornful smile etc.

A snowdrop.

sneeze *vb.* a sudden rush of air through the nose, caused by an irritation of the mucous membrane. *n.*
sniff *vb.* draw in air quickly and noisily through your nose. *n.* act of sniffing.
snippet *n.* a small piece. *He read a snippet from the newspaper.*
snob *n.* someone who admires people only if they are rich or important. **snobbish** *adj.*
snooker *n.* a game played on a billiard table, using balls, and a cue.
snooze *vb.* & *n.* (take) a short sleep; nap.
snore *vb.* & *n.* (make) a noise through the nose or mouth when asleep.
snorkel *n.* a tube for breathing air through when you are under the water.
snort *n.* noise made by forcing air inwards through the nose. *vb.*
snout *n.* an animal's nose.
snow *n.* & *vb.* flakes of frozen water that fall from the sky in very cold weather.
snowball 1. *n.* a ball of compressed snow. *The children were having great fun throwing snowballs at each other.* 2. *vb.* grow or increase rapidly.
snowdrop *n.* a green and white flower that grows in early spring.
snowstorm *n.* a heavy fall of snow with a high wind; a blizzard.
snug *adj.* warm and cosy.
soak *vb.* leave something in liquid for a very long time.
soap *n.* a substance made from oil or fat and used for cleaning

things. *vb*. lather with soap.
soar (rhymes with *door*) *vb*. fly high in the sky.
sob *vb*. cry noisily.
sober *adj*. sensible, level-headed; not drunk.
soccer *n*. Association Rules football, a ball game played between two teams, each with 11 players.
social *adj*. 1. living together in groups. *Ants are social insects.* 2. to do with people and how they live. *My aunt works in the social services office in our town.*
socialism *n*. a political doctrine which places the means of production and distribution in the hands of all the people.
society *n*. all the people who live in a group or country, and the way they live and meet.
sock *n*. an article of clothing worn on the lower part of the leg beneath a shoe; a short stocking.
socket *n*. a hole into which something fits. *Jack put the bulb into the electric light socket.*
soda *n*. washing soda (*sodium carbonate*), baking soda (*sodium bicarbonate*), caustic soda (*sodium hydroxide*).
sodium *n*. a silvery-grey metal (symbol Na) that is so soft that it can be cut with a knife.
sofa *n*. a soft seat for two or more people.
soft *adj*. not hard; having a shape that is easily changed; comfortable. **soften** *vb*. make soft.
soft spot *n*. sentimental liking. *I have a soft spot for lambs.*
soil 1. *n*. the earth in which plants live and grow. 2. *vb*. stain with dirt.
solar *adj*. to do with the sun. *Some people heat water with solar energy.*
sold *vb*. past of **sell**.
solder *n*. an alloy, usually of tin and lead, having a low melting point, used for joining (**soldering**) certain metals.
soldier *n*. a member of an army.

Soldiers on parade.

sole 1. *n.* the flat part underneath your foot or your shoe. 2. *n.* a flat sea fish. 3. *adj.* just one thing or person. *He was the sole member of the class to fail the test.*

solemn *adj.* serious, thoughtful.
solicitor *n.* lawyer.
solid 1. *n.* anything that can be touched, and is not a liquid or a gas. 2. *adj.* not hollow, with no space inside. *The ball was made of solid rubber.* **solidify** *vb.* make or become solid.
solitaire *n.* 1. a precious stone such as a diamond, set on its own. 2. a board game for one person, played with marbles.
solitary *adj.* alone, lonely.
solo *adj.* on your own. *Jane gave a solo performance on her guitar.*
soluble *adj.* capable of dissolving.
solve *vb.* find the answer to a problem or puzzle. **solution** *n.* the answer.
sombre *adj.* gloomy.
some *pron.* & *adj.* part of something; not all; not everyone; a certain amount.
somebody *n.* a person, particularly when you are not sure who it is. *Somebody has stolen my purse.*
someplace *adj.* (USA) somewhere.
somersault *vb.* & *n.* turn head over heels.
something *n.* anything; any object. *I've got something in my eye.*
sometime *adv.* at an unknown time in the future. *I hope we meet again sometime.*
sometimes *adv.* occasionally; rarely; from time to time; not often. *I sometimes play tennis at the weekend.*
somewhere *adv.* at some place. *I've left my pen somewhere but I can't remember where.*
somnolent *adj.* sleepy.
son *n.* someone's male child.
sonar *n.* a way of using sounds and their echoes to locate objects in deep water.
sonata *n.* musical composition, especially for piano, generally having three movements.
song *n.* a short poem set to music and sung.
sonic boom *n.* disturbing bang, like an explosion, heard on the ground when an aircraft flies faster than the speed of sound; caused by shock waves set up by the aircraft.
son-in-law *n.* the husband of someone's daughter.
sonnet *n.* a poem of 14 lines with a fixed rhyme scheme. e.g. ababcdcdefefgg.
soon *adv.* in a short time. *I'll have to go soon.*
soot *n.* black flakes or powder left behind, particularly in a chimney, after a fire.
soothe *vb.* make someone calm when they are upset or angry. **soothing** *adj.*
sophomore *n.* second year student (USA).
soprano *adj.* & *n.* the highest female or boy's singing voice.
sorcerer (*saw-ser-er*) *n.* a

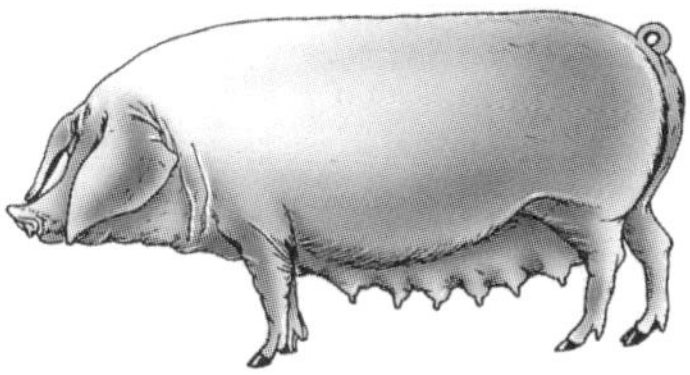

The sow is the female pig; the boar is the male.

magician; someone who can cast magic spells.

sore *adj.* & *n.* something that hurts when it is touched, like a bruise; painful.

sorrow *n.* sadness, grief. **sorrowful** *adj.*

sorry *adj.* regretful. *I'm sorry I'm late.*

sort 1. *n.* a type or group of things or people. *What sort of car did your father buy?* 2. *vb.* arrange things in sets or groups. *Pat tried to sort out her clothes from Jan's.*

sought *vb.* past of **seek**.

soul (rhymes with *hole*) *n.* the part of a person that is thought to live for ever, especially by religious people.

sound *n.* anything that you can hear.

sound barrier *n.* the speed of sound. *When a plane travels faster than sound, it goes through the sound barrier.*

soup (rhymes with *loop*) *n.* a liquid food made from meat or vegetables mixed together.

sour *adj.* sharp-tasting like lemons, not sweet; bad tempered.

source *n.* the starting point, the beginning.

south *n.* the direction opposite north on a compass.

souvenir *n.* something that you keep to remind you of a place, person or an event.

sovereign *n.* a king or queen; supreme ruler; a former coin.

sow (rhymes with *how*) *n.* a female pig.

sow (rhymes with *so*) *vb.* (past **sowed**, past part. **sown**) put seeds in the ground so that they grow.

soya *see* **soybean**.

soybean *n.* a bushy plant, native to Asia, grown for its seeds (beans) which are rich in protein.

space *n.* 1. the distance between things. *There is very little space left on the bookshelf.* 2. a place with nothing in it. *Tony took the empty space on the platform.* 3. all the places beyond the Earth in the Universe. *The Sun, Moon and stars are all in space.*

spacecraft *n.* a vehicle that carries people and things out into space, away from Earth.

Spaniels are often trained to find and retrieve game birds.

spade *n.* 1. a tool for digging the ground. 2. a playing card of suit of spades.
spaghetti *pl. n.* long thin rods of pasta (dried paste made of flour).
span *vb.* reach from one side of something to the other. *The bridge had to span a very wide river. n.* distance between piers of bridge etc. Also **life-span** the normal length of a life.
spaniel *n.* any of a number of kinds of dog having feathered tail and legs and large drooping ears.
spank *vb.* hit, usually on someone's bottom, as a punishment.
spanner *n.* a tool for turning nuts on bolts. (US **wrench**.)
spare 1. *n.* & *adj.* extra to what is needed. *You can use my spare pen.* 2. *vb.* do without. *I can spare you the afternoon.*
spark *n.* a tiny glowing bit from a fire; a flash of light.
sparkle *vb.* flash with light, send out sparks, glitter.
sparrow *n.* a small seed-eating bird.
spasm *n.* involuntary and abnormal muscle contraction.
spastic *n.* a person who suffers from spasms caused by cerebral palsy.
spat *vb.* past of **spit**.
spawn *n.* the eggs of fish and other water animals, such as frogs. *vb.* cast spawn.
speak *vb.* (past **spoke**, past part. **spoken**) talk; communicate by using words.
spear *n.* a weapon made from a long pole with a sharp point on the end. *vb.* pierce with a spear.
special *adj.* different from others and usually better than them. *My birthday is a very special day for me.*
speciality *n.* 1. something a person is specially good at. *Tina's speciality was cooking.* 2. a special or distinctive product.
specialize *vb.* study and become an expert in one subject etc. *This college specializes in science.*

A spanner and nut.

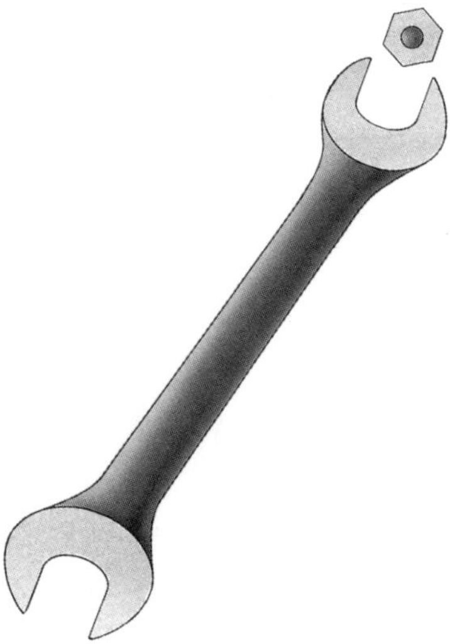

species *n.* a group of animals or plants that are alike in some way. *Mice are a species of rodent, and so are rats.*

specific gravity *n.* the density of a substance compared with the density of water at 4°C (39°F). If, for example, a substance is twice as dense as water, then it has a specific gravity (S.G.) of 2.

specify *vb.* name or state in detail. **specification** *n.* detailed description of an item or of work that needs to be done.

specimen *n.* a sample, a small amount or an example of something that shows what the rest are like.

speck *n.* a tiny amount of something, usually dust.

An ancient Egyptian sphinx carved in stone.

spectacles *n.* a pair of glasses worn in front of your eyes to help you see better.

spectator *n.* someone watching a game or other entertainment, a looker-on. *The spectators cheered when Kevin scored a goal.*

spectrum *n.* when a ray of light passes through certain materials, especially glass, it splits into a band of colours called a spectrum which looks like a rainbow.

speculate *vb.* 1. guess. 2. buy or sell shares on the stock market in the hope of making a profit.

speech *n.* 1. speaking. 2. a talk given to a group of people.

speed *n.* how fast something or someone moves. *vb.* go fast.

speedometer *n.* an instrument for measuring how fast a vehicle is moving.

spell 1. *vb.* write the letters of a word in the correct order. 2. *n.* magic words that are supposed to make something happen in a strange way. *The witch's spell turned the prince into a frog.* 3. *n.* a period of time. *A spell of fine weather.*

spend *vb.* (past **spent**) 1. use money to buy things. *How much do you spend on bus fares each week?* 2. stay a period of time. 3. use a period of time for some activity.

spew *vb.* be sick, vomit.

sphere *n.* a round object like a ball.

sphinx *n.* in mythology, the sphinx was a fabulous monster of the ancient world with a winged lion's body and a human or animal head.

spice *n.* part of certain plants used to flavour and preserve food. *vb.* flavour with spice.
spider *n.* a small animal with eight legs. *Some spiders make webs to catch insects.*

spied *vb.* past of **spy**.
spies plural of **spy**.
spike *n.* a long thin object with a sharp point; a large headless nail. *vb.* fix with spikes.
spill *vb.* let something fall out of its container. *Did you spill the salt on the table?*
spilt *vb.* past of **spill**. Also **spilled**.
spin *vb.* (past **span**, past part. **spun**) 1. turn around quickly in one place like a top. *n.* 2. make thread by twisting fibres together; make a web.
spinach *n.* a leafy green vegetable with a high iron and vitamin A and C content.
spinal column *n.* see **spine**.
spine *n.* the long line of bones down the middle of your back, the backbone; spinal column. **spineless** *adj.* lacking character.
spinster *n.* an unmarried woman.
spiral *n.* the shape a line makes when it circles around, like the thread of a screw. *vb.*
spire *n.* the tall pointed part of a church or other building.
spirit *n.* 1. the same thing as a soul. 2. a ghost. 3. alcohol. 4. courage.
spiritualist *n.* someone who believes that it is possible to communicate with the spirits of the dead.
spit *vb.* (past **spat**) throw out saliva from mouth.
splash *vb.* throw water about. *n.* sound of splashing; a patch of colour.
splashdown *n.* the landing of a spacecraft in the sea on completion of a mission.
splendid *adj.* very good; very impressive in some way; magnificent. *We saw a spendid castle when we visited Mexico.*
splinter *n.* a small sharp piece of wood or other material. *vb.* break into splinters.
split *vb.* break something into parts. *The class split up and went off in different directions. n.* a splitting.
spoil *vb.* 1. harm. *That electricity pylon spoils the view.* 2. treat a child or another person indulgently. *The kind*

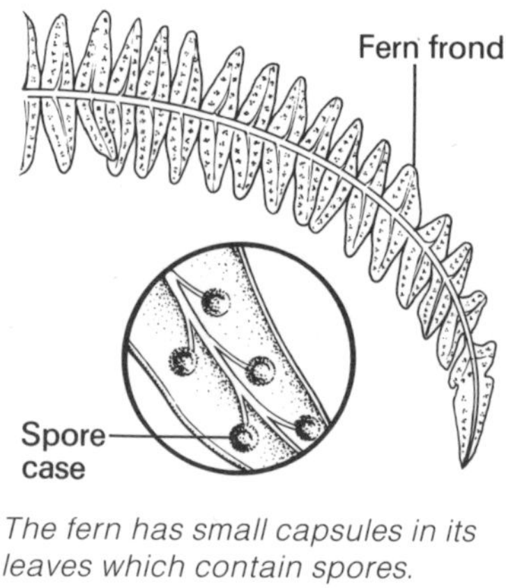

The fern has small capsules in its leaves which contain spores.

old man tended to spoil his grandchildren.

spoke *vb.* past of **speak**.

spoke *n.* radiating bar connecting hub and rim of a wheel.

sponge *n.* 1. a sea animal with a very light, soft body. 2. a soft object used for washing, once made from the sea animal, but today usually made of plastic. *vb.* wipe with a sponge.

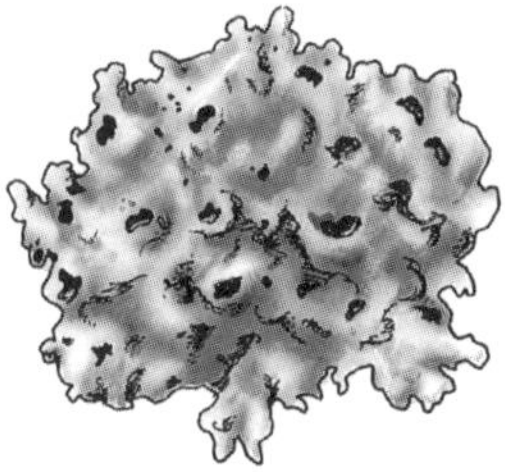

sponsor *n.* 1. a godfather or godmother. 2. a person or company paying for radio or TV advertising; a person or company who supports financially a sportsperson etc.

spoon *n.* a device with a handle and bowl for eating liquids and other food. *vb.*

spore *n.* the tiny dust-like cell from which some plants grow. *Ferns and mushrooms have spores instead of seeds.*

sport *n.* games and other activities, usually ones that happen outside. *Football and tennis are sports.*

spot 1. *n.* a place. *This is a pleasant spot.* 2. *vb.* pick out someone or something. *Can you spot your friend in the crowd?* 3. *n.* a blob. 4. *n.* a bit of something. *How about a spot of lunch?* 5. *n.* a pimple.

spotlight *n.* a strong beam of light that can be moved around.

spouse *n.* husband or wife.

spout 1. *n.* the part of something, such as a teapot, where the liquid comes out. 2. *vb.* gush. *Whales spout when they get to the surface to get rid of stale air.* 3. *vb.* (*casual*) go on speaking. *He could spout poetry for hours.*

sprain *vb.* damage a joint, such as your ankle, by tearing or straining the ligaments. *James sprained his ankle roller-skating.* *n.* such an injury.

sprang *vb.* past of **spring**.

sprawl *vb.* & *n.* spread out carelessly. *Adrian's books are sprawled all over the office.*

spray *vb.* & *n.* (squirt) a liquid in a fine mist.

spread *vb.* extend; cover something. *There's no need to spread the butter so thickly on your toast.*

sprightly *adj.* light and live. *Grandma is a sprightly old girl for her age.*

spring 1. *vb.* move suddenly upwards. *The tiger springs quickly at the goat.* 2. *n.* one of the seasons of the year, when plants begin to grow again after winter. 3. *n.* a place where water comes out of the ground. 4. *n.* a piece of metal able to return to its original shape or position after being forced into another.

sprinkle *vb.* scatter or pour out in small drops or particles. *He sprinkled salt over his food.*

sprint *vb.* & *n.* (run) very fast indeed. *He won the race by putting in a sprint at the finish.*

sprout *vb.* start to grow.
spruce 1. *n.* a tree belonging to the pine family. 2. *adj.* smart.
spud *n.* 1. slang for potato. 2. a type of small spade.
sprung *vb.* past part. of **spring**.
spun *vb.* past of **spin**.
spur 1. *n.* a sharp device worn on a rider's boot and used to prod the horse into going faster. 2. *vb.* prod or encourage someone. *I hope my advice will spur you into action.* 3. *n.* a projection, particularly a short piece of motorway that comes off the main route.
spurt 1. *n.* an extra effort, particularly in a race. *vb.* 2. *vb.* gush or spout.
spy *vb.* find out something by secret methods. *n.* (plural **spies**) a person who does that, usually for a government.
squad *n.* a small group of soldiers or people working together; a football team plus reserves.
squalor *n.* filth, dirt. **squalid** *adj.*
squander *vb.* spend wastefully. *She squandered a week's wages on a lot of worthless rubbish.*
square 1. *n.* an area with four equal sides and four right angles; an open space enclosed by houses. *adj.* in the shape of a square. 2. *vb.* & *n.* multiply a number by itself; the result of such multiplication. *4, 9, 16 and 25 are all squares.*
squash 1. *vb.* press something so that its shape flattens out. 2. *n.* a game played by two players in a special room (court) with a small, black rubber ball and racket. 3. *n.* fruit juice mixed with water and sugar.
squat 1. *vb.* crouch on the ground with your knees bent. 2. *vb.* settle in an unoccupied building.
squaw *n.* an American Indian name for a wife or woman.
squeak *vb.* make a high-pitched noise like a mouse. *I must oil that door to stop it squeaking.* *n.* shrill cry.
squeal *n.* a long shrill sound. *vb.*
squeeze *vb.* press something very tightly. *n.*
squid *n.* a sea mollusc related to the octopus.

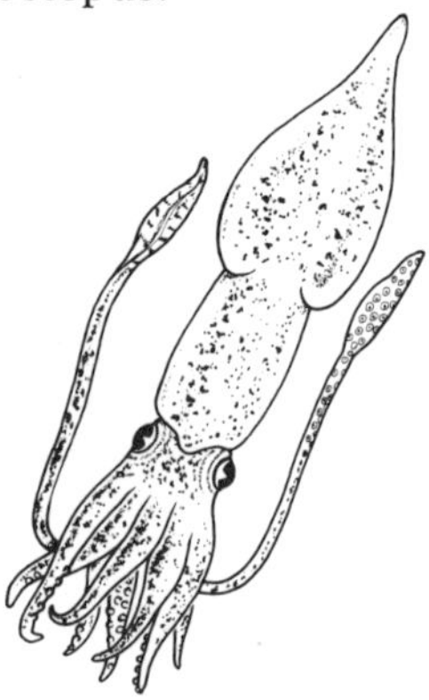

squint *vb.* & *n.* look with eyes partly closed.
squirrel *n.* a small grey or red animal with a bushy tail.
squirt *vb.* shoot out from a narrow opening. *The toothpaste squirted out of the tube.*
St *n.* 1. an abbreviation for saint as when you write 'St Francis of Assisi'. 2. an abbreviation for street, as when you write 'Chestnut St'.
stab *vb.* wound someone with a knife or another sharp weapon. *n.* a wound.

stable 1. *n.* a building for horses and cattle. 2. *adj.* steady, firmly fixed.
stack *vb.* arrange things on top of each other in a pile or stack. *n.*
stadium *n.* a large building where people can gather to play or watch sports, or to have meetings. They are usually open to the air in the middle.
staff *n.* 1. a group of people who work together. *There are four teachers on the staff of this school.* 2. a thick stick.
stag *n.* a male deer.
stage 1. *n.* the raised platform in a theatre on which people perform plays. *vb.* put on a play. 2. *n.* a point in the development of something. *What stage have you reached with your project?*
stage-coach *n.* a horse-drawn passenger vehicle running regularly between established stops or stages.
stagger *vb.* 1. walk unsteadily. 2. arrange to be at different times.
stagnant *adj.* water that is standing still and is not fresh. **stagnate** *vb.*
stain 1. *n.* a mark or coloured patch on something. *The teacher had an egg-stain on his tie.* 2. *vb.* mark; change the colour of something; dye.
staircase *n.* a set of stairs, complete with banisters etc.
stairs *pl. n.* a series of steps in a staircase.
stalactite *n.* an icicle-shaped stone structure hanging from the roof of a cave. **Stalagmites** are similar but grow upwards from the floor.

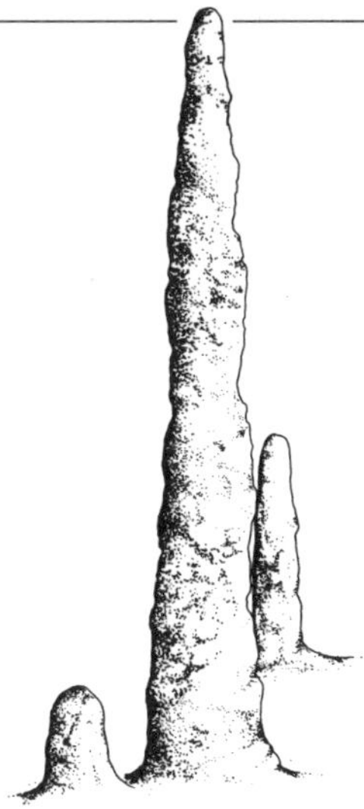

Stalagmites are found in limestone caves.

stale *adj.* not fresh; old.
stalk (rhymes with *walk*) 1. *n.* the stem of a plant. 2. *n.* & *vb.* follow something or someone so quietly that your presence is secret.
stall 1. *n.* a table or a stand in a market-place. 2. *n.* a division of a barn or stable for one animal. 3. *vb.* stop a car engine by mistake.
stallion *n.* a male horse.
stamen *n.* the male part of the flower that holds the pollen.
stamina *n.* staying power, endurance.
stammer *n.* a speech fault in which the person repeats the sound at the beginning of words, like this: 'I c-c-can't s-s-see'. *vb.* speak with a stammer.
stamp 1. *vb.* bang your foot on the ground. 2. *n.* a small label bought at a post office, which has to go on letters and parcels.

stand 1. *vb.* (past **stood**) be upright, in place. *The statue stands in the middle of the square.* 2. *n.* something on which things can be displayed, like a small, high table.

standard *n.* 1. something by which things can be compared or measured. *This ruler is not the standard size. It's much too short.* 2. a flag on a pole, usually raised to show loyalty to a country or its government.

stand in *n.* someone who acts for another person when that person cannot be there.

stand out *vb.* be conspicuous.

standstill *n.* complete stop.

stand up to *vb.* defend oneself against.

stank *vb.* past of **stink**.

stanza *vb.* a division of a poem, a group of lines.

star *n.* 1. one of the tiny shining lights you see in the sky at night. Stars are really very large, and all except our Sun are many millions of miles away. 2. a famous singer or actor.

starboard *n.* & *adj.* the right-hand side of a ship when you are facing towards the front, or bow.

starch *n.* an important food substance formed in plants. *vb.* stiffen with starch.

stare *vb.* & *n.* look hard at something for a long time.

starfish *n.* a creature of the sea-bed with a disc-shaped body and five or more arms.

starlight *n.* light from the stars.

starling *n.* a common bird with glossy black, brown-spotted feathers.

Stars and Stripes *n.* the US flag.

start 1. *n.* the beginning of something. 2. *vb.* begin. 3. *vb.* make a vehicle go. *He was unable to start his car.*

startle *vb.* surprise someone.

starve *vb.* grow ill from not having enough food, or from not having any at all. **starvation** *n.*

state 1. *n.* how something or someone is. *The garden is in an untidy state.* 2. *n.* a country, or division of a country. *There are 50 states in the United States of America.* 3. *vb.* say that something is true. *This book states that the king is dead.*

stately *adj.* dignified, grand.

statement *n.* a formal description or detailed account of something.

station *n.* 1. a place with platforms and buildings where trains stop to pick up and set down passengers. 2. a base for operations, such as a fire station. 3. an Australian stock-farm.

stationary *adj.* standing still, not moving.

Starfish.

Early steamers had sails as well as an engine.

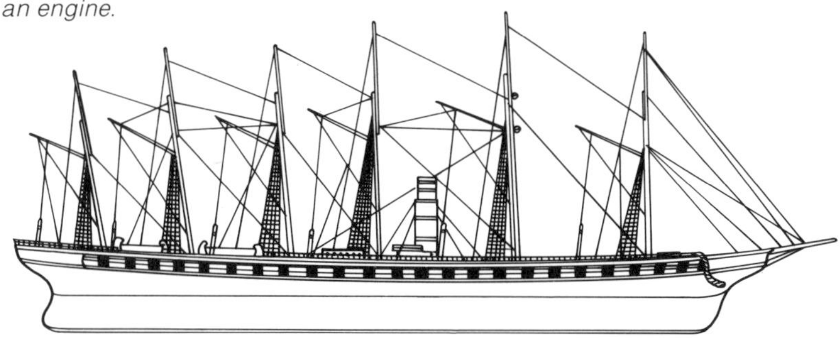

stationery *n.* the paper, pens, pencils, ink and other materials used for writing.
statistics *pl. n.* the science of collecting figures, studying them and drawing conclusions about their meaning. For example, a bus company might count how many people travel by bus to work each day to help decide what kind of buses and how many to run on its routes.
statue *n.* a model in stone or metal, of someone famous, an animal etc.
stay *vb.* remain; live somewhere for a time. *n.* a period of staying.
steady *adj.* firm; well-balanced. *vb.* make steady, stable.
steak (rhymes with *break*) *n.* a thick slice of meat or fish.
steal *vb.* (past **stole**, past part. **stolen**) take something that does not belong to you by theft.
steam *n.* water that is so hot it has turned into water vapour, or gas.
steam engine *n.* an engine or locomotive powered by steam.
steamer *n.* a boat driven by the power of a steam engine.
steel *n.* a strong metal made from iron in a furnace.
steel wool *n.* a mass of steel fibres used for cleaning.
steep *adj.* sloping sharply.
steeple *n.* a tall pointed tower on a church or other building.
steer *vb.* control the direction of a vehicle, ship etc.
stem *n.* the stalk of a plant, the part that grows up from the ground.
stench *n.* unpleasant smell.
stencil *n.* a flat sheet of metal, plastic or special paper. Words, patterns etc. are cut in it, and they can be copied by passing ink or paint through the holes on to paper or other materials. *vb.* use a stencil.
step *n.* 1. one of the movements you make when you walk, run or dance. *vb.* 2. one of the flat parts of a stair or ladder, where you put your feet when you climb them. 3. a stage in doing something.
step- *prefix* indicating a relationship through remarriage. e.g. **stepchild, stepdaughter, stepfather** etc.
steppe *n.* vast grassy plain in USSR.

stereo or **stereophonic sound** *n.* sound that is put through two or more loudspeakers.

sterilize *vb.* destroy all germs with heat or strong antiseptic. **sterile** *adj.* free of germs; unable to bear offspring.

sterling *n.* the money of Great Britain.

stern 1. *adj.* strict or severe. 2. *n.* the back end of a boat or ship.

stethoscope *n.* an instrument used to listen to people's heartbeats and the sound of their breathing.

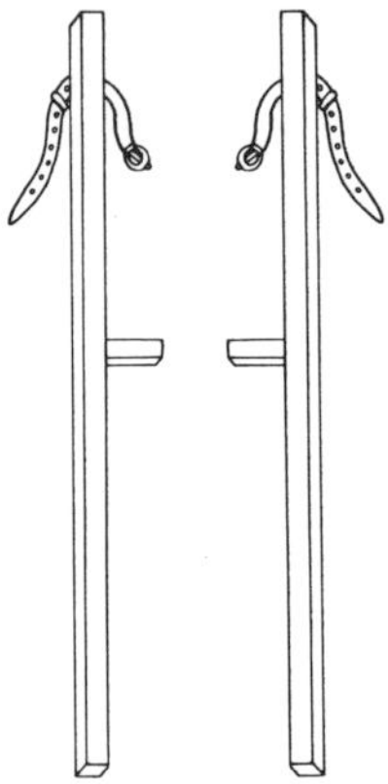

A pair of stilts.

stetson *n.* a hat with a wide brim, worn by cowboys.

stew *n.* & *vb.* a meat and vegetable mixture, usually boiled slowly for a long time.

steward *n.* a man who looks after people, often on a train or plane.

stewardess *n.* a woman who looks after people, often on a train or plane.

stick 1. *n.* a wooden rod or twig. 2. *vb.* glue or fix things together.

sticker *n.* an adhesive label.

stickleback *n.* a small freshwater fish with spines on its back.

stick up for *vb.* support someone who is in trouble. *I knew it wasn't Ted's fault so I tried to stick up for him when the others blamed him.*

stiff *adj.* not easily bent, rigid.

still 1. *adj.* & *adv.* without movement. *Still waters run deep. Please keep still.* 2. *adv.* even so, however. *I can still hear them talking.* 3. *n.* apparatus used in distilling alcohol.

stilts *pl. n.* a pair of poles on which you can stand and walk above the ground. **stilted** *adj.* stiff, pompous.

stimulus *n.* something that makes you active or energetic; an incentive. **stimulate** *vb.*

sting *n.* a sharp defence that some animals and plants have to protect themselves with. *Wasp stings hurt.* *vb.* wound with a sting.

stingy *adj.* not generous, mean.

stink *vb.* & *n.* smell bad.

stir *vb.* 1. move liquid around with something. *Steve forgot to stir the soup, and it burned.* 2. rouse.

stirrup *n.* a metal support that hangs on each side of a horse's saddle, into which the rider puts his or her feet.

stitch *n.* (plural **stitches**) one of the loops made in cloth when you are sewing or in wool when you are knitting. *vb.* sew.

stoat *n.* a small slim mammal of the weasel family with reddish brown fur.

stock *n*. 1. goods kept to be used or sold. *I keep a large stock of paper in that cupboard.* 2. a share in a company.
stocking *n*. a covering for the leg; a long sock.
stole *vb*. past of **steal**.
stomach *n*. organ in the middle part of your body, into which food goes after it is swallowed and where digestion begins. *vb*. endure, tolerate, put up with.
stone *n*. 1. a kind of rock. *The statue was made from stone.* 2. a small piece of rock. *I've got a stone in my shoe.* 3. the hard seed of some fruits, like plums. 4. a gem, a precious stone. 5. a measure of weight, the same as 14lb.
stood *vb*. past of **stand**.
stool *n*. a seat or chair without a back.
stoop *vb*. bend the body; condescend. *n*. a habitual bend in the body. *My grandfather has a slight stoop.*
stop *vb*. 1. come to a halt. *The car stopped at the traffic lights.* *n*. a halt, pause. 2. prevent.
store 1. *n*. a large shop. 2. *vb*. keep things until they are needed. *Squirrels store nuts. n.*
storey *n*. (plural **storeys**) one floor of a building. *My bedroom is on the third storey of the house.*
stork *n*. a tall white bird with a long beak and legs and wide wings.
storm *n*. a very strong wind with rain or snow.
story *n*. a tale. *Please tell me a story.*
stout 1. *adj*. thick and heavy. 2. *n*. a heavy, dark beer.
stove *n*. a device for heating a room; an oven.
stowaway *n*. someone who hides in a ship, aircraft or some other form of transport, in order to travel in secret or without paying.
straight 1. *adj*. not bent or crooked. *You can draw a straight line with a ruler.* 2. *adv*. directly. *Did you come straight home from school?*
straightaway *adv*. at once, immediately.
straighten *vb*. make something right or correct. *Henry asked me to help him straighten the carpet.*
strain *vb*. 1. push, stretch or try too hard; injure by over-using. *n*. 2. pass liquid through a fine cloth or net of small holes. **strainer** *n*.
strait *n*. a narrow channel of water joining two larger stretches of water.
strand *n*. a thread.
strange *adj*. odd; unusual.
stranger *n*. someone you don't know.
strangle *vb*. kill by pressing hard on the throat, choke. **strangulation** *n*.

Storks sometimes nest on rooftops. This is thought to bring good luck to a house.

strap *n.* a strip of leather or some other material used to fasten or hold things. *vb.* fasten with straps.

strategy *n.* the art of planning a military campaign. Also, in other planning.

stratum *n.* (plural **strata**) a layer (of rock, clouds etc.).

straw *n.* 1. dry stalks of corn. 2. a thin tube for drinking through.

strawberry *n.* a small plant belonging to the rose family, with white flowers and delicious red fruit.

stray *vb.* wander away. *The fence was broken and so the cows could stray on to the road.*

streak 1. *n.* irregular band of colour. *The white marble is streaked with red.* 2. *vb.* rush past.

stream *n.* 1. a brook; a small river. 2. a flow of anything. *vb.*

streamline *vb.* design (a vehicle etc.) with a smooth shape to cut down wind resistance. **streamlined** *adj.*

street *n.* a road lined with buildings, particularly in a town.

strength *n.* how strong something or someone is. *Walter did not have the strength to lift the barrel by himself.* **strengthen** *vb.* make or become stronger.

stress *n.* 1. tension, strain. 2. (in mechanics) pressure or force exerted on a body. 3. emphasis. *vb. I cannot stress too much the importance of a good diet.*

stretch 1. *vb.* pull something out so as to make it bigger. 2. *n.* a length of time or a distance. *Janet could see a long stretch of road ahead of the car.*

stretcher *n.* a movable bed for carrying sick or injured people.

strict *adj.* stern, severe, unkind. *The teacher was very strict.*

stride *vb.* (past **strode**) walk with long steps. *n.* a long step; a pace.

strife *n.* conflict, struggle.

strike 1. *n.* hit hard. 2. *vb.* stop work as a protest against the people who employ you. *n.* when people strike. *The workers have been on strike for six weeks now.*

string *n.* thin cord or rope.

strip 1. *n.* a long narrow piece of

The car's streamlined shape enables it to travel faster, using less fuel.

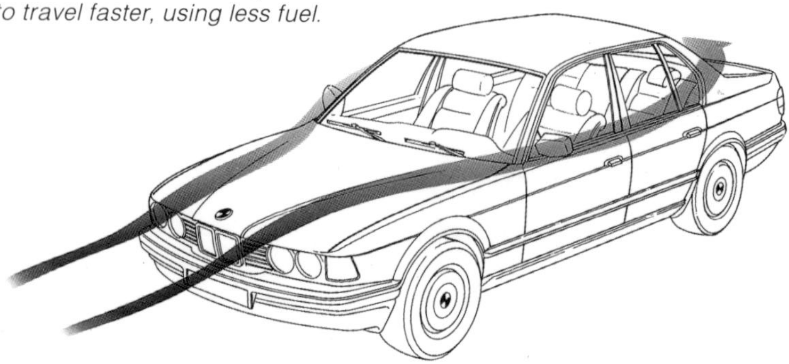

material. 2. *vb*. take off all your clothes; deprive; tear off.
stripe *n*. a band of colour, especially on clothing and other fabric. **striped** *adj*.
strive *vb*. (past **strove**) try hard. *You must strive to do better*.
strode *vb*. past of **stride**.
stroke 1. *vb*. move your hand gently over something. *Carol liked to stroke her cat's soft fur*. 2. *n*. a serious illness which can result in *paralysis* (being unable to move all or part of the body).
stroll (rhymes with *pole*) *vb*. & *n*. walk along slowly.
strong *adj*. powerful; having great strength; difficult to break.
stronghold *n*. a castle; fortified place.
strongpoint *n*. what a person is particularly good at doing.
struck *vb*. past of **strike**.
structure *n*. anything that has been built. *A house is a structure, and so is a table*.
struggle *vb*. fight, usually when you use your whole body. *Jenny had to struggle to free herself from the rope*. strive. *n*. hard contest.
strum *vb*. play a musical instrument carelessly.
strut *n*. a wooden or iron bar which strengthens a framework.
stub 1. *n*. short piece left after the main part has been used or removed. *A cigarette stub*. *vb*. put out by pressing the lighted end on something. 2. *vb*. bump on something. *Donald stubbed his toe on the rock*.
stubborn *adj*. not willing to change, or to do what other people want.
stucco *n*. & *vb*. (apply) a plaster coating to wall surfaces.
stuck *vb*. past of **stick**.
student *n*. someone who is studying, usually at a school or a college.
studio *n*. an artist's workroom; a place for recording, broadcasting, or making films.
study 1. *vb*. read and learn; look at something hard. *He had to study the map for a long time before he made the journey*. *n*. 2. *n*. a room in which someone works alone.
stuff 1. *vb*. fill something with some kind of material. *My teddybear is stuffed with wool*. 2. *n*. anything you don't know the name of. *What's the stuff your Dad mended his cup with?*
stuffy *adj*. having no fresh air, smelling stale and airless.
stumble *vb*. miss one's footing; come near to falling.
stump *n*. the short, stubby remains of something, such as the part of a tree that is left in the ground after the rest of it has been cut down.
stun *vb*. 1. make senseless with a blow on the head. 2. astonish.
stung *vb*. past of **sting**.
stunk *vb*. past part. of **stink**.
stunt 1. *vb*. stop the growth of. 2. *n*. a difficult feat, a showy performance (often for publicity).
stupid *adj*. foolish; not clever.
sturdy *adj*. strong, well built.
sturgeon *n*. a toothless, shark-like fish valued for its roe (eggs) which are sold as a delicacy under the name of caviar.

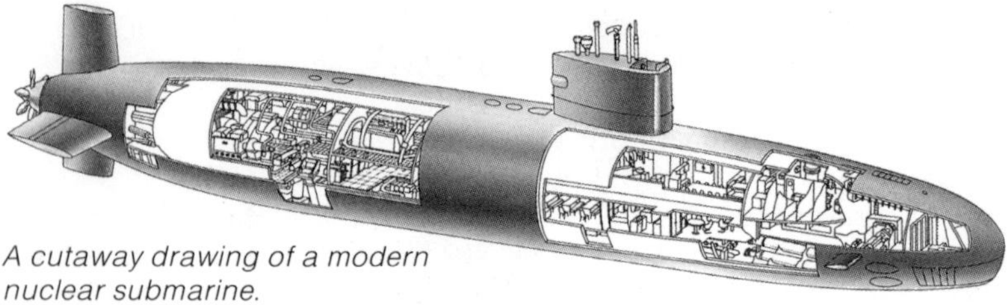

A cutaway drawing of a modern nuclear submarine.

stutter *vb.* stammer.

sty *n.* 1. (also **stye**) a painful red swelling on the eyelid. 2. a pen in which pigs are kept; a pigsty.

style *n.* the way something is done or made. *Tim's shirt is the latest style, but he doesn't like it.*

stylish *adj.* fashionable; having a good sense of style.

stylus *n.* a fine point used for playing records etc.

sub- *prefix* meaning under, inferior, lower, e.g. **subhuman; subnormal; subsoil** etc.

subject *n.* 1. the thing that is being talked about or written about. *John is the subject of everyone's interest.* 2. someone who is ruled by a government, or a king or queen.

submarine *n.* a kind of boat that can move under the water instead of on the surface. *adj.* under the sea.

submerge *vb.* plunge, go or put under water.

subscribe *vb.* contribute, sign one's name to. **subscription** *n.*

subside *vb.* settle, sink back to normal. *The flood gradually subsided.*

subsidy *n.* financial help from a government to industry, farming etc., to keep prices down. **subsidize** *vb.* pay a subsidy to.

substance *n.* anything that can be seen or touched. **substantial** *adj.* solid, considerable.

substitute 1. *vb.* put in place of something else. *Peter substituted oil for butter when he cooked the onions.* 2. *n.* a player in a game who joins in for someone else. *Paul was only a substitute but he scored the winning goal.*

subtle (*sut-il*) *adj.* delicate, refined; difficult to understand.

subtract *vb.* take something away (a part from a whole). **subtraction** *n.*

suburb *n.* the outside parts of a town, usually where people live. **suburban** *adj.*

subway *n.* an underground tunnel, particularly one for pedestrians; an underground railway in the USA.

succeed *vb.* 1. achieve something you set out to do. **success** *n.* achievement, a good outcome. 2. come after (a king or other important person). *He succeeded his father as Duke of Dorset.* **succession** *n.*

successful *adj.* able to do what you want to do or try to do.

such *adj.* of that kind. *How can you believe such stories?*

suck *vb.* take in air or liquid. *We had straws to suck our milkshakes through.*

suckle *vb.* feed (a newly born or young mammal) from its mother's teats.
sudden *adj.* quick; happening quickly and without warning. *A sudden idea struck her.*
sue *vb.* take legal action.
suede (swade) *n.* leather made from skin of young goat (kid) with flesh side out.
suet *n.* fat that protects kidneys of cattle and sheep, used in cooking.
suffer *vb.* experience pain or unhappiness. **suffering** *n.*
sufficient *adj.* enough; just right; not too much.
suffix *n.* syllable(s) added at the end of a word to make another word. e.g. host host**ess**; red redd**ish**; king king**ship**, etc.
suffocate *vb.* die from being unable to breath. **suffocation** *n.*
sugar *n.* a sweet-tasting food.
suggest *vb.* put forward an idea. **suggestion** *n.* plan, thought.
suicide *n.* die by killing yourself on purpose. **suicidal** *adj.*
suit 1. *n.* a jacket with trousers or a skirt that are made to be worn together. 2. *vb.* be right for a certain purpose, convenient, appropriate. *It will suit me to go now, because I am not busy.* 3. *n.* a legal process. 4. *n.* one of four sets in a pack of cards.
suitable *adj.* correct, right for what is needed. *That dress will be very suitable for travelling.*
suitcase *n.* a large bag or case for carrying clothes etc. on a journey.
suite (*sweet*) *n.* a set of rooms or furniture. *A three-piece suite.*
sulk *vb.* be in a bad temper. **sulky** *adj.*
sullen *adj.* silently bad tempered.
sulphur *n.* a non-metallic element often found in the form of yellow crystals. (symbol S).
sulphuric acid *n.* an extremely corrosive, colourless, oily acid widely used in the chemical industry.
sultan *n.* a king or sovereign of a Muslim state.
sultana *n.* a light-coloured seedless raisin (dried grape) used in cakes and puddings.
sum *n.* 1. the whole amount. 2. the answer to an addition problem.
summarize *vb.* give a short account, sum up. **summary** *n.* a brief account of the main facts.
summer *n.* the warmest season of the year, between spring and autumn.
summit *n.* top, highest point, peak.

Sugar cane is one of the main sources of sugar. The other is sugar beet.

summon *vb.* call together.
sum up *vb.* summarize.
Sun *n.* The Sun is the central body in the Solar System and the nearest star to the Earth.

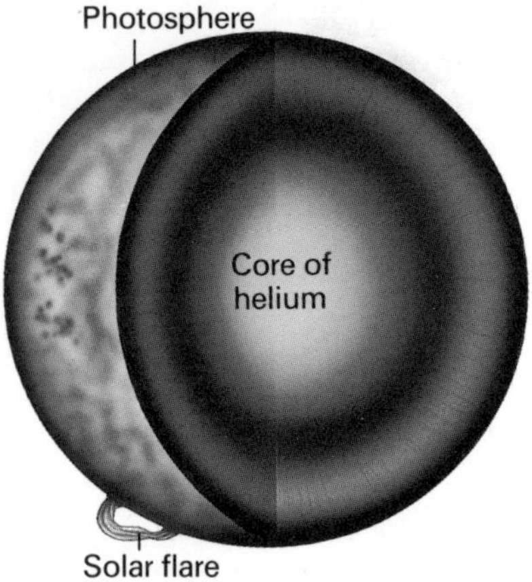

sunburn *n.* red or brown colouring of the skin caused by exposure to the sun.
Sunday *n.* the first day of the week, named after the Sun; the Christian day of worship.
sundial *n.* a kind of clock that shows the time by the shadow of the Sun on the dial.
sunflower *n.* a tall plant with a large, flat flower edged with yellow petals.
sung *vb.* past part. of **sing**.
sunk *vb.* past part. of **sink**.
sunlight *n.* the light of the Sun.
sunny *adj.* bright with sunshine.
sunrise *n.* dawn (early morning); the time when the Sun comes up.
sunset *n.* dusk (early evening); the time when the Sun goes down.
sunshine *n.* bright light from the Sun.
sunspots *pl. n.* dark patches that appear from time to time on the surface of the Sun.
super- *prefix* meaning above, over, more than, on top (of).
superb *adj.* excellent, magnificent.
superficial *adj.* on the surface.
superior *adj.* better than others.
superlative *adj.* the best.
supermarket *n.* a large self-service shop where customers can buy many different sorts of goods.
supernatural *adj.* something that does not have an ordinary explanation.
supernova *n.* a star which explodes and becomes very bright.
supersede *vb.* take the place of.
supersonic *adj.* faster than the speed of sound.
superstitious *adj.* someone who believes in luck, chance and magic happenings is superstitious. **superstition** *n.*
supervise *vb.* oversee, watch over, control. **supervision** *n.*
supper *n.* a meal eaten at the end of the day.
supple *adj.* easy to bend; not stiff. *Athletes have to be supple.*
supplied *vb.* past of **supply**.
supply 1. *vb.* give what is needed. *I will supply you with a book.* 2. *n.* things that are kept to be used later. *We have a large supply of pencils.*
support *vb.* 1. hold up. *n.* 2. help. 3. supply with a home and food. 4. regularly watch or attend (football etc.). **supporter** *n.*
suppose *vb.* think that something is true, although it

may not be. *Let's suppose that it will take us two hours.*
suppress *vb.* put down, crush; (of information) conceal. *The enemy suppressed the news of their defeat.*
supreme *adj.* the greatest; most excellent etc.
sure *adj.* & *adv.* certain; accurate. *Are you sure that what you say is true? We leave tomorrow for sure.*
surf *n.* large waves breaking on the shores of a beach.
surface *n.* the all-over covering of something, the outside. *The astronauts landed on the surface of the Moon. vb.* rise to the surface of water etc.
surgeon *n.* a doctor who operates on people.
surgery 1. *n.* a place where any kind of doctor sees the people who are patients. 2. *n.* treating disease or injuries by operating.
surly *adj.* bad tempered.
surname *n.* your family name. *My name is Anne Bell, so my surname is Bell.*
surpass *vb.* excel, do better than.
surplus *n.* what is left over when need or use is satisfied. *adj.*
surprise *n.* something that happens unexpectedly. *The party was a lovely surprise. vb.* attack or come upon suddenly; astonish. **surprising** *adj.*
surrender *vb.* give in. *The soldiers had to surrender when they lost the battle.* to give up possession of.
surround *vb.* enclose, be all around. *Flower gardens surround our house.*
surroundings *pl. n.*
survey *vb.* 1. take a look at a view. 2. look carefully at a house or other building before it is sold, to check that there is nothing wrong with it. *n.* 3. measure an area of land. **surveying** *n.* the measurement and mapping of parts of the Earth's surface.

A surveyor uses a theodolite to measure angles and planes.

survive *vb.* live through changes or difficult times. **survivor** *n.* a person who survives.
suspect *vb.* (*su*-**spekt**) have a feeling that something is true, although you are not sure; doubt. *I suspect that someone has worn my bathing suit because it seems damp. n.* (**sus**-*pekt*) a person who is suspected of having done something (usually bad).

suspend *vb*. 1. hang something up. 2. stop, cancel or postpone something.
suspense *n*. state of anxiety or excitement while waiting for something to happen.
suspicion *n*. mistrust, a feeling that something is wrong.
sustain *vb*. 1. hold up, support. 2. suffer (an injury etc.)
swallow 1. *vb*. make food go down your throat. 2. *n*. a small bird with long, slim wings and a forked tail.
swam *vb*. past of **swim**.
swamp 1. *n*. a bog or marsh. 2. *vb*. overwhelm with numbers of people etc.
swan *n*. a graceful long-necked water-bird with paddling feet.
swank *vb*. & *n*. (a) show off.
swap *vb*. (or **swop**) exchange one thing for something else. *Will you swop your lunch for mine?*
swarm *n*. a large group of bees or other insects. *vb*. form a swarm.
swastika *n*. two kinds of cross, one the symbol of the Nazis in Germany, the other a religious symbol in India.
sway *vb*. move from side to side.
swear *vb*. 1. use bad language, words that many people do not think right. 2. make a solemn promise. *The knight had to swear to obey his king*.
sweat (rhymes with *wet*) *n*. the liquid that comes out of your skin when you are hot or nervous. *vb*.
sweater *n*. a garment for the top of your body, a jumper.
swede *n*. a variety of turnip.
sweep *vb*. (past **swept**). 1. clean with a brush. 2. glide majestically.
sweeping *adj*. extensive, wide. *The government took sweeping measures to improve the economy*.
sweet 1. *adj*. having a sugary taste. 2. *n*. a sweetmeat such as a toffee or piece of chocolate. 3. *n*. the pudding at the end of a meal. 4. *adj*. charming. **sweeten** *vb*. make sweet.
swell *vb*. get bigger, increase. **swelling** *n*.
swept *vb*. past of **sweep**.

Swans are the largest water-birds. They are often seen on our lakes and rivers.

swerve *vb*. & *n*. (make) a sudden violent turn; a swerving motion. *The car driver had to swerve to avoid hitting a dog*.
swift 1. *adj*. fast, quick, **swiftness** *n*. 2. *n*. a fast-flying bird with long wings.
swig *vb*. drink greedily. *n*.
swill 1. *n*. part-liquid pig food. 2. *vb*. pour water over, rinse.
swim *vb*. (past **swam**, past part. **swum**) move yourself along while afloat in water. *n*.
swindle *vb*. cheat. *n*. fraud.
swine *n*. a collective word for pigs; (casual) unpleasant person.

swing *vb.* (past **swung**) move yourself or something else backwards and forwards. *The monkey was swinging from branch to branch. n.* a seat slung by ropes.
switch 1. *n.* a device for turning lights and other electrical appliances on and off. *vb.* switch on, switch off. 2. *vb.* change from one thing to another.
swivel *n.* a device joining two parts which enables either one or both parts to turn freely. *vb.* pivot, turn on a swivel.
swollen *vb.* past part. of **swell**.
swoop *vb.* rush down (out of the sky). *The eagle swooped on its prey. n.*
swop see **swap**
sword *n.* a hand weapon with a long blade.
swordfish *n.* a big tropical fish, with a sword-shaped bony snout.
swore *vb.* past of **swear**.
swot *vb.* study hard. *n.* a person who studies hard.
swum *vb.* past part. of **swim**.
swung *vb.* past of **swing**.

The swordfish gets its name from its long, sharp snout.

sycamore *n.* a tree belonging to the maple family.
syllable *n.* one section or part of a word, which can be said by itself. *Ambulance has three syllables: am-bu-lance.*
syllabus *n.* a course of studies.
symbol *n.* a sign. *In arithmetic the symbol + means 'add'.* **symbolize** *vb.*
symmetrical *adj.* having the same shape and size on both sides of a central line. *All these capital letters are symmetrical, even the second one: A E H M O T X.* **symmetry** *n.*
sympathy 1. *n.* a feeling for another person's distress or unhappiness. **sympathetic** *adj.* **sympathize** *vb.* 2. **in sympathy** in tune with another person.
symphony (**sim**-*fon-ee*) *n.* a form of long musical composition for a full orchestra, usually consisting of three or four movements.
symptom *n.* some indication, sign or mark on the body – e.g. a rash or high temperature – pointing to a disease.
synagogue *n.* a meeting place for Jewish religious worship and teaching.

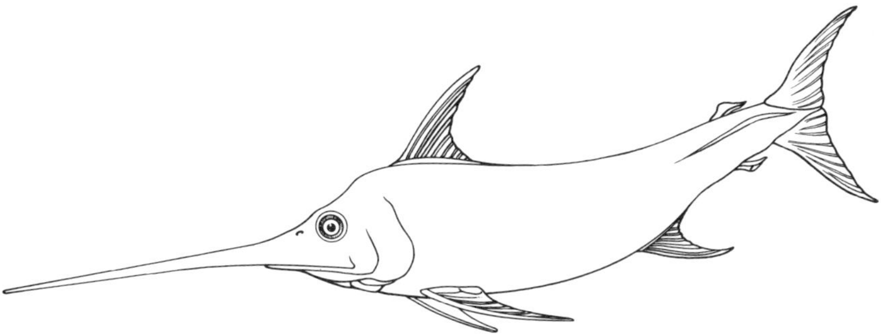

synod *n.* a meeting or council of clergy (and laity) of a Church.
synonym *n.* a word that has the same meaning as another word.
synopsis *n.* a summary or precis, especially of a story or play.
synthetic *adj.* & *n.* made artificially.
syringe *n.* an instrument for sucking a liquid in, and forcing it out again, in a thin stream.
syrup *n.* a sticky sweet liquid, made from sugar, that tastes a little like honey.
system *n.* 1. an organized set of ideas or way of working. **systematic** *adj.* 2. a set of things which together make up a complicated unit or whole. *A computer system. The body's nervous system.*

T

tab *n.* a label, tag.
tabernacle *n.* a tent used by the Jews in Bible times; a place of worship; a receptacle for consecrated hosts.
table *n.* 1. a piece of furniture with a flat top supported by legs. 2. a way of arranging figures, such as a multiplication table.
tablespoon *n.* a large spoon used for serving food. *A tablespoon is often used to measure amounts in cooking.*
tablet *n.* 1. round, compressed drug or medicine. 2. a flat slab. *Pass me the tablet of soap.*
table tennis *n.* a game played on a table, using bats and a celluloid ball.
tabloid *n.* small-sized newspaper that contains news etc. in a condensed form and which has many photographs.
taboo *n.* something that must not be talked about, touched etc; set apart.
tack 1. *n.* a small flat-headed nail. 2. *vb.* sew with long loose stitches. 3. *vb.* sail a boat on a zig-zag course into the wind.
tackle 1. *n.* equipment for a sport or some other activity. *Dad keeps his fishing tackle in the garage.* 2. *vb.* start work on a problem. *John decided to tackle the washing up alone.* 3. *vb.* intercept an opponent, especially in football.
tact *n.* knowing what to say or do to avoid offence. **tactless, tactful** *adj.*
tactics *pl. n.* the science of using military forces in a war. **tactical** *adj.*
tadpole *n.* a young frog or toad, at the stage between the egg and the adult.

Tadpoles develop into frogs or toads.

tag *n.* 1. a small label. *vb.* 2. a game in which one person chases the others, and catches them by touching or 'tagging' them.
taiga *n.* subarctic forests that thrive south of the 'tree line'.
tail *n.* a projection at the back of many kinds of animal. *Some monkeys use their tail as a fifth limb. vb.* follow close behind.
tailor *n.* a person who makes suits, coats and other clothes.
take *vb.* (past **took**; past part. **taken**) get possession of something; catch or gain.
take after *vb.* resemble. *Doesn't Tina take after her mother?*
take in *vb.* 1. be tricked. *I was taken in by what he said, but it was really a lie.* 2. bring someone in to your house. *The hotel was full, so the manager found a motel to take us in.* 3. understand. *I'm sorry but I didn't quite take in what you said.* 4. make something narrower. *The skirt was too big, but I took it in at the waist.*
take off *vb.* & *n.* 1. take to the air (of an aircraft). 2. a parody, humorous mimicry.
take over *vb.* assume control of. *n.*
take up *vb.* start doing something which is new to you. *My father has decided to take up pottery.*
talc *n.* a mineral with a soapy feel which is ground to a powder to make talcum powder for dusting the body after a bath.
tale *n.* a story; mischievous gossip.
talent *n.* an ability to do something well. *Nell has a natural talent for skating.*
talk 1. *vb.* speak. *n.* **talkative** *adj.* 2. *n.* a short lecture.
tall *adj.* having greater than average height, often used of people and buildings. *Simon is not as tall as his brother.*
tallow *n.* melted animal or vegetable fat, used for candles and soap.
talon *n.* the long claw of a bird of prey, such as a hawk.
tambourine *n.* a musical instrument shaped like a shallow drum, with discs around it. It is shaken, and beaten with the hand.

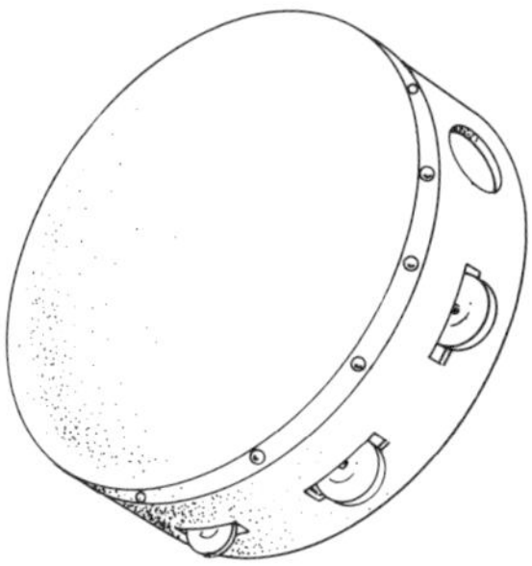

tame 1. *adj.* (of animals) not wild, used to being with humans. *vb.* make tame. 2. uninteresting, dull.
tamper *vb.* meddle with.
tan 1. *n.* a light brown colour. *vb.* go brown in the sun. 2. *vb.* make animal skins into leather.
tandem *n.* a bicycle with two seats.
tang *n.* a sharp taste or smell.
tangerine *n.* a small loose-skinned kind of orange.
tangled *adj.* confused and mixed up. **tangle** *vb.* & *n.*
tango *n.* Latin American dance. *vb.* music for this dance.

tank *n*. 1. large container for liquids. 2. an armoured fighting vehicle with guns, which moves on tracks instead of wheels.

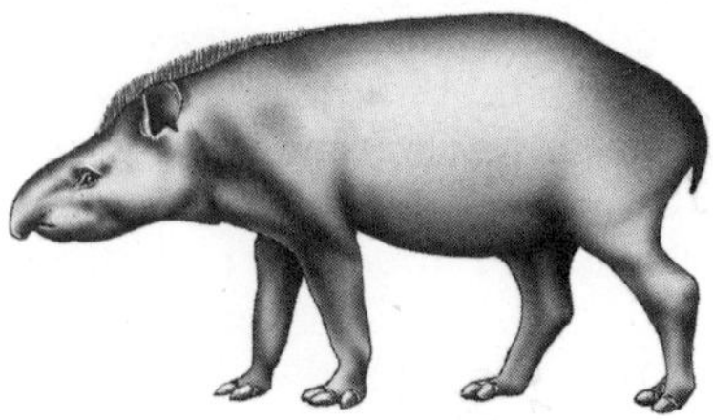

The tapir is a shy animal which lives in the forests of South America.

tankard *n*. drinking vessel (made of silver or pewter) with a handle.

tanker *n*. a ship or lorry used to carry liquids, such as oil.

tannin *n*. a substance made from tree bark, used in preparing leather.

tantrum *n*. a sudden fit of bad temper.

Taoiseach *n*. prime minister, Republic of Ireland.

tap 1. *n*. a device for turning on and off the flow of water into a sink, bath etc. 2. *vb*. knock gently but repeatedly. 3. *vb*. take water, information etc. from a source. *I think that my telephone has been tapped.*

tape *n*. 1. a narrow length of material used for typing or in dress-making. 2. a strip of plastic which is used to record sound. *vb*. record on magnetic tape.

taper 1. *n*. long thin candle used for lighting lamps etc. 2. *vb*. make or become smaller towards the end. *A church spire tapers.*

tape-recorder *n*. an instrument for recording sounds on tape and playing the sound back again.

tapestry *n*. a picture on cloth, made by sewing or weaving in coloured threads.

tapir *n*. a nocturnal animal of tropical America which is related to the horse.

tar *n*. a dark, thick, sticky substance that comes from oil, wood etc.

tarantula *n*. large black south European spider, named after the town of Taranto in Italy; it has a slightly poisonous bite.

target *n*. anything that has a missile shot or thrown at it. *An archery target is usually made of straw covered with canvas.*

tariff 1. *n*. price list; list of custom duties. 2. sum of money that must be paid, usually as a customs duty.

tarmac *n*. a road surface of broken stones mixed with tar (short for tar-macadam).

tarpaulin *n*. waterproof cloth, originally of tarred canvas.

tart 1. *adj*. sharp or sour tasting. 2. *n*. a pie with pastry underneath the filling but not on top of it.

tartan *n*. a traditional Scottish

The bite of the tarantula was once believed to be fatal to man.

woollen cloth, woven in one of a variety of square patterns.

task *n.* a job, a piece of work. *It was her task to make the beds in the morning.*

tassel *n.* a bunch of hanging threads used as an ornament.

taste 1. *n.* the sense by which you can tell the flavour of food and drink; the flavour itself. *vb.* try food or drink to see if you like it. 2. *n.* good or bad judgement in art, clothing etc. *I admire her taste in clothes.*

tattered *adj.* torn or hanging in shreds.

tattoo 1. *n.* a military pageant which takes place at night under floodlights. 2. *vb.* mark or colour the skin with patterns. *n.*

taught *vb.* (*tawt*) past of **teach**.

taut (*tawt*) *adj.* when something has been stretched so that it is firm. *Pull that rope until it is taut.* **tauten** *vb.*

tavern *n.* an old-fashioned word for an inn or pub where food and drink are served.

tawny *adj.* yellowish-brown colour.

tax *n.* (plural **taxes**) money paid to the government by people and organizations.

taxi 1. *n.* a car with a driver that can be hired for journeys. 2. *n.* the long run an aircraft makes to or from the runway. *vb.*

tea *n.* the dried leaves of an evergreen shrub. The leaves are soaked in boiling water to make the drink called tea.

teach *vb.* instruct other people; give them knowledge and encourage them to think for themselves. **teaching** *n.* the profession of teaching.

teacher *n.* a person who instructs (teaches) other people, usually in a school or college.

teak *n.* an evergreen tree with very hard wood grown in India, Burma and Thailand.

team *n.* 1. a group of people in a game or sport who are all on the same side. *There are 11 players in a football team.* 2. a group of people who join together to do a job.

teapot *n.* a vessel with a curved handle and spout for making and pouring out tea.

tear (*tare*) *vb.* (past **tore**; past part. **torn**) rip something such as cloth or paper, pull apart; move at great speed.

tears (*teers*) *pl. n.* drops of salt water which fall from your eyes when you cry.

tease (*teeze*) *vb.* make fun of someone, often unkindly.

tea-set *n.* matching teapot, cups etc. for use at teatime.

technical *adj.* to do with machinery or how things work.

technology *n.* the study of technical ideas.

tedious *adj.* boring because of its length or dullness.

tee *n.* place from which a golfer drives the ball at the beginning of each hole; small peg on which the golf ball is placed to drive off.

teenager *n.* a young person between the ages of thir*teen* and nine*teen*.

tee-shirt *n.* a short-sleeved shirt, like a vest, with no collar or buttons. *Tee-shirts sometimes have a joke written on them.*

teeth n. plural of **tooth**.

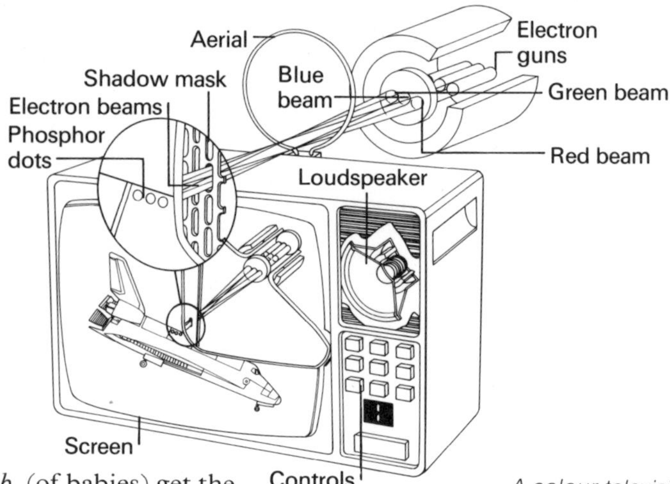

A colour television.

teethe *vb*. (of babies) get the first teeth.

teetotal *adj*. never drinking alcohol. *n*.

telecommunications *pl. n*. long distance signals by telephone, radio, telegraph and television.

telegram *n*. a word message sent by telegraph or radio.

telegraph *n*. a system of sending long-distance messages by electric current.
telegraphy *n*.

telephone *n*. an instrument for talking to people over long distances by turning speech into electrical impulses, which travel along wires, and then back again into speech. *vb*. use the telephone.

telescope *n*. a tube-like instrument with special lenses, which makes distant things appear larger.

television *n*. a way of sending and receiving pictures and sounds by radio waves.
telly and **TV** *abbreviations*.
televize *vb*.

tell *vb*. give information to somebody. *Tell me about your holiday*.

temper 1. *n*. your mood (usually when bad). *Gareth was in a bad temper because his parents refused to let him watch TV*. 2. *vb*. make a metal harder and more pliable by heating it and then cooling it rapidly.

temperament *n*. a person's character and way of feeling, thinking and behaving. *She has a gentle temperament*.

temperamental *adj*. sudden changes of mood.

temperate *adj*. (of a climate) neither too hot nor very cold. *New Zealand has a temperate climate*. moderate; avoiding excesses.

temperature *n*. the measurement of heat. *Temperature can be measured with a thermometer*.

tempest *n*. violent storm.

temple *n*. 1. a building used for meeting and worship in some

religions. 2. flat part of the side of the head between ear and forehead.
tempo *n.* the speed at which a piece of music is played.
temporary *adj.* lasting for a short time, not permanent. *We had a temporary teacher while ours was sick.*
tempt *vb.* try and persuade someone to do something they ought not to; entice.
tenant *n.* a person who rents and occupies someone else's property.
tend *vb.* be likely to do something. *This car tends to steer to the left.* 2. look after. *Shepherds tend their sheep.*
tender 1. *adj.* delicate, soft, easily hurt. 2. *vb.* offer. *The minister tendered his resignation.* 3. *n.* a small boat in which you get to a larger one.
tendon *n.* tough fibrous tissue connecting muscle to bone.
tennis *n.* a ball and racket game for two or four people, which is played on a specially marked court.
tenon *n.* piece of wood which fits into a hole (*a mortise*) to join two parts, of a piece of furniture etc.
tenor *n.* & *adj.* highest natural adult male singing voice.
tense *adj.* taut; showing mental or physical strain.
tent *n.* a shelter made from waterproof material, such as canvas, stretched over a frame of metal poles, and held up with ropes.
tentacle *n.* a long, snake-like 'arm' of an animal like the octopus.
tepee *n.* American Indian tent.
tepid *adj.* slightly warm.
term *n.* 1. a period of time. *The spring term lasts for ten weeks.* 2. word or expression which is used to describe particular ideas in different professions etc. e.g. medical terms, legal terms. 3. *pl.* conditions applying.
terminal 1. *n.* a building where you start or finish a journey by plane etc. 2. *adj.* final; particularly of an illness which someone will not survive.
terminate *vb.* bring to an end.
terminus *n.* an end station on a bus, train or air route.
termite *n.* an insect like an ant that builds large hills of earth and mud.
tern *n.* a seabird.
terrace *n.* 1. a level area cut out of a slope; 2. a row of houses built as a single block.
terracotta *n.* brownish-red baked clay used for statues, pottery, tiles and as a covering material on buildings.
terrapin *n.* a name for a small kind of turtle.
terrestrial *adj.* of the earth.
terrible *adj.* very bad, frightening, dreadful.
terrier *n.* one of various kinds of small dog that can dig out or drive out small game animals.
terrific *adj.* very great; excellent. *We had a terrific time in Norway.*
terrify *vb.* make someone very frightened.
territory *n.* an area of land.
terror *n.* great fear. (*casual*) a tiresome person.
terse (*turse*) *adj.* brief, concise.

test 1. *vb.* try out something. *I want to test the car before I buy it.* 2. *n.* a set of questions to be answered; a kind of small exam.
testes *pl. n.* (singular **testis** also **testicle**) egg-shaped glands contained in the scrotum, a bag hanging behind the penis in male mammals. The testes produce sperm which the penis releases.
Test Match *n.* a match between two countries, especially a cricket match.
tetanus *n.* a dangerous disease in which the muscles become rigid.
tether *n.* a rope for fastening an animal so that it can only move within a set radius.
Teuton *n.* a member of the Germanic race.
text *n.* the main part of a printed book.
textbook *n.* a book giving information for study in a school or college.
textile *n.* woven cloth of any sort.
texture *n.* how the surface of something feels when you touch it.
than *conj.* introducing second part of a comparison. *Jill is taller than Jack.*
thank *vb.* tell someone that you are grateful to them. *Thank you for the lovely party.*
thatch *n.* a roof covering, popular on cottages, made from layers of straw or reeds. *vb.*
thaw *vb.* melt (especially of ice or snow). *n.*
theatre *n.* 1. a place where plays are performed by actors and watched by an audience.
theatrical *adj.* 2. an operating theatre, a place where surgical operations are carried out.
theft *n.* stealing.
their *pron.* belonging to them.
theme *n.* the main subject. *The theme of the book is love.*
then *adv.* at that time. *I didn't know you so well then.* after that; next.
theology *n.* the study of religion.
theory *n.* an idea to explain something. *I have a theory about why he ran away.*
there *adv.* in or to that place. *Put the box down there.*
therefore *adv.* for that reason; and so.
thermometer *n.* an instrument for measuring temperature.

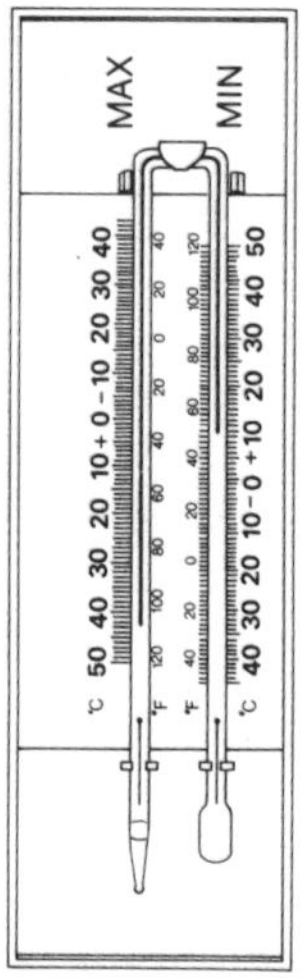

A maximum-minimum thermometer measures both high and low temperatures.

thermos *n.* a vacuum container for keeping liquids at the same temperature.

thermostat *n.* an instrument that automatically controls the amount of heat.
thesaurus *n.* a book like a dictionary, but without definitions, and with words of similar meaning listed together in groups.
thick *adj.* wide; not thin or slender. *The walls of the ancient castle were several metres thick.* 2. (of a liquid) flows more slowly. 3. an impolite word meaning 'stupid'.
thicket *n.* a dense growth of small trees and shrubs
thief *n.* (plural **thieves**) a person who steals.
thigh (rhymes with *my*) *n.* the part of your leg between your hip and your knee.
thimble *n.* a small covering, often made of metal, worn on the finger to avoid pricking it when sewing.
thin *adj.* lean, slim; not thick.
think *vb.* 1. use your brain to work out a problem; consider, reflect. 2. believe. *I think that's the right direction, but I'm not absolutely sure.*
think over *vb.* consider.
third 1. *adj.* next after second. 2. *n.* one of three pieces that make the whole thing. *There were three of us, so we each had one third of the cake.*
thirst *n.* an unpleasant feeling caused by the lack of anything to drink. **thirsty** *adj.*
this *pron. & adj.* (plural **these**) the one here, not a different one.
thistle (**this**-*sel*) *n.* one of a family of plants with prickly leaves. *The thistle is the national emblem of Scotland.*
thorax *n.* part of an insect that bears the wings and legs; (in humans) the chest.
thorn *n.* a sharp spiky projection on some kinds of plant, such as the rose.
thorough (**thur**-*a*) *adj.* proper and careful. *Fred gave his room a thorough clean.*
thoroughbred *n.* a pure breed of horse.
thoroughfare *n.* a public main road or street.
thou *pron.* an old form of the word you.
though (*tho*) *conj.* even so; even if; although.
thought *vb.* past and past part. of **think**.
thought (*thawt*) *n.* an idea or an opinion; meditation. **thoughtless** *adj.* unthinking, inconsiderate. **thoughtful** *adj.* being careful, considering other people.

Creeping thistle.

thousand *n.* the figure 1000; 10 hundreds.
thrash *vb.* beat; defeat.
thread (rhymes with *bed*) *n.* a length of spun fibre. *vb.* put a thread through a hole, such as the eye of a needle.
threadbare *adj.* with the threads showing, shabby.
threaten *vb.* warn that you will do something bad. *Michael tried to threaten his sister with a punch.* **threat** *n.*
thresh *vb.* beat the seeds from stalks of grain.
threw *vb.* past of **throw**.
thrift *n.* looking after one's money carefully; not being extravagant. **thrifty** *adj.* economical.
thrill *vb.* make someone excited.
thriller *n.* a novel or play with a lot of suspense and usually about crime.
throat *n.* the front of your neck, and the tubes inside that take food and air into your body.
throb *vb.* beat strongly and rhythmically like the heart.
thrombosis *n.* a blood clot in the heart or a blood vessel.
throne *n.* a special chair for a king or queen, or some other important person.
throttle 1. *vb.* choke, strangle. 2. *n.* a device for controlling the flow of fuel in a motor car etc.
through (*thru*) *prep.* from one side to another. *The stone went right through the glass.*
throw *vb.* (past **threw**. past part. **thrown**) fling or hurl an object, such as a ball.
throw up *vb.* be sick, vomit.
thrush *n.* 1. member of a family of small songbirds. 2. a disease affecting horses' feet. 3. a disease of the mouth and throat caused by infection by a fungus.
thrust *vb.* push, force, shove; pierce. *They thrust their way through the crowd.* *n.* a stab. *A sword thrust.*
thug *n.* a gangster, cut-throat or ruffian.
thumb (*thum*) 1. *n.* the short, thick finger on each hand. 2. *vb.* flick through the pages of a book or magazine. *That dictionary looks well-thumbed.*
thunder *n.* the noise that follows lightning in a storm.
thunderstorm *n.* a rainstorm with thunder and lightning.
Thursday *n.* the fifth day of the week, between Wednesday and Friday, named after Thor, Norse god of thunder.
thus *conj.* and so, as a result, therefore. *Monica did not study hard enough and thus failed her exam.*
thy *adj.* an old form of the word 'you' used when addressing one person. *Thy Kingdom come.*
thyme (*time*) *n.* a herb used in cooking.
thyroid *n.* an important gland in the neck near the larynx.

tiara *n.* a jewelled head ornament worn by women.

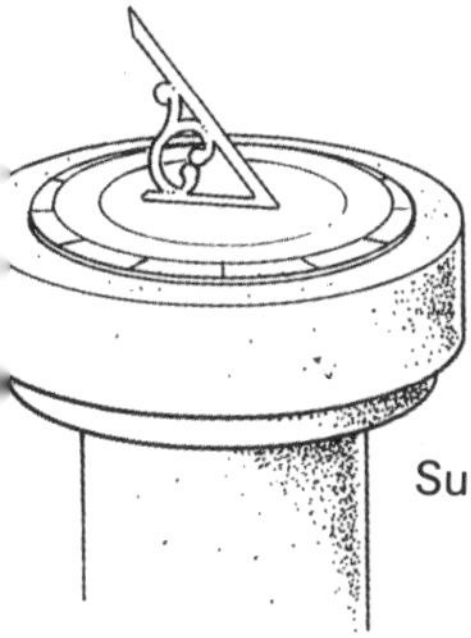

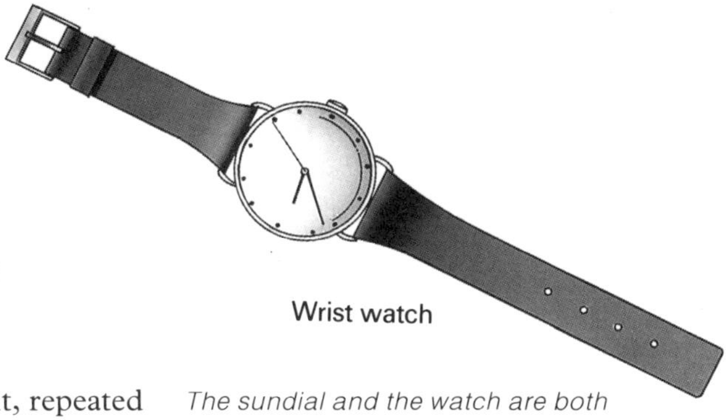

The sundial and the watch are both ways of telling the time.

tick 1. *vb.* make a light, repeated sound like a clock. 2. *n.* a small animal that burrows into the skin of animals and sucks their blood. 3. *n.* (*casual*) credit. 4. *n.* a small mark, like this one ✓.

ticket *n.* a piece of printed card or paper that allows you to go in to somewhere, such as a cinema, or travel on public transport. *Tom had to pay his bus fare again as he'd lost his ticket.*

tickle *vb.* touch someone lightly. *I tickled the baby's feet and made her laugh. n.* sensation of tickling.

tiddler *n.* a small fish or anything very small.

tide *n.* the regular rise and fall of the sea. **tidal** *adj.*

tidy *adj.* neat, in order. *vb.* make tidy.

tie 1. *vb.* fasten something with string or rope. 2. *n.* a thin piece of cloth worn knotted around the neck of a shirt.

tier (rhymes with *ear*) *n.* two or more ranks or layers placed above one another. *The wedding cake had four tiers.*

tiff *n.* a small quarrel.

tiger *n.* a large, striped animal belonging to the cat family.

tight *adj.* 1. close-fitting; difficult to remove. 2. (*slang*) drunk.

tights *n.* a close-fitting piece of clothing that covers your feet, legs and body up to your waist.

tigress *n.* a female tiger.

tile *n.* a flat piece of hard material used to cover floors, walls or roofs.

till 1. *n.* a machine used for adding and storing money in a shop. 2. *vb.* dig the land. 3. *prep.* up to, as late as.

tiller *n.* the handle or lever for turning a boat's rudder from side to side.

tilt *vb.* make something slope or slant. *n.* a slope.

timber *n.* the sawn and prepared wood from trees, ready to be used for building.

time *n. seconds, minutes, hours, days, months and years are all ways of measuring time. vb.* record time of; choose the right time; an exact point in time; portion of time.

timetable *n.* a list of times at which certain things will happen. *The timetable showed us when the music lesson would begin.*

timid *adj*. shy, not brave.
tin 1. *n*. a soft, pale metal (symbol Sn) which is mixed with other metals, or sometimes used to coat metal objects. 2. *n*. a container for food, a can. 3. *adj*. made of tin. 4. *vb*. put fruit etc. in a can.
tinge *vb*. give a slight colour to; tint.
tingle *vb*. a sensation like 'pins and needles'.
tinker *n*. a person who goes from place to place mending things, such as pots and pans.
tinkle *n*. a short ringing sound like a bell.
tinsel *n*. glittering and sparkling material used for decorations.
tint *n*. a slight or pale colour. *vb*.
tiny *adj*. very small.
tip 1. *n*. the point of something. *You can only see the tip of an iceberg above the sea*. 2. *vb*. knock over or spill something. 3. *n*. a rubbish dump. 4. *vb*. give someone, such as a waiter or taxi driver, a small present of money. *n*.
tipsy *adj*. slightly drunk.

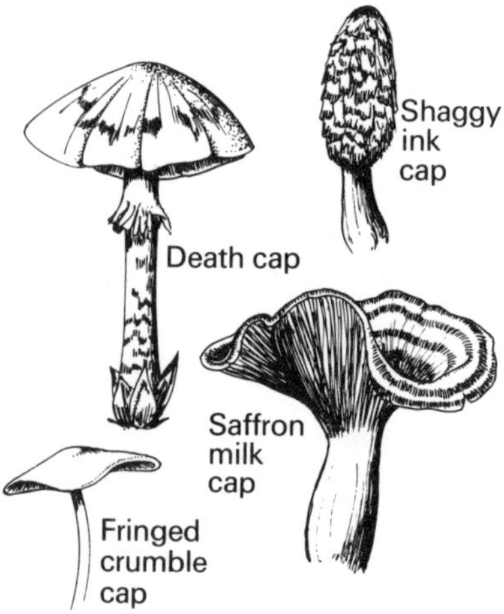

tiptoe *n*. the end of your toes. *vb*. walk on tiptoe. *She tiptoed out of the room*.
tire *vb*. become weary. **tireless** *adj*. seemingly incapable of becoming tired.
tissue *n*. any kind of very fine fabric or material. 2. a paper handkerchief. 3. the mass of cells that make up the body of an animal or plant.
tit or **titmouse** *n*. any of a variety of small, active birds, e.g. blue tit, etc.
titanium *n*. a silvery metallic element found in various ores and used mainly as an alloy (symbol Ti).
title *n*. 1. the name of a book, play, film and so on. 2. the words used to show a person's rank, such as 'lord'.
titter *vb*. & *n*. giggle.
toad *n*. a frog-like amphibian that has a rough warty skin. It lives mainly on land.
toadstool *n*. a kind of fungus like a mushroom, many of which are poisonous.
toast 1. *n*. a slice of bread browned on both sides by grilling. *vb*. 2. *vb*. & *n*. drink someone's health, success or happiness. *We drank a toast to Rob on his birthday*.
tobacco *n*. a plant; the leaves of the plant *nicotiana* which are dried and used in cigarettes, pipes and cigars.
toboggan *n*. a long flat sledge for sliding down snowy hills. *vb*. travel by toboggan.
today *n*. & *adv*. this day.
to-do *n*. unnecessary fuss.
toe *n*. one of the five finger-like digits on the foot.

toffee *n.* a sticky kind of sweet made from sugar and butter.
toga *n.* a flowing garment worn by men in ancient Rome. Made of a large circular piece of woollen cloth.
together *adv.* in company with someone or something.
toil *vb.* & *n.* work very hard. *She toiled all day for little pay.*
toilet *n.* a lavatory, or the room in which the lavatory is.
token *n.* a symbol; a coin or something used to represent something else.
told *vb.* past of **tell**.
tolerate *vb.* allow to happen; endure or put up with. *I will not tolerate bad manners.*
toll (rhymes with *coal*) 1. *n.* money paid in some places for crossing a bridge or for using a road. 2. *vb.* sound of a large heavy bell especially one used for funerals.
tomahawk *n.* a Red Indian war hatchet.
tomato *n.* (plural **tomatoes**) a round, red, juicy fruit eaten as a vegetable.
tomb n. place usually underground for burial of a corpse. **tombstone**.

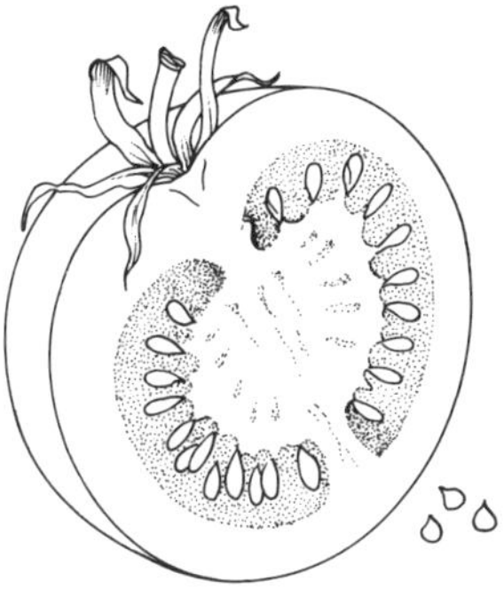

The tomato is eaten as a vegetable, but it is really a fruit.

tom-cat *n.* a male cat.
tomorrow *n.* & *adv.* the day after today.
ton *n.* 1. measure of weight, in Britain 2240 lb (1016 kg); in USA 2000 lb (907 kg); metric ton = tonne = 1000 kg. 2. (slang) speed of 100 mph on roads.
tone 1. *n.* the musical quality of a sound. 2. *vb.* match (of colours etc.).
tongs *pl. n.* (a pair of) an implement similar to pincers for grasping and holding objects, especially when hot. e.g. *coal tongs.*
tongue *n.* the flap of muscle inside the mouth that we use for tasting, swallowing and speaking.
tonight *n.* & *adv.* the night of this day.
tonne *n.* a metric measure of weight (1000 kilogrammes).
tonsils *pl. n.* a pair of glands at the back of the throat, one on each side.
too *adv.* as well as; also; in addition to something. *Can I come too?*
took *vb.* past of **take**.
tool *n.* a device such as a hammer or screwdriver that helps you to do a job; an implement.
tooth *n.* one of the hard, bony parts in your mouth which are used for chewing food. **toothache** *n.* a pain in one or more teeth.
top *n.* 1. the highest point of something, summit. 2. a spinning toy. *adj.* of or at the top.

topaz *n.* a semi-precious stone of varying colours, yellow, white, blue or pink.
topic *n.* a subject of conversation etc. **topical** *adj.* relating to what is of interest at the moment.
topple *vb.* overbalance, fall headlong.
topsy-turvy *adv.* & *adj.* upside down.
Torah *n.* the scroll of the first five books of the Bible – the Pentateuch – used in a synagogue for religious purposes.
torch *n.* a portable light, often electric.
tore *vb.* past of **tear**.
torment *vb.* tease, annoy, cause distress. *n.*
torn *vb.* past part. of **tear**.
tornado *n.* (plural **tornadoes**) a violent storm with heavy rain.
torpedo *n.* a cigar-shaped explosive weapon used against ships.
torrent *n.* 1. a rushing stream. 2. a heavy flow of something.
torso *n.* the trunk of a body or statue (without head or limbs).
tortoise *n.* a slow-moving land reptile with a hard shell.
torture *n.* & *vb.* treating someone very cruelly on purpose.
toss *vb.* throw into the air.
total 1. *adj.* complete, all of something. 2. *n.* the answer when a series of numbers is added together.
totem *n.* an emblem or symbol of a clan, tribe, family or a person.
totem pole *n.* a large wooden pole carved with totems by Indians of N.W. America.

The toucan is a fruit-eating bird.

toucan *n.* a large bird with an enormous orange beak.
touch 1. *vb.* be close enough to feel something. *I reached out until I could just touch the wall.* 2. *n.* the sense of feeling.
touching *adj.* sad; pathetic. *The film had a very touching ending.*
tough (*tuff*) *adj.* not easily cut, strong and rough.
tour *n.* a journey during which a number of places are visited. *vb.*
tournament *n.* a series of games etc. in which the skills of the competitors are tested.
tow *vb.* pull a vehicle, boat etc. behind another. *Our car's broken down. Can you tow us to a garage?*
towards, toward *prep.* in the direction of something. *The car was coming towards us much too fast.*
towel *n.* absorbent cloth for drying or wiping off wetness.
tower *n.* a kind of tall building, or the tall part of a building such as a church.
town *n.* a large group of houses

and other buildings that is larger than a village.

toy *n.* a child's plaything.

trace 1. *vb.* copy something by covering it with very thin paper and drawing around the outline that shows through. **traceable** *adj.* 2. *n.* a small sign or mark left by something.

trachea (*track*-**e**-*a*) *n.* the windpipe.

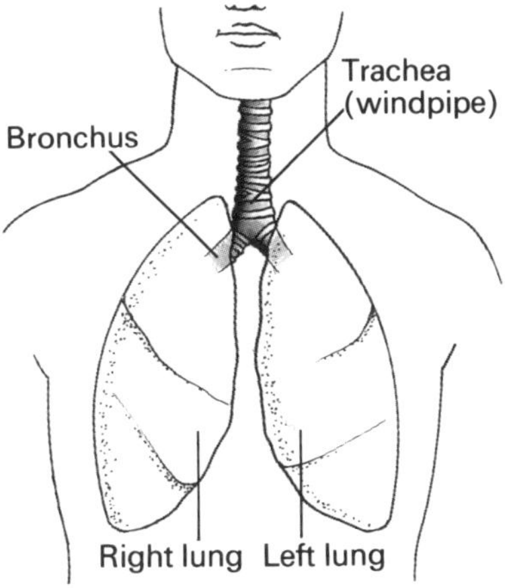

track *n.* 1. a series of marks left by an animal or a vehicle. *vb.* follow something by watching for the signs, or tracks, it has left behind. 2. a railway line. 3. very strong chains of steel which are used instead of wheels on tanks and some kinds of tractor. 4. section of a recording.

tract *n.* 1. a stretch of land. 2. a pamphlet or leaflet.

tractor *n.* a strong motor vehicle used to pull farm machinery.

trade *vb.* buy and sell, or exchange. **tradable** *adj.*

trademark *n.* a special mark or sign used to show who made something and prevent illegal copying.

trade union *n.* an organization of people who work in the same sort of job.

tradition *n.* beliefs, customs etc. which are handed down from one generation to another.

traffic *n.* vehicles such as cars and trucks that can travel along roads. *The traffic is very heavy today, because many people are driving out into the countryside.*

traffic jam *n.* a situation when the traffic has come to a standstill or slowed down to a crawl.

traffic lights *pl. n.* a crossing signal of coloured lights on a pole, which tells drivers when to go on and when to stop.

tragedy *n.* (plural **tragedies**). 1. a kind of play, usually with a sad ending. 2. any very sad event. *His death at such an early age was a terrible tragedy for his parents.* **tragic** *adj.*

trail 1. *n.* a series of marks left to show the way to somewhere. 2. *vb.* pull something along behind you. 3. *vb.* (of plant) grow along the ground.

trailer *n.* 1. a vehicle that is towed along behind another one. 2. extracts from a film etc. shown in advance as an advertisement.

train 1. *n.* a group of carriages or wagons joined together and pulled along the track by an engine. 2. *vb.* practise something. *The team trains three times a week.*

traitor *n.* someone who betrays country or friends.

tram *n.* a streetcar: a kind of bus that runs on rails like a train.

tramp 1. *vb.* walk heavily. 2. *n.* a long walk, a hike. 3. *n.* a homeless person who wanders, or tramps, from place to place.

trample *vb.* tread heavily on something, *thus* crush or destroy.

tranquil (**tran**-*kwill*) *adj.* calm, peaceful. **tranquillizer** *n.* a calming drug.

trans- *prefix* meaning across or beyond, e.g. *Trans-Siberian Railway*.

transaction *n.* business that is carried out.

transfer *vb.* move from one job or place to another.

transistor *n.* 1. a very small electronic device that is used in radios and other electrical equipment. 2. a radio that uses transistors.

translate *vb.* change from one language into another. *Pam had to translate a poem from Italian into English.* **translator** *n.*

transmission *n.* the passage of radio waves from the transmitting to the receiving station.

transmit *vb.* pass on, send out; broadcast.

transparent *adj.* something that is clear enough to see through.

transplant *vb.* move a plant from one bit of soil to another; move an organ, such as a heart or kidney, from one person's body to another.

transport (*trans*-**port**) 1. *vb.* carry people or goods from one place to another. 2. (**trans**-*port*) the vehicles in which people are carried.

transpose *vb.* change the order of.

trap 1. *n.* & *vb.* a device for catching animals. 2. *n.* light two-wheeled horse-drawn vehicle.

trapdoor *n.* a kind of door covering an opening in the floor.

trapeze *n.* a bar hung on ropes far above the ground, and from which acrobats can swing.

Trapeziums are always irregular in shape.

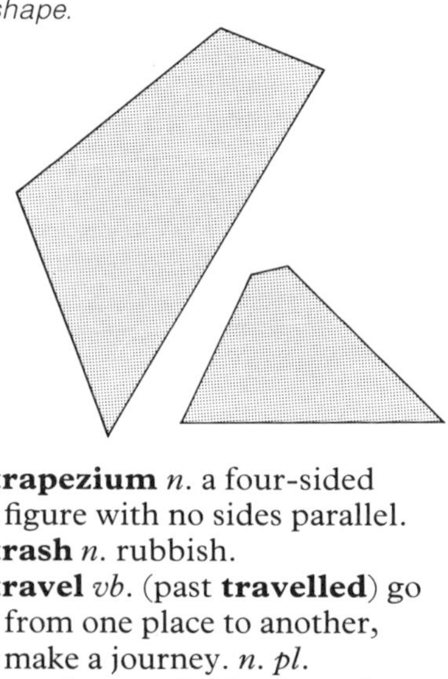

trapezium *n.* a four-sided figure with no sides parallel.

trash *n.* rubbish.

travel *vb.* (past **travelled**) go from one place to another, make a journey. *n. pl.*

trawler *n.* a fishing boat that drags (or trawls) nets along the bottom of the sea to catch fish. **trawl** *n.* a large net. *vb.* to fish with a trawl.

tray *n.* a flat object for carrying crockery etc.

treachery *n.* betraying the trust a person has in one.

treacle *n.* a dark kind of syrup, produced as a by-product of

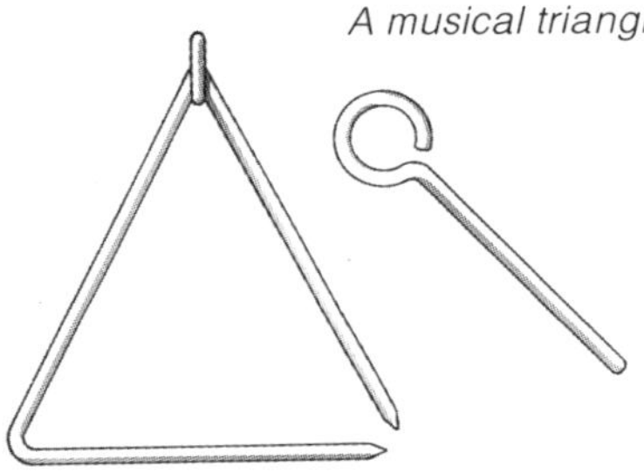

A musical triangle.

sugar refining.

tread 1. *vb*. (past tense **trod**; past part. **trodden**) put your feet down on the ground. 2. *n*. the rubber and its raised pattern on the outside of a tyre. 3. *n*. top surface of a step.

treason *n*. giving away important information to an enemy, especially in wartime.

treasure 1. *n*. a store of valuable things, such as gold and jewels. 2. *vb*. value something very highly. *Alan treasures signed photos of several pop stars*. **treasury** *n*. a place where valuable things are kept; the funds of a state.

treat 1. *vb*. behave towards someone in a certain way. *Caroline treats her baby brother very kindly*. 2. *vb*. put something right. *You can treat this stain with salt*. **treatment** *n*. 3. *n*. something that gives you special pleasure. *My aunt took us to the play for a treat*. *vb*.

treaty *n*. a written and signed agreement between countries relating to alliance, commerce etc.

tree *n*. the tallest kind of plant with a thick central stem or trunk.

tremble *vb*. shake gently all over.

tremendous *adj*. of great size or power; excellent.

trench *n*. a ditch, often used in warfare to protect troops.

trend *n*. the general direction or course.

trendy *adj*. following the latest fashions.

trespass *vb*. go on somebody else's land or property unlawfully. **trespasser** *n*. person who trespasses.

tri- *prefix* meaning three or threefold, e.g. **tricolour** meaning having three colours.

trial *n*. 1. an examination in a court of law. 2. a test of something to see how good it is. *We watched the trial of the new helicopter*. 3. a hardship, affliction.

triangle *n*. 1. a flat shape with three sides. **triangular** *adj*. 2. a musical instrument, like a triangle of metal, that is hit with a stick.

tribe *n*. a group of people who have the same customs and language. **tribal** *adj*.

tributary *n*. a small stream or river that flows into a larger one.

trick *n*. 1. a joke or prank; a deceitful act or scheme. 2. a piece of 'magic' done by a conjuror. 3. a round played in some card games, such as bridge and whist. *vb*. deceive, cheat.

trickle *vb*. flow in a thin stream.

tricolour *n*. a three-coloured flag, especially the blue, white and red flag of France.

tricycle *n*. a three-wheeled cycle.

tried *vb*. past of **try**.

trifle *n.* 1. an unimportant thing. 2. a sweet pudding made from cake, custard, fruit and cream. **trifling** *adj.* of small importance.

trigger *n.* the lever on a gun that is used to fire it.

trigonometry *n.* a branch of mathematics concerned with the properties of triangles.

trim *adj.* neat and tidy. *vb.* cut something so as to make it neat and tidy. *The barber was asked to trim my hair.*

trinity *n.* a group of three.

trinket *n.* a small ornament or jewellery of little value.

trio *n.* three people working together, especially musicians.

trip 1. *vb.* catch your foot on something and fall over. *n.* 2. *n.* a journey. *Have a good trip.*

tripe *n.* 1. the stomach of a cow eaten as food. 2. rubbish, worthless stuff.

triple *adj.* made of three parts. *vb.* become three times as great or many.

triplet *n.* one of three babies born to the same mother at the same time.

triumph *n.* great victory or achievement. *vb.* rejoice in victory. **triumphant**, **triumphal** *adjs.*

troika *n.* Russian vehicle drawn by three horses abreast.

troll *n.* a goblin or dwarf, usually evil, in Scandinavian legends.

trolley *n.* (plural **trolleys**) a small hand cart.

trombone *n.* a musical wind instrument made of brass.

troops *pl. n.* a body of soldiers; armed forces in general.

trophy *n.* something taken in victory especially when kept as a memorial; a prize; a memento.

tropical fish *pl. n.* fish that live in the warm seas of tropical regions, often along the edges of coral reefs.

Tropics *pl. n.* the area of land and sea around the equator in between the Tropics of Cancer and Capricorn. **tropical** *adj.*

trot *vb.* & *n.* run with short steps like the slow run of a horse.

trouble *n.* problem; difficulty; disgrace or punishment. *Jerry got into trouble for breaking a window.* *vb.* disturb; put to inconvenience.

trough (*troff*) *n.* a long shallow container for the drinking water or feed of animals.

trousers *pl. n.* an article of clothing for the lower half of the body, divided into two sections, one for each leg.

trout *n.* (plural **trout**) a silvery-brown speckled freshwater fish belonging to the salmon family.

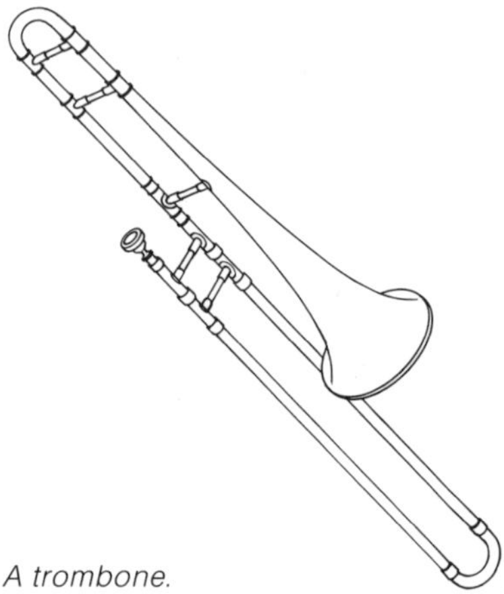

A trombone.

trowel *n.* 1. a garden tool like a small spade. 2. flat bladed tool for spreading mortar.
truant *n.* a child who stays away from school when he or she is supposed to be there. *vb.* **truancy**. *n.*
truce *n.* a period when two sides in a war or quarrel etc. agree to be at peace.
truck *n.* an open railway wagon or a lorry.

The tuatara is a rare reptile from New Zealand.

trudge *vb.* plod; walk with great effort.
true *adj.* correct; accurate; not false; genuine. *I hope what you say is true.*
truffle *n.* 1. edible fungus that grows underground. 2. soft sweet made of chocolate mixture.
trumpet *n.* a brass wind musical instrument, played by pressing valves. *vb.* proclaim.
trump up *vb.* invent, fabricate.
truncheon *n.* a short thick stick carried by policemen.
trunk *n.* 1. the main stem of a tree. 2. the body of an animal apart from the head or limbs. 3. a large box. 4. the long nose of an elephant. 5. the boot of a car (in the USA).
truss 1. *n.* a bundle of hay or straw. 2. *vb.* tie up by binding fast.
trust *vb.* & *n.* believe that something or somebody is good, or will tell the truth; confidence in a person.
truth *n.* correctness, accuracy; something that is true. *I'm telling you the truth.*
try 1. *vb.* attempt to do something. 2. *n.* scoring touch-down in rugby football. **trying** *adj.* exhausting, difficult to bear. *He is a trying person.*
tsar (*zar*) *n.* (also **tzar** and **czar**) the emperor of Russia.
tsetse (**tet**-*si*) *n.* brownish fly found in tropical Africa.
tuatara *n.* lizard-like reptile found only on certain islands off the New Zealand coast.
tub *n.* 1. a small barrel. 2. a bath (bathtub). 3. a slow and clumsy ship or boat.
tuba *n.* a large musical wind instrument that gives a low note.
tubby *adj.* short and fat.
tube *n.* a long, hollow cylinder, especially for transporting liquids. **tubular** *adj.*
tuber *n.* the large part of an underground stem, from which new plants grow. *A potato is a tuber.*
tuberculosis *n.* a disease caused by bacterial infection.
tuck *vb.* fold under. *Sheets are tucked under the mattress. n.*
Tuesday *n.* the third day of the week, between Monday and Wednesday, named after Tiu, Norse god of war.

tuft *n.* a bunch, cluster or clump. *A tuft or lock of hair.*

tug 1. *vb.* pull hard. 2. *n.* a small boat that tows larger ships in and out of port.

tulip *n.* a brightly coloured, spring flowering garden flower which grows from a bulb.

tumble *vb.* fall down suddenly in a helpless or clumsy way.

tumble dryer *n.* a machine for drying wet clothing.

tumbler *n.* 1. a large drinking-glass without a stem. 2. an old-fashioned word for an acrobat.

tummy *n.* (*casual*) stomach.

tumour *n.* a lump or swelling in the body made up of abnormal cells.

tuna *n.* a large fish, also called a tunny, of the mackerel family.

A tuna.

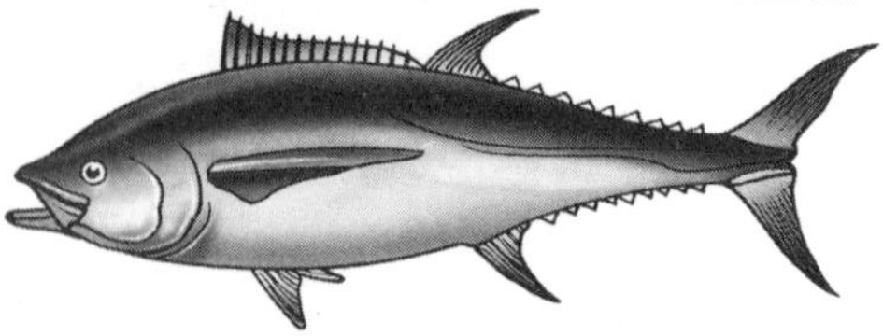

tundra *n.* the cold, treeless plains in the arctic and subarctic regions.

tune *n.* a musical melody, especially the music that goes with a song. *He hummed a cheerful tune.*

tungsten *n.* also called wolfram, a hard white metallic element (symbol W).

tunic *n.* a close-fitting jacket, often part of a uniform.

tunnel *n.* an underground passage. *vb.* dig under the ground.

turban *n.* a head-covering, consisting of a long strip of cloth wound round and round the head. Turbans are worn in some Eastern countries, often for religious reasons.

turbine *n.* an engine with a driving wheel (or screw) which is turned by water, steam or air.

turbo-jet *adj.* & *n.* a type of gas turbine in which hot gases produced by the burning of fuel turn the blades of a fan whose shaft works the blades of a compressor which sucks in air and forces it into the combustion chamber.

turbot *n.* a large flat fish.

tureen *n.* a large deep bowl for serving soup etc.

turf *n.* 1. grass-covered ground. *'The turf' is an expression sometimes used to mean 'horse-racing'.* 2. a piece of earth with grass attached to it, cut from the ground.

turkey *n.* a large bird of the pheasant family, bred in many parts of the world for its meat.

turn 1. *vb.* revolve; go round. 2. *vb.* change direction; change into something. 3. *n.* a go in a game. *It's my turn next.*

turn down *vb.* refuse an offer or ideas. *I wanted to turn down the job, but I needed the money so I agreed to do it.*

turnip *n.* a plant grown for its roundish, white, edible root, which is cooked and eaten as a vegetable.

turn-out *n.* 1. the number of people attending a function. *There was a big turn-out for the president's visit.* 2. outfit, dress.

turn up *vb.* 1. arrive, usually unexpectedly. *Emma turned up just before dinner.* 2. increase something by using a control. *That knob on the radio turns up the sound.*

turquoise *n.* a blue or green semi-precious stone.

turret *n.* 1. a small tower, usually in a larger building. 2. a revolving part of a warship, tank etc. that holds a gun.

turtle *n.* a sea reptile with a hard shell.

tusk *n.* a long pointed tooth.

tutor *n.* a private teacher; a person in a British university who gives individual instruction to the students.

tutu *n.* the short frilly skirt worn by a ballerina.

twice *adv.* two times.

twig *n.* a small branch on a tree or bush.

twilight *n.* the dim light between sunset and night time.

twin *n.* one of two children born to the same mother at the same time.

Turnips are a popular ingredient in stews and vegetable dishes.

Turtles are related to tortoises.

twinge *n.* a sharp, shooting pain.

twinkle *vb.* send out little flashes of light. *n.*

twirl *vb.* spin, turn round and round.

twist *vb.* wind around; turn and curve. *n.*

tycoon *n.* a very rich businessperson.

type 1. *n.* a kind, a sort. *Tulips are a type of flower*. 2. *vb.* use a typewriter. 3. *n.* the letters used to print words.

typewriter *n.* a machine that prints letters.

typhoid *n.* an infectious disease in which the intestines become inflamed.

typhoon *n.* a tropical *cyclone* (storm) or hurricane.

typhus *n.* a severe feverish disease marked by eruptions on the skin.

typical *adj.* a good example of its kind.

typist *n.* a person who uses a typewriter.

tyrannosaurus *n.* a huge, flesh-eating dinosaur that lived more than 70 million years ago.

tyrant *n.* a cruel, unfair ruler.

tyre *n.* a rim of metal or rubber around the edge of a wheel. (US spelling **tire**.)

U

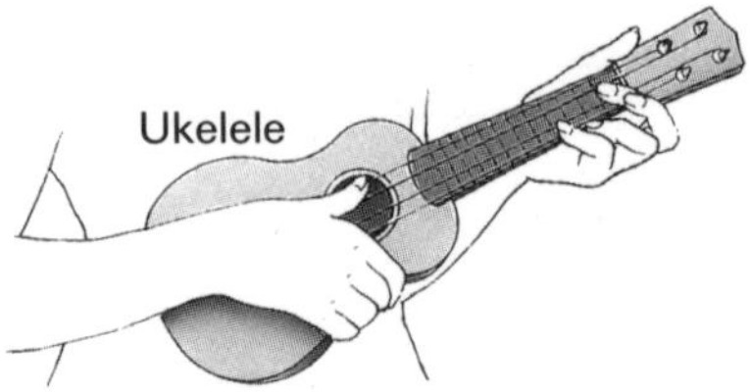

U-boat *n.* German submarine in both World Wars.
udder *n.* the bag-like part of a female mammal, such as a cow, from which milk comes.
ugly *adj.* unpleasant to look at; not beautiful or handsome. **ugliness** *n.*
ukulele *n.* a small guitar with four strings.
ulcer *n.* an open sore, usually with a flow of pus (infected fluid).
ulna *n.* the inner of the two bones of the forearm.
ultimate *adj.* last, final, eventual. *Our ultimate aim is to be successful.*
ultra-violet *adj.* (of light) beyond the visible spectrum at its violet end.
umbilical *adj.* of the navel. The umbilical cord connects the developing foetus with the mother's placenta and the foetus feeds through it. When the child is born the cord is cut leaving the 'belly button'.
umbrella *n.* a fabric shade, supported by a handle and wire frame, which people carry to keep the rain off. *You can fold up an umbrella when you're not using it.*
umpire *n.* the person who sees that the rules are obeyed in certain games. *Important tennis matches have an umpire to watch them. vb.* act as umpire.
un- *prefix* expressing negation, lack of etc., used before adjectives, adverbs and verbs. If the meaning of the main word is known then the sense of the word with the added prefix should usually be clear, e.g. **unaccompanied** not escorted or accompanied; **unbalanced** not balanced; **unchristian** not in accordance with Christian beliefs or practices etc.
unadulterated *adj.* pure; unmixed with any other material.
unanimous (*you*-**nan**-*imus*) *adj.* when everyone agrees.
uncanny *adj.* strange, mysterious.
uncivil *adj.* rude, impolite.
uncle *n.* the brother of your

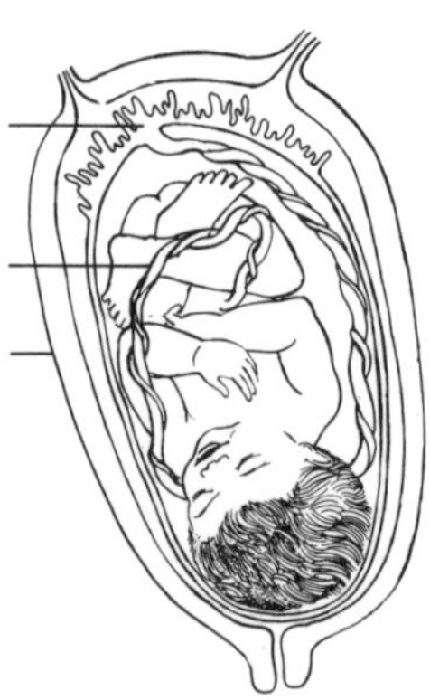

The umbilical cord supplies blood and nutrients to the unborn child.

mother or father.
uncompromising *adj.* unyielding; stubborn.
unconscious *adj.* not conscious, not knowing what is happening around you, unaware of.
uncouth *adj.* clumsy and awkward in manners and language.
uncover *vb.* take the cover off something, or show it.
undemonstrative *adj.* a person who does not show feelings openly is undemonstrative.
under *adj., adv.* & *prep.* beneath.
under- *prefix* meaning below, beneath, less than, lacking in. When the meaning of the main word is known the sense of the prefixed word should in many cases be clear, e.g. **underweight, understate** etc.
undercarriage *n.* the landing gear of an aircraft, including its wheels.
undercover *adj.* not in the open, secret.
underdog *n.* a loser or someone who will almost certainly lose in any fight or contest.
undergraduate *n.* a student at a university who has not yet taken a degree.
undergo *vb.* suffer, experience.
underground railway *n.* a railway which runs mainly underground.
underline *vb.* draw a line under words on a page to make them stand out, like this: Danger; emphasize, stress.
underneath *adv.* & *prep.* beneath. *The mechanic was lying underneath the car he was repairing.*
underpass *n.* a place where one road passes under another one.
understand *vb.* (past **understood**) grasp the meaning of something with your mind, know. *Did you understand what the teacher was saying?* **understanding** *n.* the ability to know; an agreement.
understanding *adj.* gentle, kind.
understudy *n.* an actor who takes over from the usual performer of a part in an emergency.
undertake *vb.* agree to do; be responsible for. *John undertook to look after the herb garden.*
undertaker *n.* a person who arranges funerals.
underwrite *vb.* (in insurance) accepting the risk or liability for what is insured.
undo *vb.* 1. untie (a knot); unbutton; remove. 2. reverse; bring to nothing. *This government says it is going to undo the damage caused by the last government.*
undress *vb.* take clothes off.
undue *adj.* too much, excessive. *They gave him undue praise.*
undulate *vb.* rise and fall like waves.
unearth *vb.* dig up or discover something. *Granny managed to unearth some old family photos from her desk.*
unemployed *adj.* without a paid job: out of work; not being used. **unemployment** *n.* the state of being unemployed.
unequal *adj.* not the same; not equal.
unfair *adj.* not just or according to the rules.

unfortunate *adj*. unlucky.
unfounded *adj*. not based on fact. *Your doubts about my honesty are unfounded.*
unfrock *vb*. remove a person from being a priest.
unfurl *vb*. unfold and display. *The flag was unfurled.*
ungainly *adj*. awkward, clumsy.
ungulate *n*. a hoofed animal. (Cows and sheep are ungulates.)
unhappy *adj*. miserable; not happy; unfortunate.
unhealthy *adj*. in poor health, bad for the health.
uni- *prefix* meaning one, e.g. **unicellular** having only one cell.
unicorn *n*. an animal in stories and legends with a body like a horse and a single horn in the middle of its forehead.

uniform 1. *n*. matching clothes worn by all the members of a group of people, such as a school or an army. 2. *adj*. unvarying, plain; to one standard. *The books are of uniform size.*
unify *vb*. make one; bring together; unite.
union *n*. joining together of a number of things or people. *The union of England and Scotland began in 1707.*
unique (*yoo*-**neek**) *adj*. the only one of its kind; having no equal.
unison *n*. 1. two notes of the same pitch 2. complete agreement.
unit *n*. a single thing, or a group of things that are thought of as being one thing. *A metre is a unit of length, made up of 100 centimetres.*
unite *vb*. join together, combine. **unity** *n*.
universal *adj*. general, common, done by most people. *Listening to the radio is a universal habit.*
universe *n*. everything in existence; all space.
university *n*. a place where people go on studying after they have left school; an *institute* (college) of higher education with the power to award degrees.
unkempt *adj*. untidy in appearance.
unkind *adj*. not kind; treating other people badly. **unkindness** *n*.
unknown *adj*. not known; unexplored. *n*.
unless *conj*. if not. *I'm not coming unless you come too.* except when.
unload *vb*. empty a load from something, such as a ship or lorry; remove charge from gun.
unlucky *adj*. not lucky; unfortunate. *Anne played so well that her team was unlucky not to win.*
unnecessary *adj*. not necessary; something that can be prevented.
unpack *vb*. remove things from a container, particularly a suitcase.

unpleasant *adj*. not pleasant; nasty or disagreeable.
unsavoury *adj*. unpleasant.
unscathed *adj*. unharmed.
unseemly *adj*. not suitable for the time and place; improper.
unsightly *adj*. ugly.
untidy *adj*. not tidy, not orderly; leaving things in a mess. *Adrian's bedroom was incredibly untidy*.
until *prep*. & *conj*. till; as far as; till such time as. *The dentist cannot give you an appointment until next week*.
untold *adj*. too many to be counted.
unusual *adj*. not usual; strange or peculiar, remarkable. *Caroline was wearing a most unusual dress*.
unwell *adj*. ill; sick; not well.
unwieldy *adj*. awkward to handle.
unwitting *adj*. unaware of; not knowing.
unwrap *vb*. take the wrapping off something, such as a parcel or present.
up *adv*. & *pref*. to, in a high place, mount etc.
upheaval *n*. great disorder, change.
uphill 1. *adv*. going up a hill or slope. *Riding a bicycle uphill can get very tiring*. 2. *adj*. difficult. *Life can sometimes be an uphill struggle*.
upholstery *n*. the padding and covering of chairs and sofas. **upholsterer** *n*.
upkeep *n*. cost of keeping in good repair.
upon *prep*. on; on top of.
upper *adj*. above, in a higher place.
upright *adj*. vertical, standing straight. *We put the pole upright in the sand*. honest. *She is an upright woman*.
uproar *n*. a violent noise or disturbance.
upset *vb*. (past **upset**) 1. knock something over. *Mark upset the milk*. 2. make someone unhappy. *The bad news upset Jan*.
upshot *n*. the outcome, final result. *The upshot of the argument was that we agreed to do nothing*.
upside down *adv*. the 'wrong' way up. *Sloths spend most of their time hanging upside down from branches of trees*. in total disorder.
upstage *adv*. back of the stage away from the footlights.
upstairs *adv*., *adj*. & *n*. above the round floor of a building. *Go upstairs to your bedroom*.
upstart *n*. a person who has risen suddenly to a position of power or wealth.

An example of traditional upholstery.

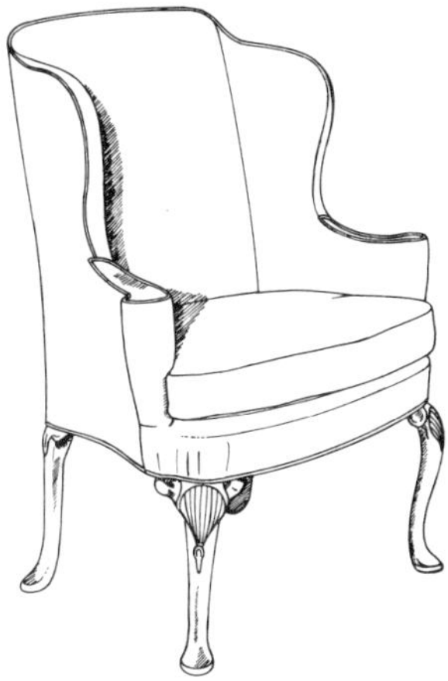

upstream *adv.* & *adj.* in the direction opposite to the flow of the stream or river, higher up the river.
uptight *adj.* nervous, annoyed.
uranium *n.* a hard, silvery, metallic element that is radioactive.
urban *adj.* to do with towns or cities. *A city is an urban area.*
urchin *n.* a mischievous, shabbily dressed child.
urge *vb.* encourage, drive on. *n.* strong force or desire.
urgent *adj.* so important that it needs to be attended to at once. **urgency** *n.*
urine *n.* an amber-coloured liquid waste that is excreted by mammals from the bladder.
urn *n.* a vase or container for storing the ashes of the dead; large vessel with a tap for holding hot drinks.

usage *n.* customary practice or manner of doing things.
use (rhymes with *views*) 1. *vb.* employ something for a particular purpose. *You use a saw for cutting wood.* 2. *n.* (rhymes with *juice*) the way in which something is used. *Plastics have many uses.*
used *adj.* not new; second-hand.
used to *vb.* 1. know some experience well because it has often happened. *We are used to waiting a long time for the bus.* 2. referring to the past. *Her parents used to live in Australia but then they moved to New York.*
useful *adj.* helpful, valuable.
useless *adj.* not useful; no good to anyone. *A broken watch is useless.*
usual *adj.* the way in which something happens, or is done, most of the time. *Dan wore his usual clothes to the party.*
usually *adv.* in an ordinary or a normal way. *We usually go to school together.*
usurp *vb.* seize or take possession of by force or illegally (especially the throne or power).
usury *n.* money-lending at an enormous rate of interest. **usurer** *n.* a person who practises usury.
utensil *n.* a tool or instrument, especially one that is used in cooking. *An egg whisk is a very handy utensil.*
uterus (**yoo**-*ter-us*) *n.* the womb, the organ in which a developing mammal is carried.
utilize *vb.* make use of.
Utopia *n.* an imaginary and perfect place. **Utopian** *adj.*
utter 1. *adj.* complete or total, especially something bad. *The room was an utter mess.* 2. *vb.* say something, make a sound. *The kitten tried to utter a faint mew.*

U-turn *n.* when a vehicle changes direction through 180° by turning on a U-shaped course; a complete change of policy.

V

vacant *adj.* empty; not filled. **vacancy** being vacant; unoccupied job. *There is a vacancy in the Post Office.*

vacate *vb.* give up, leave. *Customers are asked to vacate the premises as soon as they have finished their business.*

vacation *n.* holiday period (especially USA); time when universities and lawcourts are closed.

vaccinate (**vak**-*sin-ate*) *vb.* inoculate against a disease, notably smallpox. **vaccination** *n.* **vaccine** *n.*

vacuum 1. *n.* an absolutely empty space. 2. *n.* & *vb.* apparatus for cleaning by suction.

vagabond *n.* a person without a fixed house; also a **vagrant**.

vague *adj.* not clear, indefinite, indistinct. **vagueness** *n.*

vain *adj.* 1. showing too much pride. 2. unsuccessful. *They searched for the dog in vain.* **vanity** *n.*

vale *n.* a valley.

valence (**vay**-*lence*) *n.* also called **valency**, the number of chemical bonds with which an atom or a radical (group containing different atoms) can link with other atoms.

valet *n.* a manservant, especially one who looks after the clothes and personal needs of his employer.

valiant *adj.* brave.

valid *adj.* legally acceptable. *Is your driving licence valid for all countries?*

valley *n.* a hollow between hills; a U-shaped or V-shaped depression in the Earth's surface.

valuable *adj.* of great value or worth.

value 1. *n.* the amount of money the something is worth. 2. *vb.* estimate value of; think highly of.

valve *n.* 1. a device that controls that flow of liquid etc. allowing it to go in one direction only. 2. one half of a hinged shell.

vampire *n.* 1. a dead person in old stories who is supposed to suck the blood of living people. 2. a small bat found in the forests of Central and South America.

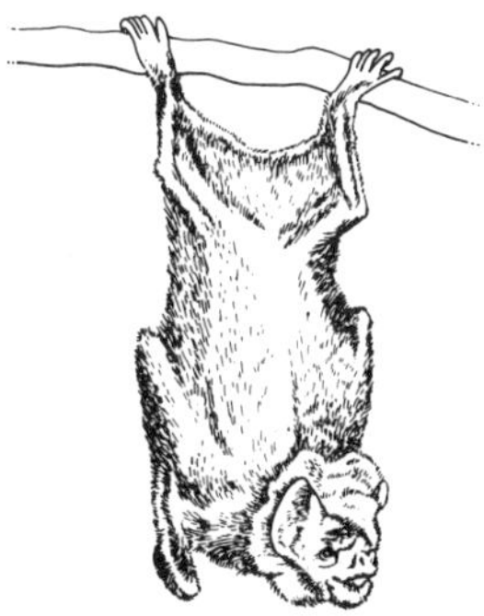

van *n.* a covered vehicle for carrying things.
vandal *n.* a person who stupidly destroys or damages things or buildings for no obvious reason. **vandalism** *n.*
vane *n.* a weathercock that revolves in the wind and indicates wind direction. *Weather-vanes are often put at the top of buildings.*
vanilla *n.* & *adj.* the pod of a tropical climbing plant used to flavour ice-cream and other foods.
vanish *vb.* disappear suddenly.
vanquish (**van**-*kwish*) *vb.* defeat, conquer.
vapour *n.* a substance such as gas, mist or smoke. *Steam is water vapour.*
variety *n.* 1. a number of different things or kinds of. *You can buy this blouse in a variety of colours.* 2. a form of popular entertainment, involving comedians, singers, dancers etc.
various *adj.* having different varieties; several. *Michael has worked in various different jobs since he left school.*
varnish *n.* a kind of shiny, transparent liquid made from chemicals like resins and which is used like paint. *vb.* coat with varnish.
vary *vb.* change, become different.
vase *n.* a glass, china or pottery container, often used to hold flowers.
vast *adj.* very large in size. *The circus tent covered a vast area.*
vat *n.* a large container for holding liquids.

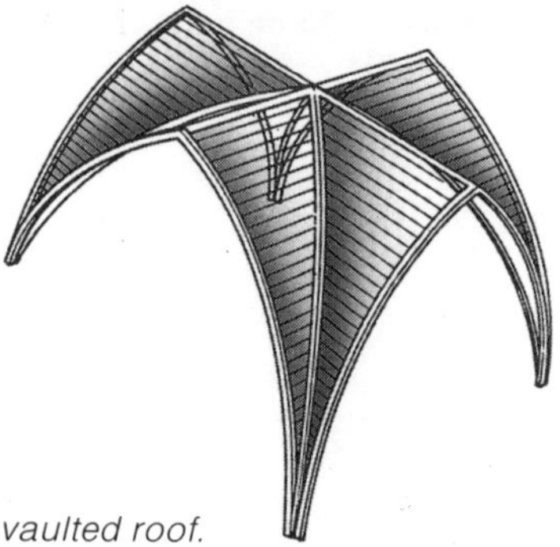
A vaulted roof.

vault 1. *vb.* jump with your hands resting on something for support. *Denise tried to vault over the fence.* 2. *n.* an underground room, often used to store valuable things. 3. *n.* an arched roof.
veal *n.* the meat of a calf.
veer *vb.* change direction, especially of the wind; change one's mind.
vegetable *n.* a plant grown for food. *Vegetables taste less sweet than the plant foods we call fruit.*
vegetarian *n.* a person who does not eat meat or fish. *Some vegetarians do not eat milk or eggs either.*
vegetation *n.* all the plants that grow in a certain place.
vehement (**vee**-*a-ment*) *adj.* violent, energetic.
vehicle *n.* anything that is used to transport people or things from one place to another. *Trains, cars and carts are all vehicles.*
veil *n.* a covering for the face or head. *Women wear veils in some Eastern countries.* a nun's headdress.
vein (rhymes with *lane*) *n.* 1. one of the blood vessels that take

blood back to the heart from various parts of the body. 2. a layer or streak of mineral.

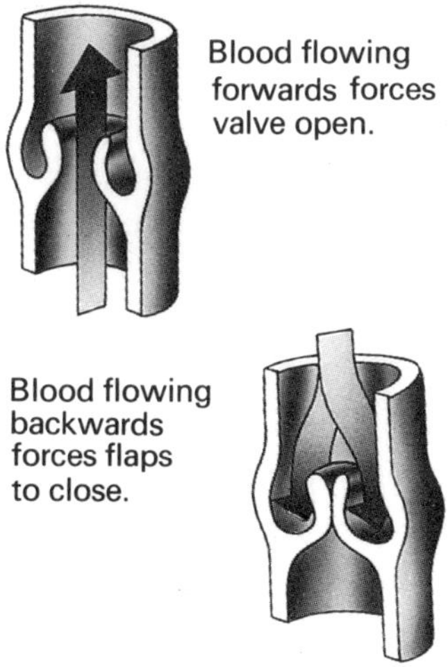

velocity *n.* the speed of a body measured in a given direction.
velvet *n.* a fabric with a thick, soft pile of short, raised threads all over its surface.
vendetta *n.* an Italian word meaning a feud or violent hostilities, especially between families.
veneer *n.* a thin layer of good quality wood covering wood of poorer quality; superficial appearance.
vengeance *n.* punishment inflicted on someone to pay back harm or wrong done; revenge.
venison *n.* the meat of a deer.
venom *n.* the poison of certain snakes and other poisonous animals, injected by biting or stinging. **venomous** *adj.*
vent *n.* an outlet or opening through which gas etc. can escape.
ventilate *vb.* circulate air to freshen a room etc; discuss something openly and freely.
ventriloquist *n.* someone who can make their voice seem to come from somewhere else.
venture *vb.* & *n.* risk, dare to. *'Nothing ventured nothing gained', as the proverb says.*
venue *n.* a meeting place.
veranda, verandah *n.* a covered patio or terrace on the ground floor of a house.
verb *n.* a word for something that is done, or happens. *In 'the cat ate the rat', the verb is 'ate'.*
verdict *n.* the decision of a judge. *The verdict was 'not guilty'.*
vermin *n.* (plural the same) any animals from insects to rats which cause harm to crops etc. or which spread disease.
versatile *adj.* having an ability to carry out different skills.
verse *n.* one section or part of a song or poem.
version *n.* one form or type of an original (book, incident etc.). *That is your version of what happened. My version is totally different.*

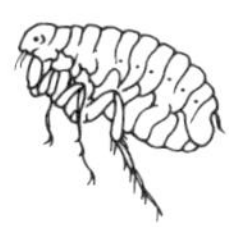

Rats and fleas are both vermin.

A railway viaduct constructed over a river.

versus *prep*. a Latin word that means 'against'. It is shortened to *v*. in the results of football matches, such as England *v*. Spain.

vertebra *n*. (plural **vertebrae**) the small bones in the backbone.

vertebrate *n*. an animal with a backbone, or spinal column.

vertical *adj*. straight up and down, upright, perpendicular.

vespers *n*. an evening church service.

vessel *n*. 1. a container, especially one for liquids. 2. a large ship or boat.

vest *n*. an undershirt like a tee-shirt. (A vest is a waistcoat in the USA.)

vestige *n*. a slight trace or evidence of something that once existed.

vestment *n*. ceremonial robes worn by priests etc.

vestry *n*. a room in a church where vestments are kept.

vet *n*. an abbreviation for veterinary surgeon.

veteran *n*. someone with a lot of experience.

veterinary surgeon *n*. a doctor for animals.

veto *n*. (plural **vetoes**) the power to forbid something. *vb*. refuse to agree to.

vex *vb*. annoy or irritate someone.

via (**vie**-*a*) *prep*. by way of. *Today the train went via Oxford instead of Banbury*.

viable *adj*. workable.

viaduct *n*. a long bridge that is built to carry a railway, road or canal across a valley.

vibrate *vb*. move very quickly back and forth, throb.

vicar *n.* a parish priest in charge of a church and parish.
vice 1. *n.* a very bad habit or immoral conduct. 2. *n.* a tool that holds things steady, and in one place, so they can be worked on. 3. *prefix* (**vice-**) in place of, next in rank to, e.g. Vice-President of the United States.
vicinity *n.* neighbourhood.
vicious (rhymes with **wish** *us*) *adj.* fierce, bad, cruel.
victim *n.* someone who suffers harm or danger.
victor *n.* one who defeats an enemy or opponent; winner.
Victorian *adj.* belonging to the reign of Queen Victoria.
victory *n.* success, winning.
victorious *adj.*
vicuna *n.* a small South American camel without a hump.
videotape *n.* a magnetic tape used for recording the pictures and sounds from films and television programmes.
vie *vb.* compete with someone.
view *n.* 1. what is seen; a landscape. 2. opinion. *Have you any views on this topic? vb.* look at.
viewfinder *n.* device to help photographer aim the camera, indicating the part of the scene that will appear in the final photograph.
Vikings *n. pl.* Scandinavian seafarers who raided and plundered many parts of Europe between the 700s and 1100s.
vile *adj.* horrible, unpleasant.
villa *n.* a country house in Roman times; a small house in a suburban or residential district.
village *n.* a group of houses and other buildings that is smaller that a town and usually has a church.
villain *n.* a wicked or evil person.
vine *n.* a climbing plant, the fuit of which is the grape.
vineyard *n.* a place where grapes are grown.
vinegar *n.* an acid liquid use for flavouring and preserving food.
viola *n.* a stringed musical instrument that looks like a large violin.
violence *n.* great physical force.
violent *adj.*
violet 1. *n.* & *adj.* a colour, like a mixture of blue and purple. 2. *n.* a small plant with violet-coloured or white flowers.

A Viking longship. The Vikings came from Norway, Sweden and Denmark.

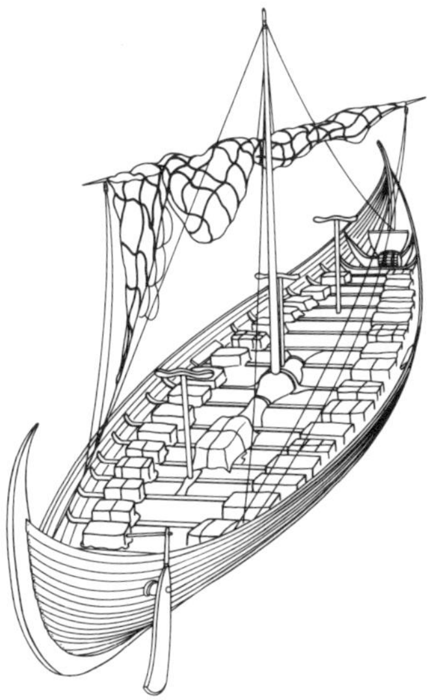

violin *n.* a stringed musical instrument played with a bow. **violinist** *n.* player of a violin.
viper *n.* one of a group of poisonous snakes.
virago *n.* a strong and aggressive woman.
virtue *n.* goodness; moral excellence.
virtuoso *n.* a highly skilled person, especially in playing a musical instrument.
virus *n.* a tiny living particle that can carry and cause disease.
visa (**vee**-*za*) *n.* a stamp on a passport allowing a person to enter a particular country.
viscount (**vie**-*count*) *n.* title of a nobleman (peer) ranking between an earl and baron.
viscountess *n.* the wife of a viscount.
visible *adj.* capable of being seen. *The ship was still just visible on the horizon.*
vision *n.* 1. the power of seeing, eyesight. 2. something seen in a dream etc. 3. great power of imagination.
visit *vb.* pay a call on someone; go to see a place; stay with or at. *n.* a journey made in order to visit a place or person.
visitor *n.* a person who comes to see, or stay with someone; a traveller who is staying in a place for a short time only.
visor *n.* the part of a helmet, usually moveable, that covers the eyes; a shade, such as the flap inside a car windscreen, that protects your eyes from the sun.
vista *n.* a view.
visual *adj.* concerned with sight and seeing. **visualize** *vb.* imagine, form a picture. *She tried to visualize what the dress would be like without pleats.*
vital *adj.* 1. of great importance. 2. lively, energetic.
vitamin *n.* one of a group of chemical substances that our body needs in order to stay healthy.
vivid *adj.* lively; bright and clear. *Dickens wrote vivid descriptions of London life.*

vixen *n.* a female fox.
vocabulary *n.* all the words known or used in a certain language.
vocal *adj.* to do with the voice.
vocation *n.* a calling (by God) to do special work; a career or

The volcano Vesuvius during an eruption in March 1944.

particular profession.

vodka *n.* type of alcohol made in Russia and Poland – a strong drink, with no colour and little flavour.

vogue *n.* the fashion at a particular time. *Hats are again in vogue.*

voice *n.* the sound produced when you speak or sing; your ability to make such a sound.

void *adj.* 1. containing nothing; empty. *n.* 2. having no legal force; not valid.

volcano *n.* (plural **volcanoes**) an opening in the surface of the Earth from which *magma* (molten rock), gas and steam is forced out; a mountain formed from hardened magma. **volcanic** *adj.*

vole *n.* a small rodent that looks like a mouse.

volley *n.* 1. return of a tennis ball before it has hit the ground. *vb.* 2. a number of guns fired at the same time.

volt *n.* a unit for measuring electrical pressure or electromotive force.

volume *n.* 1. the amount of space something takes up. 2. a single book, particularly one of a set. 3. loudness. *I can't hear the radio properly; could you please turn up the volume?*

voluntary *adj.* doing something without being forced to; without payment.

volunteer *n.* a person who offers to do something without being asked; a member of the armed services who joined up from his or her own choice. *vb.* offer one's services. *Jim volunteered to mow the lawn.*

vomit *vb.* be sick; throw up food from your stomach through your mouth.

vote *vb.* show what you want from a group of choices by supporting one of them. *n.*

voucher *n.* a coupon; a free pass.

vow *vb.* & *n.* (make) a solemn promise. *The politician vowed to cut taxes.*

vowel *n.* one of the sounds represented by the letters a, e, i o, u and y.

voyage *n.* a journey, particularly by sea.

vulgar *adj.* crude, coarse, bad taste.

vulnerable *adj.* unprotected and easily wounded; open to attack and liable to have feelings hurt.

vulture *n.* one of a family of large birds of prey which feed largely on *carrion* (dead animals).

W

waddle *vb.* walk in a clumsy way like a duck. *n.*

wade *vb.* walk through water (with some difficulty); progress slowly. *The river was just shallow enough for us to wade across.*

wadi *n.* an Arabic word meaning the dry bed of a river.

wafer *n.* a thin crisp biscuit, often eaten with ice-cream.

waffle 1. *n.* a small, crisp kind of pancake. 2. *vb.* talk or write nonsense. *n.*

wag *vb.* nod or wave part of your body from side to side. *A dog wags its tail when it is pleased.*

wage *vb.* carry on, take part in. *They waged war for five years.*

wages *pl. n.* the money you get for working, usually paid weekly.

waggle *vb.* wave or wag; wobble. *The pilot waggled the wings of his aircraft.*

wagon, waggon *n.* an open cart with four wheels; an open railway truck.

wagtail *n.* one of a family of small birds with sharp beaks and long tails.

waif *n.* a homeless, abandoned child.

wail *n.* a cry, usually loud and shrill. *vb.* cry in wails.

waist *n.* the narrow part of the

body between the chest and the hips.

waistcoat *n.* a sleeveless jacket, sometimes worn as part of a suit.

wait *vb.* stay in one place, expecting something to happen. *We will wait here until you come back. n.*

waiter *n.* a man who serves food in a restaurant.

waitress *n.* (plural **waitresses**) a woman who serves food in a restaurant.

wake 1. *vb.* (past **woke,** past part. **woken**) stop sleeping; rouse from sleep. 2. *n.* the track left in water by a ship.

walk *vb.* & *n.* (of a person or animal) move along at a steady pace, travel on foot.

walkie-talkie *n.* a portable radio telephone.

walk-over *n.* an easy victory.

wall *n.* a barrier made of brick or stone surrounding a piece of land; the side of a room or building. *vb.* (*in*) protect with a wall.

wallaby *n.* a marsupial which is similar to but smaller than a kangaroo.

wallet *n.* a folding purse in which money or papers are kept.

Walnuts are the fruit of the walnut tree.

wallow *vb.* splash about in mud; take unrestrained pleasure in. *He wallowed in self-pity.*

walnut *n.* deciduous tree belonging to the northern hemisphere, grown for its fine wood and its edible nut of the same name.

walrus *n.* (plural **walruses**) a large sea animal with long tusks, which lives in the Arctic.

waltz (rhymes with *false*) *n.* a kind of ballroom dance in triple time. *vb.* dance a waltz.

wand *n.* a slender stick used in stories by fairies and magicians to make magic spells.

Walruses live in large families.

wander *n.* go from place to place without having a plan or a purpose. **wanderer** *n.*
wane *vb.* become smaller. *The Moon is waning.*
wangle *vb.* get something by cunning. *Fred wangled a free ticket to the show.* *n.* an act of wangling.
want 1. *vb.* wish for or desire something; need. 2. *n.* lack of something; need (of).
wanted *adj.* sought (especially by the police).
war *n.* armed conflict between two or more countries or groups of people.
ward *n.* 1. a room in a hospital where sick people stay until they are well again. 2. administrative division of a town. 3. a person, usually young, under the legal care of a court or guardian.
warder *n.* a guard in charge of prisoners in a goal. **wardress** (female).
ward off *vb.* prevent something happening.
wardrobe *n.* a cupboard where clothes are hung and stored.
warehouse *n.* a large building where goods of all sorts are kept. *vb.* store in a warehouse.
warfare *n.* the state of war.
warm *adj.* slightly hot.
warn *vb.* tell people about danger. **warning** *n.* something that tells you about danger. *There was a warning light by the bridge, so we stopped.*
warp 1. *vb.* become twisted or bent. 2. *n.* the vertical threads on a loom, used for weaving.
warren *n.* a place where a group of rabbits live in burrows.
warrior *n.* a fighter.
warship *n.* an armed ship for use in wartime.
wart *n.* a small, hard lump on the skin.
wash *vb.* clean something by soaking it in water. **wash up** clean crockery etc.
washer *n.* a small flat ring used to make a joint, such as on a tap.
wasp *n.* a flying insect with a striped body and a sting in its tail. **waspish** *adj.* spiteful.

waste *vb.* use more than you need of something, or throw something away although you could have used it. *n.* unwanted material. **wasteful** *adj.* extravagant.
watch 1. *vb.* look on. *Did you watch the football match?* 2. *n.* a timepiece, usually worn on the wrist.
watch for *vb.* be on the alert for.
watch over *vb.* guard, protect.
water 1. *n.* the most common of all liquids, formed from two gases: oxygen and hydrogen. 2. *vb.* sprinkle with water; apply water to; dilute.
water boatman *n.* a water insect with long and powerful hind legs.

water buffalo *n.* a large kind of ox, used as a beast of burden in many Eastern countries.
water-colour *n.* a painting done with paint that dissolves in water.
water cycle *n.* the continuous movement of water from lakes and seas via the atmosphere to land areas and back again.
waterfall *n.* a rush of water which falls from a high place in a river or stream.
watermark *n.* a special design on paper which can be seen when held up to the light.

Water buffaloes are often used to pull carts in the rural areas of countries such as China.

water polo *n.* a game played in a swimming pool with a large inflated ball, and two teams of seven swimmers. The ball is thrown from one swimmer to another, and each team tries to score goals.

Water is continuously circulating in a cycle. Water rises from the land and sea by evaporation and falls again by precipitation.

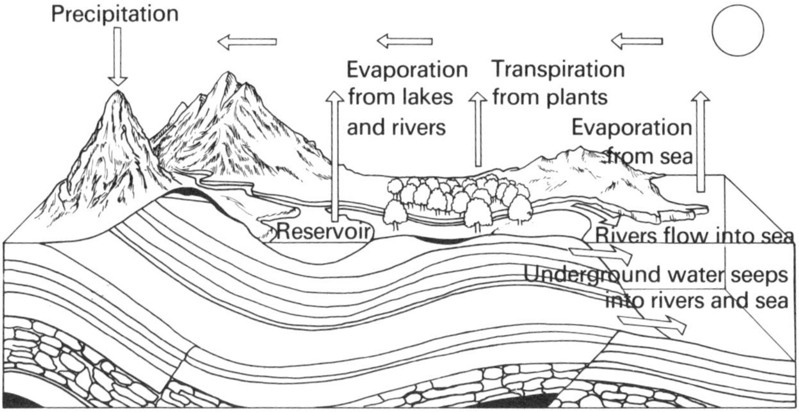

water power *n.* mechanical force derived from weight or motion of water.

waterproof *n.* & *adj.* a material that does not let water through it.

An Australian wattle tree.

water-skiing *n.* skiing on water, in which the person is towed along by a motor boat. As a competition, water-skiing includes slalom (steering round markers), distance jumping and figure skiing.

water supply *n.* the obtaining and distribution of water to houses, farms, factories etc.

water table *n.* the level below which the earth is saturated with water.

watertight *adj.* something that water cannot get into or out of; leak-proof.

waterwheel *n.* a wheel that uses the force of falling water to run machinery.

watt *n.* a unit of electric power.

wattle *n.* a plant found in Australia belonging to the acacia family, which produces branches suitable for interwoven (wattle) roofs and fencing. Its golden flower is Australia's national emblem.

wave 1. *n.* a moving ridge on the surface of the sea. 2. *n.* a curve or curl in your hair. 3. *vb.* signal to someone by moving your hand.

waver *vb.* hesitate, be undecided.

wax *n.* a soft, yellowish material which melts easily into an oily liquid, used for making things waterproof, and for polish and candles.

way *n.* 1. a method. *Can you show me the right way to do this sum?* 2. a path. 3. direction. *Do you know your way home?*

weak *adj.* fragile, easy to break, not strong. **weaken** *vb.* make (or become) weak.

wealth *n.* a great amount of money or property. **wealthy** *adj.* rich.

wean *vb.* change a baby animal from drinking its mother's milk to eating solid foods; free gradually from a habit.

weapon *n.* an object, such as a gun or sword, used for fighting.

wear *vb.* 1. be dressed in, have on your body. *Penny wanted to wear her new dress and her pearl necklace to the party.* 2. become less good through being used. *The car brakes have begun to wear quite a lot.*

weary *adj.* tired; tired (of).

weasel *n.* a small meat-eating animal related to the badger and the otter.

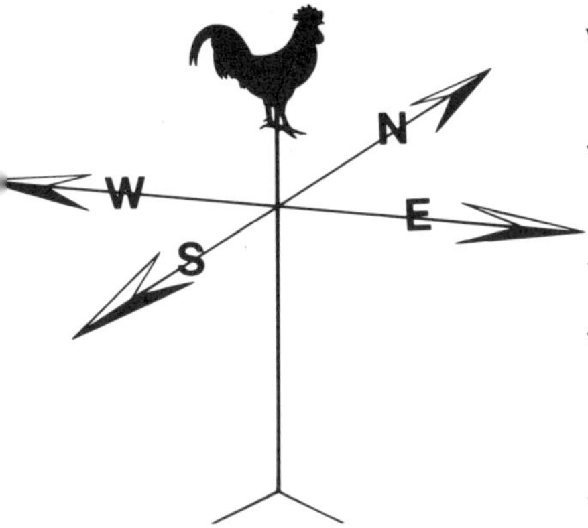

A weathercock shows which direction the wind is blowing from.

weather 1. *n*. conditions in the atmosphere, which may be wet or dry, hot or cold etc. 2. *vb*. come safely through (storm) etc.

weathercock *n*. vane in shape of a cock.

weave *vb*. (past **wove**, past part. **woven**) make cloth on a loom with a pattern of threads.

Young boys weaving a carpet on a giant loom.

web *n*. a loose set of threads. *A spider makes a web with threads from its body*.

web-foot *n*. a foot, like the ones on ducks and frogs, which have skin joining the toes together.

wedding *n*. a marriage ceremony. **wed** *vb*.

Wednesday *n*. the fourth day of the week, between Tuesday and Thursday; named after Woden, Anglo-Saxon god of war.

wee *adj*. a Scots word meaning 'tiny'.

weed *n*. a wild plant that grows where it is not wanted, such as in a flower bed. *vb*. remove weeds. **weedy** *adj*. full of weeds; (*casual*) weak and lanky.

week *n*. the sequence of seven days from Sunday to Saturday; any seven-day period.

weekday *n*. a day other than Sunday.

weekend *n*. the period between the end of one working week and the beginning of the next, usually Saturday and Sunday. A long weekend might include Friday and Monday.

weekly *adj.* & *adv.* once a week.
weep *vb.* cry with tears coming from your eyes.
weevil *n.* type of beetle distinguished by its long snout.
weft *n.* the horizontal threads on a loom, used for weaving.
weigh *vb.* measure the weight of something, perhaps on scales.
weight *n.* 1. how much something weighs. *What is the weight of that parcel?* 2. a heavy piece of metal or other substance. *A deep-sea diver has lead weights on the diving suit to help descend more quickly.*
weight-lifting *n.* one of the sports included in the Olympic Games in which competitors lift very heavy weights from the floor to above their heads.
weird *adj.* strange; peculiar; odd.
welcome *vb.* do or say things which show you are pleased when someone arrives. *n.*
weld *vb.* join metals by heating or pressure or a combination of both. *n.*
welfare *n.* people's health and happiness.

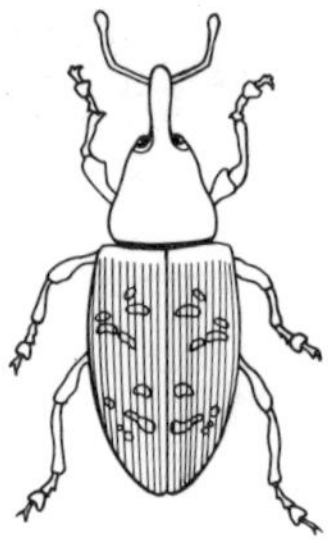

Many weevils are garden pests.

well 1. *adj.* healthy. 2. *adv.* to do something in a good or successful way. *Emma swims very well.* 3. *n.* a deep hole for underground water.
wellington *n.* the name for a kind of boot, nowadays a rubber or plastic boot. *Wellingtons get their name from the riding boots worn by the Duke of Wellington.*
Welsh *adj.* & *n.* of Wales; the people and language of Wales.
went *vb.* past of **go**.
wept *vb.* past and past part. of **weep**.
west *n.* one of the points on a compass; the direction in which the sun sets. *adj. adv.*

A set of weights.

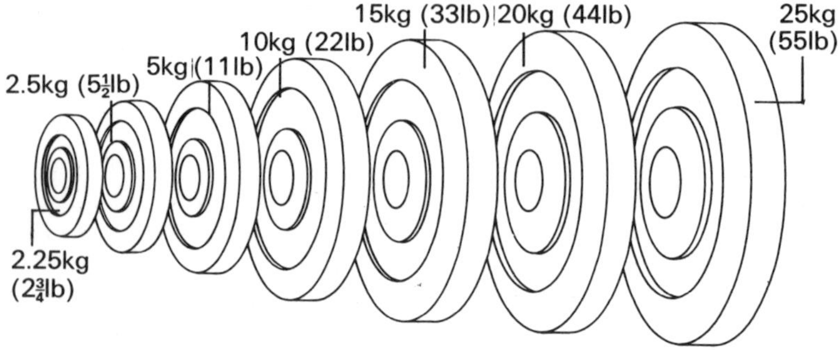

Whales are warm-bloodied animals. They cannot breathe under water.

western 1. *adj*. of Western (i.e. West European and American) countries; belonging to, or coming from, the west. 2. *n*. a film or book about the American Wild West. **westernize** *vb*.

wet *adj*. damp; consisting of or soaked with liquid; rainy. *vb*. make wet.

whack *vb*. hit heavily. *n*. a hard blow.

whale *n*. a very large sea mammal that looks like a fish. *vb*. hunt whales.

whaler *n*. a person or ship that hunts whales.

wharf *n*. a place where ships are loaded and unloaded.

what *interrogative adj*. used in questions which ask for a selection from an indefinite number or quantity.

whatever *pron*. no matter what. *Whatever he may say, I still don't believe him.*

wheat *n*. the grain from which most flour is made.

wheedle *vb*. coax or persuade.

wheel *n*. a circular structure that revolves around an axle. *vb*. push or pull a bicycle, pram etc.

wheelbarrow *n*. small garden cart, with one wheel in front, and held by two handles.

wheeze 1. *vb*. breathe with difficulty and making a hissing sound. 2. *n*. (*casual*) a clever plan.

whelk *n*. a type of edible mollusc with a spiral shell.

whelp *n*. a puppy or young dog.

when *adv*. & *conj*. at the time when; at what time? *When is our next meeting?*

whenever *conj*. at every time; at any time. *Come whenever you like.*

where *adv*. & *conj*. in such a place; in which place? *Where did you leave your case?*

wherever *adv*. & *conj*. in whatever place. *I shall find him, wherever he is hiding.*

whether *conj*. if. *Do you know whether we are late?*

which 1. *interrogative adj*. used in questions which ask for a selection from a limited number or quantity. 2. *relative pronoun* stands for a previous noun. *This is the book which you asked for.*

whiff *n*. a puff of air or a faint smell.

while 1. *n*. a period of time. *I've been waiting all this while.* 2. *conj*. during the time when (also **whilst**). *Did anyone phone while I was out?* 3. *vb*. pass away the time. *Joan whiled away the time by reading a book.*

whine *vb*. 1. make a high-pitched cry. 2. grumble (especially of a child).

whinge *vb*. (casual) to cry or complain in a feeble way. **whinger** *n*.

whinny *n*. & *vb*. a low neighing sound made by a horse.

whip 1. *n*. a long rope or strip of leather joined to a handle, and used to hit animals. *vb*. 2. *vb*. beat cream or other liquids until they thicken.

whirl *vb*. turn around fast in circles; rush along. *n*.

whirlpool *n*. a place in a river or ocean where the water spins around.

whirlwind *n*. a fierce wind that blows in circles.

whisk 1. *n*. an instrument for beating eggs. *vb*. 2. *vb*. go or carry off quickly. *The waiter whisked our plates away*.

An egg-whisk.

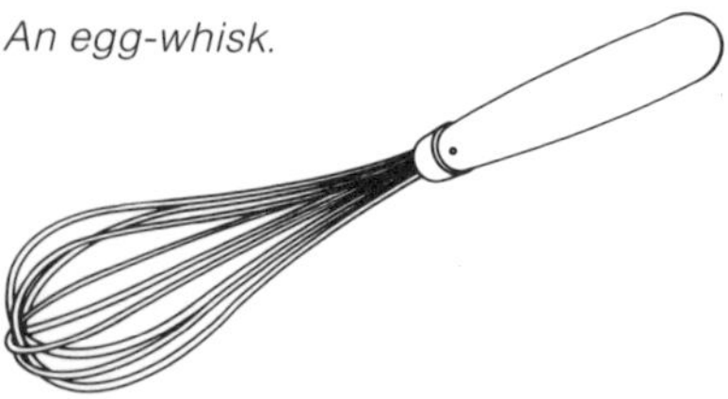

whisker *n*. 1. one of the long, stiff hairs that grow on either side of the mouth of some animals. 2. (*pl.*) beard or hairs growing on sides of a man's face.

whisky *n*. an alcoholic spirit made from grain, especially in Scotland. (Whiskey in the USA and Ireland.)

whisper *vb*. talk in a low voice, without vibrating the vocal cords. *n*.

whist *n*. a card game for four players using all 52 cards and a trump suit.

whistle 1. *vb*. make a shrill sound by blowing through your tightened lips. 2. *n*. an instrument for blowing through to make a whistling sound. *vb*. to blow a whistle.

white *n*. & *adj*. the colour of snow.

white elephant *n*. a possession that is more trouble than it is worth.

White Ensign *n*. the flag of Britain's Royal Navy.

White Paper *n*. a document printed on white paper for the information of Members of Parliament.

whiting *n*. a small sea fish.

Whitsun *n*. short for 'Whit Sunday'; a Christian festival held on the seventh Sunday after Easter. Also known as Pentecost, it celebrates the day when Christians believe the Holy Spirit comforted the apostles.

who 1. *interrogative adj*. which person? *Who did that?* 2. *pron*. the person that... *I know who was speaking to you*.

whoever 1. *interrogative adj*. what person? *Whoever would have thought it?* 2. *pron*. any

The whiting is an edible fish.

A 17th-century man's wig.

person. *Ask whoever you like to the party.*

whole (rhymes with *hole*) *adj.* all of something, a complete thing; uninjured. *n.*

wholefood *n.* natural food which has been processed as little as possible.

wholesale *n.* & *adj.* selling things in large quantities, usually to be sold again. *vb.* sell wholesale. (See also *retail*.)

whooping-cough *n.* an infectious disease marked by strange and terrible coughing.

whose *interrogative adj.* of whom. *Whose book is this?*

why *interrogative adv.* for what reason? *Why are you looking at me like that?*

wick *n.* the thread or material put into a candle or lamp which is lit with a flame.

wicked *adj.* bad, evil.

wide 1. *adj.* broad; having the sides far apart. 2. *n.* a ball in cricket bowled too far away from the batsman.

widow *n.* a woman whose husband is dead and who has not married again.

widower *n.* a man whose wife is dead and who has not married again.

width *n.* how thick something is; the distance from one side to the other.

wield *vb.* 1. use with the hands. 2. exercise power etc.

wife *n.* (plural **wives**) the woman to whom a man is married.

wig *n.* false hair to cover a bald head, or to cover your own hair with different hair.

wigwam *n.* a tent used by North American Indians, made of a frame of poles covered with cloth or skin.

wild *adj.* not tame; original or natural state; living in a natural way; out of control.

wilderness *n.* an uninhabited and uncultivated area of land.

A wigwam.

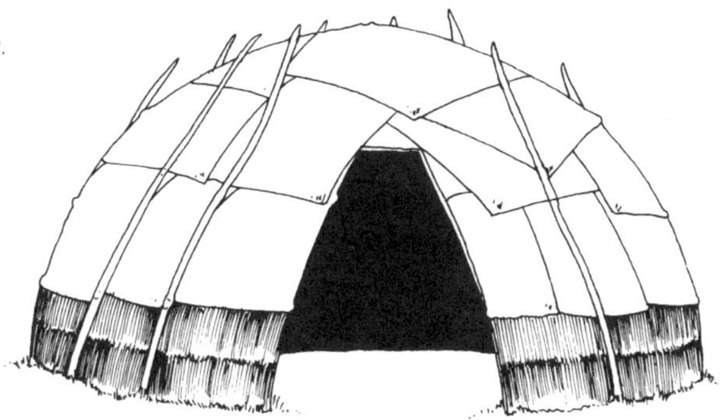

will 1. *vb.* a form of the verb 'to be' indicating determination or future action. *What will you do next?* 2. *n.* intention, determination, desire. 3. *n.* a document that says what will happen to someone's property when they die.

willing *adj.* ready to do what is wanted or needed.

willow *n.* one of a family of deciduous trees found in many parts of the world, generally near water.

wilt *vb.* droop like a plant without water, to be limp.

wimp *n.* a feeble and ineffective person. **wimpish** *adj.*

win *vb.* come first in a contest or game; gain. *n.* victory in a game. **winner** *n.*

wince *vb.* & *n.* (make) a movement of pain.

wind (rhymes with *kind*) *vb.* 1. turn the handle of a clock so that it will work. 2. wrap thread or wool around something.

wind (rhymes with *sinned*) *n.* the movement of large masses of air. **windy** *adj.*

wind instrument *n.* a musical instrument that is played by blowing into it.

windmill *n.* a mill powered by the action of the wind on 'arms' called *sails*.

window *n.* an opening, usually covered by glass, in the wall of a building to let in light and sometimes air.

windscreen *n.* the front window of a car. (US **windshield**.)

wine *n.* an alcoholic drink usually made from the juice of grapes.

Wistaria is a climbing wall plant.

wing *n.* 1. the part of a bird or insect used for flying. 2. the 'arm' of an aircraft. 3. side extension of a building. 4. mudguard of a car.

wink *vb.* close one eye rapidly, perhaps as a signal to someone.

winter *n.* the coldest season of the year, between autumn and spring. *vb.* spend the winter in, at etc.

wipe *vb.* rub something clean or dry.

wipe out *vb.* destroy completely. *A bad earthquake can wipe out a whole village.*

wire *n.* a long thread of metal that can be bent and twisted.

wisdom *n.* knowledge and understanding.

wise *adj.* able to understand many things.

wish *vb.* & *n.* want or desire something. *I wish it wasn't raining.*

wish-bone *n.* a small bone (the *furcula*) in front of a bird's breast-bone. *People sometimes break a chicken's wish-bone between them. The person with the bigger piece gets a wish.*
wistaria *n.* an ornamental climbing plant with purple or white flowers.
wit *n.* intelligence; humour.
witch *n.* (plural **witches**) a woman in stories who uses magic to make things happen.
witchcraft *n.* the magic skills of a witch.
with *prep.* connected to; possessing; in the company of. *Robin was playing with his little sister.*
withdraw *vb.* (past **withdrew**, past part. **withdrawn**) pull back from something, or take back. *Sally is going to withdraw from the match.*
wither *vb.* become dry, decay.
withers *pl. n.* the ridge between the shoulder blades of a horse.
withhold *vb.* keep back, refuse to give.
without *prep.* not having something. *James came to school without his books.*
withstand *vb.* still keep one's position, oppose, resist.
witness *n.* a person who sees something happen, particularly a crime. *vb.*
wizard *n.* a man in stories who uses magic to make things happen.
wobble *vb.* move from side to side like a jelly; hesitate.
woke *vb.* past of **wake**.
wolf *n.* (plural **wolves**) a wild animal of the dog family. *vb.* eat greedily.
woman *n.* a grown-up female human.
womb *n.* the organ in which the young of mammals are carried and developed until they are born; the uterus.
wombat *n.* a burrowing marsupial (pouched mammal) related to the koala, and found in the wild only in Australia.
won *vb.* past of **win**.
wonder *vb.* ask yourself something; feel surprised.
wonderful *adj.* a happening that is so good it surprises you.
won't *abbreviation* for **will not**.
wood *n.* 1. a number of trees growing together in one place, a small forest. 2. the trunk and branches of trees cut up and used to make things; timber. **wooden** *adj.* made of wood.
woodcut *n.* a picture printed from a wooden block.
wooden *adj.* made of wood.
woodpecker *n.* one of a family of tree-climbing birds found in most parts of the world.

Woodpeckers use their beaks to dig out nest holes in trees.

woodwind *n.* a family of musical instruments, played by blowing through a mouthpiece and into a hollow tube. Different notes are made by opening and closing holes in the instrument.

woodwork *n.* making things out of wood.

wool *n.* the natural covering found on sheep.

woollen *adj.* & *n.* (cloth) made from wool.

word *n.* a unit of written or spoken speech, made up of a number of letters. *We leave spaces between words when we write them down.*

word-processor *n.* typewriter that displays typed matter on a screen so the matter can be edited before it is printed.

wore *vb.* past of **wear**.

work 1. *n.* anything that requires effort; a job. 2. *vb.* do a job.

worker *n.* someone who works for a living.

workshop *n.* a place where things are made or mended.

world *n.* the Earth and universe.

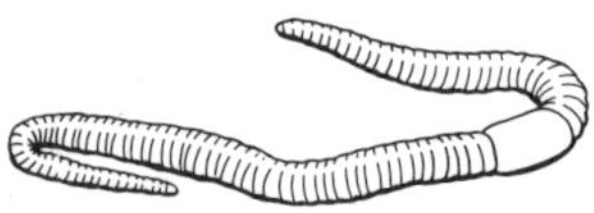

worm *n.* the common name for a large group of animals with long, thin, limbless bodies.

worn *vb.* past part. of **wear**.

worry *vb.* be upset or anxious about something or someone.

worse *adj.* not as good as. *This hamburger is not great, but I have tasted worse.*

worsen *vb.* make or become worse.

worship *vb.* praise God. *n.*

worst *adj.* the least good.

worth *n.* the value of something.

worthless *adj.* something that has no value.

would *vb.* a word that implies both possibility and the desire to do something. *I would like to help you.*

wound 1. (*woo-nd*) *n.* an injury or cut. *vb.* inflict a wound. 2. (rhymes with *round*) *vb.* past of **wind**.

wrap *vb.* cover something completely; make a parcel. *n.* a loose garment such as a shawl.

wreath *n.* an arrangement of flowers or leaves tied together in a circle.

wreck *vb.* damage something so badly that it cannot be used again. *n.* a ship or building that has been badly damaged.

wren *n.* one of a family of insect-eating songbirds that are found in most parts of the world.

wrench *vb.* pull or twist violently. *n.*

wrestle *vb.* fight using your body as a weapon.

wretched *adj*. very miserable or sad.
wriggle *vb*. twist and turn your body around.
wring *vb*. squeeze liquid out of clothing etc. by twisting.
wrinkle *n*. a crease on the skin or other flat surfaces. *vb*. become marked with wrinkles.
wrist *n*. the joint between your arm and your hand.
write *vb*. (past **wrote**, past part. **written**) put down words on paper.
write off for *vb*. send a letter asking for or ordering something, often something from an advertisement. *John will write off for that chair*.
written past part. of **write**.
wrong 1. *adj*. incorrect. *You gave the wrong answer*. 2. *n*. an old-fashioned word meaning 'evil' or 'wickedness'.
wrote *vb*. past of **write**.
wrung *vb*. past of **wring**.

X

xenophobia (*zen-o-***foab***-ya*) *n*. a great dislike of foreigners.
xerography (*zeer-***og***-ra-fee*) *n*. a means of photocopying documents, widely used in offices.
X-ray *n*. a form of electromagnetic waves which can pass into or through most living things.
xylophone (*zy-lo-fone*) *n*. a musical instrument made up of rows of wooden or metal bars that are struck by hammers.

Y

yacht *n*. a light sailing boat.
yak *n*. a large kind of ox, with a shaggy black coat and long horns.

yam *n*. the edible root of various tropical climbing plants, in particular several varieties of sweet potato.
yank 1. *vb*. & *n*. pull suddenly. 2. *n*. affectionate nickname for US American. Also **Yankee**.
yap *n*. a short shrill bark, like the sound small dogs make. *vb*.

yard *n.* 1. a measurement of length (0.914 metres, 3ft or 36in). 2. an open space surrounded by walls and buildings. 3. spar slung from mast to support sail.

yardstick *n.* a yard measure; a standard of comparison.

yarn *n.* 1. fibres of wool used in knitting and sewing. 2. a tale.

yashmak *n.* veil worn by Muslim women over the face.

yawn *vb.* open your mouth wide when you are bored or sleepy. *n.* the act of yawning.

ye *pron.* an old-fashioned word for you.

year *n.* the amount of time it takes the Earth to travel around the Sun; period from 1 January to 31 December; any period of twelve months.

yearly *adj.* every year; once a year.

yeast *n.* a substance used to make bread and beer rise.

yell *vb.* shout loudly. *n.* a loud cry.

yellow *n.* & *adj.* the colour of the primary colours. vb. turn yellow.

yen *n.* the currency unit of Japan.

yesterday *n.* & *adj.* the day before today.

yet 1. *adv.* up to the present time. *Have you finished your work yet?* 2. *conj.* nevertheless.

yew *n.* an evergreen conifer often planted in churchyards.

Yiddish *n.* the international language used by Jewish people.

yield 1. *vb.* give in, give up. 2. *n.* the amount of grain or fruit on a plant or within an area of a farm. *We got a good yield of plums from that tree.*

yodel *vb.* & *n.* sing(ing) in the manner of Swiss mountaineers, the voice going from normal to falsetto.

yoga *n.* a Hindu spiritual system of meditation. *The form of yoga popular in western countries uses special postures and breathing exercises to give control of mind and body.*

yoghurt *n.* a liquid food made from soured milk.

yoke *n.* a wooden harness which joins a pair of oxen at the neck for working together. *vb.* link together.

yolk (rhymes with *soak*) *n.* the yellow part inside an egg.

Yom Kippur *n.* the Day of Atonement, a Jewish feast marking ten days of penintence and abstinence at the start of the Jewish New Year (mid-September).

Yorkshire pudding *n.* a batter of eggs, flour and milk cooked in dripping and traditionally eaten with roast beef.

you *pronoun* used for the second

person singular and plural. *Could you please lend me your pen, John?* or *Can you all hear me?*

young 1. *adj*. not old. 2. *n*. baby animals. *Mammals feed their young on milk*. **youngster** *n*. a young person.

your *pronoun* & *adj*. belonging to you.

youth *n*. (plural **youths**) the time when one is young; a young man; (collective) young people. *The youth of today do not like smoking*.

yo-yo *n*. a toy that consists of a reel that winds and unwinds from a string held in the hand.

Z

zany (**zay**-*nee*) *adj*. absurd, eccentric; strangely funny.

zeal *n*. an old-fashioned word meaning enthusiasm or keenness.

zebra *n*. an African animal like a horse with dark stripes on a light body.

zebra crossing *n*. a pedestrian crossing, marked with beacons, and with black and white stripes painted on the road.

zebu (*zee-boo*) *n*. a humped ox of Asia and Africa.

zenith *n*. point of the sky immediately overhead; highest point; acme.

zero *n*. nought; the figure 0.

zest *n*. enthusiasm, lively enjoyment; gusto.

ziggurat *n*. a type of pyramid built in ancient Babylonia, the sides of which were built in huge 'steps', each storey set in from the one below. Ziggurats were used as temples and for observing stars.

zigzag *adj*. & *n*. going one way and then another, like the letter Z. *vb*. move in a zigzag way.

zinc *n*. a hard, bluish white metal element (symbol Zn).

zip *n*. a fastener with two sets of teeth that lock together. *vb*. fasten with a zip. (US **zipper**.)

zither *n*. a stringed musical instrument that is played in a flat position by being plucked with the fingers.

zloty *n*. principal money unit of Poland. The word means 'golden'.

zodiac *n*. a name given by the ancient astrologers to the band of the sky through which the Sun, Moon and the five planets then known, all appear to move.

zombie *n*. a corpse said to be brought back to life by witchcraft; a person with no mind of their own and who behaves like a robot.

zone *n*. part of a town or larger area that is special in some way. *vb*. divide into zones.

zoo *n*. a place where wild animals are kept (short for zoological gardens).

zoology *n*. the study of animals.

zoom *vb*. 1. fly suddenly upwards. 2. focus a camera quickly from long-shot to close-up.

International abbreviations

Abbreviations – usually just the initial letter of words – are a quick and easy way of writing long or complicated names. Here are some common abbreviations that are used and understood wherever English is read or spoken.

AA Automobile Association
AC Alternating current
A.D. *Anno Domini,* in the Year of Our Lord.
adj. Adjective
Adm. Admiral
adv. Adverb
a.m. *Ante meridiem,* before noon
AM Amplitude modulation
anon. Anonymous
Apr. April
assn., assoc. Association
Aug. August
A.V. Authorized Version (of the Bible)
Ave Avenue
A.W.O.L. Absent without official leave

b. Born
BA Bachelor of Arts
BBC British Broadcasting Corporation
B.C. Before Christ
Brig. Brigadier
BSc Batchelor of Science
BST British Summer Time

c. *Circa,* about; *centum,* one hundred; cent
C Celsius, Centigrade
cap. Capital; capital letter
Capt. Captain
CB Citizen's band
ch., chap. Chapter
Chron. Chronicles
CIA Central Intelligence Agency
CID Criminal Investigation Department
cf. *Confer,* compare
cm Centimetre
co. Company; county
c/o Care of
CO Commanding officer
c.o.d. Cash (or collect) on delivery
coll. colloq. Colloquial
com. Common
Con. Conservative
conj. Conjunction
cont., contd. Continued
Cor. Corinthians
corp. Corporation
Cpl Corporal

d. Died; *denarius,* a penny before 1971
DC Direct current
D.C. District of Colombia
dec. Deceased
Dec. December
Dem. Democrat
dept. Department
Deut. Deuteronomy
Dr Doctor

E East
Eccl. Ecclesiastes
EC European Community
ed. Edition; edited; editor
EFTA European Free Trade Association
e.g. *Exempli gratia,* for example
Eph. Ephesians
eq. Equal; equation
Esth. Esther
esp. Especially
et al. *Et alii,* and others
etc. *Et cetera,* and so forth
et. seq. *Et sequens,* and the following
Eur. Europe(an)
Ex., Exod. Exodus
Ez. Ezra
Ezek. Ezekiel

F Fahrenheit
FBI Federal Bureau of Investigation
Feb. February
ff. Following (pages)
FM Frequency modulation
fig. Figure
Fri. Friday
ft Foot

g Gram
Gal. Galatians
GB Great Britain
Gen. Genesis; general
GMT Greenwich Mean Time
govt. Government

h Hour
ha Hectare
hi-fi High fidelity
hist. Historical
HMS Her (or His) Majesty's Ship
Hon. Honourable
hp Horsepower
HQ Headquarters
hr. Hour
ht Height
Hz Hertz

I. Island
IBA Independent Broadcasting Authority
Ibid. *Ibidem,* in the same place
i.e. *Id est,* that is
ill. Illustrated
IMF International Monetary Fund (UN)
inc. Incorporated, including
IQ Intelligence quotient
IRA Irish Republic Army
Is. Isaiah; island(s)
ISBN International Standard Book Number

Jan. January
Jer. Jeremiah
Josh. Joshua
Jr Junior
Jud. Judges

kg Kilogram
kHz Kilohertz
km Kilometre
km/h Kilometres per hour
KW Kilowatt

£ *Libra,* pound (money)
l Litre
L Liberal

Lab. Labour
lat Latitude
lb *Libra*, pound (weight)
Lev. Leviticus
Lib. Liberal
Lieut. Lieutenant
log. Logarithm
long. Longitude
Lt. Lieutenant
Ltd Limited

m Metre
M Monsieur
Maj. Major
Mar. March
Matt. Matthew
max. Maximum
mg Milligram
MHz Megahertz
min. Minute; minimum
misc. Miscellaneous
ml Millilitre
Mlle Mademoiselle
mm Millimetre
Mme Madame
Mon. Monday
MP Member of Parliament; military police
mph Miles per hour
Mr Mister
Mrs Mistress
Ms Miss or Mrs
MS Manuscript
Mt Mount

n. noun
N North
NASA National Aeronautics and Space Administration
NATO North Atlantic Treaty Organization
N.B. *Nota bene*, note well
NCO Non-commissioned officer
no. *Numéro*, number
Nov. November
NT New Testament
Num. Numbers

ob. *Obiit*, died
Oct. October
OK, O.K. Correct
op. *Opus*, work
op. cit. *Opere citato*, in the work cited
OT Old Testament

p Penny, pence
p. Page
pen. Peninsula
per cent, % *Per centum*, by the hundred
Pet. Peter
PhD Doctor of Philosophy
pl. Plural
plc Public limited company
PLO Palestine Liberation Organization
p.m. *Post meridiem*, afternoon
PO Post office
pop. Population, popular (not technical)
POW Prisoner of war
pp. Pages
Prov. Proverbs
PS *Post scriptum*, postscript
PTO Please turn over
Pvt. Private (rank)

QED *Quod erat demonstrandum*, which was to be shown
q.v. *Quod vide*, which see

R *Rex*, king; *regina*, queen; river
RAC Royal Automobile Club
RAF Royal Air Force
Rd. Road
ref. Reference
Rep. Republican
Rev. Revelations; Reverend
RIP *Requiescat in pace*, rest in peace
RN Royal Navy
Rom. Romans
rpm Revolutions per minute
RSVP *Répondez, s'il vous plaît* (Fr.) Reply, if you please

s Second
S South
s.a.e. Stamped addressed envelope
Sat. Saturday
sec. Second
Sept. September
sing. Singular
soc. Society
Soc. Socialist
sp. Species; spelling
sq. Square
Sr. Senior
SS Steamship
St. Saint; strait; street
Sun. Sunday
syn. Synonym

temp. Temperature
Thess. Thessalonians
Thur. Thursday
TNT Trinitrotoluene
tr. Transpose; translation
TUC Trades Union Congress
Tues. Tuesday

UFO Unidentified flying object
UK United Kingdom of Great Britain and Northern Ireland
UN United Nations
UNESCO United Nations Educational, Scientific and Cultural Organization
univ. University
USA United States of America
USSR Union of Soviet Socialist Republics

v. Verb
v., vid *Vide*, see
v., vs. Versus
V Volt
VAT Value-added tax
VHF Very high frequency
VIP Very Important Person
viz. *Videlicet*, namely
vol. Volume

W West
W Watt
w. with
Wed. Wednesday
WHO World Health Organization (UN)
wt Weight

Xmas Christmas

YHA Youth Hostels Association
YMCA Young Men's Christian Association
YWCA Young Women's Christian Association

zool. Zoology

Weights and measures

LENGTH

Metric units
millimetre (mm)
10mm = 1 centimetre (cm)
100cm = 1 metre (m)
100m = 1 hectometre (hm)
1,000m = 1 kilometre (km)

Imperial units
inch (in)
12in = 1 foot (ft)
3ft = 1 yard (yd)
1,760 = 1 mile = 5,280ft

AREA

Metric units
square millimetre (sqmm)
100sqmm = 1 square centimetre (sqcm)
10,000sqcm = 1 square metre (sqm)
100sqm = 1 acre (a) = 1 square decametre (dm)
100a = 1 hectare (ha) = 1 square hectometre
100ha = 1 square kilometre (sqkm)

Imperial units
square inch (sqin)
144sqin = 1 square foot (sqft)
9sqft = 1 square yard (sqyd)
4,840sqyd = 1 acre
640 acres = 1 square mile (sqmile)

WEIGHT

Metric units
milligram (mg)
1,000mg = 1 gram (g)
1,000g = 1 kilogram (kg)
100kg = 1 quintal (q)
1,000kg = 1 metric ton, or tonne (t)

Imperial units (Avoirdupois)
grain (gr); dram (dr)
7,000gr = 1 pound (lb)
16dr = 1 ounce (oz)
16oz = 1lb
14lb = 1 stone
28lb = 1 quarter
112lb = 1 hundredweight (cwt)
20cwt = 1 ton = 2,240lb

CAPACITY

Metric units
millilitre (ml)
10ml = 1 centilitre (cl)
1,000ml = 1 litre (l)
100l = 1 hectolitre (hl)
1,000l = 1 kilolitre (kl)

Imperial units
gill
4 gills = 1 pint
2 pints = 1 quart
4 quarts = 1 gallon = 277.274cuin
Dry
2 gallons = 1 peck
4 pecks = 1 bushel
8 bushels = 1 quarter
36 bushels = 1 chaldron

VOLUME

Metric units
cubic millimetre (cumm)
1,000cumm = 1 cubic centimetre (cucm)
1,000cucm = 1 cubic decimetre (cudm) = 1 litre
1,000cudm = 1 cubic metre (cum)
1,000,000,000 = 1 cubic kilometre (cukm)

Imperial units
cubic inch (cuin)
1,728cuin = 1 cubic foot (cuft)
27cuft = 1 cubic yard (cuyd)
5,451,776,000cuyd = 1 cubic mile (cumile)

TECHNICAL TERMS

CHEMISTRY AND PHYSICS • THE EARTH AND SPACE • COMPUTERS • ECONOMICS • THE NATURAL WORLD • HUMAN BIOLOGY AND MEDICINE • THE ARTS

CHEMISTRY AND PHYSICS

absolute zero The lowest temperature possible in theory. Zero on an absolute scale is −273.15°C (−459.67°F).

alternating current Electric current that rapidly goes from maximum in one direction through zero to maximum in the other direction.

amalgam A compound of mercury and a metal. It may be either liquid or solid.

ampere (*am-pair*) A unit of electric current equivalent to the flow of 6 × 10 electrons per second (i.e. 6 million million electrons).

annealing A way of toughening metal by heating it and then cooling it slowly.

anode A positive electrode through which current enters an electrolytic cell or a vacuum tube.

Archimedes' principle When a body is immersed or partly immersed in fluid, the apparent loss in weight is equal to the weight of the fluid displaced.

base A substance that reacts chemically with an acid to form a salt and water.

benzene A liquid hydrocarbon that comes from coal and petroleum. It is used as fuel and as a solvent.

Bessemer converter A large container used in the steel-making process. In it, air is blown through molten pig-iron to remove impurities.

boiling point The temperature at which liquid turns into vapour.

carbohydrate A compound of carbon, oxygen and hydrogen producing energy. Starches and sugars are carbohydrates.

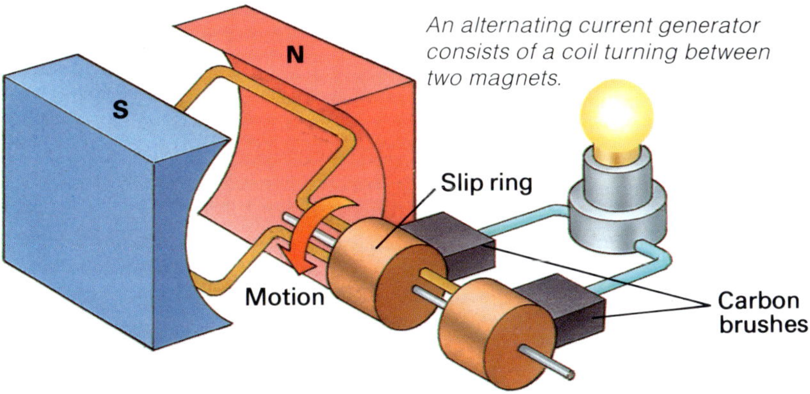

An alternating current generator consists of a coil turning between two magnets.

A chain reaction of neutrons splitting by nuclear fission into other uranium atoms.

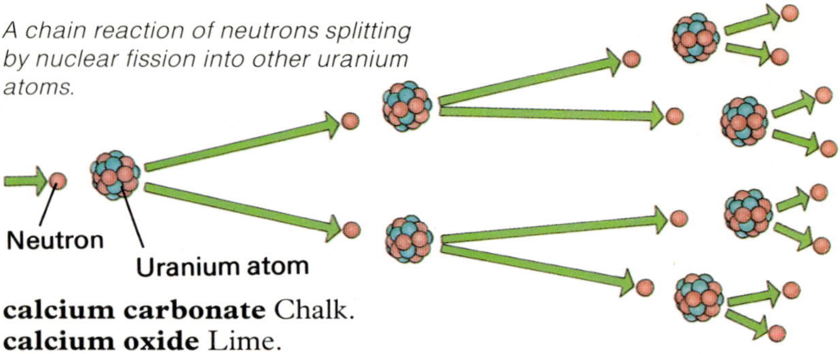

calcium carbonate Chalk.
calcium oxide Lime.
calcium sulphite Plaster of Paris.
chain reaction A reaction whose products start another reaction, the products of which start yet another reaction and so on.
circuit, electrical The complete path taken by an electric current.
compound A substance consisting of two or more elements in chemical combination in definite proportions.
cosmic rays Radiation which reaches the earth from outer space.
condensation The change from a gas to a liquid which takes place when pressure is applied to it or the temperature is lowered.
diffraction The spreading out of light by passing it through a narrow slit or past the edge of an obstacle.
direct current Current that always flows in the same direction.
elasticity The property of a material that makes it go back to its original shape after a force pushing it out of shape is removed.
electrolyte A substance which, in solution, can conduct electric current.
electromagnetic Being both electric and magnetic in character.
focus The point at which converging rays of light meet.
force Anything that can act on a stationary body and make it move, or make a moving body change speed or direction.
fusion (*few-shun*), **nuclear** The joining of the nuclei of light atoms together with the release of vast amounts of energy. This is the process that occurs in stars.
gravitation The force of attraction between any two objects because of their masses.
hydrocarbon A compound of hydrogen and carbon.
hydrochloric acid Hydrogen chloride.
insulator A substance that does not conduct electricity.
integrated circuit A complete electrical circuit, usually on a silicon chip.
laser A device which produces an intense, thin beam of light; abbreviation for Light Amplification by Stimulated Emission of Radiation.

litmus A blue colouring which is turned red by acid substances and becomes blue again if alkaline substances are applied.
mass The amount of matter in an object.
melting point The temperature at which solid turns to liquid; equal to the freezing point of the liquid.
methane A gas which occurs when vegetable matter rots.
momentum The product of the mass and velocity of a moving body.
proton A positively charged atomic particle found in the nucleus of every atom.
radiation, heat The transfer of heat by means of waves; infra-red rays.
radioactivity The giving out of radiation, in the form of alpha-particles, beta-particles and gamma-rays, when the nuclei of atoms are split.
semiconductor A substance which conducts electricity better than an insulator, but less well than a conductor. Much used in modern electronics.
solvent Something which will dissolve or form a solution with another substance. Water is a solvent.
static electricity Electricity which is not flowing, in contrast to electric current.
surface tension The property of the surface of a liquid which makes it behave as though it were covered with a thin elastic skin.
thermodynamics The study of the relationship between heat and other forms of energy.
ultrasonic waves 'Sound' waves beyond the range of human hearing.
velocity The rate at which a body changes position equal to its speed in a particular direction.
volume The measurement of a space occupied by an object.
wave Regular disturbances that carry energy. Light and radio travel as electromagnetic waves.

Lasers create and store light energy. This is then released in a burst of powerful light.

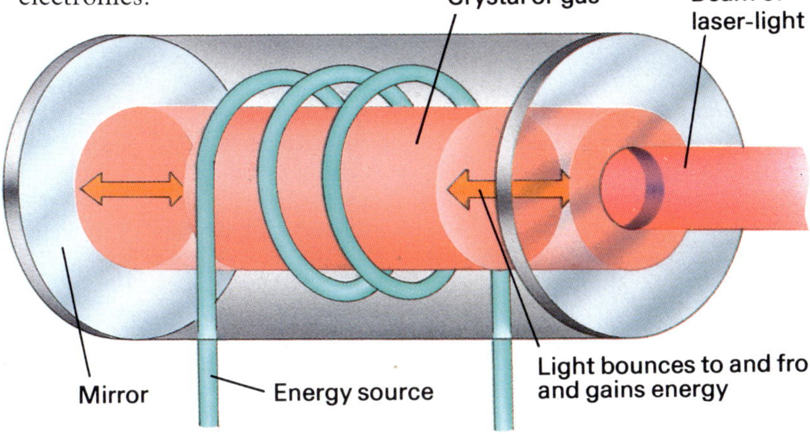

THE EARTH AND SPACE

asteroids Thousands of small bodies that orbit the sun between the orbits of Mars and Jupiter.

aurora (*awe-roarer*) The colourful displays of lights seen in the sky around the polar regions. Northern Lights – *Aurora Borealis*; Southern Lights – *Aurora Australis*.

axis An imaginary line straight through the centre of the earth from the North Pole to the South Pole.

big-bang theory A theory about the origin of our universe which suggests that it is constantly expanding.

caldera (*cal-deer-a*) A crater formed by a volcano.

continental shelf The seabed to a depth of 200m (600ft) surrounding Earth's land masses.

core The inner part of the Earth.

crust The outer layer of the Earth.

epicentre The point from which the shock waves of an earthquake radiate outwards.

fault A more or less vertical break in the Earth's crust along which the rocks have moved.

fold mountains Mountains formed by folding layers of rock. This happens when parts of the Earth's crust move together from each side.

ice sheet A solid layer of ice and snow which erodes and alters the land.

interstellar space Beyond the Solar System, amongst the stars.

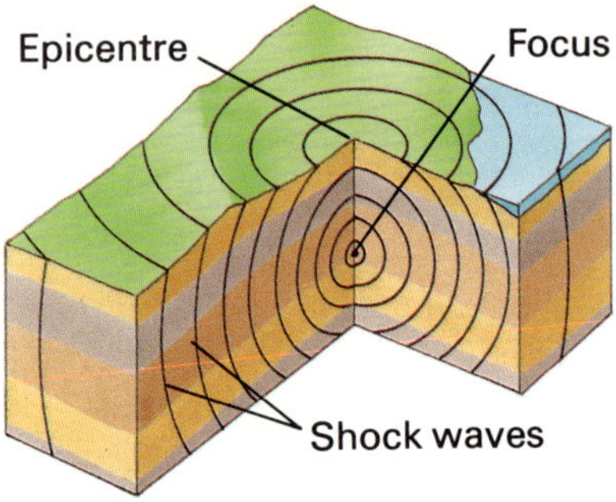

The epicentre of an earthquake is the point on the ground where the shock waves are strongest.

light year The distance travelled by light in one year: 9.46 million kilometres (5.88 million miles).

midnight sun The sun when it can be seen during both day and night. This happens in the areas nearest the North and South Poles.

Milky Way Our galaxy, containing an estimated 200,000 million stars.

radio telescope An instrument that collects radio waves from space.

sedimentary rocks Rocks like clay, sandstone and limestone, formed from sediments (small rock particles).

shooting star A type of meteor.

solar system The sun and its satellites.

solstice The time when the sun is furthest from the Earth's Equator.

tsunami (*tsew-narmi*) A tidal wave.

zenith The point in the heavens directly overhead.

COMPUTERS

access To connect to a computer in another place, usually by telephone line.
backup A copy of a program or file, made for safety.
BASIC Beginner's All-purpose Symbolic Code: a computer language which uses common English terms.
bug An error in a program, causing it to fail.
COBOL Common Business Orientated Language: a programming language designed for business and commercial use.
compatible A computer or program which is able to work with another computer.
cursor A highlight on the computer screen which picks out the character or block which is being worked on.
daisywheel A kind of printer.
data The general term for information processed by a computer.
debug To remove the bugs from a program.
disk The most common way of storing programs and data. A hard disk is rigid, a floppy disk is not.
dot matrix (*may-tricks*) A kind of printer in which characters are built up from a series of dots.
drive Part of the computer that accepts disks, writes to them and reads them.
file A collection of data stored in the computer's memory or on a disk.
format To mark a disk electronically so that it can receive data, and to erase any data which has already been entered.
graphics Pictures and diagrams, on the computer screen or printed out.
hacker A person who breaks into other people's computer systems.
language A defined set of characters used to communicate with a computer.
mainframe computer A powerful, high-speed computer.

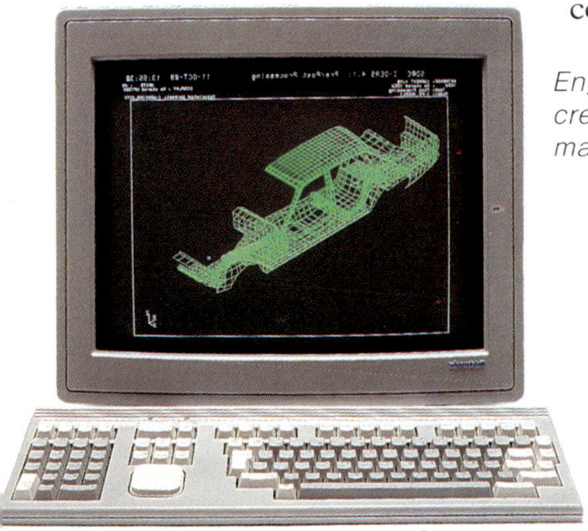

Engineers use computer graphics to create models when designing new machinery.

microchip A small silicon chip which provides memory for the computer.
modem A device which enables one computer to communicate with another over a telephone line.
monitor The device like a television set on which data is displayed.
mouse A small hand-held device which, when moved across a desktop, causes a pointer to move on the screen.
printer A typewriter-like machine that produces printed sheets from a computer.
programming Writing a program to carry out a specific task.
RAM Random Access Memory, the computer's memory available for work in progress. The work is lost when the computer is switched off unless it is stored on a disk.
ROM Read Only Memory: instructions or programs kept in the computer's memory and retained when the computer is switched off.
software The programs which give instructions to a computer and simplify its operation, usually available on disk.
terminal Another name for a work station.
VDU Visual Display Unit: a monitor for use with a computer.
work station The combination of screen, keyboard and printer linked to a mainframe computer.

ECONOMICS

assets The resources which a business owns.
balance of payments The balance between the goods a country exports and those it imports.
bank rate The rate at which a country's central bank will lend money to other banks within the country.
base rate The minimum rate of interest at which a bank will lend money.
capitalism A system under which people are free to own private property and to work for themselves. Britain is a capitalist country.
devaluation To lower the value of a currency.
exchange rate The cost of exchanging one currency for another.
free trade Trade between different countries without tax barriers.
hard currency A currency belonging to a country with a strong economy.
income tax A tax on the amount of money a person earns.
indirect taxes Taxes on goods and services, e.g. VAT.
inflation A rise in the cost of living as money buys less.
PAYE Pay As You Earn: a system of collecting income tax.
retail price index A guide to the level of prices in the shops.
VAT Value Added Tax: a tax on goods and services.

THE NATURAL WORLD

absorption The taking in of water and food by a plant.

acid rain Rain with a high level of acidity caused by pollution from the burning of coal and oil – it damages growing plants, especially trees.

adaptation Any characteristic that a species of plant or animal has developed to help it survive in its environment. For example, animals which live in cold climates have adapted by growing thick furry coats.

aerial root A root growing from above ground level.

annual ring The new ring of wood around the trunk which a tree grows in a single year. Counting the rings can tell a tree's age. Also called a growth ring.

arachnid (*a-rack-nid*) A class of animals which includes spiders, scorpions, ticks and mites. Most have four pairs of legs.

arthropods Animals without backbones with jointed legs and an external skeleton. Insects, spiders, shrimps, crabs and lobsters are all arthropods.

axil The angle formed where a leaf joins a stem.

biennial A plant which completes its life cycle in two seasons and then dies.

calyx The name for the sepals of a flower.

canine teeth The large sharp pointed teeth found in animals which eat meat.

carapace The hard shell of crustaceans like crabs and lobsters. Also the shell of a tortoise.

capillary action The way in which plants draw up water through their roots.

carpel The female reproductive organ of the flower. It is made up of stigma, style and ovary.

cephalopod A group of marine molluscs including the octopus, squid and cuttlefish.

cetacean (*set-ay-shun*) A whale, dolphin or porpoise.

chlorosis (*klor-owe-sis*) Yellowing of plants due to lack of chlorophyll.

Acid rain is caused by industrial pollution of the atmosphere.

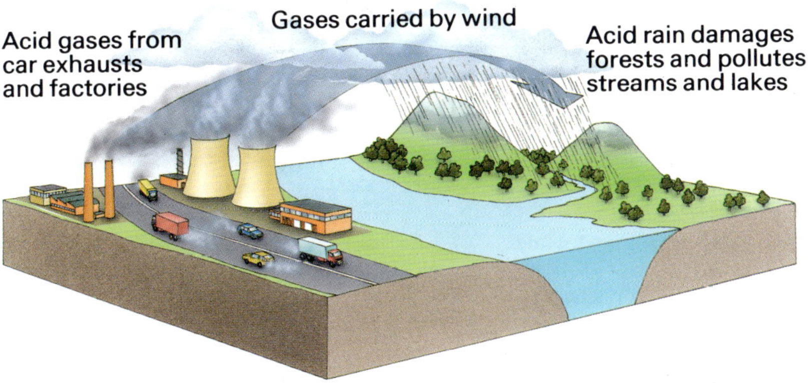

cold-blooded animals Animals which cannot control their own body temperature. Their temperature is the same as the air or water which surrounds them. Fish and reptiles are cold-blooded.

compound leaf A leaf made up of separate leaflets.

coppicing Cutting trees back to the ground to encourage new growth from the base.

corolla The petals of a flower.

cotyledon A seed leaf. The first pair of leaves of the embryo plant in a seed, often providing a food store.

cultivar A variety of a plant which is produced by man, not found naturally.

deficiency disease A plant disease caused by lack of nourishment.

dicotyledon A member of the class of flowering plants with two cotyledons in each seed.

epidermis The outer layer of skin.

floret A small flower.

frond A large leaf, such as a palm leaf.

genus (*jen-us*) A group of very similar plants or animals. Families of plants and animals are often divided into several genera.

germination The beginning of growth of a seed or spore.

grassland An area where the main plants are grasses.

herbaceous (*herb-ay-shus*) **perennial** A plant which lives for a number of years, whose leaves and flowers die back each winter and reappear in the spring.

humus Decaying organic matter in the soil.

hybrid A plant produced when pollen from one species fertilizes the flower of a different but usually closely related species.

incisors The front teeth of mammals.

insectivore An animal which feeds on insects.

kingdom A major division of living things. Most biologists recognize three kingdoms: Protista, single-celled organisms; Metaphyta or Plantae, plants; and Metazoa or Animalia, animals.

lactation Producing milk, as mammals do.

legume A type of dry fruit formed from a single ovary which splits down two sides when ripe, for example pea or bean.

life cycle The complete life history of a plant or animal from the fertilization of an egg or seed to death and the beginning of the next generation.

loam A fine, easily dug soil.

mammary gland The gland which produces milk in a female animal.

mandible The lower jaw of an insect or other invertebrate.

melanin A dark colouring which is found in the skin.

metamorphosis (*meta-morf-owe-sis*) The big changes that many animals undergo between the stages of being a larva and being an adult, as when a tadpole becomes a frog or a caterpillar becomes a butterfly.

mimicry A protective device in which many harmless and defenceless animals are shaped and coloured like poisonous or dangerous ones. This makes it likely that animals which might eat them will leave them alone.
molar A tooth used to chew or grind food.
monocotyledon (*mono-cotty-lead-on*) A member of a class of flowering plants with only one cotyledon (seed leaf) in each seed.
monotreme A rare type of primitive mammal which does not give birth to live young ones but lays eggs instead. The duck-billed platypus is a monotreme.
mutualism A relationship between two different kinds of living creature which has advantages for both. Mutualism is another word for 'symbiosis'.
nymph A stage in the development of some insects, such as the dragonfly.
omnivore An animal which eats both plants and animals. Man is an omnivore.
oviparous Describes an animal which lays eggs.
parasitism When one living thing lives on another living thing and takes its food from it.

Greenflies are parasites, they suck the sap of plants.

pistil Another word for the female part of the flower – the carpel or group of carpels.
placental mammal The largest group of mammals. Their young ones grow inside the mother's body before they are born.
radicle The part of a plant in the seed which develops into the first root.
roundworms Simple worms which have no rings or segments on their bodies. Many are parasites and live inside other animals.

Life cycle of a butterfly.

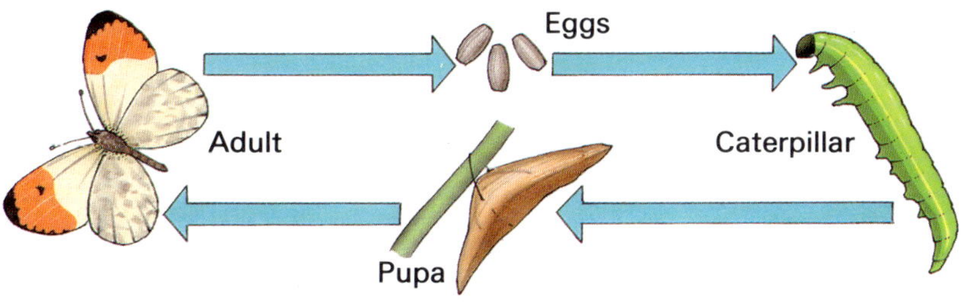

scavenger An animal which feeds on dead plants or animals. Vultures are scavengers.

self-pollination The transfer of pollen from the male to the female organs of the same flower.

social insects Insects that live in communities, with different insects doing different jobs. Social insects include honeybees, wasps, ants and termites.

stigma The tip of the carpel of a flower, which receives the pollen.

style The stalk-like part of the carpel with the stigma at its tip.

symbiosis (*sim-bye-owe-sis*) 'Living together'. Used to describe an association between two living creatures which has advantages for both. Another word for 'mutualism'.

tap root The main root of a plant.

tendril The thin, twining stem or leaf which a climbing plant such as a sweet pea uses to cling to a support.

territory An area of land which an animal marks out as its own home and which it will defend against other animals of the same kind.

thorax The middle section of the body in insects, or the part of the body containing the heart and lungs in animals with backbones.

transpiration The evaporation of water from the surfaces of a plant's leaves. As this happens, more water is drawn up into the plant through its roots.

warm-blooded animals Animals that control their own body temperatures so that they do not become too hot in hot surroundings or too cold in cold surroundings. Man is an example.

The parts of a flower.

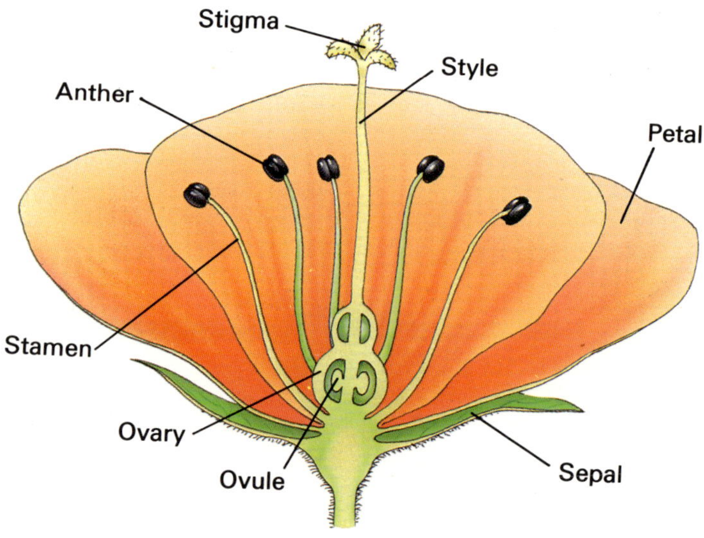

HUMAN BIOLOGY AND MEDICINE

Adam's apple The piece of cartilage which sticks out over the front of the larynx. More prominent in men than in women.

adrenalin A hormone which stimulates the heart and increases muscular strength and endurance.

alimentary canal The tube running from the mouth down to the stomach and intestines, along which food passes and is digested.

amino acids The chemical substances which make up proteins.

analgesic (*anal-gee-sic*) A pain-relieving drug.

antibody A substance produced by the body's immune system which destroys harmful bacteria and viruses.

benign A word used to describe a growth or tumour which is harmless and not likely to become worse.

bile A greenish liquid produced by the liver. It helps to digest fat in the small intestine.

blood vessels The tubes which carry blood round the body. Veins, arteries and capillaries are all blood vessels.

bronchus (*bron-kus*) One of the branches of the windpipe, leading to the lungs.

capillaries The smallest type of blood vessels.

cholesterol A fatty substance, which can build up in the blood vessels and block them.

coronary arteries The arteries which supply blood to the heart.

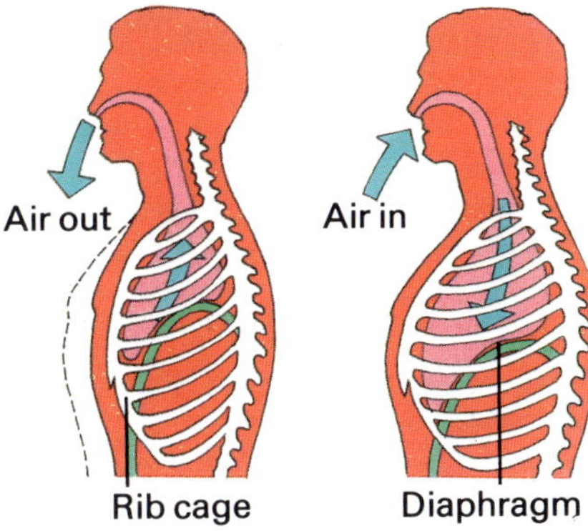

The diaphragm rises and falls with breathing.

diaphragm (*die-a-fram*) The flat muscle which separates the chest from the abdomen.

DNA (Deoxyribonucleic acid) A complicated chemical which makes up genes and chromosomes.

enzyme A chemical substance which speeds up chemical reactions within the body and controls processes such as digestion.

epiglottis A small flap at the back of the tongue which blocks the windpipe when you swallow and prevents food 'going down the wrong way'.

follicle A small pocket in the skin from which a single hair grows.

gall bladder The small sac below the liver which stores bile.

haemoglobin (*heem-o-globe-in*) The substance which carries oxygen around the bloodstream and gives red blood cells their colour.

hypertension High blood pressure.
immune system The body's own defences against infection.
inflammation The reddening and swelling, usually painful, which appears when part of the body is injured or infected.
jugular Of the neck.
ligament A tough band of tissue which holds the bones together at a joint.

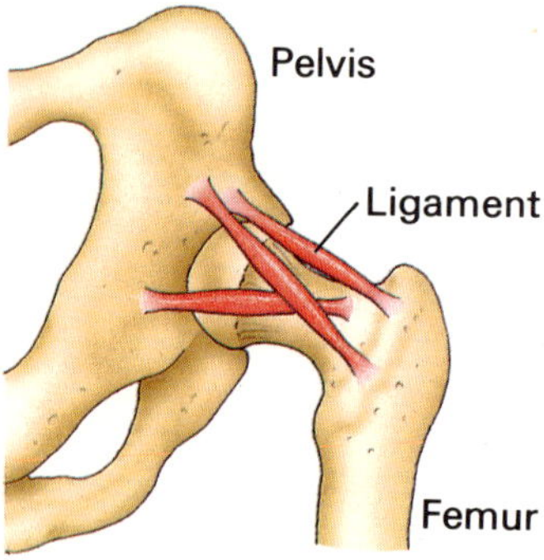

Ligaments hold bones and joints together.

lymph A clear liquid which contains white blood cells.
membrane A thin layer of cells which lines or covers various parts of the body.
malnutrition A lack of the food needed to stay healthy.
oesophagus (*es-of-a-gus*) The gullet or food pipe leading to the stomach.
pituitary (*pit-yew-it-ary*) An important gland, which amongst other things, controls growth.
plasma The liquid part of blood.
poultice A hot, soothing substance put on an inflamed part of the body.
pulmonary Of the lungs.
renal Of the kidneys.
reflex actions Actions which are automatic and which cannot be controlled by thinking about them.
sebaceous (*see-bay-shus*) **gland** An oil-producing gland in the skin.
sinuses Four sets of cavities in the skull where the air you breathe is warmed.
senility Changes brought on by old age.
sperm The male cells.
spinal cord The thick cord of nerves which begins at the base of the brain and ends to the bottom of the back.
temperature The level of heat in the body. A normal temperature is 36–37.5°C (97–99°F).
thyroid A gland in the neck which produces a hormone called thyroxine. This controls the speed of chemical processes in the body.
tourniquet (*torn-i-kay*) A band which is twisted tightly about an arm or leg to stop bleeding from an artery.
toxin A poisonous substance.
ultrasound A way of using sound waves to build up a picture of what is happening inside the body.
urethra The tube which leads from the bladder to the outside of the body.
vaccinate (*vaks-in-ate*) To treat with a mild form of a disease in order to prevent someone from catching the disease in its serious form.
vascular Of the blood vessels.

THE ARTS

LITERATURE

autobiography A book about oneself, written by oneself.

bibliography (*bib-lee-og-rafi*) A list of books about a subject.

blank verse Poetry which does not rhyme.

biography A book about someone, by another person.

couplet Two lines of verse, one after another, which rhyme with each other.

figure of speech A recognized type of expression used in speaking or writing, for example a simile.

foreword A short introduction to a book.

ghost writer Someone who writes on behalf of another person and under their name. For example, a film star's autobiography is often written by a ghost writer.

linguistics (*ling-wist-ix*) The study of language.

hyperbole (*hy-per-bol-ee*) A figure of speech which uses exaggeration to make a point. For example, 'I've told you a million times, don't do that.'

pseudonym A name used by an author which is not his or her real name.

simile (*sim-ill-ee*) A figure of speech which compares one thing to another. For example, 'My love is like a red red rose.'

tautology Saying the same thing more than once in different words.

translation Turning something written or spoken in one language into another language.

THEATRE AND CINEMA

apron The front of the stage, extending beyond the proscenium.

arch, proscenium (*pro-seen-e-um*) The archway between the stage and the auditorium.

cast The group of actors performing a play.

close-up A picture taken near a subject.

curtain call When actors return to take a bow after the curtain has fallen at the end of a play.

dolly The mobile carriage which carries a camera.

dress rehearsal The last rehearsal of a play, with the actors in full costume, before it is performed in public.

epilogue (*epi-log*) A speech at the end of a play, after the main action is over.

flash-back An interruption in the story of a film to show a past event.

flat A large canvas screen on which scenery is painted.

freeze To hold a shot so that the action seems to stop.

lines The words an actor speaks.

melodrama A play with a sensational plot.

mystery play A medieval religious play presenting a scene from the bible. Also called a miracle play.

pan Short for panoramic shot. A sideways sweep with the camera.

prologue A speech made at the beginning of a play by one of the characters or by an actor representing the author.

props The small objects needed on stage to make a scene realistic such as cups, flowers or newspapers, but not scenery or furniture. Short for properties.
repertory The collection of plays that a theatre company performs in a season.
read through The reading of a play by the cast, without actions.
revue (*re-view*) A series of songs, dances and short acted scenes.
set The scenery for a play or the area where filming takes place.
shooting Filming a scene.
soliloquy (*sol-ill-o-kwe*) A speech which is not supposed to be heard by other characters in the play, in which an actor speaks his thoughts out loud.
take Part of the scene of a film shot without interruption.
wings The areas, hidden from the audience, on either side of the stage.

MUSIC

a capella Not accompanied by instruments.
adagio (*add-adge-i-owe*) At a slow pace.
allegro At a fast pace.
andante At a quiet, peaceful pace.
anthem A work to be sung by a choir in church.
aria A solo sung in an opera.
arpeggio (*ar-pedge-i-owe*) Notes of a chord played in quick succession.
brass instruments Metal musical instruments sounded by blowing into a mouthpiece.
counterpoint Two or more tunes which are played at the same time.
crescendo Increasing in loudness.
electronic music Music where the sounds are produced by the use of electronics, not with ordinary musical instruments.
folk music Music and ballads of the people.
forte Played or sung loudly.
fortissimo Very loud.
fugue (*fewg*) A composition which has different tunes in different keys.
largo At a slow pace.
libretto The words of an opera or oratorio.
lieder German songs written in the 19th century.
madrigal A song for several voices, unaccompanied by instruments.
mezzo-soprano Female singing voice between soprano and contralto.
operetta A light opera.
stringed instruments Instruments with strings that are played with a bow, like the violin and cello.
pianissimo Very softly.
piano Played or sung softly.
pizzicato (*pit-see-ka-to*) To play a note by plucking the strings of an instrument.
soprano The highest female singing voice.
spiritual A religious folk song, usually of Black American origin.
theme A tune which is heard more than once in a piece of music.
vivace (*viv-ah-chay*) Lively.

ARCHITECTURE

architrave (*ark-i-trayve*) The beam which lies across the top of the columns in classical architecture.

Art Nouveau (*noo-vo*) A style of art and architecture of the late 19th and early 20th centuries, using curving forms, often of flowers and leaves.

buttress A structure built on the outside of a wall in order to support it.

Byzantine An ornate style of architecture used in the Eastern Roman Empire between 400BC and AD1453.

campanile A bell tower.

capital The broad top part of a column which supports the entablature.

caryatid A draped female figure used as a pillar in classical architecture.

classical The style of Greece and Rome, or any style based on these.

cornice The top section of the entablature, supporting the roof.

Elizabethan The style of architecture of England in the 1500s.

entablature In classical architecture, the part of a building between the top of the columns and the roof. It consists of architrave, frieze and cornice.

frieze The central part of the entablature, between the architrave and the cornice. Usually decorated.

Georgian A classical style of architecture used in England in the 1700s.

Gothic A style of architecture developed in France in the 1100s.

lintel The horizontal stone over a doorway or window which supports the wall above.

oriel A type of bay window.

pedestal The block of stone used to support a column.

portico An area with a roof supported by rows of columns.

vault An arched roof or ceiling built of brick or stone.

Parts of a classical building.

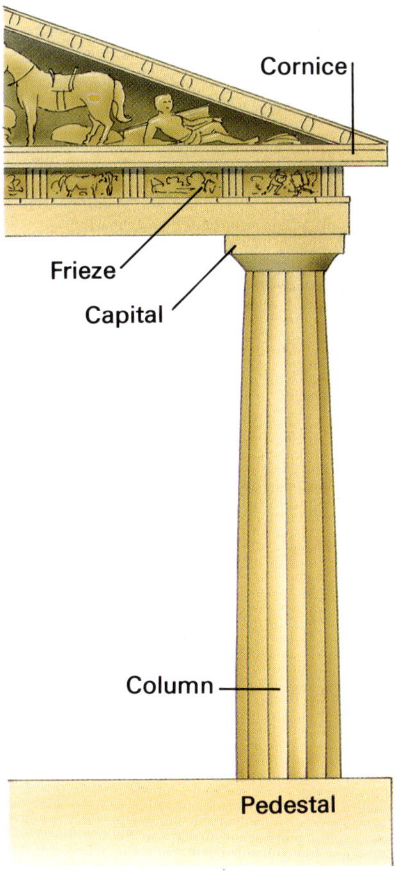

ART

abstract art A form of art which uses geometric designs instead of natural forms.

airbrush A device used by artists to spray paint, varnish or fixative. It is worked by compressed air.

aquarelle (*ak-wa-rel*) A water-colour painting.

armature The wood or metal framework used to support a model made by a sculptor.

chiaroscuro (*kyaro-skewro*) The balance of light and shade in a picture.

Cubism A style of modern painting started by Picasso and Braque in 1907. Cubists used simple shapes like cubes, spheres and cones.

Dutch School The art and artists of the Netherlands in the 1600s. Important painters included Rembrandt and Hals.

Expressionism A style of painting which tried to express the artist's inner feelings.

finger painting A way of painting using a finger instead of a brush.

The spray in this picture has been created with an airbrush.

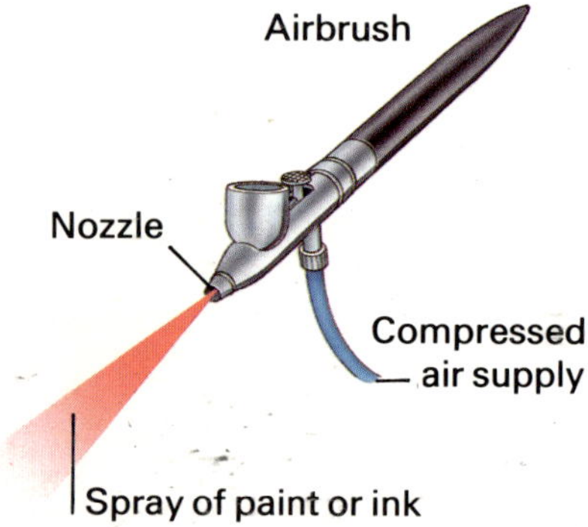

A triptych is a painting in three parts.

gouache (*goo-ash*) A type of water-colour painting.

Impressionism A style of painting where the painter is interested in light and its effects. Impressionism began in France in the mid-1800s, and the most important impressionist painters include Manet, Monet, Renoir and Degas.

landscape painting Pictures whose main subject is the landscape, not the human figure.

maquette (*mack-et*) A small wax or clay model made by a sculptor in preparation for a larger work.

miniature A tiny painting, usually a portrait.

oil painting A way of painting using pigments ground up in oil.

representational art Pictures which try to show objects in as lifelike a way as possible.

still life A painting or drawing of a non-living object or objects such as a vase of flowers or a bowl of fruit.

triptych A series of three paintings, linked together.